D0154436

AMERICAN
STATESMEN

AMERICAN STATESMEN

Secretaries of State from John Jay to Colin Powell

Edited by Edward S. Mihalkanin

GREENWOOD PRESS
Westport, CT • London

Library of Congress Cataloging-in-Publication Data
American statesmen : secretaries of state from John Jay to Colin Powell /
edited by Edward S. Mihalkanin.
      p. cm.
  Includes index.
  ISBN 0-313-30828-4
    1. Statesmen—United States—Biography. 2. Cabinet officers—United States—Biography.
3. United States—Foreign relations. I. Mihalkanin, Edward S.
E176.A596 2004
327.73'0092'2—dc22   2004010871

British Library Cataloguing in Publication Data is available.

Copyright © 2004 by Edward S. Mihalkanin

All rights reserved. No portion of this book may be
reproduced, by any process or technique, without the
express written consent of the publisher.

Library of Congress Catalog Card Number: 2004010871

ISBN: 0–313–30828–4

First published in 2004

Greenwood Press, 88 Post Road West, Westport, CT 06881
An imprint of Greenwood Publishing Group, Inc.
www.greenwood.com

Printed in the United States of America

The paper used in this book complies with the
Permanent Paper Standard issued by the National
Information Standards Organization (Z39.48–1984).

10 9 8 7 6 5 4 3 2 1

Copyright Acknowledgment

Every reasonable effort has been made to trace the owners of copyright materials in this book, but in
some instances this has proven impossible. The author and publisher will be glad to receive information leading to more complete acknowlegments in subsequent printings of this book and in the meantime extend their apologies for any omissions.

William Jennings Bryan is reprinted with permission of Nebraska History.

To the memory of Kinley Brauer, Richard Fanning, and the other scholars who have gone before us and to our contemporary colleagues who have done so much to enrich our understanding of the diplomatic history and foreign policies of the United States of America.

CREDO

Time in its irresistible and ceaseless flow carries along on its flood all created things and drowns them in the depths of obscurity. . . . But the tale of history forms a very strong bulwark against the stream of time, and checks in some measure its irresistible flow, so that, of all things done in it, as many as history has taken over it secures and binds together, and does not allow them to slip away into the abyss of oblivion.

—Anna Comnena

The historian has a duty both to himself and to his readers. He has to a certain extent the cure of souls. He is accountable for the reputation of the mighty dead whom he conjures up and portrays. If he makes a mistake, if he repeats a slander on those who are blameless, or holds up profligates or schemers to admiration, he not only commits an evil action; he poisons and misleads the public mind.

—Albert Mathiez

The greatness of today is built on the efforts of past centuries. A nation is not contained in a day nor in an epoch, but in the succession of all days, all periods, all her twilights and all her dawns.

—Jean Jaurès

We are reminded by William James . . . that everyone . . . has in truth an underlying philosophy of life . . . a stream of tendency . . . which gives coherence and direction to thought and action. . . . All their lives, forces which they do not recognize and cannot name, have been tugging at them—inherited instincts, traditional beliefs, acquired convictions; and the resultant is an outlook on life, a conception of social needs, a sense in James's phrase of "the total push and pressure of the cosmos," which, when reasons are nicely balanced, must determine where choice shall fall.

—Benjamin N. Cardozo

CONTENTS

Contents

PREFACE

American Statesmen: Secretaries of State from John Jay to Colin Powell is intended to introduce readers to the persons who have held the office of secretary of state of the United States throughout its history. As a biographical dictionary, this volume provides neither a detailed narrative of U.S. diplomatic history nor a comprehensive analysis of the foreign policies of our republic. However, because the secretary of state is legally charged with at least some responsibility for the actions of the U.S. government as it pertains to foreign affairs, most of the important issues in U.S. diplomatic history are discussed in the essays of this book.

Some readers may question the need for such a book, given the decline in influence of the secretary of state and the State Department in U.S. foreign policy formulation, especially since World War II. In *The Politics of United States Foreign Policy*, Jerel Rosati has argued that the decline in the State Department's policy-making role is due to four global and historical patterns, or what one could call structural changes: (1) the increasing importance of international affairs, (2) the growing power of the United States in the world, (3) innovations in communication technology, and (4) an increase in the use of force to attain U.S. foreign policy goals. The U.S. government, in the face of the increasing importance of foreign affairs, fashioned instruments that displaced the State Department's bureaucratic monopoly in the executive branch in the area of foreign policy. The establishment of new institutional tools to aid the United States in the defense of its foreign policy interests begun by President Franklin D. Roosevelt with such agencies as the Export-Import Bank, the Office of Strategic Services (OSS), the International Monetary Fund (IMF), and the International Bank for Reconstruction and Development (IBRD), more commonly known as the World Bank, was not a temporary aberration due to the extreme conditions of the Great Depression and the Second World War.

Rather, Roosevelt's agencies were the harbingers of a new burst of institution building carried out by his successor, Harry S Truman, in the face of the newly perceived threat from the Soviet Union specifically and the continued importance of foreign affairs in the postwar world generally. With the establishment of the Department of Defense (DOD), the Central Intelligence Agency (CIA), the National Security Council (NSC), and the other agencies during and after the Truman administration, the State Department and secretary of state have had to share major responsibilities in U.S. foreign policy formulation and implementation. The loss of the department's institutional monopoly position appears permanent.

The increasing threat and use of force exacerbated the decline of the State Department, which was originally prompted by the increasing importance of foreign policy and the establishment of these new government institutions. Under post–World War II policies, the United States put itself on a permanent war footing. The U.S. government developed nuclear weapons and delivery systems, a large peacetime conventional military, counterinsurgency forces, and covert capabilities. The reliance on the threat and use of force by the U.S. government by definition reduced the importance of the State Department and subordinated it to DOD, the CIA, and other agencies.

The secretary of state also has lost power to the office of the president. As the United States became more powerful and technological innovations occurred in transportation and communication, the U.S. presidency became more powerful, and presidents viewed foreign policy as too important to be left in the hands of the State Department. A presidential foreign policy bureaucracy was developed to oversee State's handling of foreign policy and, at times, to take over the management of U.S. diplomacy from the department. The development of air transportation and instant communication allowed the president to remove the "middleman" and actually conduct diplomacy on a day-to-day basis.

Many argue that the State Department and, by extension, the secretary of state should be given less importance, not just as a consequence of structural changes in the international and domestic environments, but as a matter of policy. Many critics of State point to the subculture of Foggy Bottom and the individuals who comprise the personnel there. The subculture at State is considered to be elitist, loyal, cautious, and apt to "go native" in opposition to U.S. interests. Others complain that the State Department is incapable of advising the president in foreign policy formulation and implementation because of bureaucratic defects. They stress that State is unresponsive, averse to change, unable to lead, slow, and inefficient.

Yet, although the secretary of state has had to share foreign policy with other executive department officials, the secretary is still considered one of a handful of key U.S. government personnel when it comes to U.S. foreign policy. The secretary is the senior member of the cabinet and considered bureaucratically to be the chief spokesperson on foreign policy. The secretary is expected to define and carry out the foreign policy of the United States. In fact, no matter how diminished the status of secretary of state is, the secretary, under law, is understood to be the executive branch official most responsible for the foreign policy of the United States.

As early as Thomas Jefferson's complaints about Alexander Hamilton's interference with his department, secretaries of state have been complaining about such poachers—the struggle for control of U.S. foreign policy is therefore as old as the United States itself. Yet, unless there is a revolution that destroys the current international system or a radical change in the organization of the federal government of the United States, the secretary of state will continue to be seen as the official spokesperson on questions of U.S. foreign policy.

To borrow words from the historian Samuel Flagg Bemis, this book seeks to provide, through its essays on "the career and the diplomacy of each of the several Secretaries of State, a readable and authoritative narrative of the more important phases of American foreign relations, particular in so far as they are to be connected with any one secretary."

Due to the constraints of fitting the biographies of the secretaries of state into one volume, *American Statesmen* does not, with but two exceptions, include those persons who held the office on an *ad interim* basis. The exceptions are John Jay and Hugh S. Legaré. Jay was an important transitional figure bridging the foreign policy of the Continental Congress during the Revolutionary War and the foreign policy of the United States under the Articles of Confederation on the one hand and the foreign policy of the United States under the Constitution of 1789 on the other. Legaré, who served in the Tyler administration, would have been nominated by President John Tyler and confirmed by the Senate as secretary except for Legaré's insistence that he would be better able to achieve the annexation of Texas and other foreign policy goals of the administration as an interim rather than as a permanent secretary. For these reasons, both men were deemed necessary inclusions in *American Statesmen*.

Immediately following this preface is a short introduction designed to provide an overview of U.S. diplomatic history and foreign policy from the time of Benjamin Franklin to the present. The 65 biographical essays of the secretaries of state are arranged alphabetically, and each begins by giving the secretary's birth and death dates, dates in office, administration(s) served, and political party. Each essay covers the secretary's early life and background; education and influences; career before becoming secretary of state and any expression of ideas relating to foreign policy; appointment as secretary; relations with the president, cabinet, and Congress; foreign policy ideas, especially as expressed in policies while secretary of state; major foreign policy issues during this tenure; circumstances of leaving office; career after leaving secretaryship; and general assessment as secretary. The most important parts of the essays deal with the subjects' foreign policy ideas before becoming secretary; foreign policies while secretary; and major foreign policy issues during the subjects' tenure as secretary. Each essay also concludes with a Bibliographical Essay listing the most important primary and secondary sources available for each secretary's term of office. *American Statesmen* also includes a detailed subject index and a Quick Reference Chronology of Secretaries of State that lists American secretaries of state in chronological order with their dates of service and the administration(s) they served.

It is hoped that this book may be of some value both to general readers and to scholars interested in the great issues facing the United States during the tenures of these secretaries of state.

BIBLIOGRAPHICAL ESSAY

For a general overview of U.S. foreign policy, especially in terms of politics, institutions, and processes, see Jerel A. Rosati, *The Politics of United States Foreign Policy*, 3rd ed. (1997). See also John Franklin Campbell, *The Foreign Affairs Fudge*

Factory (1971); Anthony Lake, *Somoza Falling* (1989); and Burton M. Sapin, *The Making of United States Foreign Policy* (1966).

For a general discussion on bureaucratic decision making applicable to governmental institutions, see Morton H. Halperin, *Bureaucratic Politics and Foreign Policy* (1974); James Q. Wilson, *Bureaucracy: What Government Agencies Do and Why They Do It* (1990); and a new edition of a classic, Graham Allison and Philip Zelikow, *Essence of Decision: Explaining the Cuban Missile Crisis*, 2nd ed. (1999).

For a negative interpretation of the State Department's policymaking role, see Duncan Clarke, "Why State Can't Lead," *Foreign Policy* (spring 1987); I. M. Destler, *Presidents, Bureaucrats and Foreign Policy* (1972); Robert Pringle, "Creeping Irrelevance at Foggy Bottom," *Foreign Policy* 29 (fall 1977); and Bert A. Rockman, "America's Department of State: Irregular and Regular Syndromes of Policy Making," *American Political Science Review* (December 1981).

For those who emphasize bureaucratic defects at State, see Andrew M. Scott, "The Department of State: Formal Organization and Informal Culture," *International Studies Quarterly* (March 1969); Harry Crosby (pseudonym), "Too at Home Abroad: Swilling Beer, Licking Boots and Ignoring the Natives with One of Jim Baker's Finest," *The Washington Monthly* (September 1991); and Barry Rubin, *Secrets of State: The State Department and the Struggle over U.S. Foreign Policy* (1985).

ACKNOWLEDGMENTS

I want to take this opportunity to thank many people without whom this volume would not have been possible. First, I want to thank James T. Sabin and Cynthia Harris of Greenwood Press, who showed their confidence in me, a political scientist, by assigning me the editorship of this book. Also, I need to thank John Wagner, development editor at Greenwood. John's kindness, professionalism, consideration, and assistance were invaluable to the completion of this book. It could not have been done without him. I also need to thank James Broussard, who introduced me to the project.

I also need to thank the many people who assisted me in the preparation of the manuscript. Rayana Gonzales, Mark Hatfield, Nicholas Johnson, Jennie Tomme, and Dodie Weidner all worked on the manuscript at different times. In addition, Nicholas Johnson helped oversee the progress of all the essays. David Fernandez III and Amy Portwood worked with me on the page proofs. All of them have my sincere thanks.

I also want to thank all the scholars who contributed to this book. Many of them advised me on different facets of the book, including suggestions for potential contributors to the volume. They were unfailing in their encouragement and support, and for this and their contributions I thank them.

By editing this book, I was introduced to the community of U.S. diplomatic historians, and to a person they gave of themselves to help me with this project. A senior historian told me early on: "Be the editor! Don't be shy about being the editor." Regardless of the differences in age or discipline, they welcomed me, and for this I will always be grateful. Specifically, I also need to thank Edward Crapol and the late Kinley Brauer for reading and commenting on my Seward essay and Walter LeFeber for reading and commenting on my Sherman and Day essays. Their insights made the essays better.

Finally, I want to thank my 10-year-old nieces, Elizabeth and Ashley, who reminded me that sometimes an uncle needs to stop and play for a while to keep a sense of perspective critical to finishing a big job. Thanks.

Edward S. Mihalkanin
San Marcos, Texas

INTRODUCTION

Expansion, if not empire, has been a consistent goal of the leaders and citizens of the United States throughout its history. This expansionistic impulse has been defined both territorially and commercially, and it has not been limited to the geographic contours that the United States has ended up having. Such expansion has been seen, for the most part, as being integral to the safety and viability of the United States as a state in the global environment comprised of other territorial states and to the safety and viability of our experiment in representative government. At the same time there have been recurrent cautions expressed about the threat to our republican institutions from such expansionism, even if such cautions have not proved to be the dominant refrain through most of our national history.

As to the question of means, unilateralism, not multilateralism, has been the common strategy of U.S. expansionism and the perceived way to protect the institutions of our representative government throughout most of our history. It was only during the presidency of Franklin D. Roosevelt that multilateralism, in effect, was adopted by the United States and became the dominant method for the achievement of the historic goals of the United States, albeit with some unilateralist variations, throughout the post–World War II period. Yet, the administration of George W. Bush has appeared to reject multilateralism and has become the most unilateralist administration the United States has had in over 60 years. This unilateralism has been coupled with a major and sustained projection of U.S. power into southwest Asia and the old southern littoral of the former Soviet Union, which is new in terms of its extent and duration. The United States and its citizens are facing a major crisis to their national security internationally. Permit me to sketch an outline of how the United States arrived at this crossroads.

To begin to understand the U.S. drive for expansion, it is helpful to erase from our minds the current geographical extent of the United States. If we keep the current map in our minds, then the expansion of the United States appears to be merely the placing of the missing pieces, in chronological order, of an already existing geographic jigsaw puzzle. Thus, it appears that our policy makers had a preconceived plan to "fill out" the country within the current borders of the United States. For example, the Gadsden Purchase of 1853 becomes a "rounding out" of the continental expansion of the United States. This perception distorts the picture by limiting U.S. expansionism to rather narrow, although substantial, geographic limits. Instead, U.S. statesmen conceived the entire North American continent, if not the whole Western Hemisphere, as the main arena for U.S. expansionism, which would itself then become a springboard for even greater expansion across the Pacific and on into Asia. The canvas U.S. statesmen wanted to paint the history of their country on was larger than the current territorial extent of the United States.

This expansionist sentiment was present in Britain's North American colonies before the Seven Years War. Although many of the land grants awarded by the British to its Atlantic colonies extended to the Pacific Ocean, Benjamin Franklin was the first statesman of what became the United States who systematically argued for the necessity of the settlement of new lands and the development of new territories as early as 1751, irregardless of who or what in Britain or the colonies controlled such expansion. Further, Franklin's arguments on the need for the British acquisition of Canada in the 1750s and early 1760s became a fundamental component of diplomatic and military strategy of the United States during its War of Independence.

The armies of the Continental Congress made repeated attempts to conquer Canada and thereby bring it into the revolutionary fold. Further, states like Virginia had not forgotten their pre–Revolutionary War activities west of the Appalachians. Settlement of what is now Kentucky and Tennessee by Virginians continued at about the same pace as the prewar flow, whereas the government of Virginia, not the Continental Congress, authorized, organized, and supplied the expedition led by George Rogers Clark, which in 1778–1779 captured Kaskaskia, Cahokia, and Vincennes, thereby laying the foundation to the U.S. claim of the land west of the Appalachians.

The desire for territory undergirded U.S. diplomacy with France. Franklin was able to sign a treaty of alliance with France in February 1778. By the treaty, France recognized the sovereignty of the United States and promised to guarantee the possessions and any additions or conquests the United States was able to obtain during the war from Great Britain. By the Treaty of Paris in 1783, Britain not only recognized the sovereignty of the United States but also recognized the western border of it at the Mississippi River and the northern border at the Great Lakes. Franklin, exhibiting an Anglo-Saxon version of chutzpah, had suggested to Britain that it cede Canada to the United States, without a formal U.S. request, as part of the peace treaty as a way of restoring the good feelings between the two peoples and had suggested to France that it make a new loan to his country so as to give lie to rumors that the Franco–U.S. alliance had ended over the U.S. treaty of peace with Britain. The British demurred while the French made the loan. Even with these rather extensive borders, given the relatively small population of the new country, U.S. statesmen in the 1780s and 1790s were already eyeing New Orleans, the Floridas, and Cuba.

The acquisitions of new territories would have to wait a generation, but the administration of George Washington established the firm foundations for a strategy of unilateralism or, in his thought, neutrality, which would enable the United

States to gain tactical advantages as a result of the competition among the European Great Powers. Washington's Neutrality Proclamation of 1793, no matter how hotly debated its constitutionality, was confirmed by the Neutrality Act passed by Congress in 1794. Further, it enabled the United States to negotiate and ratify Jay's treaty of 1795, which in turn made possible the advantages obtained by the United States by Pinckney's Treaty. Washington's foreign policy negated the aberration that the French alliance represented, and by it Washington tried unsuccessfully to reduce the growth of factions and to establish a foreign policy above partisan politics.

Washington's foreign policy of neutrality was supported at home by many because it was seen as a bulwark of U.S. representative government. The reasoning was as follows. It was against the interest of the United States to enter an alliance with a European power because all the Great Powers were a part of the balance of power system. The states of this system used war as a tool of statecraft to enhance the power of their states. These European wars would drag the United States into these conflicts against countries with whom the United States had no competing interests. Thus, U.S. wealth would be used, not to further U.S. national interests, but the interests of European countries. Further, wars that the United States engaged in because of an alliance would necessitate the establishment of a standing army, which would constitute one of the gravest threats to the continued existence of representative government in the United States. And it was for the protection of its republican governments that the United States declared its independence in 1776.

No matter how much Jefferson had worked against the Washington administration after he left it in 1793, Jefferson continued the broad outlines of his predecessor's policies and reaped the benefit of them with the purchase of the Louisiana Territory in 1803. Brushing aside any constitutional qualms he may have had if the Federalists had proposed the purchase, Jefferson sent the treaty to the Senate, which approved it after four days of debate. From the beginning of the acquisition of Louisiana, the United States pushed for the broadest claim to it, including land east of the Mississippi River along the Gulf Coast. Although it has been said that the purchase secured the security and independence of the United States, neither looked certain during the Second War of U.S. Independence. The war in effect was fought because Britain was insisting that the United States accept protectorate status, whereas the United States was demanding equality as a sovereign state. What is striking again is that the United States organized military expeditions against Canada in the hopes of grafting it in toto to the country while being completely open to invasions by the British at multiple points on the Atlantic and the Great Lakes. Due to a series of events occurring in Europe beyond the control of the United States, and to the excellence of its small navy, the young republic was able to survive the war. If the British government had not been so willing to end the war, the United States might have lost the Old Northwest and parts of New York and Maine. As it was, both Britain and the United States decided on a peace based on *status quo ante bellum*, including all territorial issues.

A war that had led to British armies marching almost at will through the United States might be one that would have sobered the American imagination. Instead, Jackson's victory at New Orleans in early 1815 acted as a spur to even further territorial expansion. It is instructive to note that while U.S. diplomats and citizens were pushing for expansion south into the Floridas, north into the Red River Valley, northwest into the Oregon Country, and southwest into Texas, by the time of the Transcontinental Treaty of 1819, only one state had entered the Union from the Louisiana Purchase—Louisiana itself. So, in the face of literally hundreds of millions of acres of territory, even more land beckoned from across the miles.

Under President James Monroe's and Secretary of State John Quincy Adams's stewardship, the United States was able to acquire the Floridas, establish the 49th parallel to the Rockies as a boundary between the United States and Canada (with the hope of further U.S. expansion up the Red River Valley and beyond), open the Oregon Country to settlement by U.S. citizens, and establish the 42nd parallel as the northernmost boundary of Spanish America, thereby laying a U.S. claim to the Pacific Coast.

The empire for liberty that first Franklin and then Jefferson envisioned and that had formed the basis for the national consensus in favor of territorial expansion began to be redefined in the 1830s with the rise of slavery as an issue in national politics. President Jackson only extended diplomatic recognition to the Republic of Texas in the final days of his presidency to limit the political fallout to the Democratic Party and his successor, Martin Van Buren. Yet, the agitation over Texas became more, not less, heated as President John Tyler raised the issue of U.S. annexation of Texas, and it became tied to the full-throated cry in favor of a Manifest Destiny proclaimed by John L. O'Sullivan and others as a U.S. demand for the whole North American continent.

Mexico, refusing to be reconciled to the loss of Texas in 1836, fearful that the United States was going to attempt the seizure of Texas and California, attempted to secure British support against the United States and finally agreed to extend *de jure* recognition to the Texas Republic in May 1845. It was too late. The United States and Texas had just signed an annexation agreement approved by the U.S. Congress in March and a Texas Convention in July 1845.

Having compromised with Britain over the Oregon Country after deciding that California, in effect, was more important than British Columbia, President James K. Polk, elected on an expansionist platform, arranged a war with Mexico over Texas and California. The relative ease of U.S. arms over Mexico whetted the appetites of Polk and many others, who began to consider annexing all of Mexico and integrating it into the American commonwealth. Nicholas Trist ignored his recall order from Polk and negotiated the Treaty of Guadalupe Hidalgo. By the treaty Mexico agreed to the Rio Grande as the border between Mexico and the United States and ceded the lands west of the Rio Grande, including California. The treaty was approved by the U.S. Senate, although most of the "no" votes were cast by senators who wanted even more Mexican territory.

Jefferson's democratic vista had envisioned new territories providing a place for the yeoman farmer as an independent producer to stake his claim to the rights and duties of citizenship. The self-reliance and intelligence necessary to successful agriculture were the same characteristics needed by a citizenry for a republican government to sustain itself. If a person was not free and independent economically, then the person could not be free and independent politically. For others, such as the Whigs and later Republicans, the success of the experiment in representative government was not proved by how extensively the institutions had spread territorially but by how much the institutions had been improved internally over time. The Whig–Republican criticism of territorial expansion became dominant when they were able to convince the great bulk of their fellow citizens that territorial growth could fatally threaten representative government because the growth was tied to the strengthening of slavery and the slave power—a power willing to subvert the institutions of representative government to protect and expand the institution of slavery.

If Polk was the best representative of the Democratic version of Manifest Destiny, William Henry Seward was the premier exponent of its liberal political economy variant. Seward eschewed violence and argued that a continental federated republic centered in the United States would evolve peacefully. Countries in the Western Hemisphere following the U.S. example would reform their political institutions to conform to U.S. political practice. Concomittaly, the greater integration of their economies with the U.S. economy would lead to those countries joining the American Union. Seward's and Polk's dream would be in the main shelved for decades due to domestic political developments in the United States. Although many U.S. statesmen and citizens fixed their eyes on new territories after the Treaty of Guadalupe-Hidalgo had been approved, this time the forces in favor of new acquisitions did not command a national consensus. Rather, they represented the sectionalization of Manifest Destiny by tying territorial expansion to the interests of slavery. After the Mexican War, the empire for liberty became transmuted into an empire for slavery as filibusters, or soldiers of fortune, organized expeditions from the late 1840s to the early 1860s to conquer Baja California, Cuba, and Nicaragua, financially supported by and often composed of U.S. citizens. Also, the U.S. government under Presidents Polk, Pierce, and Buchanan offered Spain millions for Cuba but to no avail.

The United States only made one territorial gain from the presidencies of Taylor to Lincoln—the Gadsden Purchase—which the Senate reduced before approving it, making it the first time in U.S. history that the Senate reduced the amount of land obtained by the United States in treaty negotiations. The antagonism to Mr. Gadsden's purchase ushered in an era that was very hostile to new territorial acquisitions that stretched to the mid-1890s. This antagonism to territorial expansion was strengthened with the events of the Civil War, Reconstruction, the growth of industrialization, and the changing attitudes on race. While the country turned its back on territorial expansion, it increasingly embraced commercial expansion as a means to further the natural interest of the country. The interest in the growth of commercial possibilities dates from colonial times and found expression in the treaties of commerce Franklin and other U.S. diplomats negotiated with many European countries. Although U.S. policy makers were sure that their country's goods would be very competitive in an open market and that trade with Europe would continue to be of major importance to the United States, statesmen and citizens also looked to the east for markets yet undeveloped by U.S. merchants. As early as 1780, the *Empress of China* sailed for the Far East and returned to the United States with a handsome profit.

As the United States grew westward territorially, its interest in Asia grew commercially. Just as the territorial acquisition of Pacific Coast territories was a goal in its own terms and as a means to an expanded U.S. role in the Asian trade, so, too, was U.S. control of Hawaii seen to be a goal in itself and as a means to expand U.S. trade with Asia. In fact, U.S. interest in Hawaii as a springboard for increased trade with Asia, especially China, developed earlier than such an interest in California. More U.S. citizens lived in Hawaii than California in the 1830s, for example. The concerns that the United States had about potential British expansion in North America were reinforced by the concerns that U.S. statesmen had about British and French penetration of the Pacific, which were perceived to threaten U.S. trade with the Pacific and Asia. The Tyler Doctrine was enunciated in response to the French annexation of Tahiti and the beginning of British control in Hong Kong. Perry's expedition to Japan was designed to counter British moves in China. Even the U.S. purchase of Alaska from Russia in 1867 was seen to have a commercial component. Besides removing another European power from the North American continent, many saw the purchase as a way of increasing U.S. trade with China. (President John Tyler's diplomatic note to Britain and France, warning that the annexation of Hawaii by either would be considered a hostile act toward the United States, is even more remarkable considering that the U.S. territorial boundaries in the west bordered Mexico's province of Texas and the Continental Divide. In short, U.S. territory in its northwest ended hundreds of miles from the Pacific, and U.S. territory in its southwest ended over a thousand miles from the Pacific.)

The greatest systematic exponent of a commercial diplomacy for the United States during the Gilded Age was James G. Blaine. Blaine, having witnessed as a member of Congress Seward's failed attempts at acquiring the territories of or naval bases in the Dominican Republic, the Virgin Islands, Haiti, and Samoa and President Ulysses S. Grant's failure to obtain Samaná Bay in the Dominican Republic, developed a vision of commercial expansion aided by active government sponsorship domestically and by an active diplomacy internationally. For Blaine, trade didn't follow the flag, the flag followed trade. Especially in his Pan-American initiative, Blaine called for improving transportation and communication links between countries, the exchange of commercial information, and the establishment of reciprocal trade agreements, all designed to open areas to U.S. trade.

The concern for new commercial outlets for U.S. products grew as a second great wave of imperialism swept the globe. From roughly 1871 to 1902, all the Pacific, all of Africa save Ethiopia and Liberia, and all of Asia were colonized, save the Ottoman Empire, the Himalayan states, Siam, and Japan, whereas China and Persia were divided into spheres of influence. Coupled with the concern this territorial division of the world would have on U.S. trade was the stark realization that the American frontier had closed in 1890. What had been a political and economic safety valve no longer existed, and so the question became more urgent of where the United States would find new markets for the increasing number of goods produced by its industrial economy. The long recession of the mid-1870s to mid-1890s made the discussions on trade vitally important to both foreign and domestic policy. Issues of trade and tariffs were major campaign issues during the 1880s and 1890s.

A revolt close to the United States in Cuba in the 1890s helped tie the consensus on the need for commercial expansion to what had been the discredited idea of territorial acquisition. President William McKinley implemented policies that led to the United States jumping into the Great Game of colonial expansion and control, which it followed for decades. If McKinley saw the end of war in Cuba as a prerequisite to economic recovery at home, he appears to have seen Hawaii, Guam, and the Philippines as necessary to the continued, if not perpetual, economic prosperity of America by increasing U.S. access to the China market.

The U.S. acquisition of Puerto Rico and the establishment of its protectorate over Cuba laid the foundations for the transformation of the Caribbean into an American lake. From Theodore Roosevelt to Herbert Hoover, the Dominican Republic, Guatemala, Haiti, Honduras, Nicaragua, and Panama were ruled either directly by the United States or became U.S. protectorates, while Mexico was subject to U.S. military intervention during its revolution in 1915 and 1916–1917, all in the name of the Roosevelt Corollary to the Monroe Doctrine, under which the United States claimed the right to exercise international police powers in the Western Hemisphere.

President Woodrow Wilson's foreign policies continued those laid down by his Republican predecessors and expanded the meaning of Roosevelt's corollary. Wilson was convinced that continued U.S. prosperity was dependent on U.S. access to overseas markets, be they in Latin America or Europe. Thus, Wilson used the U.S. military in the Caribbean basin to ensure the safety of U.S. investments. Some have argued that Wilson used the U.S. military for the same reasons in Europe in 1917–1918. As it progressed, the Great War was seen to threaten the European balance of power. The victorious side, whichever it was, would be able to dominate the continent and close the European market to U.S. goods. In addition, the U.S. economy, which had been in a recession in 1914, rebounded due to war orders from the Allies, and in 1916, the president lifted the ban on private bank loans to belligerents, which overwhelmingly helped the Allies. Through these war orders and loans U.S. prosperity became tied to the success of the Allies in the Great War.

The resolutions adopted by the Allied countries of Belgium, Britain, France, Italy, Japan, and Russia at the Paris Economic Conference of 1916, if implemented, threatened to close Europe and Japan off from not only German trade but also from U.S. trade as well. Wilson's response was to deepen the involvement of the United States on the side of the Allies by having the country enter the war on their side. Wilson's decision to have the United States enter the war reduced the possibility that the Paris resolutions would apply to the United States after the war and legitimized Wilson's articulation of U.S. war aims, the Fourteen Points, which were antithetical to and which he hoped would supersede the economic nationalism of the Paris conference.

As is well known, U.S. participation in the Great War and the resulting peace soured mass and elite opinion alike in the country and ushered in an era in which the United States attempted to liquidate its overseas responsibilities, even in such traditional areas of concern as the Caribbean basin. President Hoover and his secretary of state, Henry L. Stimson, refused to send troops to Latin America during the economic upheavals caused by the Great Depression. President Franklin D. Roosevelt continued and deepened Hoover's "Good Neighbor" policy by removing U.S. troops from Haiti, abrogating the Platt Amendment, which permitted U.S. intervention in Cuba, and accepting the principle of nonintervention.

Yet, Roosevelt's policy toward Japan was part of a different mind-set and forms a link in a steel chain stretching back at the least to Secretary of State John Hay. By Hay's Open Door diplomatic notes, the United States refused to recognize spheres of influence in China and further committed itself diplomatically to the independence and territorial borders of China to protect future and potential U.S. interests in China, which were primarily commercial.

Working within the framework of the vagueness of the Open Door, President Theodore Roosevelt, playing the mediator in 1905, blocked the Japanese claims for a large indemnity and territorial concessions in Manchuria from Russia. Again in 1919, U.S. officials interfered with Japanese claims for German territory in the Pacific during the Versailles Conference and set naval tonnage limits on the Japanese Navy at the Washington Naval Disarmament Conference of 1922. The great link, however, between the Open Door and Pearl Harbor was the Stimson Doctrine, named after Hoover's Secretary of State, Henry L. Stimson. Japan had invaded Manchuria in 1931 and set up the satellite state of Manchukuo. The territory, rich in resources that Japan needed and a buffer against Soviet Communism, was considered a vital Japanese interest. Arguing that the Japanese action violated the Washington Conference treaties, the Open Door agreements, and the Kellogg–Briand Pact, Stimson announced in January 1932 that the United States refused to recognize Manchukuo or any other arrangements concerning China imposed by force.

The basis of U.S. policy toward Japan may be understood in two different ways. First, the United States viewed itself as playing the role of the balancer in the northwest Pacific, similar to the role played by Britain in Europe, without, though, committing any substantial resources to support that balancer effort. In that light, U.S. efforts to limit Japanese power were seen to be a "necessary" consequence of the chaos in China and the then perceived Russian/Soviet weaknesses in East Asia. Second, the United States appeared to be able to view Japan only in terms of it being a junior partner to the United States in the latter's efforts to regulate the affairs of East Asia. In that light, the United States seemed to want East Asia, particularly China, to be under the influence of the United States and for Japan to be content with the role the United States was willing to concede to it there. One could argue that in its treatment of Japan, the United States displayed the worst characteristics of both views, exhibiting the condescension a superior feels toward a subordinate and expressing the hostility that a power feels toward a potential rival.

With Stimson's appointment as secretary of war in 1940, the U.S. commitment to the Stimson Doctrine deepened, leading the country to impose economic sanctions on Japan. The Japanese government, facing the choice, from its point of view, of subordinating itself to the United States or maintaining its independent foreign policy, chose the latter, and as is well known, attacked the United States in December 1941. The Japanese–United States war became a German–United States war within days of December 7, when Germany declared war on the United States.

The German decision for war against the United States allowed Roosevelt to continue his strategy of working to defeat Hitler before defeating Japan. For Roosevelt, a German defeat of Britain and the Soviet Union would put the United States on the defensive globally, with no important allies, thereby increasing the risk for the United States of losing a future war against the combined forces of the Third Reich and the Japanese Empire.

Due to Roosevelt's concern that an isolationist backlash could occur after World War II similar to what occurred after World War I, Roosevelt chose to limit U.S. battlefield deaths (for every U.S. citizen who died in the war, 53 Russians died, for example) by not implementing a containment-like strategy against the Soviet Union during World War II. Such a strategy would have necessitated increasing the numbers of U.S. divisions from the 90 actually organized to the 215 that had been originally estimated as the number required to defeat Germany.

Roosevelt rejected the unilateralism of past U.S. foreign policy and embraced multilateralism during World War II through such mechanisms as the creation of a combined Allied command structure for Operation Overlord, the United States and British conferences leading to the establishment of the United Nations and its associated agencies, and the Bretton Woods agreement establishing an international monetary regime that lasted for decades. This multilateralism launched by Roosevelt was continued and increasingly institutionalized by his successor, Harry S Truman, but decoupled from the Grand Alliance of the Second World War and used instead to bind countries together into what became known as the Western Alliance, an alliance opposed to any expansion of Soviet power or influence. This new U.S. strategy of containment was first announced publicly as the Truman Doctrine in March 1947. Containment continued as the basis of U.S. foreign policy throughout the history of the Cold War.

Roosevelt and Truman together laid down the foundation for the multilateralism, which became the dominant approach to U.S. foreign policy after World War II with such initiatives as the United Nations, the International Monetary Fund, the World Bank, the North Atlantic Treaty Organization, the General Agreement on Tariffs and Trade, and the Marshall Plan, which itself substantially aided the economic integration efforts culminating with the European Community. Although a few post–World War II presidents tended to be more unilateralist, Richard Nixon and Ronald Reagan come to mind, in the main postwar U.S. policy makers embraced multilateralism with the same fervor that their predecessors had embraced unilateralism.

The United States used four general policies to achieve the goals set by its containment strategy. The policies were bilateral and multilateral military alliances, covert action, direct use of U.S. troops, and economic aid. Under the first policy, for example, the United States helped establish the Rio Pact in 1947, the North Atlantic Treaty Alliance in 1949, the Japanese–United States Defense Treaty in 1950, the Southeast Asian Treaty Organization in 1954, and the Baghdad Pact in 1955. It soon became apparent, though, that regional military collective security agreements would not themselves provide the security demanded by U.S. policy makers.

Although there is some evidence of covert U.S. interference in French and Italian elections in the mid and late 1940s, an early example of covert action that most historians discuss is the Central Intelligence Agency covert operation that aided the overthrow of Iranian Prime Minister Mohammed Mossadegh and restored the Shah to the throne. Covert operations followed in Guatemala in 1954, Cuba at least in 1960 and 1961, and in Chile from 1970–1973. The longest and strangest such operation was the overt covert action against Nicaragua from 1981 to 1990.

The direct use of U.S. troops has, of course, generated the most amount of concern and interest. In the name of the United Nations, Truman sent U.S. troops to Korea in response to the North Korean invasion of South Korea in June 1950. Although the war destroyed Truman's presidency, his successors also made the decision to send U.S. troops into conflict or potential conflict situations, such as President Dwight D. Eisenhower in Lebanon in 1958, President John F. Kennedy in Vietnam from 1961 to 1963, Lyndon B. Johnson in the Dominican Republic in

1965 and, most importantly and tragically, in Vietnam from 1963 to 1968, and President Richard Nixon in Cambodia in 1970. During the last decade of the Cold War, Reagan sent U.S. troops to Lebanon and Grenada, and President George H. W. Bush ordered two U.S. military operations, one to Panama in 1989 and the second to Iraq in 1991.

Except for the Marshall Plan, most post–World War II U.S. leaders have been opposed to multilateral aid programs, preferring instead economic bilateral aid programs. Also, nonmilitary economic aid from the United States usually has flowed to those countries that were also the major recipients of U.S. military assistance. After the disbursement of the Marshall Plan monies, South Vietnam, Cambodia, and Laos became the largest recipients of U.S. aid up the mid-1970s. From roughly the mid-1970s until today, countries in North Africa and the Middle East, such as Egypt and Israel, have been major recipients of U.S. aid, whereas Saudi Arabia and Iran were major buyers of U.S. arms from the 1950s to the 1990s for the former and from the 1950s to the 1970s for the latter. Occasionally, the United States has reluctantly provided other regions with economic aid, such as Latin America with the establishment of the Inter-American Development Bank in 1959 and the operation of the Alliance for Progress from 1961 to 1966, but such efforts have not proved to be substantial in the long run.

The administration of President George H. W. Bush straddles the last years of the Cold War and the first years of the post-Soviet era. The Bush administration executed a brilliant diplomacy in its construction of the global coalition that forcibly removed Iraq from Kuwait in 1990–1991, and it was able to convince the Soviet Union to accept a reunited Germany in NATO in 1990 in exchange for a promise of economic aid. A year later Bush prudently handled the hard-line communist-led coup attempt against Gorbachev by not ordering any sudden military moves that could be perceived as threatening the Soviet Union. Within months of the failed coup, the Soviet Union ceased to exist, and Boris Yeltsen became the president of an independent Russia. The demise of the Soviet Union in 1991 literally presented the United States with an unprecedented opportunity. Never before had any country held such global power without also facing rivals of substantial strength. The first U.S. president elected in the post–Cold War world, William J. Clinton, launched policies that established U.S. interests in regions heretofore not seen to be critical to U.S. national security. Clinton announced his support for NATO expansion in 1994, and the U.S. Senate in 1998 approved the Czech Republic, Hungary, and Poland entering the alliance. Also, Clinton authorized U.S. troop deployment to Bosnia from 1996 on and also authorized bombing raids against Yugoslavia.

Of more import were Clinton's decisions supporting many of the new countries of the southern littoral of the old Soviet Union. In 1994, the Ukraine relinquished its nuclear arsenal while the United States promised to uphold Ukrainian independence and paid Kazakhstan for its nuclear weapons grade fuel. Further, the United States entered into a train and equip program with Georgia in 1995 whereby the U.S. military agreed to train and arm the Georgian army. These actions have not gone unnoticed because the Russian government since Yeltsen has viewed the former Soviet republics as making up its "near abroad" and lying within a Russian sphere of influence.

The current administration of George W. Bush has deepened U.S. interests in southwest Asia and the southern littoral of the former Soviet Union. The administration has also embarked on unilateral means by which to achieve its foreign policy objectives. After the evidence was made clear that al-Qaeda used Afghanistan as a base of operations and the Afghan government refused to aid in the apprehension of those who had been part of the terrorist attacks on the United States on September 11, 2001, the U.S. government, supported by the world, invaded Afghanistan in 2002. To aid its military operations, the Bush administration secured a military base in Turkmenistan and deployed troops to Pakistan in the same year. Later in 2002, in exchange for $500 million, the U.S. government secured a military base in Uzbekistan. Crowning the projection of U.S. power into greater southwest Asia was the U.S. invasion of Iraq in 2003. Despite the opposition of such countries as France, Germany, and Russia and the lack of any credible evidence that the Iraqi government of Saddam Hussein had had any role in the terrorist attacks against the United States on September 11, 2001, or had stockpiles of weapons of mass destruction, the United States invaded Iraq to destroy the government of Hussein.

The U.S. use of force is troubling for many reasons. First, it is the first time in U.S. history that the U.S. government has invaded a country on the basis of the doctrine of preemptive war. By this same logic, the United States could be seen to have cause to invade North Korea or Iran, for example. Second, the military occupation of Iraq in the heart of the Middle East reinforces the concern that the Bush administration is planning on having the United States maintain a permanent military presence in that region. The United States is now militarily occupying Iraq and Afghanistan, has military bases in Turkmenistan and Uzbekistan, has pledged to defend the independence of the Ukraine, is training the Georgian army, and has troops in Georgia and Pakistan. Southwest Asia and the Black Sea littoral are beginning to look like the Caribbean basin when Wilson was president. And third, because the official reasons for the invasion of Iraq have been proved false, there is a growing cynicism that the real reasons for the invasion may have had more to do with oil than weapons of mass destruction and with establishing a precedent for a U.S. right to exercise unilaterally an international police power globally.

It is understandable that the countries who had been the Great Powers of Europe are uneasy and distrustful of a country that asserts its right to project its power anywhere in the world, regardless of how many countries are against such a deployment of power. There has been much talk in the United States about the projection of U.S. power globally, but too little discussion domestically about how the United States can establish its leadership in the world. For the United States to work with its allies to take their concerns into account is not weakness. Diplomacy is not insisting that all other countries agree to a policy that has been decided on unilaterally but working together to create honorable compromises that serve the interests of all the allies. To order is not to lead, and power is not authority.

The argument that justice requires the equality of power to be a factor in international relations was made long ago and recorded by Thucydides in the Melian Dialogue. If the Athenians were correct that the strong do what they will and the weak accept what they must, the Melians spoke a greater wisdom in their response to the Athenians. The Melians cautioned that it was dangerous to destroy a principle that aided the general good, namely that justice should check the demands of power, for this principle affected all countries, and if the Athenians ignored it, then they could make no appeal to it when they faced a stronger enemy. When that future time came, they would be visited by the most terrible vengeance and be made an example to all the world. The people of the United States need to ask what example they want their country to set—an example of unrestrained power or an example of equity and justice.

BIBLIOGRAPHICAL ESSAY

It's difficult to do justice in a bibliographic essay to all the literature that deals broadly with the main issues in U.S. diplomatic history. This essay will provide a brief and chronological overview of works that have dealt with important, long-standing issues and themes in the area of U.S. foreign policy. For a comprehensive review of U.S. foreign relations issues, please consult Bruce W. Jentleson and Thomas G. Paterson, *Encyclopedia of U.S. Foreign Relations* (1997); and Richard Dean Burns (ed.), *Guide to American Foreign Relations Since 1700* (1983).

For the colonial, revolutionary, and confederation periods, please see Felix Gilbert, *The Beginning of American Diplomacy: To the Farewell Address* (1965); Lawrence S. Kaplan, *Colonies into Nation* (1972); Walter LaFeber, "Foreign Policies of a New Nation," in William A. Williams (ed.), *From Colony to Empire* (1972); Max Savelle, *The Origins of American Diplomacy* (1967); Richard W. Van Alstyne, *The Rising American Empire* (1960); Samuel Flagg Bemis, *The Diplomacy of the American Revolution* (1957); Jonathan R. Dull, *A Diplomatic History of the American Revolution* (1985); Bradford Perkins, *The Creation of a Republican Empire 1776–1865* (1993); Reginald C. Stuart, *United States Expansionism and British North America, 1775–1871* (1988); Richard W. Van Alstyne, *Empire and Independence* (1965); and Gerald Stourzh's excellent *Benjamin Franklin and American Foreign Policy* (1969).

General histories of the United States from Washington to Madison include Reginald Horsman, *The Diplomacy of the New Republic, 1776–1815* (1985); Daniel G. Lang, *Foreign Policy in the Early Republic* (1985); Perkins (cited earlier), *Republican Empire* (1993); Jacques Portes (ed.), *Europe and America: Criss-Crossing Perspectives, 1788–1848* (1987); and Paul A. Varg, *Foreign Policies of the Founding Fathers* (1970). For the issues of the 1790s, please consult Joseph Charles, *The Origins of the American Party System* (1956); and Glenn A. Phelps, *George Washington and American Constitutionalism* (1993).

For Jefferson, Madison, the War of 1812, and the Treaty of Ghent, read Lance Banning, *The Jeffersonian Persuasion* (1978); Alexander De Conde, *This Affair of Louisiana* (1976); Malcolm J. Rohrbough, *The Trans-Appalachian Frontier* (1978); Robert W. Tucker and David C. Henrickson, *Empire of Liberty* (1990); Clifford L. Egan, *Neither Peace nor War: Franco-American Relations, 1803–1812* (1983); Reginald Horseman, *The Causes of the War of 1812* (1962); Julius Pratt, *Expansionists of 1812* (1925); Steven Watts, *The Republic Reborn: War and the Making of a Liberal America, 1790–1820* (1987); Harrison Bird, *War for the West, 1790–1813* (1971); Fred L. Engleman, *The Peace of Christmas Eve* (1962); Donald R. Hickey, *The War of 1812* (1989); Jonathan Goldstein, *Philadelphia and the China Trade 1682–1846* (1978); and Frank L. Owsley, Jr., and Gene A. Smith, *Filibusters and Expansionists* (1997).

For Manifest Destiny and expansionism from Monroe to Polk generally, please see George Dangerfield, *The Awakening of American Nationalism, 1815–1828* (1965); Norman Graebner (ed.), *Manifest Destiny* (1968); Howard Kushner, *Conflict on the Northwest Coast: America–Russian Rivalry in the Pacific Northwest, 1790–1867* (1975); Fredrick Merk, *Manifest Destiny and Mission in American History* (1963); Christopher Morris and Sam W. Haynes (eds.), *Manifest Destiny and Empire* (1997); Anders Stephanson, *Manifest Destiny* (1995); William Earl Weeks, *Building the Continental Empire* (1996); and Albert Weinberg, *Manifest Destiny* (1935).

Monroe, John Quincy Adams, and the range of foreign policy issues during Monroe's administration are covered in Samuel Flagg Bemis, *John Quincy Adams and the Foundations of American Foreign Policy* (1949); Walter LaFeber (ed.), *John Quincy Adams and American Continental Empire* (1965); William E. Weeks, *John Quincy Adams and American Global Empire* (1992); Philip C. Brooks, *Diplomacy and the Borderlands* (1939); Lester D. Langley, *The Americas in the Age of Revolution* (1996); Ernest R. May, *The Making of the Monroe Doctrine* (1975); Dexter Perkins, *The Monroe Doctrine 1823–1826* (1927), and *A History of the Monroe Doctrine* (1963).

Issues dealing with Anglo–U.S. relations, California, Texas, and the Mexican War are covered in Ray A. Billington, *Far Western Frontier* (1956); Norman A. Graebner, *Empire on the Pacific* (1955); Wilbur D. Jones, *The American Problem in British Diplomacy, 1841–1861* (1974); Frederick Merk, *The Oregon Question* (1967); Charles G. Sellers, *James K. Polk, Continentalist, 1843–1846* (1966); Richard Griswold del Castillo, *The Treaty of Guadalupe Hidalgo* (1990); Robert W. Johannsen, *To the Halls of Montezuma* (1985); David M. Fletcher, *The Diplomacy of Annexation* (1973); and John H. Schroeder, *Mr. Polk's War* (1973).

The dominant diplomatic and political issues and leaders of the 1850s are covered in Frederick M. Binder, *James Buchanan and the American Empire* (1994); Charles H. Brown, *Agents of Manifest Destiny* (1980); William H. Freehling, *The Road to Disunion* (1990); Michael H. Hunt, *Ideology and U.S. Foreign Policy* (1987); Lester D. Langley, *Struggle for the American Mediterranean: United States-European Rivalry in the Gulf-Caribbean 1776–1894* (1976); Robert E. May, *The Southern Dream of a Caribbean Empire, 1854–1861* (1973); Dexter Perkins, *The Monroe Doctrine, 1826–1867* (1933); Thomas B. Schoonover, *The United States in Central America* (1991); James T. Wall, *Manifest Destiny Denied* (1982); and Ernest N. Paolino, *The Foundations of the American Empire* (1973).

For the leaders and the diplomatic issues of the U.S. Civil War, please refer to Kinley J. Brauer, "The Slavery Problem in the Diplomacy of the American Civil War," *Pacific Historical Review* (1977); Lynn M. Case and Warren F. Spencer, *The United States and France* (1970); David P. Cook, *The North, the South and the Powers, 1861–1865* (1974); Norman B. Ferris, *The Trent Affair* (1977), and *Desperate Diplomacy: William H. Seward's Foreign Policy, 1861* (1975); Charles M. Hubbard, *The Burden of Confederate Diplomacy* (1998); Brian Jenkins, *Britain and the War for the Union* (1974–1980); Howard Jones, *Union in Peril: The Crisis over British Intervention in the Civil War* (1992); Robert E. May (ed.), *The Union, the Confederacy and the Atlantic Rim* (1995); James M. McPherson, *Battle Cry of Freedom* (1989); Frank L. and Harriet Owsley, *King Cotton Diplomacy* (1959).

For the period from Andrew Johnson to Benjamin Harrison generally, please see Robert L. Beisner, *From the Old Diplomacy to the New* (1986); Charles S. Campbell, *The Transformation of American Foreign Relations 1865–1900* (1976); John A. S. Grenville and George B. Young, *Politics, Strategy and American Diplomacy* (1967); David Healy, *U.S. Expansionism* (1970); Walter LaFeber, *The American Search for Opportunity, 1865–1913* (1993), and *The New Empire*, new ed. (1998); Milton

Plesur, *America's Outward Thrust* (1971); Robert Wiebe, *The Search for Order* (1967); and William A. Williams, *The Rise of the Modern American Empire* (1969).

For economic issues and U.S.–British relations, consult David Pletcher, *The Diplomacy of Trade and Investment* (1998); Tom Terrill, *The Tariff, Politics and American Foreign Policy, 1874–1901* (1973); Harold and Margaret Sprout, *The Rise of American Naval Power, 1776–1918* (1966); Kenneth Bourne, *Britain and the Balance of Power in North America, 1815–1908* (1967); and Edward P. Crapol, *America for Americans: Economic Nationalism and Anglophobia* (1973). For relations with Latin America, Hawaii, and East Asia, please refer to Jules Davids, *American Political and Economic Penetration of Mexico 1877–1920* (1976); Luis Martinez-Fernandez, *Torn Between Empires* (1994); Dexter Perkins, *The Monroe Doctrine, 1867–1907* (1937); Thomas D. Schoonover, *The United States in Central America, 1860–1911* (1991); Merze Tate, *The United States and the Hawaiian Kingdom* (1965); Jerome Ch'en, *China and the West* (1979); Michael Hunt, *The Making of a Special Relationship* (1983); and Thomas A. Tweed, *The American Encounter with Buddhism, 1844–1912* (1992).

There are many fine works that discuss the issues that arose from the New Imperialism. Please consult Richard Challener, *Admirals, Generals, and American Foreign Policy, 1898–1914* (1973); Ernest R. May, *Imperial Democracy* (1961); Louis A. Perez, Jr., *The War of 1898* (1998); Julius Pratt, *Expansionist of 1898* (1938); Howard K. Beale, *Theodore Roosevelt and the Rise of America to World Power* (1956); William C. Widenor, *Henry Cabot Lodge and the Search for an American Foreign Policy* (1980); E. Berkeley Tompkins, *Anti-Imperialism in the United States* (1970); Thomas McCormick, *China Market* (1967); R. G. Neale, *Great Britain and United States Expansionism, 1800–1900* (1966); and Joseph Smith, *Illusions of Conflict: Anglo-American Diplomacy Toward Latin America, 1865–1896* (1979).

Progressive era diplomacy, the Great War, and the debates over peace are covered in William H. Becker, *The Dynamics of Business-Government Relations: Industry and Exports, 1893–1921* (1982); Lester H. Brune, *The Origins of American Security Policy* (1981); Robert C. Hilderbrand, *Power and the People: Executive Management of Public Opinion in Foreign Affairs, 1897–1921* (1981); see Challener and Beale (listed earlier); Frederick S. Calhoun, *Power and Principle: Armed Intervention in Wilsonian Foreign Policy* (1986); Mark T. Gilderhus, *Pan American Visions* (1986); Warren G. Kneer, *Great Britain and the Caribbean, 1901–1913* (1975); Lester Langley, *The United States and the Caribbean, 1901–1970* (1980); Thomas Schoonover, *The United States in Central America, 1860–1911* (1991); John M. Hart, *Revolutionary Mexico* (1988); Alan Knight, *U.S.–Mexican Relations, 1910–1940* (1987); Dennis L. Noble, *The Eagle and the Dragon* (1990); Holger H. Herwig, *Politics of Frustration: The United States in German Naval Planning, 1889–1941* (1976); Ellis W. Hawley, *The Great War and the Search for a Modern Order* (1992); Bernadotte E. Schmitt and Harold C. Vedeler, *The World in a Crucible, 1914–1919* (1984); Kendrick A. Clements, *The Presidency of Woodrow Wilson* (1990); Edward H. Buehrig (ed.), *Wilson's Foreign Policy in Perspective* (1957); David M. Esposito, *The Legacy of Woodrow Wilson: America War Aims in World War I* (1996); Lloyd E. Ambrosius, *Woodrow Wilson and the American Diplomatic Tradition* (1987); Keith Nelson, *Victors Divided: America and the Allies in Germany, 1918–1923* (1973); Stuart I. Rochester, *American Liberal Disillusionment in the Wake of World War I* (1977); John Lewis Gaddis, *Russia, the Soviet Union and the United States* (1990); Manfed F. Boemeke, et al. (eds.), *The*

Treaty of Versailles (1998); and Arthur S. Link (ed.), *Woodrow Wilson and a Revolutionary World, 1913–1921* (1982).

For U.S. foreign policy from Harding to Franklin D. Roosevelt up to 1939, please consult Selig Adler, *The Isolationist Impulse* (1957); Justus D. Doenecke and John E. Wilz. *From Isolation to War* (1991); Robert Ferrell, *American Diplomacy in the Great Depression* (1957); Arnold Offner, *The Origins of the Second World War* (1975); Raymond Sontag, *A Broken World, 1919–1939* (1971); Robert Dallek, *Franklin Roosevelt and American Foreign Policy, 1933–1945* (1979); Willard Range, *Franklin D. Roosevelt's World Order* (1959); Derek H. Aldcroft, *From Versailles to Wall Street, 1920–1929* (1977); Charles P. Kindleberger, *The World in Depression, 1929–1939* (1986); Joan Hoff Wilson, *American Business and Foreign Policy, 1920–1933* (1971); Warren I. Cohen, *The American Revisionists* (1967); James V. Compton, *The Swastika and the Eagle* (1967); Brian McKercher (ed.), *Anglo-American Relations in the 1920s* (1991); Wolfgang Mommsen and Lothar Kettenacker, *The Fascist Challenge and the Policy of Appeasement* (1983); Arnold Offner, *American Appeasement* (1983); Edward Bennett, *Franklin D. Roosevelt and the Search for Security* (1985); John Lewis Gaddis, *Russia, the Soviet Union and the United States* (1990); George F. Kennan, *Russia and the West Under Lenin and Stalin* (1960); Cole Blasier, *The Hovering Giant* (1976); Alton Frye, *Nazi Germany and the American Hemisphere, 1933–1941* (1967); Irwin F. Gellman, *Good Neighbor Diplomacy* (1995); Walter LaFeber, *Inevitable Revolutions* (1993), also very helpful for U.S. policy toward Central America throughout the post–World War II era; and Robert F. Smith, *The United States and Revolutionary Nationalism in Mexico* (1972).

The following works are helpful to understanding United States and World War II: Silvo Hietanen (ed.), *The Road to War* (1993); David Reynolds, *The Creation of the Anglo-American Alliance, 1937–1941* (1982); D. C. Watt, *How War Came* (1989); Akira Iriye, *The Origins of the Second World War in Asia and the Pacific* (1987); Hilary Conroy and Harry Wray (eds.), *Pearl Harbor Revisited* (1994); Youli Sun, *China and the Origins of the Pacific War* (1993); Robert Beitzell, *The Uneasy Alliance* (1972); Robert Devine, *Roosevelt and World War II* (1969); Gary R. Hess, *The United States at War, 1941–1945* (1986); Gaddis Smith, *American Diplomacy During the Second World War* (1978); John J. Sbrega, *Anglo-American Relations and Colonialism in East Asia* (1994); David Rock (ed.), *Latin America in the 1940s* (1994); and Verne Newton (ed.), *FDR and the Holocaust* (1995).

For overviews of the developments in post–World War II foreign policy and the evolution of the Cold War, please read Douglas Brinkley, *Rise to Globalism* (1997); John Lewis Gaddis, *The Long Peace* (1987), *The United States and Origins of the Cold War* (1982), *Strategies of Containment* (1982), and *We Now Know* (1997); Walter LaFeber, *America, Russia and the Cold War* (1993); Geir Lundestad, *The American "Empire"* (1990); Kendrick A. Clements (ed.), *James F. Byrnes and the Origins of the Cold War* (1982); John Kent, *British Imperial Strategy and the Origins of the Cold War* (1993); Michael J. Hogan, *The Marshall Plan* (1999); Alan S. Milward, *The Reconstruction of Western Europe, 1945–51* (1984); Lawrence S. Kaplan, *The Long Entanglement: NATO's First Fifty Years* (1999); Akira Iriye and Warren Cohen (eds.), *American, Chinese and Japanese Perspectives on Wartime Asia, 1931–1949* (1990); Yonosuke Nagai and Akira Iriye (eds.), *The Origins of the Cold War in Asia* (1977).

For the Korean War and U.S. foreign policy under Eisenhower, please consult Robert M. Blum, *Drawing the Line* (1982); Rosemary Foot, *The Wrong War* (1985);

Peter Lowe, *The Origins of the Korean War* (1997); H.W. Brands, Jr., *Cold Warriors* (1988); Robert Devine, *Eisenhower and the Cold War* (1981); William B. Picket, *Dwight David Eisenhower and American Power* (1995); Richard H. Immerman (ed.), *John Foster Dulles and the Diplomacy of the Cold War* (1990); Thomas Risse-Kappan, *Cooperation Among Democracies: The European Influence on U.S. Foreign Policy* (1995); Jerome H. Kahan, *Security in the Nuclear Age* (1975); Roger Buckley, *U.S.–Japan Alliance Diplomacy, 1945–1990* (1992); Gordon H. Chang, *Friends and Enemies: The United States, China, and the Soviet Union, 1948–1972* (1990); Melvin Gurtov, *The United States Against the Third World* (1974); George Lenewzowski, *The Middle East in World Affairs* (1980); Stephen G. Rabe, *Eisenhower and Latin America* (1988); and Bryce Wood, *The Dismantling of the Good Neighbor Policy* (1985).

The Kennedy, Johnson, and Nixon administrations and Vietnam are ably discussed in Michael Beschloss, *The Crisis Years* (1991); Douglas Brinkley and Richard T. Griffiths (eds.), *John F. Kennedy and Europe* (1999); Seymour Hersch, *The Other Side of Camelot* (1997); Timothy P. Maga, *John F. Kennedy and New Frontier Diplomacy* (1994); H. W. Brands, *The Wages of Globalism*, (1995); and (ed.), *The Foreign Policies of Lyndon Johnson* (1999); Paul K. Conkin, *Big Daddy From the Pedernales* (1986); Robert Dallek, *Flawed Giant* (1998); Larry Berman, *Planning a Tragedy* (1982); and *Lyndon Johnson's War* (1989); William J Duiker, *U.S. Containment Policy and the Conflict in Indochina* (1994); Frances Fitzgerald, *Fire in the Lake* (1972); Michael Genovese, *The Nixon Presidency* (1990); Joan Hoff, *Nixon Reconsidered* (1994); David Halberstam, *The Best and the Brightest* (1972); Jeffrey Kimball, *Nixon's Vietnam War* (1998); Gabriel Kolko, *Anatomy of a War* (1985); *The Pentagon Papers: The Defense Department History of the United States Decisionmaking on Vietnam* (the Gravel Edition) (1971); James R. Rosenau, *American Leadership in World Affairs: Vietnam and the Breakdown of Consensus* (1984); and Marilyn B. Young, *The Vietnam Wars, 1945–1990* (1990).

For Latin America and the Cuban Missile Crisis, please consult Graham Allison and Philip Zelikow, *Essence of Decision: Explaining the Cuban Missile Crisis* (1999); Herbert Dinerstein, *The Making of a Missile Crisis* (1976); Jerome Levinson and Juan de Onis, *The Alliance That Lost Its Way* (1970); James A. Nathan (ed.), *The Cuban Missile Crisis Revisited* (1992); and L. Ronald Scheman (ed.), *The Alliance for Progress* (1988); and Lars Schultz, *Beneath the United States* (1998).

Soviet–United States relations, détente, and the last years of the Cold War are analyzed in Richard Barnet, *The Giants* (1977); Michael B. Froman, *The Development of the Idea of Détente* (1992); Alexander L. George, et al. (eds.), *Managing U.S.–Soviet Rivalry* (1982); Richard W. Stevenson, *The Rise and Fall of Détente* (1985); Gene T. Hsiao (ed.), *Sino–American Détente and Its Policy Implications* (1974); Raymond L. Garthoff, *Détente and Confrontation* (1985); Robert C. Gray and Stanley J. Michalak, Jr. (eds.), *American Foreign Policy Since Détente* (1984); A. Glenn Mower, *Human Rights and American Foreign Policy* (1987); Jerel A. Rosati, *The Carter Administration's Quest for Global Community* (1987); Coral Bell, *The Reagan Paradox* (1989); Robert Dallek, *Ronald Reagan* (1984); Beth A. Fischer, *The Reagan Reversal* (1997); Haynes Johnson, *Sleepwalking Through History* (1991); Seweryn Bialer and Michael Mandelbaum (eds.), *Gorbachev's Russia and American Foreign Policy* (1988); Michael Mandelbaum and Strobe Talbot, *Reagan and Gorbachev* (1987); Steven K. Smith and Douglas A. Wertman, *U.S.–Western European Relations*

During the Reagan Years (1992); Daniel P. Bolger, *Americans at War 1975–1986* (1988); and Walter LaFeber, *Inevitable Revolutions* (1993).

For overviews and works on the post–Cold War world, please consult James Chace and Caleb Carr, *American Invulnerable: The Quest for Absolute Security from 1812 to Star Wars* (1988); J. Gary Clifford and Kenneth J. Hagen, *American Foreign Policy: A History, 1900 to the Present* (1988); George F. Kennan, *American Diplomacy: 1900–1950* (1952); Don Oberdorfer, *From the Cold War to a New Era* (1998); Randall B. Ripley and James M. Lindsay (eds.), *U.S. Foreign Policy After the Cold War* (1997); Ronald Steel, *Temptations of a Superpower* (1995); Thomas G. Patterson, *American Foreign Policy: A History since 1900* (1988); Paul Kennedy, *The Rise and Fall of the Great Powers* (1987); Robert W. Tucker and David C. Henrickson, *The Imperial Temptation* (1992); Tony Smith, *America's Mission: The United States and the Worldwide Struggle for Democracy in the Twentieth Century* (1994); David P. Calleo, *Beyond American Hegemony* (1987); Jim Hansen, *The Decline of the American Empire* (1993); Henry Nau, *The Myth of America's Decline* (1990); Joseph S. Nye, Jr., *Bound to Lead* (1990); and Hans J. Morganthau, *Scientific Man vs. Power Politics* (1946), especially chapters 5–8.

For a sobering account of the destruction of one people's greatness, which has lost none of its power, please see Thucydides, *The Peloponnesian War.*

DEAN ACHESON (1893–1971)

Served 1949–1953
Appointed by President Harry S Truman
Democrat

As a boy in Middletown Connecticut, during what he later described as "the golden age of childhood," Dean Gooderham Acheson had a pony that didn't share its master's passion for imaginative games. "Mean, as well as lazy, and uncooperative," Acheson wrote of the animal, "he knew who was afraid and who would fight back. The timid did well to feed him sugar on a tennis racquet; but he was gentle as lamb if one had one's fist cocked for a fast punch in the nose." The lesson stayed with Acheson throughout his life, and when he became the most gifted secretary of state in the twentieth century, he would often approach his adversaries with that same fist cocked, ready to bargain but equally ready to deliver a fast punch. He was not merely present at the creation, as he called his memoir of his state department years; he was the prime architect of that creation.

It would be Acheson, first as Under Secretary, then as Secretary of State, who would be a prime architect of the Marshall Plan to restore economic health to Western Europe, who refashioned a peacetime alliance of nations under the rubric of the North Atlantic Treaty Organization, and who crafted the Truman Doctrine to contain any Soviet advance into the Middle East and the Mediterranean. It was Acheson who had already been instrumental in creating the international financial institutions at Bretton Woods that helped ensure global American economic predominance. And it was Acheson who would stand by Truman in deciding that the United States must respond to the North Korean invasion of South Korea, who urged the firing of General Douglas MacArthur for insubordination, and who stood up to the vilification of Senator Joseph McCarthy.

Above all else, it was Acheson who created the intellectual concepts that undergirded Truman's decisions, who had the clearest view of the role America might play in the postwar world, and who possessed the willpower to accomplish these ends. Despite later appearances Dean Acheson was not an American patrician. Nor was he born to great wealth. His father, who was born in Kent, England, in 1857, basically ran away from a wicked stepmother in his teens and emigrated to Canada.

He worked for a dry goods company in Toronto, then enlisted in the army, and fought in the Northwest Territories to put down a rebellion by a Canadian of part-Indian descent who wanted to establish a separate nation. Later he found a way to put himself through a seminary at the University of Toronto and married the daughter of a prominent distiller. The young clergyman, however, was so poorly paid that his father-in-law settled some money on the new couple, who then lived comfortably in Middletown, Connecticut, where he became a rector of the Episcopal Church—and who in 1915 was named Bishop of Connecticut. In 1893, their first child, Dean, was born.

Growing up for young Dean was, by his description, idyllic, in an uncomplicated world of the small-town pleasures in the late nineteenth century. He was an independent boy, who habitually got into scrapes. But his independence cost him dearly in the years ahead, for, at the age of 12, he was sent to Groton School, largely because the wealthy families of Middletown were Episcopalians and recommended the school to his father. Acheson simply hated Groton, its strict discipline and anti-intellectualism, and he rebelled—so much so that his mother was asked to come to see the formidable rector, Endicott Peabody. Dean graduated at the bottom of his class, an incorrigible boy, who was not fearful of expressing the independence of his opinions. Acheson prided himself on his ability, then and later, to amuse, shock, dazzle, or discomfort.

At Yale, he was essentially a playboy. He earned so-called gentlemen's Cs, but was renowned as a wit, a Yale blade, and a swashbuckler. He also had a serious run-in with his Victorian father, whose rather muscular Christianity dealt with ethics and conduct rather than salvation and redemption. During the 1912 presidential campaign when Acheson, as a sophomore at Yale, supported Theodore Roosevelt who was running on the third-party ticket as a Bull Mooser, and he got into an argument with his father who called him a fool. For this offense, Acheson was banished from the house for one year, though he was permitted to continue at Yale. This draconian punishment was symbolic to some degree of Acheson's relationship to his father, whom he admired, but whose approval he craved and often found lacking. Time and again he would search for affirmation where he could find it—if not in his father, then within the larger circle of friends whose applause he sought.

After Yale he entered Harvard Law School, with no particular sense of calling, and shared a place in Cambridge with Cole Porter who had been a couple of years ahead of him at his club at Yale. Yet, in his second term at the Law School, all of Acheson's native brilliance came alive under the teaching of a young professor, Felix Frankfurter. By the time he graduated, Acheson ranked fifth in his class and had been elected to the prestigious Harvard Law Review. In later years, Frankfurter was named to the Supreme Court by FDR and became one of Acheson's closest friends.

Recommended by Frankfurter to Supreme Court Justice Louis Brandeis, Acheson went to Washington, where he remained for the rest of his life. Although he clerked for Brandeis for two years, the person who most affected him and was his last truly formative influence was Justice Oliver Wendell Holmes, then a legendary figure who had fought in the Civil War. Holmes was emblematic of the pragmatism that Acheson believed was the essence of the law. It was judge-made common law to which Holmes was devoted. Absent some specific constitutional provision, Holmes never doubted that the U.S. Congress and the state legislatures had the supreme right to legislate as they pleased. Most important of all, Acheson encountered with

Holmes the shock of recognition that a young person undergoes when a mentor of exceptional eminence ratifies one's own intellectual and moral inclinations.

After his clerkship, he married Alice Stanley, a painter from Detroit. He and his wife and his first two children, David and Jane, settled in Georgetown. Later, a third child, Mary, completed the family circle. For more than a decade, he practiced law with the firm of Covington and Burling; he served briefly in FDR's first administration as Under Secretary of the Treasury, then resigned within a year over a dispute with FDR over the right of the president to set the price of gold. But in 1941, Acheson, who had been supporting Roosevelt's efforts to aid the allies prior to America's entry into the war, was asked to join the government as Assistant Secretary of State for Economic Affairs. In this post, he was instrumental in enforcing the oil embargo against the Japanese on the eve of World War II. With the end of the war, Acheson expected to return to the law firm, but Truman and Secretary of State James F. Byrnes urged him to stay on as second-in-command, at that time with the title of Under Secretary of State.

Although Acheson was a convinced anticommunist, he rejected extremes and was far from being a Cold Warrior at the end of World War II. On the contrary, he sought cooperative agreements with the Soviet Union as a great power that had shared in the victory over the Axis powers with the United States and Great Britain. However, when he determined that it was imperative to contain what he considered an expansionist Soviet Union, he was prone at times to employ a rhetoric of anticommunism that, in his own words, made his arguments "clearer than truth" to get them accepted by the Congress. These were Faustian bargains, and during his last years in office Acheson would be savagely attacked by the conservatives as an appeaser of an ideologically threatening Soviet Union.

In his essence, however, Acheson was a realist. He never intended, as he testified later, that the United States should embark on a "crusade against any ideology." Although he did not come to high office with an elaborate plan to establish an American imperium, more than any of his contemporaries, including Roosevelt, Truman, and General Marshall, he perceived what the interests of the United States and its allies required. In this respect, he did the most to create the world that endured from the outset of the Cold War to the collapse of communism almost half a century later.

Nor did Acheson's influence end with the Truman presidency. Out of office, Acheson sat as a member of President John F. Kennedy's Executive Committee during the Cuban Missile Crisis. Then, in the twilight of his career, he was asked by President Lyndon B. Johnson to head a group of senior statesmen, the so-called Wise Men, to see how the United States could extricate itself from the Vietnam quagmire. Although other senior statesmen and military leaders had earlier urged Johnson to avoid a land war in Asia, it was only when Acheson turned against the Vietnam War and told the president that it was time to "take steps to disengage" that Johnson knew it was all over. Later, even President Richard Nixon sought Acheson's counsel, and Acheson reiterated his policy recommendation for Vietnam—to move out steadily; he finally broke with Nixon when the president extended the war into Cambodia.

Arguably, the most important figure in U.S. foreign policy since John Quincy Adams, Dean Acheson was the quintessential American realist who most fully understood and mastered the exercises of American power in the American era. Five turning points shed significant light on Acheson's career in office. These are, first of all, the Acheson–Lilienthal plan to share international control of atomic weapons with the Soviet Union. Second, the Iranian crisis when the Soviet army did not evacuate Iran. Third, the Soviet designs on the Dardanelles at the mouth of the Black Sea in 1946, when the Truman administration brought the country to the brink of war with the Soviet Union. Fourth, the Truman Doctrine, when Acheson employed universalist rhetoric for limited ends. And last, the China policy, when Acheson's desire to recognize Mao was frustrated by McCarthyite domestic opposition.

Secretary of War Henry L. Stimson, a Republican supported by FDR to create a bipartisan cabinet, had been deeply perturbed over the implications for the international community of the U.S. monopoly of the atom bomb. Vacationing in the Adirondacks in the summer of 1945, he concluded that if the United States tried to keep scientific knowledge of how to create an atom bomb secret and then endeavored to use its monopoly to pressure an increasingly truculent Soviet Union to follow domestic and foreign policies that the United States dictated, it was bound to fail. That strategy might even lead, as he later put it, to "a secret armament race of a rather desperate character." At the core of Stimson's thinking was his belief that the United States did not possess scientific atomic secrets as such—only the American technological ability to construct a bomb.

Returning to Washington on September 3, Stimson had a long and rather distressing talk with Secretary of State James F. Byrnes. "I took up the question I had been working on, namely how to handle Russia with the big bomb," he wrote. "I found Byrnes was very much against any attempt to co-operate with Stalin." Later that day, Stimson had a meeting with the President and told him that he was unhappy about Byrnes' approach. He also realized he needed more time to explain his own position, and so he arranged for a longer meeting with Truman on September 12 to discuss a memorandum he was working on.

The heart of the memorandum was that a direct approach to Stalin would be the best way to avoid a devastating arms race. Regardless of how long it might take the Soviets to develop their own bomb, it was vital that the United States work to ensure their cooperation in the postwar world. What Stimson was after was to obtain Soviet cooperation in controlling the use of atomic energy and weaponry. Stimson wrote, "for if we fail to approach [the Russians] now and merely continue to negotiate with them, having this weapon rather ostentatiously on our hip, their suspicions and their distrust of our purposes and motives will increase."

He concluded by urging a one-on-one approach to the Russians. An offer through the medium of the United Nations, or any other "international group of nations" would not be taken seriously by the Soviets." It must be "peculiarly the proposal of the United States."

Truman encouraged Stimson to present his views to the whole Cabinet on September 21, 1945, the day Stimson turned 78 and his last day in office.

To prepare for the meeting, Stimson sent his memo over to Under Secretary Acheson, who, he believed, "is evidently strongly on our side on the treatment of Russia." Acheson's first reaction to the destruction of Hiroshima had been horror: "The news of the atomic bomb is the most frightening yet. If we can't work out one sort of organization of great powers, we shall be gone geese for fair." From now on, the Stimson approach would be in the hands of Acheson, in many ways his moral successor.

Dean Acheson's verdict on the fateful cabinet meeting at which Stimson presented his views on the atom bomb and the Soviet Union was that the discussion was unworthy of the subject. To begin with, no one in the Cabinet had had an opportunity to consider the implications of the proposal. The discussion soon veered away from the central issue of how to approach the USSR on questions raised by America's development of the bomb—directly, or through the United Nations. In essence, was Stimson's one-on-one approach to Moscow the right one? Instead the debate, such as it was, centered over the spurious issue of whether or not the United States should "give" the bomb to the Russians.

Four days later Acheson sent an unusually passionate memorandum to the President. He then argued that the joint development of the bomb by the United States, Britain, and Canada "must appear to the Soviet Union to be unanswerable evidence of an Anglo-American combination against them." His logic was impeccable. For America to declare itself a "trustee of the development for the benefit of the world will mean nothing more to the Russian mind than an outright policy of exclusion."

Acheson proposed approaching the USSR directly. Byrnes, however, did not favor dealing directly with the Soviets and embraced a UN approach. In Acheson's view, however, by bringing the discussion of atomic energy control to "a large group of nations that included many small ones of no demonstrated power of responsibility," Byrnes was following a course that was "the opposite pole" from what he and Stimson had advocated.

What exactly did Byrnes want? The best approach, as Byrnes saw it, was to appoint Acheson to head a committee to formulate American policy. As Acheson tells the story, Byrnes phoned Acheson, who was in bed with the flu, and asked him to chair a group to devise a plan for the international control of atomic energy. Acheson protested, "Mr. Secretary, I don't know anything about this." But Byrnes was about to depart for London on January 7, 1946, for the first meeting of the UN General Assembly. He said, "My plane's going in a few minutes, and I have no time to argue. The President wants it done, and you are appointed."

Despite Acheson's grave reservations about exploring the international control of atomic energy through a UN commission rather than first approaching the Soviets directly, he nonetheless labored wholeheartedly with David Lilienthal, who had headed the Tennessee Valley Authority, to come up with a workable plan.

On March 17, 1946, the Acheson–Lilienthal report was ready. The key to the plan was an Atomic Development Authority that would control the whole field of atomic energy. In essence, the Committee recommended that the United States abandon its monopoly on the atomic bomb and rest its hopes on cooperative control of the terrible weapon.

On the very day that Acheson presented the Secretary of State with the formal report, Byrnes told him that Truman had asked Bernard Baruch to sell the plan to the rest of the world. Baruch, a self-styled "park bench" philosopher and self-promoting "adviser to presidents," was 75 years old and had made a fortune speculating on Wall Street. Baruch soon made it clear he was not about to accept the report as written and present it to the United Nations; as he put it, he was not going to be "a messenger boy."

He made two key changes in the Acheson–Lilienthal report that proved fatal. There should be "immediate and sure punishment" for violations of the plan; and such punishment should *not* be subject to a veto by any member of the UN Security Council. Such conditions for a treaty, Acheson believed, "were almost certain to wreck any possibility of Russian acceptance of one."

In a talk with Truman, Baruch said that punishment meant "war." Acheson certainly understood that any effective punishment of a great power did mean war, but he also believed that no one would go to war over such an issue. The whole idea of such punishment was an illusion, and Acheson was too much of a realist not to detest "paper police sanctions," as he called them. Controlling uranium through the international authority was the best way to prevent cheating.

Truman, however, endorsed the no-veto provision, and the plan was effectively dead. Truman later confessed to Acheson that choosing Baruch was "the worst mistake I have ever made." Acheson described Baruch's role more succinctly: "It was his ball and he balled it up."

Was there any real hope of serious negotiation over the control of atomic energy? Once Truman agreed to put the issue in the hands of the United Nations rather than approach the Russians personally, the idea of controlling the future of atomic energy may well have been doomed. But Truman never really concentrated on these issues: otherwise, how could he have both approved the Acheson–Lilienthal report and also backed Baruch's veto?

There is also no evidence that Truman really understood the report or even read it with care. Truman's policy, as Kennedy's former national security adviser McGeorge Bundy described it, "seldom went beyond the counsel he had to choose from. He was not an initiator but a chooser; the buck stopped here, but he waited for the buck to arrive."

As long as the United States possessed atomic bombs, Stalin was determined that the Soviet Union would also have them. Yet, even if we accept that after Hiroshima Stalin was determined that the United States would not retain its monopoly over atomic weapons, this does not mean that his views could not have been changed. Stimson and Acheson were doubtless right in September 1945 to press for an early direct approach to Moscow precisely to avoid perpetuating a threatening monopoly. Had Roosevelt lived, this might well have occurred. Bundy makes the case that "Roosevelt would have taken to heart the quest for a workable international agreement" and "made the matter his most pressing business." Truman did not.

Had the Soviets responded favorably to the Acheson approach, the history of the Cold War might have been substantially different. Soviet behavior would likely have been far less confrontational, especially after Stalin's death in 1953. A bilateral effort, which Stimson had originally urged, would have provided an even more solid basis for postwar cooperation on a broad range of security issues.

In the end, the Acheson–Lilienthal plan was the best that anyone could develop. Then, despite Acheson's best efforts to reopen the path to Moscow, Baruch threw up his final barrier. Perhaps the direct approach would not have worked in any case—nonetheless, a true test of the approach was never made.

There was, in essence, no grand strategy at this time. Acheson was very much aware of the limitations as well as the abundance of American power. He believed that he had to rein in Truman's initial inclination to confront Soviets as aggressor, even while he himself grew increasingly uneasy at the truculence of Soviet diplomacy and the unwillingness of Stalin to hold free elections in Poland or withdraw his troops from northern Iran.

"Once slowly," Acheson wrote in his memoir, "did it dawn upon us that the whole world structure and order that we had inherited from the nineteenth century was gone and the struggle to replace it would be directed from the two bitterly opposed and ideologically irreconcilable power centers."

In this situation, the practical objective of getting the Soviets to abandon aggressive moves without making undue threats to their legitimate interests would be tested in Iran, with Acheson in a leading role. The Iranian crisis unfolded over the winter and spring of 1946. As the March 2 deadline for withdrawal of Soviet troops passed with no Soviet action, George Kennan delivered on March 6 a protest to the Soviet government over its unwillingness to pull out its troops. Cables from the American vice-consul in Tabriz, reporting "exceptionally heavy Soviet troop movements" in northern Iran became so ominous that State Department officials had to consider the possibility of using force against the USSR.

Byrnes was now taking a tough line toward the Russians. On March 7, looking at the blown-up map of Azerbaijan, which showed bold arrows representing Soviet forces moving in the direction of Turkey, Iraq, Teheran, and southern Iranian oil fields, he beat one fist into his other hand and said, "Now we'll give it to them with both barrels."

Two days later, Acheson chaired a State Department meeting to deal with the Iranian crisis. Hawks from the Division of Near Eastern Affairs wanted to take a strong line that Moscow had violated its treaty obligations. Charles Bohlen, as a Soviet expert, pointed out that the United States was in no position to confront the Soviets in Iran. America had no substantial forces in the region. Nothing would be more self-defeating than a bluff.

As was his habit, Acheson, did not divulge his own position until he had heard all sides of the argument. Then he said firmly that the department should let Moscow know that it was aware of Russian movements in Iran but "leave a graceful way out" if the Russians wanted to avoid a showdown. What Acheson did not want to do was threaten force, which the United States did not possess, over an issue that he believed could be resolved by a show of U.S. firmness, without jeopardizing relations between Washington and Moscow.

In Moscow, Kennan delivered Acheson's message on March 9, demanding an explanation for the movement of additional Soviet forces into Iran. Truman later declared that he sent Stalin an "ultimatum" on Iran. But there is no record of this. It was Acheson's note that brought the crisis to an end by encouraging Stalin to work out a deal with the Iranians.

By early May the Soviet forces were gone. There was no doubt that American pressure had been instrumental in furthering the settlement. Yet, Acheson's desire to let the Soviets have a graceful way out showed he was far from an unreconstructed Cold Warrior.

In that same spring, however, there were USSR troop concentrations pointed toward Turkey, with at lest 200 Soviet tanks crossing the Iranian border, about a third of them mobilizing along the Turkish–Iranian frontier. Despite these intimidating deployments, Ankara stood firm against Soviet demands, while approaching London and Washington for support.

As the crisis deepened, former Soviet foreign minister Maxim Litvinov, who had been associated with a more friendly policy toward the United States in the 1930s, gave a surprisingly revealing interview on June 18, 1946, to the CBS correspondent in Moscow, Richard C. Hottelet. The old Bolshevik explained that there "has now been return in USSR to outmoded concept of "geographical security." When Hottelet asked if Soviet policy would be mitigated if the West were to give in to Soviet territorial demands, Litvinov insisted that "it would lead to West being faced after period of time with new series of demands."

On August 7, 1946, the Soviet Union sent a detailed note to the Turkish government, with a copy to Washington. Moscow now demanded a joint Turkish–Soviet defense of the Straits, which would necessarily require Soviet bases.

In the absence of Secretary Byrnes, who was in Paris, Acheson called a series of meetings of the Departments of State, War, and Navy, along with the Chiefs of Staff, to study the situation and agree on a course of action. In Acheson's mind, the worst policy would be one of bluff: the Soviets must be certain that America would support Turkey if it were attacked.

To that end, Navy Secretary James Forrestal ordered a naval task force, which included a new aircraft carrier, the *Franklin D. Roosevelt*, and two destroyers, to rendezvous off Lisbon with two cruisers and three more American destroyers, and thence to join the *USS Missouri*, which had already arrived in the Dardanelles on April 5.

The interdepartmental meetings, leading up to a crucial meeting with the president on August 15, produced one of the toughest recommendations for policy yet offered to Harry Truman. Flanked by Forrestal and the top military brass, Acheson presented the joint report. "In our opinion," the report read, "if the Soviet Union succeeds in its objective of obtaining control over Turkey, it will be extremely difficult, if not impossible, to prevent the Soviet Union from obtaining control over Greece and over the whole Near and Middle East." Should this happen, Moscow would be in a much stronger position to threaten India and China. "The only thing which will deter the Russians will be the conviction that the United States is prepared, if necessary, to meet aggression with the force of arms." The report then concluded: "In our opinion therefore the time has come when we must decide that we shall resist with all means at our disposal any Soviet aggression and in particular, because the case of Turkey would be so clear, any Soviet aggression against Turkey."

The President did not hesitate: "We might as well find out whether the Russians were bent on world conquest now as in five or ten years." He was prepared to pursue the policy to the end.

Unfolding the map of the Middle East and eastern Mediterranean, he gave a short lecture on the historical background and current strategic importance of the region. It was vital to protect the Straits from any Russian incursion; otherwise, Soviet troops would soon be used to control all of Turkey, and in the natural course of events Greece and the Near East would fall under Soviet domination.

Four days later Acheson, with Truman, rejected the Soviet demand of August 7. The message dismissed any notion that the USSR should share responsibility with Turkey for the defense of the Straits.

Confronted by American resolve and the naval task force in the Turkish Straits, the Soviets backed down. A month later their tone on the Dardanelles was much softer.

A week after Acheson had sent the U.S. reply to Moscow, *New York Times* reporter James Reston noted a shift in Acheson's thinking. Although Acheson had previously held out for a "liberal policy" toward the Soviet Union, Reston wrote, "when the facts seemed to merit a change—as he seems to think they do in the case of the Soviet Union—he switched with the facts."

On Monday morning, February 24, 1947, Acheson handed Secretary of State Marshall a recommendation for aid to Greece and Turkey telling him that the papers contained "the most major decision with which we have been faced since the War."

By this time, Acheson believed that there were only two powers—the United States and the USSR—but was concerned that Congress would not support a substantial aid plan. Persuading a Republican Congress to vote the funds to shore up Greece and Turkey turned out to be a formidable task. Truman scheduled a conference over Greece and Turkey with congressional leaders on Thursday, February 24, a meeting that Acheson viewed with foreboding: "I knew we were met at Armageddon."

Among those present for the meeting with Truman, Marshall, and Acheson was Republican Senator Arthur Vandenberg, chairman of the Senate Foreign Relations Committee. General Marshall led off the discussion, but his rather summary and even cryptic presentation fell flat. He seemed to imply that the United States should provide aid to Greece for humanitarian reasons and to Turkey to bolster Great Britain's position in the Middle East. The reactions of the congressional leaders to these reasons were cool.

Things were going badly. In desperation, Acheson whispered to Secretary Marshall, who was sitting beside him, "Is this a private fight or can anyone get into it?" Marshall asked the President to let Mr. Acheson have the floor.

For Acheson, as he recalled later, "This was my crisis. For a week I had nurtured it. These congressmen had no conception of what challenged them; it was my task to bring it home." In the past eighteen months, he said, Soviet pressure on the Dardanelles, on Iran and northern Greece had brought the Balkans to the point where a Soviet breakthrough might open three countries to Soviet penetration. He went on to suggest that if Greece fell, "like apples in a barrel infected by one rotten one, the corruption of Greece would infect Iran and all to the east. It would also carry infection to Africa through Asia Minor and Egypt, and to Europe through Italy and France, already threatened by the strongest domestic Communist parties."

Not since Rome and Carthage had the world been so polarized between the two great powers, he continued. Therefore, it was not a matter of bailing out Britain and responding to Greece and Turkey on humanitarian grounds, but rather a strengthening of free peoples against communist aggression. America had no choice, he concluded. It had to protect its own security—it had to protect freedom itself.

A deep silence followed Acheson's passionate call to arms. Then Senator Vandenberg said gravely, "Mr. President, if you will say that to Congress and the country, I will support you and I believe that most of its members will do the same." Others recalled that Vandenberg may have put the message more bluntly: "Mr. President, the only way you are ever going to get this is to make a speech and scare the hell out of the country." This is precisely what Truman was prepared to do.

On March 12, 1947, Truman addressed the Congress. After laying out the physical, financial, and economic condition of war-torn Greece and the need to sustain an independent and economically viable Turkey, the President proclaimed what would come to be known as the Truman Doctrine: "I believe that it must be the policy of the United States to support free peoples who are resisting attempted subjugation by armed minorities or by outside pressures."

By using universalistic rhetoric to attain more modest ends, Acheson and Truman laid the groundwork for the belief, which would become ever more widely shared by government officials as well as the larger public, that the United States saw little alternative but to embark on the global containment of communism. Acheson had made the arguments, as he later put it, "clearer than truth."

In fact, Acheson had a more pragmatic and temperate worldview. He was well aware that the economic and military means to embark on a broader crusade were neither available nor needed. When he appeared before the Senate Foreign Relations Committee in the last week of March, he began his testimony by asserting that aid to Greece and Turkey did not establish a pattern for future American assistance elsewhere. This was not, Acheson declared, "an ideological crusade."

America's decision to intervene, and the threat that this posed to the neighboring communist regimes intensified Stalin's growing rift with Tito. On February 10, 1948, in his office in the Kremlin, Stalin met with the top-ranking Bulgarian and Yugoslav communists (though not with Tito, who prudently declined the invitation to travel to Moscow). After haranguing the Yugoslavs and Bulgarians over their differences with the Soviet Union, he suddenly turned to the Greek civil war. "What do you think," he demanded, "that Great Britain and the United States— the United States, the most powerful state in the world—will permit you to break their line of communication in the Mediterranean Sea! Nonsense. And we have no navy. The uprising in Greece must be stopped and as quickly as possible." And so it was.

On the very day Dean Acheson assumed the office of Secretary of State on January 1, 1949, Generalissimo Chiang Kai-shek resigned the presidency of the Republic of China. His Nationalist armies, badly led and demoralized, had collapsed before the onslaught of well-disciplined Chinese communist troops.

Finally, on Sunday morning, April 24, 1949, the communists easily crossed the great Yangtze River—which U.S. General Albert Wedemeyer had once said could be defended with broomsticks by an army willing to fight.

As a total communist takeover of China mainland now appeared inevitable, the Republican opposition bitterly tried to pin the "loss" of China on the Democrats. And as the Republican attacks mounted in fury, Acheson would find it increasingly difficult to carry out the policy which he believed was best for the United States— to wait until the communists had fully consolidated their power on both the mainland and the island of Taiwan, where Chiang Kai-shek and the remnants of his forces hung on, to recognize Mao's new regime and to try to prevent it from becoming subservient to the Soviet Union.

The problem that constantly bedeviled him was the willingness of the Republican opposition to hold up appropriations for European recovery to force the administration to support Chiang Kai-shek. Acheson's strategy at home therefore was to try to placate pro-Chiang conservatives while the president mobilized support for containment in Europe.

How had all this come to pass? In 1946, Truman had sent General Marshall to mainland China to see if he could mediate a settlement between the communists and the nationalists. For Acheson, the U.S. Congress and public deserved an explanation of U.S. policy for the past four years, and in the spring of 1949, he had his staff prepare a 1,000-page document known as the White Paper. It was designed to provide a dispassionate history of U.S. efforts to hold China together after Japan's surrender, while portraying the increasing disenchantment of U.S. officials before Nationalist corruption and incompetence, along with the evidence of communist determination and discipline.

Marshall had remained in China for one year and had utterly failed to achieve an end to the civil war. Concluding that the Nationalists were determined to use force to further their aims, he virtually accused Chiang's government of duplicity in regard to its further military activity in the north. Continued efforts at mediation would be fruitless. Neither the Communists nor the Nationalists trusted one another. The Marshall mission had clearly collapsed, and the General returned home in the New Year to become Truman's new Secretary of State.

Consistent with his belief that the communists would overwhelm the Nationalists, even if they retreated to Taiwan, Marshall had decided by October 1948 that the United States would not defend Taiwan, a decision "unanimously recommended" by all the departments concerned.

By May, the Nationalist resistance on the mainland was virtually at an end. Mao officially announced the founding of the People's Republic of China, with Beijing as its capital, on October 1, 1949.

On February 7, 1949, Dean Acheson as the Secretary of State, self-confident after years of experience dealing with Congress, met with thirty Republican congressmen to discuss the likely final collapse of the Nationalist government. Asked to predict the course of events, Acheson replied that "when a great tree falls in the forest one cannot see the extent of the damage until the dust settles."

The next day the press reported that his China policy was to "wait until the dust settles." Though Acheson vainly protested that this was not a policy, but rather a confession of his inability to see very far into the future, the China bloc found his imagery invaluable in assaulting the administration's foreign policy.

Eventually Acheson predicted, "most all of China will come under Communist rule." The last thing the Truman administration should do would be to give any further military aid to the Nationalists, for this would simply solidify the support of the Chinese people for Mao's regime and "perpetuate the delusion that China's interests lies with the USSR."

By the end of February 1949, the National Security Council presented a paper to the president that called for the government to "maintain its freedom of action" by pursuing a policy designed "to create serious rifts between Moscow and a Chinese Communist regime."

In this respect, Washington should restore "ordinary economic relations between China on the one hand and Japan and the western world on the other." Such an approach would make it possible for the United States "to exploit frictions between the Chinese Communist regime and the USSR should they arise." This Titoist strategy might keep Mao from aligning himself to closely too Stalin.

In early April, Acheson and his advisers met with British Foreign Minister Ernest Bevin, who was told that the administration had abandoned "the idea of supporting the [nationalist] regime," but it was difficult "publicly to withdraw support for Chiang." Nonetheless, Acheson, hoping that he would eventually be able to recognize Mao's government, assured Bevin that the "U.S. henceforth will pursue a more realistic policy respecting China."

However, Acheson was worried; like General Marshall he was deeply troubled over the power of the China bloc to influence the rest of the Senate. To win passage of European recovery aid for fiscal year 1950, Acheson therefore agreed to permit the unexpended portion of the funds provided for in the China Aid Act to be spent beyond the Act's expiration date of April 2, 1949; the Senate extended that date to February 15, 1950.

This was clearly a signal that Acheson would be flouting the wishes of Congress by abandoning support of the Chinese Nationalists. Time, it seemed, was running out for a realist policy of establishing relations with Beijing on the basis of who represented the effective government of China.

No sooner had the aid bill been modified than Mao Zedong declared on June 30, 1949, that China would align itself with the Soviet Union. To assure the Soviets that he was not about to become an Asian Tito, he asserted, "We must lean to one side. . . . Sitting in the fence will not do; nor is there a third road."

If Mao and Zhou, fearful of a continuing alliance between Chiang and Washington and even a possible U.S.-backed Nationalist landing in the mainland, were moving closer to Stalin, they nonetheless hoped to have correct relations with the United States, which could eventually lead to recognition. In this respect, their policies did not differ greatly from what Truman and Acheson were trying to do. The Americans saw trade as a means of weaning away the Chinese communists from Moscow's embrace; Mao and Zhou saw trade as a hedge against too close an alignment with Stalin. At the same time, Stalin, alarmed at the signing of the North Atlantic Treaty on April 4, 1949, perceived China as an increasingly valuable asset in the Cold War.

On August 5, 1949, Acheson released the 1,000-page document known as the White Paper, as an explanation of U.S. policy from 1945 to 1949. Though the White Paper still holds up as a model of scholarship, it failed to achieve its purposes: its bulk of 1,000 pages simply does not lend itself to serious study except by scholars. More accessible but ultimately more disastrous was Acheson's Covering Letter of Transmittal, which engendered a great deal more controversy than Acheson had intended.

The Letter was essentially a political document that portrayed the Chinese communists as tools of Moscow. This was a position that Acheson did not hold, according to a key adviser on China affairs, who had written the draft of the White Paper. Indeed, Acheson would have done far better had he pointed out that a communist-run China did not pose a major threat to the United States because Washington still controlled Japan and the Western Pacific. Instead, Acheson had approved the language to appease the China bloc.

Once again, as he had in 1947 when he used the heightened rhetoric of the "rotten apples" to gain support for the Marshall Plan—evoking a world of communist states should aid to Greece and Turkey fail—Acheson stirred up the fires of the growing anticommunist consensus. By asserting Beijing's submissiveness to Moscow, Acheson made it more difficult for his government to pursue a policy of recognition, even should Mao eventually conquer Taiwan and eliminate all domestic opposition.

Republican Senators Knowland, Style Bridges, and Kenneth Wherry—along with antiadministration Democrat Pat McCarran—assailed the White Paper as "a 1,054-page whitewash of a wishful, do-nothing policy which has succeeded only in placing Asia in danger of Soviet conquest."

Diplomatic recognition of the Communist Chinese government, which Mao officially proclaimed as the government of China on October 1, 1949, was an absolute necessity in Acheson's view. Yet, it was almost impossible to accomplish, not only because of the strength of the China bloc, but also because Chiang Kai-shek had now established his Republic of China government on Taiwan. Moreover, every abuse by Mao's government, including the detention of the American Consul in Mukden, Manchuria, from late 1948 to late 1949, added to Acheson's difficulty in proceeding with recognition.

As long as Chiang was in power on Taiwan, the China bloc could present an alternative to recognizing Mao's government in Beijing. What, then, should be the policy of the Truman administration? Should the United States protect Taiwan from invasion from the mainland? Or should it wait for Taiwan to fall, in which case recognition might come more easily.

George Kennan, head of the Policy Planning Staff, proposed a drastic scheme to rid the island of the Kuomintang but then retain it as strategically valuable to the United States. He urged the use of U.S. forces to throw Chiang's troops out of Taiwan and the adjoining islands and, under U.S. auspices and protection, create an independent country. This was the way "Theodore Roosevelt might have done it," he suggested, with "resolution, speed, ruthlessness and self-assurance."

Acheson rejected these proposals and recommended that the United States abandon any effort to prevent the island from falling to the communists. In August 1949, the Joint Chiefs of Staff (JCS) also agreed that military measures would be unwise. At a meeting in December between members of the State Department and the Joint Chiefs, Acheson argued that "Mao is not a true satellite in that he came to power by his own efforts and was not installed in office by the Soviet army." By the end of the year the JCS defined an American defensive position based on the Philippines, north to the Ryukyu Islands and to Japan itself.

On January 10, 1950, Acheson testified in executive session before the Senate Foreign Relations Committee. So far as recognition of Mao's government was concerned, he saw no reason to move too swiftly at this time. He wanted to see how the Chinese communists would behave toward Americans in China and their attitude toward the foreign debts of the Nationalist government, but he warned the senators not to get "this thing mixed up with approval or disapproval." Above all, "we should not [use] military forces of the United States to take, secure, or defend Formosa [Taiwan]."

Two days later, Acheson delivered an important address on Far Eastern policy to the National Press Club in Washington. Tossing aside the speech the Department had prepared, which he felt lacked life and had "no continuity of thought," he had made extensive notes for a new one at his house in Georgetown. He reminded his audience that nobody says "the Nationalist Government fell because it was confronted by overwhelming military force which it could not resist." On the contrary, Chiang's "support in the country has melted away," and he noted the U.S. defensive perimeter as the JCS had defined it. As for South Korea, which was clearly not within the American defense perimeter, Acheson declared that the United Nations might well come to its aid should it be threatened; he also urged that U.S. aid to Korea be continued. Soon after Acheson's statement, the House rejected further aid for Korea.

Above all, he warned Americans against "the folly of ill-conceived adventures on our part," which could "deflect from the Russians to ourselves the righteous anger, and the wrath, and the hatred of the Chinese which must develop. It would be folly to deflect it to ourselves."

Acheson's press club speech had also been reported to Stalin and Mao in Moscow. When Acheson declared that the USSR was going to annex parts of China, a process "nearly complete in Manchuria," this outraged Stalin because it was very close to the truth.

Stalin now had to demonstrate to Mao that he had no intention of seizing Chinese territory; Mao, in turn, could not allow himself to be portrayed as a weak leader who allowed himself to be used as a puppet of Stalin. For Mao, Acheson's hands-off stand on Taiwan was welcome news; for Stalin, it might portend a tacit understanding between Beijing and Washington.

A month later, Moscow and Beijing signed the Sino-Soviet Treaty of Friendship, a defense pact. Yet despite this rapprochement between the Soviet Union and China, Acheson did not give up on the hope of abandoning Chiang, recognizing the People's Republic of China, and then weaning it away from a Soviet alliance.

On March 29, 1950, Acheson once again testified in executive session before the Senate Foreign Relations Committee. "If the devil himself runs China," he said, "if he is an independent devil, that is infinitely better than if he is a stooge of Moscow, or China comes under Russia." Despite the Sino-Soviet agreement signed in February, he said, "the Chinese, inevitably, we believe, will come into conflict with Moscow."

As far as Acheson was concerned, Chiang was actually inviting Mao to invade Taiwan. "The Communists would be criminally crazy," he advised the senators, "if they did not put an end to [Chiang's island bastion] just as soon as possible." Had this happened, Acheson believed that he could have overcome opposition to recognizing communist China.

Acheson miscalculated, however; time was running out. His approach of waiting for the dust to settle, moving slowly in hopes that events in the Far East would ease his task of recognizing communist China, of driving a wedge between Moscow and Beijing, and of containing communism on the periphery of the Middle Kingdom, was each day made far more costly by accusations by the China bloc at home that Truman administration had "lost" China. The outbreak of the Korean War in June 1950, followed by intervention by Chinese communist forces later that year, doomed any possibility of reconciliation with Beijing for the next twenty years.

Acheson believed, with the theologian Reinhold Niebuhr, that power could not be divorced from morality. This meant that during the Cold War U.S. power had to oppose Soviet power. By disavowing the responsibilities of power, the United States would invoke far worse guilt than whatever guilt came from wielding it.

As Acheson wrote to Truman in early 1954, "Power is at the root of most relationships—by no means the only factor, but one of vast importance. A balance of power has proved the best international sheriff we have ever had."

In his book, *Power and Diplomacy*, published in 1958, Acheson inveighed against unlimited force and unlimited objectives, which were, he believed, too often occasioned by "moralism of an outraged pacifism."

Acheson's warnings against excessive moralizing did not arise out of a belief that "moral principles can, or should be, excluded from the relations of states to one another." But "to characterize conduct between nations as moral or immoral will involve us in confusions of vocabulary and thought." He made the classic realist distinction between relations between individuals and those between states: "The substance of all discussion, which concerns the conduct of individuals within a society toward one another, is more likely to be misleading if applied to the relations of one society to another."

In his own way, Acheson tried to elaborate a view of America's role in the world that was deeply grounded in his realist approach to foreign policy. Acheson was fully aware of the limitations of U.S. power and purpose. On October 20, 1949, he said at the annual Al Smith dinner in New York City: "We cannot direct or control; we cannot make a world, as God did, out of chaos."

A few weeks later, Acheson spoke at the National War College. Once again, he tried to explain that the Cold War was not a struggle between good and evil. America had to deal with the Soviet Union as a great power, and not as a monster that had to be destroyed. "Today you hear much talk of absolutes . . . that two systems such as ours and that of the Russians cannot exist in the same world . . . that one is good and one is evil, and good and evil cannot exist in the world." But—"Good and evil have existed in this world since Adam and Eve went out of the Garden of Eden."

After he left office, Acheson missed what he called "the habit-forming drug of public life." It was not the trappings of power he desired, but he was always eager to be active, to be doing something. Senator McCarthy's attacks on him for "losing China" and for his alleged softness toward communism, the vilification heaped on him for his famous remark that he would not turn his back on Alger Hiss when Hiss's case was under appeal—a statement that was made out of Christian compassion, not because Acheson believed Hiss was necessarily innocent—these attacks took their toll on him. When Truman left office in 1953 and Acheson returned to Covington and Burling, he found it hard to get good cases; to a large extent the law firm carried him, and he was even shunned socially after having been tainted by McCarthy's charges.

It was only toward the end of decade that he once again was able to make his voice heard as the Democratic Party's spokesman for foreign policy, and when Kennedy was elected, he consulted Acheson on cabinet appointments. It was Acheson who recommended Dean Rusk to JFK as secretary of state, a recommendation Acheson came to regret. Rusk, he saw later, was an able lieutenant but not a leader. Acheson was especially influential in NATO policy, but he was not heeded when he urged the president not to become obsessed with Castro. After the Bay of Pigs disaster, Acheson commented that "Brains are no substitute for judgment."

In the Cuban missile crisis, Acheson was consulted as member of the Executive Committee and urged a quick air strike to take out the missiles rather then a naval blockade, as he feared that a blockade would give the Soviet troops on the island time to make the missiles operational. When his plan was not followed, however, he nonetheless agreed to brief General de Gaulle on Kennedy's decision to institute a naval blockade of Cuba.

Later, under Johnson, Acheson was frequently consulted on the Vietnam War; he generally supported LBJ, although he also worked on a peace plan for Vietnam with the dovish George Ball, who was Under Secretary in the Johnson cabinet. Finally, Acheson became increasingly suspicious of the canned military briefings with which LBJ was providing him.

Just after the disastrous Tet offensive in January–February 1968, Acheson was once again called to the White House. At this time, LBJ went on and on with a tirade against those who were criticizing his conduct of the war. Acheson abruptly excused himself and walked out of the Oval Office to his law firm across Lafayette Park. The phone rang almost immediately on his return. It was LBJ's national security adviser, Walt Rostow, who asked why Acheson had left so abruptly. "You can tell the President and you can tell him in precisely these words," Acheson said coldly, "that he can take Vietnam and stick it up his ass." The president soon came on the line and asked him to come back, and Acheson said bluntly that the JCS didn't know what they were talking about. If the president wanted any more advice, then Acheson had to have no more canned briefings but the full run of the shop. LBJ agreed: He could have access to all top-secret information.

A few weeks later, his study of Vietnam complete, the old pragmatic Acheson resurfaced. He told Johnson that he was being led down the garden path by his generals, and at a later meeting of the "Wise Men" Johnson senior advisers, Acheson said that it was now time to disengage. When the chairman of the joint chiefs, General Wheeler, tried to contest his view, explaining that the Pentagon was not bent on a classic military victory, but only helping the Vietnamese to avoid a communist victory, Acheson answered with a characteristic flash of his old style: "Then what in the name of God are five hundred thousand men out there doing—chasing girls?"

Two weeks later, in a televised speech to the nation, LBJ followed Acheson's advice. He ordered a bombing halt above the 20th parallel in North Vietnam and offered to negotiate. The escalation of the war had ended.

Even his old antagonist, Richard Nixon, sought his views, especially on European matters, and Acheson was both flattered at the attention Nixon and Kissinger paid him and eager to help stem any tendencies toward isolationism. He was also convinced that Nixon was serious about pulling out of Vietnam as soon as possible. Yet, when Nixon secretly expanded the war to Cambodia, Acheson broke with the president. The Nixon–Acheson honeymoon came to an abrupt end.

On a beautiful Columbus Day afternoon at his farm in Maryland, Dean Acheson was felled by a massive stroke at the age of 78. He died in seconds, and three days later more than 1,000 people attended his funeral at the Washington Cathedral. There were no eulogies. It was a brief service for the burial of the dead from the Episcopal Book of Common Prayer.

A little over a quarter century later Madeleine Albright moved the official portrait of Dean Acheson to a prominent place in the large outer office of the Secretary of State.

As head of the state department, Acheson was a towering figure. And he had in Truman a president who rarely questioned his views. As both men shared a disposition for decisive action, their teamwork lent an extraordinary dynamism to the furthering of U.S. foreign policy goals.

Even in his later years Acheson's brilliance in argument did not falter. He always wanted to show his panache, the grand manner, a D'Artagnan who grew up to become a Richelieu, the foreign statesman he most admired. Above all, he was a builder, and it is not surprising that his most rewarding avocation was his cabinet-making and architectural drawings. Like those of John Quincy Adams, the secretary of state whose portrait hung in his office, Acheson's achievements were enshrined in the structures he built. He was not merely present at the creation; he was the prime architect of that creation.

In the end, his actions not only defined American power and purpose in the postwar era, but also laid the foundations for U.S. predominance at the end of the twentieth century. He was, as his friend, British ambassador Oliver Franks, described him, "a pure American type of a rather rare species," imbued "with a love of cabinet making and gardening, never forgetting and ever going back to the roots from which it all sprang"—but above all and always, "a blade of steel."

BIBLIOGRAPHICAL ESSAY

Dean Acheson's papers are housed in the Harry S Truman Presidential Museum and Library. Other paper collections of value to an understanding of Acheson include the James V. Forrestal papers in the Seeley Mudd Library at Princeton University, the George F. Kennan papers also in the Mudd Library at Princeton, and the Harry S Truman papers at the Harry S Truman Presidential Museum and Library. Important bibliographic and historiographical works on the Truman era include Richard S. Kirkendall (ed.), *The Truman Period as a Research Field* (1967) and *The Truman Period as Research Field: A Reappraised* (1974). See also Richard D. Burns (ed.), *Harry S Truman, The Man and the Presidency: A Guide to References* (1984).

Important works on Acheson include his own autobiography, *Present at the Creation: My Years in the State Department* (1969). See also his *Morning and Noon* (1965). Important biographies of Acheson include Gaddis Smith, *Dean Acheson* (1972), part of *The American Secretaries of State and Their Diplomacy series;* David S. McLellan, *Dean Acheson: The State Department Years* (1976); Douglas Brinkley, *Dean Acheson: The Cold War Years, 1953–1971* (1992), and *Dean Acheson and the Making of U.S. Foreign Policy* (1993); James Chace, *Acheson: The Secretary of State Who Created the American World* (1998); and Walter Isaacson and Evan Thomas, *The Wise Men: Six Friends and the World They Made: Acheson, Bohlen, Harriman, Kennan, Lovett, McCloy* (1986).

Important biographies and memoirs of other high ranking officials of the Truman Administration include James F. Byrnes, *Speaking Frankly* (1947) and *All in One Lifetime* (1958); Richard L. Walker and George Curry, *E. R. Stettinius, Jr. and James F. Byrnes* (1965); Patricia Dawson Ward, *The Threat of Peace: James F. Byrnes and the Council of Foreign Ministers, 1945–1946* (1979); Walter Mills (ed.), *The Forrestal Diaries* (1951); Robert H. Ferrell, *George C. Marshall* (1966); Elting E. Morison, *Turmoil and Tradition: A Study of the Life and Times of Henry L. Stimson* (1960); Henry L. Stimson *On Active Service in Peace and War* (1948); Frederick H. Schapsmeier, *Prophet in Politics: Henry A. Wallace and the War Years, 1940–1965* (1970); and John Morton Blum (ed.), *The Price of Vision: The Diary of Henry A. Wallace, 1942–1946* (1973).

For other important people connected with the Truman Administration please see Charles E. Bohlen, *Witness to History, 1929–1969* (1973); Jean Edward Smith (ed.), *The Papers of Lucius D. Clay*, 2 volumes (1974); Frederick J. Dobney (ed.), *Selected Papers of Will Clayton* (1971); W. Averell Harriman with Elie Abel, *Special*

Envoy to Churchill and Stalin, 1941–1946 (1975); George F. Kennan, *Memoirs, 1925–1950* and *1950–1963* (1967, 1972); Clark M. Clifford with Richard Holbrook, *Counsel to the President: A Memoir* (1992); Warren I. Cohen, *Dean Rusk* (1980); Douglas MacArthur, *Reminiscences* (1964); and William Manchester, *American Caesar, Douglas MacArthur, 1880–1964* (1978).

Important works on the Truman presidency include Robert J. Donovan, *Conflict and Crisis: The Presidency of Harry S. Truman, 1945–1948* and *Tumultuous Years: The Presidency of Harry S. Truman, 1949–1953* (1977, 1982); Cabell Phillips, *The Truman Presidency: The History of a Triumphant Succession* (1966); and Robert H. Ferrell, *Harry S. Truman and the Modern Presidency* (1983). See Arthur M. Schlesinger, Jr., *The Imperial Presidency* (1973), for a liberal critique of the Truman presidency.

For Acheson's role in affecting U.S. policy toward Japan and for U.S. foreign policy generally under Roosevelt, please consult Waldo Heinrichs, *Threshold of War: Franklin D. Roosevelt and American Entry into World War II* (1988); Robert Dallek, *Franklin D. Roosevelt and American Foreign Policy, 1933–1945* (1979); Robert A. Divine, *Roosevelt and World War II* (1969); Willard Range, *Franklin D. Roosevelt's World Order* (1959); Walter LaFeber, *The Clash* (1997); Herbert Feis, *The Road to Pearl Harbor* (1950); Daniel Yergin, *The Prize: The Epic Quest for Oil, Money, and Power* (1991); and Ronald H. Spector, *Eagle Against the Sun* (1985).

For insight into the development of the Marshall Plan and the reconstruction of Europe generally, please see Gregory A. Fossedal, *Our Finest Hour: Will Clayton, The Marshall Plan, and the Triumph of Democracy* (1993); John L. Harper, *American Visions of Europe: Franklin D. Roosevelt, George F. Kennan, and Dean G. Acheson* (1994); and Michael J. Hogan, *The Marshall Plan: America, Britain, and The Reconstruction of Western Europe, 1947–1952* (1989).

A substantial literature is available on the origins and development of the Containment Strategy of the United States and the origins and evolution of the Cold War. Important works include William Appleton Williams, *The Tragedy of American Diplomacy* (1962), which led the academic research and debate on the issues; John L. Gaddis, *Strategies of Containment: A Critical Appraisal of Postwar American National Security Policy* (1982); *The United States and The End of the Cold War: Implications, Reconsideration, Provocations* (1992), *We Now Know: Rethinking Cold War History* (1997), and *The United States and the Origins of the Cold War 1941–1947* (1972); Joseph M. Jones, *The Fifteen Weeks (February 21–June 5, 1947)* (1955); Bruce R. Kuniholm, *The Origins of the Cold War, Great Power Conflict and Diplomacy in Iran, Turkey and Greece* (1994); Deborah W. Larson, *Origins of Containment: A Psychological Explanation* (1985); Thomas G. Paterson, *On Every Front: The Making of the Cold War* (1979), and Daniel H. Yergin, *Shattered Peace: The Origins of the Cold War* (1990).

For NATO and the Western Alliance see Alfred Grosser, *The Western Alliance: European-American Relations Since 1945* (1980); Avi Shlaim, *The United States and the Berlin Blockade, 1948–1949* (1983); Nicholas Henderson, *The Birth of NATO* (1982); Lawrence S. Kaplan, *The United States and NATO: The Formative Years* (1984); Timothy P. Ireland, *Creating the Entangling Alliance: The Origins of the North Atlantic Treaty Organization* (1981); and Robert McGeehan, *The German Rearmament Question: American Diplomacy and European Defense after World War II* (1971).

Concerning issues of importance to the United States in the Middle East and Latin America, please see Michael Stoff, *Oil, War and American Security: The Search for a National Policy on Foreign Oil, 1941–1947* (1980); Irvine H. Anderson, *Aramco, The United States and Saudi Arabia: A Study in the Dynamics of Foreign Oil Policy, 1933–1950* (1981); John Snetsinger, *Truman, The Jewish Vote and the Creation of Israel* (1974); David Green, *The Containment of Latin America: A History of the Myths and Realities of the Good Neighbor Policy* (1971); and Robert D. Cuff and J. L. Granastein, *American Dollars—Canadian Prosperity: Canadian–American Economic Relations, 1945–1950* (1978).

For discussion of the Cold War in East Asia and the Korean War please consult Robert M. Blum, *Drawing the Line: The Origins of the American Containment Policy in East Asia* (1982); Yonosuke Nagai and Akira Iriye, eds., *The Origins of the Cold War in Asia* (1977); Russell D. Buhite, *Soviet-American Relations in Asia, 1945–1954* (1981); Dorothy Borg and Waldo Heinrichs, eds., *Uncertain Years: Chinese-American Relations, 1947–1950* (1980); Rosemary Foot, *The Wrong War: American Policy and the Dimensions of the Korean Conflict, 1950–1953* (1985); and William Whitney Stueck, Jr., *The Road to Confrontation: American Policy toward China and Korea, 1947–1950* (1981).

James Chace

JOHN QUINCY ADAMS (1767–1848)

Served 1817–1825
Appointed by President James Monroe
Democratic-Republican

Scholars seem to agree that John Quincy Adams was the most accomplished diplomat and statesman in the country's history. Behind his unsurpassed career was a totally unique upbringing and exposure to learning. As the son of John and Abigail Adams, he lived in a universe of high expectations, devotion to duty, Christian faith, and classical virtue. He spent much of his youth abroad in the company of American and European leaders of distinction and renown. Born on July 11, 1767, he was scarcely 10 years old when he accompanied his father on a brief diplomatic mission to Paris. When John Adams returned to Paris as minister plenipotentiary in 1779 to negotiate a peace with England, Abigail insisted that John Quincy again accompany his father. "In all human probability," she wrote, "it will do more for your education to go back to France with your father than to prepare for college at Andover."

John Quincy's next six years comprised a phenomenal learning experience. For six months he studied at Passy, transferred to the Latin School in Amsterdam, and then pursued classical studies at the University of Leyden. Already he had read many classics in history, politics, and philosophy. His father had recommended *Thucydides's History of the Peloponnesian War* for his enlightenment on war and diplomacy. Adams's apprenticeship in diplomacy began in July 1791 when, at 14, he became private secretary to Francis Dana, the newly appointed U.S. representative to the court of Catherine the Great of Russia. Finding Russian education hopeless, he turned to English and European history. In 1782–1783, having returned to his father's residence at The Hague, Adams embarked on a seven-month trip through Sweden, Denmark, and Germany. Back in Paris, where his father helped to negotiate the Treaty of Paris (1783), he served as his father's private secretary, observed the diplomatic protocol and extravagances at Versailles, discussed science and politics with Franklin and Jefferson, attended Lafayette's weekly dinners, and read the works of France's famed eighteenth-century philosophers. In London, where in 1785 his father became America's first minister to the English court, he spent days listening to such great orators as Fox, Pitt, and Burke in the House of Commons. In March 1786, with his mother's admonition to study well, John Quincy Adams entered Harvard as a member of the junior class.

Upon graduating from Harvard in 1787, Adams spent three years studying law under Theophilus Parsons of Newburyport, later Massachusetts's chief justice. Having adopted his father's Federalist approach to national politics, Adams favored the new U.S. Constitution, opposed the French Revolution, and, in his "Marcellus" letters, joined Alexander Hamilton in defending President Washington's neutrality policy toward the European war. Washington, in 1794, appointed the 27-year-old John Quincy Adams U.S. minister to the Netherlands. Three years later, his father assigned him to Prussia. Washington approved. "Mr. Adams," he wrote, "is the most valuable public character we have abroad, and . . . there remains no doubt in my mind that he will prove himself to be the ablest of all our diplomatic corps." Upon his return to Massachusetts, Adams entered the Massachusetts senate in 1802 and the U.S. Senate in 1803.

In 1809, President James Madison appointed him minister to Russia, where he established a trusting friendship with Tsar Alexander. Alexander's offer to mediate a treaty of peace to end the War of 1812 between the United States and Great Britain brought James A. Bayard and Albert Gallatin to St. Petersburg. There, on July 21, 1813, they joined Adams for the negotiation. The British rejected the mediation, but suggested a meeting for the following year. Adams, Bayard, and Gallatin, joined by Henry Clay and Jonathan Russell, opened negotiations with the British in Ghent in August 1814. At Ghent, the American commissioners gained no British concessions on the issues that led to war: a maritime code that recognized neutral rights or an end to impressment. Otherwise they protected all previously acknowledged American rights, including those to the Newfoundland fisheries. They successfully challenged the British–Indian ties that curtailed the movement of American pioneers into the Ohio country. Adams defended the American "perpetual encroachments upon the Indians" by claiming "the moral and religious duty of a nation to settle, cultivate, and improve their territory—a principle . . . recognized by the law of nations." For Adams, it was incompatible with the natural order of things to "condemn vast regions of territory to perpetual barrenness and solitude: when countless American farmers were pressing to enter them for subsistence." What happened to the Indian was not Adams's concern.

From 1815 to 1817, Adams remained in London as U.S. minister to the English Court. He achieved little during his tenure beyond setting in motion the deliberations that led to the Rush–Bagot Treaty in 1817. This agreement limited naval armaments on the Great Lakes and demilitarized the U.S.–Canadian frontier, the first reciprocal naval disarmament of modern times. Adams's long residences abroad, added to the changing political climate in the United States, gradually undermined his earlier devotion to the Federalist Party. He acknowledged to his father, in August 1816, that the longer he lived, the more nationalistic and the less parochial his allegiances had become. In London he heard rumors that the incoming president, James Monroe, might appoint him secretary of state. On April 16, 1817, he received a letter informing him of his appointment and requesting that he return to the United States. John Adams advised his son to accept: "You are now approaching fifty years of age. In my opinion you must return to [your country], or renounce it forever." Monroe explained his selection of Adams in a letter to

Andrew Jackson: "Mr. Adams, by long service in our diplomatic concerns appearing to be entitled to the preference, supported by his acknowledged abilities and integrity, his nomination will go to the Senate." Jackson replied that the President could not have chosen better.

The two men functioned as an effective team, which reflected not only Monroe's republican conversion to Federalist principles of diplomacy, but also Adams's acceptance of a subordinate role in policymaking. Adams recognized the bureaucratic impediments he would face; in practice, he worked independently, often as a minority of one. Far more learned, energetic, and forceful than Monroe, he tended to dominate cabinet meetings when foreign policy was at issue. He alone among the country's leaders knew Europe's leading statesmen personally, especially Tsar Alexander, France's Talleyrand, and Britain's Castlereagh. Still, Adams's powerful cabinet associates opposed him on numerous occasions. Recognizing both the secretary's independence of mind and refusal to accept views he regarded rash, Baron Hyde de Neuville, the French minister, wrote of Adams in December 1817: "I know that he has dared to declare himself very strongly on many occasions against indiscreet and purely speculative ideas."

Physically and temperamentally, Adams scarcely resembled the classical diplomatist—suave and reassuring. He was short and bald, with a rheumy affliction that caused his eyes to run incessantly. Adams's childhood among adults, much of it abroad, deprived him of the association with peer groups that might have adjusted him to normal social intercourse. "I went out this evening," he said, "in search of conversation, an art of which I never had an adequate idea. . . . I am by nature a silent animal, and my dear mother's constant lesson in childhood, that children in company should be seen and not heard, confirmed me irrevocably in what I now deem a bad habit." When not simply uncommunicative, he was often argumentative, a shortcoming that he recognized. Following a dinner at the home of the president of the Bank of the United States, he confided to his diary: "I am not satisfied with myself this day, having talked too much at dinner. . . . Nor can I always (I did not this day) altogether avoid a dogmatical and peremptory tone and manner, always disgusting, and especially offensive in persons to whose age or situation others consider some deference due." On another occasion he noted in his diary: "I am a man of reserved, cold, austere, and forbidding manners. . . . With a knowledge of the actual defect in my character, I have not the pliability to reform it." Adams had countless acquaintances, but very few friends.

Beyond his deep-seated convictions, which neither time nor circumstances would alter, Adams possessed every quality essential for diplomatic distinction. His knowledge of Europe and its relationship to the New World was profound, and he understood the limits of effective diplomacy. For Adams, no less than for Washington and Hamilton, U.S. foreign policy had one major purpose: to serve the interests of the country, defined in commercial and geographic terms. He recognized, as did Hamilton, the natural separation of the New World from the old and the essential advantages that geography bestowed on the United States. Adams managed the technical aspects of diplomacy with remarkable skill. He read all dispatches sent out or received by the State Department. The experienced Monroe maintained a close surveillance over Adams's correspondence. When, on occasion, Adams objected to presidential statements, it was because the president reacted to events abroad from the standard of simple republican virtue, rather than a clear recognition of the country's interests, possibilities, and genuine intentions. Ultimately, it was Adams and not Monroe who gave leadership and direction to U.S. foreign relations during the eight years of their close association.

If Adams often faced opposition in the cabinet, Congress, and the press, he towered over the Washington diplomatic corps. Those compelled to negotiate with him never ceased to admire his intelligence and learning, his industry and self-discipline, and his unwavering pursuit of his country's interests, grasped more surely by him than any other man of his age. British envoy Stratford Canning wrote of Adams in his memoirs: "He was. . . . much above par in general ability, but having the air of a scholar rather than statesman, a very uneven temper, a disposition at times well-meaning, a manner somewhat too often domineering." Adams often revealed his capacity for annoyance toward those who impeded his diplomatic efforts, especially when he believed his protagonist had no choice but to accept his demands. His description of Luis de Onís, the Spanish minister, as a swindler was not uncommon. The president and members of the cabinet often modified the severity of Adams's language. Monroe, for example, challenged an Adams attack on Tsar Alexander and the principles of the Holy Alliance as unnecessarily irritating.

As secretary of state, Adams operated on three fundamental assumptions. The first was his belief in the economic and moral necessity of international trade, an interest, he believed, that all nations shared. His father had taken an early lead in condemning Europe's mercantile system in his advocacy of equality of access to foreign markets, reciprocity in commercial practices, and open sea-lanes for the vessels of all nations. The principles of freedom of the seas was the means whereby an inferior naval power could compete commercially with the world's dominant states. For John Quincy Adams, the free flow of international commerce would create a sense of community and create ties and mutual interests that might diminish the prospects of war. As Secretary of State, Adams claimed that "the principles of justice, humanity, and Christianity demanded, in particular, that free or neutral ships should make free goods and the neutral goods should be safe in enemy ships." Despite his efforts, Adams failed to establish a commercial world based on free trade principles. In wartime neutral rights remained elusive; a strong naval power, such as Britain, would not readily permit a neutral carrier to undermine its belligerent interests in the name of neutral rights—unless the neutral possessed some effective means of retaliation.

Second, Adams viewed the North American continent as the proper and ultimate domain of the United States. His territorial ambitions did not contemplate war, but recognized the enormous discrepancies in power between the country and its neighboring regions. During November 1819, Secretary of the Treasury William H. Crawford informed Adams that many British and French observers regarded the United States as dangerously ambitious and encroaching. Adams retorted that to argue otherwise would be useless:

Nothing that we could say or do would remove this impression until the world shall be familiarized with the idea of considering our proper dominion to be the continent of North America. From the time when we became an independent people it was as much a law of nature that this should become our pretension as that the Mississippi should flow to the sea. Spain had possessions upon our southern and Great Britain upon our northern border. It was impossible that centuries should elapse without finding them annexed to the United States; not that any spirit of encroachment or ambition on our part renders it necessary, but because it is a physical, moral, and political absurdity that such fragments of territory, with sovereigns at fifteen hundred miles beyond the sea, worthless and burdensome to their owners, should exist permanently contiguous to a great, powerful, enterprising, and rapidly growing nation. . . . Until Europe shall find it a settled geographical element that the United States and North America are identical, any effort on our part to reason the world out of a belief that we are ambitious will have no other effect than to convince them that we add to our ambition hypocrisy.

The Canadian–American border settlement, as defined by the Convention of 1818, followed the 49th parallel from the Lake of the Woods to the Rocky Mountains. The Oregon territory west of the Rockies would be occupied jointly up to ten years. In December 1820, a House Committee issued a report that announced U.S. claims to the entire Pacific Northwest as far as 60 degrees. British Minister Canning asked Adams to explain U.S. interests toward such vast expanses when Britain claimed no less than the Columbia River as Canada's southern border. Adams replied that Britain had no claims to the Columbia boundary; he then proceeded to challenge Britain's imperial claims elsewhere. Certainly, Adams declared, the London government had come "to the conclusion that there would be neither policy nor profit in caviling with us about territory on this North American continent." When Canning asked if the secretary included Canada in his claims, Adams responded: "No, there the boundary is marked, and we have no disposition to encroach upon it. Keep what is yours, but leave the rest of the continent to us."

Third, even as Adams championed the expansion of global trade and the cause of continental expansion, he resolutely opposed U.S. involvement in the affairs of other nations. Toward the European continent, emerging from a quarter century of war, he urged a posture of strict neutrality. Unconvinced that Europe's peace would be long continue, he recommended that the country "persevere in the system of keeping aloof from all their broils, and in that of consolidating and perpetuating our own union." To underwrite his hopes for national peace and security in a still-challenging world, he looked to an ever-stronger union and a reasonable level of military preparedness. He steadfastly opposed material and diplomatic aid to peoples struggling for independence. He expressed his total disapproval of foreign crusades in his famed speech of July 4, 1821, declaring that the United States "goes not abroad, in search of monsters to destroy. She is the well-wisher to the freedom and independence of all. She is the champion and vindicator only of her own." Any shift from liberty to force, Adams warned, might make the United States the dictatress of the world, but no longer the ruler of its own spirit. He, like others, would limit the country's contribution to human progress to the creation of a model republic worthy of emulation.

In 1815, the burgeoning revolutionary upheaval of South America threatened the peace and stability of the Atlantic world. Napoleon's invasion of Spain in 1808 had terminated Madrid's effective control of Spanish America. Provisional juntas maintained by Spain's ruling classes continued to claim jurisdiction over the empire, but by 1815 their New World influence was purely nominal. Freed of Spain's commercial restrictions, the various regions of Latin America opened their commerce to the world. When war broke out between the restored Spanish monarchy and the now rebellious colonies, the struggling South Americans looked to the United States for economic, military, and moral support. American editors, congressmen, even some administration officials embraced the cause of South American independence. Determined to sever Europe's ties with the New World, editors led by William Duane of Philadelphia's *Aurora* demanded American guardianship of Latin America independence. In Congress, the powerful Henry Clay denounced the administration for neglecting American interests and the cause of liberty in Latin America. Adams was appalled at the widespread defiance of the official U.S. policy of neutrality, for Spain continued to claim sovereignty over its Latin American empire. "There seems to me," he complained in June 1816, "too much of the warlike humor in the debates of Congress—propositions even to take up the cause of the South Americans, . . . as if they were talking of the expense of building a light house."

During 1818, the course of the U.S. policy toward Latin America began to emerge. In March, Monroe requested a congressional appropriation to defray the expenses of a commission of inquiry to South America. Clay attached an amendment to add $18,000 for a U.S. legation in Buenos Aires, thereby compelling the president to recognize the independence of the Argentines. Clay stepped down from the speaker's rostrum to enter a strong plea for his amendment, which lost 115 to 45. Adams expressed his contempt for Congress in his diary: "The present session will stand remarkable in the annals of the Union for showing how a legislature can keep itself employed when having nothing to do. . . . The proposed appropriation for a minister to Buenos Ayres has gone the way of other things lost upon earth, like the purchase of oil for light houses in the western country." In July, the president's fact-finding commission returned to Washington, hopelessly divided. Still the administration continued to respond to the changing conditions both in Europe and in Latin America. By the summer 1818, Monroe and Adams concluded that the great European states would never restore Spanish sovereignty in South America. At the conference of Aix-la-Chapelle, which opened in September 1818, England opposed the use of force against the Latin Americans, but Foreign Secretary Lord Castlereagh rejected Adams's suggestion of a concerted British–American policy.

By 1817, Spain's growing weakness in the New World raised the question of Florida's future. The Madrid government was too plagued with disorders elsewhere to maintain order in the region. British adventurers perennially armed and incited the local Indians to raid north of the Florida border. Monroe dispatched General Andrew Jackson to punish the Indians for their destruction of American lives and property. Carrying out his orders with vigor, Jackson pursued a band of marauding Indians into Florida where he captured and executed two British agents as well as two Indian chiefs. Spain protested the action; Jackson's enemies in Congress demanded his dismissal. Monroe and all members of the cabinet, except Adams, agreed that Jackson had exceeded his instructions and committed war against Spain, an act that required an official disavowal. Adams reminded the cabinet that Jackson's actions were defensive and that he had entered Florida, not to war on Spain, but to terminate the Indian depredations. Jackson had discretionary powers; to disavow them was unthinkable. Adams's argument carried. He reminded the complaining Spanish minister, Onís, that Spain had an obligation, under treaty, to keep order in Florida. If it could not control the Indians, it had no choice but to cede the colony to the United States. Spain acknowledged its dilemma. In July 1818, French Minister Hyde de Neuville informed Adams that Spain would cede Florida to the United States, provided that Washington would assume the claims of American citizens against Spain, estimated at $5 million.

Ever conscious of its growing weakness, the Madrid government recognized the necessity of creating a barrier between the United States and the Spanish borderlands in the Southwest, even if it required a boundary to the Pacific. In Washington, Onís had not received authority to negotiate a western boundary, but on July 11, 1818, he offered a Spanish proposal for a boundary between the United States and Spanish Mexico along a line running northward near Natchitoches to the Red River, and from there to the Missouri. Adams found the offer unacceptable; when Madrid remained uncompromising, he threatened to terminate the negotiations. Then on October 31, Adams presented Onís a note outlining what he termed the final U.S. offer:

> Beginning at the mouth of the River Sabine, on the Gulf of Mexico, following the course of said river to the thirty-second degree of latitude; the eastern bank and all the islands in said river to belong to the United States, and the western bank to Spain; thence, due north, to the northern-most part of the thirty-third degree of north latitude, and until it strikes the Rio Roxo, or Red River, thence, following the course of the said river, to its source, touching the chain of the Snow mountains, in latitude thirty-seven degrees twenty-five minutes north, longitude on hundred degrees and six degrees fifteen minutes west, or thereabouts, as marked on Melish's map, thence to the summit of the said mountains, and following the chain of the same to the forty-first parallel of latitude; thence, following the said parallel of latitude forty one degrees, to the South Sea. The northern bank of the United States, and the southern bank of the same to Spain.

For Madrid, determined to push the boundary eastward and northward as far as possible, Adams's demands were totally unacceptable. Through the deadlocked negotiations of late 1818, Adams resorted to the South American recognition issue to coerce a satisfactory treaty from Spain. On December 12, he suggested to Hyde de Neuville that France join the United States in recognizing the government of Buenos Aires. The French minister, hoping to forestall recognition to prevent a rupture in the Adams–Onís negotiations, asked Adams to give Spain three to four months before deciding on recognition. Adams declined to offer any assurance, arguing that Spain should have come to terms on the boundary issue earlier. Adams instructed the U.S. minister in London to inform the entire diplomatic corps of the importance of early recognition of the South American states. He instructed the cabinet that the United States had cause for recognition even as he asked Congress for legislation authorizing the president, under certain contingencies, to seize Spanish Florida. By the year's end, Adams began to wonder how long he could resort to such efforts at diplomatic coercion without endangering the peace or suffering humiliation.

Finally, on January 3, 1819, Hyde de Neuville informed Adams that Onís had received instruction to negotiate a transcontinental boundary. The instructions advocated a line to the Pacific along the 43rd parallel as well as a larger barrier for Santa Fe than Adams's Red River line. On January 16, however, Onís called for a boundary running from the mouth of the Missouri River to the Columbia, and down that river to the Pacific. Adams rejected that proposal, but responded favorably to Madrid's request regarding Santa Fe. He modified his ultimatum of October 31 by substituting for the Red River to its mouth a line to run due north from the Pawnee bend of the Red to the Arkansas, following that river to its source in the Rockies. When Adams discovered that the Pawnee bend was four or five degrees west of his initial reading of 97 degrees west longitude, he informed Hyde de

Neuville that he would accept the 100th meridian. On January 24, Onís received instructions from Madrid that granted him full powers to settle all remaining points of controversy. Thereafter Onís's counterproposals began to approach the American demands. On February 4, Onís accepted Adams's modified proposal along the Red, but demanded the 43rd parallel to the Pacific.

Monroe was now prepared to concede all remaining points of conflict. But Adams observed that "if Onís intends to conclude at all, we can obtain better." On February 12, the cabinet authorized him to accept the 100th meridian from the Red to the Arkansas and the 43rd parallel if he could not obtain more. Adams still advocated the 41st parallel at the Pacific as well as the southern and western banks of rivers to deny Spain access to their navigation. Monroe instructed Adams to make his counteroffer. Onís preferred a compromise at the 42nd parallel, but insisted that the boundaries follow the center of the rivers, permitting Spanish navigation. Adams accepted the 42nd parallel, but observed that the United States, unlike Spain, would soon have settlements along the rivers, rendering the issue of Spanish navigation moot. Determined to settle the Florida issue as well as the transcontinental boundary, Onís, on February 9, presented Adams a treaty project that included the cession of East and West Florida to the United States, as Britain ceded them to Spain in 1783. Adams rejected Onís's supposition that West Florida was not part of the Louisiana Purchase. Onís accepted Adams's demand that American claims against the Spanish government, to be assumed by the United States, be limited to $5 million. This eliminated an open-ended U.S. liability for claims against Spain. On February 20, 1819, Adams and Onís reached final agreement on the transcontinental boundary, but postponed the signing until February 22, Washington's birthday.

Monroe and Adams feared that the acceptance of the Sabine River boundary, enabling Spain to retain Texas, would face serious public and congressional disapproval. Monroe believed that the acquisition of the Floridas, the extension of the boundary to the Pacific, giving the United States frontage on the ocean, and the resolution of the claims issue would mitigate any condemnation of the Sabine boundary. Adams might have acquired a portion of Texas; even Onís's instructions of October 10, 1818, authorized him to offer the Colorado River of Texas. Adams may not have known this, but unlike his uncompromising pursuit of objectives elsewhere, he acquiesced passively in the cession of Texas. Monroe's letters reveal his disinterest in the acquisition of Texas, not to gain territory elsewhere, but to prevent the potential expansion of slavery. Ultimately both Adams and Monroe had reasons to see positive good in the Sabine decision. In 1820, when Missouri statehood raised the question of slavery and the sectional balance, both Adams and Monroe could rejoice that Texas did not augment the burgeoning sectional controversy. The Senate approved the Transcontinental Treaty unanimously on February 24, 1819, permitting the opposition no time to coalesce.

What soon troubled Adams was Spain's reluctance to ratify the treaty. The king seemed agreeable, but members of the Consejo de Estado complained that Onís had given away too much territory and failed to secure a U.S. pledge of nonrecognition of the new South American states. Adams, in his repeated employment of the recognition issue, had convinced too many in Madrid that he did not regard Washington bound by the American policy of neutrality. Monroe, troubled by adverse domestic opinion as well as Europe's known determination to support Spanish interests in the New World, doubted the wisdom of precipitate action. When the cabinet met on November 26, Adams insisted that Spain had no legal right to procrastinate and advocated military action. Monroe resented such advice. As Adams noted: "Lately, and particularly yesterday, I saw that my advice had become irksome to the president—that he was verging on the suspicion that I was spurring him to rash and violent measures."

As the drift continued month after month, Adams feared that Henry Clay's Western opposition, as well as the Northern fear of Florida statehood unleashed by the Missouri debates, would prevent another Senate approval. Adams concluded as early as January 1820: "The Treaty is gone forever . . . all the benefit which was hoped from it for the administration is lost." In May, Monroe announced plans to delay implementation of the treaty until the new Spanish government, the creation of a military revolt, had time to organize itself. The new Spanish minister, General Dionisio Vives, arrived in Washington during April 1820, demanding that the United States guarantee the integrity of Spain's territorial possessions in Latin America and promise not to recognize the new rebel governments. Adams and Monroe had no intention of adhering to Vives's demands, but had no idea how to proceed. Suddenly, on October 5, 1820, the administration's forbearance triumphed. That day the new Spanish government ratified the treaty. The troubling Spanish land grants in Florida, issued just before the initial signing of the treaty in 1819, were declared null and void. Monroe resubmitted the treaty to the Senate; again it passed, but without four Western votes. On February 22, 1821, precisely two years after the initial vote, the Adams–Onís Treaty became effective.

During the period between the two signings of the Treaty, Adams upheld the policy of strict neutrality toward South America's revolutionary struggles, one totally in harmony with that of the European powers. To that end, he resisted congressional demands to recognize the independence of the South American republics before "the chances of [Spain] . . . to recover [them] had become utterly desperate." He objected when the House of Representatives passed a resolution in 1820 expressing "the deep interest which [Americans] feel for the success of the Spanish Provinces . . . which are struggling to establish liberty and independence." In cabinet discussions, he opposed plans to sell arms to the South American rebels. Adams was distressed that the idea of shipping secret aid to the revolutionaries, while openly professing neutrality, appeared acceptable to the cabinet. Such behavior, Adams warned, would appear an act of war against Spain, which the chief executive could not undertake, under the Constitution, without the authority of Congress. Adams opposed any reference to the wars for South American independence in Monroe's annual messages of 1819 and 1820, arguing that such references would antagonize the governments of Europe. For him, the American principle of neutrality left no room for intervention. Nor did the justice of the cause alter the rules that governed the behavior of third parties.

Ratification of the Transcontinental Treaty in February 1821 eliminated the one remaining impediment to recognition. Adams had not satisfied Vives on the question of American recognition, but he hinted that if Spain ratified the treaty, the United States would not "precipitately recognize the independence of the South Americans." By early 1821, the striking victories of the revolutionary forces all but destroyed Spain's remaining authority in South America. Clay secured passage of two House resolutions, one expressing interest in South America independence, the other encouraging the president to recognize the independence of the new states whenever he believed it expedient. In a special message to Congress on March 8, 1822, Monroe recognized the changing conditions by declaring Chile, the United Provinces of the Plata (Argentina), Peru, Colombia, and Mexico fully independent and thus rightful claimants to recognition by other nations. Adams kept his word by waiting a decent interval before advocating the step that Spain had feared and Europe opposed. Congress responded by appropriating funds to meet the expense of "such missions to the independent nations on the American continent as the President might deem proper."

Spain's internal anarchy set the stage for Adams's final contribution to America's external relation: erecting the framework for the famed Monroe Doctrine. When Spanish revolutionaries captured King Ferdinand VII and proclaimed a constitutional monarchy, the Holy Alliance of Russia, Austria, and Prussia refused to accept this threat to Europe's monarchial order. At the Congress of Verona in 1822, it persuaded France to dispatch an army to Spain to restore the king. With ample support among Spanish people, France quickly reestablished order, thereby enhancing its own prestige and the predominance of the Holy Alliance. Lord Castlereagh's successor, George Canning, feared that France, encouraged by Tsar Alexander, might attempt to restore the Spanish Empire in America. In August 1823, Canning informed U.S. Minister Richard Rush that Britain would counter any French move to interfere in the Spanish colonies. He suggested that Britain and United States issue a joint declaration, warning France and other Continental powers against any Latin American involvement, while reassuring Spain that neither country had any designs on the Spanish Empire. Rush received Canning's letter on August 22 and forwarded it to Adams. Rush agreed to sign a joint declaration, without instructions, if Britain would recognize the New Latin American republics. This Canning refused to do. Convinced that he would obtain no support from the United States, Canning approached the French ambassador, Prince de Polignac, directly. France had no interest in opposing Latin American independence and, in the secret "Polignac Memorandum," assured the British that it had no intention of dispatching an expedition to the New World. For Canning, that resolved the issue.

In Washington, France's unopposed invasion of Spain troubled Monroe as an assault on Spanish human rights, which demanded some U.S. response, but Adams assured Rush that the U.S. policy of neutrality still held. Rush's long communication of late August reached Washington on October 9. Monroe was inclined to accept the British offer, but first sought the advice of Jefferson and Madison, both of whom endorsed Canning's proposal. Meanwhile, Adams had responded to the French invasion of Spain by asserting the American doctrine of *no transfer*. He feared that Spain might cede Cuba to Britain to secure an Anglo-Spanish alliance. In April 1823, he sent a long message to Hugh Nelson, the U.S. minister in Madrid, warning the Spanish government against the transfer of Cuba to another European power. When Canning assured Washington that London had no intention of acquiring the island, Monroe recommended to the cabinet that the United States also issue a statement of self-denial. Adams objected; for him the United States had no reason to bind itself permanently against the possibility that Cuba one day might solicit a union with the United States. Monroe assured London informally that the United States also had no designs on Cuba.

Russia provoked another historic Adams response when the Tsar, in 1821, issued a ukase that excluded foreigners from trading, fishing, or navigating within 100 Roman miles of the northwest coast from Bering Strait to the 51st parallel. Both Britain and the United States objected. On June 28, 1823, Adams recommended to the cabinet that the United States should formally contest the Russian ukase. Adams informed Baron de Tuyall, the Russian Minister, in July that the United States would challenge the right of Russia to any territory on the continent under the principle that "the American continents are no longer subjects for *any* new European colonial establishment." Then on July 22, Adams instructed Henry Middleton, the American minister in St. Petersburg: "With the exception of the British establishments north of the United States, the remainder of both the American continents must henceforth be left to the management of American hands." Thus Adams asserted the principle of *noncolonization*.

When Monroe returned to Washington with the opinions of Jefferson and Madison corroborating his own, Adams objected to a joint U.S.–British warning against European intervention in Latin America. He doubted that France entertained any such intention and suspected that Canning's self-denying proposal was aimed less at Europe than at future U.S. expansionism toward Texas and the Caribbean. When the cabinet met on November 7, Adams proposed that the United States take its stand against the Holy Alliance unilaterally. "It would be more candid, as well as more dignified," he said, "to avow our principles explicitly to Russia and France, than to come in as a cock-boat in the wake of the British man-of-war." Adams remained untroubled by the continued rumors of European encroachments on South America. Spain, he averred, had no more power to restore its control in the Western Hemisphere than had the Chimborazo to sink to the bottom of the sea. He warned that "if the South Americans were really in a state to be so easily subdued, it would be but a more forcible motive for us to beware of involving ourselves in their fate." To strengthen U.S. opposition to European encroachment, Adams suggested that the United States disclaim all interference in the affairs of Europe under the supposition "that the European powers will equally abstain from the attempt . . . to subjugate by force any part of these continents to their will." Adams thus formulated the principle of *nonintervention* in Latin American affairs by Europe; Monroe accepted it and announced that he would proclaim this American intention toward the Western Hemisphere in his December message to Congress.

On November 21, Monroe read to the cabinet a preliminary draft of his forthcoming message. Adams was shocked at its "tone of deep solemnity and of high alarm, intimating that this country is menaced by imminent and formidable dangers. . . ." Adams was especially troubled by the President's open endorsement of Greek independence. The Greek revolution had gathered momentum until by 1821 it posed an immediate threat to Ottoman rule. Turkey's Sultan Mahmud II retaliated against the Greek revolutionaries with such violence that he aroused anti-Turkish sentiment throughout Western Europe and the United States. Monroe expressed regret over Turkey's despotic rule over Greece in his annual message of December 1822. Then in 1823, Edward Everett, professor of Greek literature at Harvard, championed Greek independence in a long essay appearing in the *North American Review*, a journal that he edited. Adams was not impressed and argued strongly against any American meddling in the affairs of Greece and Turkey, especially because the country was not prepared financially or militarily to intervene.

Adams considered it essential that Monroe not antagonize the Holy Alliance needlessly by interfering in the affairs of Europe. To meet a forceful European interposition in America, Adams warned, would be difficult enough "without going to bid them defiance in the heart of Europe." The secretary summarized his views before the cabinet: "The ground that I wish to take is that of earnest remonstrance against the interference of the European powers by force with South America, but to disclaim all interference on our part with Europe; to make an American cause, and adhere inflexibility to that." Adams added to nonintervention the principle of *abstention*. This concept of two worlds Monroe embodied in his celebrated message to Congress on December 2, 1823. The Monroe Doctrine declared specifically that the United States would regard any effort of the European powers to extend their rule to any portion of the Western Hemisphere as a threat to its peace and safety. Monroe assured the nations of the Old World that the United States would not interfere with their dependencies in the New World or involve itself in matters purely European.

In London, Canning regarded Monroe's principle of noncolonization extravagant. He assumed, with Rush, that the doctrine was directed principally, if not specifically, against the equally extravagant claim of the Russian ukase of 1821. During the spring of 1824, Adams resolved the far Northwest conflict with Russia. When New England traders demanded access to the fur seals and sea otters in the Aleutians far north of 51 degrees, he reminded Stratford Canning in Washington that the United States had no territorial claims as far north as the 51st parallel and assumed that British interests would be sufficient to counter Russia's demands. Adams suggested a boundary at 55 degrees north latitude. The Russian government accepted Adams's noncolonization principle as well as the U.S. right to unsettled areas north of the line of division. To keep all of Prince of Wales Island under their control, the Russians proposed the boundary of 54–40 degrees. In the Convention of April 1824, Russia gained its preferred boundary, but gave up all pretensions to a *mare clausum* in the north Pacific.

Even as the April convention disposed of the Russian challenge in the far Northwest, Adams's allies in Congress disposed of the Greek issue. Among Everett's converts was Daniel Webster, then congressman from Massachusetts. Webster introduced a resolution into the House in December 1823, which provided that "provision ought to be made by law, for defraying the expense incident to the appointment of an Agent or Commissioner to Greece, whenever the President shall deem it expedient to make such appointment." On January 19, 1824, on this apparently noncommittal text, Webster launched into an eloquent appeal to American humanitarian sentiment. He asked nothing of Congress; courage and spirit, properly expressed by the passage of the resolution, would achieve more than money. The Greeks, he declared, look to "the great Republic of the earth—and they ask us by our common faith, whether we can forget that they are struggling, as we once struggled, for what we now so happily enjoy?"

John Randolph's reply to Webster, on January 24, revealed the conservatism that the nation expected of him. He attacked Webster's effort to commit the nation abroad to what it could not accomplish, except at enormous cost to its own interests. Why, he asked, would Webster launch a crusade against slavery in the eastern Mediterranean when slavery existed by law within the United States? Why would he fix on Turkey as the enemy of America's democratic values when Turkey's external behavior had been preferable to that of the Christian nations of Europe? How, Randolph wondered, would the United States operate effectively in a country distant as Greece? "These projects of ambition surpass those of Bonaparte himself." Finally, he attacked the resolution itself: "We are absolutely combatting shadows. The gentleman would have us believe his resolution is all but nothing. . . . Either it is nothing, or it is something. If it is nothing, let us lay it on the table . . . but if it is that something which it has been . . . represented to be, let us beware how we touch it." Such argumentation, much to Adams's delight, eliminated the issue of Greek independence from the nation's consideration.

Adams detected more assuredly than his contemporaries that European influence in the Western Hemisphere was on the decline. This assumption underlay his confident and consistent course on Latin American independence, his vision of an expanding republic on the North American continent, and his disinclination to compromise on issues purely American. Recognizing the limits of U.S. power outside the Western Hemisphere, he argued against verbal commitments that transcended demonstrable national interests or the intention to act. Rejecting resorts to threats or war, he settled for what diplomacy could achieve. Where he possessed the diplomatic advantage, as in the Rush–Bagot and Adams–Onís treaties, he pursued the American interest as he defined it. Where the country's advantage was doubtful, as on the questions of Oregon and commercial reciprocity, he either postponed settlement until the superior interests and advantages of the United States became apparent or simply accepted less than he desired. Where the issue was revolution in Latin America, Greece, or Spain, he established the principles of U.S. abstention in European affairs and European nonintervention in the Western Hemisphere. Monroe relied heavily on Adams's acute sense of the possible, but rejected Adams's advice when it appeared unnecessarily demanding. Together Monroe and Adams stretched the possibilities of success in external relations as far as wise judgment and the avoidance of serious error would permit.

BIBLIOGRAPHICAL ESSAY

There are two rich primary sources for the life of John Quincy Adams. One is the vast trove of Adams family papers in the Massachusetts Historical Society, Boston; the other is *Memoirs of John Quincy Adams, Compromising Portions of His Diary from 1795 to 1848*, edited by Charles Francis Adams (12 vols., 1874–1877). Allan Nevins published a useful one-volume edition of the *Memoirs* (1951). Worthington C. Ford edited Adams's correspondence and public addresses to 1823 in seven volumes, *Writings of John Quincy Adams* (1913–1917). Most of Adams's official correspondence as minister to St. Petersburg and London, as well as secretary of state, appears in *American State Papers, Foreign Relations*, volumes III–V. Walter LaFeber has prepared an excellent compilation of Adams's letters, speeches, and diary excerpts in *John Quincy Adams and American Continental Empire* (1965).

First among studies of Adams's diplomatic career is Samuel Flagg Bemis's *John Quincy Adams and the Foundations of American Foreign Policy* (1949). William H. Seward's *Life and Public Services of John Quincy Adams* (1850) is a laudatory biography by a distinguished disciple. On the young Adams see Robert A. East, *John Quincy Adams, The Critical Years: 1785–1794* (1962). A general account of Adams's secretarial years is in Dexter Perkins, "John Quincy Adams" in Samuel Flagg

Bemus (ed.), *American Secretaries of State and Their Diplomacy, IV* (1928). The best general account of James Monroe's presidency is George Dangerfield's judicious and well-written *The Era of Good Feelings* (1952). Albert Weinberg's *Manifest Destiny* (1935) analyzes American nationalism during Adams's secretarial years. George A. Lipsky's *John Quincy Adams: His Theory and Ideas* (1950) and Greg Russell's *John Quincy Adams and the Public Virtues of Diplomacy* (1995), analyze Adams's thought regarding diplomacy and international relations.

For Adams's secretarial relations with important American contemporaries, see Harry Ammon, *James Monroe: The Quest for National Identity* (1971); Raymond Walters, Jr., *Albert Gallatin: Jeffersonian Financier and Diplomat* (1957); Richard Rush, *A Residence at the Court of London* (1833); and J. H. Powell, *Richard Rush, Republican Diplomat, 1780–1859* (1942). For the views of European diplomats toward Adams, see Stanley Lane-Poole, *Life of Stratford Canning* (2 vols., 1888) and "Correspondence of the Russian Ministers in Washington, 1818–1825," *American Historical Review, XVIII* (January, April, 1913), 309–45, 537–62.

Among the many writings on specific aspects of Adams's diplomacy are the analyses of Adams's relationship to American commercial policy in Vernon Stetser's *The Commercial Reciprocity Policy of the United States, 1774–1829* (1937) and F. Lee Benn's *The American Struggle for the West India Carrying-Trade, 1815–1830* (1923). Edward H. Tatum, Jr., stressed U.S. animosity toward England after 1815 in his *The United States and Europe, 1815–1823* (1936). Bradford Perkins traced Adams's diplomatic relations with Britain's Lord Castlereagh in *Castlereagh and Adams: England and the United States, 1812–1823* (1964). P. C. Brooks's *Diplomacy of the Borderlands: The Adams–Onís Treaty of 1819* (1939) and Williams Earl Week's *John Quincy and the American Global Empire* (1992) deal fully with the Transcontinental Treaty of 1819.

Volumes on Adams's reaction to the Latin American independence movements are C. C. Griffin's *The United States and the Disruption of the Spanish Empire, 1810–1822* (1937), Arthur Preston Whitaker's *The United States and the Independence of Latin America, 1800–1830* (1941), J. Fred Rippy's *Rivalry of the United States and Great Britain over Latin America, 1808–1830* (1929), and William W. Kaufmann's *British Policy and the Independence of Latin America, 1804–28* (1951). The standard work on Adams and the Monroe Doctrine is Dexter Perkins, *The Monroe Doctrine, 1823–1826* (1927). Richard Van Alstyne's *The Rising American Empire* (1960) contains a thoughtful discussion of the Monroe Doctrine. George Dangerfield, *Awakening of American Nationalism, 1815–1828* (1965), contains excellent chapters on the Transcontinental Treaty and the Monroe Doctrine. J. A. Logan, Jr., *No Transfer: An American Security Principle* (1961), discusses Adams's role in the development of that American principle.

Norman Graebner

MADELEINE ALBRIGHT (1937–)

Served 1997–2001
Appointed by President Bill Clinton
Democrat

During his two terms in office William Jefferson Clinton, the 42nd president, was served by two secretaries of state. The second of these was Madeleine Albright, who was born Marie Jana Korbel on May 15, 1937, in Prague. On January 23, 1997, she made history by becoming the first woman secretary of state, after unanimous confirmation by the Republican-dominated Senate. Albright is the highest-ranking woman in the history of the U.S. government and was one of the most publicly recognized modern secretaries of state. Prior to achieving this position, her career service was primarily in academia and Democratic Party circles, and she served in relatively low-level positions in the Carter administration, the only Democratic administration between Lyndon Johnson and Bill Clinton. As Clinton's second secretary of state, she was the 64th in the history of the United States.

Her family background represents a reaction to two of the twentieth century's most terrifying regimes: Hitler's Germany and Stalin's Soviet Union. Her great-grandfather escaped from a Polish Jewish ghetto by getting a job with a railroad. Her grandfather began his career as a railroad employee and became a prosperous Prague businessman. Her father dropped Judaism in favor of Catholicism, was a Czechoslovakian diplomat, and fled communism for the academic world of the University of Denver when Albright was 11 years old. Having experienced her family's struggles with these great pariahs influenced Albright's strong patriotism, incrementalism, and anticommunism.

Albright evidently was unaware of her Jewish roots until a reporter uncovered them at the time of her nomination to become Secretary of State, and it has been suggested that this obliviousness is part of a pattern of behavior, including her lack of awareness of the impending doom of her marriage of 23 years in 1982. More severe critics accused Albright of prevarication.

Albright earned a B.A. in political science from Wellesley College. She studied at the School of Advanced International Studies at Johns Hopkins University and received a Certificate from the Russian Institute at Columbia University. She also received her master's and doctoral degrees from Columbia. Her master's thesis was entitled *The Soviet Diplomatic Service: Profile of an Elite* (1968), and her dissertation was entitled *The Role of the Press in Political Change: Czechoslovakia 1968* (1976).

As a research professor of international affairs and director of the Women in Foreign Service Program at Georgetown University's School of Foreign Service, Albright taught courses in international affairs, U.S. foreign policy, Soviet foreign policy, and Central and Eastern European politics. Her publication record in academic journals is rather thin, with "The Role of the United States in Central Europe" published in *Proceedings of the Academy of Political Science* in 1991 and no books to her credit.

From 1981 to 1982, Albright was a fellow at the Woodrow Wilson International Center for Scholars at the Smithsonian. She also served as a Senior Fellow in Soviet and Eastern European Affairs at the Center for Strategic and International Studies. From 1978 to 1981, Albright served as a staff member of President Jimmy Carter's National Security Council and as a White House staff member. From 1976 to 1978, she served as chief legislative assistant to Senator Edmund Muskie of Maine. In 1972, a reception Albright hosted for then-presidential candidate Muskie was the victim of pranks perpetuated by the Nixon campaign to sow dissent among the Democratic presidential candidates.

Albright was a member of the Clinton administration from its beginning in 1993. Prior to her appointment as Secretary of State, Albright served as the United States' Representative to the United Nations and as a member of Clinton's Cabinet and National Security Council. She was from the beginning a major contributor to the basic theory informing Clinton's foreign policy.

Albright participated in some controversial actions during her tenure as U.S. ambassador to the United Nations. She persuaded President Clinton that the United States should use its veto to deny UN Secretary-General Boutros Boutros-Ghali a second term. Although outvoted 14 to 1 in the Security Council, the U.S. prevailed through the use of its veto power.

The situation in Bosnia was very important to Albright as well. Albright disagreed with then-Chairman of the Joint Chiefs of Staff Colin Powell about the use of force to prevent ethnic cleansing in the former Yugoslavia. Albright's vision emerged victorious, and the United States abandoned the policy of creating UN-defended safe havens for Bosnian Muslims and instead the United States committed itself to the creation of a multiethnic Bosnia. The NATO mission to Bosnia consisted of 50,000 troops in total, of which 20,000 were Americans. The United States also launched a cruise missile attack against Serb positions in Bosnia.

Despite her academic credentials, Albright has not been considered a great thinker in the history of international relations scholarship and practice. She has earned the respect of Democratic elected officials through her loyalty, determination, and reputation for telling it like it is.

While a UN representative, Albright helped frame the aims of the Clinton foreign policy: promoting economic security, backing diplomacy with military force, encouraging democracy, and respect for human rights. In several speeches in 1993, Clinton's national security team spoke of moving from "containment" to "enlargement." Formerly, the major objective of foreign policy had been limiting the influence of communism, but with the end of the Cold War the objective became the enlargement of the number of free-market democracies.

As the first completely post-Cold War administration, the Clinton foreign policy team was in a unique position, and one that presented many difficulties. U.S. military and economic power was essentially unchallenged, yet this freedom came with its own set of problems. Without a clear enemy, U.S. use of power remained restricted because of the freedom allies now felt they had to reject what they perceived as bullying by the United States. In other words, without the threat of a common enemy, allies of the world's remaining superpower felt more empowered to reject U.S. influence without suffering consequences.

Also, without the threat of Soviet communism, foreign policy naturally became less significant to the public. This lack of public concern, coupled with a president who at least at the outset did not much care about foreign policy, contributed to the episodic and reactive appearance of policy.

Few Americans of any mainstream ideological stripe found much with which to disagree among the objectives as framed by the Clinton foreign policy team. Still, critics of the administration, especially some of its traditional supporters among organized labor, faulted the administration for its stress on the enlargement of markets rather than democracies.

The Republican Congress faced by Albright was led by one of the more isolationist majorities in recent history. Since 1995, the Clinton foreign policy team faced a Congress bent on cutting the State Department budget. Congress was not willing to pay the $1 billion in dues and peacekeeping bills owed to the UN.

Senator Jesse Helms, chairman of the Senate Foreign Relations Committee, personified the intransigence of Congress. Albright enjoyed relatively cordial relations with Congress, especially with Helms, even though the two disagreed on most significant issues. One criticism Congressional Republican leaders often leveled at the Clinton team regarding foreign policy was that their policies lacked cohesion and they merely reacted to crises. This criticism is not entirely justified because foreign policy makers must react to events as they occur. However, Albright herself contributed to the potential for such criticism, when in a 1993 speech as UN Ambassador she indicated that the United States would make decisions about intervention on a case-by-case basis.

Preventing the spread of weapons of mass destruction was a major goal of the Clinton foreign policy team, which in the second term included Sandy Berger as national security advisor, William Cohen as secretary of defense, and Bill Richardson as UN ambassador. However, the administration suffered three failures during Albright's watch as secretary of state. First, in 1998 the administration failed to convince India and Pakistan not to test nuclear weapons. Albright strongly warned the antagonists against the acquisition of such weapons and suggested that none of their interests was sufficiently important to risk such a high level of potential destruction and certain regional destabilization as nuclear weapons were capable of producing.

The India–Pakistan nuclear question contributed to another problem as well. The Clinton administration had hoped to keep warm relations with India, not only because it is the world's most populous democracy (with about 1 billion people), but also because it represents a major potential market for U.S. exports. India's GDP is a mere $390 billion, but its growth rate is high. Also, trade with India does not carry the same stigma as trade with China. The President's national security team spoke of moving from the old policy of "containment" to "enlargement."

Clinton recognized that with the end of the Cold War the major U.S. foreign policy objective needed to become increasing the number of free-market democracies, not just for the benefit of foreign nations, but for the benefit of the U.S. economy as well.

Second, in 1999 the Clinton administration failed to win Senate approval of the Comprehensive Test Ban Treaty. The Senate voted 51–48 against the treaty, which would have required support of two-thirds of the Senate, or 67 votes, to pass. However, Albright pledged that the United States would continue to honor the nuclear test ban, which had been put in place by former President George Bush in 1992, despite Senate rejection of formalizing the test ban in treaty form. Again, this conflict interweaves with the India–Pakistan situation because U.S. refusal to ratify the treaty likely undermined the ability of the United States to persuade India and Pakistan to sign the treaty.

Also, United Nations nuclear weapons inspections in Iraq collapsed, and attempts to restart them failed. Holding together the coalition that fought the war against Iraq to continue inspections and sanctions was naturally quite difficult, even among allies and potential allies more dependent on Middle East oil than the United States. Moreover, France, Russia, and China had continually pushed for a softening of sanctions under a reduced weapons inspection plan and continued promoting the soft line during 1999 talks about restarting inspections. Great Britain and the United States insisted on inspections under the same conditions that governed the previous team and continued sanctions until Iraq fully complied with disarmament. At the end of the Clinton administration there were no UN weapons inspectors in Iraq.

In 1998 Albright, Berger, and Cohen attended a "town meeting" at Ohio State University to explain policy toward Iraq. The event degenerated into a debacle when critics of U.S. policy got the best of the secretary in questioning and heckling, and she lost her composure. This event more than any other is credited with ending the Albright honeymoon.

Clinton signed the National Missile Defense Act of 1999, which committed the United States to deploying such a system as soon as it becomes technologically feasible and to spend $128 billion on the project over 30 years. Albright tried to reassure Russian leaders that the missile-defense system would not abrogate the Anti-Ballistic Missile Treaty and that the system would only protect the United States against rogue states, which may only be able to launch a small number of missiles at one time, and that it could not possibly stop the much larger Russian arsenal.

Clinton rejected China's request in April 1999 to join the World Trade Organization, but by November of that year he changed his mind. The bilateral deal the Chinese accepted to enter the WTO required them to open several previously closed markets such as insurance and telecommunications. Moreover, Albright consistently made it clear that, despite campaign pledges to do otherwise, it was Clinton administration policy not to link trade and human rights. The House finally passed a bill to give China permanent normal trade status by a 237–197–1 vote on May 24, 2000, which solidified China's position with the WTO.

Another important foreign policy situation during Albright's tenure was the WTO summit in Seattle. Violence erupted in the streets when a small minority of the protesters attacked some chain stores, turned over newspaper boxes, and clashed with police. UN Secretary-General Kofi Annan, U.S. Trade Representative Charlene Barshefsky, and Albright were unable to leave their hotels because tens of thousands of protesters blocked their way. This action prevented the summit's formal opening. The AFL-CIO, a traditional ally of the Democratic Party, organized the largest single protest. The 20,000 or so people gathered under AFL-CIO banner in Seattle to protest the power of the WTO indicated the difficulties faced by a Democratic administration in pursuing expansion of international trade while trying not to offend its labor base. The long-term effect of the Seattle meeting in mainstream foreign policy circles is unlikely to be significant, although opponents of further global economic integration felt strengthened by the Seattle situation.

The Clinton administration wanted to make environmental concerns a part of its foreign policy. In December 1997 the administration negotiated the Kyoto Protocol on Global Climate Change, which required the United States, the European Union, and Japan to reduce greenhouse gas emissions. The administration never submitted the treaty to the Senate because it faced certain rejection in that it did not limit China's and other underdeveloped countries' emissions. Albright argued in favor of the agreement by saying developed countries ought to act first on greenhouse gas emissions and wait for developing countries to limit emissions later. Late in 2000 multinational talks about how to implement the standards ended with disagreement between the European Union and other developed countries.

In 1999 the United States tried to use an air bombardment as a means of ending the Serbian army's alleged expulsion of Albanians from Kosovo, after the Serbian government had rejected a diplomatic solution to the crisis. During negotiations, Albright may have set up the Serbs, and the diplomatic agreement she tried to get them to accept may have been drafted to guarantee rejection by Serbia. Albright was pleased that the process of assembling NATO power to oppose Serbia in Kosovo was achieved more quickly than it had been in Bosnia. Eventually, because airpower alone was insufficient to end Serbia's alleged purging of Albanians from the province, NATO ground forces helped move Serbian forces out of Kosovo, but both the refugee situation (estimates are that no fewer than 1.5 million people were forced from their homes in the disputed province) and ultimate resolution of the Milosevic situation remained the Serbian people's problem exclusively.

In October 2000, the Serbian people peaceably forced Milosevic from power, despite his attempts to retain power after losing an election to Vojislav Kostunica. Previously Albright had spoken positively of Milosevic and had even called him a peacemaker. But trying to steal an election in the year 2000 made those diplomatically necessary perceptions from 1995 outdated and Milosevic indefensible.

At the end of 1999, the United States had 253,000 soldiers deployed in other countries. Most of these were stationed in 11 countries belonging to NATO, plus Japan and Korea. The smaller deployments were among the more controversial. In Bosnia and Herzegovina there were 5,800. In Serbia, including Kosovo, there were 6,400; in Macedonia there were 1,100, and in the Middle East there were 13,000. These deployments became an issue during the presidential campaign between Republican George W. Bush and Democrat Al Gore, with Bush sometimes arguing that the U.S. military was overextended in missions not serving the national interest and also underfunded. However, the foreign policy goals of candidate Bush were not significantly different from those pursued by the Clinton administration.

The Clinton administration made the peace process in the Middle East a priority during Albright's tenure as well. Whereas former Secretary of State Warren

Christopher made peace in the Middle East a significant personal priority, Albright did not invest the same level of personal commitment to the troubled region. PLO leader Yasser Arafat and Israeli Prime Minister Ehud Barak did negotiate at Camp David in during the summer of 2000, but the results were disappointing. Barak offered more than any previous Israeli government in terms of the formation of a Palestinian state. He agreed to a U.S. compromise proposal that would have given Palestinians sovereignty over some parts of East Jerusalem, despite domestic pressure to sacrifice nothing of the ancient Israeli capital. Arafat could not accept compromise on the Jerusalem question because of pressure from other Arab leaders. East Jerusalem remains a sore point for Arab leaders because it was captured from Jordan during the 1967 Arab–Israeli War. The Clinton team was unable to forge a compromise acceptable to both sides.

After the Camp David talks failed, some of the worst ever clashes between Palestinians and Israelis occurred. Less than a month after the talks failed in late July, Israeli Foreign Minister Shlomo Ben-Ami announced that Israel would not give sovereignty of holy sites to the Palestinians. In a move that might have been expected to reduce tensions, the PLO voted to defer a unilateral declaration of Palestinian statehood, which had been slated for September 13. About two weeks later Israel's opposition leader, Ariel Sharon, visited a disputed holy shrine in Jerusalem. One day later 6 Palestinians were killed in clashes at the shrine. Days later clashes erupted in the West Bank and Gaza Strip, where 14 Palestinians were killed. Several supposed cease-fire agreements were reached, but each collapsed. Albright worked to defuse the situation and met with Barak, Arafat, and French President Jacques Chirac in France. Both sides ordered military forces away from controversial areas. Albright also met later with Arafat and Egyptian President Hosni Mubarak in Egypt. In all, more than 100 people were killed in these clashes.

In 1998 the United States launched cruise missile attacks on Iraq, Sudan, and Afghanistan. The attacks on Afghanistan and Sudan were aimed, respectively, at alleged terrorist training camps and a pharmaceutical factory suspected of producing chemical weapons. These attacks were in retaliation for terrorist attacks on U.S. embassies in Kenya and Tanzania.

The attacks on Iraq were designed to weaken Saddam Hussein's war-making capacity and to punish the regime for defeating UN arms investigations. The attacks on Iraq, Sudan, and Afghanistan occurred sufficiently near the impeachment proceedings that there was speculation they were as much designed to distract the public from those unseemly events as they were for strategic or military purposes.

The normalization of relations with Vietnam was an important issue during Albright's tenure. The United States has maintained an embassy in Hanoi since diplomatic relations were established in 1995. In 1999 Albright dedicated a $3.3 million consulate building in Ho Chi Minh City (formerly Saigon) near the site of the former embassy from which U.S. diplomats scrambled into helicopters in a famously photographed retreat in 1975. In 2000, President Clinton visited Vietnam.

Former Portuguese colony East Timor was invaded by Indonesia in 1975. The people of Timor struggled for nearly a quarter century to prevent absorption of their tiny country into Indonesia. In 1999 Australian troops led a 2,500-soldier UN peacekeeping mission to East Timor after the populace had voted for independence from Indonesia, and Timorese militias, perhaps with the support of the

Indonesian military, terrorized pro-independence groups on the island. Officials estimated that 300,000 refugees fled to West Timor. The United States threatened to cut off aid to Indonesia if it did not help protect the refugees.

Another indication of the kind of threats the world's remaining superpower faces in its global extensions is the October 12, 2000, bombing in Yemen of the USS *Cole* that killed 17 U.S. sailors and injured another 39. Albright asserted the United States would find the terrorists responsible for the bombing and not retreat into isolationism because of it.

Madeleine Albright became the 64th secretary of state with great fanfare and high expectations. She did not achieve greatness in her role, but neither did she fail. The strategic position of the United States as the world's lone remaining superpower did not diminish significantly on her watch. Basically U.S. relations with foreign nations remain much as she found them when she took office early in 1997.

BIBLIOGRAPHICAL ESSAY

Thomas Lippman's *Madeleine Albright and the New American Diplomacy* (2000) is a good journalistic account of Albright's tenure as secretary of State. Excerpts of Lippman's book were published in the *National Journal* (Vol. 32, No. 23, 2000, p. 1,736). Ann Blackmann's *Seasons of Her Life* (1998) and Michael Dobbs' *Madeleine Albright: A Twentieth Century Odyssey* (1999) are comprehensive and well-received biographies. Dobbs published a piece based on the research for the book in the May 2, 1999, edition of the *Washington Post Magazine. Madam Secretary: The Biography of Madeleine Albright* (1997), by Thomas Blood, a Democratic Party activist, has been criticized for being excessively praising of Albright. Stephen M. Walt's "Two Cheers for Clinton's Foreign Policy" (*Foreign Affairs*, Vol. 79, No. 2, March/April 2000, pp. 63–79) is a clear and comprehensive (to 1999) analysis of the goals and achievements of the Clinton foreign policy team. Finally, see Madeline Albright, *Madam Secretary* (2003), for a defense of her secretaryship.

David Jackson

ROBERT BACON (1860–1919)

Served 1909
Appointed by President Theodore Roosevelt
Republican

Robert Bacon was born at Jamaica Plain, Massachusetts, on July 5, 1860, and descended from a long line of Puritans. The second son of his father William's second marriage, Robert was educated at Hopkinson's School and then Harvard. Theodore Roosevelt was a classmate, and the friendship that developed between them there lasted their whole lives. Bacon was an excellent athlete and participated in baseball, football, lacrosse, and rowing, among other sports.

Graduating from Harvard in June 1880, the youngest of his class, Bacon took a trip around the world. After returning to the United States, Bacon joined the banking firm of Lee, Higgenson & Company. He left the company in 1883 to become a partner in the firm of E. Rollins Morse & Brother. He married Martha Waldron Cowdin the same year.

Bacon left the Morse Company in 1894 to accept a partnership in J. P. Morgan & Company, and soon Morgan himself involved Bacon in some of the most important actions of the firm. These actions included the Morgan loan of almost sixty-five million dollars to the U.S. government during the panic of 1895, the establishment of the United States Steel Corporation, and the transactions that led to the formation of the Northern Securities Company, both in 1901.

Secretary of State Elihu Root, with President Theodore Roosevelt's support, asked Bacon to take the office of Assistant Secretary of State. Bacon took the oath of office on September 5, 1905, and served during Root's whole secretaryship.

Bacon served as acting Secretary of State when Root was out of the country to attend the Pan-American Conference at Rio de Janeiro and to travel throughout Latin America on a goodwill tour in 1906. During this time, Bacon oversaw U.S. participation in a Central American peace conference held to end hostilities between El Salvador and Guatemala. He also was part of a peace mission, which included Secretary of War William Howard Taft, that Roosevelt had sent to Cuba to try to find a formula agreeable to all warring Cuban factions that would restore civil peace and forestall U.S. intervention. The mission failed, and the United

States governed Cuba until January 1909. Bacon opposed the U.S. intervention because he feared such intervention would become habitual.

Upon Root's resignation from state, Bacon became Secretary of State on January 27, 1909. In the few weeks left to him, Bacon tried to shepherd approval of a tripartite treaty, signed by Colombia, Panama, and the United States, designed to settle all outstanding issues arising from Panamanian independence. The treaties failed due to the hostility of Colombia public opinion. Bacon left office on March 5, 1909.

President Taft appointed Bacon ambassador to France on December 21, 1909, and he served ably until he resigned in January 1912. At the outbreak of World War I, Bacon was convinced that U.S. participation in it was inevitable and constantly urged U.S. preparedness. He protested publicly against the German violation of Belgium neutrality and worked for the American Ambulance service in France. Late in 1915 he joined the U.S. Army as a private and in 1916 ran for the U.S. Senate from New York on a platform of preparedness, narrowly losing in the primary.

Bacon was commissioned a major in the Quartermaster Corps and sailed with General John Pershing in 1917. Bacon served as chief of the American Military Mission at British General Headquarters. He was promoted to the rank of lieutenant colonel late in the war and returned home in March 1919, physically exhausted from overwork and stress. Bacon died on May 29, 1919, a few months after his old friend and college classmate, Theodore Roosevelt.

BIBLIOGRAPHICAL ESSAY

Robert Bacon's papers dealing with his service to the United States as secretary of state and ambassador to France are in the manuscript archives of the State Department. A sympathetic and scholarly biography by a friend of Bacon's, James Brown Scott, is *Robert Bacon, Life and Letters* (1923). A short version of the Bacon biography is Scott's essay "Robert Bacon" in Samuel Flagg Bemis (ed.), *The American Secretaries of State and Their Diplomacy* (1928). For an understanding of Bacon's views on Latin America, see his *For Better Relations with our Latin American Neighbors: A Journey to South America* (1915).

Edward S. Mihalkanin

JAMES BAKER III (1930–)

Served 1989–1992
Appointed by President George H. W. Bush
Republican

James Addison Baker III served as the 61st Secretary of State under Republican President George H. W. Bush. A distinguishing characteristic of Baker is that he had spent many years in politics and election campaigns prior to his tenure as the president's chief diplomat. The Baker years coincided with a dramatic change in the international system. The Cold War ended and with the collapse of the Soviet Union, the world went from bipolarity to unipolarity in a surprisingly short period of time. Baker worked to maintain stability and to protect U.S. interests during this transition.

Baker was born on April 28, 1930, in Houston, Texas. He earned his undergraduate degree from Princeton and then served in the Marine Corps from 1952 to 1954. Baker earned his law degree from the University of Texas Law School and began practicing law in Houston in 1957 with the firm Andrews, Kurth, Campbell and Jones. He practiced law until his appointment as Undersecretary of Commerce in 1975.

A defining element in Baker's public career has been his friendship with George H. W. Bush. Their friendship dates back to the late 1950s and their Houston Country Club days as tennis partners. Baker worked on his first Bush campaign when the latter ran unsuccessfully for the U.S. Senate in 1970. In 1972 Baker was the leader of the Republican presidential campaign in 14 Texas counties. Baker served as Undersecretary in the Commerce Department in 1975 and was the National Chair of President Gerald Ford's unsuccessful presidential campaign in 1976. Following Ford's unsuccessful effort, Baker ran for Texas Attorney General in 1978 and lost.

In 1979 Baker worked on Bush's presidential nomination effort and encouraged Bush to pull out of the race as Ronald Reagan's victory became assured. Following Reagan's nomination for president in the summer of 1980, Baker became a senior aide in that campaign. After Reagan's win over Jimmy Carter in the presidential election, Baker accepted the job of White House chief of staff. Baker was also given a seat on the National Security Council, a position he held until 1985. Most observers credit Baker, in his role as chief of staff, with helping to make Reagan's first term a political success.

Baker left his chief of staff position to serve as Reagan's Treasury Secretary from 1985 to 1988. His tenure at Treasury has generally been regarded favorably. He helped direct the administration's second-term tax reform agenda. The tax reform package was welcomed by business and industry as it simplified the code and was investment friendly. By most accounts Baker worked effectively with the Democratic-controlled Congress. Baker also helped craft the U.S.–Canada Free Trade Pact and helped restructure Third World debt. Despite these successes, Baker left office with unprecedented budget and trade deficits. According to a 1998 *Business Week* story on his legacy at Treasury, Baker is remembered for "recognizing that the USA had lost the power to dictate economic policy for the industrial world." Baker left Treasury in 1988 to work on Bush's successful presidential bid.

A common theme by those remarking on Baker is that he is a brilliant campaign strategist. Baker is credited with closing the gap between Ford and Carter in the 1976 election, whereas the Reagan electoral victories in 1980 and 1984 and the Bush win in 1988 all benefited from Baker's involvement. Baker effectively linked politics and foreign policy in each of these campaigns.

After winning the 1988 presidential election Bush selected Baker to be his secretary of state, and he took this position the following year. Baker proved to be an effective diplomat. A speech Baker gave in December 1991 at his alma mater presented his underlying foreign policy philosophy. He expressed a strong identification with a post–Cold War foreign policy that sought a "world free from the shadows of war, of political tyranny, of economic distress." In this sense he was more like Henry Kissinger than John Foster Dulles. He saw an opportunity to build constructive relationships with the Soviets/Russians through active engagement.

Baker is not known for deep philosophical undertakings, but is seen as a conservative with tremendous political instincts. He is a pragmatic political operative who is very focused and a hard worker. A Soviet report commissioned by the Soviet Foreign Minister Eduard Shevardnadze recognized these traits of Baker. He has identified himself as a "doer," rather than one who contemplates weighty theories and debates. In this vein, he has identified himself as a realist. This pragmatism is evident in his choices and actions during the waning years of the Cold War, the Persian Gulf War, and other key events of 1989–1992.

The Bush–Baker years came at a time of great international crisis and change. The Cold War ended, Germany was reunified, Central America attempted to move toward peace, and war broke out in the Persian Gulf. In his memoir, Baker says, "We in the Bush administration sought to harness, shape, and manage those seismic geopolitical changes in the strategic interests of our country." The president gave his old friend a great deal of latitude as secretary of state, and their relationship was close. Baker capitalized on this level of trust and used it to let the career officers at the State Department know that he would be in charge.

The events in the Persian Gulf in 1990–1991 helped shape the Bush–Baker legacy. On August 2, 1990, Iraq invaded Kuwait. Iraq's timing, according to Baker, was maladroit because on this day Bush was meeting with Prime Minister Margaret Thatcher, and Baker was in Siberia meeting with Shevardnadze. The serendipitous timing of these meetings with the invasion allowed the United States to have a "running start" in forming the coalition that would compel Iraq to withdraw months later. The secretary himself was unsure of Iraqi intentions when Kuwait was invaded. Michael Beschloss and Strobe Talbott argue that Baker did not know whether the Iraqis were "going all the way" to Kuwait City, or whether they were "just taking the disputed stuff," such as the islands and oil-rich land that Kuwait and Iraq had historically argued over.

The invasion was due in part to misperceptions. The United States did not believe that Iraq would invade Kuwait, and Iraq did not receive a clear indication that the United States would strongly disapprove of such an action. This perception is likely to have been encouraged by the emphasis the United States had placed on strengthening relations with Iraq. Prior to the invasion, Baker had sought stronger U.S.–Iraq relations. For instance, he successfully helped gain White House approval in November 1989 for $1 billion in government-backed agricultural credits for Iraq, regardless of concerns over their use.

Moreover, immediately before the invasion the United States did not strongly warn Iraqi leader Saddam Hussein against invading Kuwait, a mistake for which Baker is at least partly responsible. On April 2, 1990, Hussein made an inflammatory speech against Israel. On July 25 Iraq moved troops to forward positions along the Kuwait border. Later that day, U.S. Ambassador to Iraq, April Glaspie, had been summoned to meet with Hussein. Glaspie, reflecting the position of Baker and the State Department, stated to Hussein that the United States did not have an opinion on conflicts between Arabs, such as the Iraqi border disagreement with Kuwait.

After the meeting between Saddam and Glaspie the United States did not expect an Iraqi invasion. Glaspie concluded that Iraq would not invade Kuwait and that joint naval maneuvers between the United Arab Emirates and the United States currently underway would sufficiently deter Iraq. Bush then sent a message to Hussein on July 28 stating that "I was pleased to learn of the agreement between Iraq and Kuwait to begin negotiations in Jeddah. . . . The United States and Iraq both have a strong interest in preserving the peace and stability of the Middle East." Coming three days after the Glaspie meeting, Baker has suggested that this rather mild letter conveyed a signal to Iraq that the United States lacked resolve. It was during this time that the United States was heavily involved in the collapse of the Soviet bloc and German reunification. Baker has argued that no amount of American resolve short of troop movement would have slowed Saddam because in Baker's opinion, Saddam was a crazed dictator.

After the August 2 invasion of Kuwait, Bush sent troops to Saudi Arabia to deter an Iraqi attack on that country. Throughout the crisis, from the Iraqi invasion to the liberation of Kuwait, Baker was part of the select group of key officials involved in the making of U.S. foreign policy. Apart from Baker, this group, or the "gang" as they have been termed, consisted of Bush, Vice President Dan Quayle, White House Chief of Staff John Sununu, National Security Advisor Brent Scrowcroft, Secretary of Defense Richard Cheney, and the Chairman of the Joint Chiefs of Staff Colin Powell. Scowcroft's deputy, Robert Gates, was also a member, and he acted as a link with the Deputies Committee, the routine crisis management group.

At least initially, Baker worried that the United States was acting too swiftly and that the vulnerability of American troops deployed in Saudi Arabia meant that they would be in grave danger if Hussein attacked. Another concern for Baker was the presence of Americans in Kuwait and Iraq. Baker believed that the plight of the hostages should be a key focus of the American Gulf policy, as it was an issue that would unite Americans and the international community against Iraq. Nor was Baker overenthusiastic with regard to using the U.S. military to force the withdrawal of Iraq. Baker wanted diplomacy rather than a military offensive to force Iraq's withdrawal and supported a policy of containment.

However, although Baker still hoped to avoid war, as the crisis continued he increasingly realized that force might have to be used against Iraq. On October 19, Baker had a private meeting with Powell. The two agreed on a policy of "building a deliberate offensive capability" that would be designed to compel Iraqi withdrawal. They also agreed that domestic politics would not allow a conflict that would result in many U.S. casualties. To decrease the number of potential American losses, Baker and Powell discussed a coalition approach. Alongside the military coalition's buildup there would be a diplomatic front. On October 31, Bush authorized 200,000 more troops for Saudi Arabia. Despite Baker's acceptance of the U.S. military buildup in the Middle East, he questioned the timing of White House announcements on the troop increases. Baker was concerned over whether such announcements were being hurried and whether there had been adequate consultation.

Baker played a significant role in building and maintaining the international coalition of countries against Iraq. Of particular importance was Baker's ability to forge an agreement with the Soviets to cooperate during the crisis. Baker's close friendship with Shevardnadze made this cooperation possible. In addition to presenting a strong face to Hussein, this agreement helped consolidate the new post–Cold War thaw between the two superpowers. Baker and Shevardnadze made a joint statement on August 3, "jointly calling upon the rest of the international community to join with us in an international cut-off of all arms supplies to Iraq." Similarly, Baker developed wording acceptable to the Soviets, allowing him and Shevardnadze to agree on United Nations (UN) Resolution 678 passed by the Security Council on November 29. This authorized "all necessary means" to uphold the eleven resolutions already passed against Iraq and to "restore international peace and security in the area."

As the coalition against Hussein developed, Baker still hoped that diplomacy would prevent war and was determined to ensure that all means of resolving the crisis peacefully had been exhausted before force was used. In line with this thinking, Baker sought to meet Hussein to ensure that the Iraqi leader clearly understood the U.S. position. Although no such meeting occurred, Baker met with Iraqi Foreign Minister Tariq Aziz in Geneva on January 9, 1991, in one last effort to prevent war. However, after the six-and-a-half-hour meeting, Baker told the waiting media that there was no Iraqi flexibility. Iraq had refused to back down and accede to Bush's demands.

Operation Desert Storm, the operation to force the Iraqi withdrawal from Kuwait, was launched on January 17, 1991, with an air offensive against Iraq and Iraqi forces in Kuwait. The air offensive successfully destroyed Iraqi forces while sustaining minimal losses. On February 24 the ground war started, with Bush declaring that the liberation of Kuwait was entering a final phase. Iraqi resistance succumbed to coalition forces and swiftly subsided, and on February 27 Kuwait City was liberated. After 100 hours of the land war, Bush declared a cease-fire effective from February 28.

During the conflict Baker remained an important figure behind the coalition. Baker was in direct contact with Israel to discourage it from launching retaliatory attacks against Iraq in response to Scud missile strikes. Baker discouraged such retaliatory attacks because he feared that members of the coalition against Iraq, especially the Arab members, would find such acts unacceptable. Vice President Dan Quayle and Secretary of Defense Cheney were more sympathetic to Israeli retaliation than Baker. After the victory against Iraq, a Kurdish uprising was staged, which Hussein brutally suppressed, and soon a humanitarian disaster was unfolding as Kurdish refugees fled Iraqi forces. Baker was reluctant to commit U.S. forces to help the Kurds, as he feared that the United States could become mired in a civil war. International pressure for action mounted, however, especially from the European community. Consequently, relief efforts were accelerated, and safe havens were established for the Kurds.

Despite his overall caution during the crisis, Baker did show initiative, not always to his advantage. Illustrative of this is the joint statement made during the coalition air offensive by Baker and Alexander Bessmertnykh, Shevardnadze's successor. This statement offered a cease-fire in return for an Iraqi commitment to withdraw from Kuwait and promised joint Soviet–U.S. efforts to promote Arab–Israeli peace and stability. This statement outraged both President Bush and Israel, as neither had been consulted. The State Department was forced to deny any change in U.S. policy, and Baker was embarrassed by the incident.

The Iraqi defeat in Kuwait had occurred much more quickly and with drastically fewer U.S. casualties than predicted. Baker today still steadfastly defends the president's decision to stop the fighting with Hussein still in power. Essentially, Baker argues that the United States did not want to get involved in the type of civil war that had taken place in Lebanon a decade earlier. Furthermore, the Bush administration wanted to preserve the Gulf War coalition and pursue postwar weapons inspections.

The coalition against Iraq had included Arab states, and this cooperation stimulated further attempts to establish peace in the Middle East. Symbolic of this was the late 1991 peace conference in Madrid, Spain. Baker worked for eight months to bring the Arabs and Israelis together. For instance, Mikhail Gorbachev in his memoir noted the "enormous amount of work" Baker put in during his shuttle diplomacy. The conference was widely praised as an important step toward peace and was followed by unprecedented talks on peace between Israel, its Arab neighbors, and the Palestinians. Baker also actively tried to ease tensions in the region by opposing the building of Israeli settlements on disputed land, such as the Golan Heights.

There were other important events during the Baker years. In December 1989, the United States launched Operation Just Cause, the forceful removal of Manuel Noriega from power in Panama. In 1988 Baker had taken a tough, public anti-Noriega stance and opposed Reagan's plan of lifting two U.S. drug indictments against Noriega if he resigned from power. As secretary of state, Baker supported Operation Just Cause but ensured that Bush knew that the action would have some negative consequences. These included the opposition to the operation that would be heard both inside and outside Central America. However, Baker believed that generally such opposition would not be strong, and he anticipated that privately most governments would be neutral or even pleased with the U.S. action. Baker was actively involved in notifying other governments of the operation, and after

Noriega sought refuge in the Vatican Embassy, contacted the Vatican to ask that Noriega be turned over to the United States. Noriega was successfully taken into U.S. custody in January 1990.

Baker recognized the significance of the changes occurring in the Soviet Union. Gorbachev had taken power in March 1985 and soon initiated wide-ranging political and economic reforms. Baker believed that Gorbachev was central to the success of Soviet reforms and so attempted to help Gorbachev. Gorbachev writes that he concluded after his first talks with the Bush administration that Baker's general attitude was "constructive," and that "we had established quite a good rapport." Moreover, in June 1991 Baker warned Gorbachev that hard-liners were planning to stage a coup against him.

Baker initially was cautious in dealing with the Soviets and believed that former Secretary of State George Shultz had paid for Soviet concessions that Gorbachev might have made for free. However, Baker gradually changed his opinion as his friendship with Shevardnadze developed. Baker himself believes that his close friendship with the Soviet Foreign Minister started in July 1989 after he was moved when Shevardnadze talked openly of the Soviet Union's internal problems. Baker became increasingly optimistic that Gorbachev would remain in power and his reforms would succeed. Baker's opinions were more progressive than those of other senior members of the administration.

Baker actively sought better U.S.–Soviet relations, and this is reflected by the joint efforts in arms control. In September 1989, Baker and Shevardnadze reached agreement for the exchange of U.S.–Soviet data on chemical weapons, the provision of advance notification of military exercises involving long-range bombers, and the limiting of mobile intercontinental ballistic launches. The following year Baker moved to revamp the military structure of the North Atlantic Treaty Organization (NATO) to allay Soviet fears, and in 1991 Bush and Gorbachev signed the Strategic Arms Reduction Talks (START) Treaty.

Similarly, during Baker's tenure major developments occurred in Eastern Europe as Communist regimes fell and states fragmented. Baker supported political and economic reforms instigated in the region, but their speed surprised both himself and Bush. The administration was also concerned over the resultant instability. Of particular concern was Romania, where mass protests against its dictator, Nicolae Ceausescu, were met with brutal repression during December 1989. Indeed, Baker remarked on December 24 that the United States would not object if the Soviets intervened in Romania, a suggestion that Shevardnadze rejected. Baker also worked desperately to keep Yugoslavia together. When the country broke up the Bush administration announced in August 1992 that it would establish full diplomatic relations with Croatia, Slovenia, and Bosnia-Herzegovina. During the conflict Baker denounced Serbian attacks on Bosnia and sought to isolate the aggressor country.

Of particular significance was the fall of the Berlin Wall in November 1989 and the official reunification of Germany in October the following year. Baker played an important role in supporting and facilitating the reunification of Germany. The secretary had assumed that German reunification would be gradual, and that the Bush administration would not have to commit itself to an approach on the issue before the East German elections that were scheduled for May 1990.

However, with the rapid changes after the fall of the Berlin Wall, the question of reunification arose. Baker supported German reunification, attempted to allay Soviet fears of a resurgent Germany, and gradually persuaded Gorbachev to support reunification. Baker also played a key role in supporting the "Two-plus-Four" mechanism for dealing with the issue of German reunification. ("Two-plus-Four" formula referred to the process that all East–West German agreements had to be approved by the Allied Occupation Powers: France, Great Britain, the United States, and the Soviet Union.) Despite this, Baker was surprised that during a meeting in the Soviet Union between Gorbachev and the German Chancellor Helmut Kohl, the Soviet leader publicly accepted the prospect of German reunification. Baker had believed that there would be no major decisions at the German–Soviet meeting and had not expected Gorbachev to accept reunification this early because of hard-liners in the Soviet Union.

In August 1992, Baker resigned as Secretary of State, apparently reluctantly, to become the White House chief of staff and to manage President Bush's reelection campaign. When Baker left the State Department to take over the reins of President Bush's reelection campaign, many Democrats asserted that Baker's departure would seriously undermine continuity in the wake of the collapse of the Soviet bloc. Others suggested that Baker was leaving at a critical juncture in the Middle East peace process. Perhaps the severest criticism that has been leveled at the Baker tenure is that the administration was caught off guard by the Iraqi invasion of Kuwait. In his memoir Baker says, "We should have given Iraqi policy a more prominent place on our radar screen at an earlier date." In his defense in 1990, Baker was considerably preoccupied with German reunification, U.S.–Soviet relations, and the Middle East generally.

Baker was not a traditional Cold War warrior. He recognized the importance of democracy and did not see the world entirely in terms of capitalism versus communism. He saw the potential for cooperation and forged important relations at the diplomatic level that fostered international cooperation and hastened the end of the Cold War. It would seem that Baker was the right person for the position at a time of great geopolitical flux and upheaval. Symbolic of this is Baker's close friendship with Shevardnadze. Moreover, although the swiftness of change in Eastern Europe and the invasion of Kuwait surprised Baker, as was the case among many at the time, he recognized the seriousness of Gorbachev to undertake major reform before many other members of the Bush administration. Baker's shuttle diplomacy in the Middle East also brought the various opposing groups together. Baker calmly charted a course for the United States during this eventful time. In less capable hands, events could have proceeded less favorably.

Over the years, Baker has won many awards. He received the Presidential Medal of Freedom (1991), the Princeton University Woodrow Wilson Award, the Harvard University John F. Kennedy School of Government Award, the George F. Kennan Award, the Department of the Treasury's Alexander Hamilton Award, and the Department of State's Distinguished Service Award.

After his term in office ended in January 1993, Baker became a private consultant with the Carlyle Group and is senior partner in the law firm Baker & Botts. Baker serves on the boards of Rice University and the Woodrow Wilson International Center for Scholars. Baker is also involved with his namesake, the James Addison Baker III Institute for Public Policy created at Rice University in Houston, a school his grandfather helped found. The Institute is a "nonpartisan organization focusing on the study, formulation, execution and criticism of public policy."

After the presidential election of 2000, Baker again answered the Bush family call when he became lead spokesman for George W. Bush's campaign during the controversial recounts and Supreme Court rulings. George W. Bush justified Baker's involvement by acknowledging Baker's skills as a tough articulate lawyer and an excellent strategist. Interestingly, one of the two lead spokesmen for the Al Gore campaign was former Secretary of State Warren Christopher.

In addition to Baker's involvement in domestic politics since 1993, the former Secretary has maintained an active interest in international relations. In 1997 Baker was appointed a UN special envoy to resolve the West Sahara dispute and has provided public analysis of significant international events.

BIBLIOGRAPHICAL ESSAY

There is no scholarly full-length biography of Baker at this time, but there are a stable of memoirs from members of the Reagan and Bush administrations, 1981–1993. James Baker's *The Politics of Diplomacy* (1995) cover his years as Secretary of State. Other memoirs that discuss Baker and different elements of his government service include Colin Powell, *A Soldier's Way* (1995); Dan Quayle, *Standing Firm—A Vice Presidential Memoir* (1994); Ronald Reagan, *An American Life* (1991); and Casper Weinberger, *Fighting for Peace* (1990).

For the Bush administration, see Colin Campbell and Bert Rockman (eds.), *The Bush Presidency* (1991); Mike McNamee and Paul Magnusson, "The Bottom Line on Baker: Not Bad for a 'Bright Amateur'," *Business Week*, No. 3065 for a generally sympathetic review of Baker's years as treasury secretary. Christopher Madison, "Jim Baker's Legacy," *The National Journal* (Vol. 24, 1992); and Bob Woodward, *The Commanders* (1991), are good accounts of how Bush Sr. and his high command made decisions for the use of force.

For Baker's relationship with Bush see Maureen Dowd and Thomas L. Friedman, "The Fabulous Bush and Baker Boys," *The New York Times Magazine* (May 6, 1990); and Micheal Kramer, " Playing for the Edge," *Time* (February 13, 1989).

For the Gulf War, see Deborah Amos, *Lines in the Sand* (1992), which discusses Baker only in regards to his January 1991 meeting with Aziz; Rick Atkinson, *Crusade: The Untold Story of the Persian Gulf War* (1993); Laurence Freedman and Efrain Karsh, *The 1990–1991 Gulf Crisis* (1993); Gary Hess, *Presidential Decisions for War: Korea, Vietnam, and the Persian Gulf* (1991); Ken Mathews, *The Gulf Conflict and International Relations* (1993); and Jean Smith, *George Bush's War* (1992).

For U.S. relations with Panama during the Bush presidency, see Fredrick Kempe, *Divorcing the Dictator* (1990); and R. M. Koster and Guillermo Sanchez, *In the Time of Tyrants* (1990).

For U.S.–Soviet relations, see Michael Beschloss and Strobe Talbott, *At the Highest Levels* (1993); Mikhail Gorbachev, *Memoirs* (1996); and David Remnick, *Lenin's Tomb: The Last Days of the Soviet Empire* (1993).

For general analyses of the transition from bipolarity to unipolarity and the emergence of a post–Cold War world, see James Chace, *The Consequences of the Peace* (1992); Michael Cox, *U.S. Foreign Policy After the Cold War* (1995); John Gaddis, *The United States and the End of the Cold War* (1992); Michael Hogan (ed.), *The End of the Cold War* (1992); and Allen Lynch, *The Cold War Is Over—Again* (1992).

Karl DeRouen and Paul Bellamy

THOMAS F. BAYARD (1828–1898)

Served 1885–1889
Appointed by President Grover Cleveland
Democrat

Thomas Francis Bayard was born in Wilmington, Delaware, on October 29, 1828, to James Asheton Bayard and Anne Francis Bayard. His father served successive terms in the U.S. Senate in 1850, 1856, and 1862. Among his ancestors, his grandfather, great-grandfather, and an uncle were also members of the Senate. Thomas was educated at a private school in Flushing, New York, worked in mercantile houses in New York City and Philadelphia, and in 1851 was admitted to the Delaware bar. A lawyer for 18 years in Wilmington and relatively briefly in Philadelphia, Bayard engaged in a thriving legal practice, particularly being involved in administering estates. In 1853–1854 he served as federal district attorney in Delaware. By then Bayard was a strikingly handsome man, over six feet tall and powerfully built. In October 1856, he married Louise Lee, daughter of a wealthy Baltimore banker. They had nine children. During the Civil War, he, like his father James, was a peace Democrat, opposing secession but preferring peaceful departure of the Southern states to civil war.

When in 1869 James Bayard resigned his Senate seat, the Delaware legislature chose Thomas to succeed him. A member of the electoral commission of 1877, appointed by Congress to decide the contested Hayes–Tilden election, Bayard gave his full support to Democratic presidential candidate Samuel J. Tilden. He fought Radical Reconstruction policies, claiming that they were far too harsh and involved undue centralization of executive power. Racism was by no means absent. For example, in opposing the Force Bill of 1870, he accused the Republicans of maintaining their power by manipulation of "ignorant and semi-barbarous" blacks. Standing firmly in his party's laissez-faire tradition, he opposed as "class legislation" bills fostering ship subsidies, railroad land grants, or tariff protection. A hard-money man, he maintained that all currency must be based on gold or silver. He received some support for the Democratic presidential nomination in 1876 (when Buffalo attorney Grover Cleveland favored his candidacy), 1880, and 1884 as a favorite son. Standing second only to Cleveland as party leader, Bayard ran just behind the New York governor at the 1884 Democratic convention, receiving 170 votes on the first ballot.

Once elected, President Cleveland appointed Bayard secretary of state. He accepted the post reluctantly, admitting his ignorance of foreign affairs and fearing the expense accompanying his new social duties. In office he was close to the president and was respected for such qualities as diligence, patience, courtesy, and a keen intelligence. His reserve could work against him, as it was often perceived as snobbery. In negotiation he could be infuriatingly vague, thereby creating unnecessary confusion. At one point Bayard's secretaryship was marked by personal tragedy. In January 1886, he lost in rapid succession his daughter Kate and his wife, the latter an invalid for years.

Though besieged by hordes of Democratic office seekers, Bayard usually made superior appointments. Among them were the able Vermont lawyer Edward J. Phelps as minister to Britain, civil service advocate George H. Pendleton as minister to Germany, and seasoned diplomat Robert M. McLane as minister to France. Bayard was ably served by Alvey A. Adee, second assistant secretary of state, who had been in the department since 1870; legal scholar John Bassett Moore, whom Bayard recruited to the department and made third assistant secretary of state; and Francis Wharton, an Episcopal priest who was department solicitor.

One flagrantly political appointment ended disastrously. Bayard made Anthony M. Keiley, the brother of an important Brooklyn politician, minister to Italy. When Keiley, at a mass meeting of Roman Catholics in Richmond, Virginia, referred to the "cruel and causeless invasion of the Papal States," the Italian government declared him persona non grata. Bayard sought to appoint him to Austria-Hungary, but Keiley met with a similar rebuff there, at least in part because his wife was Jewish.

Problems soon arose over Canadian fisheries, one of the world's great natural resources. According to the Treaty of Washington (1871), Canada was permitted to export its fish to the United States without duty, "free fish," in return for allowing Americas valuable fishing rights within its three-mile limit, "free fishing," the latter a provision that had given New England fishermen generous use of bays and inshore waters in eastern Canada. Included were broad reaches of the Gulf of St. Lawrence, the more restricted Bay of Fundy, the Labrador coast, and the offshore banks of Newfoundland and Nova Scotia. For various reasons—the desire of New England fishermen to exclude Canadian fish, a general tendency toward protectionism, irritation remaining from the Civil War controversies—strong sentiment existed to abrogate "free fish" as early as possible. Two years before Cleveland's election, Congress did so, the prohibition to take effect on July 1, 1885. Retaliating Canadian authorities reverted to a legalistic interpretation of the previous treaty covering such matters, a woefully outmoded agreement made in 1818. U.S. fishermen were suddenly harassed with local police regulations; refused bait, supplies, and transshipment of their catch; and finally excluded from certain great bays of Canada, which the United States had claimed were parts of the high seas and hence not under Canadian jurisdiction.

Conservative Lord Salisbury, who personally handled foreign affairs, headed the British government, which ultimately determined Canadian foreign policy. He was relatively indifferent to the whole matter. Furthermore, communication between British and Canadian officials was most cumbersome, and even trivial matters took months to settle. Therefore, the Canadian government, which was headed by Prime Minister Sir John MacDonald, often had surprising leeway in policymaking.

By the spring of 1886, the Canadians were seizing U.S. fishing crafts that were exceeding their rights, as defined by the antiquated convention of 1818, to fish in Canadian waters or dry their catch on Canadian soil. Acting through Minister Edward J. Phelps in London, Bayard urged the British government to stop condoning the boarding and seizure of Yankee schooners, which, the secretary claimed, threatened "the peace of two kindred and friendly nations." On March 3, 1887, Cleveland signed a harsh Retaliation Act that was spearheaded by a newly elected Republican Senate. It empowered the president to bar Canadian goods and ships from U.S. ports if U.S. fishing received unjust treatment. Cleveland did not enforce the measure but used it as a bargaining chip for a new agreement.

That May, MacDonald sent Sir Charles Tupper, Canada's finance minister, as his emissary to Washington. When Tupper proposed a joint conference over the fisheries matter, Bayard welcomed the bid. British-Canadian representatives included Tupper, who, as a Nova Scotian, was familiar with the fisheries matter; Joseph Chamberlain, a potent force in British politics who had recently resigned from the third Gladstone cabinet; and the uninspiring Sir Lionel Sackville-West, British minister to the United States. Bayard himself was part of the U.S. delegation. So was James B. Angell, president of the University of Michigan and a Republican friendly to the Cleveland administration. The third American was Judge William L. Punt, an outstanding lawyer from the fishing state of Maine, who had been serving for several months as special counsel to the State Department on the fisheries issue.

In February 1888, the Bayard–Chamberlain treaty, as it was called, was completed. It defined fishing boundaries and promised the United States additional privileges if it ever agreed to continue the "free fish" practice. A mixed commission would delimit the territorial rights of U.S. fisherman in Canadian waters, so long disputed under the treaty of 1818. Article XV tacitly held out a bribe: whenever the United States removed the import duty on Canadian fish, Canada would let U.S. fishermen buy supplies, transship catches, and take on crews in offshore waters. Until the bill was passed, a modus vivendi, that is, a temporary arrangement pending final settlement, would be in effect.

The treaty met with much criticism. The fishery interests, who wanted the March 1887 law enforced, deemed it a "shameful surrender." As U.S. ships and fish were still excluded from Canadian ports, they called for stiff penalties. Republican senators attacked Cleveland for not submitting the three U.S. members for senatorial approval. They also called Article XV the opening assault on the entire U.S. protectionist system.

On August 21, just a few weeks before the presidential elections, a Republican majority in the Senate vetoed the treaty 30–27. One Republican senator told Tupper, "We cannot allow the Democrats to take credit for settling so important a dispute." Bayard was caustic in the matter, calling the rejection an "unheard-of thing within the pale of civilized government."

Although the Senate blocked the Bayard–Chamberlain treaty, the modus vivendi went into effect. By its terms U.S. fishing vessels could buy bait and dry fish in Canadian and Newfoundland after purchasing an annual license at a fee of $1.50 per ship ton. U.S. fishermen willingly purchased the proffered licenses. Britain kept renewing the agreement every two years until she and the U.S. reached a definite settlement in 1912.

For generations the sealing industry in the Northern Pacific had centered around the Pribilof chain, four small islands located in the Bering Sea. Here the great fur seals mated during a breeding season that lasted from early May to mid-November. A California firm, the North American Commercial Corporation, held a monopoly on the hunting. Included in the Alaska purchase of 1867, the Pribilofs were recognized as part of the United States.

Canadians ships, too, engaged in seal hunting in the region, insisting that the Bering Sea was an open sea and that "pelagic sealing" (the killing of seals in the waters off the islands) did not endanger the herd. Americans differed strongly, claiming that for every seal's skin secured by Canadian pelagic hunters, nine others were wantonly butchered. In 1886 Cleveland, convinced that pelagic sealing was fast depleting the fur-seal herd, ordered revenue cutters to arrest the Canadian offenders. In 1886 an American revenue cutter, the *Corwin*, seized three Canadian sealing schooners. Authorization for such capture had been given without the knowledge of Secretary Bayard, who reported to Cleveland that the seizures were all made on the "high seas" and hence "outside our jurisdiction." He persuaded Cleveland to cancel the pending proceedings against Canadian vessels and release those arrested. Within a year, however, other seizures followed, accompanied by increasingly sharp protests from the British and Canadians.

Seeking international regulation, not unilateral policing, Bayard authorized Minister Phelps in London to negotiate. The Canadians refused to accept international restraints on their sealers and thereby terminated the conversations, largely because of the secretary. U.S. cutters did not arrest a single pelagic sealer in 1888. On March 2, the day before he left office, Cleveland signed a bill that instructed the president to warn all poachers entering "all the dominion of the United States in the waters of the Bering Sea." Bayard's efforts at settlement had failed.

Bayard's greatest controversy was centered on Samoa, a land racked by civil war and foreign intervention. Early in 1885, the German consul, disturbed by native actions that threatened Germany's economic position in Samoa, ordered the seizure of the town of Apia and of the nearby Mulinuu peninsula, where the king, Malietoa Laupepea, resided. Until this time, the United States, Germany, and Britain, acting through their respective consuls, had joint jurisdiction over such matters and law enforcement, public works, sanitation, and taxation. In November, the German consul at Samoa imposed a treaty on Malietoa, which virtually made the government of Samoa a German protectorate. Directly after signing the agreement, Malietoa along with 48 other chiefs, appealed to Britain to annex the islands so as to prevent "other governments" from seizing his nation.

On June 19, 1885, Bayard told Berthold Greenebaum, American consul to Samoa, that "the moral interests of the United States with respect to the islands of the Pacific" would cause the United States to "look with concern on any movement by which the independence of those Pacific nationalities might be extinguished by their passage under the domination of a foreign state." Moreover, the United States had a "moral right to expect that no change in native rule shall extinguish the independence of the islands."

In May 1886, Malietoa, desperate over the growing rebellion, invoked U.S. good offices, something proffered in an 1878 treaty with the United States that was never approved by the Senate. On May 14, Greenebaum, acting without authorization, flew the U.S. flag over Samoan public buildings and announced a temporary U.S. protectorate. Bayard immediately disavowed the move, recalled the consul, and claimed that he desired "no separate protectorate for any nation."

On June 1, Bayard proposed that all three consuls be replaced and that he, along with the British and German ministers in Washington, devise a new government for Samoa. Within three weeks, he met with Sackville-West and his German counterpart, Friedrich von Alvensleben. Bayard proposed the recognition of Malietoa as king; the appointment of a council composed of the king, the vice-king, and three foreigners selected by the treaty powers; an assembly elected by the natives; and the submission of confused land titles to a court. By Bayard's plan, there would be an independent Samoan kingdom, admittedly one guided by foreign advisers but with no single foreign power predominant. The Germans wanted a rival chief, Tamalese, as king; he would rule with the assistance of a German adviser. In reality Germany would administer Samoa. The British, who had just reached a détente with Germany over colonial jurisdiction in the Pacific and Africa, backed the German proposal. Given the deadlock in late July, Bayard proposed adjournment until autumn. The three would never meet again over the matter.

In August, Germany sent four warships off Apia, landed 700 marines, deposed Malietoa, and recognized Tamasese as king. A German named Brandeis, whom Tamasese named prime minister, ruled the country. Not surprisingly, the new regime favored the interests of the German Commercial Company and discriminated heavily against the British and Americans concerning such matters as land titles, taxes, and local improvements. On September 23, when asked by Alvensleben to approve Germany's actions, Bayard replied that "the first allegiance of this Government" was "to right and justice," a matter that not only involved the rights of the German, Britain, and U.S. governments in Samoa, but "the natives" as well. Implying the German was playing the role of bully, he said, "as to Germany declaring war against Malietoa, of course the thing had but one side; that it was utterly impossible for the weak King and that little, scattered handful of subjects to contend with Germany." Five days later, he told Alvensleben that "the trouble" was "caused by the greed of that commercial company of Germans who virtually represented the German Government in those Islands."

During 1888, the turmoil continued, particularly when, on September 4, Samoan chief Mataafa successfully rebelled against the Brandeis–Tamasese regime. On October 1, Bayard cabled Minister George H. Pendleton in Berlin that the United States intended to respect Mataafa as "the choice of the Samoan people." Yet the secretary of state remained cautious throughout, declaring that under no condition could "unjust and even cruel treatment by the Samoans by the Germans" be casus belli for the United States.

That December, Germany landed a force at Fangalili, not far from Apia. In meeting Mataafa's resistance, the Germans began "shelling and burning indiscriminately," according to the American vice-consul, "regardless of American property." Early in 1889, powerful elements within the American press played up German insults to the American presence. Cleveland ordered Admiral Lewis A. Kimberly, commander of the U.S. naval forces in the Pacific, to Apia on his flagship, the *Trenton*, to protect American lives and property as well as protest against Germany's displacement of the indigenous government. In January, the president warned

Congress against the preponderance of German power there. Congress responded by appropriating half a million dollars to protect American interests and a hundred thousand to develop a naval station at Pago Pago, a right granted in the 1878 treaty.

On February 4, Count von Arco Valley, Germany's new minister to the United States, told Bayard that his government sought a three-power conference to stop the fighting. Bayard immediately accepted. Although the conference was held after Bayard left office, the worst of the crisis was over. In June, the Unites States signed a treaty in Berlin with Germany and Britain establishing a tripartite protectorate over Samoa, which at the same time recognized limited independence for that nation.

Hawaii also preoccupied Bayard during his secretaryship. In January 1887, the United States renewed a reciprocity treaty, adding an article giving it exclusive right to maintain a naval coaling and repair station at Pearl Harbor. A few months later Bayard opposed a proposed two-billion dollar loan by Britain to the Hawaiian royal government. The loan, the secretary feared, would risk control "by foreign creditors, over the financial measures and administration of the Hawaiian government." Because Bayard lacked confidence in the integrity of Hawaii's ruler, King Kalakaua, the former also opposed Hawaiian efforts to form a Polynesian League to be initially based on a union with Samoa.

On July 7, 1887, after a one-day revolution, Kalakaua proclaimed a new constitution giving greater powers to Hawaii's wealthy white residents. Despite the major role played by U.S. residents there, Bayard disclaimed any effort to control the native government. At the same time, he opposed a British proposal to have a joint British-German-American guarantee of "the neutrality and equal accessibility of the islands and their harbors to the ships of all nations without preference."

International tension was also created by the presence of a massive number of Chinese laborers, particularly on the U.S. west coast. Following assaults on Chinese workers in Seattle, Tacoma, and Rock Springs, Wyoming, in 1885, Bayard expressed his "strong feelings of indignation" to Cheng Tsao Ju, the Chinese minister in Washington, but denied government responsibility, claiming that these outrageous acts were committed by private individuals, not federal officials. On March 12, 1888, in a treaty signed by Bayard and the new Chinese minister, Chang Yen Hoon, the two governments agreed to prohibit the entry of Chinese laborers into the United States for 20 years. Any Chinese immigrant, however, who had a lawful wife, child, or parent in the United States or who owned a thousand dollars worth of property in the United States, could return. The Chinese government would receive the sum of $276,619 to compensate those Chinese who had suffered injuries through mob rule. When the Republican-controlled Senate, with its eye on the forthcoming national elections, delayed confirmation, the outraged Chinese government demanded that the duration of the ban be reduced and that the proviso barring reentry be revised. President Cleveland, with his own eye on the electorate, signed a bill prohibiting the return of any Chinese laborers who left the United States. For Bayard, to foster such legislation while a treaty was pending, violated "international courtesy, good faith, and self-respect."

For the most part, Bayard did not have to involve himself extensively with Latin America. When, in January 1885, a Colombian revolution reached Panama, Bayard declared that U.S. reinforcements were sent to the isthmus only to protect American interests; the United States would not interfere in the domestic struggle.

Bayard met Guatemala's effort to force federal union on the states of Central America by endorsing voluntary union but opposing any coercion. "We strongly reprobate such plotting," he said in July 1885, "against each other's peace by Central American States." In November 1888, he challenged the right of Britain to defend Mosquito Indians, who lived under sovereignty of Nicaragua, as the United States "can never see with indifference" the "assertion of a British protectorate in another form."

For many years Venezuela and British Guiana had contested their boundary. Controversy intensified because of the presence of British settlers in the disputed area and the discovery of the largest gold nugget ever found. Several times between December 1886 and February 1888, when it appeared that the two nations might go to war, Bayard offered the good offices of the United States. Yet, suspecting that Venezuela was attempting to maneuver the United States into interceding on its behalf, he backed off before leaving office.

During the presidential campaign of 1888, Sackville-West intimated that Cleveland's election victory would be of greater benefit to Britain than would that of Republican candidate Benjamin Harrison. Although the British minister's letter was a private communication, it soon became public. Bayard felt himself forced to demand the minister's recall, a response that so infuriated the British government that it did not replace Sackville-West until Cleveland left office.

Upon leaving office, Bayard resumed his law practice in Wilmington. In November 1889, he married Mary W. Clymer, the daughter of a navy physician. In the same year, Cleveland, again elected president, asked Bayard to resume his old post. Bayard declined, but accepted the ambassadorship to Britain. In so doing he was the first chief of mission to London to hold ambassadorial rather than ministerial rank. He remained in London until 1897, working on such familiar matters as North Atlantic fisheries, Bering Sea fur seals, and the Venezuela boundary. On November 7, 1895, in addressing the Edinburgh Philosophical Institution, he assailed the protective tariff as form of state socialism, an event that caused the U.S. House of Representatives to censure him. On September 28, 1898, Thomas Francis Bayard died in Dedham, Massachusetts.

BIBLIOGRAPHICAL ESSAY

Bayard's papers are in the Library of Congress and the Delaware Historical Society in Wilmington. Material on his role as secretary of state may be found in *Foreign Relations of the United States*. Biographical material may be found in Lester G. Shippee, "Thomas Francis Bayard, Secretary of State, March 7, 1885 to March 6, 1889," in *The American Secretaries of State and Their Diplomacy* (1963), vol. 8, edited by Samuel Flagg Bemis and in Charles C. Tansill, *The Foreign Policies of Thomas F. Bayard, 1885–1897* (1940). Superior general accounts include Allan Nevins, *Grover Cleveland: A Study in Courage* (1932); Charles C. Campbell, *The Transformation of American Foreign Relations, 1865–1900*; and Richard E. Welch, *The Presidencies of Grover Cleveland* (1988).

Justus Doenecke

JEREMIAH S. BLACK (1810–1883)

Served 1860–1861
Appointed by President James Buchanan
Democrat

Jeremiah Sullivan Black was born on a farm in Somerset County, Pennsylvania, on January 10, 1810. Although he attended a variety of local schools, Black was largely self-educated. At 17, Black began the study of law with a local politico and prominent Somerset attorney, Chauncey Forward, and was admitted to the bar in 1830. Black was appointed president judge of the courts of common pleas in the 16th judicial district of Pennsylvania. He was elected to the state supreme court in 1851 and reelected in 1854, serving three years as its chief justice.

In 1857, President James Buchanan appointed Black attorney general of the United States. Black's most significant action as attorney general before the secession crisis was his successful challenge of questionable Mexican land grants in California.

Black's and Buchanan's professional relationship was based on a long-standing friendship and a sharing of essentially conservative political views. Friends for decades, Buchanan valued Black for his honesty, forthrightness, devotion, and competence. Further, both men were against any kind of radicalism, including, in their minds, free-soilism, strongly defended party discipline, and believed in legal solutions to political problems. Finally, Black had defended Buchanan's Kansas policy, and both men had warmly supported the Dred Scott decision and John Breckenridge's candidacy in 1860.

After Abraham Lincoln's election, but before any Southern state had seceded, Buchanan, on November 17, 1860, asked Black what powers the president had concerning a range of issues if a state or states were to secede. Black's response, delivered on November 20, argued that the South had no legal right to secede and so the president had a duty and right to collect duties, defend public property, and execute the laws, based on the military act of 1795. At the same time, Black believed that because there was no federal common law, Congress needed to enact new statutes for the federal government to collect revenues during the abnormal political situation. Further, Black said that although the federal government could enforce its decrees on individuals, to enforce the law against the complete opposition in a state would constitute "an offensive war," which had no constitutional sanction.

Buchanan based his annual message to Congress on December 3, 1860, in part, on Black's constitutional arguments. In addition to declaring secession unconstitutional and arguing that the federal government had no authority to force any state to remain in the Union, Buchanan blamed the crisis on the Republicans for increasing the possibility of slave rebellions, opined that the South was justified in secession if Northern states did not repeal their personal liberty laws, and advocated the calling of a constitutional convention, which he recommended should pass an amendment protecting slavery where it existed.

After Buchanan refused to send reinforcements to Fort Sumter requested by Major Robert Anderson, Secretary of State Lewis Cass resigned on December 12, 1860. Buchanan was angry and refused Black's suggestion that Cass be readmitted to the Cabinet. Black agreed to succeed Cass if Edwin M. Stanton would be appointed attorney general. Buchanan reluctantly agreed to the arrangement.

As secretary of state, Black, along with Stanton and Secretary of War Joseph Holt, were strong advocates against secession. Secretary of Interior Jacob Thompson believed that Black was responsible for Anderson having discretionary authority to move his troops as he thought best. In response to the vehement Southern protest of Anderson's moving his troops to Fort Sumter on December 27, Black defended Anderson as having followed the president's orders and to Secretary of War John B. Floyd's demand that Anderson be ordered out of Sumter, Black hotly retorted that "there never was a moment in the history of England when a minister of the Crown could have proposed to surrender a military post which might be defended, without bringing his head to the block."

After meeting unofficially with South Carolina commissioners on December 28, 1860, Buchanan met with his cabinet twice the next day. The president presented the cabinet with a draft reply to the commissioners. In it, Buchanan was willing to order Anderson to return to Fort Moultrie if South Carolina pledged not to occupy any other federal forts and to recommend that Congress treat with the commissioners.

Black was completely against the draft message. Supported by Stanton and Holt, Black wanted the message to deny that any presidential promise had been made earlier concerning Sumter and did not want any hint that South Carolina could be represented diplomatically. Black also refused to approve a statement, wherein Buchanan expressed his opinion that Congress lacked the constitutional authority to force a state to remain in the Union, thereby contradicting the legal advice he gave Buchanan on November 20, 1860. At the end of the second cabinet session, Buchanan announced that he would send his draft to the commissioners.

After spending a sleepless night, Black informed Secretary of Navy Isaac Toucey and Stanton on December 30 that he would resign. Stanton said they would stay or leave together, and Toucey informed Buchanan. When Black met with Buchanan at the latter's request, Buchanan quietly accused Black of desertion, and Black told Buchanan that the president was on a course that nobody could defend. Uncharacteristically, Buchanan asked Black to modify the draft as he saw fit before sundown. Black, with Stanton's help, listed his objections, and Buchanan rewrote the letter to meet Black's objections. In the final letter sent to the commissioners, Buchanan refused to evacuate Sumter, said only Congress could decide the proper relations between the commissioners and the federal government, and that he would see them only as private citizens. Buchanan and the cabinet considered the commissioners' response to the president's message to be so rude that they all agreed that it should not be received officially.

Black urged the reinforcement of Anderson in Sumter, even after the *Star of the West* was unsuccessful. On February 28, 1861, Black sent instructions to U.S. diplomatic representatives that they should warn foreign governments against recognition of the Confederacy, his most important diplomatic action as secretary of state.

Black left office practically penniless and resumed the private practice of law to recoup his fortunes. He soon developed a lucrative law practice. Black successfully attacked the constitutionality of the government's wartime acts while representing Milligan and McCardle before the U.S. Supreme Court, and his arguments in favor of a narrow interpretation of the rights conferred on citizens by the Fourteenth Amendment were accepted by the Court in the Slaughterhouse Cases (1873). Black also represented Samuel J. Tilden before the Electoral Commission in 1877. Black continued to practice law until his death in Brockie, Pennsylvania, on August 19, 1883.

BIBLIOGRAPHICAL ESSAY

Black's papers are in the Library of Congress, and the Buchanan papers in the Historical Society of Pennsylvania are also helpful. Chauncey F. Black published a collection of his father's essays and speeches, *Essays and Speeches of Jeremiah Black* (1886), and his daughter, Mary Black Clayton, wrote *Reminiscences of Jeremiah Sullivan Black* (1887).

There is no biography of Black. Older but still useful works that deal with Black's actions during the secession crisis are Samuel Wylie Crawford's *The Genesis of the Civil War; The Story of Sumter: 1860–1861* (1887); James Buchanan's *Mr. Buchanan's Administration on the Eve of the Rebellion*, (1866); George Ticknor Curtis's *Life of James Buchanan, Fifteenth President of the United States, Volume II* (1883); Philip G. Auchampaugh's *James Buchanan and His Cabinet on the Eve of Secession* (1926, reprinted 1965); and John Bassett Moore's (ed.) *The Works of James Buchanan, Volume XI* (1910).

See also Roy F. Nichols's biographical sketch, "Jeremiah Sullivan Black," in *The American Secretaries of State and Their Diplomacy*, edited by Samuel Flagg Bemis (1958). Elbert B. Smith's *The Presidency of James Buchanan* (1975) is helpful in discussing Black's relationship to Buchanan, Black's actions concerning secession and the threats of secession as attorney general and secretary of state, and his actions as secretary of state generally.

Edward S. Mihalkanin

JAMES G. BLAINE (1830–1893)

Served 1881; 1889–1892
Appointed by President James Garfield
Continued in office under President Chester A. Arthur
Reappointed in 1889 by President Benjamin Harrison
Republican

James Gillespie Blaine, member of the U.S. House of Representatives (March 4, 1863–July 10, 1876), U.S. Senator (July 10, 1876–March 5, 1881), and secretary of state under Presidents James A. Garfield and Chester A. Arthur (March 5–December 19, 1881) and Benjamin Harrison (March 5, 1889–June 4, 1892), was born in West Brownsville, Pennsylvania, on January 31, 1830. The son of Ephraim Lyon Blaine, a successful investor in land and trading goods, and Maria Louise Gillespie, he graduated from Washington and Jefferson College (Pennsylvania) in 1847. He then taught at the Western Military Institute in Georgetown, Kentucky. In June 1850, Blaine married Harriet Stanwood; the couple raised seven children, four of whom survived him. Blaine's dislike of the South and ambition to study law caused him to return to Pennsylvania. From 1852 to 1854, he taught at the Pennsylvania Institute for the Blind in Philadelphia and studied law.

In 1854, Blaine moved to Augusta, Maine, his wife's hometown. He became part owner and editor of the *Kennebec Journal*, the state's most prominent Whig newspaper, and served on the editorial staff of the *Portland Advertiser*. Blaine's association with both newspapers provided him with an opportunity to pen editorial comments on foreign policy issues of the day. In so doing, he sharpened his firm sense of American mission, dating back to his support for the Mexican War, and acquired an internationalist outlook in advancing American interests in Latin America and Asia. He developed an interest in annexing Hawaii and criticized the Clayton–Bulwer Treaty for its failure to remove Britain from Central America. Yet, Blaine's resistance to the extension of slavery tempered his support for "manifest destiny," as demonstrated by his opposition to acquiring Cuba.

A Whig and an admirer of Henry Clay, Blaine, a delegate to the first Republican convention in 1856, was one of the founding fathers of the Republican Party. He eventually became the most prominent Republican politician in the United States between 1865 and 1900. He began his political career as a representative in the Maine legislature (1859–1862), serving as its speaker during his second and third terms (1861–1862). At the same time, he began his long service as chair of the Republican State Committee (1859–1881). Drafted to serve in the Civil War, Blaine hired a substitute and pursued national office. He won election to the U.S. House of Representatives seven consecutive times beginning in 1862. Although he enthusiastically supported President Abraham Lincoln and the Union, Blaine later opposed Radical Republican Reconstruction measures. He served as Speaker of the House (1869–1875) and focused on economic questions such as the currency and tariff. He remained interested in foreign affairs as evidenced by his opposition to French influence in Mexico and his heightened Anglophobia stemming from Britain's "benevolent neutrality" toward the Confederacy during the Civil War and its continued commercial supremacy in the Western Hemisphere. Indeed, by the mid-1870s Blaine had few doubts that the United States should be the leader of the Western Hemisphere and that American expansion in the Pacific should be governed by economic and commercial considerations, not territorial acquisition.

By the late 1870s, Blaine's magnetism made him the Republican Party's most commanding figure and a leading candidate for his party's nomination in every presidential contest from 1876 to 1892. Blaine's chances of securing his party's presidential nomination in 1876, however, were ruined by allegations of financial misconduct. Specifically, Blaine was accused of using worthless bonds of the Little Rock & Fort Smith Railroad as collateral to secure a $64,000 loan. James Mulligan, a bookkeeper for Warren Fisher Jr., the builder of the railroad, possessed Blaine letters to Fisher that were assumed to contain damaging information against the presidential aspirant. Blaine confronted Mulligan and demanded that he turn over the private correspondence. Mulligan did so, but Blaine's subsequent actions seemed to confirm the charges. Blaine, in an effort to clear his name, read selected excerpts from the letters on the floor of the U.S. House of Representatives. This only fueled questions about his character that thwarted his pursuit of the White House throughout the remainder of his political career. In immediate terms, his political enemies rallied behind Ohio Governor Rutherford B. Hayes to deny Blaine the Republican presidential nomination in 1876. Though he would never again openly campaign for his party's presidential nomination, Blaine remained the "Plumed Knight" to his loyal legions of supporters and would continue to receive significant support for the presidency.

Shortly after the Republican National Convention of 1876, the governor of Maine selected Blaine to fill the vacancy in the U.S. Senate caused by the resignation of Lot Morrill. Blaine remained in the U.S. Senate until he served as secretary of state under Presidents Garfield and Arthur in 1881. During his tenure in the U.S. Senate, Blaine encouraged U.S. export trade to Latin America by supporting the construction of a merchant marine fleet and by becoming a leading advocate of reciprocity treaties. He hoped that such trade could foster Pan Americanism and help America achieve political and commercial hegemony in the Western Hemisphere without further territorial acquisitions.

By 1880, the Republican Party had split into two factions, Stalwarts and Half-Breeds, primarily over the issue of distributing the spoils of office. Within the context of this heated intraparty squabble, Blaine's supporters (Half-Breeds) pushed him for the presidency to stop Ulysses S. Grant's supporters (Stalwarts) from returning the former president to the White House for an unprecedented third term. After denying Grant the nomination through thirty-five ballots, Blaine threw his support to James A. Garfield, a Civil War general and nine-term member of the U.S. House of Representatives from Ohio, who won the Republican Party nomination and subsequent election. Garfield, in turn, appointed Blaine secretary of state.

Blaine, with Garfield's consent, would function as the "premier" of Garfield's short-lived administration. The assassination of Garfield and the succession of Arthur to the presidency effectively ended Blaine's influence in the cabinet. Yet, despite serving as secretary of state for only nine and a half months, Blaine, a nationalist, would establish a reputation as "Jingo Jim," one of the architects of a new, aggressive American foreign policy to advance U.S. interests in Latin America and the Pacific. In advocating a policy of "America for Americans," which he termed the "American System," Blaine insisted on U.S. control of a Central American canal and sought to expand American trade and influence throughout Latin America and thus deny Europe any opportunity to intervene in the affairs of the Western Hemisphere.

According to political supporters and enemies, Blaine used his final months in office to build a reputation as a statesman in preparation for yet another run for the White House in 1884. Until Garfield's death, Blaine focused all his attention on denying federal patronage to his political opponents, the Stalwarts, led by Blaine's political nemesis, New York Senator Roscoe Conkling. Then, in a late burst of activity following Garfield's death on September 19, 1881, Blaine tried to assert hemispheric leadership through offers of good offices and arbitration. Blaine, aroused by a recent Colombian concession to a French company to build a canal across Panama, informed the British government that the United States sought to void, unilaterally if necessary, the Clayton–Bulwer Treaty of 1850, which provided for joint Anglo-American control and construction of any Central American canal. The British government ignored the threat, but Blaine's Anglophobia, which during his first tenure at the State Department included a spirited defense against the arrest of Irish-Americans in England, won him much praise from Democratic Irish voters as well as from his own party. At the same time, he promoted the construction of a U.S.-controlled canal across Nicaragua. Frederick T. Frelinghuysen, Blaine's successor, supported this policy, but the Cleveland administration reversed Blaine's canal policy, arguing that the project should not come under the exclusive control of any one power.

In his efforts to assert U.S. hemispheric leadership to eliminate opportunities for European intervention, Blaine also sought to prevent French seizure of Venezuelan customhouses over unpaid debts. In a move that anticipated the Roosevelt Corollary to the Monroe Doctrine two decades later, Blaine urged Venezuela to pay its debt through an American agent and threatened that if no payment was made within three months, the United States would seize the customshouses and collect the money to pay the debt.

Blaine also exhibited an aversion to European interference in Western Hemispheric affairs through his efforts to make the United States the sole arbitrator of territorial disputes throughout Latin America. Blaine's efforts to mediate territorial disputes between Guatemala and Mexico, Costa Rica and Colombia, as well as ending the War of the Pacific between Chile and Peru, however, earned him a reputation for aggressive and reckless diplomacy that only reinforced Latin American suspicions toward the "Colossus of the North." In the boundary dispute between Mexico and Guatemala over control of the province of Chiapas, Blaine feared that

Mexico planned to take advantage of its weak neighbors to extend its boundaries far beyond the territory in dispute, namely, to absorb Central America into the Mexican federal system. Blaine asked Mexico to accept impartial arbitration while all too obviously taking Guatemala's side. When Blaine left office in December 1881, this dispute stood about as he found it. His successor, Frederick T. Frelinghuysen, decided not to press the matter. In the end, Blaine had managed only to offend an important neighbor. Farther south, when Costa Rica and Colombia agreed to a European proposal to submit their boundary dispute to Spain for arbitration, Blaine bellowed loudly against Old World intrusions in the hemisphere, again accomplishing little more than lowering U.S. stock in Latin America.

Blaine's efforts to mediate an end to the War of the Pacific demonstrated how political opportunism and lack of diplomatic experience undercut U.S. leadership in hemispheric affairs. The war, which began in 1879, pitted Chile against Peru and Bolivia in a struggle to control coastal areas rich in nitrates and guano. By 1881, Chile had won the military contest handily but could not conclude the peace because Peru refused to accept Chile's large territorial gains. The United States had already tried mediating the impasse without success, but Blaine was willing to give it another try. Counting on political capital for himself in any diplomatic victory, he wanted the United States to stand opposed to armed expansion in the hemisphere. He also hoped to curb pro-British Chile's rising power and offer aid to Peru before it sought European assistance. Throughout his handling of the situation, Blaine exaggerated British efforts to influence the region, which sharpened his anti-Chilean prejudice as he sought to end the war. Blaine's personal choices for ministers guaranteed the failure of this mediation effort: Hugh Judson Kilpatrick took Chile's side in Santiago, Stephen Hurlbut championed Peru's cause in Lima, and the two men publicly voiced their disagreements in the press. The ministers proved to be too ill-trained and ill-tempered to resolve the matter. Worse, Blaine failed to control them or even to answer their dispatches.

Blaine tried desperately to rescue his diplomacy. First, he sent a special agent, veteran diplomat William H. Trescot, to South America to pressure Chile to drop its demands for annexation of Peruvian territory and persuade Brazil and Argentina to back the U.S. position. Meanwhile, Blaine convinced Arthur to invite all Latin American nations except Haiti to a Pan-American conference in Washington, D.C. While claiming that the conference sought to expand trade and develop mechanisms to maintain hemispheric peace, Blaine probably hoped that encouraging inter-American cooperation would accomplish three goals: recoup his political fortunes, restore a facade of success to the shambles of his failed mediation policies, and force Mexico and Chile to retreat from their hard-line diplomatic positions.

Trescot's mission and the proposed Pan-American conference were doomed to fail, however. Shortly before Trescott arrived in Chile, Frelinghuysen succeeded Blaine at the State Department. Unwilling to follow Blaine's policy, he limited Trescott's powers with new instructions that eliminated the need for the mission. When the U.S. Senate called for the correspondence relating to Blaine's mediation effort to end the War of the Pacific, Frelinghuysen turned over the entire correspondence, including communications of the most confidential nature. Furthermore, Frelinghuysen withdrew the conference invitations. Nor did Blaine's humiliation end there. Shortly after the publication of the Chilean–Peruvian correspondence, charges were made that one or more of the ministers who served under

Blaine were improperly connected in business ventures that strongly suggested they stood to profit financially from an anti-Chilean settlement of the War of the Pacific. The House Committee on Foreign Affairs investigated the matter, clearing Blaine of any charges of malfeasance. In so doing, the committee allowed Blaine to defend his mediation effort in the War of the Pacific as an attempt to prevent European, particularly English, intervention in the war. However, Blaine's defense of his policy did not end the matter. Hurlbut, the former U.S. minister to Peru, accused Blaine of improper financial dealings with that government, which reaffirmed Blaine's tainted image as the "tattoed man" during the presidential campaign of 1884.

These difficulties aside, Blaine, during his first term as secretary of state, deserves credit for preparing the way for U.S. expansion in the Pacific at the turn of the century. He authorized the voyage that led to the 1882 commercial agreement negotiated by Commodore Robert W. Shufeldt with Korea. In addition, he extended the U.S. security perimeter to Hawaii, using the 1875 U.S. reciprocity agreement with the island kingdom to check possible British advances in the North Pacific that could pose a threat to America's Pacific commerce and to the projected Central American canal.

Blaine appeared to retire from politics in 1881 when he withdrew from his only remaining political post as chair of the Republican State Committee in Maine. Although concerned with his declining health, he remained the most popular Republican in the country. He turned his attention to writing his memoirs, *Twenty Years of Congress: From Lincoln to Garfield*, published in two volumes in 1884 and 1886. Meanwhile, the Democrats had won control of the U.S. House of Representatives and appeared ready to capture the White House in 1884 behind the candidacy of New York Governor Grover Cleveland. With many Republicans fearful that Arthur could not defeat Cleveland in the upcoming election, Blaine received his party's nomination for the presidency.

In the bitter campaign that followed, several problems derailed Blaine's third presidential bid. The Mugwumps, a small but influential group of reform-minded Republicans, criticized Blaine as a "tattoed man" whose involvement in questionable financial transactions such as the Mulligan Letters demonstrated a lack of moral character they expected from a president of the United States. This criticism seemed justified when Blaine joined 200 of the wealthiest men in America at a lavish diner at Delmonico's restaurant in New York near the end of the campaign. A *New York World* cartoon depicted "Belshazaar Blaine and the Money Kings" dining on the finest food and wine while a poor family begged for scraps from the table. In addition, Blaine failed to react quickly against a Protestant clergyman's description of the Democratic Party as the party of "rum, Romanism, and rebellion." This cost Blaine the Democratic Irish vote, which he had courted by his habit of "twisting the lion's tail," or standing up to Great Britain in foreign affairs. These factors, together with Blaine's long-standing personal rivalry with Roscoe Conkling, cost Blaine New York's 36 electoral votes, which proved decisive in his defeat to Cleveland.

Although still recognized as a leader of the Republican opposition to President Cleveland, Blaine again appeared to retire from politics. He visited Europe from June 1887 to August 1888. Cleveland, however, saw to it that Blaine would assume some role in the presidential election of 1888 by devoting his entire third annual message (December 1887) to a call for tariff reduction. Blaine immediately defended existing tariff rates as beneficial to business, labor, and farmers alike and urged fellow Republicans to unite against tariff reduction to recapture the White House. Blaine, however, insisted that he would not be a candidate for the presidential nomination nor did he give his supporters a chance to draft him by supporting Benjamin Harrison, who eventually won the party nomination. Harrison's debt to Blaine increased when Blaine returned to the United States in August 1888 to campaign for him. Harrison, having little choice other than to acknowledge Blaine's standing in the party, asked Blaine to become secretary of state again. Yet, the two men never shared the close relationship that Blaine had had with Garfield. Blaine appeared upset that Harrison had waited several months before offering him the portfolio to run the State Department. Harrison, for his part, did not want a "premier" for his administration. Indeed, he did not consult Blaine about filling other cabinet positions. When Harrison declined to allow Blaine's son, Walker Blaine, to serve as first assistant secretary of state, it was clear that Blaine's influence and power in the Harrison administration would be limited.

Blaine and Harrison have been credited with contributing to the strategic formation of the new empire that the United States created by the end of the nineteenth century. They agreed on two key objectives of late nineteenth-century U.S. foreign policy: American control of a Central American canal and establishing an assertive U.S. presence in the Caribbean and the Pacific. Yet, the Harrison administration enjoyed few concrete advances in accomplishing either goal. It failed in its effort to encourage the Nicaraguan government to agree to the construction of a U.S. canal across that country, and it also failed in each of its attempts to secure U.S. naval bases in the Pacific and the Caribbean. In Korea, Blaine hoped to take advantage of the Shufeldt Treaty to secure a coaling station for the U.S. navy. This, he perceived, would ensure an open door for American interests against Russian and Chinese influence in the hermit kingdom. Korea rejected the offer. Across the globe, Blaine tried to take advantage of a revolution in Haiti to secure a lease for a naval base at Môle Saint Nicholas. He helped the Haitian opposition gain power, but then became impatient with the slow pace of the negotiations and replaced the American negotiator, U.S. Minister Frederick Douglass, with a white naval officer, Rear Admiral Bancroft Gerhardi. Threats to use naval force to secure the concession failed to move the Haitians, and the United States came away empty-handed. American efforts to secure a lease for the use of Samaná Bay in the Dominican Republic proved equally fruitless. The administration also tried in vain to secure a lease for Chimbote in Peru and to purchase the Danish West Indies. Blaine accepted these defeats rather well, as he expected Cuba, Puerto Rico, and the projected isthmian canal to come under U.S. control within a generation.

Blaine experienced further disappointment at the first International Conference of American States, which met in Washington, D.C., between October 1889 and April 1890. The Democrats had revived Blaine's original plans for the inter-American meeting, and Cleveland issued the invitations, though fittingly Blaine convened the conference and presided as president over the proceedings that delegates from eighteen hemispheric states attended. He was eager to attack British domination of Latin American markets by persuading the conferees to establish a customs union that set common tariffs against outsiders and preferential duties within the union. Enthusiastic support came from important sectors of American manufacturing, agriculture, and shipping, some of whose leaders served in the U.S. delegation. Aside from his commercial objectives, Blaine also hoped the conference would produce the machinery for arbitrating armed conflicts among hemispheric states. While achieving the admirable object of abolishing war in the hemisphere, arbitration also would reduce occasions for European intervention.

Blaine first arranged a tour through major industrial cities that would advertise U.S. products to the Latin delegates and publicize the conference at home. The results of the meeting itself, however, came as a great letdown. Throughout the deliberations, Argentina and Chile were suspicious, aloof, and generally uncooperative; most of the other Latin American states did their share of foot-dragging, too. The U.S. public soon grew impatient with so much talk and so few results. The conference finally disbanded without establishing a customs union or arbitration apparatus.

To stimulate trade, interested nations were encouraged to conclude reciprocity agreements with one another. Blaine, who viewed commercial reciprocity to promote hemispheric trade as a politically safe middle ground between high tariffs and free trade, had earlier pushed for a commercial reciprocity amendment to the McKinley Tariff (1890), convinced that this policy would open markets in the hemisphere to American exports. The Harrison administration offered to remove five major Latin American exports from tariff duties—animal hides, coffee, molasses, sugar, and tea—and expected similar treatment for exports from the United States. Of all the South American nations, only Brazil, a major exporter of coffee to the United States, agreed to a reciprocity treaty. Nevertheless, Blaine accomplished one of his key objectives, strengthening hemispheric economic ties, at least with the nations of Central America and the islands of the Caribbean. The United States concluded reciprocity treaties with El Salvador, Guatemala, Honduras, and Nicaragua in Central America, and with the Dominican Republic, Great Britain for its West Indian colonies and British Guiana, and Spain on behalf of Cuba and Puerto Rico. The reciprocity agreements, however, were given little chance to increase U.S. exports to these countries. When the Democrats won control of the White House and both Houses of Congress in 1892, they abandoned reciprocity for the Wilson–Gorman Tariff of 1894. Thus, aside from setting a precedent for later meetings and creating an information bureau, the future Pan American Union, the long-awaited conference passed without significant accomplishments.

The complexities of the American federal system caused Blaine his next headache. In 1891, a New Orleans jury acquitted eleven Italians suspected of Mafia ties on charges of murdering the city's police superintendent. A local mob rejected the ruling and lynched the suspects while the police looked the other way. The Italian government demanded redress and punishment of the offenders, but Blaine shunned any responsibility because the federal system did not authorize him to act on a problem concerning local justice. When the Italians rejected this argument, Blaine delivered a bombastic lecture on American civics and, in effect, told Italy that the federal government could offer it no remedy. The Italian government recalled its minister to the United States, Washington reciprocated, and in both countries there was talk of war. Fortunately, Blaine then demonstrated unusual patience and helped resolve the matter by pointing out to the Italian government that only three of the victims had retained their Italian citizenship at the time of their deaths. Harrison inserted a tacit apology in his annual message, and Blaine quietly sent $25,000 to the bereaved Italian families through the State Department's secret service fund.

Blaine had a more difficult time defusing a U.S.–Chilean war scare in 1891–1892. The spark that nearly ignited a U.S.–Chilean conflict occurred in Valparaiso, in October 1891, when approximately 100 American sailors on shore leave from the USS *Baltimore*, most of them intoxicated, were suddenly attacked by local residents. Two sailors were killed, seventeen badly wounded, and many others beaten by police, who joined in the assault before putting most of the Americans in jail to dry out. The brawl nearly led to war. Chile, in 1891, needed no reminder that Harrison's secretary of state had tried to reduce its territorial gains from the War of the Pacific. Moreover, many Chileans were upset over the U.S. role in the recent revolution, just concluded a few weeks before the Valparaiso riot, in which the Congressionalists had defeated the incumbent President Balmaceda. The United States had made several errors: supporting Balmaceda against a parliamentary claim to power, offering to mediate just as the rebels began to win, attempting to seize a rebel ship employed on legal business shipping arms bought in the United States to Chile, and granting asylum in the U.S. embassy to Balmaceda supporters. Simply put, the U.S. had backed the losing side. To add further insult to injury, when the new president took office, the U.S. minister, Patrick Egan, boycotted the ceremony and deliberately delayed recognizing the new Chilean government.

To make matters worse, the Harrison administration viewed the close ties between the Congressionalists and Great Britain as a threat to vital American interests throughout the hemisphere. The new Chilean government did not help matters when it was slow to act decently toward the victimized sailors. Its first responses to U.S. protests were unrepentant, and Harrison threatened retaliation. This led Chile's foreign minister to insult Harrison and his administration, which inflamed U.S. public opinion. The Chilean government aggravated the situation by denouncing Minister Egan and demanding his recall. Harrison issued an ultimatum, threatening to break diplomatic relations unless Chile apologized promptly and made amends. Finally realizing the danger, Chile's government framed a conciliatory reply, which Washington received immediately after an impatient Harrison sent Congress a request for a declaration of war. It seems clear that Harrison was not bluffing, so Chile acted just in time. Its message was an abject apology and promise of an indemnity for the injured seamen and families of the dead, later set at $75,000. Harrison reluctantly accepted the settlement.

Blaine lay ill throughout the crisis, further weakened by his grief over the death of three of his children within a year. Several times during the crisis, he dragged himself to the White House to urge caution and restraint. Yet, Harrison remained in charge throughout the crisis, drafting all correspondence and ultimatums. Although the rationale for Harrison's hypersensitive nationalist stance in the dispute remains unclear, the results are not: greater friction in U.S.–Chilean relations, a blow against the spirit of Pan-Americanism, and a growing suspicion of Yankee diplomacy in other Latin American capitals, all of which harmed Blaine's twin objectives of promoting peace and trade in the Western Hemisphere.

The sudden U.S. effort to annex Hawaii in 1893 represented the Harrison administration's most important diplomatic venture. Fearful that the reciprocity agreements of 1875 and 1887 would not protect Hawaii sugar growers from having to pay tariff duties to export their product to the United States, Hawaii's minister to Washington, Henry A. P. Carter, and Blaine worked out an agreement in 1889 that would basically establish Hawaii as a U.S. protectorate. The proposed agreement promised complete trade reciprocity between the United States and Hawaii. In addition, the United States would guarantee Hawaii's independence provided that the Hawaiian king did not enter into any treaty with foreign governments without prior American consent. Additionally, the agreement granted the United States the power to use military force to preserve domestic peace and protect Hawaiian sovereignty from foreign threat. The Hawaiian monarch, fearful that the Harrison administration would use this provision to take control of the island, refused to approve or revise the agreement. A year later, Congress adopted the McKinley Tariff, placing sugar on the free list, costing Hawaii its advantage under the earlier reciprocity agreements. Blaine understood the impact of the tariff on Hawaii's economy and privately told Harrison that the United States should be prepared for the possibility of annexing the island.

Blaine might have been trying to accelerate matters when he appointed John L. Stephens as U.S. minister to Hawaii. Stevens, a partner and coeditor of the *Kennebec Journal*, had been a strong advocate for annexing Hawaii since the 1850s, when Luther Severance, then U.S. commissioner to Hawaii, convinced him and Blaine of Hawaii's importance to America's future position in Asia. Without instructions, Stevens arrived in Honolulu in the summer of 1889.

In January 1893, Stevens supported the coup d'état led by American sugar growers that overthrew the Hawaiian monarchy of Queen Liliuokalani. Specifically, Stevens had promised the Americans military support if they did rebel and ordered 150 marines from the USS *Boston* to guard locations in Honolulu that the rebels had to control once their coup began. The revolutionaries then proclaimed a republic, which Stevens recognized even before Queen Lilioukalini's main defenses had a chance to surrender. He also declared a U.S. protectorate over Hawaii and raised the American flag over Honolulu.

There is no written proof that Stevens acted under orders from Blaine or his successor, John W. Foster. Stevens's dispatches addressing the issue of an American-supported coup remained unanswered in Washington. Blaine's failure to respond might be interpreted as a tacit approval for Stevens's plan of action to annex the island to the United States. Meanwhile, Americans had taken the lead in forming the Annexation Club, whose leader, Lorrin Thurston, plotted with Stevens to bring Hawaii under U.S. control. He even met with Blaine once in 1892 to inform the ailing secretary of state of the political unrest in Hawaii caused by Queen Liliuokalani's rule. Thurston later claimed that Blaine told him that he did not see how the United States could reject an application for annexation. If true, Stevens's intervention in January 1893 should hardly be a surprise. At minimum, he acted with some knowledge that the Harrison administration was interested in annexing Hawaii.

The Harrison administration disavowed the protectorate, approving everything else Stevens had done. Shortly thereafter, Secretary of State Foster and a party of Hawaii's provisional government, without any Hawaiians, discussed terms of annexation. They finished their work on February 14, and President Harrison, though lukewarm to the idea, sent the treaty to the Senate the next day. The Senate slowed down proceedings because of its own doubts and President-elect Cleveland's request for delay. President Cleveland withdrew the treaty from the Senate, Stevens was relieved from his post, and Hawaii was not annexed to the United States until 1898.

Blaine failed to solve two additional diplomatic problems, the fur seals controversy and Samoa. The Anglo-American controversy over fur seal fisheries in the Bering Sea centered around two points of dispute: whether the United States had any right to exclusive jurisdiction in the Bering Sea and whether the United States had any right of protection or property in the fur seals outside the three-mile territorial limit off the Alaskan coastline. While Russia remained in control of Alaska, neither the United States nor Great Britain challenged Russian monopoly control over the profitable fur sealing trade. Upon purchasing Alaska, the United States assumed complete control of the trade, leasing the privilege of taking fur seals at their breeding places in the Pribilof Islands to the Alaska Commercial Company. The lucrative trade attracted Canadians, who respected U.S. jurisdiction over the waters within three miles of the islands by capturing the fur seals on the open sea. When such operations soon threatened to destroy the herd, U.S. officials declared the Bering Sea a mare clausum, closed sea, and American revenue cutters began to seize Canadian ships engaged in the trade operating as far as 115 miles from the islands. An attempt to settle the matter in the mid-1880s failed, due in large part to Canadian opposition to recognize any U.S. jurisdiction over the Bering Sea.

With no chance of an agreement, Blaine, in the summer of 1889, instructed U.S. revenue cutters to prevent open sea sealing operations, leading to the seizure of British and Canadian vessels. In response to British protests, Blaine justified his policy as an attempt to prevent the extinction of the herd stemming from *contra bonos mores* (a pursuit involving serious injury to the rights of the government and people of the United States). He also relied on the precedent of Russia and later the United States having enjoyed exclusive control of the fur seal trade until the 1880s but without pressing the claim of mare clausum. After failing to agree on a solution after three years, Blaine in 1892 accepted an arrangement to settle the matter through arbitration

By the early 1870s, Californian businessmen looked to the Samoan harbor of Pago Pago as a potential coaling station for U.S. steamships involved in South Pacific trade. In 1878, a U.S. presence was established at Samoa with a treaty that secured the right to a coaling station at the port as well as trading privileges. Great Britain and Germany each secured similar treaties, and all three powers began to press their claims to the island. Blaine, upon inheriting this unresolved dispute over Samoan autonomy, supported a proposal for tripartite control to guarantee Samoan autonomy. At the same time, he pressed a demand for a naval station at Pago Pago to meet the needs of America's increasing Pacific trade. An 1889 agreement safeguarded U.S. interests on the island but failed to provide self-government for the Samoans. To Blaine's critics, the agreement violated America's tradition of nonentanglement. Blaine, in contrast, viewed it as the only viable solution to the dispute. The implication of European recognition of America as a world power in this arrangement probably made it easier for Blaine to accept it.

Blaine's deteriorating health limited his ability to function as secretary of state on a day-to-day basis. As early as April and May 1889, while the United States participated in the Berlin Conference with Germany and Great Britain that established a three-power protectorate over Samoa, Blaine was confined to his bed with lumbago. After the tragic deaths from pneumonia of his son Walker in mid-January 1890 and his daughter Alice less than three weeks later, Blaine was never the same. He became ill in March 1891 and collapsed in April. Blaine did not return to the State Department until October. In the interval, he exhibited all the symptoms of a nervous breakdown.

Despite his declining health stemming from both Bright's disease and lung problems, a group of powerful Republicans hoped to use Blaine to block the nomination of President Harrison for a second term. Harrison's independence had alienated several party bosses, especially Thomas C. Platt of New York and Matthew Quay of Pennsylvania. Following the Democratic Party's overwhelming success in the congressional elections of 1890, which gave it control of both houses, the bosses insisted that Harrison could not win in 1892 and pressured Blaine to become a candidate for the presidential nomination.

Blaine suddenly resigned as secretary of state on June 4, 1892, just a few days before the opening of the Republican National Convention. He never explained why he resigned, but contemporaries described him as feeble, overwhelmed by the constant badgering of those involved in the scheme to remove Harrison from power, and seemingly unable to resist being drawn into the machinations of the bosses. Blaine's recent disagreement with Harrison on handling the *Baltimore* affair probably influenced his decision to leave the State Department as well. In any case, Harrison easily won the nomination. Just a few days after the convention, another of Blaine's sons, Emmons, died from appendicitis. This may have been the final blow for Blaine. He made one brief speech during the campaign in October, and early in January became ill for the last time. He died in Washington, D.C., on January 27, 1893.

Blaine contributed more than any other political figure of his time to the power and prestige of the Republican Party in the post–Civil War era. In so doing, he became the symbol of the party's successes and failures during the Gilded Age. Although he enjoyed few successes in directing U.S. foreign policy in 1881 and again from 1889 to 1892, he developed a vision of America's place in world affairs, especially concerning U.S. supremacy in the Western Hemisphere, which shaped the country's expansionism at the turn of the century in several ways. His push for a U.S. canal across Central America anticipated the abrogation of the Clayton–Bulwer Treaty. His reciprocity treaties foreshadowed the implementation of Dollar Diplomacy. Finally, Blaine's emphasis on developing an "American System" set the stage for employing the Monroe Doctrine to justify American military, political, and economic intervention in Latin America in the early twentieth century.

BIBLIOGRAPHICAL ESSAY

The papers of James G. Blaine are in the Manuscript Division of the Library of Congress. The Family Correspondence series, General Correspondence series, and scrapbooks contain references to U.S. foreign policy during Blaine's two terms as secretary of state, especially concerning Latin America. Other collections that offer some insight include the Papers of Benjamin Harrison and Whitelaw Reid, both at the Library of Congress. Some interesting insights concerning Blaine's Latin American policy can also be found in Harriet S. Blaine Beale (ed.), *Letters of*

Mrs. James G. Blaine, 2 vols. (1908). For Blaine's published diplomatic correspondence, see *Papers Relating to the Foreign Relations of the United States* (1881, 1889–1892), and Albert T. Volwiler (ed.), *The Correspondence Between Benjamin Harrison and James G. Blaine* (1940).

Two of Blaine's published writings contain references to U.S. foreign policy. Blaine's *Twenty Years of Congress: From Lincoln to Garfield*, 2 vols. (1884–1886), focuses almost exclusively on U.S. politics between 1861 and 1881 except for a single chapter on the Canadian fisheries question and brief discussions on Chinese immigration, foreign trade, and Santo Domingo. Blaine's *Political Discussions: Legislative, Diplomatic, and Popular, 1856–1886* (1887) is more useful in studying Blaine's foreign policy. This collection of speeches and newspaper/periodical articles addresses numerous foreign policy topics, including the Halifax award, trade with South America, Chinese immigration, the Clayton–Bulwer Treaty, the War of the Pacific, U.S.–Mexican relations, United States interest in Hawaii, the Pan American Conference, and Blaine's reflections on the objectives and accomplishments of the Garfield administration.

David S. Muzzey, *James G. Blaine: A Political Idol of Other Days* (1934), is the only scholarly biography on Blaine. Gail Hamilton, *Biography of James G. Blaine* (1895), Charles Edward Russell, *Blaine of Maine: His Life and Times* (1931), and Edward Stanwood, *James Gillespie Blaine* (1905), read much like Blaine's campaign biographies in 1884, such as Russell H. Conwell's *The Public Services of James G. Blaine*. Hamilton's biography nevertheless contains numerous correspondences that help in understanding Blaine and his public life.

Of the various full treatments of Blaine's foreign policy, both Alice Felt Tyler, *The Foreign Policy of James G. Blaine* (1927), and Richard C. Winchester, "James G. Blaine and the Ideology of American Expansion" (1966) view Blaine as a significant transitional figure in late nineteenth-century U.S. diplomacy between Seward's expansionism and later economic expansionism. A similar condensed view of Blaine can be found in Lester D. Langley, "James Gillespie Blaine: The Ideologue as Diplomat," in *Makers of American Foreign Policy: From Benjamin Franklin to Henry Kissinger* (1974), edited by Frank J. Merli and Theodore A. Wilson. Edward P. Crapol, *James Gillespie Blaine: Architect of Empire* (2000), examines Blaine's goal of achieving global economic supremacy through energetic government action, explains his desire to displace Britain from the Western Hemisphere in pursuit of U.S. economic nationalism, and concludes, much like Tyler and Winchester, that Blaine was the most important architect of American empire in the late nineteenth century. David F. Healy, *James G. Blaine and Latin America* (2001), examines Blaine's vision of America's standing in world affairs through his Latin American policy. He concludes that Blaine had a clear vision of national greatness and that his nationalist rhetoric prepared the ground for America's emergence as a world power by the end of the nineteenth century. Joseph B. Lockey, "James G. Blaine" in Samuel Flagg Bemis (ed.), *The American Secretaries of State and Their Diplomacy*, Volumes VII and VIII (1928), provides an uncritical, overly favorable assessment of Blaine's diplomacy.

Three studies on the Garfield administration cover Blaine's diplomacy in the early 1880s. As one might expect, Justus D. Doenecke, *The Presidencies of James A. Garfield and Chester A. Arthur* (1981), and Allen Peskin, *Garfield* (1978), argue that Garfield deserves greater credit for the major ventures of his short-lived administration, particularly Pan Americanism. David M. Pletcher, *The Awkward Years: American Foreign Policy under Garfield and Arthur* (1962), places Blaine's policies within the context of the confusion and frustration of U.S. foreign policy of the period.

For Blaine's "limited" role in shaping foreign policy in the Harrison administration, see Homer Socolofsky and Allan Spetter, *The Presidency of Benjamin Harrison* (1987); Allen Spetter, Harrison and Blaine: Foreign Policy, 1889–1893," *Indiana Magazine of History* 65 (1969):215–27; and Albert T. Volwiler, "Harrison, Blaine, and American Foreign Policy, 1889–1893," *Proceedings of the American Philosophical Society* 79 (1938):637–648.

For specific aspects of Blaine's diplomacy, including Pan Americanism; reciprocity agreements; U.S. relations with Britain, Chile, Germany, and Italy; and American interest in Hawaii, see Wilgus Curtis, "James G. Blaine and the Pan American Movement," *Hispanic American Historical Review* 5 (1922): 662–708; Russell H. Bostert, "A New Approach to the Origins of Blaine's Pan American Policy," *Hispanic American Historical Review* 39 (1959): 375–412; Russell Bostert, "Diplomatic Reversal: Frelinghuysen's Opposition to Blaine's Pan-American Policy, 1882," *Mississippi Valley Historical Review* 42 (1956): 653–71; David M. Pletcher, "Reciprocity and Latin America in the Early 1890s: A Foretaste of Dollar Diplomacy," *Pacific Historical Review* 47 (1978): 53–89; Tom E. Terrill, *The Tariff, Politics, and American Foreign Policy, 1874–1901* (1973); Mike Sewell, "Political Rhetoric and Policy-Making: James G. Blaine and Britain," *Journal of American Studies* 24 (1990): 61–84; Edward Crapol, *America for Americans: Economic Nationalism and Anglophobia in the Late Nineteenth Century* (1973); Paul M. Kennedy, *The Samoan Tangle: A Study in Anglo-German-American Relations, 1878–1900* (1974); David A. Smith, "From the Mississippi to the Mediterranean: The 1891 New Orleans Lynching and Its Effects on U.S. Diplomacy and the American Navy," *Southern Historian* 19 (1998): 60–85; Joyce S. Goldberg, *The Baltimore Affair: United States Relations with Chile, 1891–1892* (1986); Tate Merz, *The United States and the Hawaiian Kingdom: A Political History* (1965); Charles S. Campbell, Jr., "The Anglo-American Crisis in the Bering Sea, 1890–91," *Mississippi Valley Historical Review* 48 (1961):393–414; Charles S. Campbell, Jr., "The Bering Sea Settlements of 1892," *Pacific Historical Review* 32 (1963): 347–68; and John W. Foster, *Diplomatic Memoirs*, 2 vols. (1909).

George H. Mayer, *The Republican Party, 1854–1964* (1964); Robert Marcus, *Grand Old Party: Political Structure in the Gilded Age, 1880–1896* (1971); and H. Wayne Morgan, *From Hayes to McKinley: National Party Politics, 1877–1896* (1969) cover Blaine's role as a leading political figure in the late nineteenth century. For Blaine's failed presidential run in 1884, see Mark Walgren Summers, *Rum, Romanism, and Rebellion: The Making of a President, 1884* (2000).

Dean Fafoutis and Edward S. Mihalkanin

WILLIAM JENNINGS BRYAN (1860–1925)

Served 1913–1915
Appointed by President Woodrow Wilson
Democrat

William Jennings Bryan looked as little like a secretary of state as anyone who has ever occupied the office. His baggy, countrified clothes were always rumpled, his hair a long untidy fringe around his bald dome. His pockets were stuffed with official dispatches, letters, and memoranda scribbled on the backs of old envelopes and with radishes, his favorite snack. Informal and gregarious, he preferred farmers to foreign dignitaries. Each summer he left Washington to deliver inspirational speeches before rural audiences, who gathered by thousands to hear his rolling baritone voice. To urban critics, his appearances on those Chautauqua stages, along with magicians, comedians, and ventriloquists, were proof that he was unfit to be secretary of state. When he refused to serve wine at official functions, many people derided his "grape juice diplomacy."

That Woodrow Wilson chose such a seemingly inappropriate person to be secretary of state was, of course, a result of time-honored tradition. Bryan was appointed because he was the most prominent figure in the Democratic Party, and Wilson asked him to serve to have him "in Washington and in harmony with the administration rather than outside and possibly in a critical attitude."

Bryan's influence on Wilson administration policy resulted from his personal relationship with the president. Although Wilson had earlier opposed Bryan politically, the two had hardly met before 1912. Bryan's support for Wilson's presidential candidacy and their agreement that Christian principles ought to guide policy gave them common ground on which to stand while they discovered that they liked each other. "My father . . . ," Bryan recalled, "saw no necessary conflict—and I have never been able to see any—between the principles of our government and the principles of Christian faith." Wilson might well have said the same thing. Moreover, Wilson's adherence to reforms that Bryan had long championed and Bryan's loyal support of the president's domestic policy drew them together. Had they not disagreed over the proper response to German submarine warfare, Bryan might well have served eight years in the cabinet rather than a little more than two.

Born in Salem, Illinois, on March 19, 1860, Bryan's Baptist father and Methodist mother both taught him that God expected Christians to serve Him by serving their fellow men. Perhaps to avoid taking sides in the family Bryan chose the Presbyterian church and subsequently became an important lay leader in it, but aside from a belief in the literal interpretation of the Bible, denominational ties were never as important to him as the broad ideal of Christian service.

After graduating from Illinois College at Jacksonville in 1881 and from the Union College of Law in Chicago in 1883, Bryan married and practiced law for four years in Jacksonville. In 1887 he moved to Lincoln, Nebraska, where his law practice quickly became secondary to his main vocation, politics. For the rest of his life his income came more from writing and lecturing than from law. His magnificent voice and eloquent defense of religious and cultural values of the Midwest made him a favorite on the Chautauqua circuit, and for almost 30 years his lectures drew enormous audiences and paid large fees. Even while secretary of state he continued these lectures, and he also supplemented the considerable income from them with a stream of books and articles on political and moral topics.

For Bryan there was no sharp line separating moral and political issues, and it was precisely that blending of the issues that made him a natural leader for Western farmers when he entered politics as a Congressman in 1890. During two terms in the House, as a senatorial candidate in 1894, and as a presidential candidate in 1896, he defended farmers' values and expressed their conviction that their troubles were the result of urban influences over the tariff and the monetary system. When he proclaimed to the Democratic convention in 1896, "You shall not press down upon the brow of labor this crown of thorns, you shall not crucify mankind upon a cross of gold," it was no accident that he used religious imagery. He was defending a way of life as well as advocating political policies.

Bryan's defiance of the established order won him both the Democratic and Populist presidential nominations in 1896, but even in that depression year, defiance alone was not enough. William McKinley, the Republican nominee, was backed by the moneyed and respectable men of the nation and conducted a dignified, well-financed campaign, while Bryan crisscrossed the country in a lonely attempt to appeal personally to voters. His words fell on deaf ears in the nation's growing cities, where owners and workers alike feared that his monetary proposals would cause inflation, and McKinley won a narrow victory. Declaring that 1896 was only "the first battle," Bryan vowed to renew the fight four years later.

Before he could do so, however, the nation recovered from the depression and plunged happily into a "splendid little war" with Spain in 1898. Together, prosperity and war transformed the nation beyond anything Bryan had imagined in 1896 and made his old issues irrelevant. Opposed to the war, Bryan nevertheless volunteered loyally and served as a colonel in Nebraska's Third Regiment, a unit that never saw battle. When the conflict ended, he resigned his commission and raced to Washington, where his support for the Treaty of Paris, transferring the Philippines to the United States, may have tipped the balance in favor of the treaty. Renominated for the presidency in 1900, Bryan tried to combine the old and new by opposing both the gold standard and imperialism. Americans, prosperous and self-confident, found his message negative and irrelevant, and he was defeated by McKinley more soundly than in 1896.

In the long run, even imperialists like Theodore Roosevelt and Woodrow Wilson came to believe that taking the Philippines had been a mistake, but that conversion was several years in the future. Meanwhile, Bryan, seemingly discredited, was forced out of party leadership. Democratic conservatives returned to power, only to be humiliated in 1904 by Theodore Roosevelt, who took over many of Bryan's progressive reform proposals and built for them a broader national consensus than Bryan had ever been able to secure. After seven years of Roosevelt's ebullient presidency, it was obvious to Democrats in 1908 that they must nominate a strong reformer if they were to have any chance of defeating Roosevelt's hand-picked successor, William Howard Taft. For the third time they turned to Bryan. Taft, instinctively conservative, seemed an easy target, even with Roosevelt's endorsement, but Bryan could not find an effective campaign issue, and the portly Ohioan rolled over him because the Republicans were the dominant party and people were satisfied with conditions in the United States.

Bryan's three electoral defeats never made him bitter or self-doubting. Issues, he believed, were more important than personal victories, and by 1912, when he relinquished party leadership to Woodrow Wilson, he knew that both parties had adopted ideas he had been among the first to support. Regulation of big business, the direct election of senators, the income tax, women's suffrage, and other reforms he had long championed had won bipartisan backing and were being enacted into law. Imperialism, which he had denounced since 1898, was being questioned in both parties, and his proposal, first offered in 1905, that the nations abolish war by agreeing to international investigation of all disputes, was winning international support. When Wilson offered Bryan the appointment as secretary of state in December 1912, plans were already being laid for a great international exposition to be held in 1914 to celebrate the opening of the Panama Canal and a century of peace in Europe. To Bryan the moment seemed opportune to bring to fruition both his dreams of domestic reform and of international peace.

Bryan hoped to use the State Department to create an international structure of trust and order that would make war obsolete, to liquidate the vestiges of American imperialism and to encourage other nations to do likewise, and to establish international relations on a basis of morality and integrity. These were ambitious plans, and the outbreak of World War I made them ludicrous, yet when Bryan took office on March 4, 1913, they did not seem absurd to the members of the new administration nor to outsiders. Western society was permeated with confidence in material and moral progress, and Americans never doubted they could reshape the world. As Woodrow Wilson's League of Nations plan showed, not even the shock of war could undermine this benevolent arrogance.

Yet if Bryan sought to reshape the world, he was also a practical politician who had been leader of his party during the sixteen years the party had been out of power. Democrats all over the country looked to him for the rewards of victory, and he was eager to oblige. "I am glad to have the public know that I appreciate the services of those who work in politics and feel an interest in seeing them rewarded," he said frankly and set out to find as many federal jobs as possible for "deserving Democrats." The common notion of Bryan as a spoilsman determined to flood the federal civil service with party hacks is, however, inaccurate. He had relatively few appointments at his command, and although he was tireless in seeking jobs for his supporters, most of his diplomatic appointees served about as well as their Republican predecessors, and almost all were more sympathetic to the new administration's policies than the old hands would have been. Although Bryan's appointees included some incompetents and at least one outright crook, Democratic diplomats measured up reasonably well to the challenges of representing their country amid war and revolution.

Often complicating Bryan's task and undermining State Department morale were Wilson's tendencies to direct foreign policy personally and to bypass regular diplomats by using personal agents. The president had not studied foreign policy in detail before entering office, but he had very clear ideas of what he wanted to achieve, and he often took more personal interest in foreign issues than in details of domestic administration. His closest friend, Edward M. House, fancied himself a subtle and effective diplomat, and when crisis erupted in Europe, Wilson often relied on House rather than Bryan. For the most part the secretary accepted this situation with astonishing good humor, and his basic agreement with the president on principles enabled him to maintain a constant influence, but there were times when his policies were abruptly and embarrassingly reversed, or when House was given some assignment the secretary particularly wanted, such as a peace mission in Europe in 1915.

Latin American policy typified the relationship between Wilson and Bryan. The two men concurred on broad goals, which were to free the region from European domination, to promote the peaceful settlement of conflicts, to enlarge legitimate U.S. trade and investment opportunities, and to encourage democracy and constitutionalism. Wilson issued a statement outlining these principles in March 1913 and renounced American imperialism in a speech at Mobile that autumn. The president also took personal charge of relations with Mexico, then undergoing a great revolution, but he left Bryan to handle diplomacy with the rest of the region and entrusted the administration's trade and investment programs to Treasury Secretary William G. McAdoo and Commerce Secretary William C. Redfield.

Bryan's personal projects for Latin America included the negotiation of a series of bilateral treaties providing for the investigation of all disputes (never used), the signing of a treaty with Colombia expressing regret for American involvement in the 1903 rebellion of Panama (ratified years later in a diluted form), the negotiation of Western Hemisphere nonaggression treaty (never signed), and a scheme to reduce the risk of European intervention in the region by replacing private European loans with loans made by the U.S. government (vetoed by Wilson). All were benevolently intended, but none amounted to much, and all were overshadowed by actions that, whatever their intentions, are difficult to defend on the basis of results.

The besetting weakness of both Wilson's and Bryan's approach to Latin America was paternalism. Confident that the world's nations were evolving toward constitutional democracy, and aware that America had acquired vast new military and economic strength, they could not resist the temptation to push the evolutionary process. In Mexico, where Wilson interfered militarily and politically, an indigenous revolutionary movement with definite goals blunted the impact of American meddling, but elsewhere in the Caribbean intervention produced more damage.

The most striking examples of these problems were in the Dominican Republic and Haiti. Both countries were heavily indebted to foreigners and politically unstable. When this combination seemed likely to provoke foreign intervention, Theodore Roosevelt had intervened to impose an American customs collectorship on the Dominican Republic in the hope that economic order would beget political stability. The hope proved futile, and by the time Wilson and Bryan entered office, both the Dominican Republic and Haiti were sliding toward chaos.

In the Dominican Republic Bryan found a provisional president facing an incipient revolt. Warning the rebels that the United States felt "profound displeasure" at their "pernicious" activities, the secretary secured a ceasefire by promising U.S.-supervised elections to the Dominican congress. The following year, 1914, the United States also supervised a presidential election, and Bryan believed that all problems had been solved. "The election having been held and a Government chosen by the people having been established," he instructed the American minister, "no more revolutions will be permitted."

Dominicans did not share his optimism, and bitter conflicts between the congress and the president led to a breakdown of order in 1915 and 1916. A year after Bryan left office, U.S. troops landed and began a lengthy military occupation of the nation. Although Bryan was not immediately responsible for that event, his belief that the United States could and should organize the Dominicans' affairs for them led inexorably toward intervention and occupation.

Likewise in dealing with Haiti, benevolent motives led Bryan toward intervention. Convinced that Latin America would be stabilized if its economic problems were solved, Bryan listened sympathetically to arguments advanced by Roger Farnham, a New York banker with large interest in Haiti. Farnham insisted that American control over the Haitian customs service would solve all problems and would avert threatened intervention by Haiti's French and German creditors. By the time the outbreak of World War I in the summer of 1914 obviated the danger of Franco-German intervention, the administration was committed to straightening out Haiti's affairs. In the spring of 1915, as revolution followed revolution, Bryan began to consider "forcible interference" to impose political and economic order on Haiti. At the end of July, not long after the left office, U.S. Marines landed and imposed a military government that lasted twenty years. Ironically, although he sought to promote democracy, Bryan's policies laid the basis for a later dictatorship.

The other area of the world where Bryan's influence on policy was greatest was Asia. His most notable success in that region was in persuading Wilson to promise Philippine independence. As is turned out, that was not difficult, for the president, like many other Americans, had come to believe that taking the islands had been wrong and that holding them was dangerous because they were so vulnerable to attack in the event of war between the United States and Japan. Passage of the Jones Act officially promising independence came after Bryan left office, but soon after becoming secretary he had had the great satisfaction of assuring the Filipinos that the administration was committed to independence.

In regard to China, Bryan and Wilson shared a confidence prevalent among American Protestants that the great Asian nation was moving rapidly toward democracy and Christianity. The Taft administration had labored mightily to have the United States included in international development schemes for China, believing that in that way American economic interests would be safeguarded while China's development proceeded. Bryan and Wilson viewed these multilateral schemes as imperialistic, however, and over the objections of Republican experts in the State Department withdrew the United States from the international loan consortium and extended unilateral diplomatic recognition to the new Chinese Republic. They hoped that in so doing they would encourage others to follow the American lead and stimulate desirable tendencies within China. Instead their policy exposed American businessmen to ruinous foreign competition while American influence on events within China declined. The situation worsened after the beginning of World War I, because whatever moderating effect the European nations had had on each other and on Japan was then removed, and the United States found itself facing Japanese expansionism alone.

Bryan was especially worried about the Japanese threat in the spring of 1915, because he was keenly aware of how bad Japanese–American relations already were. Indeed, one of the first problems to face him after he became secretary of state was a crisis with Japan over California's efforts to ban land ownership by Oriental aliens. The Japanese resented this discrimination bitterly, and there was a war scare in the spring of 1913. Bryan did everything in his power to defuse the issue, making a trip to California to plead unsuccessfully with the legislature not to pass discriminatory legislation and spending endless hours with the Japanese ambassador seeking a formula that might solve the problem. The issue proved intractable, largely because there was little the federal government could do about a state law and because Democratic leaders were reluctant to interfere with a state's rights, especially on a racial question. When World War I began, therefore, relations between Japan and the United States were already strained.

The war rapidly worsened the situation. Japan, an ally of Great Britain, declared war on Germany to take over German concessions in China, even though the British opposed their entering the conflict. "When there is a fire in a jeweler's shop," a Japanese diplomat admitted frankly, "the neighbors cannot be expected to refrain from helping themselves."

Bryan thought there was little the United States could do about Japanese aggression in China without taking unacceptable risks. In a note sent on March 13, 1915, the secretary protested mildly against Japanese actions but added the damaging concession that "territorial contiguity creates special relations between Japan and these districts" of China. Delighted, the Japanese seized on the "territorial contiguity" phrase to justify their actions.

By this time in the spring of 1915 Bryan and Wilson were disagreeing over several issues arising from the war, with Wilson steadily taking a stronger, more assertive position than the secretary. Although the president accepted the March 13 note, he soon decided a more vigorous stand was needed. "We shall have to try in every practicable way to defend China," he told the secretary, and on May 3 Bryan loyally drafted a note protesting Japan's demands on China as violations of China's sovereignty and infringements on American treaty rights. The note was sent to Japan on May 5, and on May 11 another American protest declared that the United States would not "recognize any agreement of undertaking" that violated American treaty rights, China's integrity, or the Open Door policy.

Thus at the time of Bryan's resignation it appeared that the United States might be headed for a confrontation with Japan as well as with Germany. That possibility may have contributed to Bryan's decision to step down, but he need not have worried. Nothing came of the 1915 friction, except that when the United States entered the war in 1917, the Japanese immediately sought American recognition of their Chinese acquisitions. The administration conceded as little as it could, but Wilson realized America's weakness in Asia. At the end of the war he attempted to revive the international loan consortium from which he had withdrawn in 1913. Belatedly, he came to Bryan's opinion that American hopes of influence in Asia had to yield to the realities of power.

The issue that ultimately disrupted the harmony between Wilson and Bryan was the war in Europe. When it began in the summer of 1914, Wilson's wife was dying, and he willingly left the details of American neutrality to the secretary. An ardent peace advocate, Bryan recommended that Americans be discouraged from loaning money to the belligerent governments, to prevent the formation of economic and emotional ties to either side. At the same time he urged Wilson to make repeated offers of America's services as a peacemaker.

Bryan's hope of financially starving the war ran head-on into the self-interest of American manufacturers and farmers, who saw war as an opportunity to escape from a recession. Over the following months, the desire of Americans to sell and the eagerness of the British and French, in particular, to buy led to an erosion of Bryan's loan ban and to a vast increase in trade between the United States and the Allies. Inevitably, the growth of trade led, as Bryan had feared, to emotional commitments to the Allies, and it also led the Germans to the conclusion that the trade must be cut off if they were to win the war. Early in 1915 Germany moved to do just that, announcing the establishment of a "war zone" around the British Isles in which submarines would attack Allied ships and which neutral shippers were advised to avoid.

Bryan and Wilson agreed that the German declaration required a protest, and on February 10 they informed Berlin that the United States would hold Germany to "strict accountability" for harm to American ships or citizens. If anyone in the administration knew what that phrase meant or how it was to be enforced, no record of it remains. When U.S. ships were attacked and U.S. citizens killed and injured in a series of attacks during late March and April, no one knew what to do. Not until May 7, when the British passenger liner *Lusitania* was sunk with the loss of 128 American lives, did Wilson reach a clear decision. Overriding Bryan's contention that Americans who traveled in the war zone were guilty of "contributory negligence" and the secretary's plea to postpone demands for reparations until after the war, on May 13 Wilson sent a brusque note to Germany demanding the end of submarine warfare.

The issue between Wilson and Bryan was now clear. Wilson believed the United States must protect its trade and its rights as a neutral, even at the risk of war; Bryan was willing to sacrifice some trade and postpone legal issues until after the war. Both had hoped that a peace mission to Europe by Colonel House earlier in the year might avoid the dilemma by bringing the conflict to an end, but by May that hope had disappeared. With peace prospects dark and Wilson's opinion hardening, Bryan was convinced that the nation would be dragged into the war. On June 8, in a gesture rare among secretaries of state, he resigned in protest against the president's policy.

Although the United States was able to avoid war for almost two years after Bryan's resignation, in the end he was right. By demanding that Germany cease submarine warfare, Wilson had surrendered to Berlin the decision on whether or when the United States would enter the war. For the next two years Bryan struggled to awaken the country to the danger and to change Wilson's course, but failed as he had before his resignation. Nevertheless, when the United States declared war in April 1917, he volunteered his services loyally, although he continued to believe the decision a mistake.

Once the United States entered the war, Bryan shifted his concern to the postwar settlement and hoped that Wilson might choose him to seek such a peace at the postwar conference. The hope was hardly realistic, especially when Wilson was determined to attend the conference himself. From the United States Bryan watched the Paris conference attentively, agreeing with Wilson that the time had come for the Untied States to give up isolationism and join the new League of Nations. Bryan urged Senators to approve the Treaty of Versailles without amendments. Later, when it became obvious that the Senate would not approve the treaty without changes, he urged Democrats to ignore Wilson's stubborn insistence on unqualified ratification and to accept whatever reservations were necessary to secure a favorable vote.

Diabetic and aging, Bryan concentrated in the 1920s on such issues as prohibition and the struggle against the teaching of evolution rather than on politics or international affairs. He applauded the Washington Naval Conference of 1921–1922 and supported the movement to make war illegal, but such issues did not occupy the center of his attention. On July 26, 1925, five days after helping to convict John T. Scopes of illegally teaching the theory of evolution at Dayton, Tennessee, he died peacefully in his sleep during an afternoon nap.

Bryan was neither a great nor terrible secretary of state. Little fitted by background, training, or temperament for the position, he often aroused the ridicule of critics for his personal quirks and naïveté, but his attitude toward foreign policy was typical of his countrymen at the time. Much impressed by the nation's new economic and military strength, he assumed innocently that American power could reshape the world, yet at the same time he feared the possible consequences of long-term involvement. The result of these contradictory impulses was an inconsistent policy combining rash interventionism with fearful isolationism. Like many Americans, Bryan wanted his nation to serve others, but he had neither a realistic understanding of the limits of national power nor much comprehension of how little most other peoples wanted to be Americanized.

BIBLIOGRAPHICAL ESSAY

The main collection of Bryan's papers is in the Manuscripts Division of the Library of Congress, but there are also Bryan papers at the Nebraska Historical Society in Lincoln and a small but important collection, sometimes called the Bryan–Wilson Correspondence, in the National Archives. For the State Department period, the department's records in the National Archives, the Woodrow Wilson Papers in the Manuscripts Division of the Library of Congress, and the published *Papers of Woodrow Wilson*, Arthur S. Link et al. (eds.), 69 vols. (1966–1993) are also essential.

Bryan's books include *The Memoirs of William Jennings Bryan* (1925), *The First Battle: A Story of the Campaign of 1896* (1896), *Republic or Empire? The Philippine Question* (1899), *The Second Battle* (1900), *Letters to a Chinese Official, Being a Western View of Eastern Civilization* (1906), *The Old World and Its Ways* (1907), and *The Forces That Make for Peace*, in World Peace Foundation Pamphlet Series, no. 7, pt. 3 (1912), among others. He also wrote a large number of articles that were published in a variety of magazines and newspapers and, with his brother Charles, from 1901 to 1923 published a weekly (after 1912 a monthly) newspaper, *The Commoner,* which strongly expressed his outlook.

Notable early biographies of Bryan include the charmingly caustic *The Peerless Leader: William Jennings Bryan* by Paxton Hibben (1929) and the worshipful *William Jennings Bryan* by Wayne C. Williams (1936). A pioneering and still valuable study of Bryan's approach to foreign relations is Merle Curti, *Bryan and World Peace,* Smith College Studies in History 16 (1931).

Of recent studies of Bryan, the most important is Paolo E. Coletta's three-volume biography, *William Jennings Bryan* (1964–1969). Good one-volume biographies include LeRoy Ashby, *William Jennings Bryan: Champion of Democracy* (1987); Robert W. Cherny, *A Righteous Cause: The Life of William Jennings Bryan* (1985); and Louis W. Koenig, *A Political Biography of William Jennings Bryan* (1971). Books focusing particularly on Bryan's role in foreign policy include Kendrick A. Clements, *William Jennings Bryan, Missionary Isolationist* (1982); and Edward S. Kaplan, *U.S. Imperialism in Latin America: Bryan's Challenges and Contributions, 1900–1920* (1998). Bibliographies in these works will lead readers to helpful articles and other books.

Kendrick Clements

JAMES BUCHANAN
(1791–1868)

Served 1845–1849
Appointed by President James K. Polk
Democrat

James Buchanan was born near Mercersburg, Pennsylvania, on April 23, 1791, the second of eleven children by James Buchanan and Elizabeth Speer Buchanan. His father had immigrated to Pennsylvania from Country Donegal, Ireland, in 1783, where he settled as a farmer and eventually owned a frontier trading post at Stony Batter. Young James grew up in a staunch Presbyterian household, where he learned patriotic values and acquired a love of learning. He graduated with honors from Dickinson College in 1809 and was admitted to the bar in Lancaster, Pennsylvania, in 1813, where he set up a law practice.

James Buchanan's career in politics began when he was elected to the Pennsylvania assembly in 1813 as a Federalist after serving briefly in the War of 1812. In 1820 he was elected to Congress in the wake of a personal tragedy. He was briefly engaged the previous year to Ann Caroline Coleman, daughter of a prosperous ironmaster. The family accused Buchanan of wanting her simply for her money, and Ann was forced to break the engagement; she died a week later. It was the subject of intense gossip, and Buchanan never married, later making him the first and only bachelor president. His niece, Harriet Lane, would later serve as White House hostess.

He would serve five terms in the House of Representatives, first as Federalist, and after the demise of that party in 1824, he threw his support behind Andrew Jackson. Buchanan broke with him personally in 1827, after Jackson accused him of complicity with Henry Clay in the House of Representatives in the contested election of 1824, which ultimately elected John Quincy Adams president. Buchanan denied this adamantly and remained a staunch Jacksonian Democrat.

Democratic politics would determine his next appointment, as he and fellow Pennsylvanian George M. Dallas vied for patronage. Jackson made Buchanan Minister Plenipotentiary to Russia in 1832, where he served until 1834. Although this appointment was, in effect, a political exile, it enabled Buchanan to negotiate the first commercial treaty with that country, while giving him important experience in foreign affairs. That experience made him an obvious choice to serve as chair of the Foreign Relations Committee in 1836 after he was elected to the Senate in 1834.

James Buchanan distinguished himself as a committed expansionist and nationalist, and he was instrumental in the creation of an American continental empire. As an ardent nationalist, he supported President Andrew Jackson in the Spoliation claims, where the president's bellicose insistence that France pay reparations for incursions against American shipping twenty years earlier nearly led to war between the two countries. He supported the Texas Revolution in which American settlers there overthrew Mexican rule in 1836 and favored American recognition of the Texas Republic. In 1842 he denounced the Webster–Ashburton Treaty, which settled the Maine boundary, insisting that Britain's alleged success in the Northeast would cause that country to make more outlandish claims in the Northwest. Soon thereafter he declared publicly that the United States had the right to all of the Oregon territory. When the annexation of Texas dominated national politics in 1844, he became an avid supporter of it. He agreed with then Secretary of State John C. Calhoun that British support for an independent Texas was simply a mask to achieve political influence through commercial dominance. If Texas remained independent, British abolitionists would be in a position to incite servile insurrection there with disastrous consequences for the South. Although personally opposed to slavery, he believed in the constitutional right to possess slave property. He agreed with the theory that Texas would draw slaves away from the upper South and over time would expand through Mexico. As for the argument that the annexation of Texas risked war with Mexico, Buchanan believed that the United States would not get Mexican consent to it "whilst England can prevent it." Moreover, he supported Democrat James K. Polk's vision of continental expansion, favoring both the acquisition of all the Oregon territory and the acquisition of California during the 1844 presidential election.

Thus, when lame-duck President John Tyler proposed annexation by joint resolution in 1845, Buchanan was in favor. James K. Polk then nominated him for secretary of state on February 17, 1845, two weeks before the former's inauguration on Andrew Jackson's advice. Although there had never been a personal rapprochement between the two, Buchanan was a loyal supporter of Jackson's policies throughout his career. As a leading figure in the Democratic Party, with extensive experience in foreign affairs and staunch supporter of expansion, Buchanan would also bring to the administration support from Pennsylvania, whose manufacturing interests were wary of Polk's position on the tariff.

Buchanan entered the State Department when relations with both Great Britain and Mexico were growing critical. Polk demanded all of the Oregon territory with the campaign slogan, "54° 40′ or fight." In the past, both parties recognized the 49th parallel as the basis for negotiations, but differed over such issues as the free navigation of the Columbia and access to ports. The British favored arbitration, which the administration rejected outright, fearing that a final settlement would be in Britain's favor. Buchanan presented to then British minister Richard Pakenham an offer setting the boundary at the 49th parallel and a free port on Vancouver Island. Pakenham rejected this outright, as it contained no mention of free navigation of the Columbia River. His superiors in London thought this needlessly harsh and preemptory, and indeed, the rejection did delay settlement for a year, as the administration withdrew any further offers and fell back on the position that the

United States held claim to all the territory. Here Polk and Buchanan were at odds. Although in the Senate Buchanan had positioned himself with the fifty-four forty men, in the cabinet he urged a much more moderate course. The issue nearly led to war, with the threat of Polk abrogating the treaty of joint occupation negotiated in 1827 and leaving little room for negotiations. In April 1846, the Senate voted to give the required one-year notice to abrogate the treaty, but the president would submit any British proposals to the Senate for advice. Finally, the British offered to accept Polk's original proposal to divide the territory along the 49th parallel. The British gave up free navigation of the Columbia River in exchange for all of Vancouver Island. The United States retained control over Puget Sound. Polk submitted the terms without comment, and on June 15, 1846, the Senate passed the treaty settling the issue.

In the end, the Polk administration was eager to settle the Oregon question at this time because the United States was already at war with Mexico. Buchanan, in particular, was worried about a British–Mexican alliance over Oregon and Texas. He felt California especially vulnerable to British intrigue and appointed Monterey businessman Thomas O. Larkin the U.S. consul with confidential instructions to arouse annexationist sentiment there. Meanwhile, John Slidell was appointed special agent to Mexico with instructions to purchase California and New Mexico. Mexico refused, and Polk dispatched General Zachary Taylor to the disputed territory between the Nueces and the Rio Grande rivers. Polk was already planning a declaration of war when news arrived in Washington that Mexican troops attacked a unit of U.S. soldiers. On May 13, 1846, Congress declared war.

Buchanan's position on the territory issue was somewhat inconsistent. He disagreed with Polk about making territorial objectives part of the war aims. He was also decidedly cool toward the All Mexico movement, which was gaining ground among expansionists, commenting, "How should we govern that mongrel race which inhabits it [Mexico]." Yet he was adamantly opposed to the Treaty of Guadalupe Hidalgo, arguing that Lower California (Baja) and the northern provinces of Mexico should be included in the settlement. Buchanan even distanced himself from the final Oregon Treaty in case expansionists claimed that he had settled for less than what he should have because of the war with Mexico. On the slavery issue, Buchanan favored a more moderate course, supporting an extension of the Missouri Compromise line through the territories acquired from Mexico.

A good deal of his public positions on foreign policy were motivated by personal political ambitions. Not wishing to alienate Southern expansionists, who would be his likely supporters in a presidential race, he often positioned himself in a way likely to garner their support.

In 1848 he retired to Wheatland, his country estate near Lancaster, to plan his campaign for the 1852 presidential race. Divisions within the Democratic Party gave the nomination and ultimately the election victory to Franklin Pierce, and Buchanan was subsequently appointed minister to Great Britain in 1853. An important part of his mission was to iron out differences over the Clayton–Bulwer Treaty of 1850 in which the two nations had agreed to cooperate in the construction of an isthmian canal across Central America. They also agreed that neither would acquire exclusive transit rights and to guarantee the neutrality of the canal once built.

More important, however, was Buchanan's involvement in the controversial Ostend Manifesto of 1854. Democrats North and South had long favored the acquisition of this strategically important and economically viable island. Buchanan agreed with Southern expansionists who worried about the possible "Africaniza-tion" of Cuba should Spain abolish slavery or British abolitionists incite servile insurrection there. Another "Haiti" so close to American shores would pose an intolerable threat of slave revolt in the U.S. South. Personally, he was opposed to using force either by filibuster or by U.S. conquest and favored purchasing the island instead. At the time, Spain was in economic chaos, and if European holders of Spanish bonds were in favor, perhaps Spain might be persuaded to sell.

American minister to Spain, Pierre Soule, was instructed to offer as much as 130 million dollars to Spain for Cuba. Spain refused, and in October 1854 he met with Buchanan and American minister to France, John Y. Mason, to discuss how the United States could acquire Cuba. The subsequent Ostend Manifesto asserted that Cuba was "as necessary to the North American republic as any of its present mem-bers, and it belongs naturally to that great family of States which the Union is the providential nursery." The three recommended that an "immediate and earnest effort ought to be made" to purchase Cuba, but should Spain continue in its refusal, then "by every law human and divine, we shall be justified in wresting it from Spain."

Buchanan did not agree with the implication that the United States was justified in "wresting" the island by force and signed the document reluctantly. Always the politician, he was probably anticipating the Northern outcry accusing the adminis-tration of conspiring with the slave power to add a new slave state into the Union, which is what happened when the Manifesto was leaked to the press. Although Cuba was part of Buchanan's vision of American empire, and he regarded it in nationalist terms, the question could not be separated from the growing sectional crisis over slavery. Any new addition of territory was inextricably linked to this issue.

Ironically, however, it was precisely Buchanan's distance from the domestic slav-ery issue while minister to Great Britain that made him a viable candidate in the presidential election of 1856. He was not directly associated with the troubles aris-ing out of the Kansas–Nebraska Act of 1854 and was known for his moderation on domestic political issues.

Despite the growing sectional divide, Buchanan made the annexation of Cuba and continued American expansionism a goal of his administration. Indeed, it was the most likely issue that could unite Northern and Southern Democrats. Employing the language of Manifest Destiny, he argued in 1857, "It is beyond question the des-tiny of our race to spread themselves over the continent of North America. . . . The tide of emigrants will flow to the south, and nothing can eventually arrest its progress. If permitted to go there peacefully, Central America will soon contain an American population which will confer blessings and benefits as well upon the natives of their respective governments." He then recommended that negotiations be reopened with Spain to purchase Cuba.

This nationalist and expansive vision of an American empire was consistent throughout his career. Yet the crisis of Union precluded any major foreign policy initiatives during his administration. Although an important base of political sup-port came from the South, and this constituency determined many of his foreign policy positions on key issues, he was also a firm believer in Union. He refused to recognize the legality of secession, but neither would he use coercion to bring back the states that seceded. He left office a firm supporter of the Union cause and retired completely from public life to his estate at Wheatland. He died there on June 1, 1868.

BIBLIOGRAPHICAL ESSAY

An edited selection of the public speeches, state papers, and private correspondence of James Buchanan is found in John Bassett Moore (ed.), *The Works of James Buchanan* (1960), 12 volumes. The most comprehensive treatment of Buchanan's foreign political outlook throughout his career is Frederick Moore Binder's *James Buchanan and the American Empire* (1994). David Pletcher's *The Diplomacy of Annexation: Texas, Oregon and the Mexican War* (1973) provides a detailed account of Buchanan's involvement in the diplomatic intricacies of Texan annexation, the Oregon boundary issue, and the Mexican War. An excellent general treatment of American expansionism during this period is in William Earl Weeks, *Building the Continental Empire: American Expansion from the Revolution to the Civil War* (1996). For James K. Polk's vision and involvement in these issues see Sam Haynes, *James K. Polk and the Expansionist Impulse* (2001).

Important recent biographies include Philip S. Klein, *President James Buchanan: A Biography* (1995), and Elbert B. Smith, *The Presidency of James Buchanan* (1978).

Lelia Roeckell

JAMES F. BYRNES
(1879–1972)

Served 1945–1947
Appointed by President Harry S Truman
Democrat

James Francis Byrnes was secretary of state from July 3, 1945, to January 7, 1947. Although his reputation was overshadowed by his successors, George C. Marshall and Dean Acheson, Byrnes presided at Foggy Bottom during the critical moment of transition from World War II to the Cold War. Few people, if anyone, could have felicitously handled those opening months of the Cold War. His job would not have been easy in the best of times, but at the end of the European war, with the war against Japan still ongoing and relations between the Big Three entering a delicate new stage, Byrnes faced a daunting task.

Byrnes was born in Charleston, South Carolina, on May 2, 1879. His father, also James Francis Byrnes, had died of tuberculosis seven weeks before the birth of his namesake. The senior Byrnes was descended from immigrants fleeing an Ireland gripped by the potato famine. His wife, Elizabeth McSweeney Byrnes, was from an Irish Catholic family also.

After the death of her husband and the birth of her son, Elizabeth Byrnes opened a dressmaking shop in her home and through hard work and skill raised her son and daughter Lenore and provided a home for her invalid mother, her sister, and her sister's son. Although money was tight at times, the family did not live in poverty.

After completing seventh grade, Byrnes quit parochial school and in 1896 landed a full-time job as an office boy for an old Charleston law firm. In what became a lifelong pattern, Byrnes was befriended by a senior partner of the firm, Judge Benjamin H. Rutledge, an older, more powerful man who became Byrnes's first patron. The judge supervised a course of reading for Byrnes that provided him with a better education than his parochial school could offer. During the same time, Byrnes learned shorthand at the insistence of his mother. The skill came in handy when Byrnes won first place in a shorthand competition held by the second judicial district in upstate South Carolina to fill the court stenographer position.

Byrnes moved to Aiken, which housed the office of district judge and his new boss, Judge James H. Aldrich. Like Rutledge, Aldrich befriended Byrnes, who studied law under the judge's tutelage and began to attend his new mentor's Episcopal Church. After passing the state bar exam, Byrnes relocated his mother and grandmother to Aiken. In May 1906, Byrnes married Maude Busch, the daughter of a prosperous hotelier. Soon thereafter, Byrnes formally became a member of the Episcopal Church. In 1908, Byrnes successfully campaigned for his first elective office—district prosecuting attorney.

In 1910, Byrnes ran for Congress, beating the congressional incumbent by 57 votes in the Democratic primary, which was then tantamount to election in the states of the former Confederacy. Byrnes ingratiated himself with two powerful politicians: George Legaré, head of South Carolina's House delegation, and Senator Benjamin "Pitchfork Ben" Tillman, the legendary former governor and now senior senator for South Carolina. As a congressman, Byrnes was a strong supporter of President Woodrow Wilson's New Freedom, helping to pass such bills as the Underwood Tariff and the Federal Reserve Act. Byrnes was able to secure positions on the House Banking and Appropriations committees years before most members would have been considered eligible for such committee assignments.

Although Byrnes was a moderate on race, at least by prevailing Southern standards, never "race-baiting" in any of his campaigns, he made two unfortunate speeches on the House floor, which haunted him for the next 30 years. In 1919, Byrnes accused returning black servicemen and Dr. W. E. B. DuBois of working to create a "little Russia" in the south and requested that any blacks who supported racial equality be deported. In 1925, he again used overly harsh language to oppose federal funding of Howard University in Washington, D.C. As Byrnes learned to his deep disappointment in July 1944, his observation in the 1925 speech that "unfortunate though it may be, our consideration of every question must include . . . consideration of the race question" became true for the North as well as the South.

Byrnes suffered his only electoral defeat in his campaign for the U.S. Senate in 1924. Ironically, he lost to Coley Blease, a race-baiter who had received the endorsement of the Ku Klux Klan after Byrnes had rejected the Klan's offer of support. After his defeat, Byrnes and his wife moved to Spartanburg, South Carolina, where he built a lucrative legal practice as a partner in a prominent law firm. Byrnes reentered politics in 1930 when he defeated Blease's bid for reelection. Byrnes won the race with the financial support of Bernard Baruch, a noted financier and Democratic Party contributor, who became Byrnes's lifelong patron. Senators Byron "Pat" Harrison of Mississippi and Carter Glass of Virginia became Byrnes's Senate patrons. With their aid, Byrnes soon became one of the most influential members of the Senate. To some, he was the most influential Southern member of Congress between John C. Calhoun and Lyndon Johnson.

Byrnes worked tirelessly for Franklin Roosevelt's presidential nomination in 1932, contacting FDR as early as November 1928. After Roosevelt's nomination, Byrnes ensured Baruch's financial support of the Democratic candidate during the general election campaign. After the Democratic sweep of 1932, Byrnes had himself appointed chair of the Audit and Control Committee, which gave him a "virtual dictatorship" of Senate patronage.

This patronage helped Byrnes become a key figure in Roosevelt's New Deal Congress. Byrnes was instrumental in securing passage of such landmark laws as the Emergency Banking Act, the National Industrial Recovery Act, and the statutes that established the Civilian Conservation Corps (CCC), the Agricultural Adjustment Administration, the Federal Emergency Relief Administration, and the Works Progress Administration (WPA). In 1936, Byrnes won reelection to a second term in the Senate, securing 87 percent of the vote in the Democratic primary.

Although Byrnes never broke formally with Roosevelt, and the two maintained their friendship, Byrnes opposed most of the domestic legislative program the president proposed during his second term. Byrnes led a shifting bipartisan conservative coalition, which either defeated or weakened bills concerning child labor, the CCC, new regional TVAs, and new national labor regulations. Byrnes supported Roosevelt's court packing plan, but worked for compromise from the beginning against Roosevelt's wishes. On the death of Senator Joe Robinson of Arkansas, Byrnes unsuccessfully opposed Alban Barkley, Roosevelt's candidate for majority leader.

In 1938, Byrnes quietly and effectively opposed the president on another of his major initiatives, the so-called purge attempt to rid the Democratic Party of its most conservative federal elected officials. Byrnes distributed campaign funds from Baruch's war chest to such Bourbon Democrats as Millard Tydings of Maryland and Guy M. Gillette of Iowa. All the candidates Byrnes supported won. Byrnes was also part of a successful Southern filibuster that defeated a proposed antilynching bill. During his speech opposing the measure, Byrnes verbally attacked Walter White, executive secretary of the NAACP, which called to mind Byrnes's harsh racist speeches of 1919 and 1925.

Despite these differences on domestic issues, Byrnes performed yeoman service for FDR in 1939–1941. Byrnes led the successful fight for the presidential reorganization bill of 1939 and managed FDR's unprecedented renomination to a third term in 1940. In the face of great hostility from the delegates, Byrnes also secured Henry Wallace's vice presidential nomination. After his appointment to the Senate Foreign Relations Committee in January 1941, Byrnes secured the passage of bills substantially increasing the size of the U.S. Navy and became floor manager for the Lend-Lease bill. To all observers, Byrnes's leadership was critical to the passage of the bill by a two-thirds majority.

Although Roosevelt's appointment of Byrnes to the Supreme Court in 1941 surprised many, the nomination paid back all the president's political debts to Byrnes, removed the senator from vice presidential consideration in 1944, and healed the breach with Southern Democrats, who were still angry with the attempted purge of party conservatives in 1938. The Senate unanimously approved Byrnes's nomination by voice vote within minutes of formally receiving it.

Byrnes served as an associate justice of the Supreme Court from October 6, 1941, to October 3, 1942. Byrnes was not a great Supreme Court justice, but the criticisms of his short tenure are overdrawn. Byrnes, following a pattern established when he was a congressman, sought consensus, not bold innovations, in judicial doctrine. This predilection, combined with his war work for FDR after Pearl Harbor, contributed to the fact that Byrnes never wrote a concurring or dissenting opinion. Anxious to return to active politics, Byrnes was unhappy on the Supreme Court, viewing it as a too early retirement.

His chance came with the entry of the United States into World War II. Within days of the U.S. declaration of war against Japan, Roosevelt told his advisors that all proposed legislation and executive orders dealing with war mobilization of the economy had to be cleared by Justice Byrnes. The justice jumped at the chance and was the moving spirit behind the First and Second War Powers Acts. The laws, passed by March 1942, vastly increased presidential control over the economy.

After complaints arose over the first agency created to administer war mobilization, the president established the Office of Economic Stabilization (OES) in October 1942 and the Office of War Mobilization (OWM) in May 1943. Roosevelt picked Byrnes to be director of each organization, and he proved to be an excellent choice. As director, Byrnes had the authority to set wage and price controls and adjudicate disputes between government agencies. In addition, Byrnes had authority over all civilian labor related to war production. This authority included settling disputes between branches of the U.S. military and the competing needs of the Allied militaries and the U.S. military for the same war supplies. Due to the scope of his authority, Byrnes was known throughout the war as the "Assistant President."

And yet, Byrnes was sorely disappointed in 1944 when Roosevelt twice picked other men to fill positions to which Byrnes aspired. In July 1944, after two months of intense politicking, Senator Harry S Truman of Missouri was selected instead of Byrnes to be the Democratic vice presidential candidate. Byrnes believed that FDR had encouraged him to be an active vice presidential candidate as a way to check the ambitions of the liberal incumbent, Vice President Henry Wallace. The president's choice of Truman pleased conservatives, who were happy to be rid of Wallace, and liberals, who were happy to have blocked Byrnes; both factions thus worked hard to ensure Roosevelt's election to a fourth term.

FDR's decision, as the memoirs of both Byrnes and Truman state, had been a great surprise, but Byrnes, however much he thought his hard work and loyalty deserved reward, could hardly have added much to the Democratic ticket because he was from the Deep South and a lapsed Catholic. Roosevelt passed over Byrnes again when Cordell Hull resigned as secretary of state in November 1944. With his reelection victory behind him, Roosevelt, wary of Byrnes's independence, selected Undersecretary of State Edward R. Stettinius, Jr. to replace Hull. Byrnes, bitter at being twice passed over, told FDR that he planned to resign his directorship before the total defeat of the German armies.

Knowing this, FDR convinced Byrnes to accept an invitation to be part of the U.S. delegation at the Yalta Conference in February 1945. Although Byrnes did not participate in the discussions, his attendance at the conference gave him status after the president's death as an expert on Yalta. Byrnes officially resigned as director of the OWM on April 2, 1945.

Byrnes's retirement from government service was brief. Truman, an old protégé from the Senate, asked his friend and mentor to accept the office of secretary of state pending completion of Stettinius's work dealing with the new United Nations. Truman wanted Byrnes for a variety of reasons. First, the president wanted to repay Byrnes for Roosevelt's earlier failure to nominate Byrnes as either vice president or secretary of state. Second, Truman respected Byrnes for his vast political experience, skills, and judgment, especially as they related to his reputation as a shrewd negotiator able to work well with members of Congress from both political parties. Third, Truman wanted a secretary of state who had the qualifications to succeed to the presidency should anything happen to the president, and Truman considered Byrnes as best qualified in this regard. Finally, Truman was convinced that only Byrnes knew all the secrets of the Yalta Agreement.

Byrnes accepted the appointment with the understanding that he was going to be, in effect, the assistant president for foreign policy. In 1945, Truman was unsure of himself when it came to international politics and gladly turned over responsibility for it to Byrnes. Only after the fact did Truman complain that his secretary of state had not kept him informed about the London and Moscow conferences. In fact, at no time during these conferences did Truman offer any advice more substantive than "Use your best judgment," nor did Truman evidence any interest in the negotiations.

However, in the beginning, Byrnes had Truman's complete confidence. Before Byrnes's appointment as secretary of state could take place, the new president appointed Byrnes as his personal representative to the Interim Committee, which was established to advise the president on the potential war use of the atomic bomb and the future control of atomic weaponry. At the committee meetings, Byrnes was a forceful advocate against sharing U.S. atomic research with the U.S.S.R. Byrnes also argued for dropping the atomic bomb on Japan as quickly as possible and against warning Japan first. The Interim Committee, without properly evaluating the issue of warning Japan, accepted Byrnes's recommendations as its own.

After being sworn in as secretary of state on July 3, 1945, Byrnes pressed successfully for the surprise use of the atomic bomb on Japan. Although Byrnes was himself a strong supporter of the unconditional surrender of Japan, advocating it during the Potsdam Conference in July 1945, he realized that most Americans would be angry if they came to believe that the war was unnecessarily prolonged because the United States rejected Japanese surrender terms that were less than "unconditional." Although there is substantial disagreement on this issue, it appears that Byrnes advocated dropping the bomb without warning to avoid mass U.S. casualties from a planned assault on the Japanese home islands and to increase U.S. domestic support for less than unconditional surrender by showing the U.S. public that its government was using all available force to compel Japanese capitulation. Truman accepted Byrnes's advice, and two atomic bombs were dropped on Japan in August 1945. The Soviet Union then declared war on Japan, and the Japanese sent surrender terms to the Allied governments. Byrnes opposed accepting the Japanese terms because they included reference to the "prerogatives" of the emperor as "Sovereign Ruler." Byrnes drafted the U.S. response, which, in effect, accepted the continuation of the imperial dynasty but put the Japanese government, including the emperor, under the jurisdiction of the supreme allied commander. The Japanese government accepted the U.S. terms on August 14, 1945.

In the diplomacy of the early postwar world, Byrnes was increasingly alone in continuing to accept and practice the Rooseveltian policy of "wheeling and dealing" through personal diplomacy with scant regard for professional advice. He failed to notice, perhaps because he spent so little time at the State Department, that attitudes in the administration and country toward the Soviet Union had changed and that the president, by example, had led that change.

Up to January 1946, Byrnes appears to have been committed to preserving the wartime U.S.–Soviet alliance into the postwar era, but without a well-thought-out rationale for such a policy. Byrnes was disappointed by the lack of agreement during the Foreign Ministers Conference in London in September and October 1945. As a result of this diplomatic failure, Byrnes redoubled his own efforts at compromise and on his own initiative formally reopened a second foreign ministers conference in Moscow before the end of December. Ironically, the failure of the London conference began a shift in U.S. public opinion away from supporting negotiations with the Soviets, just as the failure caused Byrnes to increase his efforts to maintain the U.S.–Soviet wartime alliance. Byrnes suggested Moscow as the site for the new conference because he, like Roosevelt, believed that personal diplomacy could build trust between American and Soviet leaders. Byrnes believed that if the intransigence of Soviet Foreign Minister Vyacheslav Molotov threatened the conference, he would be able to negotiate directly with Soviet leader Josef Stalin.

Although the Moscow Conference was relatively successful, it ended Byrnes's independence as secretary of state. Byrnes reached agreement with the Soviets in principle to a United Nations Atomic Energy Commission. In addition, the United States recognized the Romanian and Bulgarian governments in return for adding opposition ministries to their governments. The Soviet government reaffirmed its support of the Nationalist Chinese government and agreed to establish an Allied Central Council for Japan (which would only advise Supreme Commander General Douglas MacArthur), thereby securing Soviet recognition of the U.S. domination of postwar Japan.

When Byrnes returned to the United States, however, the domestic political situation had changed. Congressional Republicans were denouncing the Moscow Agreements. Specifically, Senator Arthur Vandenberg called the agreement on a UN atomic energy agency a "typical American give-away" and threatened to resign from the U.S. delegation to the first UN General Assembly meeting. Admiral William D. Leahy, White House chief of staff, denounced the whole Moscow agreement as "an appeasement document." Truman himself had become increasingly dissatisfied with both the content and style of Byrnes's diplomacy but had failed to communicate his growing concern to his secretary of state. Instead, Truman brooded over the slights, real and imagined, that Byrnes had inflicted on him. Still, all cabinet officials serve at the discretion of the president, and Byrnes forgot that he answered to a constituency of one—the president. Due to his hectic travel schedule, Byrnes overlooked the signs of Truman's resentment over the way he was being treated by his secretary of state.

Moreover, by not keeping the president informed and by planning on going to the press before he reported on the Moscow Conference to Truman, Byrnes lost Truman's trust. This erosion of trust was abetted by other Truman administration officials such as Dean Acheson, Clark Clifford, Averell Harriman, George Kennan, and William Leahy, who, for their own individual reasons, disliked Byrnes and worked to bring about his downfall. Finally, Byrnes had been willing to recognize what he considered to be the legitimate Soviet security concerns in Eastern Europe, whereas Truman was increasingly suspicious of Soviet motives in the region.

Although Truman insisted that Byrnes discuss the results of the Moscow Conference the same evening that Byrnes arrived in the United States after a 60-hour flight from Moscow, there was no contemporary evidence that Truman reproved Byrnes then or later. Truman did express his displeasure about learning of the adjournment of the conference from the public press, but Byrnes explained the circumstances leading to that situation, and Truman seemed satisfied. At no time during that evening did Truman express disagreement with Byrnes.

Neither did Truman read to Byrnes the president's memorandum of January 5, 1946, which ended with the famous line, "I'm tired of babying the Soviets." Byrnes said often that if Truman had read that to him, he would have resigned immediately. Still, it was obvious from stories in the U.S. press, which noted Truman's dissatisfaction with Byrnes, that the secretary had lost the president's confidence. From roughly January 1946, Byrnes was no longer in control of U.S. foreign policy.

George Kennan's "Long Telegram" arrived in Washington on February 22, 1946, and laid out a systematic criticism of U.S. foreign policy toward the U.S.S.R. since 1941. Kennan's analysis became the basis of a new policy that Byrnes described as "patience and firmness." According to historian John L. Gaddis, the new policy would pursue the following principles: discuss U.S. disagreements with the Soviet Union openly and fairly; end concessions to the U.S.S.R. by defending all targets of Soviet expansion without liberating any area already under Soviet control; reestablish U.S. capability and formally review economic and military aid from allies; and continue negotiations with the U.S.S.R. to win Soviet acceptance of U.S. proposals or to make public Soviet unwillingness to compromise. Byrnes implemented the policy quickly, providing valuable service at the Paris and London Conferences in 1946. By these conferences, the Soviet-sponsored regimes in Bulgaria, Romania, and Hungary were recognized while the Soviets had to settle on moderate reparations from Italy and Finland. Byrnes also provided valuable public service to the United States by his public diplomacy against the continued Soviet military presence in Iran and by his forceful advocacy of the Iranian case before the UN Security Council. Byrnes publicly warned that the U.S. government would use force to implement the legal findings of the Security Council, even if the decision went against the Soviet Union. When the U.S.S.R. withdrew its troops from Iran, the victory was seen as a personal diplomatic triumph for Byrnes.

Yet, it is obvious that Byrnes was uncomfortable in his new subordinate position to Truman and that the president was hoping Byrnes would initiate a graceful exit on his own. Byrnes submitted his resignation on April 16, 1946, to take effect at the conclusion of the peace conference in Paris. By so delaying his departure, Byrnes was able to refurbish his reputation with his diplomacy at Paris and London and by his strong defense of the Iranian position against the continuation of Soviet troops in that country. Further, Truman's and Secretary of Commerce Henry Wallace's ham-handed handling of Wallace's speech at Madison Square Garden on September 12 undercut Truman's account of his January 5, 1946, memo, as did his retreat from his initial strong support of Winston Churchill's "Iron Curtain" speech of March 5. Furthermore, Truman's initial verbal support of the Wallace speech enhanced Byrnes's hard-line position—Byrnes threatened to resign unless Wallace was removed from the cabinet. With Byrnes's diplomatic success at Paris, London, and over Iran, and with his political success in forcing Wallace's resignation, Byrnes himself resigned on January 7, 1947, to be succeeded two weeks later by George Marshall. Soon thereafter, Byrnes was named *Time*'s Man of the Year for 1946.

Byrnes publicly criticized the Truman administration's domestic policies throughout the president's second term, and in 1950 he successfully ran for governor of South Carolina. As governor, Byrnes convinced the legislature to pass laws against public mask wearing and cross burnings on private property without the consent of the owner as a way to destroy the Ku Klux Klan in the state. Byrnes also had his legislature pass the state's first sales tax. The resulting revenues were to be equally divided between black and white schools to ensure the equality of separate but equal. His actions proved to be an example of too little, too late, as the Supreme

Court, much to his surprise and anger, unanimously declared as unconstitutional the doctrine of "separate but equal" in *Brown v. Board of Education of Topeka* in 1954. In response, Byrnes so successfully helped organize the strategy of "massive resistance" to the implementation of *Brown* that by 1964 only an estimated 1 percent of schools in the states of the Lower South were integrated.

For some years after leaving the Truman administration, Byrnes tried to organize the South as an independent voting bloc to increase the region's clout in national electoral politics and veto what Byrnes saw as the continual liberal dominance of the United States. Byrnes organized Independents for Eisenhower, the 1952 Republican presidential candidate, and refused to support either Eisenhower or Democrat Adlai Stevenson in the 1956 presidential election.

Byrnes worked successfully to build a new Solid South, but this time within the Republican Party, thereby ensuring Southern Republicans as an important a place in their new party as Southerners had once enjoyed in the Democratic Party. Byrnes called on Southerners to vote Republican and supported Richard Nixon for president in 1960. Although Nixon lost to John F. Kennedy in 1960, Byrnes supported Republican Barry Goldwater in 1964 and Nixon again in 1968. In fact, Nixon's successful "Southern strategy" was based on advice freely given to him and his staff by Byrnes. Byrnes's health slowly declined in the 1960s, and he died quietly at his home on April 9, 1972. His wife Maude died in 1976.

Byrnes may have been an unfortunate choice for secretary of state, yet an understandable one, given his earlier relationship with Truman. Byrnes was still resentful that FDR had not chosen him to be the president's running mate in 1944, and the emotion came out as truculence and a desire to work on his own. Not only did Byrnes fail to keep the president informed, he infrequently consulted with his own office. Also, as Gaddis has pointed out, "patience and firmness" was not so much a strategy as it was a "set of attitudes."

Byrnes was not able to articulate a foreign policy vision independent of the Containment doctrine, and thus was ground down by the criticisms of his foreign policy by both liberals and conservatives. He was, in fact, a caretaker for most of his secretaryship.

BIBLIOGRAPHICAL ESSAY

The papers of James F. Byrnes are at the Cooper Memorial Library, Clemson University, Clemson, South Carolina. Byrnes wrote two memoirs, *Speaking Frankly* (1947), and *All In One Lifetime* (1958). Other collections of value to understanding Byrnes's career are the Bernard C. M. Baruch Papers, Mudd Library, Princeton University, Princeton, New Jersey; the Benjamin R. Tillman Papers, Cooper Memorial Library, Clemson University; the Franklin D. Roosevelt Papers, Franklin D. Roosevelt Library, Hyde Park, New York; and the Harry S Truman Papers, Harry S Truman Library, Independence, Missouri.

Jefferson Frazier's unpublished senior honors thesis, "The Southerner as American: A Political Biography of James F. Byrnes" (1964) is an excellent monograph of Byrnes's life in politics. David Robinson's *Sly and Able: A Political Biography of James F. Byrnes* (1994), is the standard biography.

Joseph Alsop and Robert Kinter's "Sly and Able" in the *Saturday Evening Post* of July 20, 1940, is an excellent contemporary review of Byrnes's career before his appointment to the U.S. Supreme Court. Byrnes's term on the Court is ably covered by Walter Murphy in his biographical sketch of Byrnes in Leon Friedman and Fred L. Israel (eds.), *The Justices of the Supreme Court, 1789–1969: Their Lives and Major Opinions*, volume 4 (1970). Two works that cover Byrnes's jobs in the executive branch during World War II are John William Partin's University of Florida dissertation " 'Assistant President' for the Home Front: James F. Byrnes and World War II" (1977), and Herbert Somers, *Presidential Agency OWMR: The Office of War Mobilization and Reconversion* (1950). Also helpful in understanding Byrnes's administrative and political activities during World War II is Robert E. Sherwood's *Roosevelt and Hopkins: An Intimate History* (1948).

The best academic piece on the machinations of the 1944 Democratic National convention is John Partin's "Roosevelt, Byrnes and the 1944 Vice-Presidential Nomination, *Historian*, 42 (1979). Memoirs by many of the participants at the convention include George E. Allen's *Presidents Who Have Known Me* (1950), Johnathan Daniels's *Man of Independence* (1950), and Edward J. Flynn's *You're the Boss* (1947).

The literature on the decision to use the atomic bomb on Japan is vast. The following are reasonably representative of the available scholarship: Barton S. Bernstein, "Roosevelt, Truman, and the Atomic Bomb 1941–1945: A Reinterpretation," *Political Science Quarterly* 90 (1975); Robert Maddox, *The New Left and the Origins of the Cold War* (1973); Gar Alperovitz, *Atomic Diplomacy: Hiroshima and Potsdam: The Use of the Atomic Bomb and the American Confrontation with Soviet Power* (1985); Robert L. Messer, *The End of the Alliance: James F. Byrnes, Roosevelt, Truman, and the Origins of the Cold War* (1982); Robert J. C. Butow, *Japan's Decision to Surrender* (1954); Herbert Feis, *The Atomic Bomb and the End of World War II* (1966); George Herken, *The Winning Weapon* (1981); and Martin Sherwin, *A World Destroyed* (1975).

For the origins of the Cold War, refer to Maddox (listed earlier). See also Barton S. Bernstein (ed.), *Politics and Policies of the Truman Administration* (1970); Kendrick A. Clements (ed.), *James F. Byrnes and the Origins of the Cold War* (1982); Herbert Feis, *From Truth to Terror: The Onset of the Cold War* (1970); John Lewis Gaddis, *The United States and the Origins of the Cold War* (1972); James L. Gormly, *The Collapse of the Grand Alliance* (1987); Michael J. Hogan, *A Cross of Iron: Harry S. Truman and the Origins of the National Security State* (1998); Donald R. McCoy, *The Presidency of Harry S. Truman* (1984); David Reynolds (ed.), *The Origins of the Cold War in Europe* (1994); Daniel Yergen, *Shattered Peace* (1977); and the aforementioned Robert Messer, *The End of the Alliance* (1982), which is also helpful in understanding Byrnes's secretaryship.

On Byrnes's tenure as secretary of state, see Messer (listed earlier) and Patricia Dawson Ward, *The Threat of Peace: James F. Byrnes and the Council of Foreign Ministers, 1945–1946* (1979). Memoirs of Byrnes's contemporaries include Charles E. Bohlen, *Witness to History, 1929–1969* (1973); George F. Kennan, *Memoirs: 1925–1950* (1967); Dean Acheson, *Present at the Creation: My Years in the State Department* (1969); and Clark Clifford, *Counsel to the President: A Memoir* (1991).

The policy of the United States vis-à-vis Iran in 1946 is covered in Bruce R. Rumholm, *The Origins of the Cold War in the Near East* (1980); Robert Rossow, Jr., "The Battle of Azerbaijan, 1946," *Middle East Journal*, 10 (1956); David Yergin, *The Prize: The Epic Quest for Oil, Money, and Power* (1991); Justus D. Doenecke's "Revisionists, Oil and Cold War Diplomacy," *Iranian Studies: A Bulletin of the Society for*

Iranian Cultural Social Studies, 3 (1970), and "Iran's Role in Cold War Revisionism," *Iranian Studies*, 5 (1972); Stephen L. McFarland, "A Peripheral View of the Origins of the Cold War: The Crisis in Iran, 1941–1947," *Diplomatic History*, 4 (1980); and Gary Hess, "The Iranian Crisis of 1945–1946 and the Cold War," *Political Science Quarterly*, 89 (1974).

For Byrnes's career after leaving the State Department, see Harry S. Ashmore, *Hearts and Minds: The Anatomy of Racism from Roosevelt to Reagan* (1982); Leslie Dunbar, "The Changing Mind of the South: The Exposed Nerve," *Journal of Politics*, 26 (1964); Ralph McGill, "What Is Jimmy Byrnes Up to Now?" *Saturday Evening Post*, October 14, 1950; and Richard Hofstadter, "From Calhoun to the Dixiecrats," *Social Research*, 16, 1949.

Edward S. Mihalkanin

JOHN C. CALHOUN
(1782–1850)

Served 1844–1845
Appointed by President John Tyler
Democrat, serving in Whig administration

John Caldwell Calhoun was born in the Abbeville district of South Carolina on March 18,1782. Although little is known about his early childhood, the back country of his youth was undergoing rapid social and political change. His father, Patrick, settled there in 1752 and soon prospered as a farmer and surveyor. He was one of a steady influx of Scotch-Irish settlers who would bring to the back country its cotton culture, Presbyterian values, and Republican politics. Patrick eventually emerged as a prominent local leader who challenged the low-country planter elite for influence. He represented the area's interests in the colonial assemblies, revolutionary congresses, and the state legislature. At the time of his death in 1790, Patrick Calhoun owned over a thousand acres and 31 slaves. John was only 13 at the time, but his father's influence would leave an important mark on his later political thinking.

Calhoun attended a local academy at age 18 and entered Yale as a junior in 1802. He graduated with distinction in 1804 and then spent a year at Litchfield Law School. He was admitted to the South Carolina Bar in 1807 and returned to his native Abbeville to practice law. His obvious intellectual gifts and political acumen earned him his father's old seat in the state legislature, where he was instrumental in ensuring that the largely Republican back country interests were evenly represented against the low-country Federalists. His marriage to second cousin Floride Bonneau Colhoun in 1811 gave him the financial independence and social prominence to continue pursuing a career in politics.

His early career was distinguished by an intense nationalism both in foreign and domestic affairs. Calhoun was elected to Congress in 1811 as relations between the United States and Great Britain were deteriorating over the impressment of American sailors and seizure of American ships. Although he would later gain greater notoriety as a champion of state's rights and Southern interests, his distrust of Great Britain was consistent throughout his career. Great Britain's actions were, according to Calhoun, an abuse of power, which could only be restrained by U.S. power. America's attempts at economic coercion were ineffectual, as Britain's motive was not simply to defeat Napoleon, but to weaken the United States. The issue was over maritime rights and national honor, which he believed could only be defended by force. He had the support of South Carolinian planters who, impatient over the loss of profits during the embargo, argued that war was a faster solution to the impasse than commercial negotiation. Calhoun quickly gained national prominence as chairman of the House Foreign Relations Committee; he presented the bill declaring war in 1812 and advocated large appropriations throughout the conflict.

In peacetime, Calhoun's nationalism was no less pronounced. He warned against too rapid a demobilization and was a vocal advocate of Henry Clay's "American System," which pushed for high tariffs, internal improvements, a national bank, and an enlarged navy for the protection and promotion of American trading interests. Underlying these policies was the principle that commercial development and economic prosperity was key to national strength and sectional unity. As Secretary of War in 1817 under James Monroe, he promoted a number of policies designed to advance these goals. In this role he was a visionary. He tirelessly worked toward the establishment of a professionally trained, expandable peacetime army as a means to strengthen national defense and promote national economic growth. He reformed West Point and established an enlarged professional officer and engineering corps to assist the states in the development of transportation systems, frontier fortifications, and harbor improvements. As part of this process, he established a Board of Engineers for Internal Improvements in the War Department, which prioritized projects in accordance with their respective commercial and military importance.

Calhoun believed that the advancement of the nation's economic interests was an important role for the federal government in its duty to promote the national welfare, but he also contended that it was equally in the national interest to protect the rights of individual states. The tension between state and national power was almost as old as the republic, but the issue gained new urgency during the 1820s. The National Bank, although designed to facilitate commercial expansion, seemed to many a bastion of undue influence, particularly to agrarian interests who suffered in the postwar economic depression. The Missouri Compromise of 1821 exposed deep sectional fissures over slavery. Planters, who were feeling the adverse effects of overproduction and low prices, blamed ongoing tariff increases for raising the costs of manufactured goods and constricting foreign markets for cotton.

Calhoun turned against the tariff for these reasons in 1824. That same year he had been elected to serve as vice president under the administration of John Quincy Adams. In 1828 he was again elected to the vice presidency, this time supporting Andrew Jackson, hoping to be named as Jackson's successor. The exceptionally high Tariff of 1828 prompted an open challenge to federal law from South Carolinian planters, who requested that Calhoun prepare a report on their position. The resultant *South Carolina Exposition* (1828), published anonymously, was the first formal statement of Calhoun's political philosophy. In it, he argued that because the Union was essentially a compact between sovereign states, each state had the right to deny or affirm federal law. When a given law was deemed harmful to an individual state, that state could call a special convention—not unlike the state conventions that ratified the constitution—to either accept the law or nullify it. This theory was put to the test against the Tariff of 1832, which retained high import duties that many in South Carolina felt was sacrificing their own well-being to Northern industrialists. A state convention was called and the tariff nullified.

Jackson initially equivocated on the tariff, but he was unambiguous in his denunciation of nullification and his determination to preserve the Union. By the Force Act, he received congressional approval to use troops to collect customs duties, while recommending further tariff reductions. Calhoun had fallen out with Jackson both personally and politically and resigned the vice presidency to enter the Senate to better represent South Carolina's interests. He worked closely with Henry Clay to pass a compromise tariff in 1833.

Although the issue was over the tariff, the principle, according to Calhoun, dealt with minority rights within the Union. Nullification provided the mechanism by which each section could protect its own majority, be it on the tariff or a question peculiar to its own interests. If the federal government could pass legislation against the tariff, what could prevent it from passing legislation against slavery? The abolitionist movement was gaining ground at this time, and he became more preoccupied with constructing a political and moral defense of the "peculiar institution." In the Senate, he worked hard for the passage of the Gag Rule, which stifled any discussion of slavery.

The slavery issue exploded on the national agenda once again over the question of Texas annexation, which Calhoun would ultimately play an important and controversial role in as secretary of state. American settlers had been migrating to the Mexican territory with their slaves since the 1820s. Frustrated by Mexican attempts to control the province more directly, settlers rebelled in 1836 and effectively overthrew Mexican rule. Texas immediately applied for annexation to the United States. Although Andrew Jackson favored annexation, he would not risk war with Mexico, which refused to concede the loss of Texas. That, coupled with Northern opposition to the addition of a slave territory, made annexation divisive and politically explosive. Jackson decided to recognize Texan independence instead, and on the last day of his administration, he signed treaties with the new republic.

With little indication that the United States would overcome its sectional differences, Texan leaders then turned to Europe for formal recognition. Diplomatic relations with Great Britain were considered to be especially important, as Britain maintained extensive commercial interests in Mexico. Texas hoped that Britain would use its influence there to mediate an effective peace settlement. That, in turn, might remove an objection to annexation in the United States or, at the very least, make Texas more attractive to desperately needed settlers and capital, while providing a market for Texas cotton.

As an avowed expansionist and champion of Southern interests, Calhoun favored annexation all along and became directly involved with the question when President John Tyler embarked on a policy of annexation in 1843. Tyler revived the long-dormant issue when reports surfaced from London and Texas that Britain was allegedly offering loans to the cash poor republic in exchange for emancipation. To Southern expansionists, these reports were not far-fetched. Britain was committed to the principle of the universal abolition of slavery after its own abolitionist experiment in the West Indies 10 years earlier. Moreover, Texas offered an attractive alternative to American cotton in British markets. Annexationists feared that Texas would become economically dependent on Great Britain and thus vulnerable to British political influence, especially on the issue of slavery, with dire consequences to the American South. Moreover, Britain's motives for doing so were less than altruistic. The fact that the two countries were competitors in the international marketplace was an economic reality. The notion that Britain deliberately sought to undermine American economic growth and prosperity had been a powerful reason for diplomatic action throughout the life of the republic. Echoing sentiments first expressed thirty years earlier, Calhoun warned then-Secretary of State Abel Upshur in 1843 that Britain's "object is power and monopoly, and abolition but the pretext." "No nation," he continued, "in ancient or modern times, ever pursued dominion and commercial monopoly" so "vehemently."

Tyler announced to Congress in 1843 that Texas was subject to "the interference on the part of stronger and powerful nations" interested in forwarding their own "peculiar views." By making the issue a question of national security, Tyler hoped to overcome sectional differences over annexation, as well as to increase his own chances for the Democratic presidential nomination in 1844 by garnering support in the South.

The outcome of the question may have been entirely different had it not been for the untimely death of Secretary of State Abel Upshur. Tyler appointed Calhoun to succeed Upshur on April 1, 1844. Although the Senate unanimously approved him, his subsequent one-year tenure as secretary of state would prove to be one of the most controversial periods of his long career.

A treaty of annexation was submitted to the Senate in April 1844 for ratification. Documents accompanying the treaty included what was to become known as the Calhoun–Pakenham correspondence, so called after a series of diplomatic notes exchanged between the secretary of state and Richard Pakenham, the British minister in Washington. British Foreign Secretary Lord Aberdeen had recommended to Mexico that emancipation be the basis of peace negotiations with Texas. He had also publicly announced to Parliament that "no one was more anxious than himself to see the abolition of slavery in Texas." The British government dropped this policy when it became apparent that it stirred annexationist agitation in the United States. At the same time, Aberdeen attempted to allay Southern fears by assuring Washington that Britain "would not act directly or indirectly in a political sense on the United States through Texas." Yet he maintained Britain's right to "counsel" Texas, but would not seek to "compel" the republic to abolish slavery.

Calhoun responded with a blistering attack on British policy in which annexation became a measure of self-defense in response to an avowed policy that was regarded by the slave-holding states as a threat to their very existence. It was the duty of the United States, he argued, "whose safety and prosperity may be endangered by her policy, to adopt such measures as them may deem necessary for their protection." Calhoun went on instruct the British government on the benefits of slavery, based largely on the racist assumption of black inferiority. "Slavery is," he declared, "a political institution, essential to the peace, safety and prosperity of those States in the Union where it exists."

Contemporaries and historians alike have attacked Calhoun's spurious defense of slavery and regarded it as responsible for the treaty's defeat in 1844 by alienating Northern support, essential for its passage. His actions make sense, considering his own concept of Union as a compact between the states, with each willing to come to the defense of the other. To Calhoun, the North's interest in Texas was only marginal, but the dangers to the South were real. He hoped for the North's support for annexation just as the South had given over the recent Maine boundary issue. He also made public the correspondence to put Great Britain "on the defensive."

There was a genuine worry that Texas, frustrated by sectional differences over annexation in the United States, might agree to a European-sponsored peace settlement guaranteeing Texan independence.

These fears were justified; a more aggressive and interventionist policy did develop among the European powers in 1844. Great Britain proposed a plan committing Texas to permanent independence with fixed boundaries guaranteed by France and Britain. Calhoun was quick to exploit the traditional enmity between the two by initiating a diplomatic correspondence with France. Emphasizing America's traditional friendship with France, he argued that British policy toward Texas was designed to gain "a monopoly in the productions of the great tropical staples, and the command of the commerce, navigation, and manufactures of the world, with an established naval ascendancy and political preponderance." And in arguments reminiscent of his correspondence with Pakenham, Calhoun warned France not to be blinded by "the plea of philanthropy."

Tyler submitted this correspondence to Congress in December 1844 with the recommendation that annexation be passed by joint resolution, which required only a simple majority in both houses rather than a two-thirds vote for a treaty in the Senate. Calhoun's effort effectively ended Anglo-French commitment to an independent Texas, largely because France did not want to appear to favor Britain at the expense of good relations with the United States. By then, the Texas question dominated domestic politics and became the key issue in the presidential election of 1844. Democrats nominated the ardent expansionist and Tennessee protégé of Andrew Jackson, James K. Polk, who ran on a platform calling for the "re-annexation" of Texas and the "reoccupation" of all Oregon. Although these issues continued to divide the nation, Tyler interpreted Polk's narrow victory as a mandate for annexation and recommended annexation by a joint resolution of Congress. The resolution passed, and on March 1, 1845, Tyler signed the measure, three days before leaving office.

That same month Calhoun left office and was succeeded by Senator James Buchanan of Pennsylvania. Calhoun reluctantly returned to the Senate the following year, in part to play a role in a peaceful settlement of the Oregon boundary, left unresolved since the Treaty of Ghent in 1814. He viewed Polk's belligerent insistence that the United States held title to all of the Oregon territory as unnecessary and dangerous. As secretary of state he put in considerable effort toward a peaceful outcome. Although Calhoun was as distrustful of British intentions as Polk, in his mind the two issues were substantively different. In Texas, the concern was over British *influence* that might bind the republic to an independent future. American claims to Oregon were well established, and patient negotiations would yield an equitable result. The alternative was war with Britain, a war Calhoun believed would result in economic disaster for the South and the ultimate loss of Oregon. Eventually a compromise was reached in 1846 along the lines first negotiated by Calhoun.

Calhoun was equally critical of Polk's provocative policy toward Mexico. Mexico had already broken off diplomatic relations over Texas and was overwhelmingly opposed to any further territory being handed over to the United States. Polk attempted to purchase New Mexico and California and sent General Zachary Taylor into the disputed borderlands between the Nueces and Rio Grande Rivers. Polk's war message to Congress in response to the Mexican raid on Taylor's forces in May 1846 prompted Calhoun to write: "Never was so momentous a measure adopted, with so much precipitancy; so little thought; or forced through by such objectionable means."

Calhoun was not opposed to the acquisition of California and New Mexico in principle, but he did not think that war was necessary to accomplish this. While secretary of state, he maintained a moderate stance toward Mexico, reviewing the possibility of pecuniary compensation for the loss of Texas, so that an agreeable boundary settlement could be negotiated. The war also brought the politically explosive issue of the status of slavery in the territories acquired by Mexico. He led the fight against the Wilmot Proviso of 1847, which would have banned slavery in the new territories, contending that this would be a violation of the property rights of slaveholders. He continued to insist on this principle in his March 7 denunciation of the Senate of the Compromise of 1850. This was his final act as senator. He died in Washington on March 31, 1850.

It may seem ironic that John C. Calhoun began his public life as a nationalist and War Hawk and ended his long and turbulent career opposed to the Mexican War and champion of slavery and Southern rights. This is explained, in part, by the rapid social and economic change during this period in which national issues were becoming more divided along sectional lines. Calhoun would not have seen himself as inconsistent. Whether in foreign or domestic affairs, principle always preceded policy, and his conception of Union, which he was clearly devoted to, meant the protection of Southern rights as he understood them. Throughout, he had admirers and detractors both North and South, and his opinions were always influential. In foreign policy, Calhoun demonstrated a keen awareness of the United States in relation to the wider world. Always eager to advance and protect America's ever-expanding global trading interests, he worked on establishing formal missions in China and Hawaii, conducted extensive negotiations with the German Customs Union, and pressed American claims in the Caribbean and Latin America. Moreover, he endeavored to establish the widest possible latitude for the United States in its foreign policy initiatives, even when motivated by sectional or partisan interests. In this sense, he was a nationalist throughout his career.

BIBLIOGRAPHICAL ESSAY

A good introduction to the wealth of primary and secondary sources available on the life and career of John C. Calhoun is found in Clyde N. Wilson, *Bibliographies of American Notables* (1990), No. 1. All the important correspondence, writings, speeches, and official documents for each phase of his public life until 1848 are found in Robert L Meriwether, W. Edwin Hamphill, and Clyde N. Wilson (eds.), *The Papers of John C. Calhoun*, (1963–) 25 vols.

There are a number of excellent biographies of John C. Calhoun. Charles M. Wiltse's *John C. Calhoun* (1944–1951), 3 vols., although somewhat partisan, achieves the greatest depth. An older but still valuable source is Margaret L. Coit's *John C. Calhoun: An American Portrait* (1950). The best and most balanced one-volume treatment is Irving H. Bartlett's *John C. Calhoun: A Biography* (1993). For some interesting insights into Calhoun's personality, see John Niven, *John C. Calhoun and the Price of Union: A Biography* (1993). For a comparison of Calhoun with the other great figures of his age see M. D. Peterson, *The Great Triumvirate: Webster, Clay and Calhoun* (1987).

Although Calhoun was influential in all the international questions of this period, there is no extensive treatment of either his foreign policy or his tenure as secretary of state. David Pletcher's *The Diplomacy of Annexation: Texas, Oregon and the Mexican War* (1973) provides a thoroughly researched and detailed account of the events and issues dealing with Calhoun's tenure at the State Department and the period following in the Senate. A lengthy account of Calhoun's role in the annexation of Texas in relation to the slavery issue is in William Freehling's *Road to Disunion: Secessionists at Bay, 1776–1854* (1990). For his opposition to the Mexican War, see Ernest M. Lander, *Reluctant Imperialists: Calhoun, the South Carolinians, and the Mexican War* (1948).

Lelia Roeckell

LEWIS CASS (1782–1866)

Served 1857–1860
Appointed by President James Buchanan
Democrat

Lewis Cass was born at Exeter, New Hampshire, on October 9, 1782, the first of six children to Jonathan and Mary Gilman Cass. The Casses were a family of moderately prosperous farmers, whereas the more affluent Gilmans sent several family members to the Continental Congress. Jonathan Cass enlisted as a private soldier in the patriot ranks following the clash at Lexington and Concord, and he saw action in the northern and middle states, rising to the rank of captain.

Lewis Cass's political moderation and social conservatism were shaped by his father. Jonathan Cass was an ardent Federalist who supported Alexander Hamilton's fiscal policies and, as marshal for the New Hampshire district, took a strong stand in maintaining order when riots erupted in Exeter at the time of Shays' rebellion. The elder Cass instilled in his son a sense of nationalism, but he was less successful in imbuing Lewis with lasting Federalist principles.

Lewis Cass was educated at Phillips Exeter Academy, under the able tutelage of Benjamin Abbott, and his classmates included a rather awkward Daniel Webster. Lewis was a headstrong, robust youth who demonstrated leadership in organizing fellow students into a military company, the Washington Whites, which he commanded and drilled. Upon leaving Phillips Exeter at the age of 17, Lewis joined his family in Wilmington, Delaware, where he taught Latin at a local academy. His sojourn at Wilmington proved to be a learning experience for the young teacher, as Lewis was first exposed to the institution of slavery. Delaware was a border state in which slaves were relatively well treated, leading Lewis to discern little difference between the bondsmen and free blacks struggling to eke out livelihoods. In short, Lewis Cass developed no moral abhorrence to slavery and would view the issue solely as a constitutional question.

Lewis's brief teaching career ended as his father left the army after receiving a grant of bounty land near Zanesville, Ohio. The Cass family arrived at Marietta in October 1800, and Lewis commenced to read law in the office of Return Jonathan Meigs, later governor of Ohio. After aiding his father in building a cabin and clearing his land at Wakatomaka, Lewis returned to Marietta to continue studying law, and in December 1802 he was licensed to practice. The following year, at the age of 20, he was admitted to the state bar shortly after Ohio entered the Union.

Lewis Cass soon developed a thriving law practice, and he amplified his social and professional standing by joining the Masonic Lodge. He later served as the first Grand Master of the Masonic Order of Michigan, but characteristically, when the political backlash against the elitist, secret organization swept the country in the 1820s, Cass recommended that the Detroit lodge members disband until the anti-Masonic feeling dissipated.

As a successful young lawyer in a new state, Lewis Cass was drawn to politics. He obviously realized that in the Old Northwest the future did not lie with the Federalists, and it took little coaxing from Meigs and other prominent Jeffersonians to convince Cass to embrace Democratic ideals. This conversion, however, was not a cynical abandonment of principle for political preferment. Lewis had grown up deeply influenced by his father's New England Federalism, whereas his early manhood was spent on the Ohio frontier, a territory imbued with the Western spirit of rough-hewn democracy. Lewis Cass not only understood the political expediency involved in becoming a Democrat, he also came to believe sincerely in such party principles as popular rule and a federal government of limited powers.

In 1804 Cass was elected prosecuting attorney of Muskingum County, and two years later the voters sent him to the Ohio legislature. This would be the last time in his long public career that Lewis Cass would be elected by popular vote to a civil office. Shortly before commencing his duties as a state representative, Cass married Elizabeth Spencer of Woody County, Virginia. This enduring union proved to be happy and fruitful; Elizabeth bore seven children before her death in 1853.

Lewis Cass played an active role in the state legislature, aiding the governor in foiling the grandiose schemes of Aaron Burr. This brought him to the attention of an approving President Jefferson, who appointed him U.S. marshal for Ohio in 1807. The post was not particularly remunerative one, and Cass continued to practice law while, during the same period, he rose to the rank of brigadier general in the Ohio militia.

As the War of 1812 approached, three Ohio regiments were formed of militiamen and volunteers, and Cass served as one of the colonels under the command of Brigadier General William Hull, a Revolutionary War veteran. Hull's force was sent to defend Fort Detroit, but the general's ineffectiveness and the inexperience of his subordinate officers and troops led to the ignominious surrender of that post. Cass ultimately gained his revenge against the British: as a brigadier general in the regular army he served as an unofficial aide-de-camp to General William Henry Harrison at the Battle of the Thames. Following that decisive victory, Harrison appointed Cass civil and military commander of Michigan Territory. President Madison concurred, and Lewis Cass served as governor for eighteen years as the territory grew from a frontier buffer to the threshold of statehood.

It was during his tenure as governor of Michigan Territory that Lewis Cass developed into an inveterate Anglophobe, a characteristic that had important consequences relating to foreign policy. The United States and Great Britain entered into an era of improved relations following the War of 1812, but tensions remained in the Northwest. British influence over the Indians caused anxiety in the American settlements, and Governor Cass frequently called on the federal government for military protection. Furthermore, Cass had many opportunities to oppose what he perceived as British pretensions. In a series of confrontations with Canadian officials, he vigorously protested against British military forces seeking deserters in Michigan. Governor Cass also emphatically condemned the British practice of boarding American vessels on Lake Erie to inspect crews and cargoes. He informed Secretary of State James Monroe of such occurrences and ominously warned that if continued, they would terminate in bloodshed. The American government pursued these and similar protests and ultimately reached the Rush–Bagot agreement. The right of search issue, however, remained unresolved; Secretary of State Lewis Cass settled it some 40 years later.

When Andrew Jackson reorganized his cabinet at the end of his first term, he chose Cass to replace John Eaton at the War Department. The major problems Secretary Cass faced were maintaining the efficiency of the army as economically as possible, while confronting various Indian uprisings such as those led by Black Hawk and Osceola. Secretary of War Cass also promoted Indian removal on humanitarian grounds, claiming it was the only practicable manner by which the natives could be protected from white encroachments. The Jackson administration faced the Bank War and the Nullification Crisis during these years as well, and Cass was only too happy to accept the post of minister to France when the president tendered it in the late 1836. Cass thus gracefully withdrew from the muddled domestic scene and improved his stature in international politics. Somewhat ironically, while in Paris Cass became further embroiled in American partisan politics.

The appointment of Lewis Cass as U.S. minister to France signaled the end of a protracted diplomatic dispute between the two countries over the spoliation claims arising from the Napoleonic wars. Cass soon established cordial relations with King Louis Philippe, but the U.S. minister continued to distrust the British government. The right of search was again at issue when France joined Britain, Austria, Prussia, and Russia in the Quintuple Treaty, signed in December 1841. This agreement was designed to suppress the African slave trade, but because the Mediterranean was specifically exempted from the provisions of the Quintuple Treaty, its primary purpose was simply to allow the signatories to declare formally their opposition to that nefarious commerce. To Cass's eye, however, the treaty appeared to be an attempt by Britain to institute a general policy of searching all ships off the African coast, and as such it represented a menace to the rights and freedoms of the United States, a growing maritime nation. The American minister therefore took it upon himself to oppose ratification by the French government of the Quintuple Treaty.

Cass launched his attack against the treaty with the publication of a pamphlet, *An Examination of the Question, Now in Discussion, Between the American and British Governments, Concerning the Right of Search*, in which he divorced the question of the right of search from British attempts to suppress the slave trade. Instead, as Cass saw it, the key issues were impressments and other potential abuses arising from a systematic searching of American ships. The pamphlet concluded on a somber note; Cass remained convinced that war between the United States and Great Britain would ultimately settle the issue.

The U.S. minister's intervention in the Quintuple debate was one of several factors that led the French government to reject ratification of the Treaty. The controversy over the right of search continued unabated, however, and was actually exacerbated by U.S. Senate ratification of the Webster–Ashburton Treaty. Cass had written Secretary of State Daniel Webster from Paris, suggesting that he negotiate with Lord Ashburton the question of the right of search in relation to the African slave trade. The final treaty was silent on that issue, to Cass's chagrin; apparently Webster and Ashburton agreed to disagree on the right of search, including in their negotiations only those matters that could be settled amicably. Disappointed with the Webster–Ashburton Treaty, Lewis Cass resigned from the Paris mission and entered into an acrimonious debate with Daniel Webster, conducted through a series of letters, which were soon made public. The argument lasted for some time after Cass's return to the United States and ended with each participant believing he had bested the other.

Upon his return to the United States, Cass found that his dispute with Webster had brought him before the public's attention, and that he was prominently mentioned as a contender for the Democratic presidential nomination of 1844. During the course of a bitter national convention in which both Martin Van Buren and Lewis Cass attained a majority of the delegate's votes while falling short of the two-thirds necessary for nomination, the Democrats finally settled on James Knox Polk.

Following the campaign, the Michigan legislature elected Lewis Cass to the U.S. Senate, and he soon became a leading administration spokesman for expansionism. Cass staunchly supported the American claim to all the Oregon country, although he acquiesced in the compromise treaty with Great Britain, which drew the boundary along the 49th parallel. Senator Cass was less inclined to compromise with America's southern neighbor, and he urged a vigorous prosecution of the war with Mexico and a territorial indemnity for the perceived wrongs she had inflicted on the United States. Anglophobia again played a motivational role; Cass believed that unless the United States annexed the entire southwestern region, it would come under the sway of Britain. It did not matter to him whether the territory in question would be slave or free, and for that reason, after an initial hesitation, Cass opposed the Wilmot Proviso as an obstacle to the acquisition of territory from Mexico. The famous letter Cass penned to Alfred P. Nicholson on December 24, 1847, was an attempt to defuse the Wilmot controversy. The Nicholson letter claimed for Cass the sobriquet "Father of Popular Sovereignty" and secured the ensuing Democratic presidential nomination.

The election of 1848 was an exciting contest, with Zachary Taylor leading the Whigs to victory over Lewis Cass and the Free-Soil candidate, Martin Van Buren. Following his defeat, Cass was returned to the Senate, where he helped fashion the Compromise of 1850. Two years later, Senator Cass again sought the Democratic presidential nomination, leading James Buchanan and Stephen Douglas during the early balloting before the exhausted convention delegates turned to Franklin Pierce.

Senator Cass then shifted his attention back to legislative matters, supporting without enthusiasm the Kansas–Nebraska Act and bemoaning the subsequent violence that erupted in "Bleeding Kansas." As the election of 1856 approached, Cass continually attacked sectionalism, focusing on the political dangers presented by the nascent Republican Party. His warnings went unheeded in Michigan; although James Buchanan was elected president, the Republicans carried Cass's home state, and Zachariah Chandler replaced Cass in the U.S. Senate.

Lewis Cass was 74 years old when President-elect Buchanan tapped him to head the State Department. Buchanan was determined to preside over a harmonious cabinet free from political extremism and sectionalism, and he originally favored a close personal friend, Howell Cobb of Georgia, for the chief cabinet post. However, the choice of Cobb as secretary of state was opposed by more vocal Southern spokesmen, led by Jefferson Davis, as well as by Northern expansionists who supported Robert J. Walker. One of Walker's prominent backers was Stephen Douglas, then engaged in a struggle with Jesse Bright of Indiana for control of the Democratic organization and patronage in the Northwest. Buchanan disliked Douglas, but the influential Illinois senator could be neither ignored nor unceremoniously antagonized during the cabinet selection process. So Buchanan seized upon Bright's suggestion: he appointed Lewis Cass to the State Department and gave Howell Cobb the important position of secretary of the treasury. Neither Douglas nor Cobb would oppose the selection of the venerable Father of Popular Sovereignty, and the Democratic-dominated Senate swiftly approved Cass's appointment. He formally took office in March 1857.

Buchanan thus selected Lewis Cass as secretary of state for political and personal reasons. As an elder spokesman acceptable to all factions of the party, Cass served as a symbol of Democratic unity in a time of increasing sectional tensions. Buchanan expected Cass to serve as a figurehead while the diplomatically experienced president personally directed American foreign policy. Buchanan even maintained an office in the State Department and personally picked the assistant secretary, John Appleton, who managed the daily affairs of the department. Lewis Cass accepted the conditions (although he preferred son-in-law Henry Ledyard as his assistant) because he no longer had the patience for routine paperwork, and he had no wish to return to Detroit after being defeated for reelection to the Senate. Nonetheless, Secretary of State Cass would be more than a figurehead; he was instrumental in carrying out foreign policy, and he convened and presided over cabinet meetings during Buchanan's frequent absences from Washington.

Freed from the responsibility of the routine functions of the State Department, Lewis Cass turned his attention to several long-standing diplomatic controversies. He strongly supported the aggressive foreign policy of President Buchanan, who sought additional territory in Latin America. Shortly after a bill was introduced in the Senate allocating thirty million dollars to facilitate the purchase of Cuba, Cass claimed that such an acquisition was of paramount importance to all sections of the country. Zachariah Chandler, however, successfully led the congressional opposition to the addition of further slave territory, and Cuba remained under Spanish control. This set the tone for foreign affairs during the Buchanan administration; sectionalism transcended foreign policy, and with only one major exception, Republicans uniformly acted to thwart the policies of the president and secretary of state.

Secretary Cass also joined Buchanan in casting acquisitive eyes toward Mexican territory. The time appeared to be propitious for additional cessions; during the 1850s a succession of revolutionary governments south of the Rio Grande resulted in the deaths of several U.S. citizens and claims of ten million dollars against Mexico. Shortly after taking office, Secretary of State Cass approved and forwarded a proposed treaty to the U.S. minister to Mexico, John Forsyth, who was instructed to offer between twelve and fifteen million dollars for Lower California and substantial portions of Sonora and Chihuahua. Furthermore, Forsyth was to seek a separate treaty expressly guaranteeing the right of transit across the Tehuantepec Isthmus. The U.S. minister approached a succession of Mexican leaders but he was consistently rebuffed and in frustration broke off diplomatic relations. Forsyth's replacement, Robert M. McLane of Maryland, was instructed to concentrate on commercial matters rather than territorial cessions, and a treaty was concluded in December 1859 with the Benito Juarez government that guaranteed the United States the perpetual right of transit across the isthmus. This treaty was submitted to the Senate, where it was soundly defeated by Republican votes. An obdurate Congress, split along sectional lines, thus prevented Buchanan and Cass from achieving their foreign policy goals regarding Cuba and Mexico.

The Buchanan administration was ultimately more successful in its dealings with Great Britain and Central America. Two days after he offered Cass the secretaryship of state, Buchanan felt obliged to inform the British foreign secretary that he need not fear Cass's alleged Anglophobia, which, stated the president, no longer existed. Indeed, drawing no doubt on his own experiences as a diplomat in a foreign nation, Secretary Cass worked smoothly with Lord Napier, the British minister to Washington. This was most fortunate, because several vexatious problems faced the United States and Britain, the most troublesome proving to be the Clayton–Bulwer Treaty, which Senator Cass had voted to approve in 1850. Cass had misgivings regarding the efficacy of that pact (by which the United States and Britain pledged that neither nation would seek exclusive control over any isthmian canal, nor would either colonize or exercise dominion over any part of Central America). The British government maintained that the Clayton–Bulwer Treaty was prospective rather than retrospective; that is, the pact sanctioned those colonies already held. Furthermore, Bulwer handed Clayton a note prior to the formal exchange of treaty ratifications, which explicitly declared that the convention did not apply to the British settlement of Honduras or to its dependencies. Acting on this construction of the treaty, Britain in 1852 proclaimed the diminutive archipelago lying off the Honduran coast to be the Colony of the Bay Islands. In a series of Senate speeches, Cass opposed such British arrogation; he similarly attacked the protectorate Britain established over the Mosquito Coast as another violation of the Clayton–Bulwer Treaty. His unchanging theme was that Britain must abide by the United States' interpretation of the treaty and allow the Central American states to govern themselves.

President Buchanan's first annual message to Congress in December 1857 concurred with Secretary of State Cass's sentiments regarding affairs in Central America. In an attempt to prod the British government into settling the controversy, Buchanan argued that the wisest course would be to abrogate the Clayton–Bulwer pact and begin negotiations anew. While thus serving notice to the British government, the Buchanan administration in the meantime attempted to negotiate peaceful settlements with individual Latin American states. On November 16, 1857, Secretary of State Cass signed a general treaty of amity and commerce with Antonio José de Yrisarri, the newly appointed Nicaraguan envoy to Washington. This treaty granted to the United States the right of transit between the oceans through Nicaraguan territory and the power to use military force to protect any such route. In return, Cass pledged his nation to guarantee the international neutrality of any railroad or canal constructed under the terms of the treaty. The secretary of state hastened to advise U.S. diplomats in London and Central America that the United States desired to keep the isthmian routes open to all nations of the world, but such assurances proved to be unnecessary because the Nicaraguan government distrusted American intentions and rejected the Cass–Yrisarri Treaty.

Nicaragua and the other Central American states had become increasingly alarmed at filibustering expeditions originating from the United States. On the same day that Cass and Yrisarri signed their pact, for example, William Walker (President of Nicaragua, 1855–1857) embarked from a southern port in hopes of again achieving supremacy in Nicaragua after being overthrown in 1857. The Buchanan administration attempted to suppress such filibustering campaigns through rather half-hearted enforcement of federal neutrality laws. Secretary of State Cass telegraphed customs officials and government attorneys at Mobile and New Orleans urging them to prevent any such illegal expeditions, but the impact of these instructions was lessened by public knowledge of a letter Cass had written praising Walker's earlier exploits. And while President Buchanan denounced the filibusterers, Central American leaders believed he did so only because their actions temporarily prevented the United States from gaining hegemony across the isthmus. In response, the presidents of Nicaragua and Costa Rica issued the Rivas Manifesto, which placed the protection of their countries under the guarantee of European nations, including France and Great Britain.

Although tensions thus increased between the United States and Central America by the spring of 1858, a solution to the controversy was in the making. The first step was the improvement of relations between the United States and Great Britain, which also had a large stake in the future of Latin America. This was accomplished with the settlement of the "right of search" issue. Secretary of State Cass addressed a long communication to the British minister at Washington on April 10, in which he dismissed as irrelevant the distinction made by the British between "search" and a "visitation" to determine the nationality of a vessel. The United States, Cass succinctly concluded, would deny any foreign naval cruisers the right to board U.S. ships in time of peace. This firm stand received strong non-partisan support in the United States, as evidenced by a Senate resolution, which denounced any visitation as a violation of U.S. sovereignty. Even outspoken anti-slavery Republicans, such as William Henry Seward, joined in unanimously adopting the resolution. Public and judicial sentiment in Britain likewise advocated acceptance of the U.S. position. (An admiralty judge, for example, denied the validity of any right to visit and search foreign ships in peacetime.) Lord Malmesbury, the foreign secretary, therefore prudently declared that his government would henceforth recognize the U.S. position on the right of search issue. Secretary Cass was deeply gratified that this long-standing controversy, with which he became entangled during his tenure as governor of Michigan Territory and again as minister to France, was settled satisfactorily.

Following the amicable adjustment of the right of search controversy, attention once more turned to the Central American quarrel. Secretary Cass sent a cordial note to Lord Napier on November 8, urging that both their nations enter into negotiations in a friendly and conciliatory manner. The British government responded in kind and promptly recalled from Central America the diplomatic agent who was blamed by the United States for rejection of the Cass–Yrisarri Treaty. His replacement swiftly negotiated a treaty with Guatemala securing the boundaries of Belize. In November 1859, a British pact with Honduras restored the Bay Islands to that republic, and three months later, Britain relinquished her protectorate of the Mosquito Coast. In the meantime, the presidents of Nicaragua and Costa Rica disavowed the sentiments of the Rivas Manifesto, claiming that it was

111

drafted precipitately in the face of filibustering expeditions. The U.S. minister subsequently concluded a treaty with Nicaragua, which essentially embodied the precepts of the Cass–Yrisarri pact. The controversy in Central America was thereby settled peaceably to the satisfaction of all concerned parties. Indeed, aside from an inability to attain territorial cessions, President Buchanan and Secretary of State Cass were invariably successful in attaining their foreign policy goals in Central America.

The Buchanan administration was not nearly as successful in dealing with internal sectionalism, and this ultimately led to a parting of the ways between the president and the secretary of state. In his inaugural address, James Buchanan endorsed the doctrine of popular sovereignty incorporated in the Kansas–Nebraska Act, and despite personal reservations, Secretary of State Cass publicly supported the president's attempts to bring Kansas into the Union under the proslavery Lecompton constitution. The Father of Popular Sovereignty realized that the unrepresentative Lecompton document made a sham of his cherished doctrine, but a greater principle was at stake—failure of the administration to support the Southern position in Kansas would lead to a breakup of the Democratic Party and threaten the Union. Despite the concerted efforts of Buchanan and his cabinet, the Lecompton constitution was not sanctioned by Congress. More importantly, a schism did occur in the Democratic ranks, and the Republicans carried the election of 1860.

The disunion, which Lewis Cass had long predicted would follow a Republican victory, was quick in coming; led by South Carolina, Southern states immediately began to implement plans for secession. When the dispirited Buchanan cabinet met a few days after the election, sectional differences were clearly delineated. Howell Cobb and Secretary of the Interior Jacob Thompson strongly endorsed the right of secession and prepared to follow Georgia and Mississippi out of the Union. Secretary of War John B. Floyd of Virginia did not consider Lincoln's election to be valid grounds for the dissolution of the republic, but he recognized the constitutional right of a state to secede. Isaac Toucey of the Navy Department opposed secession, as did most of his fellow New Englanders, but he recoiled at the thought of using armed force to maintain the Union. Kentuckian Joseph Holt, who had succeeded to the Post Office Department; Attorney General Jeremiah S. Black of Pennsylvania; and seventy-eight-year-old Lewis Cass led the Unionist faction within the cabinet. Cass did not accept the right of secession under the Constitution, and as always, he placed the welfare of the nation over that of his state or section.

President Buchanan presented his formal response to the secession crisis in his final address to Congress in early December, and Secretary of State Cass wholeheartedly agreed with most of what was said. Both men tended to blame radical antislavery men for the widening breech between North and South; both believed secession to be unconstitutional, although neither claimed the federal government had the right to coerce a state to remain in the Union. Secretary Cass, however, vehemently disagreed with Buchanan's policy regarding federal forts located in the South. He urged that they be strengthened immediately and warned that the three posts of Charleston, South Carolina, were particularly vulnerable. Cass entreated the president to reinforce Major Robert Anderson, but the secretary of war persuaded Buchanan to delay any such action until he had conferred with General Winfield Scott. In the meantime, Cass received a communication from General John E. Wool, commander of the Eastern Department, urgently pleading that relief forces be sent at once to Charleston. This advice braced Cass's resolve, and he repeated his call for reinforcements at a cabinet meeting held on December 13. When Buchanan again refused to act, Lewis Cass, who as secretary of war under Andrew Jackson had assumed responsibility for the defense of the Charleston garrison during the nullification crisis, informed the president of his intention to resign from the cabinet. Jeremiah Black subsequently delivered Cass's letter of resignation. Buchanan publicly expressed his surprise and regret and reminded Cass that the secretaries of war and the navy supported the president's position. Privately, Buchanan complained that because of his advanced age and indecisiveness Cass had been a most ineffectual secretary of state.

President Buchanan derided Cass's important contributions as secretary of state because of personal pique and the fact that the resignation damaged the president's reputation in the North. Nonetheless, he was correct in observing that his age and deteriorating health diminished Cass's decisiveness. Cass in fact postponed official notification of his resignation following his last cabinet meeting; his letter was dated December 12, but it was not submitted for several days. Whatever second thoughts regarding his resignation Cass had, however, were quickly dispelled by the reception he received. Admirers thronged his rooms following the resignation announcement, and words of lavish praise reached the former secretary from throughout the free states. Even his hometown Republican organ, the *Detroit Advertiser*, acknowledged on December 17 that although "we have in times past had occasion to differ from General Cass on questions of public policy . . . we take pleasure in giving our cordial approval of this manly act."

Lewis Cass savored the Northern acclaim, which greeted his withdrawal from the Buchanan cabinet, but he privately despaired at the sundering of the Union. The former secretary of state received small comfort from the fact that several weeks later President Buchanan finally agreed to send reinforcements to Fort Sumter. The *Star of the West* expedition vindicated Cass's position, but it was driven back by shore batteries without accomplishing its purpose.

In February 1861, Lewis Cass returned for the final time to Detroit, where, his health deteriorating, he spent the war years in quiet support of the Union cause. He subscribed thousands of dollars to equip volunteer regiments, and when Michigan infantry units returned after the first battle at Bull Run, Cass delivered a welcoming address. The former secretary of state additionally aided the North in the field of foreign affairs. In November a federal cruiser stopped the British steamer *Trent* in West Indian waters and took into custody two Confederate agents, James M. Mason and John Slidell. The Southerners were bound for Europe aboard a neutral vessel, and Britain demanded their immediate release and an official apology from the United States government. War fever ran high in both nations as, ironically, their traditional roles on the right of search issue were reversed. Cass cautioned the Lincoln administration to act prudently; he promptly cabled Secretary of State Seward recommending that the federal government use the *Trent* incident as a lever to commit Great Britain even more firmly to the American position regarding the right of search. Cass supported his arguments in a letter he sent to Seward the next day, warning that war with Britain would prevent the restoration of the Union. President Lincoln was receiving similar advice from Senator Charles Sumner of the Foreign Affairs Committee, and he defused the crisis by ordering the release of Mason and Slidell. Secretary of State Seward wrote a personal note to

Cass expressing his appreciation for his considerate and patriotic counsel in the *Trent* affair. Lewis Cass had again served his country well, and fittingly, he lived to see his beloved Union restored. He died on June 17, 1866, and was buried beside his wife in Detroit's Elmwood Cemetery.

BIBLIOGRAPHICAL ESSAY

The primary depositories of Cass manuscripts are the Burton Historical Collection, Detroit Public Library; the William L. Clements Library, University of Michigan, Ann Arbor; Library of Congress (manuscripts Division), Washington, D.C.; and the Michigan Historical Collections, Bentley Historical Library, University of Michigan, Ann Arbor. Of course, the appropriate Instructions and Dispatches sections of the Records of the Department of State in the National Archives provide a wealth of information relating to Cass's tenure as secretary of state.

Biographers of Lewis Cass generally provide a rather cursory view of his years as secretary of state: Andrew C. McLaughlin, *Lewis Cass* (1899): Frank B. Woodford, *Lewis Cass: The Last Jeffersonian* (1950); Willis Frederick Dunbar, *Lewis Cass* (1970). McLaughlin's dated work, part of the American Statesmen Series, is hampered by the lack of correspondence and personal papers available at that time. Woodford, of the Detroit *Free Press*, presents a highly laudatory biography; whereas Professor Dunbar, within the confines of ninety pages, provides a more judicious account. Two dissertations shed some light on Cass's public career: Richard G. Hewlett, *Lewis Cass in National Politics, 1842–1861* (1952); Willard Carl Klunder, "Lewis Cass, 1782–1866: A Political Biography" (1981). John Thomas Hubbell's dissertation provides an interesting look at the disintegration of the Buchanan administration: "The Northern Democracy and the Crisis of Disunion, 1860–1861" (1969). Two monographs, which discuss the broader subject of the Buchanan presidency, are Philip Shriver Klein's *President James Buchanan* (1962) and *The Presidency of James Buchanan*, by Elbert B. Smith (1975).

William Devereux Jones, *The American Problem in British Diplomacy, 1841–1861* (1974), and Paul A. Varg, *United States Foreign Relations: 1820–1860* (1979), present overviews of antebellum diplomacy; whereas Donald S. Spencer discusses Cass's impact on foreign affairs while he served in the Senate, "Lewis Cass and Symbolic Intervention: (1848–1852, 11) Michigan History 53 (1969): 1–17. Lewis Einstein focuses on Cass's tenure as secretary of state in "Lewis Cass," *The American Secretaries of State and Their Diplomacy*, vol. 6 (1928). Lewis Cass provides a personal glimpse of his role as an American minister in *France, Its King, Court, and Government; and Three Hours at Saint Cloud* (1841).

The right of search of controversy and the ensuing Cass–Webster debate over the Ashburton treaty have inspired a great deal of research, triggered by Cass's pamphlet, *An Examination of the Question, Now in Discussion, Between the American and British Governments, Concerning the Right of Search* (1842). Sir William Gore Ouseley responded with a *Reply to an "American's Examination" of the "Right of Search": with Observations on Some of the Questions at Issue Between Great Britain and the United States, and on Certain Positions Assumed by the North American Government* (1842). Hugh G. Soulsby is more dispassionate in his treatment, "The Right of Search and the Slave Trade in Anglo-American Relations, 1814–1862," *Johns Hop-*

kins University Studies in Historical and Political Science 51(1933): 115–299. Howard Jones places the debate between Cass and Webster in its historical context with *To the Webster-Ashburton Treaty: A Study in Anglo-American Relations, 1783–1843* (1977). Also contributing to the debate is Richard N. Current, "Webster's Propaganda and the Ashburton Treaty," *Mississippi Valley Historical Review* 34 (1947): 187–200, and Kenneth E. Shewmaker, "The 'War of Words': The Cass–Webster Debates of 1842–43," *Diplomatic History* 5 (spring 1981): 151–164. Shewmaker is the editor of *The Papers of Daniel Webster: Diplomatic Papers.*

In short, the involvement of Lewis Cass in American diplomacy and foreign policy remains a fertile field for scholarly research.

William Klunder

WARREN CHRISTOPHER (1925–)

Served 1993–1997
Appointed by President Bill Clinton
Democrat

During his two terms in office William Jefferson Clinton, the 42nd president, was served by two secretaries of state. The first of these was Warren Minor Christopher, who was born in Scranton, North Dakota, on October 27, 1925. From 1943 until 1946, he served in the Naval Reserve. Christopher received a bachelor's degree from the University of Southern California in 1945 and a law degree from Stanford University in 1949. Christopher is married to the former Marie Wyllis.

From 1949 to 1950, Christopher served as law clerk to U.S. Supreme Court Justice William O. Douglas. He practiced law with O'Melveny & Myers from 1950 to 1967 and became a major figure in California legal and political circles while with the firm. He became a partner in 1958, and special counsel to California Governor Edmund G. (Pat) Brown in 1959. Christopher served from 1965 to 1966 as vice-chairman of the governor's commission that investigated the 1964 Los Angeles riots in Watts.

In 1991, Christopher served as chairman of the Independent Commission on the Los Angeles Police Department, which identified several dozen "problem officers" and proposed significant reforms of the Los Angeles Police Department in the aftermath of the Rodney King beating incident. These reforms were approved overwhelmingly by a public referendum.

In 1992 Christopher directed the vice presidential search for Bill Clinton that chose Tennessee Senator Al Gore, and he served as the director of Clinton's presidential transition team. In 2000 Christopher headed Democratic presidential nominee Al Gore's vice presidential candidate search that selected Connecticut Senator Joseph Lieberman.

Christopher's national governmental career prior to becoming secretary of state is steeped in the mainstream of the Democratic Party and its national elected officials. He served in some capacity in every Democratic administration since Lyndon Johnson. He served as deputy attorney general late in the Johnson administration (from 1967 to 1969), after which he rejoined O'Melveny & Myers. Christopher served as President Carter's deputy secretary of state (under Cyrus Vance) from

1977 to 1981. In this role he helped win Senate ratification of the Panama Canal treaties, which gave control of the canal back to Panama in 1999. Christopher also assisted in the process of normalizing relations with China and in negotiating the release of American hostages in Iran. President Carter awarded him the Medal of Freedom in 1981.

Clearly the Iranian hostage crisis was one of the most important foreign policy challenges Christopher faced during his service in the Carter administration. Muslim extremist followers of the Ayatollah Khomeini seized control of the government of Iran away from the U.S.-supported Shah in February 1979, and held 52 Americans hostage for the next 444 days. What role Christopher played in creating the disaster in Iran is uncertain, but he was the chief American negotiator in the 1981 talks that ended the crisis, and he is credited with negotiating the complicated political and financial deal that led to the release of the hostages.

On January 20, 1993, Christopher was sworn in as the 63rd secretary of state. Frequently described as plodding, Christopher has rarely been hailed as a foreign policy visionary, and this reputation is probably not without merit. Christopher has been called courtly, and some described him as a father figure in an administration not particularly interested in foreign policy. Christopher defined the aims of U.S. foreign policy under President Clinton as promoting economic security, backing diplomacy with military force, and encouraging democracy and respect for human rights. He stressed the importance of maintaining productive political and economic relations with world powers and the building and maintenance of institutions to enhance international cooperation. One would be hard-pressed to find opposition to these goals in mainstream foreign policy circles.

Also, one must remember that secretary of state was not the most desirable job in the administration. This was true in part because Clinton won the presidency without a majority of the popular vote and had focused his campaign on the ills of the domestic economy. "It's the economy, stupid," became a familiar mantra of Clinton operatives in their campaign against President George Bush, whose greatest successes came in the foreign policy arena. Moreover, Clinton's relations with the military were expected to be strained, due to his avoidance of the draft and a controversial letter he wrote as a college student expressing his disdain for the service. The traditional balancing of the interests of the State Department, the intelligence community, and the military were thus made all the more difficult for the new secretary. The Clinton administration was perceived as excessively deferential to the military, and to whatever extent this may have been true, part of the blame comes from Clinton's controversial past.

Naturally however, Clinton's campaign rhetoric had not been completely void of foreign policy concerns. During the campaign Clinton espoused a good deal of idealist rhetoric about U.S. support for human rights, reduced reliance on military power in international affairs, and liberal internationalism in general. A major promise was to link Chinese progress on human rights with trade.

Early in the administration the president's national security team spoke of moving from "containment" to "enlargement," as they put it in several 1993 speeches. In other words, in the past the major objective of U.S. foreign policy had been to contain the influence of Soviet and Chinese communism, but with the end of the Cold War the objective needed to become the enlargement of the number of free-market democracies. Opponents of the administration, especially some of its traditional supporters among organized labor, criticized the administration for the stress on the enlargement of markets rather than democracies.

The theory of international relations of the Clinton administration during Christopher's tenure also has been described as assertive or aggressive multilateralism, which meant more heavy reliance on international institutions such as North Atlantic Treaty Organization and the UN in the making and execution of foreign policy. However, the United States and the UN butted heads over a number of issues. The U.S. blamed the UN for some significant failures in foreign affairs (e.g., Somalia) and helped remove Secretary-General Boutros Boutros-Ghali in 1996.

As the first completely post–Cold War administration the Clinton foreign policy team was in a unique position and one that presented many difficulties. U.S. military and economic dominance were essentially unchallenged, yet this freedom came with its own set of problems. Allies now felt empowered to reject what they perceived as bullying by the United States. Without the threat of a common enemy, allies of the world's remaining superpower felt safer in sometimes rejecting U.S. preferences. Also, without the threat of Soviet communism, foreign policy naturally became less significant to the public. This lack of public concern was coupled with a president who at least at the outset did not much care about foreign policy. In fact, Christopher offered to spend an hour per week briefing Clinton on international relations in a noncrisis format, but the president rejected his offer. It should not have been surprising that especially during the first term, Clinton foreign policy seemed episodic and reactive, rather than coherent and engaging.

Certainly Clinton's administration was not the first to shift from idealism at the outset to realpolitik as time went on, and there were reasons other than political expediency for the administration's retreat. Foreign policy looks very different from the White House than on the campaign trail. Ultimately, Clinton's foreign policy embodied an incrementalist approach. He did not confront great crises, nor seek out great achievements that might also involve major risk. Congress also cramped the administration.

In the 1994 midterm elections one of the more isolationist Congressional majorities was ushered into office. Two-thirds of the Republicans elected to Congress as the majority in 1994 did not even possess passports and took their isolationism very seriously. Therefore, after 1995, the Clinton foreign policy team faced a Congress bent on cutting the budget not only for the State Department, but for the International Monetary Fund and the peace process in the Middle East as well. Not surprisingly, they were also less than enthusiastic about paying the $1 billion in dues and peacekeeping bills that the U.S. owed to the UN.

Senator Jesse Helms, chairman of the Senate Foreign Relations Committee, in many ways exemplified the intransigence of the new congressional majority. Early in his tenure, Helms halted business meetings of the committee, froze 400 State Department promotions, and blocked the Chemical Weapons Convention from a vote in the full Senate. This level of recalcitrance from the legislature made foreign policy more difficult for the entire Clinton team (which included, during the first term, the national security adviser, Anthony Lake, and the representative to the UN, Madeleine Albright). But Christopher's tenure was not without successes.

One of the first challenges the Clinton administration faced was the North American Free Trade (NAFTA) agreement in 1993. The Bush administration had negotiated the trade agreement with Canada and Mexico, but candidate Clinton had called for approval of it only after it had been amended to reflect concerns of U.S. farmers, environmentalists, and organized labor. The administration succeeded in passing NAFTA without significant changes to the core principles of the deal, through a Democratic majority House of Representatives and against opposition from much of the Democratic House leadership. After NAFTA passed there was a good deal of enthusiasm in the Clinton administration about foreign policy. At the time, Christopher said the administration hoped to use the momentum created by the NAFTA victory to strike deals that would reduce the trade deficit with Asia and to conclude negotiations on a world trade agreement.

Clinton campaigned on a pledge to press China on human rights and specifically to use the renewal of Most Favored Nation (MFN) trading status to pressure the Chinese in this area. His administration soon abandoned that policy, which Christopher never fully supported but still tried to make work, and instead pursued an engagement policy with the Chinese. The administration consistently supported reapproval of China's MFN status, and ultimately the administration achieved legislative approval of permanent MFN status for China. This will ease its entry into the World Trade Organization.

After the passage of NAFTA, the troubled economy of Mexico required more immediate attention. Because Congress would not fund an assistance package, Clinton used money from the Exchange Stabilization Fund totaling $50 billion to bail out the Mexican peso in 1994. Although this bailout did not cost U.S. taxpayers a dime, the timing of it so near the passage of NAFTA made some Americans wary of the alleged benefits of closer trade and political ties with Mexico. However, at the time of the bailout, Christopher assured the public that Mexico would work to make border crossings more secure to reduce illegal immigration and increase efforts to curtail the illegal drug trade in part as payment for the U.S. assistance.

The Chemical Weapons Convention was negotiated by the Bush administration, but Clinton submitted it to the Senate in 1993, and the Senate ratified it in 1997, during the tenure of Secretary of State Madeleine Albright. Ratification of the deal was an important element of the Clinton administration's goal of preventing the spread of weapons of mass destruction, and its passage was a major success.

In 1994 the Clinton administration considered a preemptive military strike against North Korea's nuclear potential, but opted instead to follow a diplomatic route. North Korea agreed to stop plutonium production in exchange for U.S. assistance in building two light-water reactors for electricity production and to supply heavy fuel for power plant use while the reactors were developed. Hawks opposed the deal because it appeared to reward North Korea for defying the nonproliferation regime, yet it was unclear what alternative would have halted North Korea's drive for nuclear weapons. The deal did not require Senate approval, but members still raised objections.

Despite the death of Britain's Princess Diana, for whom it was a personal cause, the United States opposed the UN convention banning land mine use. It is estimated that there are 110 million mines planted in the field, and the same number in storage. Because women and children are often the victims of these deadly antipersonnel weapons, there has been a growing global movement since 1991 to ban their use. President Clinton promised to ban land mines in a speech before the UN General Assembly in 1994. The administration reneged on that promise, primarily due to pressure from General John Shalikashvili, then Chairman of the Joint Chiefs of

Staff. This acquiescence to the military fueled criticism that Clinton was too deferential to the services. On a 1996 visit to Angola, Christopher detonated a pile of land mines to symbolize the administration's efforts to curtail these weapons.

Naturally the United States was also interested in preventing the dissemination of old Soviet nuclear materials as well, and the administration persuaded Belarus, Kazakhstan, and Ukraine to give up their nuclear weapons during Christopher's tenure.

Several peacekeeping missions involving the U.S. military were carried out during Christopher's tenure as secretary of state. One of these occurred in the impoverished nation of Haiti. One of the major U.S. objectives in Haiti was to keep hordes of refugees from leaving the Caribbean island nation and heading for the United States. Clinton managed to achieve this outcome in 1994 and to restore President Jean-Bertrand Aristide to power (using Christopher's former boss, Jimmy Carter, to negotiate the surrender of the Haitian coup leaders). Despite the crippling poverty in Haiti, Clinton's policy toward the country has been considered a humanitarian success as the 20,000 U.S. troops dispatched to the island achieved their limited objectives. Near the end of the U.S. deployment, Christopher visited Haiti and said that such missions strengthened the diplomatic initiatives of the U.S. because they showed that the administration was willing to use force when it deemed it necessary to achieve its ends.

President George Bush sent U.S. troops to Somalia in 1992 as part of a multinational force whose mission was to prevent "warlords" from disrupting food and medicine shipments to famine victims. The warlords drew the force into gun battles that killed 132 of the peacekeepers. Then the Somalis shot down an American helicopter, took one American soldier hostage, and dragged the body of another through the streets of Mogadishu, the Somali capital.

These events helped turn the American public and Congress against the humanitarian effort, which ultimately cost 18 American lives. President Clinton persuaded Congress to allow the troops to stay in Somalia until the situation stabilized and the operation could be turned over to the UN. At the time of U.S. withdrawal in 1995, Somalia still lacked an effective government. The lesson of the intervention to the Clinton administration seemed to be that humanitarian efforts were not always in the national interest, especially if they required "nation-building" to have their desired effect. The sting of Somalia may have contributed to U.S. reluctance to intervene in Rwanda, where genocide of an epic proportion occurred in 1994.

Rwanda's Hutu regime organized the killing of approximately 800,000 members of the country's Tutsi minority and their moderate Hutu supporters. The Organization of African Unity placed part of the blame for the slaughter on the United States, which had worked in the UN to reduce the role of peacekeepers in the country. In fact, Clinton administration officials refrained from using the word *genocide* in reference to Rwanda until Christopher did so in June 1994. In all, the United States dispatched 2,350 troops to the region who helped deliver water, food, and sanitation to hundreds of thousands of Rwandan refugees in Zaire. During a visit to Africa in 1998, the first ever by an American president, Clinton apologized to Rwanda for the lack of international response to the ethnic cleansing. However, doubts remain about how much of an effect U.S. intervention could have had, in that 250,000 people were killed in two weeks.

The 1995 Dayton peace accords were designed to end the fighting in Bosnia-Herzegovina and to begin building democracy in the countries of the former

Yugoslavia. They also committed the United States to support the creation of a multiethnic Bosnia and committed Bosnia to holding fair and free elections by September of 1996. After the elections the UN would lift sanctions against Bosnia. The NATO mission to Bosnia consisted of 50,000 troops in total, of which 20,000 were Americans. The United States also launched a cruise missile attack against Serb positions in Bosnia. Christopher's early preference had been to lift the arms embargo against the Bosnian Muslims and to assist their struggle with NATO air strikes. He was unable to convince European allies of the wisdom of this plan.

During the 1992 presidential campaign Clinton promised to insist on "results-oriented" trade agreements with Japan that would cause an increase in U.S. exports to that country. Such rhetoric was probably necessary to placate labor union leaders who were uncomfortable with a governor of a right-to-work state as the party's standard bearer. However, it soon became clear to the Clinton team that U.S.–Japan relations were about more than just trade, and in 1995 the United States and Japan reaffirmed their security agreement in an important, if overlooked, foreign policy achievement of the Christopher era. This was the first revision of the pact in nineteen years, and the recommitment of the United States indicated a realization by the world's remaining superpower that it had interests to protect militarily in East Asia, especially because two of the world's largest remaining communist countries—North Korea and China—are in the region and represent a potential threat to U.S. allies.

The new deal called for Japan to possess the minimum military capability necessary for self-defense and to upgrade its military hardware. It also created guidelines for the Japanese military's role in dealing with natural disasters, as well as with acts of terrorism, which have become increasingly important roles for the militaries of advanced industrial democracies. Participation of the Japanese military in overseas peacekeeping operations was also permitted by the new guidelines. The difficult issue of the U.S. military presence in Okinawa was not dealt with in the arrangement. The U.S. troop commitment in East Asia remained at 100,000, with 47,000 of those in Japan. Thus, despite the high Japanese military budget of $50 billion per year, Japan remained dependent on the United States for protection.

President Clinton enjoyed favorable relations with Russian President Boris Yeltsin, even though Christopher often reiterated the U.S. concern that Yeltsin's pursuit of war in Chechnya hurt Russia's chances of winning full-fledged membership in the G-7. The administration also helped Yeltsin defeat ultranationalist opponents in the 1996 elections. U.S. interests in terms of Russia included assisting the transition to democracy and free-market capitalism, along with assuaging Russian fears about NATO expansion and intervention in the Balkans.

The Clinton administration pursued peace in Northern Ireland during Christopher's tenure as well. In 1994 the United States made overtures to Sinn Fein's Gerry Adams in the hope of convincing him to bring his organization to the bargaining table. The granting of Adams's visa to visit the United States was controversial, and Christopher argued against it, along with Attorney General Janet Reno. Moreover, it appeared that Clinton might have been trying to gain support among the 45 million Americans who claim Irish ancestry. Despite the controversial nature of the visa, negotiations involving all parties following Adams's U.S. visit led to a fragile peace accord in April 1998—named the Good Friday agreements for the Christian holiday on which they were signed.

Of course, the Clinton administration made the peace process in the Middle East a priority during Christopher's tenure as well. Christopher made more than twenty trips to the Middle East in his four years as secretary of state, which indicates how personally significant it was to him to contribute to peace in that troubled region. The administration achieved some early success in this area, with the historic White House handshake between Palestine Liberation Organization leader Yasser Arafat and Israeli president Yitzakh Rabin and a peace agreement between Jordan and Israel. The assassination of Rabin and the rise of Benjamin Netanyahu dampened peace efforts.

The communist Castro regime in Cuba remained a thorn in the United States' side during Christopher's tenure. Congress passed the Helms–Burton act, which imposed economic sanctions on non-U.S.-based companies that did business in Cuba, and it wrote into law the U.S. economic embargo of Cuba so that presidential action alone could not lift it. Initially the administration opposed the law, but after Cuba shot down two planes operated by a Miami-based dissident group, Christopher recommended that Clinton sign it because Congress would likely have passed it over his veto anyway.

Jimmy Carter, the president in whose service Warren Christopher made his first great mark in foreign policy, has become known as a model former president through his work as a peacemaker in international affairs. Ironically, Christopher may also become well known for his activities after leaving office, but on the domestic front. With the 2000 presidential election results in Florida in dispute, Democratic candidate Al Gore sent Christopher to that state to serve as one of his point men and spokespersons in his court challenges and attempts to force a manual recount of disputed ballots. Christopher's role diminished when the battle shifted almost completely to the courts, especially the U.S. Supreme Court, which eventually rejected Gore's challenge.

Warren Minor Christopher was neither a great nor a terrible secretary of state. Considering that he was part of an administration not very interested in foreign affairs and faced a nativist and isolationist Congressional majority, his successes—and there were many—stand out all the more. Christopher will be remembered as a loyal servant of Democratic presidents and the interests and ideals of his party.

BIBLIOGRAPHICAL ESSAY

Currently, there are no biographies of Warren Christopher in print. In terms of his service in the Carter administration, *Working in the World: Jimmy Carter and the Making of American Foreign Policy* (2000), by Robert A. Strong, is a comprehensive analysis of the administration's successes and failures, with a focus on the successes.

Stephen M. Walt's "Two Cheers for Clinton's Foreign Policy," *Foreign Affairs*, 79, no. 2 (March/April 2000, pp. 63–79), is a clear analysis of the goals and achievements of the Clinton foreign policy team. Stephen Schlesinger's "The End of Idealism: Foreign Policy in the Clinton Years," *World Policy Journal* (winter 1998/99), briefly covers the first six years of Clinton foreign policy. Christopher's own "America's Leadership, America's Opportunity," *Foreign Policy* (1995), presents his theory of foreign policy and achievements of the Clinton administration midway through its first term. Also, Christopher's *In the Stream of History: Shaping Foreign Policy for a New Era* (1998) is a collection of his speeches while secretary of state.

David Jackson

HENRY CLAY (1777–1852)

Served 1825–1829
Appointed by President John Quincy Adams
Democratic-Republican

Henry Clay is best known as a perennial contender for the presidency between 1824 and 1850 and as a giant in the House of Representatives and the Senate between 1808 and 1852. His chief claims to fame stem from his advocacy of the "American System," an elaborate nationalistic program that included protectionism, federal support for internal improvements, and a national bank; his instrumental role in ending bitter sectional controversies in 1833 over Southern nullification of the Tariff of 1828 and in 1850 over the admission of California and organization of territories acquired from Mexico; and his powerful championship of Western interests.

Clay's prominence in domestic affairs has all but obscured his important involvement in debates on U.S. foreign policy before he became secretary of state and has shrouded his activities as secretary. Before the War of 1812, Clay was a vehement advocate of war with Britain. Between 1815 and 1824, he was an eloquent champion of the recognition of the new states of Latin America. He also joined Daniel Webster in calling for active support for the Greeks in their struggle against Ottoman rule. Although his involvement in actual diplomacy had been restricted to service as a peace negotiator with Albert Gallatin and John Quincy Adams at Ghent, during these years Clay developed a sophisticated and innovative foreign policy program. His prominent position in Congress and leading role in foreign policy debates made his selection to head the Department of State both plausible and legitimate.

Clay's appointment aroused bitter partisan controversy, and his decision to accept the appointment in the Adams administration was a serious political mistake from which he never fully recovered. Clay hoped both to make a major contribution to U.S. foreign policy and to advance his chances for the presidency. He accomplished neither, and his years at the Department of Sate were, perhaps, the most unhappy and unsuccessful period of his political career.

Clay was born on April 12, 1777, near Richmond in Hanover County, Virginia. His formal education was scanty, but with the encouragement of the brilliant legal and constitutional scholar and teacher of Jefferson and Madison, George Wythe, whom Clay served as a secretary, he read law and was admitted to the bar in both Virginia and Kentucky in 1797. He opened a law office in Frankfurt, Kentucky, in that year and quickly established himself as an able champion of landholders, capitalists, and entrepreneurs. In 1799, he married the daughter of one of Lexington's most prominent and influential families and within a few years was comfortably seated among the elite in Kentucky.

Clay was active in Kentucky politics virtually from the moment of his arrival. Possessed of great charm and an outgoing personality, he became the drinking and gambling companion of a number of prominent Kentuckians and acquired a reputation as a fearless risk taker, an attribute highly regarded in the new community and especially suited to the rough and tumble of frontier politics. In Virginia, he had early developed an interest in debating and demonstrated a flair for public speaking; his success at both seems to have derived more from style than from substance. Initially, Clay honed his talents in support of various Jeffersonian Republican causes, and in Kentucky he initially achieved recognition for his support of liberal causes. By 1803, however, he had already begun to establish himself as Lexington's most promising conservative spokesman.

Clay's rise to prominence in national politics was rapid. In 1803 he entered the state legislature, which in 1806 and 1810 appointed him to fill one-session vacancies in the U.S. Senate. In late 1810, however, he won popular election to the U.S. House of Representatives, and one indication of his success and effectiveness is that, following his first election to the House, he was chosen speaker by his colleagues.

Clay remained in the House of Representatives until January 1814, when he resigned to join Gallatin and Adams in Ghent. Following the successful peace negotiations, Clay returned to the House where he remained, except for two years, until assuming duties as John Quincy Adams's secretary of state in 1825. During that time he firmly established himself as a champion of Western interests and the chief spokesman for the American System. He also emerged as the chief critic of the foreign policy of the Monroe administration and the diplomacy of John Quincy Adams.

Clay's foreign policy emerged out of his domestic policy and rested on vigorous nationalism and persistent Anglophobia, both of which were reflected in his determination to free the United States from its economic dependence on Britain. During the decade before the War of 1812, Clay promoted modest tariff protection and federally funded internal improvements to facilitate the transport of western goods to eastern markets. He also argued that although the United States would likely remain primarily an exporter of raw materials and foodstuffs and continue to import the bulk of its manufactured goods, the federal government ought to encourage local manufacturing to reduce American dependence on foreign economies wherever possible. He did not think the United States was likely to become an exporter of manufactured goods during this period.

The dramatic rise in domestic manufacturing before and during the war, combined with the withering of overseas markets for American raw materials and foodstuffs and the rise of economic nationalism on the Continent after the war, caused Clay to change his ideas. In 1816, as British goods began to flood the American market, he perceived a willful British conspiracy to destroy American industry and to maintain the United States as an economic colony. Thereafter Clay became the most eloquent and unwavering champion of protectionism and the leading advocate of full-scale industrialization. Protectionism, he thought, was necessary to save the American economy from British domination; industrialization was essential to provide a stable, secure home market to replace the decaying foreign market.

In developing these programs, Clay promoted a fundamental revision of the American political economy. He advocated a revived form of mercantilism in which all sectors of the American economy, guided, rationalized, and supported by the federal government, would prosper within a balanced, diversified, and largely self-sufficient system. Furthermore, anticipating that industrialization would soon provide Americans with a surplus of manufactured goods available for export, he also promoted an aggressive foreign policy aimed primarily at expanding future U.S. trade. In the endeavor, too, Clay regarded Britain as America's enemy.

Clay focused his attention on Latin America, which he saw as an area of extraordinary opportunity for U.S. merchants and manufacturers. Between 1815 and 1825, he insisted that the United States assume a predominant role in the Latin American insurgency and strive to preempt Britain and the Continental powers from securing primary influence and economic control of the new nations. He promoted the establishment of a hemispheric economic system similar to his domestic program in which the United States would provide a market for a wide variety of Latin American raw materials and become the chief source for Latin America's imports of manufactured products. This system, he hoped, would lay the basis for hemispheric unity, complete the separation of Latin America from Europe, and establish the New World as a counterpoise to the Old. Clay thus became America's first advocate of "Good Neighborism."

Clay's support for the Latin American insurgents stemmed from more than nationalism and the desire for a profitable economic relationship. He also fully subscribed to the notion that the United States had a clear mission to spread republican ideals and institutions throughout the world. Latin America provided the most promising immediate outlet for this task. Clay believed that in addition to struggling for political independence, the Latin American insurgents were themselves engaged in liberal revolutions, which America had a responsibility to support. Throughout the decade following the Peace of Ghent, he insisted that it was essential that the United States provide encouragement and material support for the insurgents to prevent reactionaries and agents of the European powers from dominating and guiding the newly emerging nations. Clay consistently opposed attempts by both the Madison and Monroe administrations to tighten American neutrality laws and advocated full support for the insurgents short of actual military involvement. He also established himself as the leading proponent of early recognition of the new Latin American nations.

Clay's sympathy and support for the insurgents and their cause won him a good deal of popular support but aroused the ire of the administration. Secretary of State Adams had solid practical, strategic, and economic reasons for opposing Clay. Clay's assertive policies threatened America's substantial licensed commerce with Cuba (which had not risen in rebellion), jeopardized Adams's negotiations with Spanish minister Luis de Onís over Florida and the Spanish-American boundary west of the Mississippi River, and threatened to precipitate European intervention in support of Spain. Unlike Clay, Adams doubted that the new states of Latin

American would provide any substantial market for American goods and thought it foolish to destroy a flourishing commerce with Cuba in anticipation of a not very promising substitute.

Adams and Clay also disagreed on the means of fulfilling the American Mission. Clay was optimistic and promoted an active involvement in liberal causes; Adams was pessimistic and cautious. The secretary doubted that there was much likelihood that Latin America would develop republican institutions and chose to view the struggle solely in practical terms. Yet, Adams was not hostile to the promotion of international liberalism. He merely preferred that the American Mission be undertaken slowly, realistically, and through diplomacy aimed at establishing liberal principles. Thus, whereas Clay based his policy toward Latin America on direct action in support of liberal movements and concern for American economic development, Adams based his programs on caution and patient diplomacy.

The differences between Clay and Adams were mainly differences of degree, tactics, and timing. There was no fundamental conflict in the views of the two men, and there were also broad areas of positive agreement, particularly on the role of Britain in the New World. Clay firmly supported Adams's attempts to break down British colonialism in the Caribbean, and both wanted to eliminate the special privileges British merchants had secured in Latin America. Both also wanted to ensure that neither Britain nor any other European nation acquired predominant influence or control of the economies of the new nations of Latin America in the future.

Following the ratification of the Adams–Onís treaty, Monroe began the recognition process with the new states of Latin America. And Adams and Clay began to make peace with each other. Although Clay had vehemently castigated Adams for relinquishing America's weak claims to Texas in the Spanish treaty, Clay came to understand that Adams's retreat was merely tactical. Following the enunciation of the Monroe Doctrine in 1823, which Clay warmly applauded, the two leaders moved even closer together.

In 1825, there was little of substance that separated Adams and Clay, although they were hardly good friends or firm political allies. The two men were fundamentally different: Adams was essentially a dour New Englander possessed of an almost unbearable sense of duty, responsibility, and seriousness; Clay was convivial, charming, and immensely social. On a number of occasions, beginning with their association at Ghent, the two were openly frustrated with each other. Both were also political rivals with vaunting ambition, though Adams's was far more subtle that Clay's.

The hostility between Clay and Adams between 1818 and 1821 was far better known than their rapprochement after 1821, and therefore it came as a considerable surprise when Adams chose Clay to be his secretary of state in 1825. Four candidates, Adams, Clay, Andrew Jackson, and William Crawford, had campaigned for the presidency in 1824, and Jackson had won a plurality of both the popular and electoral votes, with Adams a close second. Clay narrowly defeated Crawford in the popular vote but received fewer electoral votes and so was out of the contest when the decision went to the House of Representatives. Because Crawford had suffered a paralytic stroke during the campaign, he was not a serious contender. Although Clay was no longer a candidate, he still controlled a substantial body of votes and therefore effectively had the power to choose the next president. After considerable reflection and good measure of political calculation, and after meeting with Adams, Clay decided to instruct his political allies in the House to cast their votes for

Adams. With those votes, Adams easily triumphed, and when Adams subsequently offered Clay the leading cabinet post, opponents of both charged that the two had made a "corrupt bargain."

There is no evidence that Adams and Clay made any kind of a deal or even had come to an implicit understanding before the House vote, and Adams's intensely puritanical character makes such an agreement highly unlikely. The charges levied against Adams and Clay were essentially partisan attempts to embarrass the administration, to frustrate Clay's presidential aspirations, and to promote the candidacy of Jackson in 1828. There is also an overwhelming logic that accounts for Clay's action. In addition to Clay's hostility toward the elevation of an inexperienced military hero to the presidency, Jackson was Clay's primary political rival in the West. If Jackson's supporters were looking forward to 1828, so, too, was Clay. Furthermore, in terms of domestic issues, Jackson's position was unclear on a number of issues Clay thought crucial. Adams, on the other hand, had adopted an explicit nationalistic program that was entirely satisfactory to Clay. Furthermore, Clay's hostility towards Adams's foreign policy had all but evaporated by 1824.

Although Adams continued to have reservations about Clay's character, he had respect for his ability, and it was far better to have Clay inside the administration than outside as an articulate and popular critic. And of course, Clay did control enough votes to swing the election to Adams. Except for a few disagreements on minor issues, Adams and Clay had a harmonious relationship. Both were fully committed to American commercial and territorial expansion, and the only essential difference in their tactics was that Clay tended to be more belligerent than Adams, who in the case of negotiations with both France and Brazil had to restrain his secretary. Otherwise, Adams left foreign policy in Clay's capable hands.

By the time Clay assumed his duties as secretary of state, commercial relations with Britain had been restored by the Convention of 1815, negotiated by Clay and Albert Gallatin, which had been extended for 10 years in 1818. According to this agreement, the United States secured reciprocity in direct trade with the British Isles in goods of national origin and access to certain British ports in India and the East Indies on a most-favored-nation basis. The agreements did not include trade with the British West Indies, however, and negotiations over the terms of that trade remained a source of contention throughout the Adams administration.

Attempts to secure equal access to the British West Indies had led to retaliation by both nations that had effectively closed the British West Indies to American merchants. Clay had fully supported a firm American policy, but by 1826, when negotiations over the issue resumed, he expressed willingness to compromise. A chief obstacle to peaceful settlement had been the U.S. demand for access on terms provided all British colonials and the right to ship West Indian goods to any port around the world. The British had refused to yield on the principle of imperial preference and to allow foreigners to carry colonial goods to foreign markets. In 1826, however, under pressure from West Indian planters, Britain agreed to open its West Indian ports to general commerce, but continued to insist on imperial preference. Britain also insisted that before American merchants would be allowed to enter their ports, the United States would have to end its retaliatory discriminatory policy. Clay agreed to accept the British demand for imperial preference, but before the Congress could agree to abrogate its discriminatory policies, negotiations were suspended. In 1827, Britain opened its West Indian ports to other nations but refused to reopen negotiations with the United States. In an agreement with Britain in 1826 on other issues, the provisions of the Convention of 1818 were continued. The West Indies issue remained unresolved throughout the remainder of the Adams administration. Significant in the diplomacy was the willingness of Clay and Adams to compromise. They were frustrated by congressional obstructionism and bad timing.

Clay also failed to resolve two annoying boundary questions with Britain in the negotiation of 1827. They first dealt with the northeastern boundary of Maine, an issue not settled until the Webster–Ashburton treaty of 1842. The second concerned the Oregon boundary. Clay had instructed Albert Gallatin to attempt to secure an extension of the 49th parallel to the Pacific and to offer Britain, as part of a compromise, the right to navigate the Columbia River through American territory. Clay hoped that British agreement on the Columbia River navigation would strengthen American claims to navigation on the St. Lawrence. The British, however, were unwilling to concede on the boundary, and Gallatin chose not to press the issue of navigation of the St. Lawrence. Oregon was left open to joint occupation, and the two nations did not resolve the boundary question until 1846. Clay's negotiations with Britain, therefore, achieved little.

Clay fared no better in relations with France. Between 1815 and 1825, Franco-American relations had been stormy. In an attempt to rebuild its economy and international prestige following the end of the Napoleonic wars, France embarked on an intensely nationalistic economic program that severely reduced Franco-American commerce, and the French government would not consider the reciprocal abolition of discriminatory port duties. In addition, American merchants had levied enormous claims against France for French depredations on American shipping between 1806 and 1815 that France refused to consider. During the 1820s, Clay had adopted a belligerent position toward France, and he continued this approach as secretary of state, suggesting the use of privateers against French shipping if the French remained unwilling to negotiate a settlement. Adams, however, rejected the threat or use of force and suggested arbitration of some of the issues, but France continued to procrastinate and Franco-American issues, too, remained unresolved.

Although Clay was frustrated in dealing with Britain and France, he did have some success in negotiations with the smaller nations of Western Europe. He devoted considerable time and energy to negotiations on claim settlements for U.S. citizens with Sweden, Denmark, Naples, and Holland, and he not only secured reasonable compensation for the U.S. claimants, but he also gained official acceptance of many American liberal trade principles.

Clay was also successful in securing the reciprocal abolition of discriminating port duties and extension of reciprocity to indirect as well as direct trade in agreements with Denmark and the Danish West Indies, the Hanseatic cities, Prussia, Sweden, Norway and its West Indian colony of St. Barthelemy, and Austria. Clay also inaugurated negotiations with the Ottoman Empire that were completed during the following administration. In each of these cases, Clay enthusiastically carried forward Adams's program of commercial expansion.

Most of Clay's interest, however, centered on the new nations of Latin America. His policies aimed at opening all of independent Latin America to American merchants on terms of competitive equality with all nations and eliminating all remaining special privileges and other favoritism granted by the new nations to the nations of the Old World. This program had been clearly laid out during the Monroe administration by Secretary of State Adams in the opening of relations with Colombia; Clay's task was to implement these policies with the other nations of Latin America.

One of Clay's basic aims in relations with Latin America was to promote harmony and friendship. In this effort, he clearly failed. Throughout most of his tenure, Clay defended American claims against Brazil and the Republic of Buenos Aires arising from their seizures of American ships during a conflict between these two countries. Although American claims were settled in the favor of Americans and Buenos Aires accepted the American definition of a legal blockade, the controversies left a bitter aftertaste. For a short time during the course of discussions with Brazil, the U.S. minister demanded his passports, and relations were broken. Clay adopted a stern policy but was overruled by Adams. Relations with Mexico similarly suffered as Clay's minister, Joel Poinsett, attempted to purchase Texas, became involved in domestic Mexican politics, and was finally expelled from the country.

Clay was more successful in his commercial negotiations. He sought to secure full reciprocity in all trade except coastal and absolute equality in Latin American commerce. He therefore resisted Latin American inclinations to establish special arrangements with Spain or, in Brazil's case, Portugal or among the Latin American nations themselves. In the case of Brazil, Clay reluctantly accepted Brazil's decision to provide Portugal with special privileges. With Mexico, Clay could not gain reciprocity and had to settle for most-favored-nation status only. Elsewhere, however, Clay did secure equality with Europe and nearly perfect reciprocity. Only in negotiations with the Federation of Central America did Clay achieve all his ends—both most-favored-nation treatment and perfect reciprocity.

Clay's final frustration in implementing his Latin American policy occurred in American involvement in the Panama Congress of 1826. As early as 1821, Simón Bolívar proposed that all the new nations of Latin America meet to consider "union, association, and perpetual federation." Adams was sympathetic to the proposal and had adopted a policy of "watchful waiting." Clay was especially eager to participate in such a hemispheric meeting, and when in 1825, Mexico, Colombia, and the United Provinces of Central America formally invited the United States to participate in a conference in Panama, Clay and Adams readily agreed to participate. In addition to providing an opportunity to strengthen the bonds of friendship between Latin America and the United States, the conference also offered Clay and Adams the possibility for securing common agreement in questions of international law and liberal commercial principles and the chance to emphasize the danger of European political influence in the new nations. Central to the discussions among the Latin Americans themselves, however, were issues relating to the slave trade, relations with the black republic of Haiti, the continuing war with Spain, and the question of continued Spanish control of Cuba and Puerto Rico.

Of all the Spanish colonies in the Western Hemisphere, only Cuba and Puerto Rico had not risen in rebellion. Because Spain had opened Cuba to restricted but highly profitable commerce to American merchants, the United States did not provide the same moral and diplomatic support for the Cuban minority that wished to join the insurgents as it had for insurgents elsewhere. Of greatest concern was the prospect that Spain would cede Cuba to Britain or France, or that revolution would lead to a race war and foreign intervention. During Clay's tenure, new worries arose over the intentions of Mexico and Colombia, alone or in concert, to marshal an invasion of Cuba. In 1824 Bolívar had raised the threat of just such an invasion to apply pressure on Spain for a peace settlement.

Clay initially was ambivalent about a revolution in Cuba. He fully supported the expulsion of Spain from the New World (and accepted Jefferson's "No-Transfer" rule), but he understood that American merchants had much to lose by an extension of warfare to Cuba, and he doubted that Cuba itself was ready for independence. The latter concern predominated, and Clay decided that it was more in the interest of both the Cubans and American merchants that Spain retain its colony. He thus found himself in the awkward position of promoting Spain's retention of the island.

It was also clearly in the interest of the Untied States and the Latin Americans that Spain end its increasingly futile efforts to reconquer its lost colonies. In 1825, after momentarily supporting a British proposal to offer Spain a tripartite pledge by Britain, France, and the United States guaranteeing its control of Cuba in return for Spain's agreement to an armistice, Clay rejected the idea, arguing that such a pledge might encourage Spain to continue the war. He decided to appeal directly to Russia for mediation and to use that appeal to delay an aggressive action from Colombia or Mexico. Russia's lack of enthusiasm for the project led to delay and eventual abandonment of the scheme.

When Adams informed the U.S. Congress of his intention to have the United States participate in the Panama Congress and shortly thereafter nominated as American representatives three Clay partisans, Richard C. Anderson, Jr., of Kentucky and John Sergeant of Pennsylvania, as ministers and Williams B. Rochester of New York as secretary to the mission, an acrimonious political debate erupted. Between January and May 1826, Jacksonians denounced virtually every aspect of the project and vilified Adams and Clay. Although Adams and Clay had made it clear to the Latin Americans and Congress that the United States would not compromise its neutrality in the Latin American war with Spain or consider any formal alliance with the Latin Americans, Jackson's partisans charged that Clay had seized control of American policy and that his schemes threatened both American neutrality and political isolationism. Some charged that Clay was promoting a revolution in Cuba that portended a race war, and Southerners denounced any participation in discussion relating to the slave trade and Haiti. Following a particularly hostile attack on Clay by John Randolph of Virginia, Clay challenged Randolph to a duel in which shots were fired but neither was hurt. Although Congress eventually supported participation, the nature of the debate thoroughly alienated Latin Americans, and its length delayed the dispatch of instructions to the American delegates. Clay instructed the delegates to promote Latin American acceptance of American commercial principles, warn Latin American about European interference in the domestic affairs, and advocate adoption of republican institutions. He also restated American opposition to a Latin American invasion of Cuba. Due to pressures from Southerners, Clay remained silent on proposals for a strengthened anti-slave trade convention and recognition of Haiti.

The American delegates, however, never made it to the conference. Anderson died of tropical fever en route to the conference from his post in Bogota, and Sergeant decided to postpone his departure for Panama until the fall. Clay chose

Poinsett, a Calhounite, to replace Anderson. Meanwhile, the Panama Congress had opened without American representation, and after drawing up a number of draft agreements, adjourned in mid-July with an agreement to reconvene in Tacabaya, Mexico, in the following January. Sergeant and Poinsett arrived in Mexico in January, but the failure of the Panama draft treaties to win approval in several of the Latin American nations meant that the Congress never reconvened.

Clay's failure to secure a better relationship with the Latin Americans at Panama was compounded by awareness that in the absence of representation by the American delegates, the British representative had advanced Britain's prestige at America's expense. Adding to Clay's frustration was a loss of faith in Latin American liberalism. In 1827, Bolívar wrote Clay expressing his gratitude for Clay's support for the Latin American cause. Clay, however, had received information from Americans in Latin America suggesting that Bolívar had dictatorial intentions, and in 1828, Clay responded to Bolívar's note in a cold fashion that ended their correspondence.

Clay had arrived at the State Department with a well-developed foreign policy and the intention to continue the diplomatic programs established by his predecessor, which he integrated with his broad domestic program. The merger of Adams's foreign policy with Clay's domestic policy produced a broad national program that had distinctly modern overtones. Clay perceived a day in which an economically independent, industrialized United States would dominate the Western Hemisphere and satisfy its ideological destiny to promote republicanism abroad. His programs also anticipated the extension of American imperial power around the globe.

Clay's service, however, was marked chiefly by failure and frustration. The bitterly contested election of 1824 created a body of political rivals intent on embarrassing the Adams administration and was largely successful in its efforts. In addition, by 1828 the growth of self-conscious sectionalism replaced the nationalism of the postwar period and also thwarted attempts to establish a nationalistic program. Finally, the determination of Britain to maintain its global supremacy, of France to rebuild its status in Europe, and of the new Latin American nations to find their own places in world affairs created insuperable obstacles to the fulfillment of Clay's purposes.

Following the defeat of Adams in the election of 1828, Clay was out of office until 1831, when he returned to the Senate. There, with the support of Daniel Webster, he led the fight against Jackson and Jacksonianism and for his American System. In 1832, he campaigned again against Jackson and was defeated. After failing to win the Whig Party nomination for president in 1840, he tried once more in 1844 and was successful. His equivocal position on the annexation of Texas during the campaign contributed substantially to his defeat by James K. Polk.

Clay's most important contributions lay in his commanding role in the resolution of two major sectional crises. In 1833, he sponsored the compromise tariff bill that defused a bitter controversy between South Carolina and the federal government, and later he was instrumental in securing the Compromise of 1850, which postponed civil war for a decade. That compromise marked Clay's final triumph. He died in Washington in 1852, the same year as his great rival and also a giant in the Senate and former secretary of state, Daniel Webster.

Clay's tangible contributions as secretary of state were meager, but his role was significant in suggesting a new direction for foreign affairs and in laying the basis for modern American diplomacy. Although he lacked the seriousness and Roman sense of duty of Adams, the mythological qualities of his great rival Jackson, and the thundering presence of Webster, he possessed a national vision that was, perhaps, superior to them all. His fame justifiable rests on this vision and his service at the "Great Pacificator."

BIBLIOGRAPHICAL ESSAY

It is difficult to provide a list of primary and secondary sources that does justice to the vast amount of materials relating to Clay and his times. Yet, this essay should be able to serve as an introduction to such material. The Clay Family Papers are in the Manuscript Division of the Library of Congress. Included are the papers of Henry and Thomas J. Clay and the papers of other Clay family members. The collection includes approximately twenty thousand documents. John J. McDonough, "Kentuckiana in the Manuscript Division, Library of Congress," *Filson Club History Quarterly* LXII (July 1958), is an indispensable guide to the Library's Kentucky and Kentucky-related collections. Large collections of Clay papers are also to be found in the Chicago Historical Society, Duke University, the Filson Club, Indiana University, the New York Historical Society, the University of Kentucky, and the University of Virginia.

The Clay Papers Project in the King Library of the University of Kentucky has copies of practically all known Clay materials in public and private hands. The Project has published the most important documents in eleven volumes under the title *The Papers of Henry Clay* (1959–1992). Scholars also should consult Calvin Colton (ed.), *The Private Correspondence of Henry Clay* (1856) and Calvin Colton (ed.), *The Papers of Henry Clay*, 6 volumes (1857). Other paper collections and paper projects of great value are Harold Moser (ed.), *Guide and Index to the Microfilm Editions* (1987), which accompanies the entire corpus of the Andrew Jackson Papers on microfilm, organized by the director of the Jackson Paper Project; John Spencer Bassett, *Correspondence of Andrew Jackson*, 6 volumes (1926–1935); W. Edwin Hamphill et al. (eds.), *The Papers of John C. Calhoun* (1959–); and Charles M. Wiltse et al. (eds.), *The Papers of Daniel Webster, Correspondence*, 7 volumes (1974–1986); and *Speeches and Formal Writings* 2 volumes (1986, 1988).

Additional necessary published primary sources to consult include Charles Francis Adams, (ed.), *Memoirs of John Quincy Adams*, 12 volumes (1874–1877); Thomas Hart Benton, *Thirty Years' View*, 2 volumes (1865); Herbert Weaver et al. (eds.), *Correspondence of James K. Polk*, 7 volumes (1969–); Lyon G. Tyler, *The Letters and Times of the Tylers*, 3 volumes (1896, 1970); and John C. Fitzpatrick (ed.), *Autobiography of Martin Van Buren* (1920).

The best biography of Harry of the West is Robert V. Remini, *Henry Clay: Statesman for the Union* (1991). Older biographies, which are still useful, include Clement Eaton, *Henry Clay and the Art of American Politics* (1957); Glyndon G. Van Deusen's excellent *The Life of Henry Clay: Spokesman of the New West* (1937); Calvin Colton, *The Life and Times of Henry Clay*, 2 volumes (1856); and Carl Schurz, *Life of Henry Clay*, 2 volumes (1887). Please also see George R. Poage, *Henry Clay and the Whig Party* (1936), which covers the last part of Clay's life; and Robert Seager II, "Henry Clay and the Politics of Compromise and Non-Compromise," *Register of the Kentucky Historical Society*, LXXXV (winter 1987).

For works important to understanding Clay's political thought, including his American System and the ideologies of the Whig and Democratic parties, see

Daniel Walker Howe's excellent analysis in "Henry Clay: Ideologue of the Center," in his *The Political Culture of the American Whigs* (1979); and Howe's *The American Whigs: An Anthology* (1973); Glyndon G. Van Deusen " Some Aspects of Whig Thought and Theory in the Jacksonian Period," *American Historical Review*, LXIII (1958); Thomas Brown, *Politics and Statesmanship: Essays on the American Whig Party* (1985); Rush Welter, *The Mind of America, 1830–1860* (1975); John Ashworth, *"Agrarian δ Aristocrats": Party Political Ideology in the United States 1837–1846* (1983); Major L. Wilson, *Space, Time, and Freedom: The Quest for Nationality and the Irrepressible Conflict* (1974); Jean H. Baker, *Affairs of Party* (1983), and Marvin Meyer's classic *The Jacksonian Persuasion* (1957).

For Clay's early career, the War of 1812, and the peace of 1814, see Merrill D. Peterson, *The Great Triumvirate: Webster, Clay and Calhoun* (1987), and George Dangerfield, *The Era of Good Feelings* (1952), both of whom have insightful portraits of Clay; Fred L. Engelman, *The Peace of Christmas Eve* (1962); Donald R. Hickey, *The War of 1812: A Forgotten Conflict* (1989); Lawrence Kaplan, *Entangling Alliances with None: American Foreign Policy in the Age of Jefferson* (1987); Bradford Perkins, *Castlereagh and Adams: England and the United States, 1812–1823* (1964); J. C. A. Stagg, *Mr. Madison's War: Politics, Diplomacy, and Warfare in the Early American Republic 1783–1830* (1983); and Frank A. Updyke, *The Diplomacy of the War of 1812* (1912).

For the transition from the First to Second Party System and the dynamics of Second Party System, please see Richard Hofstadter's outstanding, *The Idea of the Party System* (1972). Ralph Katchem, *President's Above Party* (1984); Shaw Livermore, Jr.'s *The Twilight of Federalism: The Disintegration of the Federalist Party 1815–1830* (1962); Richard P. McCormick's *The Second American Party System: Party Formation in the Jacksonian Era* (1966); and *The Presidential Game: The Origins of American Presidential Politics* (1982) are critical to understanding their subjects; Robert V. Remini, *Martin Van Buren and the Making of the Democratic Party* (1959); and Michael Wallace, "Changing Concepts of Party in the United States: New York 1815–1825," *American Historical Review*, LXXV (1968) are also informative.

The scholarly works on Jackson and his era include Arthur M. Schlesinger, Jr.'s classic, *The Age of Jackson* (1945); Glyndon G. Van Deusen, *The Jacksonian Era, 1828–1848* (1959), which emphasizes Clay's role; Bruce Collins, "The Ideology of the Ante-Bellum Northern Democrats," *Journal of American Studies*, IX (April 1977); Louis Hartz, *The Liberal Tradition in America; An Interpretation of American Political Thought since the Revolution* (1955); Robert Kelley, *The Cultural Pattern in American Politics: The First Century* (1979); Lawrence F. Kohl, *The Politics of Individualism: Parties and the American Character in the Jacksonian Era* (1989); Roy Nichols, *The Invention of the American Political Parties* (1969); and Joel Silby, *The Partisan Imperative: The Dynamics of American Politics before the Civil War* (1985).

Of interest to students of the controversy that has continued to shadow the reputations of both Clay and Adams are William G. Morgan's two articles, "The 'Corrupt Bargain' Charge against Clay and Adams: An Historiographical Analysis," *Filson Club Historical Quarterly*, XLII (April 1968) and "Henry Clay's Biographers and the 'Corrupt Bargain' Charge," *Register of the Kentucky Historical Society*, LXVI (1968); and M. J. Heale, *The Presidential Quest: Candidates and Images in American Political Culture* (1982).

Mary W. M. Hargreaves, *The Presidency of John Quincy Adams* (1958), is very helpful to an understanding of Clay's role as secretary of state. In that regard, see also Theodore E. Burton, "Henry Clay" in Samuel Flagg Bemis (ed.), *The Secretaries of State and Their Diplomacy*, 17 volumes (1927–1967). For works on Clay and Latin American independence, please see Halford L. Hoskins, "The Hispanic American Policy of Henry Clay, 1816–1828," *Hispanic American Historical Review, VII* (1927); Joseph B. Lockey, *Pan-Americanism: Its Beginnings* (1920); J. Fred Rippy, *Rivalry of the United States and Great Britain over Latin America* (1928); William S. Robertson, "The Recognition of the Hispanic American Nations by the United States," *Hispanic-American Historical Review*, I (1918); and Arthur Preston Whitaker, *The United States and the Independence of Latin America, 1800–1830* (1941).

For other issues of foreign policy see Vernon G. Setser, *The Commercial Reciprocity Policy of the United States, 1774–1829* (1937); F. Lee Benns, *The American Struggle for the British West Indian Carrying Trade, 1815–1830* (1923); and Thomas B. Jones, " Henry Clay and Continental Expansion, 1820–1844," *Register of the Kentucky Historical Society*, LXXIII (1975).

For information on the election of 1828, its political consequences, and Clay's activities after his service as secretary of state, see Heale and Remini mentioned earlier and Florence Weston, *The Presidential Election of 1828* (1938, reprinted 1974); Robert V. Remini, *The Election of Andrew Jackson* (1963); Richard P. McCormick, *The Second American Party System: Party Formation in the Jacksonian Era* (1966); William J. Cooper, Jr., *The South and the Politics of Slavery, 1828–1856* (1978); and for a view counter to Cooper see George Rawlings Poage, *Henry Clay and the Whig Party* (1936, reprinted 1965).

Kinley Brauer

JOHN M. CLAYTON (1796–1856)

Served 1849–1850
Appointed by President Zachary Taylor
Whig

John Middleton Clayton, U.S. Senator (1829–1836, 1845–49, 1853–56) and secretary of state under Presidents Zachary Taylor and Millard Fillmore (8 March 1849–22 July 1850), was born in Dagsboro, Delaware, on July 24, 1796. The son of James Clayton, a tanner, miller, and farmer, and Sarah Middleton, he obtained his early schooling in academies at Berlin, Maryland, and Lewes and Milford, Delaware. Clayton then attended Yale College, graduating in 1815. Between 1815 and 1819, he served an apprenticeship in the law office of his cousin, Thomas Clayton, himself a future U.S. Senator and chief justice of the Delaware Supreme Court, and then studied law at Litchfield Law School in Connecticut. Clayton was admitted to the bar in 1819 and began his practice in Dover. In 1822, he married Sarah Ann Fisher, the daughter of a Camden, Delaware, physician. Clayton's wife died in 1825 following the birth of their second child. He never remarried.

Clayton's remarkable memory, devotion to duty, and drive, as well as his eloquence, charm, and skill at cross-examination, won him a reputation as one of Delaware's ablest lawyers and rising political stars. Influenced by his cousin and education at Yale, with its arch-Federalist college president Timothy Dwight, Clayton entered politics as an ardent Federalist and ally to John Quincy Adams. He battled Louis McLane and supporters of Andrew Jackson for political preeminence in Delaware. During the 1820s he occupied several state government posts, including clerk of both the state senate (1820) and house of representatives (1821), auditor of accounts (1821–24), member of the house of representatives (1824–26), and secretary of state (1826–28). As Delaware's secretary of state, Clayton used political spoils and oratorical prowess to advance the cause of the National Republican, or Whig, Party in helping Adams carry the state in the presidential election of 1828. Delaware Whigs rewarded Clayton's service to the party by electing him to the U.S. Senate in 1828, setting him on the road to national prominence.

During his first term in the U.S. Senate, Clayton championed Henry Clay's American System to foster economic development through a national bank, federal funding for internal improvements, and a protective tariff. A moderate Unionist, Clayton opposed the doctrine of state sovereignty expressed in South Carolina's nullification ordinance. He showed his Whig colors by accusing Jackson of exhibiting tyrannical tendencies of unbridled executive power in his veto of the recharter of the Second Bank of the United States, Indian removal policy, and use of political spoils.

Reelected to the Senate in 1835, Clayton chaired the Senate Judiciary Committee and took a greater interest in foreign affairs, where he advocated adherence to treaty provisions, commercial expansion, and a strong national defense to achieve world stability. Wary of British efforts to construct a canal across Central America closed to U.S. commerce, Clayton in 1835 sponsored a Senate resolution calling on President Jackson to open negotiations with governments in Central America and New Granada to secure a transit route open to all nations. Although little came of this resolution, it foreshadowed the negotiation of the Clayton–Bulwer Treaty of 1850. In response to the Franco-American war scare of the mid-1830s, which stemmed from France's failure to pay spoliation claims arising from the Napoleonic Wars, Clayton insisted that the French honor their treaty obligations. He also promoted a long-term national defense policy to protect the nation's security and commerce. This episode influenced Clayton's anti-French attitude during the Poussin Affair (1849–1850).

In December 1836, Clayton, weary of Democratic ascendancy in Washington and wanting to spend more time with his children, resigned from the Senate. Shortly thereafter he yielded to the urgings of local Whig leaders and succeeded his cousin as chief justice of the Delaware Supreme Court (1837–39). Sensing a Whig victory in 1840, he left the bench to campaign for the party's presidential candidate, William Henry Harrison. As a loyal supporter of Henry Clay, Clayton rejected any consideration to serve as Harrison's vice presidential running mate, a decision that proved costly when Harrison died after one month in office. Denied a cabinet post in the Harrison and Tyler administrations, Clayton focused on scientific farming at his home near New Castle, Delaware, becoming one of the country's leading agriculturalists. He maintained his power base in Delaware by practicing law and advising Whig state legislators and Governor William B. Cooper.

After failing to secure the second spot on the losing Whig ticket in 1844, Clayton returned to the U.S. Senate. He immediately focused on controversies with Great Britain and Mexico that threatened to produce war with both countries. As a Whig, he embraced Anglo-American friendship and commerce as essential to the success of the party's domestic economic policies. Accordingly, for reasons of security, economics, and politics he favored the Anglo-American Convention of 1846 that settled the Oregon boundary dispute. In voting for the agreement, Clayton believed that the United States was ill prepared for war with Great Britain, that such a conflict would damage U.S. commerce, and the treaty placed responsibility on Democratic President James K. Polk for abandoning the American claim to 54° 40′. Clayton, an opponent of territorial expansion, denounced the U.S. annexation of Texas as an immoral act that threatened to produce war with Mexico and reopen the divisive sectional debate on slavery extension. Although he believed that Polk had provoked the conflict and would not support annexation of Mexican territory, Clayton voted for war measures to ensure that the Whig Party would not suffer the same fate as the Federalist Party, which had opposed the War of 1812.

In 1848 Clayton deserted the thrice-defeated Clay and endorsed the triumphant Zachary Taylor for president. Although Taylor had never met Clayton, he appointed the Delaware Senator secretary of state on the recommendation of Governor John J. Crittenden of Kentucky, Clayton's longtime friend and Senate colleague. Unfortunately for Taylor, Clayton lacked experience, demeanor, or political clout to offer much promise of success in foreign policy or provide effective leadership in the president's cabinet. He had no experience dealing with foreign governments or formulating international policies. In the Senate, Clayton often allowed partisan considerations and political expediency, rather than national ideals, to influence foreign policy. He lacked tact, patience, firmness, and a stable character and was poorly organized. Clayton thus provided little leadership to a politically inexperienced president and the first newly elected administration in U.S. history to face opposition majorities in both houses of Congress.

As secretary of state, Clayton stressed commercial expansion, strict enforcement of American neutrality laws and treaty pledges, and defense of national honor. He achieved limited success in promoting American commercial expansion. In pursuit of trade with Pacific markets, Clayton secured only two minor commercial treaties with Hawaii and Brunei. He failed to act on recommendations to open Japan to American commerce that ultimately led to Matthew C. Perry's historic expeditions to Japan in 1853–1854 and the first U.S.–Japanese trade agreement. The leaders of Cochin China and Siam rebuffed Clayton's special mission to secure commercial treaties with both kingdoms. In the Western Hemisphere, Clayton's pursuit of trade agreements with Santo Domingo and Haiti to discourage British and French interest in acquiring Samaná Bay and Port au Prince, respectively, only produced a consular convention with Haiti. His effort to obtain guano from Peru for the restoration of agricultural lands along the Chesapeake Bay failed when the Peruvian government rejected the agreement. In Europe, Clayton urged recognition of Louis Kossuth's Hungarian revolution to take advantage of the new government's trade potential, but the infant government collapsed following a joint Austro-Russian invasion to restore Austrian control of Hungary.

Clayton's strict adherence to treaty obligations is evident in his enforcement of U.S. neutrality laws and interpretation of the Mexican Protocol. Clayton blocked the departure of a U.S. ship purchased and fitted out for war by the German Confederation until the German minister at Washington assured him that the vessel would not be used in the German–Danish war over Schleswig-Holstein. Clayton also did his utmost to prevent the departure of Narciso López's filibuster expeditions for Cuba. However, he also recognized the limits of American neutrality laws. When a group of alleged filibusters were unjustifiably seized off the Mexican Coast by Spanish authorities, Clayton vigorously contended for and ultimately secured their release. Regarding the Mexican Protocol, a document that clarified American intentions in modifying Article 9 (citizens rights) and deleting Article 10 (land grants in the ceded territories) during the negotiation of the Treaty of Guadalupe Hildalgo, Clayton held that it was merely a record of conversation lacking any legal force affecting the final terms of the treaty.

Clayton's lack of appreciation for diplomatic protocol and tendency to engage in "eagle screaming" to win popular support for the Taylor administration produced war scares with France and Portugal. The Poussin Affair, a foolish impasse, resulted from a war of words and petty name-calling between Clayton and both William Tell Poussin, the French minister at Washington, and Alexis de Tocqueville, the French Foreign Minister, over the U.S. government's refusal to compensate French claimants for tobacco seized by the U.S. Navy during the Mexican War and an American effort to salvage the French merchantman *Eugénie.* Taylor and Clayton's demand for Poussin's recall and their refusal to apologize to Tocqueville for the disagreeable correspondence between the secretary of state and the French minister at Washington made matters worse. French President Louis Napoleon, more interested in pursuing adventurist schemes in European politics, backed away from serious trouble with the United States by dismissing his entire cabinet and receiving William C. Rives, the new American minister at Paris, in a cordial manner. The General Armstrong Affair involved the destruction of an American privateer during the War of 1812. In the Treaty of Ghent, the United States renounced all war-related claims against Great Britain, but it immediately demanded reparations from Portugal for the loss of the ship. The U.S. government claimed that Portugal had violated its neutrality in the war by allowing the ship to be destroyed by British forces using the guns of a Portuguese fortress in the Azores. Portugal ignored American demands for redress for over three decades before the Taylor administration assumed an uncompromising stance in pressing for settlement of the claim. Clayton made extreme demands upon Portugal for indemnity, refused arbitration, and issued what was virtually an ultimatum for war. After Clayton left office cooler heads prevailed, and the claim was settled by arbitration in 1851 against the United States.

Clayton enjoyed his greatest success as a diplomat when he abandoned the Whig Party's aversion to the Monroe Doctrine to advance American hemispheric leadership. He referred to this axiom in opposing the transfer of Cuba to Britain. He also employed it to thwart French efforts to establish a protectorate in the Dominican Republic and to acquire extraterritorial rights in Haiti. More importantly, he used it during the negotiation of the Clayton–Bulwer Treaty of 1850 to guarantee American transit rights across Central America.

The Clayton–Bulwer Treaty of 1850, the major accomplishment of the short-lived Taylor administration, illustrates both the changing character of U.S. expansion from territorial aggrandizement to overseas commerce and the constant tension underlying Anglo-American relations throughout the nineteenth century. As secretary of state, Clayton contended that the United States should promote commercial expansion to foster a new era of progress. In accordance with the Whig Party's policy of compromise and peace with Great Britain, he deemed Anglo-American cooperation the cornerstone of this policy. The greatest challenge to this policy occurred in Central America, where American interest in acquiring a transit route to provide for the security of its recently acquired Pacific frontage (California and Oregon) and access to Pacific markets clashed with Britain's Mosquito protectorate, which might allow it to monopolize control over a proposed Nicaragua canal.

The Clayton–Bulwer Treaty, which perhaps averted a third Anglo-American war, tried to settle these differences. While recognizing the commercial importance of the proposed canal and agreeing to joint control and protection of it, the negotiators failed to adjust Anglo-American political differences on the isthmus, thus making it impossible to construct the waterway across Central America. According to the first article of the convention, the two countries pledged not to "occupy or fortify, or colonize, or assume or exercise any dominion over Nicaragua, Costa Rica, the Mosquito Coast, or any part of Central America." They also disavowed the use of "any alliance, connection, or influence that either may possess with any [Central American] State or Government through whose territory the said canal shall pass, for the purpose of acquiring or holding, directly or indirectly exclusive control of the proposed canal. . . . " Clayton believed that the agreement had terminated all British influence in the region, but the ambiguous language of Article 1 and declarations made by the negotiators immediately preceding the exchange of ratifications failed to specifically order Britain out of Central America. Furthermore, according to the British government, the vexing treaty provision recognized existing protectorates, alliances, and dominions so long as they were not employed to gain exclusive control over the proposed canal and only forbade future colonization of the region. Consequently, Britain refused to abandon the Mosquito protectorate, British Honduras (Belize), or its claim to the Bay Islands as dependencies of British Honduras. The two governments disagreed over the meaning of the treaty throughout the 1850s and experienced a war scare in 1856 before Britain began to recede from its position. With every late nineteenth-century American administration, beginning with Grant, asserting that the United States would unilaterally control any isthmian canal, the Clayton–Bulwer Treaty remained one of the most controversial diplomatic agreements in U.S. history until it was abrogated by the second Hay–Paunceforte Treaty in 1901.

During his 16-month tenure at the State Department, Clayton threatened to resign twice in the face of constant criticism from the press and Congress for his lack of political leadership during the debate on the Compromise of 1850 and distribution of patronage. The beleaguered secretary finally did so in late July 1850, shortly after President Taylor's death. Prompted by Democratic attacks on the Clayton–Bulwer Treaty as a violation of the Monroe Doctrine for permitting Britain to remain in Central America, Clayton returned to the Senate in 1853 to defend the agreement. In response to his chief critics, Lewis Cass (D-MI) and Stephen Douglas (D-IL), Clayton insisted that the treaty had evicted Great Britain from Central America by specifically prohibiting it from occupying or assuming any dominion in the region. The Pierce administration relied on Clayton to furnish arguments to deny the Mosquito protectorate, British ownership of the Bay Islands, and limit the extent of British Honduras to log-cutting rights acquired from Spain in 1786. The British government, fearful of U.S. aid to Russia during the Crimean War, appeared ready to accept the American interpretation of the treaty, but the American bombardment of Greytown in July 1854 delayed settlement of the dispute until 1860.

Recognizing that the Whig Party was doomed after its poor showing in the presidential election of 1852, Clayton hoped to build a Unionist coalition that would rally the nation around foreign policy issues, such as the enforcement of the Clayton–Bulwer Treaty. Passage of the Kansas–Nebraska Act of 1854 crushed his hopes and drove him to cooperation with the Know-Nothing Party. Alienated by the party's nomination of Millard Fillmore for president in 1856 and its inability to address the issue of slavery in the territories, Clayton became a political independent. During his final year in the Senate, he tried unsuccessfully to end the bloodshed between free and slave forces in Kansas. He died of kidney failure in Dover, Delaware, on November 9, 1856.

BIBLIOGRAPHICAL ESSAY

The most important primary source for Clayton's life is the collection of his papers in the Library of Congress. The bulk of the collection covers Clayton's tenure at the

State Department, particularly drafts and copies of letters written by him during the negotiation of the Clayton–Bulwer Treaty. In studying the treaty, one should also consult the papers of George P. Fisher, Clayton's secretary at the State Department, John J. Crittenden, and William Learned Marcy, secretary of state in the Pierce administration, which are all also located in the Library of Congress. The latter two offer valuable insight regarding Clayton's interpretation of the treaty. Clayton's correspondence with Robert Montgomery Bird, the editor of the *United States and North American Gazette*, a Philadelphia newspaper in which Clayton held part ownership and used to rally support for the treaty, are at the University of Pennsylvania. The complete collection of official dispatches between Clayton and Abbott Lawrence, the American minister at the Court of St. James's (1849–52), are found in the Abbott Lawrence Papers in Houghton Library at Harvard University. The papers of Henry Lytton Bulwer at the Public Record Office in London, England, help in understanding how the British minister overcame American objections to the Mosquito protectorate in concluding the treaty. Some of Clayton's diplomatic correspondence have been published in William R. Manning (ed.), *Diplomatic Correspondence of the United States: Inter-American Affairs, 1831–1860*, 12 volumes (1932–1939).

No published biography of Clayton exists. The most comprehensive work covering his political, diplomatic, and legal career as well as his personal life is Richard A. Wire, "John M. Clayton and the Search for Order: A Study in Whig Politics and Diplomacy" (1971). Mary Wilhelmine Williams, "John Middleton Clayton" in Samuel Flagg Bemis (ed.), *The American Secretaries of State and Their Diplomacy, Volume VI* (1927) provides a fair assessment of all aspects of Clayton's brief tenure at the State Department. Joseph P. Comegys's *Memoir of John Middleton Clayton* (1882) is eulogistic and riddled with factual errors.

For Clayton and his party's advocacy of commercial expansion and Anglo-American cooperation, see Daniel Walker Howe, *The Political Culture of the American Whigs* (1984); Michael F. Holt, *The Rise and Fall of the Whig Party: Jacksonian Politics and the Onset of the Civil War* (1999); Paul Varg, *United States Foreign Relations, 1820–1860* (1979); and John H. Schroeder, *Shaping a Maritime Empire: The Commercial and Diplomatic Role of the American Navy, 1829–1861* (1965).

The major monographic studies on the Clayton–Bulwer Treaty Mary Wilhelmine Williams, *Anglo-American Isthmian Diplomacy, 1815–1915* (1965), and Ira D. Travis, *The History of the Clayton-Bulwer Treaty* (1899), together with Richard W. Van Alstyne's "British Diplomacy and the Clayton–Bulwer Treaty, 1850–1860" *Journal of Modern History X* (1939): 149–83, focus on Anglo-American disagreement over the confusing wording of Article 1 of the treaty and whether the agreement violated the spirit of the Monroe Doctrine. These studies, based mostly on British primary sources, concentrate on intergovernmental relations following the ratification of the treaty.

In addition to Wire and Williams, other aspects of Clayton's diplomacy are discussed in Elbert Smith, *The Presidencies of Zachary Taylor and Millard Fillmore* (1988); K. Jack Bauer, *Zachary Taylor: Soldier, Planter, Statesman of the Old Southwest* (1985); Hamilton Holman, *Zachary Taylor: Soldier in the White House* (1951); and Tom Chaffin, *Fatal Glory: Narciso López and the First Clandestine U.S. War Against Cuba* (1996).

Dean Fafoutis

BAINBRIDGE COLBY
(1869–1950)

Served 1920–1921
Appointed by President Woodrow Wilson
Democrat

Bainbridge Colby, President Woodrow Wilson's third and last Secretary of State, was born in St. Louis, Missouri, on December 22, 1869, the only child of a prominent New York family. His father, John Peck Colby, was a lawyer and an officer in the Union Army, whereas his mother, Frances L. Bainbridge, was a descendant of the famous commodore.

Colby grew up with strong religious convictions. As he later recalled, "No man has more respect than I for the churches and for religion as such. I am descended, on both sides of my family, from ministers of the gospel; both my grandfathers were Baptist clergymen, and that is going some." Colby received the A.B. degree from Williams College in 1890 and attended Columbia University Law School, where Charles Evans Hughes was the Dean, for one year, completing his legal studies at New York Law School in 1892. Upon receiving the LL.B. degree, he began practicing law in New York under the name Alexander and Colby and soon gained recognition as a litigation lawyer. Among his many well-known clients was Samuel L. Clemens (Mark Twain), whom he represented in the settlement of the latter's financial affairs with his publishers, Charles L. Webster & Co., in 1894. Colby also served as counsel in the Northern Securities antitrust case of 1902.

Colby's political career was marked by independence and party irregularity. He entered politics as a Republican but was elected to the New York State Assembly on a fusion ticket in 1901, polling the largest vote ever given to a candidate in the Twenty-Ninth District. Declining renomination, he returned to his law practice at the conclusion of his one-year term. In 1912, as a young man with progressive ideas, he became prominently identified with the movement to nominate Theodore Roosevelt for president. After Roosevelt and his followers bolted the Republican Convention, Colby helped organize the Progressive Party and served as a delegate to its first convention at Chicago, which nominated the Rough Rider for president the following August. Colby also wrote "The Stolen Nomination," a widely circulated Progressive manifesto, claiming that William Howard Taft's followers had stolen the Republican nomination from Roosevelt. He later made a nationwide campaign tour, speaking in Roosevelt's behalf and gaining a reputation as a platform speaker and effective orator.

Despite Roosevelt's defeat by Woodrow Wilson, the Democratic candidate, Colby continued to work for the Progressive cause. In 1914, and again in 1916, he ran for the U.S. Senate from New York on the Progressive ticket, but was defeated both times. In the latter year he was chosen by the New York delegation to the Progressive convention to nominate Roosevelt for president, which he did. Yet when Roosevelt returned to the Republican fold and urged Progressives to support the Republican nominee, Charles Evans Hughes, Colby led the opposition. Branding Roosevelt a "traitor," he soon endorsed the cause of President Wilson. Colby formed an auxiliary committee of Progressives for Wilson, which cooperated with the Democratic National Committee during the campaign, and personally made a nationwide speaking tour in behalf of Wilson.

The effort of Colby and his group apparently was a decisive factor in the president's narrow reelection victory, particularly in Western and Midwestern states, where Progressivism had been strongest. After the victory, the grateful president offered Colby a choice of posts—assistant secretary of the treasury or a federal circuit judgeship—but Colby declined, preferring to devote himself to his law practice in New York. When the United States entered the Great War in April 1917, however, he agreed as a patriotic duty to serve on the Shipping Board, where he helped determine and supervise rates for requisitioned private shipping. He later also became vice president of the U.S. Shipping Board Emergency Fleet Corporation, continuing in both posts until 1919. Finally, in October 1917, he accompanied the House War Mission to Europe, headed by Colonel Edward M. House, and participated in the establishment of the Allied Maritime Transport Council to coordinate inter-Allied shipping allocation and supply. He spent two weeks in London in consultation with the British Admiralty and the British Ministry of Marine for the purpose of improving the coordination of effort between Great Britain and the United States in the use of their shipping. In the process, he revealed considerable ability as an administrator and acquired diplomatic experience in shipping negotiations with the Allies.

As with other prominent Americans, the war served to heighten Colby's interest in foreign affairs. In 1914, he opposed repeal of tolls exemptions for American coastal shipping using the Panama Canal and subsequently helped organize the "Provisional Committee for the Preservation of American Rights in the Panama Canal." He also supported the cause of Irish freedom and was identified with the causes advocated by the newspaper tycoon William Randolph Hearst, whose Anglophobia he shared. He even represented Hearst in 1915 in opposing the passage of a bill by the New York Legislature.

During the *Lusitania* crisis with Germany in 1915, he advocated a firm policy and criticized Wilson and Secretary of State William Jennings Bryan for failing to defend American rights and interests. In addition, he was involved in the League to Enforce Peace and became an enthusiastic supporter of Wilson's plans for a league of nations to replace the old balance of power system, which he believed was inadequate to maintain peace.

After Wilson forced Secretary of State Robert Lansing to resign on February 13, 1920, the president asked Colby to succeed Lansing. As Wilson told the departing secretary, he wanted "some one whose mind would more willingly go along with" his own. Wilson viewed Colby as an excellent administrator and a loyal supporter. He also greatly admired Colby's intelligence, eloquence, and writing abilities. Still physically impaired from a stroke he suffered in the fall of 1919, the President realized his need for a trusted assistant to write his diplomatic notes and state papers. Politically, he thought Colby would contribute strength in the continuing effort to ratify the Versailles Peace Treaty and in the 1920 presidential campaign. Despite continuing concerns about his lack of foreign policy experience and party irregularity, together with warnings by Senator Henry Cabot Lodge, Chairman of the Senate Foreign Relations Committee, that the poor health of both the president and the vice president meant that the new secretary would be their possible successor, the Senate confirmed his nomination on March 23, 1920, and he assumed his official duties the same day.

As Secretary of State, Colby was a good administrator whose relations with the White House were excellent. In contrast to the ailing Lansing, Colby ran the department efficiently, and morale greatly improved. He communicated with the president directly and worked harmoniously with Norman H. Davis, Wilson's personal choice for undersecretary, who was responsible for much of the actual direction of the department. Colby also supported the movement to reorganize the department and the Foreign Service, begun earlier by Lansing, and requested the use of technical trade experts to enable the United States to compete commercially with its rivals. Despite Colby's brief tenure, he established good relations with the press and with the business community. He was more candid and willing to release news than several of his predecessors had been. With Wilson himself, Colby's relationship was very close and warm. According to one diplomatic historian, "To a large degree he occupied the intimate position formerly held by House, although in contrast with the latter his role was confined primarily to foreign affairs."

In his policies, Colby was a committed Wilsonian internationalist who subscribed fully to the vision of a "peaceful liberal capitalist world order" within which the United States would play a leading role. Despite the Senate's second rejection of the Versailles Treaty four days before he took the oath of office, Colby continued to advocate both ratification of the treaty without reservations and membership in the League of Nations. When Republican Philander C. Knox sponsored a resolution in the Senate for a separate peace with Germany, Colby conferred with Senators Gilbert M. Hitchcock and Oscar W. Underwood to block it. Colby argued that the United States was no longer isolated, if it ever had been, and declared that the Monroe Doctrine had been enforced not by the prestige and power of the United States alone, but "by the European balance of power," and that therefore "our position had been quite the reverse of isolation." He believed that the United States should have a major role in the restoration of order in Europe and hailed the League of Nations as "the law of the world today." Only by entering the League, he argued, could the American people be assured of peace in the future. As for the alleged warnings by George Washington and Thomas Jefferson against foreign entanglements, Colby pointed out that those statesmen warned against permanent alliances only and spoke for a weak America. When Wilson decided to convert the 1920 election into a "solemn" referendum on the League and a possible third term in the presidency, Colby actively supported the plan. He served as a delegate from the District of Columbia to the Democratic Convention and lobbied for the president's renomination, only to be greatly disappointed as the nomination went to James M. Cox of Ohio and the election to the Republicans.

Despite the defeat of the League and the diminished role of the United States abroad, Colby exercised significant leadership in European affairs. When the German government requested permission to send a small number of troops into the demilitarized Ruhr to suppress Communist-instigated uprisings and restore order, Colby reiterated American willingness to permit the police action but opposed the French plan to occupy Frankfurt as a guaranty of early German withdrawal. As he explained in prophetic words, any additional Allied occupation of German territory might "cause a junction of militaristic forces in Germany and elements . . . striving for revolution and overthrow of political and economic order." He also rejected a British claim that under the Versailles Treaty only the League and its members could determine League mandates in the Middle East. In a note of November 20, 1920, sometimes referred to as the "Mesopotamia note" because it dealt with American rights in Iraq, Colby stated that because of its role in the war and despite its rejection of the Versailles Treaty and the League of Nations, the United States could not be excluded from "equal treatment to the commerce and to the citizens of all nations." He sent a similar note to the Council of the League of Nations in February 1921, regarding the former German islands in the Pacific, stating that "as one of the 'Principal Allied and Associated Powers,' the United States has an equal concern and an inseparable interest with the other principal allied and associated powers in the overseas possessions of Germany, and concededly an equal voice in their disposition." By thus insisting on a voice in both the framing of the terms of the mandate agreements, or trusteeships, and the equality of treatment within any spheres of influence, Colby reiterated the Wilsonian faith in an open door world as essential not only to America's prosperity but to world peace. His stand also contributed to Secretary of State Charles Evans Hughes's successful diplomacy at the Washington Naval Conference of 1921–1922, concerning a cable station on the island of Yap.

Colby's statements on the Bolshevik government of Russia were even stronger and became the basis of the U.S. policy of nonrecognition that lasted until 1933. In a reply to an inquiry by the Italian Ambassador on August 5, 1920, regarding the attitude of the United States toward the Soviet–Polish War, Colby stated that although the interest of the United States was in the preservation of both Polish and Russian territorial integrity and political independence, it would not favor the expansion of the armistice negotiations into a general European conference because it would probably involve recognition of the Bolshevik regime. "It is not possible," he pointed out, "for the Government of the United States to recognize the present rulers of Russia as a government with which the relations common to friendly governments can be maintained." This conviction had nothing to do with any particular political or economic system set up in Russia by the Russian people, Colby insisted. Rather, it rested on the fact "that the existing regime in Russia is based upon the negation of every principle of honor and good faith, and every usage and convention, underlying the whole structure of international law." Communist ideology and practice meant that "no compact or agreement made with a non-Bolshevik government can have any moral force for them." He further pointed out that the Bolshevik regime sought to promote revolutionary movements in other countries, working through the Third International or Comintern, aided by Soviet diplomats. "Inevitably, therefore, the diplomatic service of the Bolshevist Government would become a channel for intrigues and the propaganda of revolt. . . ." There could be no common ground, mutual confidence, or trust with "a Power whose conceptions of international relations are so entirely alien to its own, so utterly repugnant to its moral sense." Colby concluded by declaring, "We cannot recognize . . . a government which is determined and bound to conspire against our institutions; whose diplomats will be the agitators of dangerous revolt; whose spokesmen say that they sign agreements with no intention of keeping them." As the historian George Kennan has commented, the Colby note was based firmly on principle and was "a harsh position, and a negative one." It was also the most comprehensive exposition of the attitude of the Wilson administration toward Russia.

In regard to the Far East, Colby's actions were more positive. He formalized Lansing's plan for an international bankers' consortium, composed of British, French, Japanese, and U.S. bankers, to advance needed funds to the Chinese republic and made some progress toward moderating the Japanese thrust in Manchuria and Siberia. Lansing's unannounced purpose was to aid China in the defense of its integrity, prevent its reliance on Japanese sources alone for financial loans, and in effect break down all existing spheres of influence. When Japan sought to exclude its rights and options in Manchuria and Mongolia from Lansing's plan on the grounds of its special interests in those areas, Colby cooperated closely with Great Britain and France in a joint diplomatic endeavor to persuade the Japanese authorities to abandon their demands for special treatment. The State Department also obtained a large measure of British support in its determined effort to prevent the Russian-owned Chinese Eastern Railway in Manchuria from coming under exclusive Japanese control and in opposing the renewal of the Anglo-Japanese Alliance because it potentially targeted the United States. Thus, Colby furthered Anglo-American cooperation, upheld the Open Door policy, and encouraged a more cautious, moderate policy by the Japanese government. He thereby contributed to the Pacific treaty system that was to emerge from the Washington Naval Conference of 1921–1922. However, he failed to solve the immigration problem, the other long-standing issue in Japanese-American relations, although he favored revising the Gentlemen's Agreement of 1907–1908, in the face of continuing agitation within the United States, to exclude completely all Japanese immigration, a solution that would be incorporated in the Immigration Act of 1924.

As for Latin America, criticism of the Caribbean interventions by the United States and a more secure America after the defeat of Germany, which resulted in less likelihood of European intervention, led to a significant change in attitude. Colby's negotiations with the Mexican revolutionary government over American-owned oil and land interests later resulted in the signing of the Bucareli Agreement in August 1923, by which Mexico agreed not to apply Article 27 of the Mexican Constitution, reserving ownership of all subsurface mineral and oil deposits to the Mexican people, retroactively to foreign-owned oil concessions obtained prior to 1917 and on which development had begun. The negotiations also led to the restoration of normal diplomatic relations. Furthermore, Colby announced the intention to withdraw the marines from the Dominican Republic (completed in 1924) and from Haiti (completed in 1934) and avoided armed intervention in Cuba and Nicaragua when electoral disorders and revolutionary violence threatened. When similar conditions developed in Guatemala, Colby told the U.S. minister, "nothing short of the most serious menace to the lives of foreigners resident in

Guatemala City would lead the Department to consider such a step [armed intervention]. The mere fact of existence of disorder . . . would not justify so extreme a measure. . . . The Department deems it important to emphasize these fundamental principles of policy." Most important, Colby undertook a goodwill tour of South America in December 1920, to reduce Latin American suspicions and cement better relations. He visited Brazil, Uruguay, and Argentina as the personal representative of the president, returning official visits to the United States by the presidents of Brazil and Uruguay. In his public speeches and official declarations, Colby trumpeted hemispheric cooperation and disavowed the imperialistic aspects of the Monroe Doctrine. By all accounts, the tour was highly successful and contributed significantly to Pan-Americanism.

Colby left office at the end of the Wilson administration, having served almost a year as secretary of state. In contrast to his predecessors in that position, Bryan and Lansing, whose tenures ended over policy disagreements with Wilson, Colby's relationship with the former president remained very close and warm. After the inauguration of Warren G. Harding, Wilson and Colby formed a law partnership under the name Wilson and Colby with offices in Washington and New York. Wilson was admitted to the Bar in the District of Columbia by a vote of its members, and in New York by a special act of the legislature, passed in response to a special message from the governor. The partnership lasted until January 1, 1923, when it was dissolved at Wilson's request because of his poor health and disagreements with Colby over the kinds of cases Wilson thought proper to accept.

Despite his brief tenure and the unpromising domestic political situation resulting from the Senate's defeat of the Treaty of Versailles and U.S. membership in the League of Nations, Colby's record as Secretary of State was of considerable importance. He established an excellent working relationship between the State Department and the chief executive. He also enjoyed great freedom and responsibility because of the president's continued impairment. In Europe and the Far East, he opposed excessive reparations and unnecessarily harsh treatment of Germany and attempted to curtail Japanese exploitation and expansion in Manchuria and Siberia in cooperation with Great Britain, thereby strengthening the Open Door policy. He also formulated explicitly for the first time the U.S. policy of nonrecognition of the Communist government in Russia. In his most notable achievement, he retreated from interventionism and began a new era in Caribbean and Central American policy. Thus, Wilson–Colby foreign policy made significant contributions to American diplomacy and indicated the approach that the succeeding Republican administrations were to follow in the 1920s.

After serving as secretary of state, the remainder of Colby's career was largely anticlimactic. He supported Franklin D. Roosevelt for president in 1932, making a nationwide campaign speaking tour in his behalf, and later served as special assistant to the attorney general on enforcement of the antitrust acts, but his enthusiasm for Roosevelt soon waned. In 1934, he joined with such conservative Democrats as Alfred E. Smith, John J. Raskob, and John W. Davis in the American Liberty League in opposition to Roosevelt's New Deal. Colby believed in the personal and property rights of the individual and maintained that the role of government was to foster the private enterprise system against what he and others viewed as the collectivist trend of the New Deal. He even assisted plans for an independent Democratic Party. He was highly critical of Roosevelt in the 1936 election and supported Republicans Alfred M. Landon in 1936 and Wendell Willkie in 1940. He also served as counsel for the Hearst Press in its struggle with the National Recovery Administration, which sought to impose regulations on the press through the code system. Subsequently, he published articles on the freedom of the press, including an editorial for the Hearst Press that received honorable mention for the Pulitzer Prize.

Colby was divorced from his first wife, the former Nathalie Sedgwick of Stockbridge, Massachusetts, in 1929, after he complained that she had satirized him in a novel about the shallow lives of wealthy Americans. That same year, he married Anne Ahlstrand Ely of New York, a widow. Colby died at his home in Bemus Point, New York, on April 11, 1950.

BIBLIOGRAPHICAL ESSAY

The most important primary source for Colby's life is the collection of his private papers in the Library of Congress, Manuscript Division, which contains 2,500 items, including drafts of the 1912 convention call of the Progressive Party and 150 letters from Woodrow Wilson pertaining to foreign policy and personal affairs. Colby's official papers as Secretary of State are in the State Department files in the National Archives. *Papers Relating to the Foreign Relations of the United States, 1920–1921*, 5 vols. (1935–1936), includes much of the diplomatic correspondence of the United States. For the British position, see E. L. Woodward and R. Butler (eds.), *Documents on British Foreign Policy, 1919–1939*, first series, 16 vols. (1947–58). Colby's own account is *The Close of Woodrow Wilson's Administration and the Final Years* (1930), which is a reprint of an address by Colby to the Missouri Historical Society at St. Louis, April 28, 1930.

For brief biographical sketches, see John Spargo, "Bainbridge Colby," in Samuel Flagg Bemis (ed.), *The American Secretaries of State and Their Diplomacy*, 10 vols. (1927–1929), 10: 179–218, and the New York *Times*, February 29, 1920. Spargo was a well-known writer from Vermont who knew Colby. The most comprehensive study of the topic is Daniel M. Smith, *Aftermath of War: Bainbridge Colby and Wilsonian Diplomacy, 1920–1921* (1970). It includes much of the material in Smith's "Bainbridge Colby and the Good Neighbor Policy, 1920–1921," *Mississippi Valley Historical Review*, 50 (June 1963): 56–78. See also Mark T. Gilderhus, *Pan American Visions: Woodrow Wilson in the Western Hemisphere, 1913–1921* (1986). Colby's role in 1920 presidential politics appears in Wesley M. Bagby, "Woodrow Wilson, a Third Term, and the Solemn Referendum," *American Historical Review*, 60 (1955): 567–75, and *The Road to Normalcy, the Presidential Campaign and Election of 1920* (1962). See also Arthur C. Walworth, *Woodrow Wilson*, 2 vols. (1958).

On Wilsonian liberal internationalism, see N. Gordon Levin, Jr., *Woodrow Wilson and World Politics: America's Response to War and Revolution* (1968). Colby's relations with the State Department are covered in Graham M. Stuart, *The Department of State: A History of Its Organization, Procedure, and Personnel* (1949). For economic diplomacy, see Carl P. Parrini, *Heir to Empire: United States Economic Diplomacy* (1969). The fight for the Open Door in Mesopotamia can be found in John A. DeNovo, *American Interests and Policies in the Middle East, 1900–1939* (1963), and his "The Movement for an Aggressive American Oil Policy Abroad, 1918–1920," *American Historical Review*, 61 (1956): 854–76.

More specialized studies include George F. Kennan, *Russia and the West under Lenin and Stalin* (1960), and Ronald Radosh, "John Spargo and Wilson's Russian Policy, 1920," *Journal of American History*, 52 (1965): 548–65, which examines Spargo's influence on Colby's note of August 10, 1920. For a detailed account of Far Eastern problems, see Frederick V. Field, *American Participation in the China Consortiums* (1931). Negotiations surrounding Article 27 of the Mexican Constitution are dealt with in Robert Freeman Smith, *The United States and Revolutionary Nationalism in Mexico, 1916–1932* (1972). An obituary is in the *New York Times*, April 12, 1950.

Alexander W. Knott

WILLIAM R. DAY (1849–1923)

Served 1898
Appointed by President William McKinley
Republican

William Rufus Day was born on April 17, 1849. His father, Luther, had served as chief justice of the Ohio Supreme Court. His mother, Emily Spalding, was the daughter of Rufus Spalding who had served on the Ohio Supreme Court and who had helped establish the Republican Party in Ohio. Day's ancestors on both sides of his family hailed from New England.

Day graduated with a bachelor's degree from the University of Michigan in 1870. Day read law in the office of Judge George F. Robinson and returned to study law at his alma mater for a year. He was admitted to the Ohio bar in July 1872 and opened his law practice in Canton, Ohio, in partnership with William A. Lynch in October of the same year. Day met Mary E. Schaefer in Canton, and they married in 1875. The marriage was a happy one, and they had four sons. Secure in his marriage and career, Day built up his practice concentrating on criminal and corporation cases. As important to Day as his marriage and law practice was his friendship with William McKinley.

McKinley had established a law practice in Canton five years before Day. Their wives were friends before the husbands were. Day and McKinley were also drawn together by their devotion to the Republican Party, similarity of temperament, and the respect each had for the other's legal ability. When McKinley entered the U.S. House of Representatives, Day became his personal, financial, and legal advisor, and these roles continued into McKinley's presidency. An excellent example of Day's help occurred in 1893, when Robert L. Walker went bankrupt. McKinley had endorsed Walker's notes and so was in danger of bankruptcy himself. Serving as McKinley's personal counsel, Day helped establish a trust organized to discharge the debts McKinley then owed. McKinley turned over all his property to the trust, and Day served as one of the trustees. Under Day's supervision the entire debt was cleared without hurting McKinley's political career.

Before his service in the State Department, Day's public service was brief. After being nominated by both the Republican and Democrat parties, he served for six months on the court of common pleas. He resigned due to the low salary. In 1881, President Benjamin Harrison appointed Day judge of the United States District Court for Ohio's northern district, but Day resigned before ever taking up his duties on grounds of health.

Day's role as a personal advisor to McKinley continued in the hectic time of the conventions and election of 1896. Day was a party to the multitude of preconvention conferences that led to McKinley's presidential nomination by the Republican Party in June 1896 as he was to so many of the campaign conferences after McKinley's nomination. Day was a shrewd political judge and realized before McKinley or anyone else of the inner circle that with Bryan's presidential nomination by the Populists and Democrats in July, the silver issue would dominate the campaign.

Day was an integral part of the decision making that made up McKinley's cabinet selections specifically and patronage decisions in general. McKinley's choices in the main were designed to reassure the business community. After McKinley had selected Senator John Sherman for secretary of state, Ohio Governor Asa S. Bushnell refused to nominate Mark Hanna as Sherman's replacement. A personal request from McKinley carried directly to Bushnell by Day finally induced Bushnell to nominate Hanna.

During the cabinet selection process, Day had been mentioned publicly for either solicitor general or attorney general. Day turned down the top job at Justice. By April 1897, it was reported that McKinley was going to send Day to investigate conditions in Cuba. As Day was preparing to leave for Havana, however, McKinley offered his old friend the office of first assistant secretary of state.

As with most political decisions of McKinley, it is difficult to know with total certainty the president's reasons for the appointment. McKinley did not take anyone fully into his confidence to the point that most of his friends said that they did not feel that they knew him. Disingenuous at times, he did not like to say no. Also, McKinley usually had a number of reasons for making the decisions he did. Thus, we have a better sense of why Day accepted the offer than why McKinley made it in the first place.

Yet, it does appear that McKinley decided on Day for first assistant knowing he had to keep Sherman, no matter the latter's deficiencies, and because Day was a trusted friend who had worked with McKinley on a host of issues over the years. By his work, Day had proved his good sense, prudence, and cool judgment. An added bonus for McKinley, who wanted to be his own secretary of state, was that Day had no personal desire for public office in the executive branch, had no diplomatic experience, and had no set ideas on foreign policy. Therefore, it was highly unlikely that Day would ever challenge McKinley's foreign policies once the president had made clear his own preferences. Day accepted the post out of personal loyalty to McKinley although it would reduce his annual income by more than two-thirds.

One of the most difficult problems for Day was his relation with Sherman. For this McKinley bears most of the responsibility. It appears that the president had decided that Sherman was incapable of running State as it pertained to important diplomatic issues. Yet, the president did not address the issue squarely. Probably embarrassed at the thought that people who had charged him with appointing Sherman to State knowing the Senator's incapacity for the job would appear to be vindicated if he asked for Sherman's resignation only weeks after being sworn in, McKinley decided that Sherman would have the title but not the real authority of secretary of state. Routine authority would be exercised by Day, but McKinley never sat down with Sherman to explain diplomatically the situation they were in and ask for his acquiescence in, if not outright support for, the arrangement. Although it is possible that Sherman would have bristled at the suggestion if made explicitly by McKinley, the president never attempted to soften the blow to the old man's pride. Instead, McKinley's silent support of Day's usurpation embittered Sherman toward McKinley.

Within days of officially assuming his duties, the first secretary was running the State Department. Ambassadors and ministers would be presented to Sherman, and then the real diplomatic business would be conducted by Day. Substantively, Day was given authority over all the important diplomatic issues facing the administration, including negotiations over the annexation of Hawaii and the negotiations between the United States and Spain over Cuba.

Day gave the actual drafting of the Hawaiian annexation treaty to John W. Foster, who had drafted such a treaty for the lame-duck Harrison administration, which President Grover Cleveland then withdrew from the Senate in 1893. Sherman was not informed of the negotiations. In response to an official inquiry from the Japanese minister the secretary denied they were taking place. Sherman was informed of the treaty when he was asked to affix his signature to it so the treaty could be transmitted to the Senate.

It was inexcusable that McKinley did not ensure that Sherman was informed of the negotiations over Hawaii. As a consequence, Japan protested the annexation treaty to the U.S. government. Although the protest was withdrawn in December 1897, the Japanese could not help but think that the U.S. government had intentionally lied to them. A second consequence involved Sherman. It was from this incident that Sherman convinced himself that McKinley had never intended for him to play a role in U.S. foreign policy formation and had put him in the State Department to make room for Hanna. This was the beginning of the deterioration in McKinley's and Sherman's relationship, which led to Sherman's resignation, and constant criticizing of the McKinley administration after Sherman left government service.

As the Hawaiian annexation treaty episode showed, Day ran the daily operations of State and oversaw the main diplomatic issues. The question about his role in the adoption of foreign policy measures rightly should deal with not only his year as assistant secretary but also his short tenures as secretary of state and head of the U.S. delegation to the peace conference to negotiate a treaty ending the War of 1898. Although there is a range of opinion on this issue, it appears that Day's biographer, George William Duncan, has the best sense of the dynamics of the McKinley–Day relationship, albeit with some additions. McKinley and Day collaborated to reach a single judgment, after having debated their differences in private and having reached a consensus. McKinley was the senior partner in this enterprise and laid down the broad policy outlines but was open to at least Day's tactical suggestions and respectful of his judicial friend's insights. Day was at State because of his personal devotion to McKinley, but he was not a sycophant. He was an honest sounding board for the president because of his personal loyalty, honesty, and almost disinterested view of the foreign policy issues crowding in on the United States in 1897–1899. It may have been an informal, even amateur, way of doing business, but McKinley achieved nearly all of his foreign policy goals. Day helped

McKinley, in words used to describe an earlier president, to "row to his goals with muffled oars."

Cuba was the burning issue facing Day and McKinley. The island began its final struggle for independence in 1895. Spain responded tenaciously by attempting to suppress the "ever faithful isle" by military force. The Spanish could not afford the cost, but none of the major players—the Queen Regent, the Liberals, or the Conservatives—believed that they could survive politically if any of them accepted Cuban independence. Soon the conflict was dominated by guerrilla warfare. By the end of 1896, 150,000 Spanish soldiers had been posted to Cuba. By 1898 two-thirds of the force had been killed or rendered unfit for battle due to wounds or disease. The Cuban insurrectionists adopted a scorched earth policy.

In response, the new Spanish Captain-General for Cuba, Valeriano Weyler, began a policy of reconcentration on February 16, 1896. Weyler forced civilians in the countryside to move to the newly constructed camps so that the rebels would be cut off from civilian support. The camps became scenes of death as the overcrowding and unsanitary conditions killed thousands. Weyler's policies and the continued rebellion inflamed U.S. public opinion, fanned by the "Yellow Press," which printed lurid stories of the Spanish repression in Cuba.

President Grover Cleveland and his Secretary of State, Richard Olney, decided on a policy of neutrality. Cleveland refused to grant belligerency status to the Cuban rebels and appeared to think that Spain could pacify Cuba either through repression or reform. Yet, Cleveland put the United States on record as having interests in Cuba sufficient to make the situation on the island an issue properly to be raised by the United States in its relations with Spain. Madrid always denied the legitimacy of the U.S. position, arguing that Cuba was a domestic Spanish issue and not properly a subject of diplomatic discussion.

Day and McKinley were in control of U.S. policy on that issue from the time he took office. All correspondence and instructions between the U.S. government and its diplomatic personnel dealing with Cuba went through Day's office. McKinley retained Fitzhugh Lee as consul general in Havana, appointed Stewart L. Woodward minister to Spain, and sent William J. Calhoun on a secret mission to report on the conditions in Cuba. Calhoun's report on Cuba of June 22, 1897, laid out the constraints on U.S. policy for McKinley and Day. Calhoun argued that neither the Spanish nor the insurgents could defeat the other, thus prolonging a very bloody and destructive war. Although Calhoun admitted that the rebel forces were representative of all Cubans and that a majority was in favor of independence, he was against the United States granting belligerent status to the rebels and selling them arms because such actions would lead to Cuban independence, class warfare, and a continued disruption of U.S. businesses.

McKinley and Day's policy on Cuba was direct. Woodward, on behalf of his government on September 18, 1897, expressed to Spain the deep interest the United States had in an end to the Cuban War and threatened that the United States would not be able to stay neutral in the conflict because Congress wanted the U.S. government to recognize the belligerency of the rebels. Thus, the United States was willing to offer her "good offices" to aid a settlement of the conflict. Woodward made it clear that the United States would intervene if Spain did not improve the conditions and refused to change its military strategy in Cuba.

The new Spanish government realized that Woodward's demands were a turning point. Either Spain would have to accept the U.S. demands or be ready to resist increased U.S. involvement in Cuba. The Spain attempted to obtain support from the European powers so as to withstand U.S. pressure and implemented reforms in Cuban policy. The reforms were designed to reduce U.S. pressure while maintaining Spanish sovereignty on the island. At no time did Spain ever acknowledge officially that Cuba was an issue properly within the concern of United States–Spanish relations.

In October and November 1897, the Spanish government announced its reforms. General Weyler was recalled and the reconstruction order was modified. Cubans would be given autonomy. They would elect municipal and provincial councils as well as a Cuban parliament, which would have total control over domestic affairs. Spain would maintain control of foreign affairs, defense, the courts, and relations with the Catholic Church. The Queen Regent signed the autonomy decrees on November 15, 1897, but the decree establishing the new autonomous government would not go into effect until approved by the Cortes. The insurgents denounced the measures and vowed to continue the struggle for independence.

McKinley appeared to be pleased with the Spanish reforms and the role the United States had played in leading the Spanish to the reforms. In his annual message to Congress on December 6, 1897, McKinley emphasized that U.S. intervention had been considered but was not then necessary because of the reforms the Spanish were introducing in Cuba. If the Spanish did not follow through on their reform promises, however, U.S. intervention would occur. McKinley also came out against U.S. recognition of insurgent belligerency. However, a majority in Congress consisting of both Republicans and Democrats favored the recognition of Cuban belligerency. Yet, events in the New Year quickly destroyed the apparent progress on Cuba. Within two weeks of the autonomy legislation going into effect on January 1, 1898, antiautonomy riots rocked Havana and the rioters demanded the reinstatement of General Weyler. Cubans on the opposite side of the issue were against autonomy because they were determined to see Cuba independent. Lee communicated to Day on January 18 that autonomy was a failure. The next day a House of Representatives resolution supporting the recognition of Cuban belligerency was blocked by the administration with the help of Speaker Thomas B. Reed.

After Lee had recommended to Day that a U.S. warship be sent to Havana, and Second Assistant Secretary of the State Alvey A. Adee recommended to him that the whole U.S. Gulf Squadron be readied for action, McKinley met with Secretary of the Navy John D. Long, Justice Joseph McKenna, General Nelson A. Miles, and Day on January 23 to discuss the recommendations. They decided to order the USS *Maine* to Havana. McKinley was personally responsible for the decision. Day contacted the Spanish minister to the United States, Enrique Dupuy de Lôme, to inform him of the visit and that it should be considered a friendly act. Yet, de Lôme knew that the United States was assembling a fleet of warships at Key West, which was seen by the Spanish government as preparations for war. In response, Spain ordered some of its navy to Cuban waters and began purchasing ships that could be used in war by April. The *Maine* arrived in Havana harbor on January 25.

The events of the next six weeks threatened to remove the control of U.S. foreign policy from McKinley's and Day's hands. On February 9, the *New York Journal* published a letter that de Lôme had written to a friend in December 1897. In the letter, de Lôme insulted McKinley by describing him as "weak and catering to the rubble" and being a "would-be" politician. More importantly, de Lôme suggested that the Spanish government had been insincere in its autonomy reforms. De Lôme, knowing of the imminent publication, had resigned the previous day. Not wanting a personal insult to be the basis of a war, McKinley demanded through Day that the Spanish government should express regret for de Lôme's statements and disavow them. Woodward had to threaten to resign before the Spanish government issued an insolent apology a week later.

On February 10, Day received Madrid's response to McKinley's proposals of the previous December. The Spanish government insisted that the United States had no say in how Cuba was governed and that Cuba was solely a domestic, not diplomatic, issue. The note ended with a threat that Spain would fight if McKinley tried to impose a U.S. solution to the Cuban problem.

On February 16, the U.S. government learned that the *Maine* had been destroyed in an explosion the night before with a loss of 264 sailors. The United States conducted an investigation of the disaster independently of Spain. Between the sinking of the *Maine* and the issuance by the American Court of Inquiry of its report on the cause of the sinking, Day and McKinley worked to ensure that Spain would follow through on its reform promises and establish peace on the island.

In the face of congressional demands for action even before the *Maine* report was issued, McKinley requested $50 million for national defense. Two days later, on March 9, both houses passed the appropriation unanimously. McKinley's rapprochement with Congress was brief. On March 17, Senator Redfield Proctor, considered a moderate on the Cuban question, spoke on the floor of the Senate on the conditions in Cuba he had just seen. Proctor quietly and without theatrics described the starvation, the economic devastation, and the practice of reconcentration, then announced that he now supported the use of force by the United States to end the Cuban war.

McKinley received news on March 20 that the board of inquiry would report that the *Maine* had been destroyed by an external source. According to Duncan, it was during the week of March 21 that Day became convinced that war was inevitable. Yet, McKinley and Day still carried on negotiations with Spain. On March 27 Day sent Woodward the demands of the United States. The Spanish government was to revoke its reconcentration order, allow supplies to reach the Cuban people, and institute an immediate armistice to last until October 1. Finally, McKinley would be the final arbiter between Cuba and Spain if they could not reach an agreement by the October 1 deadline.

Day received the Spanish reply on March 31. Spain offered to submit the *Maine* issue to arbitration, agreed to abolish reconcentration only in the four western provinces, and agreed to a truce if asked by the insurgents. Spain refused to accept U.S. good offices and did not agree to an armistice. McKinley decided for war.

Yet, it was not until the end of April that the War of 1898 began. McKinley and Day used the time to develop the president's message to Congress, evacuate U.S. citizens from Cuba, continue war preparations, and stave off any chance, however slight, of European intervention on behalf of Spain. Day received the Spanish government's final offer on April 10. Spain's commander-in-chief in Cuba was instructed to end hostilities immediately, but for only as long as he deemed prudent. The Spanish offered Cubans autonomy but not independence.

McKinley sent his long-awaited message to Congress on April 11. McKinley stated his belief that the war in Cuba would continue until one or the other was exhausted or annihilated and that the war was no longer tolerable to the United States. McKinley refused to recognize the belligerency of the insurgents or Cuban independence. Instead, McKinley asked Congress to "authorize and empower the President to take measures to secure a full and final termination of hostilities," between Spain and Cuba and "to use the military and naval forces of the United States as may be necessary for these purposes." After more than a week of debate and parliamentary maneuvering the House and the Senate passed the same resolution that McKinley approved on April 19. The president signed the congressional resolution the next day. He ordered a U.S. blockade of Cuba on April 21. Spain declared war on the United States on April 24, and the next day McKinley asked Congress for a resolution, which it passed stating that war had existed since April 21.

Spain never accepted the legitimacy of U.S. diplomatic interest in the island. The Spanish political parties were weak and the Queen Regent would rather have lost the remnants of the Spanish Empire by war than peacefully relinquish Cuba and thereby threaten the continued existence of the dynasty. Spanish policy was directed at all times to retain its sovereignty of Cuba. McKinley had worked toward a peaceful solution to the crisis for a year in the face of Spanish obstinacy and congressional opposition.

Both the United States and Spain preferred war to compromise, which was impossible anyway, over the essential issue between them: Cuba. For Spain the violence in Cuba was a domestic matter within the jurisdiction of the Spanish government. For the United States, Spain had proved itself incapable of ending the violence in Cuba, which was important to the United States on humanitarian grounds. Thus, it was an international matter, subject to the interests of the United States.

Sherman's opposition to McKinley's foreign policies generally, and the war with Spain specifically, (in addition to his incapacities), made it untenable for him to continue as secretary of state. He resigned on April 25. McKinley announced Day's appointment to succeed Sherman while Day was in Canton because of his wife's illness. McKinley nominated Day because of the latter's familiarity with all the important foreign policy issues facing the United States and because of their deep friendship and mutual trust. Day accepted with the condition that his tenure at state would end when the war did and that John Bassett Moore, a Democrat, be appointed first assistant secretary of state.

It is difficult to say with certainty the effect Day had on McKinley's foreign policy decisions, but Day continued to be the government official in the most contact with the president. Those who attempted to convince McKinley on different foreign policy issues made it a point to see Day and discuss their concerns and preferences with him because of his influence on McKinley.

Day asked a variety of experts their opinions on the issue of contraband of war and on the rules of blockade. With the proffered advice, the State Department created an updated list of contraband and developed instructions for U.S. vessels taking part in the blockade of Cuba.

Before the outbreak of the war, Day and McKinley had been concerned about the seizure of Chinese territory by the European powers and the potential negative effect those seizures could have on U.S. trade with China. Day believed that China represented the greatest potential overseas market for U.S. products. His concern about the fragility of the Chinese market was a part of a larger concern expressed throughout the 1890s that the European powers' colonial expansion was threatening U.S. commercial interests in Asia. U.S. ambassador to the Court of St. James, John Hay, sent official word to Day in early May 1898 that Germany might demand compensation in the Philippines or Samoa if the United States did not act quickly to annex Hawaii. McKinley, with Day's support, asked Congress to approve the Hawaiian annexation agreement quickly. McKinley signed the joint Hawaiian annexation resolution on July 7, 1898.

The president's decision to demand U.S. acquisition of the Philippines appears to have formed in early May. He was ahead of Day and the rest of the Cabinet on this issue. At the request of Day, Moore drafted the first written list of U.S. conditions for a peace treaty with Spain. In this draft Spain would keep the Philippines but cede a coaling station in the islands or in the Carolinas to the United States. Madrid also would cede Puerto Rico and Guam to the United States and evacuate Cuba. This memorandum of May 9 was the accepted formulation of the U.S. position at least into early June. Yet, the final form that U.S. demands would take would be dependent on the progress U.S. arms made in the war.

Although there was near chaos in the U.S. Army's operations, Spain was more disorganized than the United States was and the U.S. Navy was vastly superior to the Spanish. Commander George Dewey's squadron defeated the Spanish fleet in Manila Bay on May 1. The U.S. Army landed in southern Cuba between June 22 and June 26. The U.S. Army defeated the Spanish at San Juan Hill on July 1–2. A naval squadron destroyed the Spanish fleet at the battle of Santiago Bay on July 3. Santiago itself surrendered on July 17. General Nelson Miles, commanding general of the army landed an expedition on Puerto Rico on July 25.

Even before the war ran its course, McKinley had made the decision to send occupation armies to both Cuba and the Philippines. Although Day was arguing, as late as mid-November, for at most a U.S. naval station in Manila, he worked with McKinley to draft orders to the Philippine Islands expeditionary force commander-in-chief sent on May 9. The orders directed the general to destroy Spanish power in the islands and to establish U.S. rule there. The Filipino people were to be made to understand that the only authority in the islands was the U.S. general acting in the name of President McKinley.

When Day learned that Emilio Aguinaldo, the leader of the Filipino rebellion against Spain, had taken control of most of the island of Luzon, Day ordered Admiral Dewey and U.S. Consul in Singapore, E. Fletcher Platt, not to enter into any negotiations with the Filipinos not expressly authorized by the U.S. government. He further instructed them to establish U.S. authority on the islands. By these and other actions Day worked consistently during the war to ensure that no U.S. representative made any commitments to Aguinaldo.

It appears that McKinley throughout May, June, and July worked quietly to ensure the postwar occupation of Cuba and the Philippines by the United States but made no public statements to that effect. In addition to being prodded by the growth of U.S. public opinion in support for the retention, Day received word from Hay that because Germany would object to the Philippines being transferred to Britain or France, Britain preferred U.S. possession of the islands in order to block possible German expansion in the Southwest Pacific.

A reflection of a hardening of U.S. resolve to keep the islands occurred in mid-May when U.S. ambassador to Berlin, Andrew D. White, informed Day of a conversation he had had with an official of the German Foreign Office. White had said the United States would keep only a few coaling stations in the East Indies and that it would be a mistake for the United States to acquire any overseas possessions. Day responded immediately with a reprimand, ordered White to inform German officials that White's statements reflected only a private opinion, and noted that the U.S. government had not made a decision on the issue.

Moore's memorandum of May 9 continued to be the basis of U.S. peace terms until the middle of June. McKinley had ordered a U.S. occupation force of 20 thousand men for the Philippines. The Cabinet met many times on the issue, but a critical Cabinet meeting directed by McKinley was held on June 26. McKinley had decided that Spain must cede Puerto Rico and other West Indies islands to the United States, relinquish all sovereignty over to Cuba, and accept the U.S. occupation of the city, harbor, and bay of Manila until a final peace conference could determine the fate of the islands.

The Cabinet agreed that Spain would lose Cuba and Puerto Rico, but on the issue of the Philippines it was badly divided. Three members of the Cabinet wanted U.S. possession of all of the Philippines. Day and two other members wanted only a U.S. naval base at Manila. Two members were undecided. McKinley later said that he did not put Day's proposal of a naval base at Manila to a Cabinet vote because he feared the Cabinet would have approved it. With the president's prodding, the Cabinet narrowly agreed to leave the final status of the Philippines to the peace commission. Yet, the direction of policy was clear when the administration decided that no person hostile to U.S. acquisition of overseas territory would be appointed to the peace commission. A Cabinet meeting on July 30 confirmed all the peace terms outlined by McKinley.

The French ambassador to the United States, Jules Cambon, had been directed by his government at the request of the Spanish to act as the representative of Spain to negotiate an armistice as a preliminary to peace negotiations. Meeting with McKinley and Day on July 26, the ambassador unsuccessfully attempted to limit the talks to Cuba. It was agreed that the talks would cover all territorial issues. McKinley and Day had a second meeting with Cambon on June 30 to present the position of the United States on the outstanding territorial issues. U.S. policy followed the terms McKinley had presented to the Cabinet on June 26 and to which it agreed on June 30. He refused to negotiate with Cambon over any Spanish territory in the Caribbean. The ambassador thought the terms harsh but McKinley was immovable.

The protocol ending the war was signed on August 12. Day represented the United States and Cambon represented Spain. By its terms Spain relinquished all claims to Cuba, ceding to the United States Puerto Rico and all other possessions in the West Indies and an island in the Ladrones to be selected by the United States; the United States was to occupy the city, bay, and harbor of Manila pending a peace treaty, which would determine the disposition of the islands; Spain was to evacuate Cuba, Puerto Rico, and all other possessions in the West Indies immediately; both countries would appoint commissioners to meet at Paris no later than October 1, 1898, to negotiate a peace treaty, and that hostilities would cease between the two countries as soon as they could inform the commanders of their armies and navies. The Spanish forces surrendered in Manila to a joint U.S.–Filipino attack on August 13, the day after the protocol was signed. With hostilities over, Day resigned as secretary of state on September 16 to be succeeded by John Hay.

Day had ensured that McKinley's policy of territorial expansion would not be compromised by U.S. actions during the war nor by the peace protocol of August 12. Neither native governments nor representatives were to be granted recognition; joint occupation forces were not allowed; no rebel representatives were present at the protocol signing ceremony. Spain surrendered only to the United States, and only Spain and the United States would be represented at the Paris Peace Conference. McKinley appointed Day to head the U.S. delegation to the conference, which also included Whitelaw Reid; U.S. Senators Cushman K. Davis (Rep.), William P. Frye (Rep.), George Gray (Dem.), and John Bassett Moore.

At the Cabinet meeting where Day submitted his resignation from the State Department, McKinley asked the commissioners present what they thought should be done about the Philippines. Day forthrightly expressed his judgment that the United States should leave the islands except, at most, the bay and harbor of Manila. In his view the United States had no other vital interests in the islands. Day held to his judgment through all preliminary meetings the U.S. delegates held to ready themselves for the peace conference.

Day and the other U.S. commissioners were able to question General Wesley Merritt, commanding officer of the first U.S. Army expedition to the Philippines, who had been sent to Paris by McKinley to confer with them and to review written reports of others in the Philippines. The commissioners' session with the general was the most significant meeting they had with experts on the Philippines. Merritt agreed with those who favored U.S. annexation of all the islands. He argued that the Filipinos were incapable of self-government and if left to themselves would degenerate into civil violence. Merritt also reasoned that if the United States took only part of the islands and permitted Spain to retain the rest that Spain would never become reconciled to the loss and would try to recover what it had lost. Conversely, if the United States held only the island of Luzon and permitted a major European power to acquire the other islands, the commercial worth of Manila for the United States would be threatened while the same problems of defense would remain.

Although he remained open to suggestions from his fellow U.S. commissioners and worked well with them, Day was always in control of his delegation. Day was able to convince the Spanish delegates that the order of the business of the conference would follow the order the issues were laid out in the August 12 protocol.

Although Day initially was in favor of the United States unconditionally accepting sovereignty over Cuba, he followed instructions from McKinley and argued against this position during the public sessions of the peace conference. After over three weeks of negotiations, Day and his delegation were able to secure Spanish agreement with the U.S. position on Cuba, Puerto Rico, and the Spanish debt relative to those islands. On October 27 the Spanish accepted the U.S. position on these issues in the hope that the United States would then compromise over the Philippines.

Day and his U.S. colleagues always anticipated that the Philippines would be the most contentious issue of the conference. In fact, the Philippines issue caused the greatest division within the U.S. delegation as well. On October 25, Day sent to Hay the differences of opinion within the U.S. delegation concerning the Philippines and asked for instructions. Whitelaw Reid and Senators Davis and Frye argued for U.S. sovereignty over the whole island group. If the United States did not acquire all of the islands, they believed Spain would hold the rest, which would lead either to revolt against Spain or Spanish sale of the islands to a commercial rival of the United States.

Day continued to argue against U.S. sovereignty over the archipelago, although he supported the acquisition of the islands of Luzon, Mindoro, and Palawan. Senator Gray argued against U.S. sovereignty over any part of the Philippines. In a follow-up confidential communication to McKinley on October 28, Day bluntly requested that the instructions should permit real negotiations with the Spanish over the Philippines and reminded McKinley of Day's opposition to U.S. acquisition of the whole island group.

On October 29, Day received McKinley's position: U.S. sovereignty over the Philippines was not subject to negotiation. Only their disposition, control, and government could be discussed. Day shared the communication with his fellow commissioners, and in response Senator Gray sent a message to Hay suggesting if Spain threatened to end negotiations over the issue the United States should offer $10–$20 million for the islands.

The commissioners received dispatches from Hay on October 31 and November 2, which argued that the United States controlled Manila and by extension the whole Philippines by right of conquest. Day responded with a vigorous confidential message to McKinley on November 2, which was supported by the entire U.S. delegation in a subsequent message sent to the president on November 4.

Day argued that the U.S. claim to the Philippines on the basis of the right of conquest was not supported by international law or diplomatic practice in any way and that the then-current U.S. occupation of the islands was made legal, not by conquest, but by terms of the August 12 protocol. To argue otherwise was "untenable." On November 5, McKinley at last permitted his delegates discretion as to what grounds they would use as the basis of the U.S. claim to the Philippines in their negotiations on the same day.

After a week of fruitless negotiations with the Spanish delegation, Day forwarded a dispatch laying out the disparate views of the U.S. commissioners and requested explicit instructions on November 11. The opinions ranged from concessions on the Philippines issue to secure a peace treaty to demanding an ultimatum and no money payment. Day reminded Hay that he was against the United States acquiring the whole island group and favored only the acquisition of Luzon. If the President demanded the archipelago, then the United States should offer Spain $15 million for it.

On November 15, Moore presented a memorandum, which became the basis for the U.S. position on the issue. It called for an ultimatum requiring the cessation of the Philippines to the United States, and, in return, the United States would offer Spain $20 million. With slight changes, Day presented this ultimatum to the Spanish delegation on November 21 along with a request of the sale of islands in the Carolinas and a resumption of the antebellum commercial treaties. A rejection of the ultimatum would end the conference. On November 28, the Spanish delegation agreed to the U.S. ultimatum.

No agreement was reached on the subsidiary issues in the days remaining to the conference. On December 10, 1898, the treaty of peace was signed. Spain relinquished sovereignty over Cuba and the United States was authorized to occupy it, Spain ceded Puerto Rico and other West Indies islands and Guam to the United States, ceded the Philippines and in return the United States paid Spain $20 million, and agreed that the civil rights and political status of the native peoples in the ceded territories would be determined by the U.S. Congress. (There were other less important articles to the treaty.)

Day had been successful in achieving all the objectives of the president in spite of his own misgivings over the Philippines. It is arguable that without Day's persistent and well-reasoned arguments to Hay and McKinley over the Philippines and McKinley's trust in his old friend's judgment, McKinley would not have accepted his commissioner's recommendation concerning the basis of the U.S. claim to the Philippines and a monetary payment for the islands. In fact, without Day as chair, it is possible that the U.S. delegation itself would not have accepted those conditions. In either case without Day, there was a real possibility that the conference would have ended without a peace treaty, thereby threatening all the gains the United States had made in the summer of 1898. Day did not take any part in the struggle over ratification of the treaty, which the Senate approved on February 6, 1899, by a vote of 57 in favor and 27 opposed.

McKinley appointed Day to a federal judgeship for the Sixth Judicial Circuit. As a federal judge, Day took no part in McKinley's successful reelection campaign. Many people assumed that Day's influence ended with McKinley's assassination, but President Theodore Roosevelt nominated Day to the U.S. Supreme Court. The Senate confirmed Day and his appointment was official on March 2, 1903.

Day was one of the Court's most active members during his almost 20 years of service except in 1911, when his wife died, and in 1915, when he had a protracted illness. Judge Day was a moderate liberal whose concept of dual federalism—each level of government had its own separate junctions independent of the other levels—rested on a literal interpretation of the Tenth Amendment and on Chief Justice Melville W. Fuller's definitions of commerce.

Fuller developed his definitions in his majority opinion in *United States v. E. C. Knight Company* (1895) when he wrote that manufacturing "for export to another state does not of itself make it an article of interstate commerce." Day always followed Fuller in the understanding that manufacturing involved the production of goods while commerce involved the transportation of goods. The most significant example of Day's definition of commerce was enunciated in his opinion for the majority in *Hammer v. Dagenhart* (1918), which invalidated the Keating–Owen Child Labor Act of 1916 outlawing the interstate shipping of products made by child labor. For Day, following Fuller, the regulation of labor used in manufacturing was totally reserved to the police power of the states.

Consequently, Day supported federal regulation of interstate transportation in such cases as *Atchison, Topeka and Santa Fe Railway Company v. Robinson* (1914), *Hoke v. United States* (1913), *Caminetti v. United States* (1917), and *Pittsburgh Melting Company v. Totten* (1918); the extension of the police power of states when they tried to protect the health, safety, and morals of their public in such cases as *McLean v. Arkansas* (1909), *Minnesota ex. rel. Whipple v. Martinson* (1921), and in his dissenting vote in *Lochner v. New York* (1905); and vigorous use of federal police powers in antitrust actions in such cases as *Northern Securities Co. v. United States* (1904), *United States v. Union Pacific Railway Company* (1912) and in his dissent in *United States v. United States Steel Corporation* (1920).

After resigning from the Court in December 1922, Day died at his summer home at Mackinac Island on July 9, 1923. Judge Day was buried in Canton, Ohio.

Day had never had any ambition in the sphere of U.S. foreign policy. He served out of personal loyalty to McKinley and as secretary of state only for the duration of the war with Spain. Day did not attempt to impose any design on U.S. foreign policies or limit his successors' future policy choices. As secretary of state and head of the U.S. peace delegation, Day loyally furthered McKinley's objectives while at the same time maintaining his opposition to the U.S. claim to the Philippines on the basis of the right of conquest. On that basis, Judge Day always defended the $20 million payment for the Philippines by the United States.

BIBLIOGRAPHICAL ESSAY

The Day papers are in the Library of Congress. Other collections of value to understanding Day's diplomatic career in the Library of Congress are the papers of George B. Cortelyou, William McKinley, John Bassett Moore, Whitelaw Reid, and John Sherman. The most complete rendition of Day's diplomatic service is George William Duncan's "The Diplomatic Career of William Rufus Day, 1897–1898" (1977), Ph.D dissertation, Case Western Reserve University. Also see Lester Shippe and Royal B. Way, "William Rufus Day" in Samuel Flagg Bemis (ed.), *The American Secretaries of State and their Diplomacy* (1958).

For McKinley's foreign policies generally, see *Papers Relating to the Foreign Relations of the United States, 1897–1901* (1897–1902). For biographies of McKinley and histories of his administration see Charles S. Olcott, *Life of William McKinley*, 2 vols. (1916); Margaret Leech, *In the Days of McKinley* (1959); Howard Wayne Morgan, *William McKinley and his America* (1963); and Lewis L. Gould, *The Presidency of William McKinley* (1980). Brief analyses of McKinley are H. Wayne Morgan "William McKinley as a Political Leader" *Review of Politics* 28 (1966); and Lewis L. Gould "William McKinley and the Expansion of Presidential Power," *Ohio History* 87 (1987). On the issue of Hawaiian annexation, see Julius W. Pratt *Expansionist of 1898: The Acquisition of Hawaii and the Spanish Islands* (1936) and William A. Russ, Jr., *The Hawaiian Republic, 1894–98 and Its Struggle to Win Annexation* (1961).

For the origins of the Spanish-American War, see Joseph A. Fry "William McKinley and the Coming of the Spanish-American War: A Study of the Besmirching and Redemption of an Historical Image," *Diplomatic History* 3 (1979); John Layser Offner, "President McKinley and the Origins of the Spanish-American War (1957); Ernest R. May, *Imperial Democracy: The Emergence of America as a Great Power* (1961); Walter La Feber, *The New Empire: An Interpretation of American Expansionism, 1860–1898,* (1963); and Howard Wayne Morgan, *America's Road to Empire: The War with Spain and Overseas Expansion* (1965). John A. S. Grenville and George Berkeley Young's *Politics, Strategy, and American Diplomacy: Studies in Foreign Policy 1873–1917* (1966) has an excellent chapter on McKinley; Robert Dallek's *1898: McKinley's Decision, The United States Declares War on Spain* (1969) has some perceptive insights on the diplomatic situation and a excellent collection of primary sources. See also Paul S. Holbo "Presidential Leadership in Foreign Affairs: William McKinley and the Turpie–Foraker Amendment," *American Historical Review* 72 (1967); and Frederick Merk, *Manifest Destiny and Mission in American History: A Reinterpretation* (1963), and Louisa A. Perez, *The War of 1898* (1998).

For the Philippines and the Paris Peace Conference, see John A. S. Grenville "American Naval Preparations for the War with Spain, 1896–1898," *Journal of American Studies* 2 (1968); Phil Lyman Snyder, "Mission, Empire, or Force of Circumstances? A Study of the American Decision to Annex the Philippine Islands (1972); Paolo E. Coletta's articles, "Bryan, McKinley and the Treaty of Paris," *Pacific Historical Review* 26 (1957) and "McKinley, the Peace Negotiations and the Acquisition of the Philippines," *Pacific Historical Review* 30 (1961); and H. Wayne Morgan (ed.), *Making Peace with Spain: The Diary of Whitelaw Reid, September–December 1898* (1965).

For Day's service on the U.S. Supreme Court, see James F. Watts, Jr., "William R. Day," in Leon Friedman and Fred L. Israel (eds.), *The Justices of the United States Supreme Court 1789–1969: Their Lives and Major Opinions*, volume III (1969) and Joseph E. McLean "William Rufus Day: Supreme Court Justice from Ohio," *The Johns Hopkins University Studies in Historical and Political Science*, LXIV, no. 3 (1946).

Edward S. Mihalkanin

JOHN FOSTER DULLES (1888–1959)

Served 1953–1959
Appointed by President Dwight D. Eisenhower
Republican

John Foster Dulles was born on February 25, 1888, the firstborn son of Reverend Allen Macy Dulles, Presbyterian pastor of the Trumbell Avenue Church in Detroit, Michigan, and Edith Foster Dulles. Foster, as his family called him, was, fittingly, born in the Washington, D.C., home of his maternal grandfather, John Watson Foster, a former secretary of state and lifelong mentor. Shortly after his birth, Dulles's parents relocated to Watertown, New York, where his father served as pastor at the First Presbyterian Church. It was there that Foster spent a remarkably happy though strictly regimented childhood with his diligent parents, precocious siblings—he had three younger sisters and a brother—and worldly grandparents. A frequent visitor was Robert Lansing, affectionately referred to by the Dulles children as "Uncle Bert." Lansing was married to Edith Dulles's sister, Eleanor, and was a successful attorney and aspiring politician who would later serve as Woodrow Wilson's secretary of state. He, like Foster's grandfather, provided advice and opportunities throughout Dulles's long march to that esteemed office.

In late 1903, Edith Dulles took Foster and a daughter, Eleanor, to spend the year in France, prior to his entrance to Princeton in the fall of 1904. Dulles's tenure at Princeton was, for the most part, unremarkable. He majored in philosophy, with the intention of fulfilling his parents' wish that he join the ministry. But as he matured, his interest in politics, international relations, and ethics grew. His senior thesis, entitled "The Theory of Judgment," won him the Chancellor Green Mental Science Fellowship, providing a year's study at the Sorbonne under Nobel Prize–winning philosopher Henri Bergson. Dulles graduated Phi Beta Kappa, second in his class, and gave the valedictory speech at graduation.

Dulles had the rare opportunity to attend the Second Hague Peace Conference during the late spring and summer of 1907. Dulles's grandfather, John Watson Foster, appealed to Princeton to allow his grandson to postpone his end-of-year junior exams to the fall. Grandfather Foster was attending as a delegate for the Imperial Government of China and assigned young Dulles, who was just a few months past his 19th birthday, as a secretary for the Chinese delegation because of his knowledge of French. While Dulles served in this first conference as a glorified clerk, his attention to detail, awareness of diplomatic protocol, and keen interest in international politics foreshadowed his long career in the conference rooms of the world.

Following his scholarship year in France, Dulles returned stateside. He enrolled at George Washington Law School in Washington, D.C., and completed all necessary course work in two years, demonstrating a voracious memory and an enviable ability for long periods of academic concentration that characterized the rest of his life and work.

During the summer of 1911, Dulles met and courted a local girl, Janet Avery, while completing job applications for several Wall Street firms. John Foster called in a favor and secured his grandson a clerkship at the well-respected firm of Sullivan and Cromwell, where he would practice for almost 40 years. His legal employment enabled him to marry Janet Avery, who would be his life's companion, bearing him three children and selflessly accompanying him on nearly every trip Dulles ever made.

Dulles's uncle, Robert Lansing, was Woodrow Wilson's secretary of state. In 1917 "Uncle Bert" called on his nephew to head a confidential mission to Panama to ensure that the countries of Central America would cooperate with U.S. policy rather than ally with Germany. Dulles carried out his assignment efficiently, and harmonious relations between the United States and the Central American countries were guaranteed.

When the United States entered the Great War, Dulles immediately volunteered for a commission. He could not serve in combat units due to his poor eyesight, a result of a near fatal bout with malaria in 1912. Therefore, Dulles was commissioned as a captain to serve as a lawyer on the War Trade Board. He served with distinction, rising to the rank of major, and gained the confidence of both Vance McCormack, head of the War Trade Board, and Bernard Baruch, head of the War Industries Board. At the close of hostilities, Baruch was selected by President Wilson to join the U.S. delegation to Versailles. Baruch, in turn, requested Dulles's service as his legal consul in his new role as U.S. Representative on the Reparations Commission. Dulles, with his wife, spent nearly a year and a half in Paris, facilitating war reparations negotiations. The British and French maintained that Germany was responsible for all "war costs," which they interpreted loosely to include not only settlements for widows and orphans and war pensions, but also compensation for all citizens who lost property or capital while fighting the war. Dulles considered such demands one-dimensional and destructive. Dulles tried until the bitter end to force a compromise. Ultimately, his attempts to achieve a reasonable statement of German responsibility as well as a fixed sum for German reparations was watered down in committee.

John Foster and Janet Dulles remained in Paris until the fall of 1919 coordinating American efforts regarding the application of the reparations decisions made at Versailles. Dulles returned from Paris having learned several valuable lessons. First, he witnessed the political decline of both his uncle, Secretary of State Robert Lansing, who was fired by Wilson for his persistent opposition, as well as that of Woodrow Wilson himself. Lansing's mistake was one that Dulles was careful to avoid during his own tenure in the office of secretary of state. Wilson's repudiation at the hands of the Senate seemed to Dulles the logical outcome of political decisions made without reference to domestic concerns and affairs. But perhaps most important was Dulles's perception that the Europeans had failed at Versailles as a result of their outdated political systems, their greed, and their unrealistic vision of the future.

Upon his return to New York, Dulles continued at Sullivan and Cromwell. Sullivan and Cromwell rewarded him with a salary increase and a firm partnership. Dulles was promoted to senior partner, responsible for the entire firm, in 1925. He was only 38 years old. During the latter 1920s and throughout the 1930s Dulles dedicated himself to the firm.

Dulles attended the Oxford Conference on "Church, Community and State" in July of 1937. The conference was intended to analyze the role of the church in modern society with particular emphasis on issues of world peace. Dulles's participation in the conference confirmed a deeply held, though long dormant, belief that Christianity could serve an integral and dynamic role in shaping moral foreign and domestic policies designed to maintain global peace and security. Building on his Presbyterian upbringing, Dulles returned from Oxford convinced that only socially moral policies could guarantee world peace. Moreover, for Dulles, the formulation and implementation of this policy was not simply a necessity but a duty. Consequently, he continued his association with the Federal Council of Churches, becoming chairman of its Commission on a Just and Durable Peace in 1940. Throughout the rest of his life, and particularly during his tenure as secretary of state, Dulles's incorporation of Christian dynamism into his political beliefs was evident.

Dulles clarified his understanding of the duty of the church in promoting and maintaining peace and security in his 1939 book, *War, Peace, and Change*. In it Dulles attempted to offer an explanation and propose solutions for the apparently inevitable return of world war. He continued to excoriate the European powers and traced the present situation directly to the failure of Wilsonian idealism at Versailles. Dulles proposed an international system of "guidance and arbitration," which would safeguard the world against subsequent violence. *War, Peace, and Change* was neither cogently argued nor realistic, yet it reflected Dulles's evolving belief that only through deep-seated morality in the hearts of all men could their most destructive creation, war, be averted.

The late 1930s were also notable because of the beginning of his relationship with Thomas E. Dewey. In 1937, Dewey, a 36-year-old rackets investigator in New York, was invited by Dulles to become a partner at Sullivan and Cromwell. The Republican Party of New York pressured Dewey to run for the office of District Attorney. In a shock to many, Dewey ran and won, with Dulles's full support, cementing a relationship that propelled Dulles more and more into the national political spotlight. Dewey unexpectedly found himself a GOP candidate for President in 1940—despite the fact that he was only 40 years old and had never held a national office. Dulles avidly supported Dewey's bids for the presidency in 1944 and 1948.

During World War II Dulles worked to create a successor to the League of Nations in concert with other U.S. intellectuals, politicians, and pacifists as diverse as Reinhold Niebuhr and John Coleman Bennett. This time, America must forcefully take the lead, must "collaborate . . . working in the muck and mire" to ensure the creation of an international system based on peace. Dulles believed the key to the establishment of international cooperation would be achieved only through

American aggressiveness—partially in atonement for their passivity in 1919 and partially because of their position of power at the close of the war. Thus he viewed U.S. leadership and international cooperation as a prescription for peace and security.

In mid-1945 Dulles was appointed as a Republican advisor to the Truman administration's State Department delegation to the Council of Foreign Ministers meeting. Soviet Foreign Minister V. M. Molotov's hard-nosed demands for Soviet control and autonomy in Eastern Europe rapidly altered Dulles's previous beliefs in the possibility of peaceful coexistence and cooperation. Upon his return from the Council of Foreign Ministers meeting, Dulles carefully stated that the consultation with the Soviets "has not created difficulties. It has merely revealed difficulties of long standing which war has obscured." Dulles immediately began an extensive, self-taught course on the political background and tactics of Communist theory. He engaged in a particularly close read of Joseph Stalin's *The Problems of Leninism*. Dulles concluded that the Soviet Union constituted a greater threat to world peace and security—the two goals of both his Christian idealism and diplomatic experience—than Hitler ever had.

In back-to-back issues of *Life* magazine in June 1946 Dulles prescribed a straightforward policy of concerted resistance to Soviet expansion. Deterrence would be made effective through superior military strength—although Dulles admitted that such an effort would have little practical impact on the Soviets—and, more importantly, through the unqualified demonstration that U.S. freedom was infinitely superior to Communism. Not surprisingly for Dulles, evidence of that fact was most significant at "the religious level." Although his formulations would be refined over the next several years, here, in 1946 is a brief but cogent encapsulation of Dulles's primary policy goals as secretary of state.

Domestic economic uncertainty and an uneven record in foreign affairs appeared to doom incumbent President Harry S Truman in the 1948 presidential election. Truman's Republican opponent was none other than Dulles's longtime ally, Thomas E. Dewey. As the election neared, most assumed that Dewey would defeat Truman and appoint his old friend Dulles as secretary of state. With Dewey's victory seemingly assured—which virtually guaranteed his appointment as secretary of state—Dulles left for Paris in mid-September of 1948 to attend the United Nations General Assembly, which planned to discuss the situation in Berlin. While in Paris, Secretary of State George Marshall entered into a private conversation with Dulles regarding the upcoming "transition," evidencing just how sure Dewey's victory appeared to be. However, Truman prevailed over Dewey in the closest presidential election since 1916. Although Dulles was appointed the nominal head of the U.S. delegation to the United Nations, it appeared that Dulles, now 61 years old, would never occupy the office of secretary of state.

The bitter disappointment in the 1948 presidential election was followed only six months later by an apparent opening. On July 6, 1949, Senator Robert F. Wagner of New York resigned, and Governor Dewey, ever in Dulles's corner, appointed his old friend to the vacancy. Dulles was unsure about the appointment, but Dewey prevailed, and Dulles was sworn in as senator from New York. On that same day he resigned from his senior partnership at Sullivan and Cromwell, citing the demands of his political career and advancing age.

Dulles entered the Senate with aplomb, giving his first speech on the floor less than a week after his swearing-in regarding the importance of senatorial ratification of the NATO treaty. For the rest of his brief tenure, Dulles focused on the dire issue of China as Chiang Kai-shek and the Nationalists fought for political survival against Mao Zedong and the advancing Communists. Dulles was instrumental in the Senate appropriation of $125 million for the Nationalist cause. Yet, his tenure in the Senate was short lived when he was defeated in the general election by Herbert Lehman. What was surprising was that Dulles lost by a mere 200,000 votes.

Following his departure from the Senate, Dulles took the opportunity to put down some of his ideas in a new book, *War or Peace*. His new book evidenced the maturation of his thoughts regarding the Soviet threat and illustrated his deepening anti-Communism. In addition, Dulles developed his moralistic Christian critique of Communism, explaining that "Soviet Communism starts with an atheistic, Godless premise. Everything else flows from that premise." Although he commended the adoption of containment as a policy of initial success—especially in regard to Western Europe—he excoriated the policy for its marked failures, particularly in China and Eastern Europe. He maintained his devotion to peace, but he stood clearly for the dual policies that would guide him as secretary of state: firm anti-Communism supported by an intractable moral critique.

Following rather lengthy negotiations, Dulles was sworn in as a "consultant" to the Department of State on April 26, 1950. Dulles's first assignment in his new post, the negotiation of a final peace treaty with Japan, thereby ending formal U.S. occupation, was a dramatic success, particularly in the context of heightening tension on the Korean peninsula. After months of careful negotiating, the treaty was signed on September 4, 1951, in San Francisco. The Japanese Peace Treaty reflected Dulles's views on international affairs. On the one hand, Dulles hewed to the lessons of Versailles in 1919, endeavoring to create a modest reparations schedule that would not economically cripple Japan or sow the seeds of vengeance. At the same time, the necessities of cooperation and mutual security arrangements in the face of Chinese aggression and Soviet threats were clearly of primary importance as Dulles set up a mutually reinforcing set of agreements to forestall Communist expansion.

The achievement of the Japanese Peace Treaty and Dulles's early support for intervention to support South Korea seemed to entrench his bipartisanship and cooperation with the Truman administration. Yet, the stalemate in Korea quickly brought old animosities to the surface as Dulles publicly rebuked the president for his lack of commitment to all-out victory over the Communists. As the Japanese Peace Treaty approached ratification in the Senate in 1952, Dulles was apparently reverting to bald partisanship once again because he anticipated a Republican victory in the upcoming presidential election and one more opportunity to hold a powerful policymaking office. He proceeded to attack the Democrats' containment policy as one "not of strength but of desperation," as he surveyed the Republican field of presidential candidates. Privately, Dulles decided early on to support General Dwight Eisenhower over his old acquaintance, Robert Taft.

However, he kept the decision to himself until he could meet with Eisenhower personally in 1952 and devoted himself to a new exposition of U.S. foreign policy. His article, "A Policy of Boldness," was published in late May 1952. It was a forthright attempt to secure a policymaking position in the anticipated incoming Republican administration while hewing closely to his Christian idealism—which was now appearing more and more as a moral mission—and his fears of the deficiencies of current U.S. policy that he believed was characterized by moral laxity, reactionary decision making, and military inadequacy. Dulles advocated a policy of determined deterrence using the entirety of the U.S. arsenal—an approach he believed appealed to Eisenhower's military background. Dulles's preeminence in the field of foreign relations garnered him the unenviable task of constructing the Republican foreign policy plank, after a joint behest by Eisenhower and Taft. The resultant platform was filled with moralistic jargon and apocalyptic visions of Communist expansion and domination. Neither Taft nor Eisenhower was particularly pleased with the final product but both endorsed it, solidifying Dulles's role as the foreign policy voice for the Republicans. The election, which was a stunning victory for Eisenhower, did not, however, assure Dulles the post he had coveted for so long.

Three tense weeks passed before Eisenhower called on John Foster Dulles to be his secretary of state. It appears that Eisenhower had to be convinced of Dulles's appropriateness for the position. Eisenhower was wary of Dulles's ability to play the partisanship game a little too well—especially given his history with the Truman administration. In addition, despite his long-standing ambition to be secretary of state, Dulles was wary of the administrative duties required in heading one of the largest departments in the U.S. government. In the end, Eisenhower invited Dulles to join the cabinet, commenting that "Foster has been studying to be Secretary of State since he was five years old."

After an initial few months of tension with President Eisenhower—Dulles was quite put off by his belief that the president found him to be boring—the two settled into one of the closest and most productive relationships ever forged between the White House and the State Department. Many historians have argued that Eisenhower was essentially a lame-duck president who relied on Dulles to formulate and carry out his administration's foreign policy. On the contrary, Eisenhower firmly controlled the policymaking reins, a fact that Dulles well understood and rarely challenged. He had learned a valuable lesson when his uncle, Robert Lansing, was fired by Wilson for disagreeing with the president one too many times at Versailles. Instead, Eisenhower and Dulles maintained a cordiality that blossomed into deep friendship. Dulles was the only cabinet member who had full access to Eisenhower, much to the chagrin of the president's schedulers and secretaries. The two talked on the phone at least three or four times a day and often took a break in the early evening to share a drink privately and discuss pressing issues.

In addition to working closely with the president, the new secretary of state was acutely aware of the crucial necessity of maintaining positive relations and an open dialogue with legislators on Capitol Hill. His predecessor, Dean Acheson, had been rendered ineffective by congressional animosity, and Dulles was determined to avoid his fate. Dulles's task was made easier by several factors. First, droves of Republicans had entered Congress on Eisenhower's coattails, and Dulles was assured of Republican committee chairmanships and legislative support. Secondly, Dulles's extensive experience in diplomacy and his tenure in the Senate, although brief, helped smooth his appeals to Congress. Yet, the Eisenhower administration was forced to overcome two serious challenges before its control of Congress was ensured. The first was the menace of the junior Senator from Wisconsin, Joseph McCarthy. While a Democratic administration sat in the White House and controlled foreign policy, many Republicans, inside and outside Congress, viewed McCarthy's machinations with responses ranging from outspoken support to tepid approval. But Eisenhower's presidential victory, the first Republican in the White House in 20 years, changed the terms of the debate. Senate Republicans attempted to quiet McCarthy, but his previous successes made him impervious to political threats, and he continued with his heated, almost always false, accusations. Eisenhower attempted to remain above the fray, claiming he would "not get into the gutter with that man," but when McCarthy attacked the army, Eisenhower could keep quiet no longer. With Eisenhower and Dulles's backing, the Senate finally moved to censure McCarthy in late 1954, though the environment of red baiting and labeling lived long after him.

In addition to McCarthy, the Eisenhower administration and the State Department in particular faced another direct threat from Congress. In 1954 Republican Senator John Bricker introduced a revised version of his proposed constitutional amendment limiting the president's power to make executive agreements with foreign countries. Obviously neither Dulles nor Eisenhower was pleased, although they acknowledged the genesis of the amendment. Dulles in particular had long been critical of secret executive agreements, such as the Yalta accords, which he argued weakened the flexibility and dynamism of U.S. foreign policy. Still, for a new Republican administration to be attacked by a Republican senator confounded logic. Together, Dulles and Eisenhower effectively mobilized support for the new administration on Capitol Hill; the Bricker Amendment was defeated by the margin of eight votes, solidifying the Eisenhower administration's control over and cooperation with Congress.

Dulles was the first secretary of state to allow and encourage reporters to quote him directly. In addition, he instituted the practice of allowing television networks to film his press conferences. Indeed, Dulles cultivated the Washington press corps, again learning from his predecessors' missteps. He spent countless hours drafting press releases and briefings, characterized by careful language and forceful pronouncements. Dulles's close relationship with the press, as well as his concise briefings, especially compared with the often rambling presidential appearances, helped buttress the false notion that he, not Eisenhower, was formulating and enacting foreign policy.

Dulles continued to rely primarily on his own judgment and was neither an inspiring nor a friendly administrative leader. The rest of the State Department, primarily regional desk officers and lower-level staffers, were almost immediately put on edge by Dulles's abrasive, formal, demanding style. Not long after his appointment Dulles held a departmentwide meeting at which he demanded in no uncertain terms "positive loyalty" from all State workers, which was tantamount to questioning their previous service and dedication to achieving U.S. policy goals. During his tenure, Dulles's combative style and inapproachability robbed the State Department of numerous competent officers.

Dulles's foreign policy ideas had been, for the most part, worked out in the years prior to his appointment as secretary of state. His implicit goals were to maintain peace through a policy of Christian moralism. During his seven years as secretary of state, Dulles, together with Eisenhower, set out to follow the dual goals of what historians later called the liberal consensus. The liberal consensus was shaped by two broad, mutually reinforcing beliefs. U.S. policy—both foreign and domestic—must be attuned to the dual goals of containing Communism worldwide while maintaining and encouraging domestic prosperity. Such a policy was labeled by the Eisenhower administration as the "New Look" and harkened back to Dulles's 1952 *Life* article, "A Policy of Boldness." For the State Department and Dulles, such goals resulted in a policy of staunch, unmitigated deterrence of Soviet threats, while not allowing military spending to cripple the economy. Achieving these policy goals required a multivalent approach consisting of overlapping security agreements with other countries, deterring Soviet advancement with nuclear diplomacy, and maintaining containment through conventional means. Dulles announced forthrightly that attempting to turn back the Soviets "man for man, gun for gun" would bankrupt the U.S. economy. Consequently, Dulles and Eisenhower moved to reduce the manpower of the standing army, cut back the production of conventional weapons such as guns, ammunition, and tanks, while forging ahead with the development first of America's nuclear arsenal and then embarking on the hydrogen bomb program while simultaneously building bombers capable of delivering nuclear munitions. Dulles viewed nuclear technology and capabilities as an effective deterrent to Soviet advancement, particularly in Southeast Asia and the Middle East.

The first major problem confronting the Eisenhower administration policy makers was the stalemate in Korea. Following diplomatic measures to induce the North Koreans and their Communist Chinese backers to solve the Korean "police action" at the conference table, which came to naught, Dulles and Eisenhower announced that the United States would "not be limited" in its choice of weapons. The threat of nuclear war was palpable. The stalemate was broken by a truce in late 1953, which Dulles attributed to his policy of "brinkmanship." It appears in retrospect that the stalemate was ended by decision makers in the Soviet Union following Joseph Stalin's death, but the lesson Dulles and the Eisenhower administration policy makers learned was that brinkmanship and the threat of nuclear war was an effective policy.

Perhaps the most important arena of Dulles's policymaking as secretary of state came in the form of his relationships with and decisions regarding possible revolutionary movements throughout the world. Following World War II many former colonies took at face value U.S. claims to support self-determination and rushed toward independence. Dulles, however, viewed his job as the preeminent U.S. diplomat to first and foremost stave off Communist expansion worldwide. Leftist movements throughout the Third World challenged Dulles and the Eisenhower administration to create a flexible and effective policy that allowed the United States to continue its rhetorical support for regional autonomy and self-determination while deterring Soviet expansion. The policy of choice was covert activity and counterinsurgency. To engage effectively in covert activity the State Department required a cooperative, efficient, and discreet Central Intelligence Agency (CIA). Thankfully for Dulles (and Eisenhower) the CIA was run by none other than Allen Dulles, the secretary of state's brother. The cooperation and effectiveness of the CIA during the 1950s was unprecedented and was due in no small part to the family ties running closely between Langley and Foggy Bottom.

The first problem spot, according to Dulles, that merited covert action, was Iran. Iran's long history of British domination through the auspices of the Anglo-Iranian Oil Company, which held a monopoly over Iranian oil, set the stage for conflict in 1953. Iranian Prime Minister Mohammad Mosaddeq, who came to power in 1951 on a nationalist platform, first demanded the nationalization of Anglo-Iranian. In the face of defiant opposition from the British, Mosaddeq pursued what he considered a compromise: requiring a 50 percent share in the profits of Anglo-Iranian—a demand based on a similar arrangement between the United States and Saudi Arabia. The British resisted, and Dulles came quickly to their defense. Dulles's opposition to the plan had less to do with the oil reserves than with his belief that Mosaddeq's power was dangerously reliant on the Iranian Communist party, the Tudeh. In the wake of a Mosaddeq fixed election, in which his party garnered 95 percent of the vote prompting comparisons with Soviet "elections," the CIA moved to increase urban unrest and arrest Mosaddeq, with the intention of replacing him with the young Reza Shah Pahlavi. As a side benefit the new regime included major U.S. oil companies in the production and profits of Iranian oil. In this first instance, it appeared to Dulles and U.S. policy makers that covert activity was an effective method in both deterring Communist expansion while simultaneously shoring up the U.S. economy.

Guatemala presented a similar conundrum. The small Central American country had long been a staunch U.S. ally, agreeing with U.S. policy while also supplying a fertile investment ground for U.S. companies, exemplified by the United Fruit Company, which controlled most of Guatemala's fruit production (its most valuable export) as well as successive governments. In 1951 Jacobo Armenz Guzmán was elected on reform platform. Arbenz began his reforms by announcing that he would seize more than 200,000 acres (most of which were uncultivated) from the United Fruit Company to effect a land distribution program for the more than 60 percent of landless peasants. Arbenz offered to pay Guatemalan market value for the seized United Fruit holdings but was rebuffed. Not surprisingly, such an initiative met with stringent opposition from United Fruit and its investors, including the Dulles brothers. In addition, Arbenz's government included numerous avowed socialists—though he professed Communism an anathema—which worried policy makers in Washington. Dulles hurriedly called and attended an inter-American conference in Caracas, Venezuela, in March 1954 to demand a unified condemnation of "international Communism." Not surprisingly, the motion passed. But the Organization of American States (OAS) refused to approve a similar condemnation. The opposition of OAS did not deter Dulles and Eisenhower, who ordered the CIA to begin training Guatemalan exiles in Honduras and Nicaragua for the overthrow of Arbenz. The invasion and overthrow occurred in June, with the help of the CIA and U.S. air support. Arbenz was forced to flee, and Dulles triumphantly crowed that Guatemala had been saved from "Communist imperialism." Given the success of covert activity and counterinsurgency in Iran and Guatemala, it became a chosen foreign policy tool of successive U.S. administrations and evidenced Dulles's willingness to turn back the Communist threat at all costs.

Covert activity and reliance on the CIA and his brother did not solve all of Dulles's policymaking problems. At the same time that the successful Guatemalan coup was taking place Dulles's attention was called to a far away and potentially more explosive situation in Southeast Asia. Ho Chi Minh, the nationalist leader of Vietnamese independence, coordinated his efforts of Vietnamese domestic resistance to Japanese occupation with the Office of Strategic Services—the U.S. precursor to the CIA. Throughout World War II, Ho's nationalist credentials during the war were sufficient to garner him the title of an official OSS agent. The reassertion of French control—and U.S. acquiescence to renewed French domination—

pushed Ho toward policies more and more in opposition with those formulated in Washington, particularly as Europe oriented policies and the Cold War dominated U.S. foreign policymakers' decision making.

By 1954 the Vietnamese, under Ho's leadership, had been fighting the French colonial administration for almost seven years. At this point the United States was funding nearly 80 percent of the French effort and was operating under the premise of the "domino theory," which Eisenhower articulated on April 7, 1954. Essentially, if one country or domino fell in Southeast Asia (or indeed anywhere in the world) others were sure to follow. Eisenhower's dour prognosis for world politics was taken directly from Dulles, who declared that the United States could not afford to allow "one rotten apple" to "spoil the whole barrel." Ho's credentials as a nationalist and his prior cooperation with U.S. officials bought him little empathy in Washington as Dulles determined to stave off revolution in Southeast Asia while offering support to a vital European ally. As the French position in Indochina deteriorated, Dulles advocated using small-scale nuclear weapons, arguing that such a course of action was the only possible way of defeating the advancing Communist threat. Eisenhower flatly refused him—one of the few times that they disagreed so vehemently on a policy—believing that the use of nuclear weapons would still necessitate the landing of U.S. ground forces, something Eisenhower was determined to avoid.

Without direct U.S. military intervention—which Dulles proposed and the French declined while requesting U.S. air support instead, which was denied—the French fort of Dien Bien Phu fell on May 7, 1954, sealing France's fate in its former colony. An international conference was already scheduled to meet in Geneva at the beginning of June, and the question of Indochina was added to the agenda over Dulles's vehement objections. Dulles himself attended the conference against his will and only once it was clear that China was sending foreign minister Zhou Enlai as its emissary. The U.S. secretary of state made a point of avoiding Zhou Enlai at all public and social functions and refused to shake his hand or otherwise acknowledge the Chinese representative at the official meetings. Ultimately, Dulles and the United States were not among the signatories of the Geneva Accords regarding Indochina, which divided the country at the 17th parallel, provided for unification elections in 1956, and prohibited international interferences or alliances until that time. The stage was set for escalating U.S. involvement in Vietnam, and Dulles was ready.

Dulles worked to install an U.S.-friendly leader, Ngo Dinh Diem. Diem had been in exile in the United States since 1950 because of his collaboration with the Japanese occupiers, studying and cultivating friendships with powerful politicians throughout the Vietnamese struggle for independence. His connected U.S. benefactors installed him as the democratic leader of South Vietnam. Dulles installed several CIA handlers in South Vietnam as well to ensure the State Department of Diem's continuing cooperation. Dulles worked closely with Diem to make sure that the 1956 elections provided for in the Geneva Accords did not occur, arguing that Communist infiltration from the North rendered a fair election impossible. In actuality, it was clear that Ho Chi Minh would win a resounding victory—in both North and South Vietnam—should the elections actually occur. The goal of U.S. policy was to create a democratic infrastructure in South Vietnam, characterized by capitalist development, educational opportunity, increased access to education, and social welfare facilities. Such a policy was, however, a complete failure. Diem was a Catholic in a region that was 90 percent Buddhist and an adept practitioner of crony capitalism, which won him the undying enmity of many Vietnamese citizens and the contingent loyalty of a few. Regardless, Dulles and the Americans were prepared to "sink or swim with Diem." The U.S. commitment continued to grow, morphing from political and economic assistance to increasing numbers of military advisors throughout Dulles's tenure at the State Department.

The United States' official support for Diem in Vietnam raised new issues for their policies in China and the rest of Southeast Asia. Fears of Communist China's expansion demanded quick responses. Consequently, Dulles formed the Southeast Asia Treaty Organization (SEATO) in 1955. The goal of the organization was to form a collective security alliance to protect the countries of that region from oppressive takeovers, ostensibly from Communist China, while also creating economic partnerships. Oddly, the member nations were the United States, France, Great Britain, New Zealand, and Australia. The only Asian countries that signed on were the Philippines, Thailand, and Pakistan. Obviously Dulles's focus on mutual security agreements demanded the creation of such an alliance in Asia—with or without the participation of Asian nations. With SEATO in his back pocket, Dulles moved to shore up U.S. influence in South Vietnam, sending military and political advisors. Both Dulles and his boss, President Eisenhower, believed that their policies in Asia prevented dominoes from falling and deterred Communist expansion, but in reality their activity did little good and fostered even less goodwill.

Dulles's and Eisenhower's attention was, not surprisingly, more focused on Europe. Events in Southeast Asia proved the relative importance of fostering positive relations with European allies rather than currying favor with Third World and emerging countries. Of primary focus for Dulles was the creation and ratification of the European Defense Community (EDC). The EDC hoped to integrate both the European militaries and economies to ease defense spending domestically while ensuring economic growth. Yet long-standing European animosities, many of which had been reentrenched during World War II, thwarted Dulles's ideal of a mutually cooperative Europe and America. The French toed the line while the United States funded their endeavors in Southeast Asia but adamantly refused the even remote possibility of German rearmament. The British, French, and U.S. statesmen wrangled over the exact definitions and responsibilities of the EDC, and it eventually went down to ignominious defeat as the British advocated limited rearmament of West Germany coupled with the stationing of British troops along French borders for protection. This was more than the French could bear, and Dulles's grand plan for European military cooperation was defeated with Eisenhower's acquiescence, which "placed military security above fiscal economy" as America and its European allies bickered about the primacy of trade arrangements over security agreements.

The failure of the EDC and the fragility of American-European relations proved costly during perhaps the greatest crisis during Dulles's tenure as secretary of state—Suez. The lingering effects of British colonialism in Egypt coupled with Arab dissatisfaction with Western policy regarding the establishment and maintenance of an independent Israel resulted in an increasingly fragile peace. Dulles sought to stabilize the region through one of his preferred methods—the creation of a cooperative security agreement. Consequently he supported Turkish and Pakistani efforts to establish a mutual security alliance. Yet when the Baghdad Pact was ratified in February 1955, it included not only Turkey, Iran, Iraq, and Pakistan, but also Great Britain. Dulles balked at the appearance of the United States as supporters of Britain's colonial interests in the region—despite its earlier intervention in Iran. Despite Britain's pressure for full U.S. participation in the agreement, Dulles would only send an "observer" to the Baghdad proceedings. Such an action appeared to contradict Dulles's intention to create overlapping security agreements throughout the world. However, in reality, it reflected the differences between British and U.S. policy. Dulles's primary concern in the Middle East was to contain Communist expansion while maintaining U.S. oil reserves. The British, on the other hand, were intent on solidifying their position—and reinforcing their colonial position—which was an anathema to Dulles. The contrast between Dulles's and the British approach would soon become obvious.

Egypt's leader, General Gamal Abdel Nasser, who was vehemently opposed to the Baghdad Pact, sought to further distance his nation from British economic control by building a dam to harness the power of the Nile River to both alleviate Egyptian farmers' dependence on unpredictable seasonal flooding and increase the fertility of lands bordering the Nile. Nasser appealed to the United States for funding the dam, and throughout 1955 Dulles proved amenable to such an investment of U.S. dollars. Dulles's reasons were twofold. On the one hand, Dulles believed Egyptian opposition to British colonialism opened avenues for Soviet encroachment. Funding the proposed Aswan Dam would prove U.S. commitment to Egyptian autonomy while simultaneously thwarting the Soviets. In addition, Dulles hoped that a cooperative U.S.-oriented Egypt—an Egypt dependent on U.S. dollars for their dam—would facilitate peace between Arab states and Israel. But Nasser proved intractable on the Israel question, and in an effort to secure his position Nasser opened channels with both the West and the Soviet bloc to secure arms. Both the British and the Americans negotiated with Nasser's emissaries, in effect trying to blackmail him into accepting Western arms in return for a pledge not to deal with the Soviet Union. Nasser refused to deal in ultimatums and eventually procured arms from the Soviet Union. Following the Egyptian–Soviet arms deal, the Soviet Union offered to finance the dam, but Nasser demurred, believing that he had already secured adequate funding from the United States and the World Bank. Dulles, in response to Nasser's decision to arm Egypt with Soviet weapons, denied Nasser funding for the dam just as the Egyptian foreign minister was landing in Washington to cement the agreement. In response, Nasser nationalized the Suez Canal—which was under joint British and French control—to fund the dam.

The Suez Canal—the causeway through which nearly all the West's oil supply traveled—was too important to let go. The French and the British secretly negotiated the beginning of hostilities against Egypt with Israel, which was intent on safeguarding its own tenuous position in the Middle East. Dulles and Eisenhower were not consulted regarding the British–French–Israeli plans but warned British Prime Minister Anthony Eden not to act rashly. Their warnings, however, came too late, as the Israelis attacked Egypt on October 29, 1956. The military intervention was a disaster as the British and French were slow to support the Israelis. Dulles and Eisenhower were, not surprisingly, furious. Their biggest fear was that the Soviets would use the situation as an opportunity to intervene directly in Egypt to support Nasser, establishing a foothold in Northern Africa and the Middle East in the face of naked Western aggression. Dulles's position was made even more difficult by the almost simultaneous rumbling of Soviet tanks into Poland and Hungary as it moved to destroy protest movements in those two countries. Dulles surveyed the possibilities and quickly determined the war in the Middle East must be ended. In an attempt to achieve this goal, he threatened to devalue British currency and cut off all oil supplies to Great Britain. In the face of U.S. opposition, Soviet Premier Nikita Khrushchev's provision of weapons to Nasser and the Egyptians, and their own military blunders, the British–French–Israeli troops quickly retreated.

Eisenhower sent Dulles to the United Nations to secure a condemnation of unilateral French–British actions and a reaffirmation of the sanctity of the United Nations. On November 2, 1956, the General Assembly passed a resolution demanding international cooperation to end the conflict, and a fragile peace resumed in the Middle East, but the fallout from the Suez Crisis was enormous. The once seemingly impenetrable Western alliance proved susceptible to intrigue and secret agreements, rendering it and U.S. dominance of it less effective. Emerging nations and Third World countries looked approvingly on Nasser's blatant defiance of the West and adroit courting of the Soviet Union to achieve economic and national autonomy. The Suez Crisis situation also allowed the Soviet Union to consolidate its power in Eastern Europe, much to the chagrin of Dulles and other U.S. policy makers.

Dulles viewed the passage of the UN resolution and the cessation of hostilities over Suez as one of his finest moments. The night after the UN vote, Dulles awoke with intense abdominal pains and went to the hospital. An exploratory operation revealed that Dulles had advanced cancer. He would not return to full duty in the State Department until January 1957 and had only 18 months left to defeat communism and safeguard his legacy of Christian moralism and a dynamic and prosperous United States.

Following his first cancer operation, Dulles quickly returned to the State Department, evidencing both his commitment to his office and his president, but also his capacity for hard work in the face of physical debilitation. The aftereffects of the Suez Crisis demanded attention, and Dulles worked hard to contain Nasser's growing power and friendship with the Soviets while attempting to patch up the sorely strained Western alliance. Consequently, in 1957 the administration put forth the Eisenhower Doctrine. Dulles requested a resolution from Congress to deter Communist aggression in the Middle East. The Doctrine called for an economic aid package as well as provisions for military equipment and training. Dulles considered the proposal another "stop sign" for the Soviets. He peppered his proposal to Congress with apocalyptic visions of "the inevitability of world war" should Communist expansion in the Middle East continue. Despite Dulles's cultivation of Congressional cooperation, many senators balked at the alarmist tone of the secretary of state's view of world affairs. The proposal was not clearly defined in its geographic impact and appeared to be a unilateral move in violation of the United Nations. The proposed magnitude of the threat and the vague military and diplomatic prescriptive responses reflected Dulles's view of the insidious nature of Communism as well as the flexibility required in U.S. responses. After weeks of debate, Congress finally passed the Doctrine, assuring the supremacy of Dulles's impact on U.S. foreign policy—the Communists now appeared surrounded by security agreements, agreements fostered, financed, and directed from Washington, the only country with the moral fiber to promote and maintain world peace.

Following the Eisenhower Doctrine, Dulles faced renewed opposition to U.S. policy in both the Middle East, characterized by troubles in Lebanon and Iraq, as well as in the Formosa Strait, as perceived threats from Communist China intensi-fied. Still, Dulles hewed to predictable policy decisions reflecting his intractable understanding of the diabolical Communist threat and strident belief in America's singular mission to meet that threat. The final crisis of his tenure as Secretary of State occurred in Berlin.

The question of Berlin had occupied U.S. policy makers for more than a decade when, in the wake of the successful launch of Sputnik and growing fears of nuclear war, a summit was proposed. The primary issues on the summit agenda were the suspension of nuclear tests, the creation of a "nuclear free zone" in West and East Germany, Poland, and Czechoslovakia, and discussion regarding the reunification of Germany. The West, led by Dulles and the United States, tentatively agreed to such a summit but supported the idea that German reunification could only be achieved through free elections. Dulles's adherence to such a plan, long considered untenable by many NATO enthusiasts, was based on both his own uncompromis-ing view of Communism and his personal friendship with West German Chancel-lor Konrad Adenauer.

According to the Soviet Union, free elections and German unification, with the underlying assumption by Dulles that the emergent Germany would be Western oriented and eventually a NATO member, was impossible. Khrushchev denounced Western militarism and stated that the only possibility was a relinquishing of occu-pation powers in Berlin. He proposed to create a neutral and disarmed Berlin, "a free city, without any state, including both existing German states, interfering in its life." Khrushchev was, in effect, attempting to trap the United States and its West-ern allies by seeming to support autonomy in Berlin.

Yet Dulles, and the rest of U.S. and Western policy makers, quickly perceived the slipperiness of Khrushchev's proposals, for Berlin was surrounded on all four sides by East Germany. To accept Khrushchev's plan, which came with a six-month deadline, was tantamount to acknowledging the sovereignty of East Germany, pos-sibly sentencing Berlin to another blockade, and ratcheting up the threat of nuclear war. In response to these ominous possibilities, NATO called a conference sched-uled for mid-December. Dulles insisted on making the trip, although he had been in the hospital for the previous five days with acute inflammation of his intestines caused by his recurrent abdominal cancer.

Dulles arrived in Paris for the NATO council pale, gaunt, and unable to hold down any solid food. The other Western diplomats were reassured by Dulles's presence despite his obvious ill health, as one emissary noted that Dulles's "granite-like" opposition to Soviet machinations was imperative. Dulles and the other NATO diplomats construed Khrushchev's proposals broadly, replying to the Soviet premier that the question of Berlin could not be settled without full negotiations over the state of Germany as a whole. Following the NATO conference Dulles returned to the United States to convalesce while continuing to hash out U.S. pol-icy options as the Soviets' May 27, 1958, deadline approached.

As the Soviet position appeared intractable and Khrushchev's deadline drew near, Dulles journeyed to Paris once more for another NATO council meeting as well as private consultations with leaders in London and Bonn. Dulles was visibly unwell, prompting British Prime Minister Harold Macmillan to remark that "In spite of all the troubles and difficulties we have had with this strange man, I had grown to have an affection and respect for him." Despite his incredible physical pain, Dulles remained committed to the principles that guided his understanding of U.S. foreign policy. He flatly refused to give an inch to the Soviets, advising Macmillian, who would be visiting Moscow in an attempt to negotiate with the Soviet Union, to defend Berlin and West Germany at all costs and deny the possibility of unification without free elections, regardless of what Khrushchev promised. Dulles returned to the United States in late February, having made his last official trip as secretary of state.

Dulles's conversations with NATO leaders and particularly with Harold Macmillan of Great Britain bore fruit as Khrushchev backed off his earlier demands and agreed to an international summit where questions of European security and disarmament agreements would be discussed while not pressing his claims to German reunification. Macmillan traveled to Washington and briefed Dulles and Eisenhower on the events of his Moscow visit. Although Dulles proved contrary to any negotiations with the Soviets, Macmillan thought this a result of his declining health. Macmillan secured Eisenhower's approval for a summit in May 1959. Dulles, however, would not be in attendance.

Dulles lingered in the hospital from February until March 22, 1959, when his wife took him home to make him as comfortable as possible. He received numerous notes and packages from friends, colleagues in the State Department, even Congressional and political opponents. He was visited at the hospital jointly by Dwight Eisenhower and Winston Churchill and reminisced over their long fight against Communist expansion. Even Nikita Khrushchev expressed his sympathies. Aware that he would not last much longer, Dulles formally submitted his resignation to Eisenhower on April 11, fearful that his commander would not take necessary precautions in sending a well-prepared envoy to the ministers meeting scheduled for May 11. Eisenhower regretfully accepted Dulles's resignation. He told Dulles in a personal note that "you have been a staunch bulwark of our nation against the machinations of Imperialistic Communism" and requested that Dulles serve "to whatever extent your health will permit, as a consultant to me and the State Department in international affairs." Dulles died on May 24, 1959, in his sleep.

Instead of courting positive domestic or international opinion, Dulles hewed intransigently to the tenets that defined his view of the world: a deeply held belief in the mission of the United States to safeguard freedom, democracy, and Christian moralism while unerringly defending the world from atheistic Communist expansion. He was alternately reviled and embraced for his inflexibility, his often-deficient administrative abilities, and single-minded defense of U.S. ideals. His policies delved into apparently un-American secrecy and covert actions but were, in his mind, fully justified in the fight for liberty. His tenure as secretary of state can best be summed up in his own words: "We are here to re-dedicate ourselves to the task of dispelling the shadows that are being cast upon the free world. . . . This is a time for greatness. . . . We pray for greatness in the spirit of self-sacrifice, so that we may forsake lesser objectives and interests to devote ourselves wholly to the well-being of all of us. . . . All of us have a vital stake in this sense of increasing sacrifice. . . . The forces arrayed against us are formidable but not irresistible."

BIBLIOGRAPHICAL ESSAY

John Foster Dulles left an expansive amount of documentation. His complete, though as yet unpublished, personal papers (1888–1959) and State Department papers (1952–1959) are available at Princeton University's Seeley G. Mudd Library. Princeton also has several collections of Dulles's State Department papers from the Dwight D. Eisenhower Presidential Library. The Oral History Collection on John Foster Dulles, a collection of interviews regarding the former secretary of state, also at Princeton University, offers valuable insights into how Dulles was viewed by other State Department officials. The Eisenhower Library itself as well as the National Archives and Records Administration have extensive holdings on Dulles's tenure in the State Department as well as some of his pre-State Department papers.

A first-rate, concise examination of Dulles's life, statesmanship, and impact on U.S. policy is Richard H. Immerman's *John Foster Dulles: Piety, Power and Pragmatism in U.S. Foreign Policy* (1999). In addition to the biography, Immerman has edited two collections of essays on Dulles, the first, *John Foster Dulles and the Diplomacy of the Cold War* (1990), which offers an archival-based reassessment of Dulles impact on policy during the Eisenhower years, and the second, *John Foster Dulles: The Leader and the Legend* (1989), which came out of papers from the John Foster Dulles Centennial Conference in 1988 at the Woodrow Wilson School of Public and International Affairs. Frederick Marks offers an interesting interpretation of Dulles's life and impact in *Power and Peace: The Diplomacy of John Foster Dulles* (1995). A useful source for understanding Dulles's early life and relationships with his family, especially his siblings, is Leonard Mosley's *Dulles: A Biography of Eleanor, Allen and John Foster Dulles and their Family Network* (1979). Townsend Hoopes offers an expansive though somewhat disorganized account of Dulles's career in *The Devil and John Foster Dulles* (1973).

For general 1950s U.S. policy a good starting place is Walter LaFeber's *America, Russia and the Cold War* (9th ed., 2002). For a more detailed account including domestic issues see James T. Patterson's *Grand Expectations* (1996). McCarthyism and its impact on the State Department is covered, though very briefly, in Richard M. Fried's *Nightmare in Red* (1990). For treatments of Eisenhower's presidency, see Stephen Ambrose, *Eisenhower: Soldier and President* (1991); and Eisenhower's own account, *Waging Peace: The White House Years, 1956–1961* (1983).

The best source on the Iranian coup is Kermit Roosevelt's *Countercoup: The Struggle for the Control of Iran* (1981), supplemented by Daniel Yergin's *The Prize: The Epic Quest for Oil, Power and Money* (1992). Herman Finer's *Dulles over Suez: The Theory and Practice of His Diplomacy* (1964) and William Roger Louis and Roger Owen (eds.), *Suez 1956: The Crisis and Its Consequences* (1989) effectively address U.S. policy during the Suez Crisis. Richard H. Immerman's excellent *The CIA in Guatemala: The Foreign Policy of Intervention* (1982) offers a detailed account of U.S. policy and supplements more general accounts such as Lars Schoultz's *Beneath the United States* (1998). Marilyn Young's *The Vietnam Wars* (1991) and Lloyd C. Gardner's *Approaching Vietnam* (1988) address America's policies toward Indochina and France during the 1950s. David F. Schmitz's *Thank God They're On Our Side* (1999) addresses U.S. policy toward Guatemala, Iran, and Vietnam during the period. Policy toward Europe can best be understood by examining James McAllister's *No Exit: America and the German Problem* (2002), William Hitchcock's *France Restored: Cold War Diplomacy and the Quest for Leadership in Europe* (1998), or Edward Fursdon's *The European Defense Community: A History* (1980).

Amy Portwood

LAWRENCE S. EAGLEBURGER (1930–)

Served 1992–1993
Appointed by President George H. W. Bush
Republican

Lawrence Sidney Eagleburger was born in Milwaukee, Wisconsin, on August 1, 1930. He received his B.S. degree from the University of Wisconsin in 1952 with a major in history. After serving as a first lieutenant in the U.S. Army from 1952 to 1954, Eagleburger received an M.S. in political science from the University of Wisconsin in 1957.

Upon graduation, Eagleburger entered the Foreign Service. His first position was in the economic section of the U.S. embassy in Tegucigalpa, Honduras. In 1959, the year of Castro's coming to power, Eagleburger was assigned as political analyst of Cuba at the State Department's Bureau of Intelligence and Research. Two years later, in 1961, he was assigned to the economic section of the U.S. embassy in the Belgrade, Yugoslavia.

In 1963, an earthquake occurred in the Yugoslav republic of Macedonia. Eagleburger led the U.S. government's efforts to provide medical and other assistance. He was recalled in 1965 to Washington to serve on the Secretariat staff dealing with European Affairs. In March 1966, he was named as special assistant to former Secretary of State Dean Acheson, who was President Lyndon Johnson's special assistant on Franco-NATO issues. In August 1966 he became acting director of the Secretariat staff. In October of that year, Eagleburger was appointed a member of the National Security Council staff. After a year in this position, Eagleburger was named in October 1967 as special assistant to Undersecretary of State Nicholas Katzenbach.

After Richard Nixon's election as president in 1968, Eagleburger was appointed as liaison to Henry Kissinger, who was to assume the position of National Security Advisor. The following January, Eagleburger was appointed Kissinger's executive assistant and helped him set up the National Security Council staff. Later, in September 1969, he was assigned to the U.S. mission to NATO in Brussels, where he would serve as political advisor and head of the political section.

Nearly two years later in August 1971, Eagleburger returned to Washington as Deputy Assistant Secretary of Defense. In 1973, Eagleburger served in a variety of positions. He became Acting Assistant Secretary of Defense for International Security Affairs and then returned to the White House under Kissinger as Deputy Assistant to the President for National Security. When Kissinger replaced William Rogers later in 1973 as secretary of state, Eagleburger followed him as executive assistant to the secretary of state. In 1975, he was named by President James Earl Carter, Jr., as Ambassador to Yugoslavia. In 1981, he was recalled to Washington by President Ronald Reagan to be Assistant Secretary of State for European Affairs. In February of 1982, Eagleburger was appointed by Reagan to the third highest position in the State Department, the Undersecretary for Political Affairs.

In May 1984, Eagleburger retired from the Department of State after serving over 27 years as a career Foreign Service officer. Prior to his retirement, he had been awarded the Distinguished Civilian Service Medal from the Department of Defense, the President's Award for Distinguished Federal Civilian Service, the Wilbur J. Carr Award for Foreign Service Career Officers with distinguished and lengthy service, and the Distinguished Honor Award from the State Department.

From 1984 to 1989 Eagleburger was elected to the boards of the Mutual Life Insurance Company of New York and Josephson International. He was also named president of Kissinger Associates, Inc., a firm founded by Eagleburger's old boss, whose mission was to serve as a consultant to various international corporations.

In 1989, Eagleburger returned to Washington at the beginning of the George H. W. Bush administration as Deputy Secretary of State, second in command to Secretary of State James Baker. During this crucial period, Eagleburger witnessed the collapse of the Soviet empire in East Europe and the subsequent conflict in Yugoslavia, the successful invasion of Panama, the unification of Germany, the implementation of Desert Shield and Desert Storm in the Middle East, and the end of the Soviet Union and the Cold War. After serving as Baker's chief lieutenant for over three years, he was named Acting Secretary of State on August 23, 1992, when Baker resigned to run Bush's doomed presidential reelection campaign. On December 8, 1992, one month after he was defeated for reelection, Bush named Eagleburger as secretary of state. The only career Foreign Service officer to be appointed secretary, Eagleburger was instrumental in convincing Bush to send U.S. forces to Somalia for humanitarian purposes.

Eagleburger received more distinctions and honors in the 1990s. In 1991, he was awarded the Presidential Citizen Medal by President Bush and in 1992 received the Department of State's Distinguished Service Award, the department's highest honor. In 1994, he received an honorary knighthood from Britain's Queen Elizabeth II. In 1997, he received an honorary doctorate from his alma mater, the University of Wisconsin. In 1999, he was named international ambassador-at-large by the American Red Cross. He currently serves as Senior Foreign Policy Advisor for the law firm of Baker, Donelson, Bearman, and Caldwell and has served on the boards of Phillips Petroleum, Halliburton, and Universal Corporation.

BIBLIOGRAPHICAL ESSAY

Eagleburger has not written his memoirs, and no critical analyses of his brief stint as secretary of state are available. The major print reference sources for Eagleburger as secretary of state are *Current Biography 1992, Who's Who in America 1990–1991*, and *Who's Who in American Politics 1991–1992*. Numerous Web sources update Eagleburger's activities since 1993, but no standard print sources are available for the period.

Theodore Hindson

WILLIAM M. EVARTS (1818–1901)

Served 1877–1881
Appointed by President Rutherford B. Hayes
Republican

William Maxwell Evarts served from March 1877 to March 1881 as secretary of state in the administration of President Rutherford B. Hayes. Evarts was born on February 6, 1818, in Boston, Massachusetts. His father, Jeremiah Evarts, was a leading Congregationalist layman, editor of the Congregationalists' *Panoplist* magazine, and a founder of the American Board of Commissioners for Foreign Missions. His mother was Mehetabel Sherman, the daughter of one of the leading figures of the American Revolution, Roger Sherman of Connecticut. William graduated near the top of his class at Yale College in 1837. He read law for a year in Windsor, Vermont, attended Harvard Law School 1838–1839, and then read law in New York City. He was admitted to the New York bar in 1841, and the next year he formed what was to become one of the most prominent New York City law firms for the next 60 years. In 1843 he married Helen Minerva Wardner of Windsor, Vermont, and they had twelve children.

Evarts was one of the leading constitutional and appellate lawyers in the United States in the nineteenth century. His intellectually forceful arguments shaped many landmark decisions in the U.S. courts. As a Whig who supported Zachary Taylor and Daniel Webster, he argued on constitutional grounds in favor of the Compromise of 1850 and the Fugitive Slave Act. He was not an apologist for slavery, as some critics suggested, but rather a strong Unionist. In 1855 he donated a fourth of his savings to support Free-Soilers in Kansas, and in 1856 he became a founder and promoter of the Republican Party. His arguments in court in 1860 on behalf of the State of New York won the latter the Lemmons Slave Case, which established the freedom of slaves whose owners brought them into the port of New York City in transit from one slave state to another. He worked for William Henry Seward's nomination for president in 1860. After Abraham Lincoln named Seward secretary of state, Evarts was disappointed that the New York legislature did not elect him to fill Seward's place in the U.S. Senate.

During the Civil War, Evarts helped organize military regiments in New York as a member of the state's Union Defense Committee. The Lincoln administration retained him to defend the government against court challenges to the legality of the Union blockade, and it sent him to London to assist U.S. Minister Charles Francis Adams in the successful efforts to gain the British government's cooperation in preventing Confederate-purchased commerce raiders from leaving British shipyards. With the death of Chief Justice Roger B. Taney in 1864, Evarts was an obvious candidate to head the Supreme Court, but Lincoln instead chose Salmon P. Chase for political reasons, rather than the attorney whom many in the profession considered the nation's best constitutional lawyer.

In 1868, a request from his longtime political colleague, Secretary of State Seward, summoned Evarts back to Washington to consider joining the counsel for the defense in the trial of President Andrew Johnson. As a Republican loyalist, he had spoken in favor of the congressional reconstruction plan over that of the president, but he agreed to join Johnson's defense team. Why Evarts said yes is unclear, but his role in the trial was pivotal. His logic demolished any pretense for the constitutionality of the Tenure of Office Act under which Congress had impeached Johnson, and he thereby helped save the president from removal from office and also helped preserve the integrity of the Constitution and the rule of law. He stayed on as attorney general through the remainder of Johnson's term.

In 1870 he was back at his firm and led in the creation of the New York City Bar Association, which headed a civic challenge to the corruption of the city's infamous Tweed Ring. In 1871 he once again returned to government service. Under terms of the Treaty of Washington of May 1871, claims by Americans against British shipyards for losses from Confederate ships built in England were submitted to five arbitrators, who met in Geneva in 1871–1872. As counsel to American arbitrator Charles Francis Adams, Evarts once again fashioned a virtually unanswerable argument, this time about Britain's international obligations that led the panel to award $15.5 million to the United States.

During the 1870s Evarts was one of the highest paid and most sought after attorneys in the United States. About two-thirds of his time was spent making arguments before the U.S. Supreme Court and the New York Court of Appeals. Many of his clients were corporations, especially railroads, but in 1875 he successfully defended the eminent Reverend Henry Ward Beecher against charges of adultery in a trial that captured public attention for six months.

In the early weeks of 1877, Evarts once again came to the legal rescue of the nation's political process as he had done in the Johnson trial of 1868. He served as chief counsel for Hayes after Congress formed an electoral commission to determine the outcome of the contested 1876 presidential contest between Republican Hayes and Democrat Samuel J. Tilden. At issue was which set of conflicting electoral votes to accept from the states of South Carolina and Louisiana, and in a strictly partisan vote, the commission approved the ballots for Hayes submitted by the Republican-controlled state governments. Evarts provided the legal rationale for the decision by making a strong argument that the commission could not infringe on the sole authority given to state governments under the Constitution to regulate voting and ballot tabulation in the states.

Even before the creation of the electoral commission, Hayes recorded in his diary that he was considering Evarts for the primary post in his Cabinet, the office of secretary of state. Evarts's loyalty to the Republican Party was well established, his legal prowess was legendary, and he had diplomatic experience. His usual sterling performance as counsel for Hayes during the commission deliberations helped seal his Cabinet appointment.

The political compatibility of Hayes and Evarts was readily apparent within the cabinet. Domestic issues, not foreign policy, were of the greatest significance to the public in the late 1870s, and on the important questions of the day Evarts became a trusted ally of the president. He supported Hayes's Southern policy—controversial within his own party—of removing the remaining federal troops from South Carolina and Louisiana and accepting the end of Republican-Reconstruction governments in those states. Evarts eagerly backed the president's civil-service reforms in the New York City Customs House, a move that reform-minded New York Republicans had long sought to break up the spoils system of state party boss Senator Roscoe Conkling. Evarts also agreed with Hayes's "sound money" policy of opposing the free circulation of silver and the issuance of paperbacks. He stood behind the president's veto of the Bland–Allison Silver Purchase Act, although Congress passed it over the veto.

In foreign policy, Evarts's legal experience clearly shaped his approach to issues. In fact, he was a prototype of many twentieth-century secretaries of state who came to that office after distinguishing themselves as eminent members of the bar. Examples include such men as Elihu Root, Philander C. Knox, Robert Lansing, Charles Evans Hughes, Henry L. Stimson, John Foster Dulles, George P. Shultz, James A. Baker III, and Warren M. Christopher. As an attorney, Evarts sought an orderly foreign policy based on reason, precedent, the rule of law, and artful compromise.

One international issue that Evarts inherited from the preceding administration of President Ulysses S. Grant and Secretary of State Hamilton Fish was relations with Mexico. In late 1876 Porfirio Diaz became president of Mexico, but Washington had not formally recognized the new regime at the time Hayes took office. Although Diaz was popular in his country and the United States had a tradition of recognizing de facto governments, the formality of initiating diplomatic contact was delayed because of the political uncertainties in Washington and Mexico City and a number of frictions along the Rio Grande border. Mexico owed claims to United States citizens for banditry and even murder committed by marauders crossing the river into the United States and retreating back again, and these serious incidents were continuing. Evarts insisted that the Diaz government offer assurances of payment of its obligations and of its intent to seek out and punish the criminals before the United States would renew normal relations. When Diaz, who was still dealing with domestic opponents, failed to respond affirmatively, the Hayes administration, at Evarts's urging, issued an order on June 1, 1877, that authorized the U.S. Army to pursue marauders across the border.

The new Mexican government strongly protested this order, and some critics in both Mexico and the United States alleged that Washington was preparing for a war of conquest. Diaz did send his troops to patrol for bandits, but he also gave them orders to repulse any U.S. forces that entered Mexico. There was war talk in Mexico City. Senator James G. Blaine, the powerful Republican leader in the Senate who had lost his bid for the presidential nomination to Hayes the year before, charged that Evarts's hot pursuit doctrine was dangerous and was intended to aid the South by claiming Mexican territory. Senator Conkling called for a congressional investigation, in part to discredit his old political foe, Evarts. The U.S. minister to Mexico, John W. Foster, warned a congressional committee that Diaz hoped to split Congress from the president, but he also advised that recognition of Diaz would produce cooperation from him on the border. In March 1878, Evarts instructed Foster to establish normal diplomatic relations with the Diaz government, but the secretary refused to rescind the pursuit order because criminal activity continued. On several occasions U.S. troops crossed the border chasing cattle rustlers, Indian bands, and thieves. By February 1880, the frontier was relatively quiet, and Evarts lifted the June 1877 order. Although Diaz had obtained recognition and never officially responded to American complaints, Evarts could with some accuracy claim that his firm action had led to improved order along the Rio Grande.

Evarts's record of accomplishment elsewhere in Latin America was mixed. Although he did not explicitly invoke the Monroe Doctrine, he opposed European involvement in Western Hemispheric affairs. He was on guard against not only any new claims to territory or concessions but also against the transfer of any rights or possessions from one European party to another. In 1879, the French entrepreneur Ferdinand de Lesseps, whose company built the Suez Canal, began planning a canal through the isthmus of Panama. Evarts declared that the United States had a "paramount interest" in any interoceanic canal and that the U.S. treaty with Colombia of 1846, which made the United States the guarantor of Colombian neutrality, gave Washington jurisdiction over any canal project in Panama. He entered into negotiations with Colombia to secure a treaty clarifying this right, but these talks were not concluded during his term in office. Evarts also argued that the Clayton–Bulwer Treaty of 1850, in which the United States and Britain agreed to cooperate in construction of an isthmian canal, did not apply to Panama. London disagreed, and it was not until the Hay–Pauncefote Treaty of 1901 that Britain relinquished its claims to share in a canal under the 1850 treaty. Secretary of State John Hay, who made that later treaty, was assistant secretary of state under Evarts. Although they did not obtain it formally, Evarts and Hayes established, in Hayes's words to the Senate in 1880, that "the policy of this country is a canal under American control." As for de Lesseps, his project ended in ruin in the 1880s.

In 1879 a serious war erupted in South America between Chile on one side and Peru and Bolivia on the other. This War of the Pacific was over possession of valuable nitrate deposits on the Chile–Peru border. Concerned about America's neutral rights in these countries' Pacific ports, Evarts made arguments to the belligerents that anticipated those later advanced by the Wilson administration in 1914 and 1915 toward Britain and Germany. Evarts also offered U.S. mediation of the War of the Pacific in October 1880, but the resulting meeting aboard an American naval vessel failed. The warring parties were too demanding, and Evarts had not given the amateur U.S. envoys sufficiently detailed instructions. The hostilities continued on until 1883, and Evarts's successors in the State Department proved no more able than he to mediate the conflict.

As an attorney with long experience with some of America's major businesses, Evarts took great interest in the advancing of the nation's foreign commerce. He took positive actions to open new markets and to expand old ones. He viewed international trade as a way to promote peace and as a means of strengthening the domestic U.S. economy. He endorsed the idea of sending U.S. Navy cruisers to Africa, Asia, and South America to ease the way for American merchants. In 1878 he made a treaty of commerce with Japan that gave greater tariff autonomy to the Japanese. This convention departed from the previous American practice of joining with the European nations in forcing Japan to set tariffs by treaty. Evarts also made a treaty with Samoa that gave U.S. naval rights in the harbor of Pago Pago in return for making available U.S. good offices in disputes between Samoa and other Western nations. Evarts also took steps to improve the quality and performance of U.S. consuls. One of his most lasting reforms was to get Congress to authorize and fund a system of monthly consular reports to give businessmen the information they needed to be successful in foreign markets.

In January 1879, Evarts's interest in advancing foreign trade and the pressures of domestic politics came into conflict over the issue of exclusion of Chinese laborers from the United States. In response to anti-Chinese agitation in California, where many workers feared competition for jobs from Chinese immigrants who supposedly would work for low wages, Congress passed a bill permitting only 15 Chinese to enter the United States on any one ship. This legislation explicitly nullified portions of the Burlingame Treaty of 1868 that protected free Chinese immigration into the United States. Hayes and Evarts were sympathetic with the concerns of the California workers, but they knew they could not sanction unilateral abrogation of a treaty. They agreed that the president had to veto the bill. For all of his other vetoes, Hayes wrote his own veto message, but in this case he decided to send Congress the reasons penned by Evarts. The secretary of state wrote that the U.S. government would seek restriction of immigration through diplomacy. The method of limitation that this legislation authorized was unacceptable to the administration because it risked setting a precedent whereby the government in Beijing could renounce the treaties on which all American commercial rights in China rested. His logic was so clear that exclusionists could not muster the votes to override the veto.

Evarts instructed Minister George F. Seward in Beijing to discuss immigration restriction with the Chinese government, but the envoy failed to press the issue. Evarts recalled Seward from his post and named James B. Angell, the president of the University of Michigan, as minister to China and as head of a commission to revise the Burlingame Treaty. Joining Angell as treaty commissioners were John F. Swift of California, who favored exclusion, and William H. Trescott of South Carolina, an experienced diplomat. Evarts had extended conversations with Angell and Trescott before they traveled west to join Swift and proceed to China. The secretary shared with the envoys his views on immigration, on extraterritoriality (legal protection of Americans in China), and on commercial prospects in China. Evarts did not provide them with a draft treaty, but he admonished them to be "just and generous" with the Chinese. On November 17, 1880, after little more than a month of negotiations, they signed a treaty with Chinese officials that allowed the United States to "regulate, limit, or suspend" but "not absolutely prohibit" the immigration of Chinese laborers. The diplomats also signed a commercial convention that prohibited U.S. citizens from participating in the opium trade and that provided for mutual consideration of expanded commerce between China and the United States. The commission's work pleased Evarts, and the U.S. Senate easily ratified the two treaties. In Evarts's view this outcome was a policy success because it resolved a sensitive political issue, preserved America's diplomatic integrity, and contributed to growth in foreign commerce.

In March 1881, Evarts relinquished his office to Blaine and the incoming administration of James A. Garfield. In his four years as secretary of state, his accomplishments had been modest in foreign affairs, but foreign affairs were not a top priority of the nation. He had protected American interests and had laid the foundation for future policies with regard to the protection of U.S. citizens, the Panama Canal, defense of neutral rights, and expansion of foreign commerce. He went back to his New York law firm and in January 1885 was elected to the Senate. He served one term but increasingly suffered from poor health and eventually lost his sight. He died on February 28, 1901, in his New York home.

BIBLIOGRAPHICAL ESSAY

Most of Evarts's significant legal arguments and speeches are to be found in Sherman Evarts (ed.), *Arguments and Speeches of William Maxwell Evarts* (1919). The three-volume work includes helpful editorial introductions.

Chester L. Barrow's *William M. Evarts: Lawyer, Diplomat, Statesman* (1941) is the standard biography and the most complete scholarly study of Evarts available. Brainerd Dyer's *The Public Career of William M. Evarts* (1933) is a good analysis of the political context of many of Evarts's actions and policies. "William M. Evarts" by Claude G. Bowers and Helen Dwight Reid in Samuel Flagg Bemis (ed.), *The American Secretaries of the State and Their Diplomacy, Volume 7* (1963), provides basic information on Evarts's diplomacy.

David L. Anderson's *Imperialism and Idealism: American Diplomats in China, 1861–1898* (1985), discusses Evarts's approach to the Chinese immigration issue.

David Anderson

EDWARD EVERETT (1794–1865)

Served 1852–1853
Appointed by President Millard Fillmore
Whig

Edward Everett was born on April 11, 1794, in Dorchester, Massachusetts, the fourth child of clergyman and jurist Oliver Everett and his wife, Lucy Hill Everett. Everett graduated from Harvard University with the highest honors in 1811. In 1814, he received a Master's of Divinity, and at only 20 years of age, became minister at Boston's Brattle Street Unitarian Church. In 1815, Harvard offered Everett a professorship in Greek literature, which he accepted with the understanding that he could undertake additional studies in Europe. In 1817, Everett received his doctorate at Göttingen University, making him the first American to earn a Ph.D., a degree not offered in the United States. In 1819, he started teaching at Harvard as well as editing *North American Review*, the nation's leading literary magazine, which he used to champion the cause of Greek independence. During this period, Everett became one of the nation's leading public orators, winning acclaim for his 1824 Phi Beta Kappa address at Harvard to an audience that included Lafayette.

In 1824, Everett was elected to the U.S. House of Representatives, where he served as a National Republican and Whig until 1835. As chair of the Committee on Foreign Relations from 1827 to 1829, he supported the Adams administration while developing a strong interest in diplomacy. By the early 1830s, he had become a leading member of the Whig Party, a protectionist, and a social conservative who advocated compromise with the South to protect the Union. In 1834, he was elected governor of Massachusetts and served four one-year terms.

Throughout his career, Everett was a protégé of his mentor Daniel Webster. In 1841, Webster became secretary of state in the Harrison administration, and knowing that Everett was interested in a diplomatic post, appointed him minister to Great Britain. Everett proved to be highly effective in London, in part because the British respected a man of such intellectual attainments and urbanity. During 1842, Webster negotiated the Webster–Ashburton Treaty in Washington, which resolved the northeast boundary dispute. During the negotiations, Everett served as his earpiece in London, sending home valuable intelligence that helped Webster understand what he could and could not hope for in a settlement.

In the wake of Webster's success, Everett sought to make his own mark in diplomacy. In late 1842, he told Webster that he might be able to resolve the Anglo-American dispute over the Oregon Territory with a compromise boundary at the 49th parallel. Much to his chagrin, Everett found little support from the administration, which hoped instead to gain British support for the American annexation of California. Everett was even less pleased when President Tyler nominated him to be a special commissioner to negotiate a trade treaty with China. The Senate quickly confirmed the nomination, but Everett declined it. Caleb Cushing accepted the mission and in 1844 negotiated the Treaty of Wangshia that opened five treaty ports to American trade. Everett remained at his post in London until August 1845.

Everett returned home and became president of Harvard University, but resigned in 1849. He found a new outlet for his intellectual energy as a confidential advisor to Daniel Webster, who replaced John Middle Clayton as Zachary Taylor's secretary of state in July 1850. In October 1850, Everett wrote a draft of the Hülsemann note that Webster later presented to the Austrian minister defending President Taylor's decision to send a special agent to monitor the progress of Hungarian revolutionaries.

Webster died on October 24, 1852. A week later President Fillmore asked Everett to serve as secretary of state for the final four months of the lame-duck administration. Fillmore's choice was probably based less on Everett's abilities than Webster's request—made some months earlier when he considered resigning—that Everett replace him if he ever left the administration. Everett accepted and began his duties on November 6. Democrat Franklin Pierce had been elected president four days earlier.

Everett experienced no major diplomatic episodes during his brief tenure and confined himself to settling a few matters that Webster had neglected in the final months of his life. The Perry expedition, for example, was ready to depart for Japan, yet President Fillmore's formal letter to the Emperor had not been written. Everett knew little about the Far East, but quickly drafted a message and the president submitted it to the cabinet, where it was approved.

Everett also cleared up a simmering dispute with Peru. Earlier in the year, Webster had foolishly decided to support the demands of American businessmen for access to the rich guano deposits on the Lobos Islands, a region long claimed by Peru. Webster claimed that Peru had no legitimate claim to the archipelago and even sent a warship to protect American ships docked there. Peru protested, and the action also raised opposition in several European countries interested in guano. Everett realized his predecessor had gone too far, that the international community recognized the Lobos as Peruvian territory, and he sought a face-saving way of backing down. On November 18, 1852, he sent a note to the Peruvian minister in Washington stating that the United States recognized Peru's sovereignty over the islands. He insisted that any injustice done to Peru was unintentional, and that Webster's actions had been based on a "transient want of information as to the facts of the case."

Everett's most important action as secretary was the rejection of a joint proposal of Great Britain and France for a tripartite guarantee of Spain's sovereignty over Cuba. In April 1852, the British and French ministers in Washington handed Secretary of State Webster identical notes calling for the United States, France, and Great Britain to disavow any desire to annex Cuba and guarantee Spanish sovereignty over the island. On December 1, Everett rejected the proposal, arguing that the Senate would never ratify such an arrangement. Furthermore, citing the guiding hands of Washington and Jefferson, he argued that the guarantee would violate American diplomatic tradition by entering into a "political" or "entangling" alliance. In addition, the proposed arrangement might keep the United States from "making an acquisition which might take place without any disturbance of existing foreign relations, and in the natural order of things"—in other words, at some future and more appropriate time. How, he asked, would the United States benefit from entering into an arrangement with two other nations about a matter in which it had much greater interest? One only had to look at a map "to see how remote are the relations of Europe and how intimate those of the United States, with this island." Everett also argued that a guarantee of Spanish sovereignty over the island would actually encourage more American filibusters to invade the island, thus undermining the Fillmore administration's efforts to contain such illegal activity. While stating that the Fillmore administration had no intention of annexing the island, the note's nationalistic tone demonstrated that Everett considered Cuba an American matter.

In 1853, the Massachusetts legislature elected Everett to the Senate. In 1854, apparently because of ill health, he failed to appear in the Senate to vote on the Kansas–Nebraska Act. His constituents were so outraged that he resigned his position, and his political career never fully recovered. In 1860, he accepted the nomination for the vice presidency on the Constitutional Union ticket, with presidential nominee John Bell. After the outbreak of the Civil War, Everett became a strong supporter of Lincoln. For all his achievements, he is perhaps best remembered for his two-hour oration at Gettysburg that preceded Lincoln's brilliant address. In 1864, he campaigned for Lincoln's reelection and served as a Republican elector from Massachusetts. He died in Boston on January 15, 1865.

BIBLIOGRAPHICAL ESSAY

The largest single collection of Everett papers is found at the Massachusetts Historical Society and is also available on microfilm. Other collections are in the Boston Public Library, Boston University, Harvard University's Houghton Library, the Library of Congress, New York Historical Society, and a number of other repositories. There is also a collection titled "Edward Everett Diplomatic Papers" at the National Archives.

The best biography of Everett is Paul A Varg's *Edward Everett: The Intellectual in the Turmoil of Politics* (1992). Also useful is Ronald F. Reid, *Edward Everett: Unionist Orator* (1990). Paul R. Frothingham, *Edward Everett: Orator and Statesman* (1925), is a rather uncritical account. For Everett's relationship with Webster, the best source is Maurice G. Baxter, *One and Inseparable: Daniel Webster and The Union* (1984). Also see Daniel Walker Howe's biographical essay, "Edward Everett," in *American National Biography* (1999).

For Everett's diplomacy see the aforementioned biographies, as well as Foster Stearns's biographical sketch, "Edward Everett," in *American Secretaries of State and Their Diplomacy*, edited by Samuel Flagg Bemis (1958). For his years as minister to Great Britain see John O. Geiser, "A Scholar Meets John Bull: Edward Everett as United States Minister to England," *New England Quarterly* (1976). A more recent study of the same period is Howard Jones and Donald A. Rakestraw, *Prologue to Manifest Destiny: Anglo-American Relations in the 1840s* (1997).

Jeffrey Mauck

HAMILTON FISH
(1808–1893)

Served 1869–1877
Appointed by President Ulysses S. Grant
Republican

Hamilton Fish, a New York political leader and secretary of state during the two terms of President Ulysses S. Grant, maintained a conservative, steady course in United States foreign policies in an administration preoccupied with the problems of Reconstruction, partisan politics, and scandals involving government officials. Although differing in background and personality, Fish and Grant developed a strong personal relationship and generally worked together effectively to implement a credible foreign policy. Fish served Grant out of a sense of *nobles oblige*, and because he brought no personal political ambitions, he could concentrate on affairs of state in a loyal manner, detached from the unethical shenanigans that characterized others in Grant's "kitchen cabinet" and circle of political hacks. Also, possibly because of his own great wealth, Fish was never tempted to join in the corruption that involved other cabinet members.

Fish was born into wealth and influence in New York, the son of Nicholas Fish, a Revolutionary War officer, and Elizabeth Stuyvesant, the daughter of a prominent family with roots in the city's Dutch colonial period. Named after Alexander Hamilton, a close friend of the family, Fish was educated in a private school supplemented by a French tutor. Fish continued his education at Columbia College and graduated with the highest honors in 1827. Following the study of law for three years in the office of Peter A. Jay, Fish was admitted to the New York bar and established a practice with William B. Lawrence. His marriage in 1836 to Julia Kean brought connections to one of New Jersey's most prominent families. Of Fish's social and financial stature, one journalist wrote: "Few men have been more the favorites of the blind goddess than Hamilton Fish."

In 1834, Fish made his first attempt to win an election, running unsuccessfully in a Democratic district as a Whig candidate for the state assembly. Fish tried again in 1842 and won because of a split among his Democratic opponents. However, he was not returned to office when he sought reelection. He was also unsuccessful four years later in a bid for the office of lieutenant governor. With the Democrats again divided, his fortunes changed the following year; and in a special election, he won the lieutenant governorship. In 1848, he was elected governor of New York.

Fish's conservative administration supported legislation establishing public schools and extending the state's system of canals. On the national issues of the day, Fish expressed views opposing the opening of California and New Mexico to slavery. His growing stature earned him consideration for the cabinet of Whig President Zachary Taylor as secretary of the treasury, but Taylor's sudden and untimely death ended any chance Fish may have had for a position in Washington at this time. In 1850, Fish was not renominated for the governorship. Fish's election to the U.S. Senate was problematic because of his refusal to commit himself to the Compromise of 1850. Nevertheless, he secured the support of Whig power brokers William Seward and Thurlow Weed, and the New York Legislature state legislature elected him to the Senate in 1851. Once in office, he joined his senior Senate colleague Seward in opposition to repeal of the Missouri Compromise embodied in the Kansas–Nebraska Act of 1854, although he was never a leader in the opposition to slavery. Amiable and dignified, Fish fit in well with his Senate colleagues, but he was not a forceful advocate on any major issue and failed to deliver a single speech during his six-year term.

With the demise of the Whig Party, Fish reluctantly became a Republican and chose not to seek reelection to the Senate. When his term ended in 1857, he took his family on a two-year tour of Europe. He seemed to be finished with politics and content to manage Glenclyffe, his estate on the Hudson River, and attend to the mundane duties of a leading citizen. Fish emerged in 1860 from obscurity to support the Republican candidate, Abraham Lincoln and, following the election, advised the new administration on the resupply of Fort Sumter and issues related to the secession of the Confederate states. He served on New York City's Union Defense Committee and was a member of a federal commission on the relief of prisoners of war. When the war ended, Fish quietly returned to private life.

Fish's surprising appointment as secretary of state in March 1869 followed a bizarre and still unexplainable set of circumstances that damaged the credibility of the new Grant administration and alienated the Senate's most formidable force in the area of foreign policy, Charles Sumner of Massachusetts. Fish was not a logical choice to head the State Department. Although Fish had supported Grant in the 1868 election, New York had gone to the Democratic candidate, so the new president owed the state no favors. In addition, Fish had expressed no particular ambition to hold office, had little foreign policy expertise, and had not held public office for more than a decade. He and President Ulysses S. Grant were not close, although the wives of the two had been good friends since 1865. In appointing Fish, Grant seemed to be acting out of a sense of desperation, and Fish, in accepting, appeared to be acting out of party loyalty to keep the administration from further embarrassment. Grant's first choice, Republican Elihu Washburne—a close friend from the president's adopted home, Galena, Illinois—and possessing minimal qualifications for the office, mysteriously resigned from the cabinet after less than a week in office to accept appointment as minister to France (another post for which his qualifications were marginal at best). Fish declined Grant's offer citing his wife's poor health, but the president submitted Fish's nomination to the Senate for consideration anyway, before receiving a reply that the nominee would accept. Grant hastily dispatched his trusted aide and private secretary, General Orville E.

Babcock, to New York to convince Fish to accept the post, at least during the first session of Congress. Meanwhile, Grant apparently never considered Charles Sumner for his cabinet and, despite the Senator's interest in foreign policy issues, did not seek his advice. Although a power as chair of the Senate Foreign Relations Committee, Sumner possessed an arrogant manner that Grant instinctively abhorred. In neglecting Sumner, however, the president set the stage for inevitable confrontations with the head of the Senate Foreign Relations Committee on the two key diplomatic issues of his first term: Santo Domingo and the *Alabama* claims.

Santo Domingo interested Grant because he viewed a naval base on the island as critical to U.S. interests in the Caribbean and to the defense of a canal through the Isthmus of Panama, which the president saw as an inevitable American venture. As a young army officer in the early 1850s, Grant had helped transport sick soldiers and families of settlers across the Panama's hostile terrain and knew firsthand of the commercial and military benefits a canal could bring. "To Europeans the benefits of the proposed canal are great. To Americans they are incalculable," Grant stated, and he ordered a half dozen survey expeditions to locate the best possible route. Like former Secretary of State William Seward, Grant envisioned securing Samaná Bay in the Dominican Republic, possibly through a lease, as an initial anchor for an enlarged United States presence in the Caribbean. Grant also hoped the island could be a haven for black freedmen. To Grant's delight, an opportunity for the easy acquisition of Samaná Bay, and possibly all of the Dominican Republic, presented itself early in his administration. However, the president's plans were frustrated by political opposition in Congress, led by Sumner, and reluctance on the part of his new secretary of state to shoulder the responsibility of governing foreign territories.

Governing a small nation that was both bankrupt and politically unstable, President Buenaventura Baez of the Dominican Republic attempted to arrange a loan from the United States, half of which Baez planned to secure for himself and his cronies as a kind of commission. When the loan fell through, he offered to sell his country to the United States, again with a considerable commission for himself, in return for U.S. support against his political rivals. Grant sent Babcock to San Domingo to investigate. He returned to Washington to present to the cabinet a treaty of annexation signed by President Baez. The deal called for the United States to pay $2 million for Samaná Bay and assume the nation's debt of $1.5 million to annex the country. Fish noted that Babcock did not have the authority to negotiate a treaty on behalf of the United States nor to commit the United States to use force to protect the Baez regime from its enemies without Congressional consent. In late 1869, Babcock again visited the Dominican Republic and on November 29 signed an agreement for a lease of Samaná Bay. He had brought with him a shipment of arms, a U.S. naval force sufficient to protect the Baez government, and a bank draft of $100,000. Newly armed, Baez's forces pursued political opponents, including rebels led by Gregorio Luperon, a black revolutionary, who had support from neighboring Haiti. At the same time, a national referendum of questionable validity demonstrated popular support for annexation. With events now seeming to move in the direction he wanted, Grant sought to build support in the Senate.

Grant took it upon himself to personally visit Sumner at his residence in Washington. In a cordial discussion, Sumner offered to provide "the most careful and candid consideration" to the issue of annexation out of a sense of party loyalty.

Grant interpreted Sumner's statement to be one of support; however, the Senator had no interest in the annexation of a Caribbean nation. Sumner, an ardent abolitionist, feared annexation of the Dominican Republic would cause Haiti to lose its independence, and he was suspicious of Babcock's scheming. He denounced the administration's endeavors in a four-hour oration in which he compared the Dominican Republic to the Biblical "Naboth's Vineyard," a bountiful place coveted by its neighbors.

At this point, Fish, who had served with Sumner in the Senate, tried to secure his support. However, his meetings with the senator went nowhere. Sumner spoke of Grant as "a colossus of ignorance" who possessed "the heart of a lackey," and Fish soon realized that he was trying to reason with a man who was losing his hold on reality. Furthermore, Fish's efforts with Sumner and others were half-hearted because he did not share the president's vision for American expansion. He was reluctant to see his nation entangled in the Caribbean and concerned about the annexation of a people foreign to the American system. Given the domestic problems of reconstruction, Fish believed the United States had all the social strife it could possibly handle. Fish went so far as to offer his resignation when the Dominican issue became a political embarrassment to the administration. After failing to secure annexation by treaty, when the Senate failed to provide a two-thirds majority, Grant sought to bring the matter to a vote of both houses of Congress in 1871, hoping to bring about annexation through a joint resolution that would have required only a simple majority. Again, his plans were frustrated. In January 1873, an American private enterprise backed by Grant's administration, the Samaná Bay Company, secured a 100-year lease for a port facility at $150,000 per year. However, within a year, the lease was rescinded when Baez was overthrown by insurgents.

Out of this imbroglio, Fish may have gained some measure of credibility for his moderate and even-handed approach. He was able to restrain the president without directly disagreeing with him. Meanwhile, Sumner incurred the president's unrestrained wrath, and his confrontation with Grant led the Republican Senate caucus to remove Sumner from his chairmanship of the Committee on Foreign Affairs, thereby opening the way for a settlement of the *Alabama* claims—an issue on which Sumner had been obstinate and uncompromising.

Other than urging Fish to settle the *Alabama* claims with Great Britain before the election of 1872, Grant appeared to have little interest in this lingering dispute with the world's premier power. Although the focus of the negotiations centered on the damage inflicted on Union shipping by five ships, including the *Alabama*, built in British shipyards, the outstanding issues with Great Britain involved myriad complex matters. These included the perennial dispute over fishing rights off the New England coast, boundaries along the coastal waterways between the United States and British Columbia, and the citizenship of former British subjects, in particular those of Irish ancestry, who returned to British territory after living in the United States. Fish inherited a diplomatic impasse following the rejection by the Senate in 1869 of the Johnson–Clarendon Convention, a treaty negotiated by U.S. Minister to Britain Reverdy Johnson and Lord Clarendon, the British Foreign Secretary. A hater of all things British, Sumner harbored a dream that the United States might some day acquire all of Canada and hoped the British might part with some or all of Canada in lieu of a payment of $2.5 billion from London for "indirect" costs to the Union and to American shipping during the Civil War. Unconcerned about the prospect of war, Sumner pursued his stubborn opposition to any reasonable compromise and insisted that the British pay a "moral debt." He held to his position with such vehemence that some of his colleagues began to question his stability and his judgment.

The *Alabama* claims were further complicated by the disruptions of the Franco-Prussian War and by the fact that a close protégé of Sumner, John Lothrop Motley, had been removed as Minister to London. Fish, negotiating in private with British minister to Washington, Edward Thornton, let it be known that despite its harsh diplomatic and public rhetoric, the Grant administration would consider reasonable terms. In late 1870, as Sumner's influence was in decline, Fish made it known to the British that the United States would accept a settlement that did not include British territory as part of a compensation agreement. In January 1871, both countries agreed to have a joint high commission address the *Alabama* claims and related issues. The commissioners, including Fish, began working in March. On May 8, the two nations agreed to the terms of the Treaty of Washington, which set forth terms to place the claims for damages inflicted by the *Alabama* and other Confederate cruisers before arbitration to be conducted in Geneva. The tribunal rendered a decision on September 14, 1872, which set the amount of damages at $15,000,000. Although the issues of fishing rights and trade remained unsettled for some time, the boundary line in the Strait of San Juan de Fuca was set in October 1872, through arbitration conducted by the German Emperor, who ruled in favor of the United States. Grant was pleased to have the matter out of the way as he successfully campaigned for a second term, and having peacefully settled the bulk of the *Alabama* claims through arbitration, the U.S. and British governments were relieved of a thorny set of problems that had hindered cooperation on important matters of mutual interest, among them trade and expansion in the Far East and Pacific.

In the Far East, American policies and interests generally coincided with those of the British, whose acquiescence was necessary for any U.S. initiatives. Since signing the 1844 Treaty of Wangxia at the conclusion of the Opium Wars, the United States had followed in the wake of Britain in its relations with China. During Fish's tenure, the administration sought successfully to preserve most-favored-nation privileges and extraterritoriality for U.S. citizens, while maintaining access to Chinese port facilities on equal terms with Britain and the other European powers. In Samoa, commissioner A. B. Steinberger, another of Grant's Civil War acquaintances, sought to secure rights to harbor facilities on that island. Unfortunately, he became involved in native politics and managed to secure the office of premier of the island for himself. British officials found him troublesome and deported him in April 1876. The British also disclosed Steinberger's correspondence with Orville Babcock, who was by this time implicated in the Whiskey Ring and Washington Safe Burglary Conspiracy scandals. Grant was forced to let Babcock go and, to Fish's relief, call an end to his Samoan endeavor. In 1871, the Grant administration responded to an attack on an American merchant ship, the *General Sherman*, by launching a punitive expedition against Korea in which over 250 Koreans were slaughtered by American guns while only three Americans were lost.

Recognizing the growing importance of the Hawaiian Islands, Fish negotiated a treaty of commercial reciprocity with Hawaii's government in 1875 that, when approved by the U.S. Senate, incorporated the island kingdom into the American commercial and economic sphere. Fish seemed to prefer securing commercial advantages and treaty privileges for the United States to the outright acquisition of new territories, which would require a commitment to govern nonwhite peoples. In the case of Hawaii, the treaty that Fish negotiated strengthened the position of American citizens, frequently missionaries, who controlled much of Hawaii's wealth. In addition, the agreement prohibited the Hawaiian monarchy from leasing or otherwise disposing of ports or other territories to any nation other than the United States.

In Latin America, unstable conditions in Cuba and Mexico provided Fish and the Grant administration with cause for concern. Throughout his eight-year tenure as secretary of state, Fish was forced to deal with problems in Spain's colony of Cuba, which was in a perpetual state of insurrection. Fish understood that American business interests would eventually dominate the Cuban economy and saw Spanish misrule on the island as a factor that would ultimately end Spain's colonial hold there. However, Fish did not favor the acquisition of Cuba any more than he had the annexation of the Dominican Republic. Having visited the island in 1855, Fish was charmed by its beauty and climate, but noted: "With its present population, the island of Cuba is anything other than a desirable acquisition to the United States, and I can see no means of getting rid of a population of some 450,000 called white but really every shade and mixture of color, who own *all* the land on the island." Fish was constantly forced to contend with political forces at home that argued for recognition of the belligerency, an action that would have led to war with Spain, and with a Spanish colonial administration angered at private filibustering expeditions launched from the United States. Meanwhile, Fish found himself pursuing the claims of U.S. citizens for reparations due to alleged abuses of the Spanish authorities and at the same time urging the Spanish to reach an accommodation with the island's rebels.

Fish strongly opposed recognition of a state of belligerency in Cuba, whereas Grant was favorably disposed to do so. Early in his administration, in August 1869, while his secretary of state was engaged in efforts to convince Spain to allow Cuban independence and abolish slavery on the island, Grant signed a proclamation of neutrality, which surprised Fish. Convinced that the president had made a mistake, he persuaded Grant to defer promulgating the document. Later, in his annual message of December 6, 1869, Grant, with Fish's advice, declared that recognition of a state of belligerency was unjustified. In June 1870, when advocates of recognition tried to push a joint resolution through Congress, Fish secured a strong message from the president, which foiled their effort. As these events were unfolding in Washington, the U.S. minister to Spain, the frequently volatile and undiplomatic civil war hero Daniel Sickles, pressed authorities in Madrid to redress the grievances of American citizens in Cuba. Spanish authorities offered promises, which generally fell short of expectations, and the Cuban situation continued to fester.

An agreement in February 1871 providing for a joint commission in Washington to determine American claims for damages suffered in Cuba appeared to have lessened tensions. Then the steamer *Virginius* was captured by the Spanish navy and taken to Cuba, where the captain and 53 of the largely U.S. crew and passengers were executed by a firing squad. Registered in the United States and owned by a Cuban revolutionary committee located in New York, the ship's purpose was clearly to assist rebel activities. Nevertheless, Fish, bowing to domestic political pressure, issued an ultimatum to the Spanish government on November 14, 1870, threatening to sever diplomatic relations if Spain did not, within 12 days, release the survivors, punish officials responsible for the ship's capture and the summary executions, and conduct a formal salute to the U.S. flag. As both countries prepared for war, Fish and the Spanish minister to Washington reached an agreement on November 17, wherein the United States would drop its demand for a salute if the Spanish could prove the illegality of the ship's registry. The crisis ended when the Spanish quickly provided the proof. The issue of punishment for Spanish officials and possible indemnities for losses was added to the ever-expanding list of unresolved problems between the United States and Spain.

The *Virginius* affair was finally put to rest in February 1874, when the U.S. minister to Spain, Caleb Cushing, a skilled diplomat who had replaced Sickles, was instructed to withhold recognition of the new regime of Alfonso XII until an indemnity award was provided. Under instructions from Fish, Cushing continued to press Spanish officials for reforms in Cuba that could lead to self-government on the island and the abolition of slavery. However, as talks continued on these matters, Spain reinforced its military in Cuba and effectively, although temporarily, suppressed rebel forces. Despite Fish's hopes for reforms in Cuba that would end the friction between the United States and Spain, nothing significant was accomplished during his tenure in office, and the troubles with Spain concerning Cuba would continue for more than two decades.

In Mexico, Fish faced incessant border problems as raids into the United States by Indians and bandits coming out of northern Mexico led to counterattacks by the U.S. military into Mexican territory. Unable to stop the raids into the United States, the Mexicans were nevertheless highly indignant when U.S. troops set foot on their land. Meanwhile, rebel forces opposed to the regime in Mexico City operated out of Brownsville, Texas, a safe haven to which they could flee from Mexican forces. In 1876, the final year of the Grant administration, Porfirio Diaz seized power in Mexico and established a new government. At first reluctant to provide diplomatic recognition to the new regime, Fish was persuaded by U.S. minister to Mexico John W. Foster (a future secretary of state) that Diaz was not a threat to American interests (despite Diaz' rhetoric) and would be open to American trade and investment.

Despite the demise of the administration's plans for the acquisition of the Dominican Republic or even a lease on Samaná Bay, Fish made two attempts to secure agreements with Latin American nations for the construction of an interocean canal. In January 1870, U.S. diplomats negotiated an agreement with Colombia for a canal through Panama. However, the treaty was amended in the Colombian senate to such a degree that the United States refused ratification. In the final days of the Grant administration, a special envoy from Nicaragua labored unsuccessfully to negotiate an agreement with the United States for a canal through his country. This effort failed when negotiators were unable to find a satisfactory status for a proposed neutral zone through which the canal was to pass.

Relations with European nations, other than Britain and Spain, involved relatively minor issues arising during the Franco-Prussian War of 1870. The United States offered its good offices in an attempt to bring about peace and an agreeable settlement. However, the offer was rejected; and during the brief war the United States assumed protection over the interests of German subjects residing in France. In addition, as French and German armies clashed outside Paris, Fish and the

American minister to France, Elihu Washburne, successfully defended to the German chancellor, Otto Von Bismark, the right of the American government to send sealed dispatches through the German lines into the besieged city.

In 1877, Fish returned to his estate in New York and occupied himself with the philanthropic and civic pursuits common for a conservative gentleman of ample means. He served as a trustee of Columbia College and as the president of the Society of the Cincinnati, the Union League Club, and the New York Historical Society. A large, sturdy man with thick sideburns and an aristocratic bearing, Fish looked on proudly as his three sons enjoyed prominence in political and business ventures. Descendants and namesakes would represent New York in the U.S. House of Representatives for many decades.

During his final years, Fish appeared content that he had loyally and competently served an administration characterized in many respects by unethical behavior and incompetence. Viewing Grant as ill advised by his less-enlightened cabinet members and political cronies, Fish had remained aloof and detached from the pressing domestic challenges faced by the administration, in particular those of Reconstruction. A cautious, patient, and conservative individual, he distrusted adventurous actions on the diplomatic front, even while he reluctantly involved himself in their pursuit. Possessing neither great vision nor great stature among international leaders, Fish nevertheless managed to maintain the Department of State on a steady course, skillfully addressing the troublesome *Alabama* claims with Great Britain, the highly charged *Virginius* affair, and the potentially diverse Dominican Republic annexation. All the while, he efficiently attended to routine diplomatic matters and kept U.S. foreign policy on a course that moved cautiously between Grant's desire for aggressive expansion in the Caribbean and Pacific and the contrary wishes of those completely opposed to any form of insular imperialism.

BIBLIOGRAPHICAL ESSAY

The most important collection of the papers of Hamilton Fish is held in the Library of Congress. The United States Department of State, *Papers of the Foreign Relations of the United States* for the years of Fish's service as Secretary of State are a rich source of material. Of particular interest is 1872: Part II, *Papers Relating to the Treaty of Washington. The Papers of Ulysses S. Grant*, ed. John Y. Simon, 26 vols. to date (1967–) contain significant material on Fish. The most recently published volumes cover the years 1874 and 1875.

Although dated in its simplistic interpretations of United States foreign policies, Allan Nevins, *Hamilton Fish: The Inner History of the Grant Administration* (1957), remains a comprehensive and useful study of Fish's role as the key member of Grant's cabinet. A highly critical analysis of Fish's tenure as Secretary of State is offered in James B. Chapin, "Hamilton Fish and American Expansion," in Frank J. Merli and Theodore A. Wilson (eds.), *Makers of Modern Diplomacy: From Benjamin Franklin to Henry Kissinger* (1974). Also see Clifford W. Haury, "Hamilton Fish and the Conservative Tradition," in Norman Graebner (ed.), *Studies in American Diplomacy* (1985).

For specific diplomatic issues, see Charles C. Tansill, *The United States and Santo Domingo, 1798–1873: A Chapter in Caribbean Diplomacy* (1938); and Sumner Wells, *Naboth's Vineyard: The Dominican Republic, 1844–1924*, 2 vols. (1928) and Rayford

Logan, *Haiti and the Dominican Republic* (1968) for accounts of the Grant administration's expansionist aims in the Caribbean, the politics related to the *Alabama* claims are thoroughly examined in Adrian Cook, *The Alabama Claims: American Politics and Anglo American Relations* (1975; Jean I. Brooks, *International Rivalry in the Pacific Islands, 1800–1875* (1941) explores the Steinberger episode; and Merze Tate, *The United States and the Hawaiian Kingdom* (1865) chronicles the rising American economic and political influence in the islands. Dale Clifford, "Elihu Benjamin Washburne: An American Diplomat in Paris, 1870–71," *Prologue*, vol. 2 (1970), 161–174, provides a good account of this unlikely diplomat; and a solid and balanced review of Grant's presidency is William S. McFeely, *Grant: a Biography* (1982).

Michael J. Devine

JOHN FORSYTH (1780–1841)

Served 1834–1841
Appointed by President Andrew Jackson
Continued in office under President Martin Van Buren
Democrat

John Forsyth is arguably the most obscure secretary of state in the early republic. The affable Georgian, an individual of modest talent and dogged determination, loyally served two presidents—Andrew Jackson and Martin Van Buren—over a seven-year period. Both chief executives, however, dominated foreign affairs, leaving Forsyth to administer their policies and languish out of the public view. Consequently, a revisionist approach to Forsyth's State Department career would be inappropriate and inaccurate. However, he does merit attention for his cool ability to handle the diplomatic tasks assigned him and for his dedicated efficiency in managing his department.

Born in Virginia in 1780, John Forsyth moved as a child with his parents to Georgia. Well educated (Princeton) and genteel, Forsyth personified the stereotypical Southern lawyer-planter aristocrat. Elected as a Jeffersonian Republican to the U.S. House of Representatives in 1813, he soon moved to the Senate. Forsyth remained there only briefly before accepting James Monroe's offer in 1819 to become the U.S. Minister to Spain. The ensuing four-year sojourn in Madrid represented the low point of his career. Bubbling over with republican self-righteousness, Forsyth committed several diplomatic gaffes, the most serious being a written lecture to the King regarding his duties to his subjects and the international community. When he came home in 1823, Forsyth was promptly returned to the House of Representatives and then elevated to the Governor's chair in 1827. He spent considerable energy during the decade promoting Cherokee removal.

The states' rights crisis of the late 1820s and early 1830s revolving around the issues of the tariff and nullification forced Forsyth into a difficult position. Entering the Senate in 1829, as a loyal Southerner he strongly opposed high protective tariffs. However, he could not endorse the destructive, anti-union doctrines of Vice President John C. Calhoun and vigorously opposed the Carolinian's positions. Forsyth's courageous stance in defense of various policies of Andrew Jackson, including the removal of the federal deposits from the Bank of the United States, won him the admiration of the president. The Georgian had already earned the friendship of Secretary of State Martin Van Buren when the two men served together in Congress.

Not surprisingly, Forsyth's name was bantered about frequently during Jackson's second term. Van Buren served as Vice President, whereas Edward Livingston and Louis McLane moved successively into the State Department, but Forsyth received no favors. An ambitious man, the Georgian expressed bitter disappointment that no rewards came his way. When disagreements over Bank policy prompted McLane's resignation, the long-suffering Forsyth was prepared to step into the State Department breach. Jackson, who conducted his own foreign policy, was pleased to have a Secretary of Forsyth's fidelity. The Georgian was well respected for his eloquence, intellect, and integrity by friend and foe alike. His selection, which won the unanimous consent of the Senate on June 27, 1834, met with widespread approbation.

During his tenure in the State Department most of the challenges Forsyth faced emerged from problems in the Western Hemisphere—with the exception of the French spoliations crisis. As part of a treaty signed in 1831, France agreed to pay the United States over four million dollars for damages inflicted on American shipping during the Napoleonic Wars. The French, however, had failed to make the first installment on the reimbursement in 1833, and the Chamber of Deputies had refused to appropriate the money in 1834.

Forsyth dealt with French Minister Louis Serurier on the matter in October 1834, informing Serurier that the president was obliged to inform Congress of the French refusal to pay. Although privately apprehensive about what Jackson might say to Congress, Forsyth remained noncommittal in his conversations with the Frenchman in November.

On December 1 the president fired the first salvo in the claims war. Reminding Congress that the French had failed in their obligations, he recommended legislation to seize French property in America if the payments were not made by the next session of the Chamber. Although Congress did not enthusiastically embrace the president's spirited message, the French reacted immediately. An irate Louis Philippe recalled Serurier, leaving the delegation in the hands of Chargé Alphonse Pageot.

Jackson's sabre-rattling produced the desired results. In April 1835 the Chamber of Deputies passed the indemnity bill, but with an amendment demanding an appropriate explanation of the president's remarks. In Paris, U.S. Minister Edward Livingston attempted to remove the tension, but the French insisted on a response from "Old Hickory" himself. Because no payments were forthcoming without the explanation, Livingston requested his papers and returned home. Sensing a stalemate, Foreign Minister Achille de Broglie wrote an informal note to Pageot discussing French sensitivity in the matter and urging that the point of honor could be easily remedied by the president. De Broglie wanted the communiqué passed along to Forsyth and Jackson. When Pageot attempted to relay the olive branch in September, the Secretary refused to accept it. The White House adopted a hard line on the note (which Pageot offered several times), claiming that it was both unofficial and unwise, constituting a meddling in U.S. internal affairs.

Instead, Jackson instructed Chargé Thomas P. Barton to again repeat the request for payment or ask for his passports. When the French held firm, Barton left

France, arriving in the United States in January 1836. Almost simultaneously, de Broglie recalled Pageot, thus totally severing Franco-American relations. Pageot leaked the De Broglie note to the American press. The *National Intelligencer* condemned the administration for its "blundering diplomacy" and attacked Forsyth for "confounding dignity and superciliousness, self respect and false pride." The maneuver also produced the desired outcry from Senate Whigs who criticized Forsyth and Jackson for suppressing vital diplomatic information from Congress and the American people.

As the situation intensified, the British nervously offered themselves as mediators. His Majesty's government was understandably concerned about an ally stumbling into a conflict with the United States, when European politics remained tense and uncertain. British assistance proved unnecessary, however, as the president moved to break the logjam. While not apologizing for his earlier remarks, he assured Congress in his December 7, 1835, message that he had not intended to menace or insult the French. This was sufficient. The Chamber had insisted on an explanation, not an apology. Jackson's strategy succeeded. In March 1836 the King instructed the Minister of Finance to begin the payments.

The French crisis passed, and a comparatively unimportant issue fortunately was resolved without conflict. In the process significant elements of the American system revealed themselves. Congress could be and was an all-important restraint on executive war-making power. Even though often revealing an inability to overcome the heated partisan climate of the period and generally lacking a constructive alternative, Congress had refused the president reprisal authority and denied him carte blanche to prepare the nation for war. Secondly, members of the Cabinet, especially Forsyth and Vice President Van Buren, restrained Jackson from harsh words that would have fanned the flames of patriotic passion. By urging moderation, these advisors contributed to preserving the peace. Certainly, Jackson did not want war, but without the counsel of men he had faith in, he might not have altered his course in the direction of conciliation.

The success with France accompanied settlements with Denmark, Naples, Spain, and Portugal. Consequently, Jackson not only gained over $7 million in claims, but also began to alter the attitude of the Europeans toward the United States. The president, his secretaries of state, and his diplomats generally displayed a determination and forthrightness that erased the smug foreign condescension of earlier years toward the weak, divided, and ineffectual national leadership and replaced it with a newfound respect for the president and his brash young republic.

The Texas issue developed into the major continental problem of the decade, frustrating Jackson and irritating Van Buren. When Forsyth became secretary of state in 1834, he entered the Byzantine world of Andrew Butler, Jackson's friend and chargé to Mexico since 1829. Butler had been attempting for five years to accomplish the president's goal of acquiring Texas. Jackson agreed to provide $5 million to secure the territory. Butler returned to Washington in June 1835 and urged the application of a $500,000 bribe to secure the favor of a clerical aide to President Antonio Lopez de Santa Anna (and likely the president himself). Jackson indignantly refused. The president unwisely allowed Butler to return to Mexico City, finally replacing him in April 1836 with Powhatan Ellis. The outbreak of revolution in Texas, however, made further dealings with the Mexicans impossible.

Although officially committed to a neutral posture based on an 1831 treaty with Mexico, most Americans were ardently pro-Texan. Jackson's arguments for neutrality evaporated amid the numerous parades, rallies, recruiting, supplying, and fundraising in behalf of the revolutionaries. Forsyth dutifully wrote to federal district attorneys in areas affected by the revolution, urging them to prosecute all violators of neutrality laws. Not surprisingly, local enforcement was lax at best. The Mexican government protested this indirect aid to the Texas insurgents. Forsyth warned that neither the Texans nor the Mexicans should attempt to use the United States as a battleground for their causes.

These pro-Texas displays technically lay within the treaty limits. However, the dispatch of American troops across the Texas border—ostensibly in pursuit of marauding Indians in the summer of 1836—ignited Mexican Minister Manuel de Gorostiza to action. Gorostiza spent the summer in an ineffectual effort to obtain from Forsyth a satisfactory explanation of General Edmund Gaines's orders and activities. The secretary testily noted how American troops were allowed to cross the border in situations where American lives or national security were threatened. By mid-October the frustrated diplomat drew up a lengthy protest and demanded an explanation and an apology. Forsyth remained calm and dispassionate, but offered no apology or promise of withdrawal. Gorostiza saw this as simply another method for guaranteeing the success of the revolution. Angry and frustrated by the Gaines expedition but also by Forsyth's attitude, he asked for his passports and departed by year's end. Simultaneously, Minister Ellis in Mexico City was unsuccessful in resolving over $6 million in outstanding American claims. When no progress appeared imminent, he, too, requested his papers and returned in December 1836.

The collapse of Mexican-American relations in the fading months of the Jackson administration correlated closely to the issue of the recognition of Texas independence and, perhaps, annexation. The battlefield success at San Jacinto and the capture of General Antonio Lopez de Santa Anna ensured the temporary success of the rebels. Texas commissioners had been lobbying for aid and recognition since the fall of 1835.

Secretary Forsyth, along with Vice President Van Buren, urged restraint. The secretary honestly believed that the United States would violate its diplomatic agreements with Mexico by moving aggressively to endorse a revolution that had been led by expatriate Americans and that would be much more advantageous if the Europeans, or ideally the Mexicans, recognized Texas independence first. Political considerations also colored Forsyth's judgment. The secretary remained optimistic that his champion, Van Buren, would be elevated to the White House in 1836. Surely there would be a place for him in the new administration. But strong anti-slave voices had already begun to cry out on Texas, and Forsyth feared the issue would become a sectional battleground dividing the Democratic Party and the Union. He wanted Van Buren to be able to formulate his own policy, not inherit a muddle created by Jackson's possible impetuosity. The Texans realized that Forsyth was a particular problem. When special commissioners were dispatched in April 1836 to solicit the administration's support, they were advised to expect reluctance from Forsyth, but to then move quickly on to the president. In fact, Forsyth met and conversed with them as individuals, but refused to recognize them officially.

Although Jackson desired Texas, he appreciated the wisdom of his secretary's cautious policy. Both agreed that the dispatch of a special agent, Henry Morfit, to investigate the Texas situation and provide additional information would be beneficial. The rebel commissioners were obliged to deal with Forsyth during the summer of 1836. They met with him on several occasions, but found the secretary "but little disposed to be communicative in anything."

Throughout the remainder of the year Forsyth continued his policy of cautious restraint. Sam Houston became President of the Texas Republic in the fall of 1836 and sent W. H. Wharton to Washington to promote concrete action. After meeting informally with Forsyth, Wharton could only repeat the litany of previous diplomats: although Texas was "a favorite measure" of the president, he would not recognize the republic now, and the matter would be referred to Congress.

In December 1836 an ailing Andrew Jackson issued two cautious messages to Congress on the Texas question. Neither urged immediate recognition. Instead, the president requested a wait-and-see posture and threw the matter into the lap of the legislature. The president, who had always preferred purchase to revolution as a means to acquiring the territory, was likely influenced by many factors, including the impending arrival in Washington of the recently released Santa Anna, who might still be persuaded to sell Texas; a complete diplomatic break with Mexico if recognition occurred; the inconclusive nature of the Morfit report on the stability of the Texas republic; the president's ill-health; and the restraining hands of Forsyth and Van Buren. Congress demonstrated its timidity on the issue by attempting to throw it back to the president. Forsyth told Wharton in January 1827 that U.S. Minister Andrew Stevenson in London was investigating the likelihood of British recognition.

The Texas lobby, championed by Mississippi Senator Robert John Walker, however, proved formidable. In late February 1837 Congress agreed to have the United States recognize the Lone Star Republic—against the wishes of Forsyth and Van Buren. Both knew that such action hinted at annexation; a sectionally explosive issue that neither wished to face.

On March 3 Andrew Jackson, sipping a glass of wine, formally received the representatives of the Texas Republic and promptly appointed a chargé. The president's seeming mercurial shift reflected the culmination of a new strategy. His temperate January exercise, focusing on talks with Santa Anna, had failed, so he now embraced recognition and perhaps even reprisals against Mexico. The failure of the Ellis mission to resolve the claims issue gave Jackson the ammunition to request the power to take action against his neighbor for its failure to pay. Congress denied the president the reprisal authority he requested. Rumors were also rife that the British indicated an unhealthy interest in the fate of the Republic.

The Van Buren administration did not share Jackson's newfound enthusiasm for Texas. Forsyth boldly told the Texans in May 1837 that he would not listen to propositions for annexation unless the Mexicans recognized the republic or ceased hostilities against her. The president did not receive Texas Minister Memucan Hunt until July 6. Hunt informed his government that "Mr. Forsyth is violently opposed to annexation!!" Following a cabinet meeting on August 25, Forsyth delivered "a chilling refusal" to Hunt's request for annexation. A treaty had been signed with Mexico that might be breached by unfriendly annexation. The constitutional legitimacy of adding a sovereign nation to the United States also loomed as an unanswered question. The Texans wanted to believe that Forsyth and other Southern administration leaders sympathized with their interests, but the opportunity for annexation was not yet propitious. Forsyth perpetuated Hunt's hopes by assuring him that annexation might occur, if matters were "properly conducted."

Grasping at the proffered straws, the Texans continued to urge annexation until June 1838. Secretary of War Joel Poinsett and Postmaster General Amos Kendall were true believers, but Forsyth remained skeptical. Should Van Buren risk a divisive war with Mexico over Texas? Equally troubling for the White House, the nation remained mired in a serious economic depression, the Panic of 1837, which consumed much of Van Buren's attention. Given the narrow majorities of the Democrats in both houses of Congress, promotion of the Texas issue would splinter the party at the worst possible time. When Congress failed to act on annexation by the fall of 1838, the Texans formally withdrew their proposition.

The tension surrounding annexation, however, did not prevent the negotiation of several treaties between the United States and Texas resolving several outstanding problems. One of the Texas treaties dealt with damage claims by American citizens incurred during the revolution; the other dealt more substantially with the boundary issue. The U.S.–Texas Treaty of April 1838 agreed on the Sabine River.

Relations with the Mexicans, although hardly cordial, allowed for some diplomatic discussion. In July 1837, Van Buren dispatched Robert Greenhow to resolve the nagging claims issue. The American met with President Anastasio Bustamente, who cordially agreed to examine the more than 50 outstanding claims. By the spring of 1838 the Mexican government recommended arbitration, and Washington agreed. (The commission was formed in 1840 and led by the King of Prussia, ultimately made a $2 million award to the Americans.)

The Texas issue revealed both the strengths and weaknesses of John Forsyth. Loyal and pragmatic, the Georgian dutifully followed Andrew Jackson to the brink of conflict with France and Mexico. Although strongly favoring a moderate course in both instances, the secretary influenced policy, but certainly never formed it. When Van Buren assumed office in March 1837, Forsyth happily accommodated himself to the New Yorker's more conciliatory style. As a loyal Southerner and slave owner, he likely favored annexation, but never pressed the issue with Van Buren, however, realizing its political divisiveness.

With little opportunity to distinguish himself under Jackson, Forsyth felt insecure about his place in the new administration. When Van Buren made an offhanded comment at a party in early 1837 about the need for cabinet harmony and putting aside "presidential fevers," the sensitive Forsyth took exception to the remark. Soon thereafter he visited the president and suggested that he be given a diplomatic post. Van Buren agreed to consider the request. Forsyth, likely disappointed that the president did not more strongly contest his withdrawal, now suspected a plot to dump him was afoot. He wrote a letter of resignation on March 9 and delivered it to the administration's organ, the *Washington Globe*. Fortunately, the president, informed of the letter, halted its publication. Quickly contacting Forsyth, he reassured Forsyth he had not intended to suggest that the Georgian was a presidential candidate or a disruptive force. Proud and impulsive, limited in political influence and diplomatic skill, Forsyth was a qualified asset to the White House. The more talented William Rives of Virginia in 1837 and James Buchanan of Pennsylvania in 1838 sought the State Department portfolio, but the president was unwilling to make a change. Forsyth, sensitive, charming, and personable, was a loyal Southern ally, a rare commodity during the Van Buren years.

Although Forsyth's tenure with Jackson involved controversies with France and Mexico, foreign policy difficulties under Van Buren often focused on Great Britain. Canada posed a particularly nettlesome problem. When a rebellion in Canada erupted in November 1837, Forsyth promptly informed state and local officials along the border to maintain strict neutrality. For the many state officials who sympathized with the rebels, however, foreign policy was a federal problem. The small U.S. army, bogged down in the quagmire of the Seminole War in Florida, could be of little assistance.

A Canadian, William MacKenzie, recruited in the United States, promising cash and 300 acres of land to volunteers, called Patriot Hunters. The Canadian-American forces led by MacKenzie and Louis Jean Papineau and numbering over 1,000 launched a series of attacks in December. The occupation of Navy Island near Niagara Falls under the auspices of New Yorker Rensselaer Van Rensselaer, who envisioned himself as a Yankee Sam Houston, lasted several weeks and brought a sharp protest from the British government. Van Buren disavowed Van Rensselaer's actions, renewed the American pledge of neutrality and dispatched General Winfield Scott to resolve the matter. Scott succeeded by mid-January in convincing the rebel forces to withdraw from the island. Scott's other sojourns along the border to Detroit contributed significantly to a quieting of the situation by mid-March 1838.

Congress assisted the President by passing a revised neutrality law empowering civilian officials to interfere in halting the flow of men and materials. British Minister Fox demanded that the Americans stop this illegal traffic. Forsyth stood helpless as events swirled around him. Forsyth characteristically carried out official policy, but played little role in determining it. He earnestly pledged his government's energies, but to his embarrassment, too often his orders were ignored or simply disobeyed by state officials. The Patriot Hunters struck once more in late 1838 along the New York and Michigan frontiers, resulting in more tragic defeats for the rebels. Again, however, Van Buren urged American neutrality, pledged cooperation, and condemned the rebels as "misguided or deluded." The second round of defeats combined with the capture, trial, and conviction of William MacKenzie crushed the rebellion and sharply reduced regional tension.

The only remaining issue breaking the calm was the failure to resolve the "*Caroline* Affair." In late December 1837, following Van Rensselaer's occupation of Navy Island, the British retaliated. On the night of the 29th, the *Caroline*, an American steamship that had been chartered to deliver supplies to the rebels, was burned on the American side of the Niagara River with the loss of an American life. The act inflamed patriotic passions along the border, prompting demands for war with England. Cooler heads prevailed, as Van Buren remained firm, but not warlike. Forsyth protested the *Caroline* incident through Minister Stevenson in London, expressing outrage and demanding indemnity. Concurrently, the president sent a private conciliatory note to Foreign Secretary Lord Palmerston so that the official tone would not be misunderstood. The two governments became involved in a lengthy legal dispute over the "piratical character" of the *Caroline*, which remained unresolved.

The issue was placed on the diplomatic back burner until 1840. In November the Americans arrested Alexander McLeod, the leader of the British raiding party, in

New York for the murder of Amos Durfee. London protested, contending that McLeod could not be tried for a public act carried out in Her Majesty's service. Forsyth rejected the argument, noting that the trial was for murder—a state offense. The federal government was powerless to intervene. Fortunately for both nations, the Court found McLeod innocent in October 1841, and the crisis passed. The British finally apologized for the incursion the following year in the Webster–Ashburton Treaty.

An equally troubling and potentially violent problem existed for the Americans along the Maine border with Canada. The Peace of Paris of 1783 ending the American Revolution provided for a boundary line. Amid claims involving ill-defined rivers and highlands in the area of Maine and New Brunswick, the "true line" became blurred. By the mid-1830s the area became the subject of increasing focus and friction as New Englanders coveted the farmlands and timber resources and Canadians desired it as the shortest transit route for a military road from St. Johns to Quebec. Numerous attempts to resolve the dispute proved unproductive. The latest, a compromise line proposed by the King of the Netherlands in 1831 that would have given the Americans two-thirds of the 12,000 square miles of territory, collapsed because of the opposition of Maine. The essential approval of Jackson and the British government was negated by the issue of states rights. Further negotiations under Jackson beginning in 1834 involving Forsyth stumbled again, largely due to Maine's insistence on its perception of the 1783 line.

The situation began to deteriorate sharply, however, in the spring of 1837 when the Maine legislature ordered a census of the territory. Census taker Ebenezer Greely was arrested in both June and September by Canadian officials while in the official exercise of his duties. Recognizing the explosive nature of the situation, both the British and Forsyth in 1838 called for a new survey of the area. When they failed to agree on a joint commission and binding follow-up negotiations, the two sides conducted independent examinations. Maine, disenchanted with Washington's lengthy delays, proceeded with its own search, as did the British. Predictably, the resultant surveys settled nothing.

Both national governments wished the matter resolved. Van Buren and Congress correctly feared irresponsible actions by Maine's residents would force the United States into an unwanted war. The British saw the issue as niggling and annoying; another manifestation of the American governmental system that obtusely allowed a state to interfere in the foreign policy making of the national government. Maine, on the other hand, became increasingly bellicose and intransigent on the matter. Accordingly, the secretary of state's credibility suffered mightily with the citizens of Maine when he was unable to get the British to concede anything. Indeed, in 1837 the New Brunswick legislature authorized a railroad across the disputed area. Forsyth protested and the English government temporarily halted the project, but this hardly satisfied the locals.

By January 1839 the Maine legislature had directed its land agents to arrest and imprison "trespassing" lumberjacks. The next month an agent and his militia force of about 200 made an ill-advised incursion into the Aroostock River area, where they arrested about a dozen trespassers. However, they soon encountered a larger force of Canadians, who in turn arrested many of them. New Brunswick Lt. Governor William Harvey protested this American invasion, and Minister Fox demanded the federal government act to control Maine. Angry state legislators responded by raising troops and $800,000 for defense and demanded assistance from Washington.

The Van Buren administration found itself in a delicate situation. The executive with the approval of Congress pledged $10 million and 50,000 volunteers to defend Maine against British aggression. London was aghast at the scope of the response. Certainly, Van Buren and Forsyth wanted to avoid war and quickly appeared as the voices of reason, urging mutual withdrawal of forces, release of prisoners, and a renewed effort at negotiation. In late February Fox and Forsyth signed an agreement to this effect. Reassuring Maine that her interests would not be sacrificed and convincing her of the need for compromise was not easy, so this joyless task was assigned to the multitalented Winfield Scott. He traveled to Augusta and New Brunswick in March, met with Democratic Governor John Fairfield and Lt. Governor Harvey, and after some difficult negotiations, miraculously achieved results. Troops were withdrawn, spheres of interest created, and tensions relieved. A temporary respite had been gained, thanks to the restrained leaders in both London and Washington, who did not allow local events to catapult them into an unwanted disaster.

In June 1839 Forsyth visited Portland in an effort to achieve a bipartisan consensus on a policy. He failed. A combination of self-righteousness and intense interparty rivalry doomed any compromise. Van Buren pressed on regardless. Within weeks, Forsyth offered a proposal to the British for a new survey commission and binding follow-up arbitration. He pressured Fox with the contention that Maine might move at any time to occupy the entire territory. Disaster could be forestalled, however, by a presidential announcement that a settlement was imminent. A troubled Fox relayed these fears to Lord Palmerston in September 1839, but noted that he failed to see any immediate danger. The Minister added that although the Georgian was not encouraging, "I never find myself able to place much confidence in Mr. Forsyth's language, except when he is under the immediate eye of the president."

Forsyth continued to press the American case into 1840, arguing that war clouds loomed and the Canadians had repeatedly violated the February 1839 agreement. The administration must protect Maine's interests, yet identify a mutually acceptable solution. London certainly wanted a settlement and was receptive to arbitration, but balked at the state's involvement. Van Buren appointed commissioners to survey the area and report to him by January 1841. The British proposed two commissions—one to survey and one to arbitrate in June 1840. The president's defeat in the fall elections terminated further discussions. Ironically, when the issue was finally resolved in 1842, the United States received one thousand fewer square miles of territory than provided in the settlement of 1831.

A final problem area with the Europeans during the 1830s involved the international slave trade. London had taken a leadership role in promoting a European alliance to end the African trade and in 1834 invited the United States to join. Forsyth, speaking for the Jackson administration, refused on the grounds that such an agreement would involve the surrender of American maritime rights and delay voyages. The secretary denounced the slave trade as piracy, but suggested that the United States could handle violators with its own patrols. Consequently, Minister Stevenson was commanded to protest illegal efforts by the English to visit and search Yankee ships. The Van Buren White House adamantly held the same views, despite increasing protests by Minister Fox that the U.S. flag served as a shield for obvious slavers.

Events took a more emotional turn with the seizure of the *Amistad* in 1839. In June the Spanish vessel departed Havana for Guana Cuba with a cargo of more than 50 slaves. At sea the blacks revolted, killed the captain, and instructed two Spanish slave traders to sail to Africa. The Spaniards surreptitiously pointed the ship in the direction of the United States. On August 26, they were intercepted in Long Island Sound by the USS *Washington* and placed in jail in New London, Connecticut.

When news of the incident reached Washington in September, the president was out of town, but vital cabinet members Levi Woodbury, Amos Kendall, Felix Grundy, and Forsyth agreed that the Pinckney Treaty of 1795 entitled the Spanish to bring the slaves to trial in Madrid. All believed that the matter was a political bombshell that must be defused by handling the case through executive prerogative. At all costs it must be kept out of the courts, where the blacks could become a cause célèbre with the abolitionists. Attorney General Grundy, following Van Buren's instructions, promptly ordered the district attorney in Connecticut to ensure that the judicial proceedings regarding the ship and cargo remained within the purview of the executive. For Forsyth and the others, the United States was under treaty obligation to return the *Amistad* and her slaves, no questions asked. This was a matter of fulfilling a diplomatic responsibility, not litigating the legal position of the blacks. To admit to flaws in the slavers' arguments or challenge the status of the Africans would have exacerbated the type of North–South tension the administration had sought to quiet and would create unwanted problems before the 1840 election.

The *Amistad* symbolized the era's growing passions and, predictably, suits were quickly filed in Connecticut and New York courts—one by Captain Gedney of the *Washington*, who sought salvage claims, the other by abolitionists accusing the two Spaniards of enslaving free Africans. In early September Spanish Minister Angel Calderon demanded the return of the ship and cargo in accordance with the Spanish-American Treaty. A frustrated Forsyth could only concur with his views, and then inform him that the matter was now out of executive control and into the judicial sphere of the American system.

Van Buren threw the weight of the Justice Department behind the Spanish position. New York U.S. Attorney Benjamin F. Butler offered to assist the slavers, but no comparable aid was extended to the slaves. Forsyth refused to cooperate with the blacks' defense attorneys. When legal delays occurred, the two Spaniards posted bail and sailed to Cuba. In Connecticut the district attorney argued the White House position that the blacks constituted Spanish property, and the United States could not take criminal action in the matter. Based on international agreement, the slaves must be returned. Forsyth did concede that the blacks were individuals and had the right to sue in federal courts.

As the trial came to its conclusions in January 1840, a confident Forsyth requested a naval vessel to anchor off New Haven in preparation for a hasty departure of the slaves. The secretary did not want to avail the abolitionists the opportunity for an appeal. The ethics and morality of such a move beg questioning, the political wisdom less so.

Additional difficulties for Van Buren and Forsyth revealed themselves in the testimony taken in district court in November 1839. The slaves apparently were recent African imports, not older chattel or "Ladinos," brought to Cuba before 1820. The licenses for transporting the blacks were therefore fraudulent. On January 10, 1840, the judge ruled that the blacks had been kidnapped and were not slaves under Cuban law. The federal government was responsible for shipping them back to Africa. Forsyth promptly ordered an appeal, but the circuit court upheld the decision.

By 1840 the *Amistad* slaves and Cinque, their leader, had become a focal point for the international antislave press, including the British. Increasingly uneasy about possible British involvement in the *Amistad* affair, Forsyth knew they objected to American recalcitrance in enforcing the slave trade and desired freedom for the captives on the *Amistad*. He suspected that the Crown might use this issue to further its designs on Cuba, an island Forsyth believed vital to the future security and economic well-being of the United States. Tempers flared in early 1841 as Forsyth informed Minister Fox that the Americans would resist advances on Cuba. Fox, in turn, assured the secretary that the British would act if the slaves were returned to Madrid for execution.

The Van Buren administration had just retired from office when the Supreme Court rendered its verdict on March 9, 1841. John Quincy Adams defended the *Amistad* slaves. The Court agreed with Adams that the papers on the blacks were fraudulent and that there was no proof under Spanish law that the Africans were slaves. A ship chartered by abolitionist Arthur Tappan took the blacks to Sierra Leone in January 1842.

The *Amistad* case agitated the Spanish, the English, and the abolitionists, a harbinger of future grief. Throughout the appeals, Calderon pressured the administration to override the courts and simply deliver the blacks to Spanish justice. Forsyth patiently explained that the Constitution prohibited the president's interference. For Van Buren and Forsyth, the case served as an unending political nuisance. The president, who did not hold slaves, and the secretary, who did, both viewed slavery as a state matter. They were burdened with border problems with Canada, the McLeod trial, ongoing economic difficulties, and—critically—an upcoming presidential contest. Van Buren's position on the *Amistad* slaves no doubt appealed to his Southern constituency, but not enough to win him reelection.

Forsyth calculated on a second term for the president and dreamed of higher office for himself. Disappointment had come in 1836, when the party ignored him for the vice presidency in favor of the "slayer of Tecumseh," Richard Johnson. As the controversial Kentuckian's personal reputation came under increasing scrutiny, Forsyth began to hint at his availability for the second slot on the 1840 ticket with Van Buren. Other contenders, however, included Senator William R. King of Alabama and Governor James K. Polk of Tennessee. Sensing political chaos, Forsyth reluctantly joined the would-be challengers in withdrawing by June 1840 in favor of Johnson. The national convention tactfully selected no one, throwing the matter back to the states. The issue mattered little, because Van Buren suffered a decisive defeat in November.

Forsyth remained in Washington after his retirement from the State Department in 1841. He thrived on the political life of the Capital. Having purchased a house in the city, he intended to return to public life. Georgia likely would have reelected him to the Senate. Tragically, Forsyth contracted a fever in the fall and died on October 21 at the age of 61, his political ambitions unfulfilled.

Historians have expressed amazing consensus in their evaluation of John Forsyth. Most scholars agree that domestic, rather than foreign policy, issues dominated the presidencies of Jackson and Van Buren. They likewise concur, as Samuel

F. Bemis noted, that the Georgian was "a satisfactory rather than brilliant" secretary of state. A magnetic individual, a dynamic orator with a melodious voice, irresistible with the ladies, Forsyth was a classic Southerner. He outgrew the rashness of his Spanish mission and provided two presidents with cool, cautious, moderating advice. Although he had a fine analytical mind, there is no indication that Forsyth possessed a creative flair for shaping foreign policy. However, he followed the commands of both Jackson and Van Buren with skill and success. Forsyth was loyal and well known in Democratic Party circles, but carried little political weight and was at best a modest asset to the New Yorker's administration.

Even Forsyth's biographer, Alvin Duckett, recognizes the inherit weaknesses of his subject. Nevertheless, he praises him as a vigorous administrator who enacted a reorganization of the State Department that lasted 35 years. Duckett notes that the dynamic Jackson overshadowed Forsyth, but the secretary did attempt to temper his views and restrain his actions. Clearly more comfortable with his old colleague Van Buren, Forsyth could pursue his duties with less restriction. The two men found themselves in agreement on most issues, allowing Forsyth maximum flexibility.

Forsyth certainly embraced the views of most Southerners on slavery and Texas expansion. However, as a career politician who aspired to higher office, he was often obliged to soften his public position. His pro-slavery ideals revealed themselves rather boldly in the *Amistad* case. The administration's need, however, to appear both constitutionally sound and pro-Southern for the 1840 election, juxtaposed itself nicely with Forsyth's own views. His predictably cautious approach to Texas annexation was not a reflection of an opposition to expansion, but rather to the politically divisive nature of the issue.

Forsyth can be criticized for dissipating his talents and energies by a whirlwind social life. Although an ambitious man, the Georgian was never aggressive. Ever the aristocrat, he refused to abandon the good life and adopt the common touch that might have carried him to a higher elevation in American politics.

BIBLIOGRAPHICAL ESSAY

Unfortunately, there exists no major collection of private Forsyth manuscripts covering his State Department career. Princeton University houses a small body of papers, and some letters are scattered throughout various libraries in the Southeast. Forsyth correspondence can be found, however, in the files of many of his cabinet compatriots, as well Presidents Jackson and Van Buren. Official correspondence is accessible at the National Archives and on microfilm.

The only biographical effort, Alvin Ducket, *John Forsyth: Political Tactician* (1962) is very evenhanded and can be supplemented with the reliable Samuel F. Bemis (ed.), *The American Secretaries of State and Their Diplomacy* (1928). Forsyth's tenure with "Old Hickory" is covered by John M. Belohlavek, *Let The Eagle Soar: The Foreign Policy of Andrew Jackson* (1985). His service with Van Buren has been more extensively documented, including James C. Curtis, *The Fox at Bay: Martin Van Buren and the Presidency* (1970), John Niven, *Martin Van Buren* (1983), Major Wilson, *The Presidency of Martin Van Buren* (1984), and Donald Cole, *Martin Van Buren and the American Political System* (1984).

Worthwhile studies on Anglo-American relations in the period include James M. Callahan, *American Foreign Policy in Canadian Relations* (1937), Henry Burrage,

Maine in the Northeastern Boundary Controversy (1919), J. Chris Arndt, "The Solid Men of Bangor: Economic, Business and Political Growth on Maine's Urban Frontier, 1769–1845" (1987), Howard Jones, *To the Webster–Ashburton Treaty: A Study in Anglo-American Relations, 1783–1843* (1977), and Howard Jones, *Mutiny on the Amistad* (1987).

For Mexican relations consult James M. Callahan, *American Foreign Policy in Mexican Relations* (1932) and for France, Richard McLemore, *Franco-American Diplomatic Relations, 1816–36* (1941).

John Belohlavek

JOHN W. FOSTER
(1836–1917)

Served 1892–1893
Appointed by President Benjamin Harrison
Republican

John Watson Foster, international lawyer, diplomat, and U.S. secretary of state, was born in Pike County, Indiana, in 1836. His English father, Matthew Foster, was a successful merchant and local politician. Foster attended local schools and then Indiana University, where he studied classical languages and graduated in 1855. After attending Harvard University for a year, Foster returned to Indiana, where he established a law practice in Evansville and became active in Republican Party politics. A strict Presbyterian and outspoken abolitionist, Foster viewed slavery and the Confederacy as the embodiment of evil. When the Civil War began, Foster felt morally obligated to enlist, despite being recently married and chronically concerned about his fragile health. During the war, Foster served as an officer with the 25th Indiana Volunteer Infantry and distinguished himself in combat at Ft. Donelson and Shiloh. He later served in campaigns in western Tennessee and Kentucky, attaining the rank of brevet brigadier general. Following the war, Foster published the Evansville *Daily Journal* (1865–73), became the city's postmaster (1869–73), and moved up in the ranks in the Republican Party. He was chairman of the Republican State Central Committee in 1872, and his successful efforts to secure Indiana's electoral votes for the reelection of President Ulysses S. Grant that year brought Foster to the attention of party leaders such as James G. Blaine, who helped secure him an appointment as minister to Mexico.

Throughout his long career in international affairs, Foster tended to appear in key roles at critical times. From 1873, when he first accepted appointment as minister to Mexico, until the end of the century, Foster was involved with most of the nation's major foreign policy issues as a diplomat, international legal counsel, or informal adviser to presidents and secretaries of state. He arrived in Mexico in 1873, just in time to encounter the revolution led by Porfirio Diaz, and he was instrumental in bringing about U.S. recognition of Diaz's regime. Furthermore, Foster initiated a relationship with Diaz that would lead to significant U.S. investment in Mexico. His close personal and professional relationship with Diaz continued until the latter's overthrow in 1910.

Following seven years in Mexico, Foster became Minister to Russia in 1880, at a time when the country was shaken by revolutionary plots and the assassination of Tsar Alexander II. Foster reported on Tsarist pogroms against Russian Jews and came to view Russia as hopelessly misruled, corrupt, and backward. Foster served as a special envoy to Spain from 1883–1884 and directed an aggressive effort to negotiate a reciprocal trade agreement for Cuba and Puerto Rico, which was a cornerstone of Secretary of State James G. Blaine's policy of Pan Americanism. Foster left diplomatic service in 1884 and built a successful legal practice in Washington, establishing a clientele that included China, Chile, Russia, and Mexico. On behalf of China, Foster argued tirelessly against Chinese exclusion legislation and for reparations to the families of the Chinese victims killed in anti-Chinese riots of 1885 in Rock Springs, Wyoming. His work for Latin American governments at times placed him in conflict with the policies of his own government.

Were it not for Blaine's extraordinary prominence in the Republican Party, Foster would have been a more logical appointment than the party's "Plumed Knight" to head the State Department under President Benjamin Harrison; both were from Indiana, and Harrison had known Foster for many years. When Harrison was putting together his cabinet, Foster was the most experienced American in the field of foreign affairs at that time. Although Foster had supported Harrison's bitter rival, Walter Q. Gresham, for the Republican Party nomination in 1884 and 1888, he and Harrison had remained on cordial terms. The events early in Harrison's term demonstrated that the president had as much, if not more, confidence in Foster than he did in Blaine. Nevertheless, following the election of 1888, Harrison selected James G. Blaine as his secretary of state, despite not being overly fond of the flamboyant, controversial, and politically ambitious figure.

Throughout Harrison's administration, Foster was close to the president whenever foreign policy issues were considered. To one Republican insider, he appeared to be the "handyman" of the State Department. Shortly after Harrison's inauguration, Foster, while maintaining his private legal practice with foreign clients, began performing for the president a variety of tasks related to reciprocal trade agreements, a key component of the new administration's foreign policy. Working the halls of Congress, Foster advised Representative William McKinley of Ohio and members of the Senate Committee on Finance on behalf of the president and the secretary of state. Once the so-called McKinley Tariff was enacted, with its provisions for reciprocal trade agreements, Foster quickly negotiated a reciprocity agreement with Brazil and received an appointment to negotiate reciprocal trade pacts in Madrid for the Spanish possessions of Cuba and Puerto Rico. Prior to departing for Spain, Foster visited Cuba as a private citizen, ostensibly for reasons of health, but more importantly as the bearer of a handwritten letter from the secretary of state stating: "He [Foster] goes to you officially with the fullest credit and confidence of the State Department. Please respond to any and all questions he may make. I give no specific direction. Mr. Foster is accredited *carte blanche*." While in Cuba, Foster met with the island's governor general, as well as with business leaders. In early 1891, Foster's efforts had produced an agreement. When Foster returned to Washington, Blaine was in seclusion at Bar Harbor, Maine, too ill to attend to matters of state. He allowed Foster to handle all matters related to the agreement with Spain and to sign the document finalizing the agreement.

Meanwhile, during Blaine's prolonged absence from Washington, in the spring of 1891, Foster attended to various tasks in a room set aside for him in the State Department. Laboring on what the president referred to as "some matters that are his charge," he negotiated reciprocity agreements with the British for their colonial possessions in the West Indies. Foster established a protocol with the German government regarding the importation of American pork and negotiated with Canadian officials about boundary disputes, Chinese immigration into the United States through Canada, jurisdiction in the Great Lakes, tolls along the Welland Canal, and reciprocal trade agreements.

Following Blaine's return to Washington, Foster continued his extensive involvement in U.S.–Canadian issues. Upon the secretary's request, he participated in informal discussions with a delegation of the Canadian Cabinet in February 1892. These meetings achieved no progress on reciprocal trade but did produce agreements for cooperation on several other matters, including the establishment of a joint survey of the boundary between Alaska and British Columbia. Toward the close of the meeting, Secretary Blaine, acting on Foster's suggestion, issued a strong protest of Canadian discrimination in the levying of tolls along the Welland Canal. Later, Foster prepared a report of the meetings, which criticized the Canadians in such strong language, that the president delayed in sending it to Congress. In June 1892, Foster again participated in meetings with Canadian officials. He advised the president to take a tough position with the Canadians with respect to canal tolls, which he believed would enhance Harrison's prospects in the coming presidential elections. By the spring of 1892, Blaine's health had declined to the point where he could devote little attention to matters of state. Harrison again turned to Foster for help in dealing with Canada, this time concerning the hunting of seals in the Bering Sea.

Foster's extraordinary influence in the Harrison administration was never more obvious than during the "Chilean Crisis," a dangerous diplomatic imbroglio that brought the United States and Chile to the brink of war. Problems between the United States and Chile arose when the transport ship *Itata*, loaded with arms purchased in the United States by Chilean rebel forces, was surrendered to American officials in Iquique, Chile, in the spring of 1891. The orders to seize the *Itata* and its cargo, which reversed earlier instructions from Secretary Blaine, were handwritten by Foster, who was at the time employed as legal counsel to the government of Chile. Chilean President Jose Manuel Balmaceda's minister in Washington had become aware of the efforts of rebel forces to buy arms in the United States and had petitioned Blaine to take measures to keep these armaments from leaving the United States. Blaine asked John Bassett Moore, then third assistant secretary of state, to draft a reply. Moore produced a document for the Secretary's signature, which stated that "such sale and shipment are permitted by law." Later, during a meeting in Blaine's home, the secretary of state was persuaded by Foster to reject this position. Then, Foster immediately wrote instructions, using plain stationery from Blaine's study, ordering the U.S. attorney general to have the *Itata* seized. Before the seizure could occur, however, the *Itata* left the United States and arrived safely in Iquique, the rebel headquarters, having eluded pursuing American naval forces. There, the Chilean authorities surrendered the ship and its cargo to representatives of the United States. However, the loss of these arms did not significantly hinder the rebels' cause.

Balmaceda was shortly afterward overthrown, and the Chilean public harbored an understandable resentment toward the United States for interfering in Chile's revolution. This anti-American sentiment erupted in a riot on the streets of Valparaiso the night of October 16. Two sailors from the USS *Baltimore* were killed, and several others were injured. Secretary Blaine urged a moderate course, which displeased Harrison, who believed that national honor was at stake. Months of crisis followed. Blaine's illness kept him away from his duties, and Harrison turned to Foster for help in negotiating a resolution to the crisis. Unlike Blaine, Foster completely supported the president's hard-line position, and Harrison's dependence on his unofficial foreign policy adviser increased.

In his dual role as adviser to the U.S. government and legal counsel for the Balmaceda government in Chile, Foster exhibited no scruples about his obvious conflict of interest. As the crisis with Chile deepened, Foster found himself involved with both sides. Assistant Secretary of State Moore noted with a sense of satisfaction that Foster's position was "getting warm" and observed that Foster was "apprehensive lest his connections with the matter might become known, and in view of his connections with the Department of State, and his great privileges and opportunities in it, be subject to comment." Although Foster employed an attorney to serve as his "go-between" with Lazcano, Foster's work for the Balmaceda government continued—to the extent that Foster drafted Chilean diplomatic notes after the overthrow of President Balmaceda. Chile's new revolutionary government, aware of Foster's seemingly unlimited influence and access, offered Foster employment as their representative. Foster declined this offer. Years later, he wrote coolly in his *Memoirs* that the "revolution which occurred in Chile . . . occasioned the government of the United States much trouble, even bringing it to the brink of war; but it furnished me some professional business."

On June 4, 1892, only a few days before the Republican National Convention, Blaine abruptly resigned as secretary of state and was quickly replaced by Foster. Although already familiar with the work of the State Department and widely experienced in diplomatic affairs, Foster brought certain political liabilities to a president about to campaign for reelection. The press criticized Foster's involvement as a lawyer for foreign governments, such as Mexico and China; the *New York Times* reported specifically on his questionable role in the Chilean crisis, using information leaked from State Department sources.

Although a possible political liability to the administration, Foster nevertheless brought to the State Department considerable administrative skills and an unflinching commitment to an aggressive and expansionist foreign policy. During his tenure as secretary of state, he took decisive action in several areas. He warned the British about their activities in Samoa and Central America that appeared to threaten American interests; attempted to secure a 99-year lease for a naval coaling station in Samaná Bay in Santo Domingo; explored the possibility of establishing a naval base in Chimbote, Peru; sought an international agreement on bimetallism at the International Monetary Conference in Brussels; and supervised the preparation of the American case to be presented before an international tribunal in Paris that would decide the Bering Sea fur seal dispute. Conscious of American prestige abroad, he raised the rank of the highest U.S. diplomats from minister to ambassador.

Foster's effort to secure the annexation of the Hawaiian Islands proved to be his most significant activity as secretary of state. For decades this beautiful chain of islands had attracted the interest of expansion-minded Americans, and the Harrison administration was prepared to annex the islands if opportunity arose. Unfortunately for expansionists in both Washington and Honolulu, when the chance for annexation came in January 1893, occasioned by a revolt led by prominent planters, the political climate had changed in the United States.

Harrison was now a lame-duck president, about to be replaced by Grover Cleveland, yet he still considered Hawaii vital to American interests, and both the president and Foster saw no reason not to attempt a treaty of annexation in the final weeks of the administration. Before the coup against the Queen, Foster had advised the U.S. Minister in Hawaii, John L. Stevens, to write two separate reports in his diplomatic correspondence, "one of which shall aim to give the narrative of public affairs in their open historical aspect, and the other to be of a strictly confidential character, reporting and commenting upon matters of personal intrigue and the like so far as you may deem necessary for my full understanding of the situation." Foster had authorized an attempt to purchase the islands in late 1892, but cautioned influential American planters in Hawaii, who had formed an Annexation Club, that any attempt to annex Hawaii in the final months of the Harrison administration could create serious political problems.

Despite Foster's earlier advice, a new revolutionary government in Hawaii, supported by U.S. naval forces stationed in Honolulu, petitioned for annexation in early 1893. Foster immediately recognized the new government and worked desperately during the final weeks of the Harrison administration to place an annexation treaty before the Senate. The Senate refused to ratify the treaty, however, because of unfavorable publicity surrounding U.S. involvement in the coup to overthrow Queen Liliuokalani and because of the antiannexationist stand taken by President-elect Cleveland. Cleveland chose as his secretary of state a Republican, Walter Gresham, who harbored an intense hatred of Harrison and had supported the Democrats in the 1892 election. Gresham wanted to embarrass Harrison by investigating the irregularities in the annexation effort and tried to restore the Hawaiian queen. This attempted restoration backfired when the Queen announced that upon restoration of her monarchy, she would behead all those who opposed her. Meanwhile, the provisional government, led by Sanford B. Dole, refused to leave office and created the Hawaiian Republic, which remained independent until 1898, when the war with Spain created a climate favorable to U.S. annexation.

When the Harrison administration ended, Foster returned to his law practice, now under the direction of his son-in-law, Robert Lansing. He immersed himself in his international legal work. He also involved himself in sporadic diplomatic assignments for the McKinley administration, taught at George Washington University (then known as Columbia College), took leadership positions with various groups advocating world peace through international law, and wrote and lectured on international affairs and U.S. diplomatic history. In 1895, Foster journeyed to Shimonseki, Japan, in the employment of the Chinese government, serving as their adviser in negotiations, which led to the conclusion of the Sino-Japanese War. Along with other leading American political and diplomatic leaders of his era, Foster became involved in the American Society for International Law, founded in 1906, and in the Carnegie Endowment for International Peace, founded in 1910. He served four times as president of the Lake Mohonk Arbitration Conference, and he played a central role in the founding of the American Red Cross. In 1907, he served as advisor to the Chinese delegation to the Second International Peace Conference at The Hague. He took with him as interpreter his 19-year-old grandson, John Foster Dulles.

In the early decades of the twentieth century, Foster emerged as a major spokesman for keeping a nationalistic, assertive, and expanded American role in foreign affairs. In his published writings, including *A Century of American Diplomacy*, *American Diplomacy in the Orient*, and *The Practice of Diplomacy*, Foster displayed an optimistic faith in the eventual triumph of the Anglo-Saxon principles of international law and the ultimate conversion of the world's people to Christianity. He expressed a firm belief in the righteousness of the U.S. expansion across the North American continent and into the Pacific (although he disagreed with the "Expansionists of '98" about the wisdom of acquiring Puerto Rico and the Philippines). He was also an advocate of promoting world peace and wrote extensively on the use of arbitration and adherence to the principles of international law. However, the lofty, idealistic rhetoric of his published writings was frequently missing in his private correspondence. Here, he often employed the language of the old warrior, the opportunistic diplomat, the partisan statehouse politician, and the hard-edged attorney. For example, in 1903, when President Theodore Roosevelt took action to separate Panama from Colombia so that work on the Panama Canal could proceed, Foster wrote to his old friend and Civil War comrade-in-arms, James Harrison Wilson: "The action of the government does look a bit premature, [however] . . . Colombia should not be permitted to stand in the way of such a great world work."

On the eve of the American entry into World War I, Foster again displayed a willingness to abandon arbitration and nonaggression in pursuit of what he saw as a righteous course. To his old friend General Wilson, he wrote: "Though a pacifist after a fashion, I am so bitter with Germany I rather hope we will get into the scrimmage."

Foster's experience in politics and diplomacy developed in him a complex blending of idealism and pragmatism. He brought to the Harrison administration an approach toward foreign affairs shaped by his wide experience in world affairs, as well as by his fundamental Presbyterian faith, his education in the classics, legal training, and unflinching loyalty to the Republican Party. A skilled and tough negotiator on international issues (John Hay once noted that "Foster's worst enemy would never accuse him of any tendency to mercy or tenderness to an opponent"), Foster brought an assertive style to an administration seeking an expanded American presence abroad. Foster's approach to politics and diplomacy was further informed by his Civil War experience, which imbued in him a fierce sense of righteous nationalism. As secretary of state, Foster provided invaluable service to a president who did not have much understanding of foreign affairs. In addition, Foster's Indiana connections and personal acquaintance with Harrison provided him with a political base and direct access to the president. Clearly, Foster had more influence in the administration than the secretary of state or any other of the senior staff in the Department of State. Foster was a principal architect, perhaps *the* principal architect, of the Harrison administration's spirited diplomacy.

BIBLIOGRAPHICAL ESSAY

Following his long diplomatic career and the completion of his two-volume *Diplomatic Memoirs* (1909), Foster burned most of his papers, and a couple of small folders in the Library of Congress are all that remain of his correspondence. Items related to the Treaty of Shimonoseki were left in the care of his eldest grandson, John Foster Dulles, and are held in the Mudd Library at Princeton University. Besides his *Memoirs*, Foster, who wrote more on U.S. diplomatic history than any other secretary of state, produced the first text on American diplomatic relations, *A Century of American Diplomacy* (1900) and a pioneering survey of U.S. relations in the Far East, *American Diplomacy in the Orient* (1904). Foster recounted his Civil War experiences in *War Stories for My Grandchildren* (1918).

Michael J. Devine, *John W. Foster: Politics and Diplomacy in the Imperial Era, 1873–1917* (1981) presents a complete biography, along with a bibliography of Foster's numerous publications. "John W. Foster and the 'Spirited Diplomacy' of the 1890s," in *Their Infinite Variety: Essays on Indian Politicians* (1982), 265–288, focuses on Indiana connections and the relationship with President Harrison; and "The Diplomacy of Righteousness: The Legacy of John W. Foster" in Kenneth W. Thompson (ed.), *Traditions and Values: American Diplomacy, 1945 to the Present* (1984), 21–42, explores Foster's influence on John Foster Dulles. Also see William R. Castle, "John W. Foster," in *American Secretaries of State and Their Diplomacy*, Samuel F. Bemis, vol. 8 (1928), 185–223; and Jack Hammersmith, "John W. Foster, A Pacifist after a Fashion," *Indiana Magazine of History* (1988), 107–113.

Of particular value on the Hawaiian annexation effort is Thomas J. Osborne, *"Empire Can Wait": American Opposition to Hawaiian Annexation, 1893–1898* (1981); and David Healy, *James G. Blaine, and Latin America* (2001) contains excellent chapters on the crisis with Chile during the Harrison administration. On the background to the Sino-Japanese War and the negotiations at Shimonoseki, see Jeffrey Dorwart, *The Pigtail War: American Involvement in the Sino-Japanese War, 1894–95* (1975), and Marilyn B. Young, *The Rhetoric of Empire: American China Policy, 1875–1901* (1968).

Michael J. Devine

FREDERICK T. FRELINGHUYSEN (1817–1885)

Served 1881–1885
Appointed by President Chester A. Arthur
Republican

Upon accepting his appointment in November 1881, Frederick Frelinghuysen brought little practical experience in foreign affairs to the Department of State. He was born in 1817 in Millstone, New Jersey, of Dutch ancestry. His father died soon after, and Theodore Frelinghuysen, a politically active uncle, adopted the three-year-old boy. Upon maturity Fredrick attended Rutgers College and subsequently practiced law. He served as Attorney General of New Jersey and as U.S. Senator (1866–1869 and 1871–1877), where his committee assignments included naval affairs, judiciary, and claims. While serving in the Senate he supported President Johnson's impeachment and was a member of the commission that certified President Hayes's election.

While secretary of state, Frelinghuysen was intermittently ill. Coupled with his cautious temperament, inexperience, and inheritance from former Secretary of State James G. Blaine, the state of Frelinghuysen's health appears to explain further a not-very-aggressive approach to the nation's foreign affairs.

Frelinghuysen's department received little aid from Congress and the battling political parties of the day. His own Republican Party was split into the familiar Half-Breed and Stalwart factions. The Half-Breeds complained often of missed opportunities or mistaken actions. This occurred noticeably with regard to Latin American affairs, which played such a dominant role in the Frelinghuysen years. Some major newspapers emphasized and exploited the intraparty differences. Democrats, denied executive power for 20 years, instinctively opposed most administration proposals. The Congressional elections of 1882 resulted in a comfortable Democratic margin of control in the House of Representatives. Although the Senate was more evenly divided, personal antagonisms and ambitions, as well as ignorance and indifference, heightened the lack of congressional consensus. Thoughtless or careless congressional meddling occasionally left its negative mark.

As did other nineteenth-century secretaries, Frelinghuysen led a small, under-funded, and patronage-oriented foreign affairs establishment. In Washington, three assistant secretaries and various clerks aided the secretary. Approximately 30 ministers plenipotentiary, ministers resident, and chargé d'affaires represented United States interests abroad. These agents abroad often made difficult situations worse by "undiplomatic" statements and behavior. It seems that on more than one occasion they deliberately misinterpreted instructions from Washington.

The arena wherein Frelinghuysen's actions were most interesting and noteworthy was Latin America. Once active U.S. involvement in seeking a solution of the War of the Pacific was concluded, the arena narrowed to the Caribbean basin and Central America. It was in this area that technology, influence, and opportunities coincided, thereby presenting a stage for U.S. initiatives. In Caribbean affairs Frelinghuysen's caution was evident, his hand unsteady and sometimes contradictory.

Former Secretary Blaine's Latin American legacy included efforts to bring the War of the Pacific to an end, plans for an inter-American congress, correspondence with Great Britain over the meaning of the Clayton–Bulwer Treaty of 1850, and support for Justo Rufino Barrios, the Guatemalan strongman who dreamed of Central American unity (under his leadership) and was disputing Mexico's claims to a border area. When Frelinghuysen assumed control of the State Department, Chile resented past U.S. interference. Defeated and partially occupied Peru believed that the United States would forcibly prevent the loss of their territory to the Chileans. Immediately prior to leaving office Blaine had dispatched William H. Trescot and Walker Blaine (the secretary's son) on a peace mission to Chile. At approximately the same time Blaine had issued invitations for an inter-American congress to devise means for preventing war between the American nations. The meetings were to take place late in the next year (1882). Blaine orally informed Trescot that he should issue the invitations to Peru, Chile, and Bolivia at an appropriate time.

While the Trescot mission was en route, Frelinghuysen took possession of his office and promptly left Washington for the Christmas season. Upon his return, Frelinghuysen cabled new instructions to Trescot, "Exert pacific influence. Avoid any issue leading to your withdrawal from Chili." Detailed instructions leisurely followed by regular mail. While awaiting clarification, Trescot learned that in Peru U.S. Minister Stephen J. Hurlbut had delivered the peace congress invitation to Peruvian authorities. Trescot quickly secured an appointment with Jose M. Balmaceda, Chile's foreign minister. While in the act of extending the invitation, Trescot was stunned to learn that the U.S. government had withdrawn the invitations. Furthermore, Balmaceda said that Trescot's instructions from Blaine and new ones not yet in Trescot's hands had been published and that copies had reached Santiago via cable from Paris. Frelinghuysen's January 9, 1882, instructions reminded Trescot, and everyone else, of the U.S.'s dilemma. The secretary wrote that were the United States to dictate terms to a Latin American nation, "even for the purpose of preventing war . . . , or to preserve the autonomy of nations, it must be prepared by army and navy to enforce its mandate, and to this end tax our people for the exclusive benefit of foreign nations." The Trescot mission ended in failure.

The blunders tell us much about the conduct of our diplomacy. Costs of long-distance telegraph and cable messages had to be considered. But, to cable vague instructions while sending detailed instructions by a ship that would take several weeks to reach its destination and then allowing publication of those instructions highlights the insensitivity and inexperience of the department. Almost lost in the embarrassment was the further question of why Hurlbut didn't withhold the peace congress invitation. Lastly, because the Chileans held the Peruvian leader Francisco Garcia Calderon under house arrest in Santiago, confusion abounded as to whether there was a practicing government of Peru.

The secretary wanted earnestly to limit Chilean territorial spoils and to keep Great Britain and other European nations from getting involved. British business interests were already far advanced in the area. Frelinghuysen knew that there was little the United States could do to support Peru, as the use of force was out of the question. The task was complicated further because Peruvian leaders proved difficult to convince that they would get nothing more than good offices from the United States while Chilean leaders had reason to suspect U.S. motives. After long delays and further embarrassments, a treaty was negotiated settling the war. The United States played no part in the final negotiations. The diplomatic interventions resulted in little but discomfort.

Frelinghuysen continued Blaine's efforts to modify and, finally, to abrogate the Clayton–Bulwer Treaty. The British could not be moved, and the initiative came to naught. President Barrios of Guatemala secured from Frelinghuysen nothing more than a promise that the United States would act as arbiter in the Mexican border dispute, and then only if both parties requested such aid. They did not. Central American union efforts ceased when President Barrios was killed in a February 1885 attempt to bring El Salvador under his control.

Whatever his legacy, Blaine cannot be connected with, or held responsible for, one of Frelinghuysen's most surprising efforts—the canal treaty with Nicaragua. As Chester A. Arthur was organizing his administration in 1881, Ferdinand de Lesseps' canal project in Panama was stimulating American interest. Congress debated whether an American transit project in Nicaragua should be built. However, arguments over canal or ship-railway schemes and whether some settlement relative to the Clayton–Bulwer Treaty with Great Britain should come first forestalled a decision. Then, in 1883 Secretary Frelinghuysen became actively interested. He had grown uneasy due to rumors of French activity in Panama as well as evidence of support by Central American governments for a Nicaraguan canal to be undertaken if need be with European assistance. Unable to come to terms with private American promoters, the secretary, early in 1884, began talks with the Nicaraguan government. On December 1, 1884, the Frelinghuysen–Zavala Treaty was signed, giving the United States some measure of control over a two-and-a-half-mile-wide canal strip. The United States and Nicaragua were to be equally represented on a board of directors. Nicaragua was to receive one-third of the profits, to maintain peacetime jurisdiction over the Canal Zone and to receive a loan for public works. American rights during wartime were not specified, but the two nations were to form a defensive alliance.

The treaty was dramatic and nearly inexplicable. The usually cautious Frelinghuysen was asking the United States to depart from tradition and to assume a relationship with Nicaragua not dissimilar from European-style protectorates. In the mid-1880s the nation's resources would be strained to fulfill such obligations. Frelinghuysen's actions were certain to outrage Great Britain, for the Nicaraguan treaty completely ignored Britain's rights as accorded by the Clayton–Bulwer agreement. Lastly, the negotiations were undertaken by an administration soon to be replaced by that of the Democrat Grover Cleveland. Finding fault with its contents and timing the Senate failed to approve the treaty, and soon after the Cleveland administration withdrew it from consideration.

Yet another Frelinghuysen initiative concerned Latin America. Beginning in 1883 the State Department negotiated a series of reciprocal trade treaties concerning Mexico, Puerto Rico, Cuba, and the Dominican Republic. It appeared that other Caribbean nations would follow suit. Frelinghuysen was hoping that reciprocal trade agreements would find congressional support by occupying a position between those of free trade advocates and protectionists. He believed that reciprocity would encourage Latin American economic growth and interdependence, which, in turn, would promote political stability. Unilateral treaties would avoid the pitfalls and potential embarrassments of a hemispheric congress. The Senate ratified the Mexican treaty in March 1884; the others, submitted to Congress in the last days of Arthur's term, were never ratified.

During Frelinghuysen's last year in office, he secured congressional approval for sending a three-man team to talk with Latin American leaders about how to bring about economic improvements and closer political ties. Reciprocal treaties, adopting silver as a common commercial exchange medium, economic development, and removal of obstacles to trade were items to be explored. Frelinghuysen cautioned his agents that the United States could not assume any control or influence over Latin America. Late in 1885, almost a year after Frelinghuysen left office, his emissaries returned and made recommendations supporting reciprocity and an inter-American conference. Congress, during the Cleveland first term, took no action.

With the exception of the canal treaty with Nicaragua, Frelinghuysen rejected opportunities to directly increase U.S. influence in the Caribbean-Central American region. The secretary spurned various overtures to acquire territory and/or guarantee security in Haiti, Venezuela, Guatemala, El Salvador, and Honduras.

Frelinghuysen's record in Latin America includes few successes. He suffered rejection of all but one of his reciprocity treaties, rejection of his Nicaraguan canal treaty, embarrassing and inconclusive involvement in the settlement of the War of the Pacific, stalemate regarding the status of the Clayton–Bulwer Treaty, and lack of opportunity to further a silver commercial coinage system in Latin America.

In East Asia Frelinghuysen's activity was more restricted—he suffered fewer setbacks but accomplished little. The secretary usually cooperated with the European powers' insistence on Chinese treaty compliance. In this way the United States risked little while the potential for gain was sizable. American traders and missionaries received what protection an aged naval presence could supply. In 1883 the American minister to China, John Russell Young, requested naval support to pressure China into allowing American firms to open new factories in Shanghai. Frelinghuysen advised Young to confer with his diplomatic colleagues before asking U.S. naval authorities for aid beyond the "moral support" afforded by the presence of a vessel of war. Young worried that the Chinese might follow up on their refusal to allow the factories by denying foreigners further commercial and manufacturing opportunities. In such a case, Young thought that China would be the loser. Frelinghuysen endorsed Young's views, but presciently wondered "whether it would be altogether for the material advantage of our people to invite what, in view of the Chinese capacity, and the extreme cheapness of their service, might result in a transfer thither of an important share of our manufacturing interests." The Chinese refused to allow the factories, the United States did not insist, and the issue was dropped.

In Japan, U.S. Minister John A. Bingham recognized that government's efforts to modernize its legal and customs systems. The Tokyo government hoped to remove or alter restrictive provisions in its treaties with Western nations. Bingham and Frelinghuysen sympathized, but European resistance to changes led the secretary to abandon Japan's cause.

Although begun earlier, it was during Frelinghuysen's tenure that Robert W. Shufeldt completed the negotiations for Korea's first Western treaty. The United States led the way in opening a previously isolated nation to intercourse with the West. Thus, an opportunity for exercising influence presented itself that would require concern, commitment, and close attention. Neither Frelinghuysen nor his successors made the effort.

U.S. relations with distant Europe remained a mixture of detachment, predictability, and occasional rancor. It is the last category that attracted attention. Several previously unresolved issues continued to defy settlement. To the dismay of exporters, Germany and France continued to ban U.S. pork products. American studies failed to convince the Europeans that the products were safe. In seeking a solution, Frelinghuysen went so far as to invite a German investigating team to study American slaughtering and packing conditions. The Germans declined. Fear of disease coupled with resentment of anxious European farmers kept the issue unsettled. The State Department found that the United States had little leverage against the European nations.

Irish-Americans strained relations with Great Britain due to continued provocations. Anti-British activities carried out by America's Irish population either in the United States or on their return to Ireland or Great Britain were a problem too political for easy solution. Frelinghuysen was unable to meet the demands of the British for curtailing an often irresponsible American press. Effective governmental monitoring of the movements and baggage of trans-Atlantic travelers was perceived to be an impossibility.

Lastly, Frelinghuysen agreed to participate in the Berlin Congo Conference of 1884–1885. The U.S. delegate, John A. Kasson, supported a settlement to open a large section of central Africa to American merchants and missionaries, and wherein he hoped the native population would receive humane treatment. However laudable the administration's intent, Kasson's presence in Berlin jarred sensibilities regarding the tradition of U.S. isolation from European affairs. This new departure met the fate of so much of Frelinghuysen's work. There being insufficient support in Congress and none by the Cleveland administration, the Congo issue died.

The diplomatic record for the years 1881–1885 is meager, episodic, and often contradictory. The implementation of what passed for policy was often amateurish, clumsy, and embarrassing. As David Pletcher has noted, these were "Awkward Years."

Frederick Frelinghuysen was ill when he left office in March. He died in May 1885.

BIBLIOGRAPHICAL ESSAY

There is no Frelinghuysen manuscript collection. The Library of Congress collection consists of three volumes containing drafts of official correspondence. Making matters worse, there are no Chester A. Arthur papers. Hence, scholars rely on the official State Department collections in the Archives, the papers of other personalities of the day, and his newspaper accounts.

Important studies dealing with the last half of the nineteenth century include Walter La Feber's *The Cambridge History of American Foreign Relations*, vol. II, *The American Search for Opportunity, 1865–1913* (1993) and his *The New Empire: An Interpretation of American Expansionism, 1860–1898* (1963), the standard "revisionist" treatment of America's search for new markets; Robert Beisner's *From the Old Diplomacy to the New, 1865–1900* (1986). Beisner suggests that the paradigm defining U.S. foreign policy changed significantly between 1865 and 1890. Unfortunately, he cites few examples from the Frelinghuysen years. Robert H. Wiebe, in *The Search for Order, 1877–1920* (1967), illustrates the lack of policy governing U.S. relations in the 1870s and 1880s. To round out the more general treatments, see: Charles S. Campbell, Jr., *The Transformation of American Foreign Relations, 1865–1900* (1976); John M. Dobson, *America's Ascent: The United States Becomes a Great Power, 1880–1914* (1978); and Milton Plesur, *America's Outward Thrust: Approaches to Foreign Affairs, 1865–1890* (1971).

Two important monographs combine the presidencies of Garfield and Arthur as well as the foreign policies of Blaine and Frelinghuysen. David M. Pletcher's *The Awkward Years: American Foreign Relations under Garfield and Arthur* (1962) is a definitive study of the era detailing clumsy and poorly focused reactions to impulses "vaguely formed and not clearly understood," which, nonetheless, form a link to aggressive policies of the 1890s. A more recent and far briefer study is Justus D. Doenecke, *The Presidencies of James A. Garfield & Chester A. Arthur* (1981), which finds coherency in the fumbling policies of Blaine and Frelinghuysen. The author describes Frelinghuysen as "being ahead of both the public and Congress." See also Edward P. Crapol, *James G. Blaine: Architect of Empire* (2000).

For U.S. relations with specific nations or regions, the following works are significant: Joseph Smith, *Illusions of Conflict: Anglo-America Diplomacy Toward Latin America 1865–1896* (1979); Lester D. Langley, *Struggle for the American Mediterranean: United States-European Rivalry in the Gulf-Caribbean, 1776–1904* (1976); Michael H. Hunt, *The Making of a Special Relationship: The United States and China to 1914* (1983); Kenneth J. Hagan, *American Gunboat Diplomacy and the Old Navy 1877–1889* (1973).

Essays contributing to understanding of the topic are found in H. Wayne Morgan (ed.), *The Gilded Age* (1970); William H. Becker and Samuel F. Wells, Jr. (eds.), *Economics and World Power: An Assessment of American Diplomacy Since 1789* (1984); and Kenneth J. Hagan (ed.), *In Peace and War: Interpretations of American Naval History, 1775–1978* (1978).

Two articles deserve special mention: Russell H. Bastert, "Diplomatic Reversal: Frelinghuysen's Opposition to Blaine's Pan American Policy in 1882," *Mississippi Valley Historical Review* 42 (March 1946), and James A. Field, Jr., "'American Imperialism': The Worst Chapter in Almost Any Book," *American Historical Review* 83 (June 1978).

William Brinker

WALTER Q. GRESHAM (1832–1895)

Served 1893–1895
Appointed by President Grover Cleveland
Democrat

Walter Quintin Gresham was born on a modest farm in Harrison County, Indiana, on March 17, 1832. His ancestors were English and Scotch-Irish. Before he was two years old, his father, who was the county sheriff, was killed by an outlaw. As he grew up, several local politicians recognized the boy's talents and superintended his education. He attended the local country schools and May's Academy at Corydon. After a year in Indiana University's preparatory department, he read law with a prominent local Whig lawyer and was admitted to the bar in 1854.

Gresham's Whig mentors pushed him toward a career in their own party, but after the Whig collapse in the mid-1850s, he enlisted in the anti-Nebraska movement and affiliated briefly with the Know-Nothings. By 1856 he had joined the Republican Party and four years later won election to the state legislature, where he served a single term during the winter and spring of 1861. In the summer he joined the Union army and by the end of the year was named colonel of the 53rd Indiana Volunteer Infantry, attached to the Army of the Tennessee. In August 1863, he won promotion to brigadier general, but his military career was cut short the following June when he was wounded during William T. Sherman's Atlanta campaign. He left the army with the rank of brevet major general.

After the Civil War Gresham resumed the practice of law at New Albany, Indiana. In 1866 and 1868 he ran for Congress in a heavily Democratic district and lost both times. He had for years been at odds with Oliver P. Morton, the leader of the Indiana Republican Party, and when his wartime friend, President Ulysses S. Grant, offered him appointment as federal district judge for Indiana, he accepted in September 1869. For the next decade he remained ambivalent about returning to active politics. In 1880 he made a clumsy bid for the U.S. Senate but lost to Benjamin Harrison, who replaced Morton as leader of the state party and as Gresham's political nemesis.

In 1883 President Chester A. Arthur surprised Gresham with appointment as postmaster general. During the year and a half he held that office, he won praise for implementing the new Pendleton Civil Service Act and for other reforms in the postal administration. On the political front, he simultaneously labored for Arthur's nomination in 1844 and cultivated a dark horse candidacy of his own. Chagrined by James G. Blaine's nomination and again generally soured by politics, he longed to return to the security of the bench. After a brief stint as interim secretary of the Treasury, in October 1884 he eagerly accepted appointment as judge of the U.S. Seventh Circuit Court, based in Chicago.

Although as a district judge Gresham had taken action both on and off the bench in defeating the 1877 railroad strike, in the 1880s his ideas toward workers mellowed, and he won favor among workingmen for his evenhanded settling of strike cases. In addition, his severe rebuke to Jay Gould for his "railroad wrecking" in the Wabash receivership case earned him a reputation as a foe of monopoly. These considerations, plus his Civil War record, his spotless personal character, and his hailing from the important and doubtful state of Indiana, made him a serious contender for the 1888 Republican presidential nomination. But his low-tariff views and opposition by the party's Blaine wing sealed his defeat, and the convention chose instead his old rival, Harrison. During the next four years Gresham became increasingly disenchanted with the Republican Party, especially after the passage of the highly protectionist McKinley Tariff. His denunciations of an emerging "plutocracy" in the United States attracted the attention of the new Populist Party, which sought to draft him for president at its 1892 convention. He refused to lead the Populist crusade, however, and instead announced his support for the low-tariff Democratic candidate Grover Cleveland, who went on to defeat Harrison's reelection bid.

Critics saw Cleveland's invitation to Gresham to head the cabinet in his second administration as the consumption of a quid pro quo arrangement from the 1892 campaign. In truth, however, fearing just such an imputation, Gresham at first declined the offer and agreed to accept only after Cleveland and other Democrats fairly begged him to do so. Cleveland's political motive was larger than a simple payoff for support. Hoping to further a realignment of parties, he saw Gresham's appointment as a way to attach the independent Republican element to the Democratic Party, appeal to labor, and undermine the Populists. The idea backfired, however, for the unpopularity of many of the secretary's policies made him an enormous political liability, an anathema to Republicans, and never fully accepted by the Democrats.

Cleveland and Gresham quickly developed a close personal and working relationship. The two men apparently had not discussed foreign affairs before Gresham's appointment, and once in office the president generally followed the secretary's lead in the formulation of policy. Gresham's dealings with his subordinates were less successful. He tried in vain to persuade international law expert John Bassett Moore to become first assistant secretary, although he did rely heavily on Moore's help as a special consultant. As a recent convert to the Democratic Party, Gresham generally refused to take part in the distribution of State Department patronage, with the result that he was saddled with a corps of diplomats in the field who owed him no political obligation for their jobs and who sometimes exhibited little disposition to follow direction from Washington. His anomalous political standing showed most clearly in his relations with Congress, where Republicans did not hesitate to condemn nearly all his acts, and few Democrats were willing to defend his controversial policies. Similarly, the Republican press was highly critical of his actions, Democratic newspapers were generally embarrassed by him, with only Mugwump journals such as *Harper's Weekly* and the *Nation* rallying to his defense.

Gresham labored under other handicaps. He lacked experience in foreign affairs. His previous career had consisted exclusively of domestic offices, and both his public utterances and private correspondence had carried almost no references to foreign policy issues. Hence, after taking over the State Department, he was compelled to devote an inordinate amount of time to studying the background of diplomatic problems he confronted. Moreover, his personality did not suit him ideally for the diplomat. He sometimes showed a tactless impatience with others' opinions, greeted foreign representatives in his shirtsleeves, and otherwise ignored diplomatic niceties. His lack of wealth deprived him of any advantage that might come from expensive entertaining. Finally, ill health frequently kept him away from the department in 1894 and 1895.

Historians once dismissed Gresham as a do-nothing secretary of state, but today most scholars recognize the painstaking attention he gave to the great volume of business that confronted his department. Although some historians allege that Gresham favored the expansion of American economic interests abroad, especially foreign markets, as a way to cure the depression of the 1890s and avert the revolution among unemployed workers, his performance as secretary followed no such design. When Gresham formulated his foreign policy, he rarely drew a connection between overseas economic expansion and the nation's labor troubles. He recognized that the labor problem antedated the depression and that it was rooted not simply in overproduction but more fundamentally in a general maldistribution of wealth. Rather than looking to economic imperialism, he saw that the solution to class difficulties must come through some change, which he never really defined, in the domestic economic system. He did defend traditional overseas interests, including economic interests, but that defense was conservative and legalistic, and he devoted little energy to trying to expand those interests. Immediately upon passage of the Wilson–Gorman Tariff he abrogated the Republican reciprocity program whose aim had been the increase of foreign markets. He gave minimal support to consular reform, which many saw as a vehicle for expanded trade. And he considered American participation in the Commercial Bureau of American Republics not a boon but a nuisance.

Instead of charting a course of either political or economic expansionism in foreign affairs, Gresham sought to reverse what he saw as the unwarranted and dangerous outward thrust launched by the Harrison administration. In the decades before he entered the State Department, he had acquired a reputation in domestic politics as a kind of political Jeremiah, constantly warning of the dangers posed to America's republican institutions by corruption, venality, and greed. He saw a general "decay of public virtue" as "the sure precursor of national ruin." After he became secretary of state, his management of foreign affairs was infused with a similar sense of a need to restore lost virtue. He argued that if the United States departed from the "warnings of its founders and earlier statesmen" and entered "upon a career of foreign acquisition and colonization, the result will be disastrous." He saw little need for a big navy for commercial or strategic purposes and feared that a burgeoning military establishment would threaten republican values. He harbored no desire to write a new "doctrine" into American foreign policy.

Because his meager background forced him to treat each new problem on an ad hoc basis, Gresham turned instinctively to established patterns of behavior. As a federal judge he had been an impartial arbiter adjusting questions brought to his attention; as secretary of state he recreated that role to a remarkable degree, relying on international law, his understanding of traditional American interests, and his sense of justice and equity to guide his opinions.

Significantly, the closest he had come to experience in foreign affairs had been as a lecturer on international law at Northwestern University while on the bench at Chicago. It was a judge's reverence for precedent, rather than any vision of territorial or economic expansion, that truly informed his conduct of foreign policy. Yet, as John Bassett Moore observed, he "soon fell into trouble attempting to decide international questions judicially."

Both Gresham's anti-imperialism and his judicial approach to foreign policy showed most obviously in his opposition to the annexation of Hawaii. In January 1893 Queen Liliuokalani had been overthrown by a coup engineered by a group of American-descended lawyers, planters, and businessmen. Harrison had quickly negotiated a treaty of annexation with the new provisional government, but the treaty failed to receive Senate approval before his term ended. When Cleveland and Gresham took office, they withdrew the treaty for reexamination and sent James H. Blount to Hawaii to investigate. Betraying little interest in the value of Hawaii as a U.S. possession, Gresham instructed Blount to determine whether U.S. officials had aided the Queen's overthrow.

Blount's reports demonstrated that the landing of American troops by the U.S. minister had led the Queen to surrender on the condition that her case would be considered by the president. Gresham concluded that this condition gave the United States the right to intervene and, as an act of justice, to undo the wrong that had been done the Queen. After lengthy cabinet discussions, the administrations settled on a plan that called for the American minister, Albert S. Willis, to use a veiled threat of force to induce the provisionals to surrender authority back to the Queen. But Willis delayed before pursuing the delicate negotiations. When leaks in the American press suggested that the United States would not really employ force, the provisionals called Willis's bluff and refused to step down. The plan had never had any real chance for success, but Gresham blamed its failure on its dilatory execution by Willis. The secretary still hoped for the new regime's collapse and implicitly encouraged the royalists to launch a counterinsurrection, which they did unsuccessfully in early 1895.

All told, the Hawaii policy was a public relations disaster. Gresham believed that he was defending the nation's morality by correcting an abuse of power and that he was preserving its institutions from the incubus of a "Roman province" that could be managed only by despotic rule. But he missed the irony in his effort to reinstate a monarchy in the name of republican virtue. Republicans in Congress and the press condemned him as quixotic and un-American. Democrats generally offered only lukewarm support or said nothing. Only the Mugwump press agreed with Gresham's continued claim that "there is such a thing as international morality." In any case, he did succeed in blocking U.S. annexation of Hawaii.

In Samoa, Gresham's aim was not to block an imperialist venture but to get out of an entanglement already consummated. In 1889 the United States had joined with Great Britain and Germany in the General Act of Berlin, whose aim was to halt international rivalry over the South Pacific island group. The Berlin treaty obligated the three powers to give close supervision to a foreign-dominated government under the nominal headship of the Samoan king. The powers appointed several government officials who held real powers, including that of taxation. The regime was highly unpopular with the natives, especially rival claimants for the kingship, and the powers frequently had to dispatch warships to the islands to maintain peace.

The outbreak of new fighting in Samoa led Gresham to call for tripartite negotiations to reconsider the terms of the Samoan condominium. When Germany refused to participate in such talks, the secretary pushed for unilateral U.S. withdrawal. In a report to Congress he argued that the Berlin treaty had brought only onerous responsibilities and troubles with no compensating advantages to the United States. Trade with the islands was minuscule, but no matter what its volume, he asserted, "We have never found it necessary to interfere in the affairs of a foreign country to trade with it." Again harkening to the teachings of the Founders, he believed the United States had reaped only "unmitigated disadvantage" from its "departure from our early and conservative policy" of avoiding foreign entanglements. Gresham succeeded in convincing Cleveland of the need to get out of the condominium, but the proposal was blocked by the Republicans on the Senate Foreign Relations Committee joined by committee chairman, Democrat John T. Morgan, who had also opposed the secretary's Hawaii policy. Gresham's Samoa policy was nearly as controversial as that in Hawaii. Still, Gresham believed the United States had no real interests in Samoa. He concluded that "the only safeguard against all the evils of interference in affairs that do not specially concern us is to abstain from such interference altogether."

As Gresham's Samoa policy showed, he generally believed that the U.S.'s interests on the far side of the Pacific Rim were minimal. Hence, when China and Japan went to war in 1894, he took the position that the conflict "endanger[ed] no policy of the United States." He steadfastly resisted calls for joint intervention with Great Britain and other nations, which would constitute a "departure from the wise policy of avoiding foreign alliances and embarrassing participation in guaranteeing the independence of distant states." After repeated pleas from China for help under the good offices clause of the 1858 Sino-American treaty, Gresham did permit the U.S. ministers in Peking and Tokyo to serve as intermediaries for peace feelers, but he cautioned them to remain absolutely neutral and to stay out of the actual negotiations. Moreover, when the U.S. minister to China suggested that the American role in the talks might lead to commercial privileges, the secretary warned him not to let "Americans anxious for valuable concessions" take advantage of his "generous and obliging nature."

Public attention regarding Gresham's Asian policy focused on his decision to turn over to Chinese authorities two alleged Japanese spies who had sought asylum with U.S. consular officials in China. Gresham believed he was following solid legal precedents, but when the Chinese executed the two men, critics castigated the secretary as a stickler for technicalities who had the blood of the Japanese on his hands.

Less noticed but of much greater significance than the spy incident were the bilateral treaties Gresham negotiated with each of the two Asian countries. The immigration treaty of 1894 with China prohibited the immigration of Chinese laborers for a period of 10 years, but it also removed some of the anomalies of the

1880 Angell treaty and placed Sino-American relations on a friendlier basis. Gresham also negotiated a new commercial treaty with Japan that removed some of the more offensive provisions of the old unequal treaty system and thereby improved relations with the rapidly modernizing Asian power.

In the Middle East Gresham's chief concern was the protection of American missionaries sojourning in the Ottoman Empire. Lobbied heavily by the American Board of Commissioners of Foreign Missions, he rendered a vigorous diplomatic defense of these Christian workers based on their traditional, treaty-based rights. Yet, he rejected all calls that the United States should take up the cause of persecuted Armenians in Turkey, who were subjects of the Sultan and hence outside the purview of any legal American right to intercede.

One of the most time-consuming issues Gresham inherited was the long-standing dispute with Great Britain over fur seal hunting by Canadians in the Bering Sea. Previous administrations had claimed an American property right in the seal because of their home base on the American-owned Pribilof Islands. In August 1893, the Paris Tribunal of Arbitration denied this claim, and Gresham entered into irksome negotiations with the British to secure the protection of the herd from destructive water-based hunting. He met with little success, however, and the dwindling of the herd continued until the negotiation of a general fur seal convention in 1911.

In the Western Hemisphere Gresham subscribed to the Monroe Doctrine insofar as it aimed to reduce European influence, but he refrained from permitting a defense of its precepts to go so far as to flout the higher dictates of international law. Nor did he see the doctrine as a vehicle for expanding U.S. influence in Latin America. In the fall of 1893 during a revolt by a portion of the Brazilian navy against the sitting government, Gresham was watchful against any attempt by European powers, particularly Britain, to influence the outcome, but he was convinced that they had little real interest in the affair. As for American policy, he adhered to a strict neutrality based on accepted precepts of international law governing insurrections in foreign countries. Because the rebels carried on fighting in the harbor at Rio de Janeiro, he was careful to ensure protection to American commerce, although he warned American merchants that their enterprises could not expect U.S. protection if they interfered with the military operations of either side. In one incident when an American merchantman was fired on directly by the rebels, a U.S. navy vessel escorted it to the docks, and no further interference was encountered. Although some observers saw this action as tilting toward the government, the U.S. had in fact maintained a neutral stance, responding only to direct assault by the rebels.

In Nicaragua Gresham adopted a policy directly opposed by American economic interests. In the Mosquito Reservation U.S. entrepreneurs controlled most of the extractive industries under concessions granted by a government ostensibly in Mosquito Indian hands but in reality under a quasi-protectorate by Britain. Although the Americans feared control by the Nicaraguans, Gresham regarded the Monroe doctrine considerations as paramount and relentlessly defended Nicaragua's sovereignty in the Reserve against British (and American) "pretensions." He witnessed the success of his policy when in November 1894 the Indians voted to place themselves under direct Nicaraguan rule.

By contrast, Gresham thought the Monroe Doctrine did not apply to the Venezuela–British Guiana boundary dispute. He urged both sides to seek a solution through arbitration, and after examining Venezuelan and British evidence, he concluded that Venezuela should settle on the basis of the line drawn in 1841 by British engineer Robert Schomburgk. Despite a heavy lobbying effort by Venezuela's agent, William L. Scruggs, the secretary refused to allow the Venezuelans to "dump the controversy upon us" in the name of the Monroe Doctrine. His position contrasted starkly with the defiant anti-British stance assumed by his successor Richard Olney.

While the boundary question was pending in early May 1895, Gresham contracted pleurisy, which soon developed into pneumonia. He died on May 28.

As the *Literary Digest* noted at his death, "His foreign policy has been denounced as un-American, unpatriotic, and treacherous, and his record for the two years of service in the State Department has been represented as humiliating and unsuccessful." Outside the department and his small circle of associates, few understood Gresham's "small policy," rooted as it was in old republican notions of virtue, justice, morality, and fair play. As many Americans clamored for empire, his calls for a return to "the conservative teachings of the founders of our government" seemed more and more out of place. Indeed, the great irony and ultimate significance of his foreign policy was that it spurred an impassioned public controversy that gave enormous impetus to the growing expansionist sentiment in the nation. Denouncing Gresham's often-quixotic diplomacy in Hawaii, Samoa, Asia, and Latin America was easy and served as the first lesson in the training of many an American imperialist. When the country finally moved toward the adoption of formal empire at the end of the nineteenth century, Gresham seemed in retrospect even more a beleaguered defender of a rapidly fading past.

BIBLIOGRAPHICAL ESSAY

The chief primary source for Gresham's career is the collection of his papers in the Manuscripts Division of the Library of Congress, which contains primarily correspondence, especially letters received, with some autograph, letterpress, and draft letters by Gresham interspersed. For his tenure in the State Department, the starting point is the published *Papers Relating to the Foreign Relations of the United States*, which must be supplemented by the unpublished official correspondence pertinent to foreign relations in the National Archives, principally the records of the State Department (Record Group 59) and the Navy Department (Record Group 45). Much revealing private correspondence is also in the papers of Grover Cleveland, Thomas F. Bayard, John W. Foster, John Bassett Moore, John T. Morgan, and Carl Schurz (all in the Library of Congress), among others.

The only full-length scholarly study of Gresham's career is Charles W. Calhoun, *Gilded Age Cato: The Life of Walter Q. Gresham* (1988), which supersedes Matilda Gresham, *Life of Walter Quintin Gresham, 1832–1895* (1919). Gresham is cast in a prominent role in the economic expansionist thesis expounded by Walter LaFeber, *The New Empire: An Interpretation-American Expansion, 1860–1898* (1963), and William Appleman Williams, *The Roots of the Modern American Empire* (1969). Eugene W. Goll's doctoral dissertation, "The Diplomacy of Walter Q. Gresham, Secretary of State, 1893–1895" (1974), takes issue with the "new empire" school, as does Thomas J. Osborne, *"Empire Can Wait": American Opposition to Hawaiian Annexation, 1896–1898* (1981).

Other works that focus on aspects of Gresham's foreign policy include Charles W. Calhoun, "American Policy toward the Brazilian Naval Revolt of 1893–94: A Reexamination," *Diplomatic History*, 4 (1980), 39–56; "Morality and Spite: Walter Q. Gresham and U.S. Relations with Hawaii," *Pacific Historical Review*, 52 (1983), 292–311, and "Rehearsal for Anti-Imperialism: The Second Cleveland Administration's Attempt to Withdraw from Samoa, 1893–1895," *The Historian*, 48 (1986), 209–224; Alfred L. Castle, "Tentative Empire: Walter Q. Gresham, U.S. Foreign Policy, and Hawaii, 1893–1895," *The Hawaiian Journal of History*, 29 (1995), 83–96; Jeffrey M. Dorwart, *The Pigtail War: American Involvement in the Sino-Japanese War of 1894–1895* (1975); Michael B. McCloskey, "The United States and the Brazilian Naval Revolt, 1893–1894," Americas, 2 (1946), 296–321; Rising Lake Morrow, "A Conflict between the Commercial Interests of the United States and Its Foreign Policy," *Hispanic American Historical Review*, 10 (1930), 213; George E. Paulsen, "The Gresham-Yang Treaty," *Pacific Historical Review*, 37 (1968), 281–297, and "Secretary Gresham, Senator Lodge, and American Good Offices in China, 1894," *Pacific Historical Review*, 36 (1967), 123–142; William Adam Russ, Jr., *The Hawaiian Republic*, 1894–1898 (1961), and *The Hawaiian Revolution*, 1893–1894 (1959); and Merze Tate, *The United States and the Hawaiian Kingdom: A Political History* (1965).

Charles Calhoun

ALEXANDER M. HAIG, JR. (1924–)

Served 1981–1982
Appointed by President Ronald Reagan
Republican

Alexander Meigs Haig chose *Inner Circles* as the title for his memoirs and in doing so may have given ammunition to the followers of C. Wright Mills and others of the elitist school of American politics who posited that decision making is dominated by a small interlocking set of elites at the highest levels of American business, government, and military. Haig circulated at the highest levels of American political life as a governmental official, as a military officer, and as a corporate executive, but he was no scion of privilege. His rise to prominence in American political life started from modest beginnings and was marked throughout by significant adversity—his short tenure as secretary of state being only one small chapter in a remarkable life that, when captious criticism is placed to one side, shows him to be a man of significant accomplishment, talent, and character.

Haig was born on December 2, 1924. His father, Alexander Meigs Haig, was a respected lawyer who died of cancer in 1933 in the midst of the Depression, exhausting much of the family's financial assets. Haig's mother, Regina, a former English teacher, struggled financially following this tragedy to provide for Alex, Jr., and his younger brother and older sister. Haig worked at numerous odd jobs to supplement the family income, and with the help of generous uncles, the family managed to get along. Haig, whose father had soldiered in World War I, aspired from his boyhood to a military career. His mother urged him to follow his father's footsteps in the law, but his own instincts prevailed. He sought an appointment to West Point on graduation from high school, but was not selected. He went to Notre Dame until his sophomore year, when he secured, through the intercession of an uncle, a congressional appointment to West Point. He graduated 214th out of a class of 310 in 1947. Although his less than stellar academic performance led no one to predict his later success, Haig embarked on a military career at a time when the heightening Cold War was changing the role of the military from a war-fighting operation into a defense and peacekeeping business, dominated by theories of limited war, peacekeeping activity, and administrative organization. In such a context, Haig's toughness of character, determination, ambition, and not a little good luck would serve him well in the face of future adversity. He proved to be a brave soldier and a good organization man, which did not escape the notice of those in higher authority.

In 1948 Haig was posted in Japan, where he met Patricia Fox. They were married in 1950. His wife was the daughter of Alonzo Fox, who served with General Douglas MacArthur during the postwar occupation of Japan. Through this connection to his father-in-law, Haig was introduced to the inner workings of military administration and worked as aide-de-camp to General Edward Almond, MacArthur's chief of staff, under whom he continued to serve during the Korean War.

After the war Haig served as an instructor in armor at West Point and captain of a tank battalion in Germany. He returned stateside for training at the Naval War College and at Georgetown, where he took a master's degree in 1961. This was followed by a series of Pentagon desk assignments, in which he worked for Cyrus Vance and Joseph Califano, important future political contacts. In 1966, he was posted to Vietnam, where he distinguished himself in action as battalion commander in the First Infantry division and was decorated for bravery. He returned to West Point as deputy commandant, prior to accepting a position as military assistant and later deputy assistant to President Richard Nixon in the National Security Council (NSC), where he served as an aide to Henry Kissinger, Nixon's National Security Adviser and later secretary of state.

Haig was tapped by Nixon in the wake of the Watergate scandal to serve as his Chief of Staff from 1973–1974 and is credited with steady management of the affairs of state during that tumultuous time. Haig avoided indictment in the Watergate affair, having navigated through the political carnage with honor. After Nixon's resignation, Haig served President Gerald Ford briefly before being named NATO Commander in 1974. He won wide respect for various reforms at NATO, where he served until 1979. He resigned from the military in that year and served as president of United Technologies Corporation, a position he held until asked by newly elected President Ronald Reagan to serve as his secretary of state.

Haig served as secretary of state for only about a year and a half. In so short a time, he could not substantially affect the course of U.S. foreign policy, and his tenure was marked by continuous battles over control of foreign policy decision making with various members of the White House Staff under President Reagan. No stranger to the NSC, to the White House, or to the bureaucracy, Haig should perhaps have weathered these internecine struggles; instead they, coupled with his personality, were his undoing.

The United States faced an increasingly hostile global situation in the early 1980s. The Soviet Union was testing the limits of its own interventionist capacity in Afghanistan, various parts of Africa and in Central America. Détente had given way to intensification of the Cold War, and the Reagan administration had indicated grimly that it was ready to meet Soviet expansionism with resolve. Haig fit the bill as the kind of secretary of state needed in such a tense and confrontational environment, and Haig's primary preoccupation during his short tenure was with the various ways in which Soviet influence affected other parts of the world. Two issues of immediate concern to Haig on taking office were the growing crisis in Poland and the steadily deteriorating situation in Central America, where Cuban and Soviet involvement stoked civil wars. Haig alone among Reagan's topmost advisors favored an open policy of direct military and economic aid to El Salvador and a "get tough" policy with Cuba, as opposed to more limited and covert measures favored by others. The department issued a report of Cuban involvement in the El Salvador insurgency in February 1981. Haig pursued meetings with the Cubans in November 1981 and sought to pressure Havana into accepting back criminal elements earlier expelled by Castro as refugees. But little headway was made, and only later would the negative implications of covert operations adopted after Haig's tenure by the Reagan administration in Central America become obvious.

Dealing with the Soviet Union in Europe involved both the problem of instability in Poland and the management of the relationship with NATO allies, especially in regard to the deployment of new missiles to counteract the Soviet deployment of SS-20 missiles. In regard to Poland, matters came to a head in December 1981 as the Polish Communist government cracked down on Solidarity. Reagan responded by imposing a list of sanctions on the USSR, including a ban on licenses for supplies for the oil and gas pipeline then in development between Western Europe and the USSR. This decision rankled Europeans, who were most directly and heavily affected by the sanctions imposed. Haig supported sanctions and a tough line against the Wojciech Jaruzelski regime in Poland, but had misgivings about the particular sanctions adopted that harmed NATO allies. In regard to missile deployment in Europe, Haig opposed the Zero Option strategy initially adopted by Reagan, which called for the United States to refrain from deploying new missiles in the European theatre as long as the Soviets would dismantle its recently deployed SS-20s. Haig, in any case, did not have the authority to negotiate on arms control issues, a job Reagan entrusted to Paul Nitze.

U.S. foreign policy in the Middle East faced new threats of terrorism, of Islamic fundamentalism, and of Soviet adventurism. Support for Israel remained a major priority, but dealing with the other threats required a measure of good relations with Arab states. Under Haig, the United States began exploring ways in which closer ties could be developed with friendly Arab regimes. Balancing military aid to Israel and to Egypt and other Arab states preoccupied Middle East policy in the early Reagan years, and it was highlighted by the approval of the sale of F-15s and AWACs to Saudi Arabia. Congressional opposition to this sale was strong, and the Senate barely approved it in October 1981.

Conflict in the Middle East centered on PLO terrorist activities in Lebanon and the military intervention of Israel to put a stop to them. This conflict persisted into Haig's last days as secretary of state, even after his formal resignation but prior to his actual departure. In those waning days of his tenure, Haig was involved in the diplomacy that led to the PLO withdrawal from Lebanon and the articulation of a peacekeeping force in which American troops would participate, with ultimately tragic consequences.

In the midst of his disputes with White House staff, perhaps the most visible and well-known initiative undertaken by Haig was his effort to mediate the Falkland Islands dispute between the United Kingdom and Argentina. Haig understood that his failure to bring a resolution to the problem could mean his demise as secretary of state. Seen by fellow members of the Reagan administration as having a propensity to grandstand, Haig's handling of the Falklands crisis reinforced the belief of some regarding his predisposition to take matters into his own hands. In the end, Haig could not prevent a conflict that was deeply rooted in the national pride of both the United Kingdom and Argentina.

Haig began his tenure as secretary of state with the understanding that he would be the point man in the formation of U.S. diplomacy, the "vicar of foreign policy," as he was fond of saying. Reagan was shot in his third month as president, and Haig stepped up to ensure an orderly response in the uncertainty that followed the assassination attempt. His claim to be "in charge" was an accurate reflection of the state of affairs at the White House in those hours, but the manner in which he made the claim led many to see Haig as too eager to command and too ambitious for the limelight. Whether true or not, this perception persisted. There is no doubt that Haig had difficulty dealing with opposition from members of the White House staff to his lead role concerning key foreign policy decisions and little doubt that Reagan was unwilling to impose the kind of discipline on foreign policy decision-making matters that he had seemingly promised when seeking out Haig's services. This ultimately, more than any single incident involving Haig, led to a clear parting of the ways in how foreign policy was being conducted. Haig's resignation came as no surprise.

His tenure having been so short, it is difficult to judge Haig's performance. His successor, George Shultz, was better fitted by temperament to advance Reagan's foreign policy agenda, an agenda that was to a very large extent eventually vindicated by the decline of Soviet influence and the collapse of communism. It is useless to speculate whether Haig's continued service would have made any difference one way or the other. In the world of diplomacy, hardly more than a year of service is but a blink of the eye in the long haul of diplomatic activity. What can be said is that Haig was in concert with the main thrust of the Reagan foreign policy agenda, which included a tough approach to the USSR.

Having retired from the military and having resigned government service, Haig returned to the private sector, where he has held numerous executive positions. He authored several books in subsequent years, including memoirs of his public life. He unsuccessfully sought nomination as a Republican to the presidency in 1988 and has remained a visible figure and thoughtful conservative voice in American political life and a senior statesman on foreign policy issues.

BIBLIOGRAPHICAL ESSAY

Perhaps the most revealing and insightful books on Haig's career are those he authored. His book *Caveat: Realism, Reagan, and Foreign Policy* (1984) is the fullest account of his tenure as secretary of state. It is a spirited defense of his own perceptions and motivations as a member of Reagan's foreign policy team and full of personal observations regarding the problems and pitfalls that marked that "team's" effort to get started on the right foot. Haig's memoirs of his career, written with Charles McCarry, *Inner Circles: How America Changed the World* (1992), is an engaging and instructive account of Haig's military career and his years in the Nixon White House, as well as an astute commentary on broader issues of foreign policy. For the reader seeking a more critical appraisal of Haig's career, see Roger Morris, *Haig: The General's Progress* (1982). Morris is relentless in portraying Haig in an unfavorable light, betraying both a political animosity for and a personal resentment of him. The book is best read in conjunction with Haig's own works for those seeking a balanced perspective on this outspoken and colorful, if short-lived, occupant of the State Department's seventh floor.

Robert F. Gorman

JOHN HAY (1838–1905)

Served 1898–1905
Appointed by President William McKinley
Continued in office under President Theodore Roosevelt
Republican

John Hay, the son of a country physician, Charles Hay, and his wife, Helen Leonard Hay, was born in Salem, Indiana, on October 8, 1838, but moved to the Mississippi River town of Warsaw, Illinois, in 1841. Growing up before the advent of public schools in Warsaw, Hay received a classical education at home and later in a private academy in nearby Pittsfield, a more cosmopolitan town. Pittsfield was important, for Hay's uncle, Milton Hay, lived there and later introduced him to Abraham Lincoln. In Pittsfield he also met John G. Nicolay, who became his close friend and with whom he later worked in the Lincoln White House and subsequently on a 10-volume "History" of Abraham Lincoln. In 1852 Hay moved to Springfield, where he enrolled in Illinois State College (later Concordia College). He received a sufficiently good education there that in 1855 he was able to enter Brown University in Providence, Rhode Island, as an upperclassman.

In Providence, Hay's literary abilities flourished, and he soon became active in various literary circles. Increasingly attracted by the culture of the east, Hay anticipated with dread his return to the barren wastelands (as he had come to view them) of central Illinois, and he composed morose poems debating the advantages of death over life. In this "slough of barbarism," there was no hope of literary accomplishment, he felt. After graduation from Brown in 1858, Hay read law with his uncle Milton, whose office was next to Lincoln and Herndon. Initially uninterested in politics, he took a small part in Lincoln's campaign for the presidency in 1860. Lincoln asked him to serve in the White House as one of his secretaries, although technically he was a clerk in the Pension Office at the Department of the Interior and then a military officer. Although Hay did not initially have a high opinion of the new president, by August 1863 Hay had become convinced that "the good of the country absolutely demands that he should be kept where he is till this thing is over . . . I believe the hand of God placed him where he is."

Hay's admiration for Lincoln deeply affected his thought in later years. Particularly in the immediate aftermath of the Civil War, Hay became an outspoken advocate of democratic reform. At least one of his poems attacked racism. A considerable part of his democratic fervor was directed at Europe, where from 1865 to 1870 he served in three diplomatic posts: first secretary of the American legation in Paris, chargé d'affaires in Vienna, and secretary of the American legation in Madrid. While in Europe, he came to abhor autocracy. Some of his poems from this period approach a genuine radicalism. "The Triumph of Order" defended the Paris Commune of 1871, and "Liberty" hinted that violence might be a necessary part of the struggle for freedom. He greatly admired the Spanish republican reformer Emilio Castelar, whom he praised in his travelogue, *Castilian Days* (1871). At home Hay's famous *Pike County Ballads* (1871), which were favorably compared to Mark Twain's writing and brought Hay considerable fame as a poet, had a strong dose of social equality in them. Hay was, in sum, on the side of change, reform, the former slaves, and the common people against despotism and a repressive status quo.

As an admirer of Lincoln, Hay believed that only Republicans could be virtuous. But if he continued to identify with Lincoln, his devotion to democratic reform lessened over time, and he became increasingly conservative. Part of the reason may be that he became a gentleman of means, particularly after he married Clara Stone, the daughter of wealthy Cleveland industrialist Amasa Stone, in 1874. His own investments, and those of his father-in-law, were directly affected by the first large industrial strike in American history, the Great Railway Strike of 1877, and Hay responded with a bitter novel, *The Breadwinners: A Social Study* (1883), which served to mark his changed attitudes. The novel, probably the first full-fledged fictional defense of unfettered American capitalism in the late nineteenth century, attacked labor unions and organizers, notably those of Irish descent. It praised the cultured aristocrats and hard-working, contented, Anglo-Saxon craftsmen, who eschewed the immoral labor organizers and were contented with their place in society.

After Hay married Clara Stone, he held few real positions until he became ambassador to Great Britain in 1897. He served briefly in the Rutherford B. Hayes administration as assistant secretary of state from November 1879 to March 1881, but left no appreciable mark on American diplomacy. Otherwise, he tended to his investments, worked on his Lincoln biography, and helped out his friend Whitelaw Reid at the *New York Tribune*. In 1886 Hay moved to Washington, living next door to his best friend, Henry Adams. Hay also helped fund the Republican Party, made occasional political speeches, criticized the Grover Cleveland administration, and in 1896 attacked the Democratic-Populist candidate, William Jennings Bryan, as a charlatan and dangerous revolutionary.

With William McKinley safely in the White House, Hay for the first time tried to secure an important position in the government: he desperately wanted to become ambassador to Great Britain and nearly lost his friendship with Whitelaw Reid, who also sought the position. But Hay prevailed, and soon after McKinley took office, Hay was on his way to the Court of St. James's.

By the time Hay sought the London appointment, he had become deeply attracted to England. Though not a fawning Anglophile, he had visited the British Isles on numerous occasions, where he enjoyed the lovely countryside and hobnobbed with the cultural and political elites. England appealed to this increasingly conservative gentleman for its culture, its manners, and its orderliness. Part of his attraction was racial. His English acquaintances—men like James Bryce, Joseph Chamberlin, Rudyard Kipling, and Cecil Spring Rice—were outspoken advocates of Anglo-Saxonism, and Hay had little reason to disagree.

Hay was not a crude racist. He had opposed slavery and continued to be a paternalistic friend of African Americans. He accepted some of the stereotypes about Jews but was not truly anti-Semitic, thinking his friend Henry Adams—a confirmed anti-Semite—daft. He thought the successful efforts to exclude Chinese immigrants were "wrong & shameless." He had little regard for Latin Americans and American Indians, and he particularly disliked the Irish. He accepted the view of most whites of that era that Anglo-Saxons stood at the peak of the racial hierarchy. Viewing the United States as an Anglo-Saxon country, he hoped as ambassador to forge a new relationship between the two "Anglo-Saxon" powers.

Great Britain and the United States had not been friends. They had fought two wars against each other, and even as late as 1891 there was a war scare when tensions erupted over fishing and sealing rights in the north Pacific. "Twisting the lion's tale" was a staple of American politics, and even in 1896 McKinley's campaign produced a pamphlet entitled, "How McKinley Is Hated in England." Hay and other farsighted Americans wanted to change this.

Fortunately for them, in the 1890s the British concluded that they ought to conciliate with the United States. Although "Anglo-Saxonism" and sentimentality may have played some role, the British decision reflected a hard-nosed assessment of potential power realities. The United States was potentially a major military power. It was already a leading industrial and trading nation. Thus British statesmen, including those who had no love for the Americans, concluded that it made sense to court the United States.

Thus, Hay's ambassadorship came at precisely the right time: the British were taking steps to attract the United States, and the political elite in the United States wanted closer ties with the mother country. Hay desired stronger ties, partly for cultural reasons, but also for well-founded strategic reasons. At first, however, Hay was not allowed to play the leading role in resolving specific problems with Britain. Paying off political debts, McKinley designated former Secretary of State John W. Foster to negotiate the complicated pelagic sealing dispute. He tapped Edward O. Wolcott to negotiate a bimetallistic agreement. Furthermore, much to Hay's distress, the president sent Reid to represent him at Queen Victoria's Diamond Jubilee. The most serious of these issues was the sealing dispute, and when no agreement was reached Hay blamed Foster, who sent harsh and threatening notes to the Foreign Office. The dispute was not settled until 1911.

Ultimately of more importance, however, were the deteriorating relations with Spain over events in its Caribbean colony, Cuba. Hay had become acquainted with the Cuban events as early as 1868, when the Cubans rebelled. As the war dragged on, Hay suggested some kind of American intervention, particularly when Spanish authorities in Cuba seized the *Virginius*, a ship flying the American flag. But he was quick to support a diplomatic settlement and was not really jingoistic. The Cuban rebellion ended in 1878, and Hay took little interest in Cuba again until the rebellion was renewed in the 1890s. Many of his friends wanted American military intervention, but Hay was cautious. Even when the *Maine* exploded in Havana harbor on February 15, 1898, he remained quiet. He saw no reason to interrupt his leisurely vacation on the Nile River to return to his post, a lapse for which Theodore Roosevelt properly criticized him.

Thereafter until war was declared in April, Hay never directly suggested more active measures, though he did ascertain from British officials that there would be no problem with them if the United States did intervene. He also passed along to Washington devastating newspaper accounts about the horrors in Cuba, which helped build the case for a humanitarian intervention. Once war was almost inevitable, Hay set aside whatever doubts remained and did what he could to secure a favorable British attitude. Important in the short run, Hay successfully used the war to further the rapprochement. Although hardly responsible alone for the Great Rapprochement, Hay's actions while in England contributed significantly to its development. When he left to take up his new responsibilities as secretary of state, there was an outpouring of compliments from the British. Henry Adams put it best in his famous *Education:* "in the long list of famous American Ministers in London, none could have given the work quite the completeness, the harmony, the perfect ease of Hay."

With the United States entering a new era, it was necessary to improve the Foreign Service, which was almost entirely unprofessional. With the Spanish-American War, pressures for imperial expansion, and demands to keep the China market open, it became increasingly important to make the diplomatic corps more competent. It was in this context that McKinley summoned John Hay from London to be the new secretary of state. It was not an honor Hay sought. He drafted a letter declining the position on grounds of fragile health. His sense of duty, however, led him to accept McKinley's request, though without pleasure. One of the most important issues facing the new secretary of state was imperial expansion. For most of his life Hay had not been a strong proponent of American overseas adventures. Although he apparently favored efforts to acquire Santo Domingo in 1868, his antiauthoritarian sentiments militated against annexationist schemes. At some point, perhaps in 1884, Hay penned a poem opposing efforts to acquire the Hawaiian Islands. But in the 1890s he became increasingly favorable to expansion. In 1893 he attacked Grover Cleveland's decision to repudiate the treaty to annex Hawaii negotiated by his predecessor. Even then, however, an important consideration for Hay was political advantage. Here was a campaign issue to defeat the Democrats, he thought. Hay's previous views that all people had the right to freedom were now muted, as he came to believe that advanced countries, particularly the "Anglo-Saxon" powers, had a duty to take care of those who supposedly could not take care of themselves. He had no objection when the United States, by a Joint Resolution of Congress, annexed Hawaii in the middle of the Spanish-American War.

Hay played no direct role in the Hawaiian annexation, but as secretary of state he was forced almost immediately to consider annexing the Philippine Islands. In England, when the issue was first raised, Hay remained cautious. It does not appear that he took much interest in the Philippines prior to the Spanish-American War. It is not even entirely clear what he thought of annexation before he returned to Washington in September 1898. But very much like McKinley, he seems to have moved gradually toward annexation. German ambitions bothered him. He also informed the State Department that the British had no objection if the United States decided to keep the islands. He also listened to those who argued that "Anglo-Saxons" could develop the islands better than the Spanish had and that the Filipinos were not capable of governing themselves. By the time Hay took up his responsibilities on September 30, 1898, the issue was nearly settled. The decision to demand that Spain cede the Philippines was McKinley's, but Hay posed no objection and in all probability fully supported it. Nor did his support waiver when

Filipinos, under the leadership of General Emilio Aguinaldo, began to fight the American occupiers. He saw no reason why "uncivilized" Filipinos should be allowed the reject the beneficence that American rule would supposedly bring to them. When Jacob Schurman, head of the first Philippine Commission sent to investigate conditions in the islands, urged Hay in a long telegram to be conciliatory and enter into negotiations with Aguinaldo, Hay dismissed the suggestion contemptuously. The Filipinos would have to accept American-imposed rule. Hay had no respect for those who resisted American efforts to occupy the islands. He was no longer a reluctant expansionist.

The acquisition of the Philippines heightened the growing American interest in nearby China, a country with whom Hay's name is forever linked because of his promulgation of the famous Open Door notes of 1899 and 1900. As interim editor of the *New York Tribune* in the early 1870s, Hay had written a few editorials about Asia, and in future years he maintained a correspondence with Edward H. House, a *Tribune* reporter with considerable expertise on Japan. Thus he was not ignorant of Asian affairs when he became secretary of state, although his knowledge was not deep. His interest in China had geopolitical and cultural dimensions, but ever since the *Empress of China* sailed for Canton in 1783, the primary American concern had been commercial, which Hay understood.

Just how to go about safeguarding those interests was the question. Traditionally, the United States had felt its interests in China best served by an independent China. In addition, the United States had generally left trade matters to those business interests concerned with the China trade. "A fair field and no favor" was the American watchword. But in the mid 1890s China's independence was under threat as the European powers and Japan began to carve out spheres of influences, and there was a growing fear that China would actually be divided up among the powers, such as Africa had recently been. These developments threatened American interests and called into question the traditional hands-off approach of the government.

Hay was flexible about methods. He immediately upgraded governmental interest and involvement in Chinese affairs. For the first time, American diplomats in China were charged with helping specific American firms. Hay was even tempted to create American outposts in China to protect American rights, but that represented too much of a departure from tradition. A more serious challenge to the traditional American approach came from those who urged Hay to acquiesce in the establishment of the European and Japanese spheres and work within them to secure an open door for American trade. In fact, the first Open Door notes of September 6, 1899, sent to Russia and Germany did not specifically attack the spheres, but only demanded equality within them. Thus Hay was willing to accommodate the new reality up to a point. But the note to England explicitly refused to recognize the spheres as legal entities, thus indicating that he still objected in principle to any actions that compromised China's independence.

The second Open Door notes of July 3, 1900, written during the Boxer Rebellion, which attacked foreign interests and threatened the lives of Western diplomats in Peking, directly attacked the spheres. American policy was to "preserve Chinese territorial and administrative entity" and to insist that American treaty rights be accepted. Hay even supported the radical idea of sending American armed forces to China to join troops from other countries to relieve the besieged Western diplomatic missions. When the crisis passed, Hay wanted to keep the troops in

China to improve his bargaining power during the negotiations. McKinley refused. In the end, China was not broken up. Hay's diplomacy may have contributed to this outcome, although the rivalries among the European powers and Japan were more fundamental. In any case, Hay's Open Door policy became an important, if not always wise, guide to the conduct of American policy toward Asia for the next several decades.

Much of Hay's diplomacy as secretary of state was related in one way or another to the rapprochement with Great Britain. The most important issues involved settling the boundary between Alaska and Canada, the Boer War in southern Africa, and the question of who would control a canal if one were built across the isthmus of Central America.

The Boer War, which paralleled the Philippine–American War, involved British efforts to suppress a revolt of Afrikaner farmers (Boers), who chaffed under British rule in the Transvaal. The Boer revolt, which bore a superficial similarity to the American Revolution, attracted widespread support in the United States. Irish-American politicians in particular used the issue to attack England. Hay would have none of it. He hoped that the British would make short work of the Boers if fighting erupted. True to his word, Hay replaced pro-Boer diplomats in southern Africa, found little to criticize in the British concentration camps, resisted and undermined Boer efforts to obtain American mediation and trade, and discouraged attempts by Transvaal President Paul Kruger to visit the United States. To Hay, the British represented civilization and should be allowed to dominate the Transvaal.

Few American interests were directly involved in the Boer War, but that was not the case in the coincident issue of the Alaska–Canadian boundary. The boundary dispute had its roots in Russian treaties with the United States and Great Britain in the 1820s and the treaty, which ceded Alaska to the United States in 1867. The boundaries were not entirely clear. No one much cared until gold was discovered in the region straddling the murky boundary between Alaska and Canada, at which point it suddenly became important to delineate the boundary exactly.

Hay was familiar with the issue. When he was ambassador a joint commission had been established to deal with several outstanding Anglo-American issues. It quickly deadlocked on the boundary question. Hay then wanted to submit the matter to binding arbitration, but the Senate's distrust of arbitration led Hay to discard the idea. He did accept a more limited arbitration proposal when the British agreed that certain important towns would remain in American hands regardless of the arbitration's outcome. But this time the Canadians killed the proposal.

Because something had to be done if Anglo-American relations were to continue to improve, Hay then proposed a modus vivendi applying to a portion of the disputed area. Then he made some further concessions to the British, including promising the Canadians some leased access to the sea, a key concern to them. Unfortunately, Hay's concessions turned the Senate against his proposal, and for the moment all he could do was to negotiate a more limited modus vivendi, which was signed on October 20, 1899. Final settlement would not come until 1903.

Even as Hay was dealing with the Boer War and the Alaska boundary, the issue of building a canal across the Central American isthmus came to a head. The dream of such a canal went back decades, and in 1850 the United States and Great Britain had negotiated the Clayton–Bulwer Treaty, which provided for joint Anglo-American control over any future canal. At midcentury the treaty was a fair compromise, reflecting the relative interest and power of the two countries. Later as the United States began to make real its theoretical dominance over affairs in the Western Hemisphere, and as it became an imperial power in its own right, the treaty seemed restrictive and unfair—at least to expansionists.

The British were willing to modify the treaty to give the Americans exclusive control, provided only that ships of all nations would be treated equally. This satisfied Hay, who asked the British ambassador, Lord Julian Pauncefote, to draft a treaty. Although Pauncefote was a recognized authority on international law relating to canals, having him draft the treaty was a political mistake because it gave ardent American nationalists cause to attack Hay as an Anglophile and urge the new treaty's rejection. The draft treaty was ready in January 1899. By the time the British signed it in February 1900, strong opposition to the treaty had developed. Particularly galling was the opposition of New York Governor Theodore Roosevelt, who called for defeat of the treaty unless it was amended to give the United States unambiguous control. Hay dispatched a scorching letter to Roosevelt, telling him to stay out of foreign affairs—advice that he was unlikely to take.

Hay continued to fight for the treaty, but the Senate Foreign Relations Committee amended it to undercut the treaty's neutrality provisions. Hay was so angry that he submitted his resignation, but McKinley refused to accept it. The Senate, in the meantime, delayed final consideration until after the election of 1900. When debate resumed, Senator Henry Cabot Lodge's opposition appalled Hay.

When the Senate approved the treaty with amendments, Hay stifled his anger and tried to persuade the British to accept it. When he was not able to do so, some of the more bumptious nationalists suggested that the Clayton–Bulwer Treaty simply be abrogated. To Hay such a course was repugnant. Consequently he fashioned a new Hay–Pauncefote treaty that took account of the Senate's concerns. By April 25, 1901 the new project was ready, and Hay sent it off to England. This time Lodge and Roosevelt expressed support, and in November the British consented. The treaty was finally approved in December 1901. It was an important victory for Hay, who had crafted a treaty acceptable both to the British and to the suspicious Senate. The United States was now free to proceed as it wished with regard to a canal, and the rapprochement was still on track.

Four months before the treaty was finally approved, Theodore Roosevelt became president when William McKinley was assassinated. Wanting to maintain as much continuity as possible with the martyred president's administration, Roosevelt kept Hay in office. He remained secretary of state into Roosevelt's second term. There were differences of style and substance between the two men, although the differences have sometimes been exaggerated. Hay was much older than Roosevelt and uncomfortable with the president's impetuous nature and his inclination at times to take strong stands against the British. This was particularly apparent in efforts to achieve a final settlement of the Alaska boundary matter. In March 1902 Hay suggested submitting the matter to a six-person commission. Roosevelt was skeptical. He wanted no real arbitration because he was convinced that the American claim was so strong as to be nonnegotiable. Nevertheless, in July 1902 he accepted the proposal, saying that the commission would only delineate the line. The Hay–Herbert Treaty of January 24, 1903, established the tribunal.

Hay was pleased with the treaty but not with Roosevelt's appointment of Henry Cabot Lodge and Elihu Root to the tribunal. They were hardly "jurists of impartial repute," which the treaty specified. Roosevelt's appointments made it impossible for Canada to use the tribunal to save face, but the president would not reconsider. He even refused to give the British a little additional time to prepare their case and threatened to "run the line ourselves." Hay offered his resignation. The president waited six days, and then asked Hay to remain.

In the end, the United States won the central point: The Canadians were kept away from access to the ocean at any point. The Canadians did get some of the disputed inland territory and two contested islands. It is probable that secret American pressure on the tribunal's lone English jurist, Lord Richard Alverstone, played some role in producing the desired verdict. The two Canadians on the panel refused to sign the award. Hay continued to believe that the United States could have won its points without ruffling British and Canadian feathers.

Despite the significant differences that emerged between Roosevelt and Hay over the Alaska boundary problem, Hay and Roosevelt actually got along quite well and had few policy differences. Some observers assumed that Hay must have objected to Roosevelt's high-handedness in acquiring the Panama Canal Zone. In fact, Hay had few if any objections. He shared Roosevelt's hope of building a canal, and if he once thought that legally Roosevelt was required to build the canal in Nicaragua, he posed no objection when the president opted for Panama. Hay objected to Roosevelt's strong words when the negotiations involved Britain, a "civilized," "Anglo-Saxon" power. Colombia, on the other hand, was in Hay's view virtually uncivilized and not entitled to the same kind of respect. When the Colombians rejected a treaty with the United States, Hay had no objection to Roosevelt's supporting a Panamanian rebellion and negotiating a favorable treaty with the new government. The Colombians were "poor creatures" and "greedy little anthropoids," he thought. Only a few days after Roosevelt acted, Hay wrote to his wife that he felt sorry for the Colombians who had lost Panama forever. "But they ought to have thought of that six months ago. . . . They will never learn that to make an omelette you must break eggs, and the eggs once broken, they can never be mended again."

Hay probably should have resigned in 1903. With the settlement of the Alaska boundary dispute, virtually all significant differences with Britain in the Western Hemisphere had been resolved. During his final two years Hay was not a mere figurehead, for he continued to advise the president and take an active role in some aspects of foreign relations. Yet, Hay's failing health led Roosevelt to assume control of more and more areas of foreign relations. Hay died in office on July 1, 1905.

Hay was one of the more important and accomplished secretaries of state. More than most of his predecessors in the nineteenth century, Hay had a relatively sophisticated understanding of international affairs and diplomacy and enjoyed a wide range of foreign acquaintances and friends—at least in the European realm. He presided over important diplomatic actions regarding Europe, Latin America, Africa, and Asia. His name is forever linked with the Open Door policy. His racial views—commonplace at the time—prevented a more sympathetic appreciation of the views of Latin Americans and Asians. Undoubtedly Hay's most important contribution was his furthering of the Great Rapprochement with Britain.

BIBLIOGRAPHICAL ESSAY

There are various John Hay manuscript collections, of which the most important is in the manuscript division of the Library of Congress. A secondary but still valuable manuscript collection is in the John Hay Library, Brown University. Minor collections of Hay materials are in the Houghton Library at Harvard University, the Butler Library at Columbia University, the New York Public Library, and the Henry H. Huntington Library at San Marino, California.

The best biography of Hay is Tyler Dennett *John Hay: From Poetry to Politics* (1933, reprinted 1963), generally sympathetic to the subject. Kent J. Clymer, *John Hay: The Gentlemen as Diplomat* (1975) is a critical assessment of Hay's views on social and international questions, as well as Hay's conduct as ambassador to Britain and as secretary of state. The work includes a thorough bibliographic essay. Anne Hummel Sherrill and Howard I. Kushner, *John Milton Hay* (1977), analyzes Hay's life, ideology, and diplomacy and emphasizes the importance of Lincoln's influence on Hay. William R. Thayer, *The Life and Letters of John Hay*, 2 vols. (1916), although dated, provides valuable details about Hay's life, reproducing many of his letters.

Robert R. Gale, *John Hay* (1978), concentrates on Hay's literary contributions, whereas Frederic Caple Jaher's "Industrialism and the American Aristocrat: A Social Study of John Hay and His Novel, *The Bread-Winners,*" *Journal of the Illinois State Historical Society* 65 (spring 1972) is the best historical analysis of the novel.

Numerous insights in Hay and his diplomacy are provided in Henry Adams, *The Education of Henry Adams* (1907). Patricia O' Toole's *The Five of Hearts: An Intimate Portrait of Henry Adams and His Friends, 1880–1918* (1990) is the best account of the secret social club to which Clarence King, John and Clara Hay, and Henry and Marion (Clever) Adams belonged.

There is a very rich literature on U.S. expansion in the 1890s. Earnest May, *Imperial Democracy* (1961), is an essential work; important, too, are William Appleman Williams's *The Roots of the Modern American Empire* (1969) and *The Tragedy of American Diplomacy* (1972). Julius W. Pratt's *Expansionists of 1898* (1935) is a classic account.

The basic work on U.S. diplomacy in China remains A. Whitney Griswold, *The Far Eastern Policy of the United States* (1938). Useful also is Thomas J. McCormick, *China Market* (1967). The Open Door notes have evoked much historical writing. Useful accounts include Roy V. Magers, "John Hay and American Traditions in China," *Social Science* 4 (May 1929); Paul H. Clyde, "The Open-Door Policy of John Hay," *Historical Outlook* 22 (May 1931); George F. Kennan, *American Diplomacy, 1900–1950* (1951) appropriate chapters; and Raymond A. Esthus, "The Changing Concept of the Open Door, 1899–1910," *Mississippi Valley Historical Review* 46 (December 1959).

General accounts of Anglo-American relations include Bradford Perkins, *The Great Rapprochement* (1968); Charles S. Campbell, Jr., *Anglo-American Understanding, 1898–1903* (1957); and Alfred L. P. Dennis, *Adventures in American Diplomacy 1896–1906* (1928).

The Alaskan boundary disputes are treated in Charles C. Tansill, *Canadian-American Relations, 1875–1911* (1943); Thomas A. Bailey, "Theodore Roosevelt and the Alaskan Boundary Settlement," *Canadian Historical Review* 18 (June, 1937).

The Hay–Pauncefote Treaty has received intensive study from J. A. S. Grenville in "Great Britain and the Isthmian Canal, 1898–1901," *American Historical Review* 61 (October 1955), whereas the best general account of the canal is Dwight C. Mines, *The Fight for the Panama Route* (1940).

Kenton Clymer

CHRISTIAN HERTER (1895–1966)

Served 1959–1961
Appointed by President Dwight D. Eisenhower
Republican

Christian Herter was born in Paris in 1895 to American parents. Both his father and mother were artists—Albert Herter being a noted painter of murals and Adele McGinnis Herter a specialist in portraiture and still life—and during his school and undergraduate years their son cultivated similar tastes. He graduated from Harvard in 1915 with a degree in art and enrolled at New York's School of Fine and Applied Arts shortly afterward. There he embarked on a course of study in architecture and interior design. Yet, Herter discovered that he had little heart for the artist's life, and when a chance meeting with a classmate-turned-diplomat resulted in an invitation to join the Foreign Service he leaped at the opportunity. Within the week he dropped out of school and had shipped off for Berlin.

Herter's tour as diplomatic attaché in the kaiser's capital included the events attending the Great War then convulsing Europe. A transfer to Brussels at the end of 1916 coincided with the onset of the protracted illness of U.S. Minister Brand Whitlock, with the result that Herter, at the age of 22, served for six weeks as acting chief of mission.

When the United States entered World War I in the spring of 1917, Herter returned to the United States to enlist in the army, only to fail the physical exam. Secretary of State Robert Lansing invited him to join the State Department, and in the autumn of 1917 he set to work on problems of prisoner exchange and repatriation of interned aliens.

At war's end Herter sailed with the U.S. delegation for Paris and the peace conference, where he assisted in drafting the charter of the League of Nations. Herter was hardly less enthusiastic about the League than was its chief sponsor, Woodrow Wilson, and when the Senate rejected the Versailles treaty, he was equally dismayed. Herter resigned from the State Department in spring of 1920.

A 1917 marriage to an oil heiress had made Herter financially independent, enabling him to indulge his belief that men of means could best fulfill their social duties in the public sector. Herter joined Herbert Hoover's relief mission to

Europe. A Republican, albeit one of low profile to this point, Herter followed Hoover to the Commerce Department in 1921, where he served as the commerce secretary's special assistant for European aid.

Herter turned to state politics in Massachusetts, after a year's lecturing at Harvard on international relations. Election to the Massachusetts House of Representatives led to appointment to the ways and means committee. There Herter gained a reputation as an efficient floor manager if a less than stirring orator, and repeated reelection made him a power among state Republicans.

When Herter ran for Congress in 1942, he defeated an incumbent and well-entrenched Democrat and went on to be reelected four times. By 1946, he had risen to a position of influence among GOP leaders in the lower chamber. With his activist credentials and his personal experience in foreign affairs, he played a prominent part in promoting the Cold War initiatives of the Truman administration, gaining for his efforts the sobriquet "Vanderberg of the House." Herter championed the Truman doctrine, the Marshall plan, and the Atlantic alliance. He took particular interest in the reconstruction of Europe, heading a task force of legislators who toured the continent in the summer of 1947.

In 1952, Herter's loyalty to internationalism and Republicanism drew him back to statewide Massachusetts politics. Promoters of an Eisenhower candidacy convinced him that a strong internationalist nominee for governor would make immeasurably more likely a victory over the isolationist Taft wing of the GOP and over the Democrats in the general election. Herter surprised most observers with the verve of his campaign and scored an upset. Two years later, he won again, capping a remarkable career of 13 election victories—six in races for the state legislature, five for Congress, and two for governor—against no defeats.

Despite considerable success as Massachusetts' chief executive, Herter found state politics confining. Consequently, he did not discourage speculation after Eisenhower's 1955 heart attack that he might be persuaded to make a run for the presidency. When Eisenhower recovered and indicated that he intended to succeed himself, Republican moderates mentioned Herter as a replacement for Vice President Richard Nixon. The "dump Nixon" initiative failed, but Herter deftly covered his tracks by personally placing the incumbent's name in nomination for the number-two slot on the ticket.

Following the resignation of Herbert Hoover, Jr., who left his post as undersecretary of state at the end of 1956, Herter seemed to Eisenhower and Secretary of State John Foster Dulles a wise choice for a successor. A solid administrator with connections on Capitol Hill, Herter appeared content to operate in Dulles's shadow, an attribute the secretary, ever vigilant against potential usurpers, especially valued. As expected, Herter's nomination sailed through the Senate, and he took over in February 1957.

Backing up Dulles turned out to be an unrewarding occupation. A commentator for the *New York Times* summarized the problem when he characterized Herter as the "Number Two man in a one-man department." Dulles refused to delegate authority on matters he deemed important, and as a result Herter was left to deal with issues Dulles considered secondary or not worth risking his own political capital.

This category included economic assistance to Third World countries. Although more of an ideological relativist than his contemporaries commonly realized, Dulles preferred to leave most battles for aid for unpopular neutralists like India's

Nehru to subordinates. This suited Herter well enough, and during 1957 the undersecretary helped spearhead the fight for what eventually emerged as the Development Loan Fund.

Herter's most important continuing responsibility as undersecretary involved chairing the Operations Coordinating Board (OCB). In 1953, Eisenhower had established the OCB to ensure that presidential decisions survived the attributive efforts of the bureaucracy and took form as policy. From its inception the OCB suffered from the reluctance of its constituents in the State Department, the Pentagon, the CIA, and the Foreign Operations Administration to surrender turf, but in the enthusiasm of Eisenhower's early years it functioned reasonably well. By the time Herter took over, however, the career staff had discovered ways to thwart policy initiatives. As a consequence Herter often found OCB sessions trying.

With Dulles's declining health Herter increasingly served as acting secretary. By April 1959, when cancer finally forced Dulles's retirement, Herter had spent a total of nearly eight months in charge of the department. The experience coupled with Eisenhower having less than two years left in his term made Herter an obvious choice to succeed Dulles. Eisenhower agreed, and the senate confirmed the nomination unanimously.

Herter inherited a number of pressing issues, but none worried Americans and their allies more than the question of Berlin. In November 1958, Soviet premier Nikita Khrushchev had delivered an ultimatum to the Western powers occupying Berlin, telling the Americans, British, and French that they had half a year to get out. The time had come, Khrushchev said, to end Berlin's anomalous situation within the German Democratic Republic.

The following months had witnessed efforts by Washington, London, and Paris to develop a coordinated response to Khrushchev's challenge. The Russians complicated matters by pursuing a divide-and-conquer policy, alternating tough talk with words of sweet reasonableness. In a single speech Foreign Minister Andrei Gromyko denied that his government had issued an ultimatum but added that if the Western powers insisted on holding on to Berlin, they would be risking a "big war."

At the beginning of February 1959, British Prime Minister Harold Macmillan flew to Moscow for what he described as exploratory conversations and what critics considered akin to Neville Chamberlain's efforts at Munich two decades before. Soon afterward Macmillan visited Washington and explained to Eisenhower and Herter that the Soviets appeared willing to settle the matter peacefully. Macmillan suggested a summit meeting of the four powers as a means of affording Khrushchev a graceful method of backing down. Eisenhower registered little enthusiasm for a summit but agreed with Herter that a top-level meeting might follow a preliminary conference of foreign ministers.

Early in May, the foreign ministers met in Geneva. Herter approached the meeting pessimistically, seeing little ground for agreement with the Kremlin. The U.S. objective remained a "free and secure Berlin."

At Geneva, the NATO allies presented the view that any settlement of the Berlin question ought to take place within the context of a broader pact involving German reunification through free elections, and that a unified Germany should have the right to join alliances if it so desired. Gromyko rejected this position out of hand. He called for making Berlin a "free city" and demanded the demilitarization and neutralization of Germany. An impasse ensued, and the conference went nowhere.

Despite summer-long stagnation at Geneva, the Kremlin gave every indication of reconsidering its policy of confrontation. At the beginning of August, Washington and Moscow agreed on a visit by Khrushchev to the United States. The announcement effectively ended the crisis.

While pressure leaked out of the Berlin issue, observant Americans came to recognize that the administration had a genuine secretary of state and not simply a post-Dulles placeholder. Herter's handling of the Berlin negotiations displayed a professionalism and sensitivity that provided reassurance that American interests were in capable hands.

Khrushchev's visit led to an invitation to Eisenhower to reciprocate in the summer of 1960 and to the scheduling of a summit conference for May. Plans for both proceeded well until two weeks before the latter, when Herter and Eisenhower learned that an American U-2 reconnaissance plane was missing over the Soviet Union. Herter assumed, as did other top administration officials, that if the plane had gone down, either accidentally or hit by a Russian rocket, it must have disintegrated, killing the pilot and destroying evidence of its mission. Consequently, he did not seriously question the wisdom of releasing a cover story describing the aircraft as a NASA weather plane that had wandered astray.

When Khrushchev revealed that Soviet authorities had both the plane and the pilot, Herter advocated a face-saving retreat. He recommended that the State Department concede that reconnaissance flight had taken place, but he urged Eisenhower to remain aloof. Initially his counsel prevailed, and the department issued a statement that an "unarmed civilian U-2 plane" engaged in "intelligence collection" had penetrated Soviet airspace. Finally, the release declared that there had been "no authorization" for the flight from the highest authority.

Unfortunately, the problem grew worse following reports that pilot Francis Gary Powers had admitted he worked for the CIA. The White House reassessed the implications of encouraging charges that the president was not in control of his own administration. Even Herter granted that there was little alternative to coming clean. On May 9, the secretary said Powers had been spying but argued that the U.S. government had a responsibility to the American people and to free people everywhere to employ extraordinary means to defend democracy against surprise attack. In a news conference two day later, Eisenhower made essentially the same points.

What the U-2 affair meant for the summit became evident as soon as the delegations from the big four powers gathered in Paris. Khrushchev opened with a blast at the United States and a demand that Eisenhower condemn the overflights and punish those responsible. When the president refused to accept such dictation, the Soviets stalked out.

The U-2 affair and the aborted summit cast a pall over the administration's last months. With the race to replace Eisenhower in full swing, the administration found itself in no position to launch new initiatives. In any event, the administration had its hands full coping with problems that did not seem willing to await a new regime.

After the flare-up in 1954, Southeast Asia had diminished as an issue in American diplomacy, but in the summer of 1959, the tenuous peace of a half-decade gave way. Contention focused on Laos, where Pathet Lao insurgents challenged the pro-Western government of Phoui Sananikone. In August, Herter told the Senate Foreign Relations Committee that the situation in Laos was very dangerous and endorsed a call by the Laotian government for United Nations intervention. Herter announced an increase in American aid to Laos.

Through the beginning of 1960, the situation remained under control, but a patently rigged election in April provoked a widespread antigovernment reaction, which in August led to a coup. Neutralist Souvanna Phouma headed the ruling group that emerged, but his hold on the capital appeared transient as right-wing military forces and the Pathet Lao slugged it out in the countryside.

Washington eyed Souvanna dubiously, unconvinced despite his personal non-communism that he could keep the leftists in line. When he accepted a Soviet offer of aid (following a temporary cutoff of American assistance) and proposed to bring two Pathet Lao representatives into a government of national reconciliation, the administration grew more skeptical still. Herter remarked that inviting the communists into a coalition would lead to a communist government in Laos.

By the time the administration turned the matter over to the Democrats, Laos was approaching the flashpoint. Briefing the president-elect, Herter advised that the optimal solution would be a new government comprising elements of the right and center and excluding communists. He expressed little optimism that the United States or anyone else could achieve such an outcome.

Even as Laos was coming to a boil, a similarly vexing situation was developing in the Congo. There the clash of East and West in a Third World context dated only from the summer of 1960 when the Belgian colony gained its independence. Murderous personal and intertribal rivalries compounded the difficulties of nation building. American leaders fretted most about the hold of the charismatic Patrice Lumumba on the imagination of considerable numbers of the Congolese, particularly when Lumumba responded to the introduction of UN forces by calling for Soviet military assistance.

In this case, as in others throughout Eisenhower's two terms, the administration pursued a dual policy. Publicly Herter and other American officials expressed support for the UN as the instrument of mediation between the contesting parties. Secretly the CIA plotted the assassination of Lumumba. The latter was killed, although not from American machinations. His death, however, did little to untangle the situation, and in the Congo as in Laos the administration passed on a problem that seem to defy solution.

Most worrisome of all was Cuba. At the beginning of 1959 Eisenhower and Herter had looked on Fidel Castro's victory with mixed emotions, realizing that Castro's predecessor, Fulgencio Batista, had hopelessly compromised himself as an agent of American influence. Castro owed nothing to the United States and consequently threatened to pursue an unsettlingly independent policy.

When Castro paid a highly publicized visit to the United States in April 1959, Eisenhower pointedly absented himself from Washington, leaving to Herter the responsibility of hosting. By summer's end, Castro had embarked on a vigorous program of nationalizing U.S. property, purging moderates from his government, and sponsoring revolutions on the Cuban model elsewhere in Latin America.

Herter understood the realities of Cuban politics sufficiently to realize that any populist leader had to denounce the colossus of the north, but as the administration entered its final year the secretary concluded that Castro's was not a garden-variety anti-Americanism. Rather, Herter believed, the Cuban revolution represented a grave threat to hemispheric security. When Castro hosted a visit by the deputy premier of the Soviet Union in February 1960, which led to the initiation of large-scale Soviet aid, the danger appeared to increase.

Herter directed the drafting of legislation to empower the president to curtail Cuba's sugar quota. Castro guaranteed passage of the measure by seizing two U.S. oil refineries. The State Department fired off a note charging "relentless economic aggression," and Eisenhower, asserting that Castro had adopted "a deliberate policy of hostility" toward the United States, slashed Cuba's quota almost to the vanishing point.

Relations spiraled downward through the end of 1960. Castro confiscated more U.S. property. Khrushchev pledged support for Russia's new ally. Eisenhower declared that the United States would not permit "the establishment of a regime dominated by international communism in the Western Hemisphere." Castro flew to New York to thunder at the United States for four hours before the United Nations. The administration imposed a trade embargo. Finally, with just weeks left in office, Eisenhower ordered a break in diplomatic relations.

Meanwhile, below the surface, the president pursued an even more forceful anti-Castro policy. The CIA laid plans for an invasion of Cuba by disaffected émigrés, so that by the time Kennedy took office the operation required little more than the approval of the new commander in chief.

Not surprisingly, Eisenhower's use of the CIA as an active instrument of diplomacy diminished Herter's influence. Dulles had managed to keep the intelligence agency largely under control by means of a jealously territorial bureaucratic style and close personal ties to the president and the agency's director, his brother, Allen Dulles. Herter enjoyed neither advantage. He was less assertive than his predecessor and did not, during his short time as secretary, succeed in cracking Eisenhower's inner circle. Consequently, he sometimes found himself little more than an observer on matters relating to the CIA.

At the same time Herter ran up against an increasing desire on Eisenhower's part for direct presidential diplomacy. With Dulles's death, Eisenhower decided to act on his inclination toward goodwill trips abroad and person-to-person discussions with such international figures as Khrushchev, Nehru, Tito, and Nasser. In this, as in the conduct of clandestine operations, Herter was not irrelevant, but neither was he at the center of American policymaking.

Herter lived nearly six years after January 1961, dying in 1966. Before his death, Herter resumed his activities on behalf of a bipartisan foreign policy, serving as a representative in various trade negotiations for the Kennedy and Johnson administrations. He also watched as the difficulties he had confronted as secretary of state blossomed, in several instances, into full-blown crises.

BIBLIOGRAPHICAL ESSAY

The only extended study of Herter's term as secretary of state is a generally sympathetic volume by G. Bernard Noble, *Christian A. Herter* (1970). Works dealing with matters engaging Herter's attention during his term in office include Jack M. Schick, *The Berlin Crisis, 1958–1962* (1971), which covers the 1959 Geneva conference; Martin E. Goldstein, *American Policy toward Laos* (1973); Charles A. Stevenson, *The End of Nowhere: American Policy toward Laos since 1954* (1972); Stephen Weissman, *American Foreign Policy in the Congo, 1960–1964* (1974); and Madeleine

G. Kalb, *The Congo Cables: The Cold War in Africa, from Eisenhower to Kennedy* (1982). The second volume of Stephen E. Ambrose's *Eisenhower* (1984), although focusing on the White House, elucidates Herter's role vis-à-vis the president.

Herter's papers are at Harvard University. Filling more than 1,400 folders, they include correspondence, speeches, articles, political papers, clippings, and photographs, mostly from the years 1943–1966.

H. William Brands

CHARLES EVANS HUGHES (1862–1948)

Served 1921–1925
Appointed by President Warren G. Harding
Continued in office under President Calvin Coolidge
Republican

The career of Charles Evans Hughes was indicative of the residual strength of Progressivism after the First World War. The goals of the State Department under Hughes reflected trends already established by Republican administrations between 1898 and 1913. American foreign policy during Hughes's tenure in office did not constitute a repudiation of Progressive foreign policy, but rather a rebuttal of Wilsonian internationalism.

Charles Evans Hughes earned the position as Warren Harding's secretary of state by virtue of his stature as a Progressive reformer. Though he had only limited foreign policy experience before 1921, Hughes was a leader in the Progressive reform movement and an important figure of conciliation in the Republican Party. After the election of 1920, the Republican Party was concerned with maintaining unity between its various factions. The position of secretary of state would be filled by someone of stature within the Progressive movement, not within the foreign policy establishment.

The early career of Charles Evans Hughes followed a typical pattern of a middle-class reformer. Hughes's father was the pastor of a Baptist church in New York. Parental authority was strong, and much attention was given to moral education. Hughes absorbed the classic Victorian virtues of diligence and reliability. His childhood was marked by a program of self-education that encouraged a voracious intellectual curiosity. He was thorough to a fault and typically worked to exhaustion. He entered Brown University in 1878 and graduated at the age of 19. After considering professions in teaching and the ministry, Hughes took up the study of law. He graduated from Columbia University's Law School and entered the New York Bar in 1884.

Hughes became a successful lawyer in the competitive environment of New York City. At the age of 25 he helped form the partnership of Carter, Hughes, and Cravath. Hughes became a skilled courtroom attorney, and the firm developed a reputation for corporate litigation. The strength of his legal practice in New York led to several invitations to join the faculty of law schools. His teaching experience, including a two-year appointment at Cornell's law school, demonstrated that Hughes was a talented legal theoretician as well as a competent courtroom attorney.

By 1905 Hughes had risen to remarkable stature in the New York legal community. He was respected for his skill in protecting corporate clients, his conceptualization of legal theory, and his adherence to strict ethical standards. When Governor Francis Higgins formed an investigating committee to examine price fixing of the gas and electricity rates in New York he invited Hughes to serve. As chief investigator, Hughes collected public testimony from a series of corporate executives and New York politicians. His search was methodical and complete. The investigation revealed long-standing patterns of stock manipulation and price fixing. Hughes recommended the creation of a state agency that would have direct regulatory authority over gas and electricity companies and the ability to regulate rates. The New York State Legislature implemented the reforms suggested by Hughes, and as a result, consumer prices for both gas and electricity were significantly reduced.

Hughes's investigation of gas and electricity rates marked a revolution in the relations between the government of New York and the corporations based in that state. This success triggered a new sense of public confidence in the political process. The press enthusiastically supported the new reformer.

The success of the "Gas Trust" investigation led to Hughes's appointment to lead the inquiry into the insurance business in New York. Once again, Hughes patiently collected testimony, which uncovered questionable stock transactions, political payoffs, and misappropriation of corporate funds for the benefit of corporate officers. The utilities investigations had been destabilizing to the unity between big business and politics, but inquiries into New York insurance corporations were far more damaging. Testimony in these investigations uncovered not only stock manipulation and price fixing, but also a pattern of campaign contributions designed to corrupt the electoral process. As a result of the Hughes investigation, the state established a powerful regulatory agency to control the insurance industry.

The leadership of the Republican Party recognized that Hughes would be a strong candidate in the upcoming gubernatorial election. President Theodore Roosevelt, de facto head of the Republican Party in New York State, argued that a Hughes candidacy would undermine the prevailing image of Republican "bossism." In 1906, Charles Evans Hughes was chosen to head the Republican ticket. He defeated Democrat William Randolph Hearst and became Governor of New York.

The Hughes governorship was characterized by the attempt to limit the power of political bosses and to encourage greater public activity in governmental affairs. Hughes hoped that he could use a tide of public indignation to end political corruption. His new government in New York State would be responsive to the general public, not the economically powerful. Reforms as diverse as the introduction of primary elections and an end to racetrack gambling were envisioned. However, the record of Hughes as a reform governor was marked by continual opposition from members of his own party. His ambitious plans for reform were undermined by the conservative leadership of the state legislature. Hughes achieved only one of his major goals—the consolidation and systemization of state regulatory agencies. Because they were industry specific, the regulatory agencies were limited in dealing with the New York corporate world. Under the Hughes governorship the agencies were merged under two Public Service Commissions, which regulated all corporate activity. His activism generally was limited to the blocking of conservative legislation through the executive veto, which he exercised 297 times. Although his record in implementing reform was limited, Hughes was able to maintain his image as a Progressive leader.

The frustrations of attempting to pass reform legislation through a conservative state legislature prompted Hughes to leave electoral politics. When President William Howard Taft offered him a position as Associate Justice of the Supreme Court in 1910, Hughes quickly accepted.

As an Associate Justice of the Supreme Court, Hughes was able to distance himself from the politics of the Republican Party. However, his position on the bench kept him involved in the political debates of the Progressive era. Hughes wrote the definitive argument for the right of the federal government to regulate commerce in his majority opinion in the *Minnesota Rate Cases*. The Hughes argument bolstered the efforts of the Interstate Commerce Commission to enforce equitable freight rates.

Hughes's appointment to the Supreme Court insulated him from the political turmoil that engulfed the Republican Party at the end of the Taft presidency. The institutional reform movement in Congress, designed to limit the power of Speaker of the House Joe Cannon, quickly erupted into a generalized war between various factions of Republicans. Members of the party divided along Old Guard—progressive lines and the progressive wing itself collapsed in a climate of bitter recrimination when Theodore Roosevelt formed a third party in 1912. This failure of party solidarity resulted in the first Democratic presidential victory in 30 years.

Woodrow Wilson's election in 1912 forced changes in the politics of the Republican Party. The party's leadership determined that a Democratic victory only occurred in the context of Republican disunity. When political infighting ceased the Republicans would return to power. The Republican presidential nominee in 1916 would have to be someone who had antagonized neither the Old Guard nor the Progressive bolters.

Hughes possessed all the qualities of a compromise presidential candidate. His political career in New York had provided him with a following in the Progressive reform movement. His refusal to condemn William Howard Taft in 1912 had earned him the respect of members of the Old Guard. As an associate justice of the Supreme Court, Hughes had stayed in government, but had withdrawn from the political intrigues of the Republican Party. He permitted himself to be drafted as the Republican presidential nominee in 1916. However, the Republican Party's policy of conciliation did not provide the foundation for a presidential victory in 1916. Residual fragmentation, combined with confusion over the Republican Party's position regarding the Great War, led to a second Wilson victory.

After the election of 1916 Hughes left electoral politics, but did not totally divorce himself from the politics of the Republican Party. He served as an intermediary figure in the Republican debates over the League of Nations. Generally supportive of the pro-League activities of the League to Enforce Peace, he maintained strong ties to Republican internationalists like William Howard Taft. At the same time, he was cautious in endorsing a new international system in which the League of Nations would possess the ability to sanction nations. These concerns made him the ally of reservationist Republicans in the Senate, who were willing to support U.S. entry into the League only if established American foreign policy practices remained unaffected.

All sides in the League of Nations debate sought support outside the Senate, appealing not only to the general public but also to the elder statesmen of both parties. As the previous Republican presidential candidate, Hughes was a man of significant stature. Hughes stayed with the Republican Party leadership. He argued that Republican-sponsored reservations to protect the U.S. government were unnecessary, but he would not join the Democrats in condemning them as dangerous. When the Versailles Treaty came to the Senate floor for debate in the fall of 1919, Hughes engaged in limited cooperation with Henry Cabot Lodge. Like other Republican supporters of the League, Hughes ultimately accepted the Lodge reservations and condemned Wilson's refusal to compromise on the Treaty text. Wilson's treaty could not be ratified, but neither could Lodge's version, as irreconcilable Republicans combined with Democrats to block ratification under Republican reservations. The final failure of the Versailles Treaty in March 1920 did not immediately end the debate over American entry into the League of Nations.

The contest for the Republican presidential nomination in 1920 was extraordinarily vicious. In this climate of recrimination, none of the major candidates could be nominated. The nomination fell to Senator Warren G. Harding, a candidate conspicuously free of political enemies. Harding defeated James Cox in November. His cabinet would be a balance of Progressive and conservatives, and to facilitate compromise, the major cabinet positions would be given to those who had remained above the political infighting.

Harding had to dispel the notion that he was the puppet of those party leaders who dominated the "smoke-filled rooms" of the Chicago nomination convention. He also had to overcome his image as someone who could not rise above politics. The appointment of Charles Evans Hughes to the position of secretary of state became an asset of incalculable worth to the Harding administration. Hughes was still regarded as one of the architects of Progressive reform. Despite his failure in the 1916 campaign for the presidency, he had kept his position as a party elder. His eloquent support of international organizations had helped to prevent the Republican Party from being branded "isolationist" during the Versailles Treaty debates. Hughes's intellect and stature would serve to overcome the president's limitations.

Hughes would prove to be an outstanding secretary of state. He possessed a clear vision of America's position in the new international system. The United States would be a world leader, not only in terms of its ability to provide material progress, but also by its advocacy of diplomacy and arbitration over military force. Hughes was fully committed to the supremacy of negotiation in the maintenance of U.S. diplomatic relations. He had extraordinary command over the details of American foreign policy. This quality was combined with an ability to maintain a clear sense of the larger goals of American diplomacy. Hughes was faced with a complex period in international relations, and he did not possess the luxury of a party that was committed to one set of foreign policy goals. Nonetheless, he was able to maintain control over U.S. foreign policy and take the country into a new role as a world power.

As secretary of state, Hughes was confronted with complex political problems. He believed that the stability of the postwar world depended on American cooperation with the European allies. He knew that most Republican politicians were willing to accept participation in the League of Nations. However, the unity of the Republican Party after the election of 1920 was still quite fragile. A small minority of Republicans were irreconcilably opposed to U.S. entry into the League, and two of the most vocal Irreconcilables, William Borah and Hiram Johnson, understood the weakness of the administration's political position. Throughout 1920 and early 1921 they threatened to lead a bolt of the Republican Party if the leadership made any attempt to sponsor American entry into the League of Nations. By the summer of 1921 Hughes understood that the primacy of Republican Party solidarity precluded American entry into the League of Nations.

As the League of Nations issue diminished in importance, Hughes was confronted with a second problem regarding international security. The Anglo-Japanese Alliance was scheduled to expire in 1921. The British government was anxious to maintain a security relationship with Japan, but wanted to include the United States in the same agreement. Several factors induced Hughes to support American participation in East Asian security arrangements. The new republican government in China had not proved stable. Furthermore, the European colonial powers had been weakened during the Great War. A climate existed that could foster either general chaos or territorial expansion by Japan. A security arrangement between the major powers in Asia would serve to mitigate these threats. However, a multilateral security pact in Asia would be opposed by the same senators who had found the League of Nations dangerous to U.S. national interests.

Senator William Borah had complicated the situation by leading a drive for massive naval disarmament by the major powers. In December 1920 he had submitted a resolution to the Senate calling for a multinational conference, which would negotiate a 50 percent reduction in naval armament. Though the resolution failed, he continued to resubmit it in 1921 to increasing popular acclaim. The Harding administration faced rising popular pressure for naval disarmament, pressure encouraged by the very same politicians who had threatened to bolt the party over the League of Nations issue. In the summer of 1921 Hughes fused this potentially divisive issue of disarmament with the problem presented by the dissolution of the Anglo-Japanese Alliance. He sought to force the supporters of Borah into a compromise and proposed the Washington Conference for the Discussion of Disarmament and Pacific and Far Eastern Questions.

The Washington Conference opened on November 12, 1921, the day after the dedication of the Tomb of the Unknown Soldier at Arlington National Cemetery. In his opening speech Hughes astonished the delegates by condemning the impending postwar naval building race and called for the strict limitation of the battle fleets of the major world navies. The presentation worked. Hughes was applauded in the American press, and the Harding administration rode on a wave of public support. The U.S. government controlled the initiative at the Washington Conference. The delegations quickly realized that refusal to negotiate a major arms reduction would result in a disastrous public image. Naval limitation became the principal objective of the conference, but to secure that objective other problems of security had to be resolved. The conference resulted in a series of treaties that provided for political stability in the Pacific.

The Four Power Treaty, signed by the United States, the British Empire, Japan, and France, declared that the signatories would respect each other's rights to insular possessions in the Pacific. In the event of conflict, the signatories were committed to a series of diplomatic negotiations to determine the appropriate response.

The Five Power Treaty, signed by the United States, the British Empire, Japan, France, and Italy, established limitations on the number of capital ships in their respective fleets. The relative strengths of the five major navies were determined, with the United States and the British Empire sharing global power and Japan guaranteed its position as a dominant power in the Pacific. The signatories agreed to upper limits in terms of ship tonnage and caliber of weapons. They committed themselves to a 10-year building holiday and a moratorium on the fortification of naval bases in the western Pacific.

The Nine Power Treaty, signed by the United States, the British Empire, Japan, France, Italy, China, the Netherlands, Belgium, and Portugal, committed the major colonial powers in Asia to protect the independence of China. China would not be partitioned into spheres of influence, nor would the integrity of the Chinese government be questioned by special economic relations with the great powers.

These three treaties were all widely supported in the United States. Only the Four Power Treaty met any resistance in the Senate, and this resistance was not great enough to prevent ratification. Taken together, these treaties provided the stability needed in East Asia and permitted American commercial expansion. Not only would American businessmen be aided by the "Open Door" provisions of the Nine Power Treaty, but Republicans also assumed that by curbing government spending under the Five Power Treaty, tax levels would be reduced to the advantage of American businessmen.

In an effort to stabilize international monetary transfers, Hughes and Secretary of the Treasury Andrew Mellon developed a policy designed to provide capital for economic development. Hughes advocated the formation of an international committee to examine the monetary problems of postwar Germany. The system of reparations established under the Versailles Treaty had triggered inflation, Germany's default on its reparations, and the French occupation of the Ruhr. Hughes hoped that the presence of Americans on a new reparations committee would encourage compromise and cooperation between the Germans and French. This new approach to reparations resulted in the Dawes Plan. Under this scheme, Germans would gain access to international loans. These loans would permit the economic stabilization of Germany, which would in turn provide the means for a national German reparations policy. Although the war debt and reparations problems were not solved completely by the Harding administration, sufficient improvements were made to provide basic levels of economic stability in Europe.

The destabilization of Europe was important to American foreign economic policy, but of equal importance was the economic development of Latin America. The centennial of the Monroe Doctrine occurred during the Hughes secretaryship, and it would have been impossible to advocate a diminution of U.S. power in Latin America. Since the declaration of the Roosevelt Corollary to the Monroe Doctrine in 1904, the U.S. government had been deeply involved in the political economy of Caribbean states. Yet, the implementation of the Roosevelt Corollary had not produced thriving middle-class democracies in the Caribbean. Attempts by the U.S. government to control the modernization process in Latin America had produced anti-American nationalism. Although Hughes accepted the basic progressive assumptions that democracies had to stifle class conflict and that order and efficiency were prerequisites for economic development, he could not deny that force had failed to transmit these values. Responding to Latin American nationalism, Hughes advocated the withdrawal of a U.S. military presence in the occupied American republics whenever practicable. Hughes initiated the process of removing American forces from both the Dominican Republic and Nicaragua as soon as it was determined that U.S. lives and property were not in jeopardy. Hughes supported the formation of strong republics in Latin America, but departed from the Rooseveltian tradition of imposing reform. He retained the progressive concept that American investment was an aid to political and economic development of Caribbean states, but was reluctant to advocate the use of American military power to protect that investment

Relations with the government of Alváro Obregón in Mexico provided a major test to this policy of economic investment without intervention. The new Mexican Constitution had put into question the ownership of subsurface natural resources. U.S. corporations were heavily involved in the Mexican mining and petroleum industries, and Hughes sought to guarantee the safety of American property in Mexico without resorting to armed intervention. After two years of negotiation on various levels, the conflict was resolved, with property rights protected and the integrity of the Obregón government intact. American investors received limited compensation for confiscated property, long-standing contracts held by U.S. oil and mining companies were guaranteed by the Mexican government, and Mexico agreed to adjudicate existing U.S. claims. The pattern of relations between the United States and Mexico, one that emphasized rational negotiation and compromise for mutual advantage, became the preferred course of U.S. diplomacy in Latin America.

The question of property rights also became a major factor in the decision not to recognize the new Russian government. The Wilson administration had refused to recognize the Bolshevik government. Hughes continued this policy of nonrecognition, despite evidence that the Bolsheviks were increasing their control over Russia and had established a functioning government. Hughes contended that the new government had repudiated the obligations undertaken before the revolution. As a result, American property in Russia had been confiscated, and legitimate debts had been annulled. The Russian government did not recognize the fundamental rights of U.S. citizens in Russia, and it compounded the problem by encouraging the spread of Communism throughout the West.

The protection of American property rights in foreign countries was not a crass bid for the support of the American businessman. Hughes believed that human progress itself depended on the universal acknowledgment that certain rights were inalienable by government. These inalienable rights were those that provided the foundation for Anglo-Saxon law—life, liberty, and property. Without the security of the right to property, economic development could not be guaranteed. Without economic development and material well-being, all other political rights were in jeopardy. It was the goal of the Department of State, consistent with the philosophy of Charles Evans Hughes, to protect the rights of American citizens under international law and to foster an international system that would favor economic and political progress.

From his first entry into politics in 1905, Hughes hoped to impose rational order on government. He did not see policy as a manifestation of the will of the powerful, but rather a means of attaining progress for all. He felt that when policy was not being implemented in an efficient manner, the institutions of government had to be systematized.

Hughes supported the rationalization of the Department of State under the Rogers Act of 1924. Officers were to be paid a competitive wage, so the Department would not have to depend on those who saw the diplomatic corps as an avocation rather than a profession. Guidelines for promotion and assignment were developed to define lines of authority within the Department. The act also combined the foreign commercial service with the State Department so that political and economic relations could be more easily coordinated.

Hughes continued as secretary of state after Harding's death. However, he stepped down in the spring of 1925 after Calvin Coolidge was elected in his own right. He resumed his private law practice, but did not stay out of government affairs for long. In 1928, in recognition of his long support of the international judicial system and his stature within the Republican Party, Hughes became a judge on the International Court of Justice.

In 1930 Herbert Hoover nominated Hughes Chief Justice of the Supreme Court, a position he held throughout the great Constitutional debates of the New Deal. During the 1930s the Court debated fundamental issues regarding economic rights and the delegation of legislative power. The period was marked by controversy over the role of the Court in American government and the attempt by President Franklin D. Roosevelt to alter the structure of the federal judicial system under "the court-packing scheme." Hughes retired from the Court in 1941 and died in 1948.

BIBLIOGRAPHICAL ESSAY

The papers of Charles Evans Hughes are located at the Library of Congress. They provide detailed insights into all facets of Hughes's public life. The collection is well indexed and has been microfilmed.

Merlo Pusey wrote the first major biography of Hughes in 1951. This two-volume study, entitled *Charles Evans Hughes*, benefits from extensive interviews with the subject. It serves as a useful reference work for any analysis of Hughes. A more recent work is Betty Glad's *Charles Evans Hughes and the Illusions of Innocence* (1966). Glad identifies "the Puritanical mould" that formed Hughes's character and intellectual outlook. His service as secretary of state is examined as a manifestation of his Puritan qualities. Dexter Perkins has written a brief, highly readable biography of Hughes that concentrates on his service as secretary of state, *Charles Evans Hughes and American Democratic Statesmanship* (1956), which is somewhat dated, but does provide a concise introduction to Hughes. Unfortunately, the new wave of scholarship concerning diplomacy of the interwar period has not produced a new biography of Charles Evans Hughes.

Hughes's early career as a reform politician is dealt with in Robert Wesser's *Charles Evans Hughes: Politics and Reform in New York, 1905–1910* (1967). This work analyzes the direction of early progressive reform and demonstrates the limitations of reform government in the complex political environment of New York. Another aspect of Hughes's career—his service on the Supreme Court—is examined in Samuel Hendel's *Charles Evans Hughes and the Supreme Court* (1951). Although this study is more useful for its explication of legal history, it does provide some insight into Hughes's conceptions of the role of the law and government.

The Washington Conference was Hughes's greatest single achievement as secretary of state. A great deal of literature exists on the subject. Thomas Buckley's *The United States and the Washington Conference* (1970) provides a detailed analysis of the American negotiating strategy and the process of ratification. Roger Dingman's *Power in the Pacific* (1976) examines the conference in light of the evolving strategic planning of the postwar period and the shifting power structure within the Republican Party.

Karen Miller

CORDELL HULL
(1871–1955)

Served 1933–1944
Appointed by President Franklin D. Roosevelt
Democrat

For a world's record 11 years, 8 months, and 26 days (March 4, 1933–November 30, 1944), Cordell Hull of Tennessee held the office of secretary of state. The image Hull presented to the public was that of a kindly southern gentleman and judge who preached the virtues of the good neighbor and Wilsonian internationalism. Behind his back he was often ridiculed for his simple-minded moralizing, for his speech impediment and profanity-filled outbursts, and because President Franklin D. Roosevelt often left Hull uninformed as he worked through his friends and conducted summit conferences alone. But in retrospect, it is Hull's statesmanlike vision rather than his shortcomings that stand out: his efforts to promote better relations with Latin America and the Soviet Union, his faith in international cooperation, and his awareness that America was foolish to confront Japan at a time when the nation was militarily weak. Had Hull been able to observe the international economic expansion in the decades after his death in 1955, he likely would have regarded that as the ultimate vindication of his faith that free trade was the route to a world of peace, prosperity, and stability.

Despite his aristocratic name, Cordell Hull was the son of a Tennessee mountain farmer who, in enterprising fashion, supported his wife and five sons by selling timber and by operating a country store and post office from which he sold goods on credit. His father named the future secretary of state, who was born on October 2, 1871, after a family friend, county judge John Cordell. As a young man Hull became skilled at all aspects of farming, and he assisted his father in the hazardous business of floating log rafts down the Cumberland River to Nashville—a virtual metropolis in the eyes of the young man from the country. For three and a half months each winter, his father employed a tutor to instruct his sons in the basics of English and history. When Hull was 15, his father sent him to Montvale Institute at Celina, Tennessee, 12 miles from the family farm. Hull recalled that his homemade clothes and socks were a source of ridicule from some of the more well-to-do students. He credited Joe S. McMillan, the school's teacher, with requiring the students to master grammatically correct English, as opposed to the country English used in everyday life. After a year of study at the normal schools at Bowling Green, Kentucky, and Lebanon, Ohio, respectively, Hull passed the entrance exam for the Cumberland University Law School. Ten months later he received his diploma, which carried with it automatic admission to the Tennessee bar. His inspiration for entering the law came from Democratic Congressman Benton McMillan, a brother of his teacher and an advocate of low tariffs. When McMillan introduced the impressionable young lawyer to President Grover Cleveland at the White House, Hull caught an incurable case of Potomac fever. By age 21, Hull had achieved entry into the legal profession, a seat in the state legislature, and a reputation in the Tennessee Democratic Party as an up-and-coming leader. And from McMillan and Cleveland he had acquired a lifelong commitment to the cause of lower tariffs.

Two terms in the fractious legislature were enough for Hull, and for two years he was out of politics developing his law practice. With the outbreak of the Spanish-American War, Hull—mindful of Tennessee's tradition as the volunteer state—raised and drilled an infantry company. By the time Hull and his men arrived in Cuba the fighting was over, but Hull's exposure to Latin American customs and modes of thought came in handy after he became secretary of state. Hull's well-known ability to swear like a trooper was likely augmented by his military service as well. Two years after returning from Cuba, Hull was appointed a state circuit judge, a position that required him regularly to travel by horse and buggy throughout a 10-county region. Hull believed that his reputation as a strict law-and-order judge who had efficiently managed his court's docket was "the largest single factor in my getting to Congress."

His chance appeared in 1906 when Benton McMillan retired after 20 years of service; by only 15 votes out of more than 15,000 cast, the 35-year-old bachelor won the Democratic nomination, which was tantamount to election. For the next 14 years, as he honed his political skills in the House of Representatives, Hull took a long-range focus. He learned that a successful congressman must be a survivor (a lesson he later applied to the office of secretary of state). Moreover, he perceived that he needed a national constituency and a national audience if he desired to exercise leadership outside the narrow confines of his district. With characteristic tenacity, Hull placed himself at the head of two progressive issues: the need for a federal income tax and a lower tariff. Hull was so zealous in pursuing his causes that he often made a nuisance of himself; congressmen such as Champ Clark of Missouri and John Sharp Williams of Mississippi found Hull's monologues so tedious that they avoided him whenever possible. Later, as secretary of state, his moralistic sermons often produced a similar reaction from members of the diplomatic corps.

During the first year of Woodrow Wilson's presidency, Hull achieved two of his objectives. In the Underwood–Simmons Tariff, Congress sharply reduced duties on foreign goods and, at the same time, included a federal income tax provision drafted by Hull. "I myself felt," he recorded in his *Memoirs*, "that if I should live two lifetimes I probably would not be able to render public service equal to my part in the long fight for enactment of our income-tax system." World War I found Hull, now a member of the Ways and Means Committee and the Democratic National Committee, advocating generous loans to the Allies, but he did not anticipate that the question of repayment would poison international relations for years to come. Regarded as an antisocial workaholic, Hull surprised his friends and colleagues in November 1917 by marrying Frances Witz, a widow from Staunton, Virginia.

Following World War I, Hull's once promising career seemed to stagnate. At age 50, defeated by the Harding landslide for reelection to an eighth term in the House of Representatives, Hull found himself out of office. To make ends meet he served for three years as the chairman of the Democratic National Committee while he prepared to regain his congressional seat. In 1922 he benefited from a reaction against the Republicans and was returned to the halls of Congress. But although he was reelected to the House in 1924, 1926, and 1928, Hull found his life more and more frustrating. His ideas on tariffs and international cooperation fell on deaf ears. Nevertheless, Hull (sounding like "Uncle Shylock") made a minor contribution to international disharmony by criticizing Republican war debt settlements as too generous to America's World War I debtors. Comparing himself to the legendary Cassandra, who had warned the Trojans to beware of Greeks bearing gifts, Hull railed in vain against overproduction and excessive tariffs. By 1930 Hull was seriously considering retirement, when both Senate seats in Tennessee became open. In a bitter, smear-filled campaign, in which he characterized his opponent as "the damnedest liar" in the state, Hull handily won the Democratic primary for a six-year term and easily vanquished his Republican opponent in November. As the depression deepened he cautiously supported New York Governor Franklin D. Roosevelt for the Democratic presidential nomination over Al Smith, the Democratic candidate in 1928. No one was more surprised than Hull when Roosevelt, following his defeat of Herbert Hoover, offered him the premier position in the cabinet. Roosevelt seriously considered only Hull, the banker Owen G. Young, and the diplomat and businessman Norman H. Davis. Hull prevailed, not due to his expertise in foreign policy, but because he had been one of Roosevelt's most reliable southern supporters and because he possessed ample reserves of dignity and bearing. The handsome six-foot-tall Tennessean looked like a secretary of state.

At age 62 Hull was "thunderstruck" to have been selected and the thought occurred to him that the office could, with luck, be an avenue to the White House itself. As late as 1940 Roosevelt was still encouraging Hull's presidential fantasies. But Roosevelt did Hull no favor by personally appointing the principal U.S. ambassadors and by naming several of his friends, including Sumner Welles and Raymond Moley, as assistant secretaries of state. Of Moley, a former brain truster, Hull noted, "I was not at all enthusiastic about this sort of appointment." Another worry for Hull was the fragile state of his health; he suffered from a mild case of diabetes and he had begun to display the initial symptoms of tuberculosis.

In contrast to the New Deal's dynamic start in domestic affairs, its initial foray in foreign affairs was amateurish. But the embarrassing failure of the London Economic Conference (June–July 1933) was not the fault of Hull, but of Roosevelt himself. Hull headed a weak, poorly instructed delegation that disagreed among itself. Furthermore, Roosevelt, who had once favored currency stabilization, changed his mind after the conference began. Hull was mortified when Roosevelt sent Assistant Secretary of State Raymond Moley to London in the middle of the conference. Thinking he was following Roosevelt's wishes, Moley agreed to a face-saving stabilization agreement, only to have Roosevelt emphatically reject it (apparently without reading it) in his famous "bombshell" message. "You had better go back home," intoned Hull to Moley. "You had no business over here in the first place and I continued to elaborate along those lines." Hull emerged as the survivor in the bureaucratic infighting as Moley was soon forced out of the State Department.

Hull rebounded from his dismal experience at London by scoring a resounding personal triumph at the Montevideo Pan-American Conference in December 1933. Demonstrating his southern hospitality and charm, Hull outlined a program of promoting hemispheric prosperity through reciprocal trade agreements and banning war throughout Latin America. He won praise from the delegates for signing a nonintervention pledge after adding a reservation, which was widely overlooked, stating that the United States retained the right to intervene under existing treaty rights. On his return via the Panama Canal in January 1934, Hull agreed to a significant revision of America's 1903 treaty with Panama. With the approval of the president, Hull was able to renounce the right to intervene in the internal affairs of Panama; at the same time the annual payment due Panama was increased from $250,000 to $436,000. With Hull running interference among reluctant senators, the revisions passed the Senate two years later. The image of the good neighbor was also enhanced in 1934 by relinquishing the right to intervene in Cuba and by the withdrawal of the last marines from the Dominican Republic, although U.S. control of Haitian customs was not terminated until 1941. In working out the details of the Good Neighbor policy, Hull heavily relied on the skills of Assistant Secretary of State Sumner Welles.

For Cordell Hull the dream of a lifetime came true on June 12, 1934, when Roosevelt signed Hull's Reciprocal Trade Agreements bill. Convinced that Congress could never be induced to repeal the Hawley–Smoot Tariff of 1930, Hull designed an end-run strategy. His bill authorized the president to increase or decrease existing rates by up to 50 percent in return for trade concessions. Once negotiated by the executive, the bilateral trade agreements required no further congressional approval. Latin America, which in 1932 had seen its trade with the United States drop to its lowest level in 23 years, was a special beneficiary of the new policy. One of Hull's most visible Good Neighbor successes came in November and December 1936 when he arranged for Roosevelt to attend the Pan American conference at Buenos Aires. Hull and Roosevelt won plaudits when they made a strategic decision to sign a categorical nonintervention pledge without reservations. As World War II approached, Hull was able to secure Latin American agreement to the principle of mutual consultation in the event of an attack on the hemisphere as well as agreement not to transfer Latin American territory to a belligerent. An obvious benefit of Hull's policy was that once war broke out a majority of the Latin American republics either declared war on the Axis or broke relations. The only serious shortcoming to Hull's policy of nonintervention, trade, and peace was that it required the acceptance of dictators such as Anastasio Samoza in Nicaragua, Fulgencio Batista in Cuba, and Raphael Trujillo in the Dominican Republic.

During his third year as secretary of state, Hull found it necessary to focus more and more on the potential threat of European and Far Eastern fascism. Hull's greatest frustration was the fainthearted response of Congressional isolationists and pacifists. Above all Hull was embarrassed by the antics of a special Senate committee appointed in 1934 to probe the activities of the munitions industry. Because none of the four Democrats on the committee wished to become chairman, the job fell by default to North Dakota Senator Gerald P. Nye, a member of the opposition. The North Dakota isolationist proceeded to complicate Hull's life by distorting the investigation into a sensational effort to show that greedy bankers and "merchants of death" had sucked the nation into World War I for profit. Furthermore, Hull was embarrassed when the Nye Committee, without asking his approval, published State Department documents furnished to it for purposes of information.

Subsequently Nye introduced neutrality legislation that required the president, at the start of hostilities, to ban loans and arms sales to belligerents and to prohibit travel by Americans on belligerent ships. Hull struck back by promoting an innocuous neutrality bill giving the president discretionary power whether to prohibit arms sales, loans, and travel so as to distinguish between an aggressor and a victim. Hull feared Nye would tie the president's hands by notifying aggressors in advance that they could attack with impunity knowing America would embargo arms to both sides. In the end Roosevelt and Hull were the losers because the "permanent" neutrality law of 1937 mandated that the president, once a state of war existed, must ban arms, loans, and travel to either side. Trade in civilian goods with belligerents was to be on a cash-and-carry basis for a two-year period at the discretion of the president. On the advice of Hull, Roosevelt decided to sign the bill, which had to be flown by seaplane to the naval vessel on which the President was enjoying a fishing trip in the Gulf of Mexico. And in January 1938, Hull was forced to undertake an all-out effort to defeat the isolationist Ludlow Amendment, which required a national referendum before war could be declared. Only dimly seen at the time, the narrow defeat of the amendment in the House of Representatives by a vote of only 209 to 188 was a turning point in Hull's fight against isolationism and pacifism.

As war clouds gathered during Roosevelt's second term, the president himself took the lead in improvising aid to Britain short of war. Thus Hull had little influence in such Rooseveltian initiatives as the Quarantine speech at Chicago (October 5, 1937), the British Royal Visit (June 7–11, 1939), the destroyer for bases deal with Churchill in the summer of 1940, and the Lend-Lease bill in the spring of 1941, and Roosevelt did not take Hull to the Newfoundland Conference with Churchill in August 1941. However, Roosevelt did enlist Hull in his efforts to modify the Neutrality Act to permit the sale of munitions to Britain and France. Roosevelt commenced the campaign in his 1939 State of the Union Address in which he criticized the Neutrality Act for failing to distinguish between an aggressor and a victim. Hull's original plan was to testify before the Senate Foreign Relations Committee in favor of granting the executive discretionary authority to sell arms to belligerents. Senator Key Pittman, the committee's chairman, urged Hull to desist on the ground that isolationists were lying in wait hoping to ask loaded questions. Instead, Hull invited key legislators to his Washington apartment arguing that they were "making the mistake of their lives" if they thought America's controversy with Hitler was just "another goddamn piddling dispute over a boundary line." The only solution, Hull argued, was to repeal this "wretched little bobtailed, sawed-off domestic statute." Not to do so would be "just plain chuckle-headed," he contended. For the time being Hull and Roosevelt were thwarted. Not until the fall of 1939, after the outbreak of hostilities, did Congress reluctantly permit the sale of munitions to belligerents on a cash-and-carry basis.

At a time when the administration's main focus was on the danger of war with Hitler, Hull concentrated increasingly on the Far East. Since the outbreak of the Sino-Japanese War in July 1937, Hull had consistently advised caution. As Japan began to promote the concept of the Greater East Asia Co-Prosperity Sphere in 1938–1939, Hull continued to enunciate basic moral concepts while opposing a tough stand that he feared could lead an unprepared America into war. Treasury Secretary Henry Morgenthau, Jr., and Interior Secretary Harold Ickes were frequently frustrated by what they regarded as weak hand-wringing on Hull's part. Hull's timidity appears less open to criticism, however, when viewed in the context of the disastrous reverses suffered by the United States and its allies in the opening months of the war in the Pacific. In retrospect Hull had a point when he told of an unarmed Tennessean who unwisely confronted a highwayman. "I leave it to you," he told his listeners, "how that conversation ended." Or, reverting to his role of a Tennessee frontiersman, Hull summed up the Axis threat to a weak America by quoting a prophetic, if crude, bit of backwoods lore: "When you're in a pissin' contest with a skunk, make sure you got lots of piss."

Therefore, Hull opposed Morgenthau's tung oil project of 1938, which proposed a $25 million loan to Jiang Jieshi (Chiang Kai-shek), the President of Nationalist China. The money would be used for completing the road then under construction from Burma to Chungking; the Export-Import Bank would be repaid by exports to America of tung oil, a component of paint and varnish. Hull was reluctant to see Japan conquer China, but he felt the loan would do little to aid China and would invite Japanese retaliation. In the bureaucratic infighting Hull was the loser, but he did not alter his opinion that a get-tough policy would be a serious mistake because it was likely to involve the nation in a war with Japan before America was ready. Hull's policy of avoiding provocation was also illustrated by his mild protests when Japan occupied Hainan Island, near Hanoi, and the Spratly Islands, near the Philippines. And in March 1939, Hull agreed to send a symbolic olive branch to Japan by returning the ashes of former ambassador Hiroshi Saito aboard the cruiser *Astoria*. As the vessel departed Tokyo, an effort to photograph the shipyard where Japan was secretly constructing its mammoth *Yamato*-class battleships miscarried when two coal-burning tugboats laid down a smokescreen and obscured the intended target.

As the Far Eastern crisis deepened, Hull saw the political wisdom of compromising with administration and congressional advocates of economic sanctions. To prevent an acrimonious Senate debate, Hull, in July 1939, accepted a resolution offered by Senator Arthur Vandenberg of Michigan that gave six months' notice that the United States intended to terminate the commercial treaty of 1911 with Japan. However, the expiration of the treaty in January 1940 did not affect trade because the State Department, on a technicality, ruled that it was not legally necessary to impose high Hawley–Smoot Tariff rates. So for the time being, Hull, who wanted to keep Japan guessing about sanctions, prevailed.

What upset Hull's calculations and the balance of world power was Hitler's lightning defeat of the Allies in the spring of 1940. Suddenly, with Europe in turmoil, Japan found itself in a position to exploit the Far Eastern power vacuum and achieve the goal of the Greater East Asia Co-Prosperity Sphere. The first economic sanctions were imposed in July 1940 following a testy debate between Morgenthau and Hull. The Treasury's position was that an embargo of strategic materials would bring Japan's war machine to a grinding halt. Hull's response was that sanctions would not alter Japan's policy. What was more likely, he contended, was that sanctions would provoke the Japanese into seizing the Dutch East Indies to fuel their expansion. Typically Roosevelt compromised between the competing administration factions and announced a limited embargo that initially applied only to high-octane aviation gasoline and number one grade scrap iron and steel. Gradually, despite Hull's misgivings, the embargo was tightened by the addition of all grades of scrap iron and scrap steel (September 1940); pig iron, iron ore, and steel (December 1940); and copper, brass, bronze, zinc, nickel, and potash (January 1941). When Japan made a diplomatic effort to improve relations with the United States in the spring of 1941, Hull played a crucial role. Beginning in mid-March, Hull began a series of secret evening meetings with Admiral Nomura Kichisaburo, the new Japanese ambassador. They never came close to an agreement, even though Hull had the advantage of being able to read Nomura's reports courtesy of code intercepts by the Army Signal Corps. Hull's critics contend that he was too moralistic and rigid in insisting that Japan abandon its new order in Asia. But Nomura, who had no instructions from his government and whose English comprehension was poor, didn't help matters by mixing up documents and failing to clearly inform Tokyo of major American proposals. A further problem was Hull's delicate health; he developed a persistent cough and suffered from complications of diabetes.

The Hull–Nomura talks were formally ended when Japan invaded French Indo-China in late July 1941. Hull did not object when Roosevelt froze Japanese assets and imposed a limited oil embargo. Subsequently, administration hardliners, lead by Assistant Secretary of State Dean Acheson, took advantage of Hull's illness and Roosevelt's absence at the Newfoundland Conference to narrowly interpret the president's executive order. By the time Roosevelt and Hull realized that no oil was being sold, they concluded it was too late to turn back because a reversal would have been interpreted as a capitulation.

Back on his feet after a vacation at White Sulphur Springs, West Virginia, Hull played a major role in the final diplomatic maneuvering prior to Pearl Harbor. Finding himself in desperate political straits at home, Prime Minister Konoye Fumimaro requested in August a face-to-face meeting between himself and Roosevelt. The president's initial reaction was favorable. He had just returned from an exhilarating bout of summitry with Churchill and briefly thought of meeting with Konoye, perhaps at Juneau, Alaska. Ambassador to Japan Joseph Grew passionately urged Roosevelt to hold the meeting, arguing that it was a last chance to avoid hostilities. But Hull, with all the force at his command, opposed the idea. Hull's basic instincts as well as his previous experience with Konoye led him to the conclusion that the Japanese leader could not be trusted. The most that could be accomplished would be the signing of vague statements that Konoye could easily stretch out of shape. On the day of Hull's 70th birthday (October 2, 1941), the United States for all practical purposes rejected the proposed summit conference (technically the United States said it was willing to hold such a meeting provided an advance agreement was reached). Thereupon, Konoye fell from power and was replaced by General Tojo Hideki.

Through code intercepts Hull knew that Japan intended in early November to submit two final diplomatic proposals. On the surface Plan A looked promising because Japan offered to evacuate Indo-China and much of the Chinese mainland. However, Japan would continue to occupy Hainan Island, Mongolia, and North China for a "necessary" period of 25 years. Moreover, Hull questioned the integrity of the proposal because code intercepts showed that Japan planned only a sham evacuation of China. Even worse, in Hull's opinion, was Plan B that required the United

States to halt aid to China and resume trade with Japan, including the critical item of oil. Under Japan's "take-it-or-take-the-consequences" proposal, the United States was being asked to surrender unconditionally, thought Hull. At this point Hull's diplomacy stalled, not because he had "burned out," but because he could not find support for a three-month truce proposal from America's allies. Instead, with Roosevelt's support, Hull dispatched to Tokyo a "comprehensive basic proposal," which required Japan's evacuation from Indo-China and Mainland China. Japan's reply was delivered at 2:20 P.M. Washington time on December 7, an hour and 25 minutes after the start of the Pearl Harbor attack. Hull, who had been alerted that the attack was in progress and who had read the intercepted Japanese note in advance, indignantly rebuked Nomura, stating: "I must say that in all my conversations with you during the last nine months I have never uttered one word of untruth. This is borne out absolutely by the record. In all my 50 years of public service I have never seen a document that was more crowded with infamous falsehoods and distortions—infamous falsehoods and distortions on a scale so huge that I never imagined until today that any Government on this planet was capable of uttering them."

Hull continued to serve as secretary of state for almost three years after Pearl Harbor, even though he had legitimate reasons for retiring. Since the summer of 1941 Hull's health had become increasingly frail. From mid-January to mid-February 1942, Hull was confined to his Washington apartment and then, on his doctor's orders, spent three months in Miami. Even after his return to the State Department in late April 1942 he was weak and exhibited more outbursts of temper than usual. Furthermore, Hull demonstrated questionable judgment by launching a vendetta against Under Secretary of State Sumner Welles. According to Hull, Welles had been guilty of disloyalty by filling the State Department power vacuum left by Hull's illnesses. Above all, Hull was appalled by the discovery of Welles' homosexuality, a condition that was then universally regarded as grounds for disqualification from government service. Reluctantly Roosevelt gave in and announced that Welles was retiring due to the poor health of his wife. Edward Stettinius, Jr., a corporate executive and former Lend-Lease administrator, filled Welles' position while the 72-year-old Hull made the strenuous and hazardous flight to Moscow to meet with the Allied foreign ministers in October 1943.

As long as the Allies shared a common enemy, the wartime partnership held together remarkably well, and Hull was swept up in the coalition euphoria. He was greatly cheered by Stalin's promises to enter the war in the Pacific and to join the United Nations organization. Upon his return, Hull received the honor of addressing a joint session of Congress, and he made the excessively optimistic claim that such traditional foreign policy devices as spheres of influence, alliances, and balance of power had been made obsolete. Viewed from the perspective of the Cold War, Hull's statements appeared hopelessly naive, although, given the nature of wartime psychology, they were commonplace enough for the times.

Despite the accolades bestowed on him by the press, Hull played only a peripheral role in wartime diplomacy. Roosevelt did not take him to the Quebec or Tehran Conferences in 1943. By the spring of 1944 Hull was considering retirement, but Roosevelt urged him to stay on to manage the Dumbarton Oaks Conference that laid the groundwork for the United Nations organization. Unstated was the president's desire to benefit politically from Hull's continued presence at the State Department while he campaigned for reelection. Hull's final battle as secretary of state was against the Morgenthau Plan for the partition and deindustrialization of Germany. In Hull's opinion, the revengeful plan, which Morgenthau had convinced Churchill and Roosevelt to initial, would inspire Germany to fight harder than ever at the cost of innumerable Allied casualties. In a final White House conversation with Roosevelt on October 1, 1944, Hull found the president in a conciliatory mood and willing to admit that he had agreed to the plan without fully appreciating its consequences. Almost immediately Hull, now 73 years old, was forced to resign as the result of a physical collapse brought about from age and his assorted aliments, which included diabetes, tuberculosis, and abscessed teeth. Officially he left office on November 30, 1944, three weeks after Roosevelt's election to a fourth term.

Much of Hull's retirement was spent in hospitals as he slowly regained his strength and contemplated writing his memoirs. Numerous honors came his way, including the Nobel Peace Prize in 1945 and the Medal of Merit presented by President Harry S Truman two years later. In November 1945 he was well enough to deliver a lengthy defense of his diplomacy prior to December 7, 1941, before the Joint Congressional Committee on the Investigation of the Pearl Harbor Attack. And Hull was greatly pleased when the committee's final report cleared him of any responsibility for the debacle. Assisted by Andrew Berding, Hull spent two years preparing his memoirs, which appeared in two massive volumes in 1948. When Hull finally succumbed on July 23, 1955, at the age of 83 he was buried at Washington's National Cathedral next to his wife, who had died a year earlier.

As the longest serving secretary of state, Hull was the ultimate survivor in the bureaucratic wars encouraged by Franklin D. Roosevelt. Possessing the hide of a rhinoceros, Hull was able to tolerate Roosevelt's cavalier habit of working through his intimates and operating independently of the State Department. With an assist from Sumner Welles, Hull shaped the Good Neighbor policy into his personal blend of nonintervention, trade, and peace. He was more consistent and effective in fighting congressional isolationists and pacifists than Roosevelt, who was often less than candid and hesitant to antagonize the isolationists during the neutrality debates of the thirties. His caution in challenging an aggressive Japan was largely validated by the embarrassing defeats suffered by an unprepared and overconfident United States military establishment at the start of the Pacific conflict. In the area of postwar planning, Hull saw the need for international cooperation through the medium of the United Nations organization, as well as the necessity of coexisting with the Soviets, even if he was eventually disillusioned by the results of his trip to Moscow. And his unceasing advocacy of free trade, as tiresome as it seemed to many of his listeners, became the foundation of world prosperity in the second half of the twentieth century. Nevertheless, although he set the world's record for longevity in the office of secretary of state, he did stay, mentally and physically, past his prime. His human shortcomings aside, Hull devoted the best years of his life, day after day and crisis after crisis, to his position. At no time had he the slightest attraction to the social side of diplomacy; his only interest and his only hobby was public service.

BIBLIOGRAPHICAL ESSAY

The Cordell Hull Papers in the Library of Congress are the logical starting point for a study of the longest serving secretary of state. Students should be aware that much of the collection consists of folders organized by country, filled with type-written memoranda written by Hull and his assistants detailing his conversations with diplomats. The Hull Papers largely justify the unkind characterization of Hull by Sir Ronald Lindsay as a man of the "utmost integrity, dignity and charm" who patiently replied at length to any question from his diplomatic visitors. "But when they return to their houses," Lindsay recorded, "they have difficulty in remembering anything he has said which deserves to be reported." The most accessible Hull source is *The Memoirs of Cordell Hull*, 2 volumes (1948). Written with the assistance of Andrew Berding, Hull's *Memoirs* are both charming and self-righteous. In 1,742 pages of narrative, Hull expresses no second thoughts about any of his decisions and exaggerates his closeness with Roosevelt.

Hull has proven to be a formidable subject for biographers. Harold B. Hinton, *Cordell Hull, A Biography* (1942), is a eulogy. The fullest scholarly account is Julius W. Pratt, *Cordell Hull*, 2 volumes (1964). Pratt provides a solid, sympathetic, if unexciting, chronology of Hull's diplomacy. Donald F. Drummond, "Cordell Hull," in Norman A. Graebner, *An Uncertain Tradition: American Secretaries of State and Their Diplomacy* (1961), describes Hull as a man with a nineteenth-century mind operating in a twentieth-century world. Hull's appointment and his first year as secretary of state are sensitively detailed in Frank Freidel, *Franklin D. Roosevelt: Launching the New Deal* (1973). Arthur M. Schlesinger, Jr., *The Coming of the New Deal* (1959), presents Hull as a complicated individual who blended economic fundamentalism with frontier vindictiveness; he was depressed and ineffective at the London Economic Conference.

Hull's Far Eastern diplomacy has a sizable literature. Herbert Feis, *The Road to Pearl Harbor* (1950), describes Hull as a cautious and competent character in an unfolding Greek tragedy. Recent accounts are not so complimentary: Jonathan Utley, *Going to War with Japan, 1937–1941* (1985), criticizes Hull for his burnout and for making a wrong decision in proposing an unworkable comprehensive peace plan in November 1941. Frederick W. Marks, III, *Wind Over Sand: The Diplomacy of Franklin Roosevelt* (1988), calls Hull a figurehead secretary of state who was ignorant about the Far East and who made no effort to understand Japan. Most critical of all is Irwin Gellman, *Secret Affairs: Franklin Roosevelt, Cordell Hull and Sumner Welles* (1995). Hull is described as petty, chronically insecure, vindictive, and homophobic.

Benjamin D. Rhodes

JOHN JAY (1745–1829)

Served 1784–1790
Appointed Secretary of Foreign Affairs by the Continental
Congress

John Jay was born in New York City on December 12, 1745. His father was Peter
Jay, a prosperous merchant. His mother was Mary Van Cortlandt, a member of one
of the great Dutch patroon landed families of the Hudson Valley. Jay further
cemented his place in high New York society when, on April 28, 1774, he married
Sarah Livingston, member of another prominent family and daughter of a future
governor of New Jersey.

Jay's family connections had great influence on his later career. His grandfather
was a French Huguenot who escaped from prison and fled Catholic persecution to
America. Jay consequently distrusted Catholicism and the French nation throughout his life and diplomatic service. Jay's politics also reflected those of his extended
family. The Jay, Van Cortlandt, and Livingston families were among the minority
of New York aristocrats who sided with the Whigs during the Revolution.

Jay himself was not an early convert to the Whig cause. He graduated from
King's College (later Columbia University) in 1764, clerked in the office of a
prominent Tory lawyer, and was admitted to the bar in 1768. He remained aloof
from politics until his marriage in 1774 and defended Whig and Tory clients without prejudice. Then, in 1774, he was elected to the committee of correspondence
in New York City to plan resistance against Parliamentary taxation measures.
Shortly thereafter, that committee nominated him to be one of five New York delegates to the First Continental Congress.

Jay generally resisted the more radical measures of the Continental Congress,
but once the Congress passed resolutions denouncing the Parliamentary actions as
unconstitutional and recommended trade sanctions against Great Britain, Jay
drafted Congress's *Address to the People of Great Britain* to justify those actions. In
the Second Continental Congress that began meeting in 1775, Jay pursued the
same course of conduct. He sought to moderate the Congress's reaction to the hostilities at Lexington and Concord, but he acceded to the request of his fellow delegates and wrote an appeal to the Canadians to join the American colonial rebellion.

He even swallowed his anti-Catholic sentiments to argue in his appeal that "the fate of the Protestant and Catholic colonies" were linked.

In these and later actions during the Revolution, Jay exhibited a pattern of conduct that he would pursue throughout his life and diplomatic career. He had strong aristocratic and conservative views, but in the end he was generally willing to compromise those views to avoid polarizing the body politic. He was then willing to champion the resulting outcome with little reservation.

Jay continued to try to moderate the quarrel with Great Britain and to resist militant calls for outright independence. As a member of the New York legislature, he was instrumental in instructing New York's representatives to the Continental Congress in Philadelphia to vote against independence. However, once the Declaration of Independence was signed and the British launched a major invasion of New York, Jay abandoned all reservations and became a leader of the war effort. He helped deliver cannons to George Washington's troops defending New York, headed a council to root out spies and traitors in the colony, and organized an espionage ring.

He also led the effort to draft a constitution for New York as that colony transformed itself into a state. Again, he showed himself a masterful compromiser and organizer. The constitution won praise from all quarters for the way in which it balanced the interests of both elites and commoners. One incident in the constitutional debate, however, showed that Jay's usual propensity to moderation and compromise could dissolve when he was faced with an issue that touched his closest personal feelings or sense of honor. He proposed a clause that denied civil rights to anyone who would not forswear allegiance to priest, pope, or other foreign power. When that affront to liberty failed, he refused to give up and offered one variant after another. Only after all those were defeated did he finally settle for a mere warning against using freedom of conscience to encourage "licentiousness."

Jay's sense of honor and rectitude could thus not only overtrump his propensity to compromise on a matter of principle, it could also slide into stubbornness, arrogance, and attempts at retribution, especially when his attempts to negotiate on what he considered a reasonable basis were spurned or his sense of personal worth was challenged. Although his private relations seem to have been warm, he protected his public dignity with a cold and formal air. He proclaimed to one person who had offended that dignity in a very minor way that he would "rather reject the friendship of the world than purchase it by patience under indignities offered by any man in it." He came close to fighting a duel with a man he had blackballed from a private club because that man's social status was too low in Jay's estimation. At least some diplomats who negotiated with him thought they could take advantage of Jay's excessive concern for his own dignity and honor. The British foreign office received a report that Jay could "bear any opposition to what he advocates provided regard is shown to his ability. . . . Mr. Jay's weak side is *Mr. Jay.*"

After serving as chief justice of the New York Supreme Court between 1777 and 1779, Jay returned to the Continental Congress and began his long involvement with American foreign affairs when he was immediately elected president of the congress in time to preside over debate about how closely the United States should cooperate with its ally, France, and on what terms it should offer to make peace with Great Britain. Members of Congress, many of them strongly influenced by the person and some by the purse of the French representative in the United States, mistakenly believed that Jay's French heritage would make him more favorable to French interests than the president he was elected to replace, Henry Laurens. Nine months later, for much the same reason, they elected Jay to be U.S. representative to Spain and to serve concurrently with John Adams and Benjamin Franklin as commissioners to make peace with Great Britain, whenever that opportunity should arise.

Whatever favor Jay might have felt for France when he left for Madrid was certainly extinguished by his experience there. Even though Spain had entered the war against Britain as an ally of France, it refused to recognize the United States or accept Jay as America's official representative. The Spanish were willing to supply some secret aid to the Americans, but they wanted no public connection with revolutionaries who condemned monarchy and coveted Spanish colonies in the Mississippi region. Even when Congress instructed Jay to give up American demands for navigation of the Mississippi in exchange for Spanish assistance in the war, the Spanish refused. Although Jay was privately relieved that the Spanish had rejected the offer of the Mississippi, he regarded Spanish conduct as an insult to himself and his country. He regarded French conduct as only slightly less insulting because he did not believe that France had done all that an ally should have done to aid his mission.

When Franklin called Jay to Paris to join him in peace negotiations with the British, Jay was seething at both France and Spain and thus eager to defy Congress's instructions that the commissioners keep the French allies fully informed about America's negotiations with the British and abide by French advice in making any final agreement. Thus, Jay refused to accept the advice of the French foreign minister, the Comte de Vergennes, that Jay and Franklin should open formal negotiations with the British envoy immediately, even though the envoy's credentials were addressed to the American colonies rather than the independent United States. Jay forced Franklin to join him in demanding new credentials for the British delegate that would recognize American independence prior to any negotiations. Jay did succeed in getting new credentials, but they did little more than the old ones to recognize American independence, and the process caused a major delay in the negotiations during which Britain strengthened its negotiating hand by defeating a French and Spanish attack on Gibraltar.

Jay's stubbornness in negotiations went even further when he heard that Vergennes' secretary had left Paris on a secret mission to London. Jay concluded that the French were negotiating separately with Britain to the detriment of American border claims and fishing rights on the Grand Banks. Without informing Franklin, he sent his own messenger to the British asking them to reject any proposals by the French that would adversely affect the United States.

When John Adams arrived in Paris shortly afterward to join his fellow peace commissioners, he supported Jay against Franklin's desire for a less-hostile policy toward France. The outvoted Franklin loyally put aside his own doubts and joined Jay and Adams in reopening peace negotiations without informing the French or seeking their advice. In the end, Jay, Franklin, and Adams secured a very favorable preliminary agreement that recognized American independence and extended the nation's borders to the Mississippi River. Technically, the agreement would not go into effect until formal treaties had been made with all participants in the war. But it clearly signaled the end of the American contribution to the war effort. The commissioners not only violated Congress's instructions to keep the French informed and abide by their advice, but they also came close to violating America's treaty agreement not to make a separate peace without the consent of France.

Jay went further even than that. Out of his intense distrust of Spain and France, he inserted an article that he tried to keep secret from France even after the commissioners revealed the preliminary agreement to Vergennes. The article provided that the border of Florida with the United States would be further north if the British retained Florida than it would if Spain regained title to the area.

Vergennes and the American Congress were both chagrined at the way in which the commissioners, under Jay's leadership, had defied their French allies. However, Vergennes was impressed by the preliminary agreement's terms and grateful that the withdrawal of the Americans gave him an excuse to push Spain toward peace without delivering on the French promise to Spain to keep fighting until the Spanish retrieved Gibraltar. In 1783, the French, Spanish, British, and Americans all signed the formal treaty that incorporated America's preliminary peace agreement and ended the war.

Although the peace terms America received were astonishingly generous, historians have long debated whether the United States could have had an even more favorable border with Canada if Jay had not delayed negotiations until the British had improved their bargaining position by defeating the assault on Gibraltar. Jay, Adams, and historians who defend them argue that only by defying the French, whose interest it was to buy off Spanish insistence on Gibraltar by offering concessions to Spanish interests in North America, did the American achieve the generous terms that they did. Even to Jay's defenders, however, the secret article on the Florida border seemed a gratuitous insult to America's allies and a misreading of the potential British threat to the United States after the war. It was another of those instances in which Jay let personal pique at supposed insults to his dignity and honor override his usual cool judgment and moderation.

Jay returned home to a hero's welcome. The generosity of the peace terms and Vergennes' moderate reaction to the preliminary agreement overrode the impulse of some Congressmen to pass a resolution condemning the commission's defiance of France and Congressional instructions. Congress then proceeded to appoint Jay as secretary for foreign affairs under the recently adopted Articles of Confederation, replacing his old friend, Robert R. Livingston. As foreign secretary, he received reports from Adams and Jefferson, America's ministers to Britain and France, respectively, that the European powers were treating American interests with contempt. Consequently, Jay chaffed at the inability of the United States to retaliate under the weak Confederation government.

After Alexander Hamilton and James Madison had failed in several attempts to gain the unanimous Congressional vote necessary to impose a tariff on foreign trade, Jay despaired of gaining the national revenue and trade leverage that he could use to secure American goals by independent action. He decided that he would have to trade away some goals to win others. Thus, in 1786 he agreed with Spanish minister Diego de Gardoqui that the United States would give up the right to navigate the Mississippi for 30 years in exchange for a Spanish trade treaty and a mutual guarantee of one another's territory in the Western Hemisphere. Such a commercial treaty would lock in the beneficial terms on which the United States was already conducting its trade with Spain. In addition, the mutual guarantee of territory might exert pressure against British occupation of several Great Lakes posts on American territory. When Jay broached the possibility of this Spanish treaty to Congress, however, Southerners were so outraged at Jay's willingness to abandon the Mississippi that they blocked any further negotiations. Many Southerners and Westerners distrusted Jay ever after.

Jay was saved from further foreign policy humiliations when the Constitutional Convention of 1787 created a new and stronger federal government. Jay was not a member of the Convention because he was busy with his duties as foreign secretary under the old government. Nevertheless, he helped secure ratification by joining James Madison and Alexander Hamilton to write the foreign policy sections of their classic defense of the new Constitution, *The Federalist Papers*. Once the states had ratified the Constitution and George Washington was elected president, Washington appointed John Jay to be the first Chief Justice of the Supreme Court.

As Chief Justice, Jay rendered several decisions that were critical to the power of the federal government. He also ran for governor of New York and demonstrated his character by discouraging his backers from extralegal challenges after a partisan election commission secured his defeat by disqualifying the returns of three counties. From his position as Chief Justice he continued to advise Washington on foreign affairs and wrote the first draft of Washington's Neutrality Proclamation after war broke out between Great Britain and Revolutionary France in 1793. When British violations of American neutral rights during that conflict brought the United States to the brink of war, Jay accepted Washington's invitation to go as a special envoy to London to negotiate a settlement. In doing so, Jay stepped into a maelstrom of partisan combat.

Former Secretary of State Thomas Jefferson and House leader James Madison, along with many of their friends in Congress who were coming to be known as Republicans, had long advocated commercial retaliation against Great Britain. They supported trade restrictions not only to force the British to respect American neutral rights, but also to make them abandon the occupied forts on the Great Lakes and to open their West Indies to American shipping on terms similar to those that had existed when America had been part of the British Empire. Secretary of the Treasury Alexander Hamilton and his so-called Federalist advocates, including John Jay, wanted desperately to avoid a conflict with Great Britain that might interrupt the extensive flow of British imports and the tariff revenue the federal government derived from them. Tariff revenue supported the whole financial system that Hamilton was using to strengthen the federal government.

Upon Jay's appointment as special envoy to London, he immediately sided with Hamilton in advising Congress against the measures of commercial retaliation that Jefferson and Madison insisted were necessary to allow America to negotiate from a position of strength. Instead, Jay relied on his best conciliatory manner, willingness to compromise, and the implicit threat that war would inevitably follow if no agreement could be found. The Jay Treaty that resulted was only a partial success. The British did agree to evacuate the Great Lakes posts and to open their West Indies to American ships, although they conceded the West Indies trade on terms so onerous that the U.S. Senate ultimately rejected that article. The British also promised to compensate American ship owners for some of the most egregious of British seizures. However, Jay could not get British recognition of America's claims to neutral rights or compensation for slaves carried away by the British during the Revolution. Neither could he avoid conceding the right of a neutral commission to force repayment of the debts contracted by Americans to British creditors before and during the Revolution. Moreover, by agreeing not to interfere with British trade for 10 years, Jay gave away the right of commercial retaliation, the one lever with which the Republicans thought they could extort a proper respect for neutral rights and other concessions from the British.

Republicans roundly attacked Jay and his treaty. They accused him of purposely selling out American interests to protect Hamilton's corrupt financial system and to support monarchical Britain against democratic France. They held mass meetings and submitted petitions to Washington to get him to refuse ratification of the treaty. When that failed, they flooded Congress with petitions to refuse the monetary appropriations necessary to implement the treaty. The Federalists at first defended Jay and his treaty only tepidly by saying that at least Jay had prevented a ruinous war. As they saw the challenge that Republicans were mounting, however, they turned to similar meetings to defend the treaty and barely succeeded in implementing it. Thus did Jay's foreign policy help expand the Federalists and Republicans from mere factions within Congress to semipermanent organized popular parties.

Jay returned from England in 1795 to find that he had been elected governor of New York. He served two terms, rejected reappointment as Chief Justice of the Supreme Court, and retired to his estate in Bedford, New York, in 1802 where he died 27 years later.

For a man so devoted to conciliation and compromise, Jay stirred enormous controversy in his service to American foreign affairs. His defiance of French interests in negotiating with Britain during the Revolution, his offer to temporarily sacrifice navigation of the Mississippi in his attempt to win Spanish support during his tenure as secretary for foreign affairs, and his compromises with Britain in the Jay Treaty all stirred fierce passions in his day, Jay responded to most of this criticism with restraint and dignity, and thus helped stimulate a spirit of civility that was and is vital to the making of a democratic foreign policy.

BIBLIOGRAPHICAL ESSAY

The Jay Papers at Columbia University constitute the largest extant collection of Jay correspondence and manuscripts. The largest collection of printed documents concerning Jay is found in H. P. Johnston (ed.), *Correspondence and Public Papers of John Jay*. 4 vols. (1890–1893). *John Jay: The Making of a Revolutionary: Unpublished Papers, 1745–1780* (1975), and *John Jay: Winning the Peace: Unpublished Papers, 1780–1784* (1980), both edited by Richard B. Morris, are excellent supplements to Johnston's work. A good multiarchival study of Jay's diplomacy is Samuel Flagg Bemis, *Jay's Treaty: A Study in Commerce and Diplomacy*, rev. ed. (1962).

Jerald A. Combs's *The Jay Treaty: Political Battleground of the Founding Fathers* (1970), sets Jay's diplomacy in a political context. The standard biography of Jay is Frank Monaghan's *John Jay: Defender of Liberty* (1935). Richard B. Morris's *The Peacemakers: The Great Powers and American Independence* (1965) is excellent on Jay and his diplomacy during the American Revolution.

Jerald A. Combs

THOMAS JEFFERSON (1743–1826)

Served 1790–1793
Appointed by President George Washington
No party designation upon appointment

Thomas Jefferson was born on April 13 (New Style), 1743 in Shadwell, Virginia, to Peter Jefferson, a county leader and self-taught surveyor. Peter's wife, Jane Randolph Jefferson, contributed her own distinguished family name to Thomas's legacy. One of eight children born to this marriage, Thomas received a classical education. After extended tutoring in Greek and Latin, he entered the College of William and Mary in 1760, where he became a dedicated and disciplined student. Jefferson especially remembered William Small, adept in science and mathematics, as an influential teacher during his two years at college and George Wythe, a distinguished attorney under whom he read law from 1762–1767.

Called to the bar in 1767, Jefferson left Williamsburg to begin his practice. An assiduous researcher though an indifferent public speaker, he handled many cases involving land titles. Elected from Albemarle County to the Virginia House of Burgesses in 1768, he quickly demonstrated his support for those who were challenging British authority to legislate for the American colonies. He formally expressed his hardening attitudes in 1774 when he wrote "A Summary View of the Rights of British America," a widely circulated disquisition that led the Virginia legislature to elect him a delegate to the Second Continental Congress. He arrived in Philadelphia in June 1775, ready to defend measures pointing toward independence.

Appointed by the Congress to a committee of five in 1775 to compose a statement explaining why a break with Great Britain was justified, Jefferson himself wrote the first draft. Most portions of the draft were modified by his colleagues, but not one word was changed of his great declaration: "We hold these truths to be self-evident; that all men are created equal; that they are endowed by their creator with certain inalienable rights; that among these are life, liberty and the pursuit of happiness; that to secure these rights, governments are instituted among men, deriving their just powers from the consent of the governed." His succinct statement presenting the concepts of inviolable rights and natural law, a convention of the day for enlightened thinkers, stood as a beacon to future generations seeking to establish democratic and egalitarian institutions.

Jefferson returned home in October 1776, where he worked with a will in the Virginia House of Burgesses to abolish primogeniture and entail. He also supported legislation requiring a complete separation of church and state and educational reforms that would encourage people to seek an education appropriate to their desire and ability. With his reputation building, Jefferson was twice elected governor of Virginia, for 1780 and 1781. Jefferson served conscientiously and well under the most trying circumstances. He returned to the Continental Congress as a Virginia delegate in December 1782. In considering America's future as an independent nation, Jefferson championed adding future Western territories as states equal to the original 13, with but few hurdles to that status. One critical condition required that slavery be abolished in the territories previous to admission to the Union. The Northwest Ordinance of 1784 stands as a monument to Jefferson's vision for governing the territory north of the Ohio and incorporating it into the national domain.

Jefferson's reputation as a spokesman for liberty, his wide learning, his interest in science, and his undoubted commitment to his new nation commended him as a replacement for Benjamin Franklin as minister to France. Though his four years in Paris (1785–1789) proved intellectually and emotionally appealing, there were few incentives to encourage France to conclude commercial treaties with the weak Articles of Confederation government, though France made concessions to American trade in tobacco and whale oil. But France would not agree to punish the commercial raids of the Barbary pirates, so damaging to American commerce carriers. Jefferson witnessed the beginning of the great revolution in France, even serving as an adviser to Lafayette and other moderates, a unique and influential experience in his life.

Meanwhile, James Madison convinced President George Washington that he should bring Jefferson into his administration as secretary of state. In Jefferson, the president secured a man with deep convictions. Jefferson was committed to the idea that an agrarian nation was most likely to be a nation of political virtue, to the expansion of liberty through expansion of the American empire, to the destruction of tyranny and its handmaiden monarchy, and to the idea that Great Britain had become a permanent enemy of the United States. France, he believed, had embarked on a road leading to an enlargement of human liberty, and thus could become an international colleague. Jefferson detested centralized governmental authority, particularly if wielded by his enemies. With no opportunity to participate in the constitutional debates because of his service in France, he returned home wishing primarily to add a bill of rights to the new constitution.

When Jefferson assumed his position in 1790 as the first secretary of state, his duties were not at all clear. Although he knew his first task concerned watch-care over the nation's external affairs, Jefferson also realized that the Federal Constitution granted the president unique responsibilities in that area. Also, because the Department of State had folded into its duties many functions that should logically have been assigned to a home department—such as supervising the mint, publishing the laws, taking the census, and supervising the Great Seal—Jefferson could not be certain how much of his energy might be devoted to domestic cares. Finally, it could not be known if Washington intended to consult cabinet members only in their special areas of expertise.

As it happened, Washington, a cautious and prudent leader, usually enlisted the opinions of all his cabinet officers on the major policy questions confronting him, often taking courses of action that deeply pained those cabinet officials whose recommendations were not accepted within their designated areas of responsibility. Washington's method of consultation and decision making invited intense competition within the cabinet where egos were large and convictions ran deep. Washington's administrative style undeniably contributed to intense contests over policy that arose between Jefferson and Secretary of the Treasury Alexander Hamilton.

Jefferson's experiences in France had been a matter of wide interest to his countrymen, raising questions about his objectivity toward France. His support for the early French republican governments has often led to assertions that Jefferson became a Francophile, one who lost his perspective on events in France and the relationship his own nation should maintain with France. This view has some merit but misses the essential Jefferson. Jefferson was a man in love with his own country, one who believed that his young nation represented progress and political virtue on the international scene. Like good nationalists everywhere, his first consideration centered on nurturing relationships and policies that could be of advantage to his own nation. France was powerful, centrally located, hostile to Britain, well disposed to the United States, and influential with Spain. Jefferson intended to use France's power and predispositions to his own nation's benefit. He hoped that France might become both a partner and a protector of the United States against the Great Satan, England. Perhaps "Great Satan" is too strong a term for Jefferson's view of England, but not by much. As he wrote to James Madison in 1789, Americans must remember that England "has moved heaven, earth and hell to exterminate us in war, has insulted us in all her councils in peace, shut her doors to us in every part where her interest would admit, libeled us in foreign nations, [and] endeavored to poison them against the reception of our most precious commodities. . . ." Jefferson witnessed the old enemy of 1776 stubbornly retaining control of large sections of the Northwest Territory granted to America in the treaty of peace, an extraordinary infringement of American sovereignty.

In the world of Oceania, the English seemed determined to grant American vessels only limited access to British and empire markets, even though their goods had captured a lion's share of American import markets following the end of the American Revolutionary War. Britain's haughty refusal to exchange diplomatic representatives with the Articles of Confederation government in the 1780s seemed a logical though irritating extension of its policy of hostility toward the United States. Clearly, some extraordinary event or a powerful counterweight to Great Britain must be found if America were to redeem its territory, expand and protect its international trade, and gain the dignity its self-perception and political maturity demanded. In Jefferson's mind, France seemed best suited to play the role of counterweight to England, and hopefully to Spain as well.

But Jefferson, a subtle and calculating man, saw another great hope for the United States to achieve its central objectives. If Europe went to war, as seemed likely to Jefferson, golden opportunities might appear to gain American territory and expand American trade. Wartime circumstances might help the United States gain its territory held by England to the north and to add lands controlled by Spain in the southwest. Because half of America's legitimate territory was still virtually controlled by these two powers in 1790, the primary task of the new government in foreign affairs must be to redeem that territory. Jefferson therefore placed his confidence in "jackal diplomacy," waiting for one's enemies to occupy themselves in war, then dashing in at an opportune moments to secure the prizes. Jefferson had learned much about the norms of nation-state conduct in the brutal eighteenth century.

Even before Jefferson assumed his office, President Washington had moved to build a constructive relationship with Great Britain. Washington sent a New York archconservative, Gouverneur Morris, to London to make discreet inquiries about opening diplomatic relations between America and Britain. As both parties knew, the United States showed promise of becoming Britain's best customer. Also, because the Americans could be very troublesome to British North America in times of international difficulty, it seemed both to Washington and Morris that the British government might now be ready to exchange diplomats and thus establish regular avenues of communication.

British wheels moved at measured pace, however, for diplomatic recognition and good-faith bargaining implied that it must be ready to consider abandoning its posts in the American Northwest Territory, stop encouraging the Indians to take positions hostile to the U.S. government, consider the question of compensation for thousands of American slaves illegally carried off by British officers during the Revolutionary War, and respond to U.S. requests that British home and Caribbean ports be opened to American goods on reciprocal terms. Each question involved some pain, for the abandoned Indian tribes, for the British treasury, or for British merchants who would certainly not welcome added American competition in the treasured West Indies. Gouverneur Morris found the British blowing hot or cold toward his mission, depending on whether England might soon become involved in war with Spain over land and fishing rights in the Pacific Northwest (Nootka Sound crisis). Morris finally reported no success to the president, a report that came to Jefferson's hand as he assumed office.

Jefferson viewed the Morris report as providing an opportunity to guide American policy toward a greater commercial independence of England and to establish closer ties with France. Under James Madison's prodding, Congress had for some months been debating the question of how to impress the British that the new nation deserved respect. Americans believed their trade should be given access to British ports on the same terms that British trade received in American ports. Madison favored punitive commercial legislation to get British attention. For one, he had been urging that tariff and tonnage duties be placed on British merchandise equal in value to charges the British placed on incoming American goods. Also, Madison asked, why not encourage the growth of the American merchant marine by lowering duties on goods imported in American ships?

As Jefferson prepared to wade into Congressional battles over trade, diplomatic recognition, territorial redemption, and compensation for past losses to England, he did so against a background of concerns raised by his energetic and brilliant cabinet rival, Treasury Secretary Alexander Hamilton. Hamilton—immigrant, Revolutionary soldier, and friend of President Washington—was no less a nationalist than Jefferson. Hamilton's priorities were establishment of a sound national credit, tying persons of wealth to the wheels of an energetic central government, and promotion of an international trade that could generate revenues for the national treasury, thus expediting debt reduction. Hamilton also believed deeply that economic expansion for a young nation demanded access to credit markets. England held potential loan resources and therefore must be accommodated. England also possessed a powerful fighting navy; if American trade and merchant marine were to prosper, the goodwill of England must be assured.

Hamilton became deeply uneasy when Jefferson submitted to Congress the report on Morris's ill-received mission to Great Britain. Congressmen expressed considerable ire and made several attempts to pass the kind of punitive commercial legislation against Britain that Hamilton believed might provoke British retaliation toward the United States. After considerable debate, the Congress took moderate actions in 1791 to encourage Great Britain to open its ports on more generous terms and to stimulate the growth of an American merchant marine. This debate was well reported to the British government. To sidetrack potentially serious punitive trade actions by the United States, the British government revealed to Hamilton and others that it would soon appoint a minister to the American government. On the American side, this intense debate and widely differing opinions led in part to the formation of political alignments that in time became political parties. Because Jefferson realized that bringing U.S. policies more fully into harmony with France might be no easy task, he thought it imperative that the United States guide or coerce British policy into more agreeable channels.

With the arrival from London in November 1791 of England's first minister, a supercilious young man of 27 named George Hammond, Jefferson hoped the process of resolving outstanding differences with Britain could begin. Britain hoped to recover the prewar debts Americans owed its merchants and financiers, debts that it charged were unpaid because the states had illegally put barriers in the way of collection. Britain also intended to recover the property of Loyalists seized following the peace and in violation of the peace treaty. Until these treaty violations were made right, Britain insisted, Americans had no business demanding that they evacuate American territory to the North, that they award compensation for slaves carried off in violation of Article VII of the treaty of peace, and that they give wider trading rights to Americans in British ports. Let the Americans act honorably first, and Britain might then be willing to consider American grievances.

Minister Hammond's instructions made clear the hard line the British intended to take. Hammond had authorization only to discuss differences. When the Americans raised the question of British evacuation of their frontier posts clearly positioned on American territory, Hammond was instructed to suggest the threatening possibility that an Indian barrier state might be created, one that would stretch from east of the Mississippi and north of the Ohio, possibly extending as far as the forts at Lake Champlain. Jefferson queried in turn what possible explanation might Britain have for refusing to abandon its frontier posts, an occupation in clear violation of the treaty of peace and a grievous assault on American sovereignty. Hammond, a lightweight, decided to take the offensive against Jefferson and his government's persistent complaints. In a lengthy note, which he smugly informed the British Foreign Office was so insightful and carefully crafted that there could be no "probability of cavil and contradiction," he indicted the U.S. government on the major British grievances.

In seven weeks of concentrated labor, Jefferson prepared a spirited, tightly argued, and effective response, perhaps his most astute paper while secretary of state. Taking advantage of Hammond's carelessness in ignoring historical context when stating Britain's case, or in overlooking Congressional actions that contradicted his assertions, or by arguing that American actions had only followed British violations of the treaty of peace, Jefferson managed to present America's grievances in a favorable light.

Alexander Hamilton lamented Jefferson's missive, falsely assuring Hammond that Jefferson's note had not been read by Washington and did not reflect his views or those of the other cabinet secretaries. Hamilton's backstage knifing of administration policy ended all immediate possibility of serious negotiations with Great Britain. In a contemptuous gesture, Jefferson's note was never even answered by the Foreign Office.

Jefferson's expectation continued that the diplomatic playing field might be leveled by a European war, one that placed England and Spain in threatened positions. Very early his expectations seemed realizable. News had arrived in 1789, before he became secretary of state, that England and Spain were circling each other over a far-off trading post on the western end of Vancouver Island, a godforsaken place called Nootka Sound. Actually, as Prime Minister William Pitt saw the situation, the issue with Spain was far greater than Nootka Sound. The issue raised was an old one: whether Spain might be allowed to forbid other nations to establish posts both in North and South America, in unoccupied areas, based only on a papal proclamation of 1493 and the Treaty of Tordesillas concluded with Portugal in 1494. Spain and Portugal's assertion of authority in the New World had been under challenge for almost three centuries, but Spain in particular found it difficult to admit its claims were ludicrous.

Even as the Washington administration settled into its duties in New York in 1789, a small coterie of British fur traders busied themselves in turning Nootka Sound into a trading base. Outraged by this British impertinence, the viceroy of New Spain sent a military party that shut down the settlement, seized two ships, and clapped their crews into a Mexican prison. The British lion, having recovered its nerve following the disaster of the American Revolutionary War, quickly made clear to Spain that it had better back down or severe consequences would follow. Spain, seeking support, found its family ally France well occupied on internal politics as the great French Revolution developed. What should Spain do? Bluff might be a dangerous game given the signals England sent of preparation for war. To fight courted disaster. Yet to retreat invited humiliation and diminished status.

As Jefferson considered the crisis, it seemed the answer to his long-held hopes. If war came, Spain might be willing to allow Western Americans access to the Mississippi River as far as the Gulf of Mexico in return for American neutrality. Britain, on the other hand, might back down on the Northwest posts if America remained only an observer. The administration began to consider its options if war came and Britain determined to attack Spanish Louisiana. To attack Louisiana, British troops would want to cross American territory in the West. What should the administration do if a transit request came from the British government? Hamilton advised Washington to yield, join in an attack on the Spanish, seize New Orleans, and defer the question of the Northwest frontier posts to a more propitious time. Jefferson's advice reflected his more cautious nature and his fundamental belief in waiting for opportune moments to occur. To Washington he counseled maintaining silence to a British request for transit rights; if British troops crossed American soil without permission, America should simply place this grievance on hold to be used when European events found England in a vulnerable position.

Neither Jefferson's nor Hamilton's advice proved necessary, for Spain decided its only choice was acquiescence to a British ultimatum. Nonetheless, Jefferson thought that circumstances were such that Spain might well be willing to consider the U.S. position on its southern border and be responsive to reasons why Americans should have virtually unhindered access to use of the Mississippi. In his thoughts on these questions, placed in his Instruction to his joint commissioners to Spain, William Carmichael and William Short, we see Jefferson as the complete nationalist. In the first part of his Instructions, he advanced reasons why Spain should be willing to acknowledge the ancient Georgia boundary of 31 degrees latitude as the southern boundary of the United States in 1789. His tortured and certainly extraordinary interpretation of a series of treaties affecting that boundary since the granting of the original charter for Georgia made it easy for Spain to believe it was negotiating with a dishonest and aggressive government.

Jefferson expanded America's case with Spain by his assertion that Americans had a "natural" right to use of the river. Historian Albert K. Weinberg has nicely described Jefferson's assertion of a "natural" right, unknown to Europeans, but certainly apt for America's needs. Jefferson argued that an upriver nation had a right to use the rivers to the sea, even if they flowed through the territory of another nation. This peculiar claim was followed by another, namely that "It is a principle that the right to a thing gives a right to the means without which it could not be used. . . ." The point here was that because Americans had a natural right to use the Mississippi, they therefore had a related right to land their goods at some transshipment point, such as New Orleans, so that their goods could find their way into international commerce. One suspects that Jefferson was himself not completely convinced by his arguments, but he knew that a vigorous presentation of the case might soften Spain for future American claims; he knew as well that his Western constituency would be pleased by his invocation of natural rights on their behalf. Jefferson tried to strengthen the American case by instructing Carmichael and Short to protest in very firm tones concerning continuing Spanish intrigue among the Creek, Choctaw, and Chickasaw Indians in the Southwest, thus adding weight to the American case.

International events brought the Spanish negotiations to an unwelcome stop. In an astonishing reversal of alignments, Britain and Spain allied in the face of a revolutionary France. Events seemed to race out of control in 1792 and 1793. In an effort to save monarchy in France, Austrian and Prussian troops tried to invade France in 1792, but were thrown back by a French nation-in-arms at the battle of Valmy and a series of lesser actions. French armies then turned aggressively to take Brussels and the Austrian Netherlands in autumn of 1792. Would France now use its new position to launch an invasion of Britain? The British moved quickly to build a coalition of powers to thwart perceived French ambitions. Louis XVI was beheaded on January 21, 1793, a final, alarming signal that the French Revolution had become a danger to monarchy throughout Europe. Only a few days later France declared war against Spain, the Netherlands, and Great Britain. On May 25, 1793, Spain formally joined hands with Britain in a treaty of alliance, linking arms with Prussia and Austria as well in the First Coalition. Thus began that great series of wars that did not end until the final exile of Napoleon at St. Helena in the South Atlantic and the settlements at the Congress of Vienna in June of 1815.

Jefferson's long-term intuition had proven to be correct: there was to be a great war in Europe, but its initial alignments presented a startling picture. Who could have anticipated that the Family Compact between France and Spain would be broken and that Spain and Britain, long bitter enemies, would become allies? But the incredible had happened and thus Jefferson's Spanish negotiations had to end, at least during his term in office. Spain need hardly back down before the small American Atlantic power while supported by its mighty British ally.

The European circumstances Jefferson envisioned in fact came about in 1795 with the end of the Anglo-Spanish alliance. Fearful of British revenge, aware that England and the United States had concluded Jay's Treaty signaling a mild rapprochement, Spain capitulated to virtually every American demand in the Treaty of San Lorenzo. Concluded by Thomas Pinckney of South Carolina on October 27, 1795, the treaty redounded to the reputations of Pinckney, Secretary of State Timothy Pickering, and President Washington. But to Jefferson must be given great credit for setting the negotiations with Spain in motion and for taking the long view that great gains for America might soon be made from impending European disasters.

Once the European powers locked in combat, tremors were felt throughout the world. How to find a safe harbor in the storm became the primary concern of Washington, who quickly set out from Mount Vernon for Philadelphia in mid-April of 1793 after news arrived of the war's onset. Washington had little doubt that his weak nation should remain neutral, so he was soon gratified to learn that his chief counselors concurred in this sentiment.

Neutrality, however, is not a concept and condition with fixed rules for nation-state conduct in time of war. Belligerents and neutrals alike recognize the wide latitude for actions and interpretations of properly neutral conduct, with no lack of precedents for justifying their course or for criticizing the conduct of another. The crucial question then becomes: What type of neutrality will best serve the interests of the nation?

In keeping with his usual procedure, Washington turned to all his cabinet officers for advice, submitting to them a list of 13 questions. Boiled down, they focused on whether and how to receive a minister from the French Republic and to what extent the treaties of alliance and commerce, concluded with monarchical France in 1778, remained valid under France's Republican regime. The two questions were interlocked, for to receive a prospective French minister with full honors strongly implied that the United States recognized the continuing legitimacy of the wartime treaties of 1778.

Hamilton, who despised the democratic thrust of the French Revolution and regarded Republican France as a destructive beast let loose on civilization, thought the present occasion a propitious one for cutting loose the French millstone. In particular he thought it awkward if not positively dangerous that the United States seemingly remained committed to the defense of the French West Indies by treaty. If honored, the United States must certainly find itself at war with England, for Hamilton the ultimate disaster. Hamilton therefore urged, in Cabinet and in writing, the qualified reception of a French minister and thus a virtual neutralization of the alliance treaty. As Hamilton argued, America's primary obligation to France was linked to the monarchy. That monarchy had been overthrown in disturbing circumstances. Furthermore, even a cursory reading of the treaty of alliance indicated that it was a defensive treaty. Could such a treaty be held as binding upon the United States when France was well known to have been the aggressor in the wars now beginning in Europe?

Jefferson's views seem more judicious than Hamilton's. Neutrality, to be sure, must be the course pursued by the United States, he counseled. But why pursue neutrality unfriendly to that nation, whose contributions during the American Revolutionary War had been decisive in achieving victory though financially ruinous to France, a nation that had now turned its back on monarchy as had the United States. With a mental reservation that the United States certainly must never defend the French West Indies, Jefferson pointed out that all political and military treaties had an awkward moment for the signatory powers. That moment had not yet arrived for the French–American defensive treaty, and thus it was not justifiable to seek means to escape the treaty, particularly during France's hour of crisis. Furthermore, every people had an inherent right to choose the form of government it wished, a principle that Americans could hardly deny; the French monarchy had been discarded, but the nation remained with whom the treaty had been negotiated. The new French minister, Edmond Genet, should therefore be received with full recognition of his diplomatic credentials.

Washington agreed with Jefferson and on April 22, 1793, issued a proclamation drafted by Chief Justice John Jay that, while not using the word *neutrality*, soon came to be known as Washington's Neutrality Proclamation. How would the powers receive this proclamation, particularly France who had claims on the United States as an ally? The initial answer, and a shaking one it was, seemed to be: with indignation. Minister Genet, sailing into Charleston with no word yet of Washington's Proclamation, assumed the United States intended to give France the widest latitude in bringing its captured British prizes into American ports, outfitting the prizes as French privateers, and recruiting American citizens to man those privateers. Furthermore, being caught up in a self-absorbed frame of mind, he proved unable to see why the U.S. government might question his commissioning and arming Americans to launch attacks on Spanish and English territories on the North American continent. Genet originally received considerable private encouragement from Jefferson, an extraordinarily indiscreet step he kept hidden from public view.

Genet's outrageous violations of American neutrality, his insolent remarks about Washington and Jefferson needing to get in tune with the sentiments of the American people, his erroneous interpretations of what the United States owed France through treaty, and his alarming attempts to turn the American people against their own government's neutrality policies all indicated that he must be recalled. Jefferson tried personally to calm Genet, but he would not listen. Finally, the Washington administration asked Genet's recall, a move Jefferson fully supported. A new French administration proved only too happy to recall this immature diplomatic firebrand. Fearing retribution from the French government, one not reluctant to separate heads from necks, Genet wisely settled in the United States. But he had done about as much damage to French–American relations as was possible in so short a time, and for this situation Jefferson was not entirely blameless.

Britain did not view with detachment Genet's activities in seizing British merchant vessels in American waters, bringing them into American ports, condemning them in prize courts he appointed, arming the ships, sending them out to seize other British merchant vessels, and recruiting Americans as soldiers to drive Spain out of Louisiana. Jefferson assured British Minister George Hammond that Genet's activities were in contravention of the administration's neutrality policy, but until passage of the Neutrality Act of June 5, 1794, little could be done legally to prosecute those cooperating with Genet.

Real difficulties with Britain did not occur over Genet's short-lived mission. The knotty problems arose because Britain determined that France and French colonies must not be fed and otherwise supplied by American vessels or those of any other neutral nation. Sensing the possibility of a long war and in possession of a fighting fleet superior to France or any other power, Britain moved expeditiously to direct high seas trade into British-controlled channels. Its de facto policies were formalized by two orders-in-council, the first dated June 8, 1793, which ordered its naval commanders to direct all ships carrying corn or flour and bound for France into British ports. Once in port the cargoes were to be paid for on a fair basis. Such a directive had two major advantages for Britain: while not going so far as to identify food as contraband, the food nevertheless would find its way into English warehouses. In addition, neutral shippers not happy with British direction of their commerce might complain little if British compensation proved to be fair.

Britain's second order-in-council, that of November 6, 1793, raised much more serious concerns for the Jefferson and the Washington administration. This directive instructed British captains to bring in for adjudication all ships carrying products of French colonies or carrying provisions for those same colonies. For America this order became threatening because American merchants had been allowed to carry on a fairly extensive trade with the French West Indies in time of peace. Britain's Rule of the War of 1756, by now becoming a firm principle, had stipulated that Britain not allow neutrals to trade in belligerent ports that had been closed to them in peacetime. Americans protested that England's second order-in-council went beyond the Rule of 1756 in that it forbade noncontraband trade to Americans in French ports that had been open to Americans in peacetime. England backed off a few months later by stipulating that only ships bound for European ports with French West Indian produce were to be seized. A little breathing spell seemed to be at hand.

Yet the orders-in-council constituted a storm warning for the years ahead. Britain had the navy to enforce its policies, however fair or unfair, yet France had certain claims on the United States through the treaties of Commerce and Alliance of 1778. Specifically, the treaties stipulated that both powers adhered to the principle that neutral ships neutralized the goods on board, except for contraband. What if France insisted that the United States defend this principle against Britain? Furthermore, the treaties provided that if France opened its ports to neutrals in time of war, both powers were obliged to, in effect, ignore the British Rule of 1756 and insist that neutral ships be allowed to trade between belligerent and nonblockaded ports in all merchandise except contraband. This provision constituted a direct challenge to the British, who had no intention of observing such stipulations convenient to the prosperity of small navy powers and of its French enemy.

Fortunately, French self-interest could not support insisting on any treaty provisions that might provide Britain an excuse to rid the ocean trade routes of neutral commerce carriers. France's empire simply could not be maintained without its lifeline, the neutral merchant marine. For the moment, therefore, the United States need not concern itself that France might call on it to honor such a treaty commitment. Yet circumstances in wartime change rapidly, so France might insist on its treaty rights from its New World ally. Jefferson was forced to consider these possibilities, as well as ominous signs that the French Revolutionary governments were showing clear intent that they intended to control ever more rigidly neutral trade in French ports and to give decided rate preference to goods in French bottoms. Fortunately for Jefferson's term as secretary of state, a second great crisis with France was avoided. As his time in office drew to an end, however, the United States became increasingly vulnerable at sea to the determination and whims of Britain. The United States might have a formidable merchant marine, but its fighting navy hardly gave Britain pause.

Jefferson dealt with two other foreign matters of importance as secretary. The first concerned repayment to France of the American Revolutionary indebtedness, a matter that could not be addressed in the Confederation period because the money for repayment simply wasn't available. France was not at first impatient to recover the 35,000,000 livres owed it, but the financial needs of the Revolutionary government as it planned to attack Spain's Florida and Louisiana territories put the American indebtedness in a new light. Washington's administration had already begun systematic repayment of the debt, certainly a mandatory act given Hamilton's determination to establish the good credit of the United States in European money markets.

Edmond Genet's mission brought the debt issue into sharper public focus, for Genet was instructed to seek advance payments on the debt. France's request was a proper one. This question became enmeshed in the struggle between Hamilton and Jefferson for control of policy. Hamilton, not wishing to help revolutionary France in any way, advised that the United States simply maintain its schedule of payments. Jefferson advised making advanced payments for 1793, but if not, at least give France a courteous explanation. Washington blended the advice, refusing advance payments but giving France the explanation Jefferson advised.

Jefferson also took to heart the plight of unfortunate Americans taken captive by the Barbary pirates and made virtual slaves in the wretched prisons of the Dey of Algiers. During his time as American minister in Paris, Jefferson advocated that the powers trading in the Mediterranean maintain a constant blockade of the key Barbary ports, to squeeze them until they went out of business. But his own country did not cooperate in the plan, so the United States, throughout the 1780s, continued to suffer at the hands of the pirates, who demanded protection money for not attacking American vessels and ransom money for captured seamen.

The situation was a cruel one; the only remedies were to pay up or to build a fighting navy that could take the action directly to the pirates. Shortly after becoming secretary of state, Jefferson argued again for creation of a league of maritime powers, suggesting as well that it was time for the United States to look to creation of a fighting navy. After due consideration, the Senate advised Washington in February of 1792 to consider construction of a navy when funds became available. In the meantime, however, it proposed continuing to pay tribute to the Dey of Algiers and to purchase ransom for captured Americans, both at knockdown prices the Dey was almost certain to refuse.

Late in March 1794, three months after Jefferson had left office, Congress authorized construction of a fighting navy, providing that peace was not soon concluded with Algeria. Peace was in fact purchased from Algeria in 1795, but by then the American navy was afloat. It became one of Jefferson's great satisfactions as president to turn this new navy on the Barbary pirates, punishing their conduct toward the American merchant marine with flashing guns and determined zeal.

As early as 1791, Jefferson had become tired of his life as secretary of state, a weariness that events did not lift. There were the constant battles with Hamilton over policy within the Cabinet and Congress, with Hamilton winning the contests all too often. As the policy battles heated up, beginning in 1791, Jefferson, a shy if not a reclusive man, personally suffered from the Congressional and personal attacks that came his way. Too, a man of conscience, Jefferson was troubled by his own questionable conduct in helping to bring journalist Philip Freneau to Philadelphia to publish a paper whose central purpose seemed to be to oppose Hamiltonian policies. Too often, as it turned out, Hamilton's recommendations became Washington's policies, so that Jefferson was in fact supporting a newspaper often disparaging to an administration of which he was a part. How long he could maintain in such a two-faced position remained a question. Washington, too, was troubled by Jefferson's relationship to the *National Gazette* and by rumors of Jefferson's ongoing political activities.

Nor was Jefferson pleased with his accomplishments while in office. He had, it is true, written distinguished state papers on the fisheries and commerce. But Spain and Britain had not given up their American territories and showed no intention of doing so. Relations with France were moving on an uncertain, unpromising course. War in Europe had taken a turn that made accomplishment of his goals impossible. He had good reason to suspect that Hamilton had poisoned the minds of British diplomats against him, making him ineffective in his negotiations with Britain. Washington, the father of his country and a man who saw himself above party, had, Jefferson believed, committed to the pro-British faction but was hardly even aware of it. Too, Washington's style of administration, of seeking advice from those both inside and outside the government, fed ambitions and seemingly made no man's advice worth more than any other's. All in all, Jefferson found himself in a highly uncomfortable position. He decided that he must plead the press of personal circumstances and withdraw from government. Despite Washington's pleas for reconsideration, Jefferson left office on the last day of 1793, to be replaced by another Virginian, Edmund Randolph.

Jefferson perhaps failed to see his contributions as secretary of state in their larger frame. To an office and department intended by Congress to be of first importance, Jefferson brought his own great reputation and talents; his presence confirmed the primacy of foreign affairs to the success of the new government and the secretaryship of state as the highest nonelective office in the land. By his conduct toward Republican France, Jefferson emphasized that ideology had its place in setting the tone in nation-state relations. He believed the world must become a better place, as well as a more secure one for the United States, when regimes triumphed whose principles were sympathetic to republicanism. This principle remains an enduring one in American foreign relations. Also, his threatening conduct toward Spain likely hastened the day of its withdrawal from the Southwest, signaling American intention to expand westward. Jefferson's policy positions, in many cases, were based on long-term considerations, reflecting both his thoroughgoing nationalism and his belief that self-inflicted European misfortunes meant American opportunities. In his view, when exploiting opportunities to aggrandize the United States, he was in reality an advocate for liberty.

Jefferson ran for president in 1796, while denying that he was doing so. Because he received fewer electoral votes than John Adams, he served as vice president from 1797 to 1801. These years were ones of intense political activity, with bitter accusations exchanged between the emerging Federalists and Republicans. Jefferson suffered deeply from Federalist charges that he had sold out his nation to French interests or that his private life had become a moral cesspool. Jefferson certainly believed poorly of his opponents, convincing himself the Federalists were contemptible lackeys of Great Britain, wishing a war with France to strengthen American ties with Britain. They intended, he believed, to aggressively enlarge the powers of the central government and thus destroy the personal liberties won so dearly during the Revolutionary years. He and his "great collaborator," James Madison, were active in organizing a network of interests and like-thinkers, which over time evolved into the Republican or Jeffersonian Party. When the Federalist "faction" overreached, tried to stimulate war fever over French conduct in the XYZ affair, and passed the Alien and Sedition Acts of 1798, the stage was set for a new round of protests against the Adams administration. Jefferson drafted the Kentucky Resolutions of 1798, claiming these acts were unconstitutional and should be resisted. His reasoning later served as justification for secessionists, nullifiers, and states' rights advocates.

A bitter presidential contest followed, exacerbated by the Quasi-War with France, 1798–1800. John Adams and Charles Cotesworth Pinckney were run for the highest offices by the Federalists whereas Jefferson and Aaron Burr were run by the Republicans. Few presidential elections have proven so perplexing. The Hamiltonian Federalists unsuccessfully conspired to get Pinckney more votes than Adams, bringing ruin on themselves. Jefferson and Burr had an electoral vote tie, so the election was thrown into the House of Representatives where Burr refused to recognize the public intent that he become vice president. It took 36 ballots and Hamilton's intervention to unravel the tie and see Jefferson elected president.

Jefferson had a Republican-dominated Congress to work with throughout his presidency, though success eventually stimulated the Republicans to quarrelsomeness within their ranks. Jefferson's highest moment as president came in 1803 when Napoleon Bonaparte decided to sell the entire Louisiana territory to the United States, rather than New Orleans, which was Jefferson's original goal. Jefferson, a believer in limited central government and a limited presidency as well, decided to ignore his serious doubts that as president he had constitutional authority to accept such a transfer. The purchase was a magnificent one, roughly doubling the national domain, and all for about 15 million dollars. Jefferson believed he had now secured an agricultural future for the American people.

His lowest moments occurred toward the end of his presidency. Not able to gain sufficient protection for American commercial vessels either from the warring French or British, Jefferson decided to take the drastic step of terminating trade with both belligerents. His high-stakes gamble became to wait and see which power came first, hat in hand, to grant American rights on the high seas and thus reopen American trade to that nation alone. For 14 months, American ports fell silent. The embargo's results: British and French merchants, particularly British, rushed in to fill the American trading void; Federalists revived as coastal merchants, once Jefferson's supporters, sank into economic despair; the federal government acted intrusively as it enforced antismuggling legislation; and the United States yielded the high seas to its tormentors. Jefferson feared, and rightly so, that policy makers in France and Britain might believe he had converted to Quaker politics. Jefferson's great experiment in economic coercion proved a decided failure, which he acknowledged by signing legislation ending the embargo just days before his presidency ended.

Jefferson returned to his beloved Monticello, where he actively supervised plantation activities. He continued his interest in science and in addition both planned and supervised establishment of the University of Virginia, a magnificent achievement. His reputation as the apostle of liberty has been questioned in recent decades as historians probed his direct involvement in the slave system. And his reputation for sterling character has been challenged by those who believe he had an extended personal relationship with his slave, Sally Hemmings. Jefferson gradually became less hopeful about his country as he watched the steady advance of commercial interests. Too, his personal debts became crushing. Some he had inherited. He had refused for many years to bring his income and expenditures into line. The embargo had added to his debts, and then a friend defaulted on a note Jefferson had endorsed. Jefferson even considered selling Monticello by lottery. A few months after he died on July 4, 1826, his home and slaves were sold to compensate his creditors. It is often noted that his onetime collaborator, later his competitor, and then his late-life correspondent, John Adams, died just hours after Jefferson.

Jefferson remains a towering figure over his own time and over American history. Never has the secretaryship of state been filled by a person of such immense talent and learning or one who so elegantly expressed the American ideals of individual rights, human equality, and confidence in the ability of well-informed citizens to govern themselves. Denied the opportunities to become a great secretary of state, Jefferson nonetheless proved himself an effective president and America's premier spokesman for liberty.

BIBLIOGRAPHICAL ESSAY

Insightful overviews of the early national period are found in Lawrence S. Kaplan's *Colonies into Nation: American Diplomacy, 1763–1801* Kaplan (1972) and Paul A. Varg's *Foreign Policies of the Founding Fathers* (1970). Forrest McDonald's *The Presidency of George Washington* McDonald (1974) ably presents the financial constraints on the Washington administration. Alexander DeConde's *The American Secretary of State* (1975) provides a useful introduction to the structure and duties of the office. All students of Jefferson must begin with Dumas Malone's masterful six-volume biography, *Jefferson and His Time* (1948–1981). Samuel Flag Bemis's essay on Jefferson in volume two of *The American Secretaries of State and Their Diplomacy* Bemis (1928) is still useful. Lawrence S. Kaplan's *Jefferson and France: An Essay on Politics and Political Ideas* Kaplan (1980) remains invaluable in understanding Jefferson. Norman K. Risjord's *Thomas Jefferson* (1994) is helpful, as is Doron S. Ben-Atar's *The Origins of Jeffersonian Commercial Policy and Diplomacy* Ben-Atar (1993). Volumes 16 through 20 of *The Papers of Thomas Jefferson* Boyd et al eds (1950–) (Julian P. Boyd, Charles T. Cullen, et. al, eds.) relate to Jefferson's service as secretary. A useful analysis is found in Walter Lafeber's *Jefferson and an American Foreign Policy*, chapter 12 in Peter S. Onuf (ed.), *Jeffersonian Legacies* Onuf ed. (1993).

Marvin Zahniser

FRANK B. KELLOGG
(1856–1937)

Served 1925–1929
Appointed by President Calvin Coolidge
Republican

Frank B. Kellogg occupied the office of secretary of state from 1925 until 1929, during the administration of President Calvin Coolidge. He began life under inauspicious circumstances. Had anyone considered his prospects in the beginning years of his life, that individual would have said at once that Kellogg would not, could not, go far. He was born in 1856 in Potsdam, St. Lawrence County, New York, and when eight years old, in the company of his family and other migrants, went out to the new and, from a distance, inviting farmland of Minnesota. The family farm did not prosper, and the life of the young man, a farmer as soon as he could work in the fields, was very difficult. Years later he described "the old, old story" of pioneering, the "far off and mysterious West, the railroad which he had never seen before, the steamship and the covered wagon on the prairies and the wilderness of the Northwest, the struggles in a wild and new land." He attended a one-room country school from his 9th to 14th year. Caught out on the prairie in the great blizzard of 1873, he nearly lost his life.

To get away from the hard work and penury he studied law in the office of a lawyer in Rochester, Minnesota, supporting himself as a day laborer on local farms. Admitted to the bar in 1877, he considered the law a veritable lifeline. After a few years he received an invitation to join a firm in St. Paul when a senior partner, his cousin, Cushman Kellogg Davis, was chosen for the U.S. Senate.

There followed an extraordinarily successful practice in which Kellogg at first represented railroads and lumbermen and, after Theodore Roosevelt became president, took on government cases against monopolies, notably the Standard Oil Company. He won the case in 1911, and the victory gave him the presidency of the American Bar Association the next year.

Elected to the Senate in 1916, he served a single term and during the fight over the League of Nations was a so-called mild reservationist, willing to vote for the Treaty of Versailles with modest amendments. A Republican, he was defeated for reelection by a Farmer-Laborite in 1922. He served as ambassador to Great Britain from 1923 to 1925.

Kellogg's appointment as secretary of state came about for several reasons. One surely was his position on the League of Nations Covenant; it was a moderate position and commended itself to President Coolidge. Even though membership in the League no longer was a major issue in U.S. politics, public opinion was against membership. Coolidge when governor of Massachusetts had favored joining the League. Another reason was his experience in foreign affairs. When his Senate term came to an end, Coolidge had appointed Kellogg ambassador to London, where he had acquainted himself with the Dawes Plan for settling both German reparations to the Allies and the war debts owed by the Allies to the United States. It is possible that Coolidge appreciated Kellogg in part because when the Minnesotan had been in the Senate, he treated the then vice president as a friend. Many senators, believing Coolidge a nonentity as vice president, had given him no attention. Also in Kellogg's favor was his eminence as a lawyer. Too, as a former senator, his nomination would easily obtain confirmation by the Senate.

Taking office on March 4, 1925, the new secretary of state generally got along well with not merely the president but also the cabinet, Congress, the press, Foreign Service, and foreign diplomats. Some of the cabinet members had been in the Senate, which helped, but Kellogg was a sensible man and so were they; Coolidge did not allow prima donnas in his cabinet. In Congress, where the secretary had to deal mostly with the Senate, he found himself at ease. Some senators privately had opposed his nomination, thinking his position on the League wrong, denigrating him as just a one-term senator, not caring for his abilities as a lawyer, but they kept quiet after the appointment. With the press his fiery temper made him attractive, for it was not difficult to get a story out of him. He was frank with the small Washington press corps of that time, and they perhaps found him a relief after his suave predecessor, Secretary Hughes. The members of the new Foreign Service, the amalgamation of the former diplomatic corps and the consular corps that was undertaken in 1924 in the Rogers Act, found him communicative and helpful, all they needed from a secretary in faraway Washington. Foreign diplomats always knew where the secretary stood, and this saved their time and that of their foreign offices. The secretary was easy to see and talk to, and his resultant memoranda for the record were as candid as the envoys might have wished.

Secretary Kellogg's four years in the department of state—he served until March 28, 1929, because his successor under President Herbert Hoover, Henry L. Stimson, had to return from the Philippine Islands where he had been governor general—were not marked by any major crises in Latin America, Europe, or what then was described as the Far East (now it is, more properly, East Asia), and the secretary hence was not called on for any large turns of policy. It is possible to contend that he occupied his office rather than advanced novelties. The times, perhaps, did not require novel turns of policy, for the latter 1920s saw a marked prosperity in the United States, indeed a notable rise in living standards, and in Western Europe, especially Germany, a seeming return to prewar stability. Germany in the early 1920s had suffered from hyperinflation and confusion over the legitimacy of the Weimar Republic, successor to the German empire. For all of Europe, including Great Britain and France, the tide of prosperity appeared to be washing away the rancors of the Great War of 1914–18. Kellogg hence dealt mainly with day-to-day problems. If one might mention the secretary of state's larger purposes and procedures, they cycled around the possibility of further limitation of naval armaments after the work of Hughes at the Washington Conference of 1921–22. Then there was the Pact of Paris of 1928 that promised to eliminate war as an instrument of national policy. Kellogg ardently believed in further limitation of naval arms and in the very real possibility of a future warless world after the losses of the late war.

If Kellogg had been asked which of the areas of the world he considered the most important for U.S. foreign relations during his tenure at the department, not necessarily what might have been the long-term importance but an area where the most problems were arising or likely to appear, he would have said Latin America. Here he would have denominated as most important relations with two countries, Mexico and Nicaragua, with Mexico foremost in his attentions. He could not understand, and in this he felt the same way as at least several of his predecessors, why the Mexican governments with their successive presidents were so hostile toward their large neighbor to the north. He might have considered the size of his own country as responsible for at least part of the anti-American feeling, in the vein of President Porfirio Diaz, who once remarked that his country was so far from God and so near the United States. Relations had deteriorated during Kellogg's era because the Mexicans desired to take over oil concessions held by foreign oil companies, notably U.S. companies. The governing officials in Mexico City adduced legal reasons and were correct in adjudging that at least some of the concessions had come through bribery and other influences, but these contentions did not faze Kellogg the lawyer, who espied despoilment. At one juncture he told the Mexican government that there was a danger of bolshevism, that the influence of Moscow, where the unrecognized Russian government had been in power since the revolution of 1917, was reaching out to overthrow or subvert governments around the world. The Mexican situation, however, eventually had its solution with the sending of a new ambassador to Mexico City, the lawyer and Morgan partner Dwight W. Morrow, whom Coolidge had met when the two men were freshmen at Amherst College and ate at the same boarding house. The president told Morrow to "go down there" and make the Mexicans his and his country's friends, and in large part Morrow did that. Although arranging an end to the conflict between the Mexican government and the hierarchy of the Catholic Church, which had closed the churches, he essentially failed with the oil issue—the latter resulted in virtual confiscation in the 1930s, after Kellogg's time.

The Nicaraguan troubles were much smaller and should have been microscopic in the concerns of Kellogg, except that the Mexicans had helped inflame them, if only to stir trouble between Nicaragua and the United States. Nicaragua was a small country, both geographically and in population, the people numbering something like 700,000. It had been in political confusion and occasional chaos for many years, and the United States had stationed a small body of marines in the capital, Managua, beginning in 1912. When in 1925 the last of the marines were withdrawn, a revolution erupted within weeks, and it proved necessary to bring them back. The revolutionary president had bought out his predecessor for the sum of $30,000 and sent him into exile in California. Coolidge resorted to a special envoy, Stimson, Kellogg's successor in 1929, who managed to forge an agreeable peace between the factions. The situation in Nicaragua gradually clarified, then it calcified, one might say, when the Somoza family took over the country in the 1930s and was only removed by a far more serious revolution decades later in 1979.

In the Far East the state of U.S. foreign relations was different, for the concern of Kellogg here—he never had visited Asia and perforce took his advice from desk officers in Washington and from able envoys in Tokyo and Nanking (legations at the time were in Nanking, having avoided Peking after the Boxer Rebellion)—was the rising nationalism in China. Until 1928 there were at least two Chinese governments and at one time in the 1920s three, and it was difficult to know with which regime to negotiate. All the governments of China were quite willing to increase their popularity by seeking an end to foreign control of the customshouse imposed years earlier and to extraterritoriality, the latter a result of the insistence of China traders who needed protection. In the 1920s the Western governments, along with Japan, were on the whole willing to threaten the Chinese, via gunboat diplomacy, as it was known. Under Kellogg, American policy makers refused to go along and adhered to the policy of Secretary Hay and his successors, who had sought no special rights but to protect China against the rapacity of the great powers. In 1925 a riot in Shanghai turned into a fury of nationalism that brought efforts by the European powers, backed by Tokyo, to punish the Chinese. Kellogg refused to go along and followed the Hay policy in favor of China.

In 1927 the soldiery of the emerging Chinese leader, Chiang Kai-shek, sacked foreign churches, residences, hospitals, and installations of trading companies in Nanking, resulting in several deaths. U.S. destroyers in the Yangtze River threw a cordon of shells around Socony Hill and brought out the residents of the city who had flocked there seeking protection. But Kellogg convened a meeting to look into tariff autonomy and another conference to examine the issues of extraterritoriality. The tariff conference was a success granting China tariff autonomy whereas the extraterritoriality conference was not, for the United States demanded establishment of laws to protect foreigners. Extraterritoriality did not end for the United States until 1943, when among other adjustments the Chinese received a quota for immigration, the first since the Exclusion Act of 1882.

As for Europe, Secretary Kellogg sought principally to advance the limitation of naval armaments beyond the Washington Treaty and for that purpose brought together the naval powers, Britain and Japan, inviting also France and Italy, in 1927 at a meeting in neutral Geneva. The two smaller powers, France and Italy, refused to attend, and the sessions of the three major powers ended in a deadlock between the British admiralty and the U.S. Navy representatives. Kellogg had thought, perhaps foolishly, that it would be possible to limit the numbers of smaller ships, smaller than battleships, especially cruisers, not to mention destroyers and submarines. The conference concentrated on cruisers, and there was dissension over the varieties of cruisers, large and small, heavy and light, as they were described, but also calibers of their guns, eight-inch versus six-inch. Tonnage of heavy cruisers was tending to approach the Washington Naval Treaty limit, which was 10,000 tons displacement. The British had built many small cruisers and did not wish them to be outgunned by the new U.S. large cruisers, of which only a few had been built. The contentions went round and round, with much ensuing ill feeling, and nothing could be done because of British and U.S. intransigence, with the Japanese looking on impassively and perhaps enjoying the spectacle. For all this Kellogg may have been foolish, but the result was for him as unexpected as for President Coolidge, who had likewise encouraged the conference. Few individuals expected the conference's abject failure over what turned out to be technicalities. In later years when a veritable cruiser race developed, all the naval powers discovered that 10,000 tons was too small a platform for eight-inch guns and that the smaller caliber displayed advantages over the larger.

Kellogg's greatest achievement by the measure of his contemporaries was the Pact of Paris, known also as the Kellogg–Briand Pact after the two negotiators, the latter being the French foreign minister, Aristide Briand. The treaty to prohibit war had an uneasy beginning in the rancors of the failure of the Geneva Naval Conference, leading some observers to think that the French foreign minister proposed the pact to place a curtain in front of his country's absence from Geneva. More to the point was Briand's effort, for such it was, although he diplomatically denied it, to bring the United States into his circle of alliances in Europe against any rebirth of German militarism. On April 6, 1927, on the 10th anniversary of American entrance into the World War, Briand began negotiations for a bilateral treaty between France and the United States to prohibit war between them, which was naught but a negative military alliance, promising U.S. neutrality in case of a French attack on Germany. Of course, Secretary Kellogg would have none of this. No dunce in regard to European diplomatic maneuvering, the secretary of state went into a rage over the proposal and apparently pressed all the buttons connected with his desk telephone, of which there were a great many, which brought a large group of his assistants into his large office, all gesticulating and shouting, with the voice of the secretary dominating the assemblage, perhaps with expletives resounding, of which he was capable. The decision was to ignore the French proposal, which Kellogg managed until December, 1927, when he learned that a cable had come into the French embassy and the ambassador would bring it over when decoded. Kellogg anticipated another of Briand's peace proposals and did not want it, and so he countered with his own proposition, which was to extend the Briand proposal to all the nations of the world and, thereby, make it worthless. Whereupon all the private peace organizations in the United States, of which there were several dozen, backed the new proposal. Further, Kellogg insisted on reservations so large that any nation signing the multilateral treaty could easily go to war despite the treaty. Eventually the antiwar treaty, suitably hedged, was signed in Paris on August 27, 1928.

As negotiations over reservations took place in the late winter and spring of 1928, the secretary of state, to the bemusement of his department officers, became ever more enamored by his own handiwork, and by the time of the treaty's signature, with Kellogg in attendance at the Quai d'Orsay, he was sure he had assisted in the advancement of peace. Many Americans felt the same way. For his work with the multilateral treaty, signed or adhered to by almost all the nations of the world, Kellogg received the Nobel Peace Prize the next year.

Upon the arrival in the United States of his successor, Stimson, Kellogg went back to St. Paul and resumed his law practice with his firm. There he basked in the admiration surrounding the Pact of Paris. He served as justice on the Permanent Court of International Justice at The Hague from 1930 to 1935 and much enjoyed the work, although the court's cases did not deal with the important issues in international relations. The caseload decreased during the Great Depression, which had begun with the stock market crash in the United States in 1929. By 1933 with the advent of the Hitler government in Germany and the increasing dominance of militarism in Japan, evidenced by the occupation of Manchuria in 1931–1932, the peace of Europe and of the Far East was in straits and by 1939 irreparably lost. Kellogg did not see all this decline in international relations, for he died in 1937. He might have been pleased, but more likely would have been astonished with the fate of his antiwar treaty. After falling into a long era of forgetfulness and disuse, it took on a virtual new life in the years immediately after World War II. At that time, American international lawyers casting about for legal support for the trials of war criminals at Nuremberg and Tokyo, based their decision to arraign the German and Japanese war criminals in part on the Kellogg–Briand Pact. Kellogg and Briand had intended the pact to apply to countries, not individuals, but the post-World War II application enlarged the pact in this novel way.

BIBLIOGRAPHICAL ESSAY

The Kellogg papers are in St. Paul at the Minnesota Historical Society. They are on the thin side. Such also is the case with the Coolidge papers in the Library of Congress. For the secretaryship of Kellogg, the best manuscript source is the diary and papers of an assistant secretary of state, William R. Castle, Jr., who was in charge of the department's European diplomacy. Castle was accustomed to walk to the department's offices each morning with his chief, during which the two discussed policy. He almost invariably informed his voluminous diary. The original is in the Houghton Library at Harvard, with copies in the Herbert Hoover Library in West Branch, Iowa, and at the Hoover Institution in Palo Alto, California.

See also David Bryn-Jones, *Frank B. Kellogg: A Biography* (1937), which had Kellogg's assistance, especially with memoranda concerning his life. For the Coolidge years, see Robert H. Ferrell, *The Presidency of Calvin Coolidge* (1998), a volume in the American Presidency Series, for which all the volumes have now been completed. Diplomacy appears in Nancy Harvison Hooker (ed.), *The Moffat Papers: Selections from the Diplomatic Journals of Jay Pierrepont Moffat* (1956) and Katherine E. Crane, *Mr. Carr of State: Forty-Seven Years in the Department of State* (1966); Moffat and Carr were notable department officers in Washington at this time. See also L. Ethan Ellis, *Republican Foreign Policy, 1921–1933* (1968) and Robert H. Ferrell, *Frank B. Kellogg and Henry L. Stimson* (1963).

For important issues and relations during Kellogg's tenure, see Hervert Feis, *Diplomacy of the Dollar: 1919–1932* (1950); Robert Freeman Smith, *The United States and Revolutionary Nationalism in Mexico: 1916–1932* (1972); Robert E. Quirk, *The Mexican Revolution and the Catholic Church: 1910–1929* (1973); William Kamman, *A Search for Stability: United States Policy toward Nicaragua, 1925–1933* (1968); Andrew J. Bacevich, *Diplomat in Khaki: Major General Frank Ross McCoy and American Foreign Policy, 1891–1949* (1989); Brian McKercher, *The Second Baldwin Government and the United States, 1924–1929: Attitudes and Diplomacy* (1984); William C. McNeill, *American Money and the Weimar Republic: Economics and Politics on the Eve of the Great Depression* (1986); Gerald E. Wheeler, *Prelude to Pearl Harbor: The United States Navy and the Far East, 1921–1931* (1963); Richard W. Fanning, *Peace and Disarmament: Naval Rivalry and Arms Control, 1922–1933* (1995); Akira Iriye, *After Imperialism: The Search for a New Order in the Far East, 1921–1931* (1965); Dorothy Borg, *American Policy and the Chinese Revolution: 1925–1928* (1947); Bernard D. Cole, *Gunboats and Marines: The United States Navy in China, 1925–1928* (1983); and Robert H. Ferrell, *Peace in Their Time: The United States and the Origins of the Kellogg–Briand Pact* (1952).

Robert H. Ferrell

HENRY KISSINGER (1923–)

Served 1973–1977
Appointed by President Richard M. Nixon
Continued in office under President Gerald Ford
Republican

Henry Kissinger was a rather remarkable individual who served as secretary of state during rather remarkable times, and scholars have yet to reach a consensus on his accomplishments and on the lasting impact he made on the conduct of U.S. diplomacy.

Henry Kissinger was born in southern Germany in May 1923. He and his family escaped Nazi Germany in 1938, eventually settling in the Washington Heights area of New York City. He interrupted his college education to serve in the U.S. Army. Later, he completed his undergraduate education with honors and then earned his MA and PhD degrees, all from Harvard University.

Kissinger was unique among secretaries of state because he held a doctoral degree in a relevant field, political science, and because he was a published if not highly regarded or particularly original scholar. His doctoral dissertation was the basis of his first book, *A World Restored: Metternich, Castlereagh and the Problems of Peace, 1812–22*, in 1957, and this interest in and understanding of national interests and balance of power politics would figure greatly in his approach to diplomacy. Scholars commonly describe Kissinger as a believer in Realpolitik, and that he admired such practitioners from early European modernity as Armand Jean du Plessis, the Duke of Richelieu (better known as Cardinal Richelieu), William of Orange, Frederick the Great, Klemens Fürst von Metternich, Robert Stewart Viscount Castlereagh, and Otto von Bismarck. He disagreed with the strain of moral diplomacy in U.S. history and favored basing foreign policy on real interests. He also, late in his scholarly career, began to doubt the willingness of the United States to bear the costs alone of international leadership and thus he would seek to introduce balance of power politics to play off the Soviet Union and to recognize the People's Republic of China.

Throughout the 1950s and 1960s, Kissinger wrote and published works on foreign policy. He rejected the massive retaliation theory of Secretary of State John Foster Dulles, believing it was unworkable, and even considered limited nuclear exchanges in his 1957 book, *Nuclear Weapons and Foreign Policy*. This willingness to consider the use of atomic weapons, along with his accent and visage, inspired Stanley Kubrick and Peter Sellers to base one of Sellers' characters in *Dr. Strangelove*—Dr. Strangelove, himself—after Henry Kissinger. Kissinger was the inspiration for the mad, wheelchair-bound, German scientist in the movie. Yet, Kissinger engaged in a narrowly constructed, very well written critique of the Dulles and Eisenhower foreign policy. He did not argue against the prevailing views that the Soviet Union was expansionistic, communism monolithic, and the Soviets controlled Third World liberation movements. He merely argued about the tactics to meet the threat.

In addition to his scholarly career, Kissinger was active in the world of diplomacy. Kissinger ran the Harvard International Seminar until he joined the Nixon Administration in 1969; he consulted with the U.S. Army's Operations Research Office and Psychological Strategy Board and with the National Security Council, the Arms Control and Disarmament Agency, and the Department of State.

During the mid-1950s, he met Nelson Rockefeller, governor of New York and a candidate for the Republican presidential nomination in 1964 and again in 1968. He became an unofficial advisor to Rockefeller, and in 1968, after Richard Nixon won the election, the two men met, and Nixon offered Kissinger the job of National Security Advisor.

Richard Nixon wanted to gain control over the conduct of foreign affairs, and he distrusted the diplomats in the State Department. He used Kissinger, who secured a small office next to the Oval Office in the West Wing. Kissinger expanded the budget of the National Security Council (NSC) and consequently greatly expanded the staff. The NSC staff would order studies and proposals from various agencies, including the State Department, to present to the president, and the staff produced a wealth of documents.

Kissinger helped Nixon achieve some of his greatest foreign policy triumphs, including détente with the Soviet Union, the opening to China, and the winding down of the Vietnam conflict. Kissinger elaborated a theory of balance of power politics and given the range of areas—military power, economic power, and political power—tried to introduce uncertainty into Soviet power politics calculations; he tried to set up five such centers of varying strength—the United States, the Soviet Union, the People's Republic of China, Western Europe, and Japan. He also believed in "linkage": the United States would expect Soviet agreement on a range of topics before agreeing to Soviet proposals on any specific topic. In a sense, he sought to reward the Soviet Union for good behavior across the globe. One result was the 1972 signing in Moscow of an agreement to bring the so-called Strategic Arms Limitations Talks (SALT) to a conclusion. Both the Soviet Union and the United States agreed to limit the number of offensive missiles, and each side pledged not to install defensive missile systems.

Kissinger had an even more spectacular accomplishment. In 1971, he eluded reporters on a trip to Pakistan, claiming a stomach ailment, and made a secret visit to the People's Republic of China, where he met with Premier Zhou Enlai and paved the way for Nixon's historic trip in February 1972, thus ending more than two decades of hostility toward the Communist rulers of mainland China. He negotiated in secret and for years with North Vietnamese diplomats, and in 1972, shortly before the U.S. presidential election, announced that he had achieved peace, although the signing of an agreement was several months away. Indeed, Kissinger and North Vietnamese negotiator Le Duc Tho received the Nobel Prize for Peace (although Tho would decline the award).

Kissinger contended with Secretary of State William Rogers, who was an old friend of Richard Nixon. Indeed, Kissinger kept Rogers and the State Department away from key matters, and limited them to the Middle East and, at the time, other areas of lower concern. Perhaps it was fitting that, in September 1973, Henry Kissinger became secretary of state.

Kissinger's rise to secretary of state (he was the first nonnative American and first Jew to achieve this position) came as the scandal of Watergate began to erode the Nixon presidency. In June 1972, burglars broke into Democratic National Headquarters offices in the Watergate, a hotel/apartment/office complex along the Potomac River in Washington, D.C. As the months passed, a series of revelations kept the scandal increasingly on the front pages of the news. In the summer of 1973, a Senate committee chaired by North Carolina Senator Sam Ervin discovered that the president used a secret taping system to record conversations in the Oval Office, presumably to help with the writing of memoirs after Nixon left the presidency. The focus became the release of the tapes, and this scandal eventually consumed Richard Nixon, forcing him to resign on August 9, 1974.

On October 10, 1973, Nixon's vice president, Spiro Agnew, had resigned as part of a plea bargain with federal prosecutors concerning allegations of extortion, bribery, and income tax violations dating back to his time as governor of Maryland. Soon after Agnew resigned, Richard Nixon nominated the well-liked if not highly regarded House Minority Leader, Republican Gerald Ford, of Michigan, as the nation's first nonelected vice president. Congress approved, and when Nixon resigned, Ford became president, the first president who was never elected to either national office. In the midst of this political instability, Kissinger remained a constant as secretary of state and reassured international leaders about the policies and intentions of the United States.

In October 1973, the Middle Eastern nations of Egypt and Syria launched a surprise attack on Israeli forces along the Suez Canal and the Golan Heights on Yom Kippur, the holiest day of the Jewish religious year. The Arab allies had Soviet-supplied, manually operated, surface-to-air missiles, or SAMs, and they extracted a heavy price on Israeli fighter planes as Egyptian forces crossed the Suez Canal and threatened advanced Israeli positions in the Sinai Peninsula. Moreover, the attack quickly drew down the ammunition reserves of all three countries. That Kissinger was Jewish was well known, and thus there was fear he had extraofficial sympathies for the Jewish state.

Nonetheless, the United States provided Israel with war materiel to balance Soviet supplies sent to Egypt and Syria. The U.S. supply and a daring Israeli attack threatened to isolate and capture the Egyptian Third Army. When the Soviet Union indicated it might send forces to help Egypt and thus widen the war, Kissinger secured a cease-fire, although the Israelis did delay acceptance to improve their position against Egypt.

Thereafter, Kissinger engaged in a step-by-step process to disengage the enemies along both fronts. His successful effort would not have been possible without support from Egyptian leader Anwar Sadat, who realized that only the United States possessed the leverage to cause Israel to give back the Sinai, which did not happen until after the Camp David Accords under President Jimmy Carter several years later.

Soon after the U.S.-aided Israeli-victory in the Yom Kippur War, the Organization of Petroleum Exporting Countries (OPEC) announced a spectacular oil embargo on the United States, presumably for its support of Israel, and before the next year was out quadrupled the price of crude oil. The OPEC action exposed a weakness in Kissinger's conduct of foreign policy, for he did not deal well with multiple situations, and this was, to be sure, a complex situation. Though the resolution was some years away, Kissinger moved to embrace the Shah of Iran, who provided plentiful petroleum despite the embargo, but the consequences would manifest themselves in the student seizure of the U.S. embassy in Teheran in 1979.

The dramatic increase in petroleum prices caused severe economic difficulties for the industrialized world, including long lines at gasoline stations in the United States and inflation, recession, and increased unemployment worldwide. For Japan, it was a particularly challenging situation, as that nation depended heavily on OPEC-produced petroleum for its energy needs. Moreover, in August 1971, Nixon and Kissinger had produced the so-called Nixon shocks, as the Japanese labeled them, informing Japan with rather scant notice of Nixon's forthcoming visit to the People's Republic of China while Japan continued to follow its U.S.-inspired "Two China" policy, of the decision to discontinue the gold standard (that is, the United States since the 1930s when it went off the domestic gold standard had maintained the price of an ounce of gold internationally as being worth $35.00), and of the decision to impose tariffs on certain imported goods—all of which seemed a punishment of a sort for Japan's hard-fought economic success. Kissinger found the Japanese difficult to understand and difficult negotiators, and thus paid them little attention. Yet, this economic challenge led, in part, to the demise of the production of television sets in the United States and the near destruction of the U.S. automobile industry and other industrial sectors of the U.S. economy.

Moreover, in October 1974, an Arab summit conference in Rabat, Morocco, declared Yassir Arafat's PLO (Palestine Liberation Organization) to be the sole representative of the Palestinians, and the PLO remained officially pledged to the use of terror against civilian targets and the destruction of the Israeli state.

As the Arab–Israeli dispute continued to simmer, a crisis occurred on the island of Cyprus, in the Mediterranean near Turkey. The population on Cyprus was more than two-thirds ethnic Greek and the remainder of Turkish ethnicity, although Cyprus is located about 40 miles south of Turkey and more than 400 miles from Greece. Greek ethnic outrages against the Turkish minority nearly caused Turkey to send troops on several occasions, and each time the United States exerted heavy pressure to avoid possible conflict between two key countries on NATO's vital southeastern border. Since the Johnson Administration, the United States had supported the Greek junta, which warred against its own population. At the same time, Nixon and Kissinger wanted to keep the vital listening posts in eastern Turkey and also have Turkish help in limiting the legal crop of opium poppies because the ultimate products often seemed destined for America's cities. The United States, including Kissinger, the State Department, and the Central Intelligence Agency (CIA), overlooked clues pointing to a Greek government-organized coup, and on July 15, the plotters took over the government of Cyprus. Despite U.S. efforts, the Turks responded, landing troops on July 20 and securing the Turkish enclave on the island. Kissinger did not fathom the depth of the ethnic and religious conflict, and talks continued in Geneva while Turkey grabbed more and more territory on the island. Kissinger looked aside to keep Turkey on board against the Soviet Union, and there was great political fallout in Congress owing to a very strong, quickly organized pro-Greek lobby and a cutoff of military aid to Turkey. Revelations about U.S. support for the right-wing coup and violence in Chile along with allegations about the administration wiretaps combined to leave Kissinger with little political standing among Congressmen anxious to reverse the rise of the Imperial Presidency.

Kissinger next had to deal with an increasingly recalcitrant Congress over the issue of the SALT negotiations with the Soviet Union. The SALT II negotiations had begun in 1972 (soon after the signing of the initial treaty, SALT I, on May 26, 1972 during a Nixon–Brezhnev summit meeting in Moscow) and continued into the Carter presidency. There were two problems—one very real and one much more imagined. There was great asymmetry between the U.S. and Soviet nuclear arsenals, for the Soviet Union had concentrated on land-based, larger missiles whereas the United States had concentrated on submarine-launched, smaller, and highly accurate missiles. There were challenges in defining the arsenals and then determining what constituted equivalent reductions. Thus there were some doubts about the benefits of the SALT I agreement to the United States.

Equally important, Congress reacted to Kissinger's celebrated secrecy. Democrats took advantage to criticize the man once called "Super K" in the media, and Republican conservatives returned to their traditional doubts about the reliability of Soviet promises and the usefulness of U.S. concessions. Moreover, there were charges, particularly by retired Admiral Elmo Zumwalt, that Kissinger largely negotiated alone on very technical matters, when it would have seemed reasonable for him to have relied on the expertise of nuclear weapons professionals.

Congressional criticism in 1975 over SALT discussions reflected the final chapter of the long, draining conflict in Southeast Asia. While Richard Nixon was able to commit overwhelming American airpower in 1972 to destroy the so-called Easter Offensive the North Vietnamese launched chiefly across the 17th parallel, there would be no repeat introduction of American support in 1975. In December 1974, the North Vietnamese launched an attack on Phuoc Binh, and its relatively easy capture convinced the government in Hanoi to prepare for a more general offensive in spring 1975. The resulting offensive beginning against the Central Highlands town of Ban Me Thuot caused panic among South Vietnamese forces. When the South Vietnamese president, Nguyen Van Thieu, ordered a retreat to the southern third of the country, the rout was on. On May 1, 1975, after a campaign of some 55 days, the North Vietnamese had won. Critics charged that Kissinger had signed away South Vietnamese independence and turned over that country to the Communists with the peace treaty he had negotiated years before and that he passively watched the collapse of South Vietnam.

When the furor over the loss of Vietnam, Laos, and Cambodia had eased somewhat, Kissinger walked into a problem in Angola in autumn 1975. Portugal finally left that country after centuries of an oppressive colonial regime. Kissinger and the CIA defined the issue in terms of the Cold War, rather than African tribal and ethnic conflicts, which likely was more appropriate, and quietly and secretly funneled aid to pro-U.S. forces, which caused the Soviet Union to provide aid to its apparently more competent, more talented clients. As Kissinger and the CIA should have expected, the war went badly, and accounts of the secret aid leaked to the media.

One can argue that, to some extent, the election of 1976 was a judgment on the diplomacy of Henry Kissinger. Gerald Ford, running for election, never had the full support of the Republican Party and had faced a rather serious primary challenge from the actor-turned-politician, former California Governor Ronald Reagan. Reagan disagreed vigorously with the underpinnings of Kissinger's foreign policy, especially the idea that the Soviet Union, at least momentarily, was ascendant, and that the United States was a slowly declining and hesitant superpower. Meanwhile, Jimmy Carter, former Georgia governor and the Democratic Party candidate, wanted to bring a morality to diplomacy that was a throwback to the years before Kissinger, and he would appoint as his National Security Advisor Zbigniew Brzezinski, who along with the election of the Polish Cardinal Karol Wojtilla as Pope John Paul II, brought a new combativeness to relations with the Soviet Union and the Communist world more generally.

Unlike most secretaries of state, Henry Kissinger, remained active in foreign policy after he left office. In addition to several volumes of memoirs about his work as national security advisor and as secretary of state, he wrote additional studies of the U.S. role in the world. He founded Kissinger Associates, an international consulting firm, with a long and impressive list of governmental and corporate clients. Although Ronald Reagan largely rejected the inherent pessimism that Kissinger felt about America's willingness to bear all the costs to remain a superpower, he appointed Kissinger to serve as Chairman of the National Bipartisan Commission on Central America (1983–1984). In November 2002, President George W. Bush appointed Dr. Kissinger to co-chair an official commission to look into all issues surrounding the terrorist attacks of September 11, 2001, on the World Trade Center towers and the Pentagon, but he decided to resign a month after being appointed because of possible conflicts of interest about or the need to provide disclosure of his firm's list of clients.

Determining the lasting impact of Henry Kissinger on the conduct of U.S. foreign policy is a difficult task. One must first recognize the disrepair in American diplomacy following the Kennedy and Johnson presidencies, particularly given Lyndon Johnson's so-called shoot-from-the-hip style. Diplomacy in that era all too often meant military intervention. Moreover, there is an old story that the State Department has two crises rooms, and if one were to ask a State Department officer what would happen if a third crisis arose, the reply would be to downgrade one of the other two crises! Richard Nixon, who had thought long and hard about the world and America's place in it, wanted to create more orderly processes both within the United States for designing foreign policy and externally for the new world order he was trying to establish. Henry Kissinger played a critical role in this Nixon grand design, and the National Security Council he strengthened and oversaw did help bring a degree of cohesion to the separate centers of U.S. foreign policy in the Department of State, the Department of the Treasury, the Department of Commerce, the Department of Defense, and the Central Intelligence Agency, among others.

Kissinger held a relatively typical view among scholars who espoused Realpolitik. He rejected the simple determinism of John Foster Dulles and "brinksmanship." He recognized the world was as more complex than it had been a decade earlier.

Regardless of which side took the very first step, he was open to discussions with the People's Republic of China, correcting a wrong that stretched back nearly a quarter century. He also recognized the continuing cost of the conflict in Vietnam and the need to end it. At the core of his beliefs was a sense that Americans were no longer willing to bear the burden of serving as the world's policeman and that the United States might lack the resources to continue in that role; he accepted a world of limits on U.S. power, which fundamentally the Kennedy and Johnson administrations did not.

Kissinger certainly had his accomplishments in foreign policy. These included the opening of relations with China and the reestablishment of friendlier relations with the Soviet Union; they also included the truce to end the Yom Kippur War and a new friendship with Egypt. Perhaps, most importantly, Kissinger deserves great credit for providing a steadiness to the conduct of U.S. foreign policy in such trying circumstances. That is, he was able to assure the nations of the world—America's friends and America's foes—that the United States would continue as it had continued despite the resignation, under fire, of the vice president, the appointment of an unelected vice president, the resignation of the president, and the succession by an unelected VP to the presidency—all remarkable events that clearly threatened the nation's international standing.

Kissinger also merits criticism for his views and policies. He agreed with the expansion of the Vietnam War into neighboring Cambodia, which sought a neutral path between the United States and the North Vietnamese. He may have participated in discussions about and approved U.S. support for the military coup on September 11, 1973, by Augusto Pinochet against the elected president, Salvador Allende, in Chile, which led to violence and the death of many suspected leftists and critics of the resulting military regime. In December 1975, he met with General Suharto of Indonesia approving his invasion of East Timor, which would lead to the deaths of tens of thousands of civilians and a long-lasting civil war.

Perhaps, most importantly, is that his efforts to achieve a balance of power, which largely meant accepting the reality of the Soviet Union and the Soviet bloc, were rejected by Jimmy Carter and his National Security Advisor, Zbigniew Brzezinski, and by Ronald Reagan, who succeeded Carter. Carter quietly brought his religion and his morality to the office and did not continue the amoral Realpolitik espoused by Kissinger. Brzezinski, who was born in Poland, apparently cooperated with Pope John Paul II to help oppose the Soviet Union. Ronald Reagan had a much more optimistic view of the United States and its capacity for world leadership, and he engaged in a great military buildup reflecting dramatic improvements in technology that the Soviet Union felt obligated to match and that led ultimately to the bankrupting of that country, the rise of Mikhail Gorbachev, his efforts to reform the system, that is, both *perestroika* and *glasnost*, and the consequent collapse of the Soviet Union and the Soviet bloc.

Any critique of Henry Kissinger, his views, his policies, and his lasting impact must take note that he was only an appointed official as national security advisor and as secretary of state, and that he reported to and was obligated to help carry out the foreign policies of the president of the United States, Richard Nixon. President Nixon was comfortable in the world of diplomacy; he had thought a great deal about the United States and its role in the world; and he maintained control of U.S. diplomacy until he was fatally weakened by Watergate. When Gerald Ford became president, maintaining the nation and restoring the damage that the Watergate scandal wrought consumed his time, and thus new or expanded diplomatic efforts took a back seat.

BIBLIOGRAPHICAL ESSAY

One should begin studying Kissinger by reading his own books, including *A World Restored: Metternich, Castlereagh and the Problems of Peace, 1812–22* (1957), in which he discussed his balance of power doctrine by discussing the great diplomat Metternich in all his glory, when the Concert of Europe truly began. In *Nuclear Weapons and Foreign Policy* (1957), Dr. Kissinger wrote persuasively but not necessarily originally that the United States must plan for a limited war and not assume that all wars will be total wars or nuclear exchanges. He claimed that this put the United States at a disadvantage in dealing with the Soviet Union. See also Henry Kissinger, *The White House Years* (1979), and Henry Kissinger, *Years of Upheaval* (1982), to see how he recounts his service in the White House of Richard Nixon and Gerald Ford. For a relatively fawning account, see Bernard Kalb and Marvin Kalb, *Kissinger* (1974).

For much more critical accounts, see Seymour Hersh, *The Price of Power: Kissinger in the Nixon White House* (1983), which argues that peace was achievable in 1968 and that Kissinger helped destroy this chance to damage the presidential aspirations of Democratic Party candidate Hubert Humphrey. William Shawcross, *Sideshow: Kissinger, Nixon, and the Destruction of Cambodia* (1987), makes the case that Nixon and Kissinger were willing to sacrifice Cambodia to save the situation in South Vietnam. Larry Berman, *No Peace, No Honor: Nixon, Kissinger, and Betrayal in Vietnam* (2001), makes the strong case that Kissinger and Nixon knew the treaty really was a sham that North Vietnam would violate, leading to the eventual collapse of South Vietnam.

More balanced accounts are Walter Isaacson, *Kissinger: A Biography* (1992). Isaacson gives Kissinger full marks for his many accomplishments in foreign policy, but he minces few words in recounting the secretiveness, devotion to Realpolitik, and personal insecurities that gained Kissinger a reputation for Dr. Strangelove-like duplicity. Robert D. Schulzinger, *Henry Kissinger, Doctor of Diplomacy* (1989), respects the circumstances internationally and at home during which Kissinger served.

Charles M. Dobbs

PHILANDER C. KNOX (1853–1921)

Served 1909–1913
Appointed by President William H. Taft
Republican

Philander Chase Knox was born in Brownsville, Pennsylvania, on May 6, 1853. He grew up in moderate circumstances as the 11th child and last son of a bank cashier. Before his death in 1921, he would serve in the U.S. Senate and the cabinets of three Republican presidents—William McKinley, Theodore Roosevelt, and William Howard Taft. He received a Bachelor of Arts degree in 1872 from Mount Union College of Ohio and read law at a Pittsburgh law office before being admitted to the bar of Allegheny County, Pennsylvania, in 1875. He served as assistant U.S. district attorney from 1876 to 1877 and then formed a successful law practice in Pittsburgh with James H. Reed. In this practice Knox built a fortune as a corporate attorney. Knox's highest honor, as an attorney, was his selection as president of the Pennsylvania Bar Association. Although his critics pegged him as pro-business, he handled many cases against corporations. In 1880, he married Lillie Smith, daughter of Andrew D. Smith, who was one of the principle owners of a controlling interest of La Belle Steele Company. The couple had four children, two of which worked for Knox briefly in the State Department. He has been described as a self-made product of an industrial society, rather than an old-world conservative who paid attention to tradition and procedure characteristic of a preindustrial society. His most important legacy comes from his foreign policy of promoting stability in underdeveloped nations by providing economic aid while encouraging political reforms.

After Knox's friend, William McKinley, won reelection to the presidency of the United States, he accepted an offer to become U.S. Attorney General. Knox held this office between 1901 and 1904 under both President McKinley and McKinley's successor, President Theodore Roosevelt. As attorney general, Knox became known as a "trust" buster and proponent of the government's right to intervene in a private damage suit to uphold federal safety appliance laws. His background as a successful corporate attorney aided him when President Roosevelt assigned him the task of enforcing the Sherman Antitrust Act of 1890. The Sherman Antitrust Act outlawed contracts, combinations, trusts, or conspiracies that restrained or monopolized trade. In the two decades following the passage of the Sherman Act, corporations ignored it as they engaged in the biggest wave of mergers in U.S. history up to that time. The resulting popular resentment toward corporate mergers and monopolies led President Roosevelt to actively enforce the law. As Attorney General, Knox became the most active of his predecessors in prosecuting corporations and trusts. Knox's greatest Sherman victory was his suit against the Northern Securities Company (a railroad holding corporation), which he personally argued before the Supreme Court. Criticism of Knox's tenure as attorney general centered on his friendly relationship, both personally and professionally, with the very corporate interests that he was responsible for regulating.

Aside from "trust-busting," Knox's tenure as attorney general was also marked by his institution of peonage-prosecution. Peonage existed in most Southern states and in the Southwest, and it affected African Americans, Mexican Americans, and poor whites. Thanks to his efforts, the courts had effectively outlawed peonage by 1910. Knox's short tenure as attorney general was remarkably active. He also drafted the law establishing the Departments of Commerce and Labor, upheld the Chinese exclusion and alien anarchist deportation laws, provided the legal argument for the U.S. position on the Alaskan boundary case, and helped shape the legislation making the Interstate Commerce Commission an effective regulator of railroad rates.

In 1904, Knox was appointed U.S. Senator from Pennsylvania to fill a vacancy. Knox's initial senatorial tour was spent serving on the Senate's Judiciary Committee and chairing the Committee on Rules and was active in the Panama Canal tolls debate. Knox had presidential aspirations, but these were extinguished after Taft won the Republican National Convention's presidential nomination on the first ballot in June 1908. He resigned his Senate seat in 1909 to accept President William Howard Taft's offer to serve as secretary of state. Knox returned to the Senate in 1917 as the first popular elected senator from Pennsylvania after spending four years as a private citizen and four years as secretary of state. He served only four years of his six-year term, dying suddenly in 1921.

As a public servant, Knox was considered helpful to progressive causes because he helped to pass the Hepburn Act of 1906, attacked peonage laws, upheld appliance safety laws, fought against corporate collusion, and supported a strong national government. During his last term as senator, Knox served on the Senate Foreign Relations Committee. He is known to have strongly disapproved of President Wilson's foreign policy and was an unyielding opponent of the Treaty of Versailles with its League of Nations Covenant. As leader of the "reservationists" in the Senate, he was successful in defeating the ratification of the treaty.

Knox's opposition to the Treaty of Versailles was based on his belief that the treaty and the League of Nations Covenant should be separated. Knox believed that the treaty's covenants would supersede the U.S. Constitution. Specifically, Knox believed that the treaty's League of Nations Covenant delegated constitutional powers and functions to an extraneous body that would impose obligations on the United States that could not be done by the treaty-making power of the president. Ex-president Taft remarked that Knox's opposition was based on his misconceived notion that the covenant conveyed U.S. sovereignty to the League's Executive Council. Knox believed that such a transfer of power could only be accomplished with a constitutional amendment. After the defeat of the treaty in the

Senate, Knox successfully guided his third resolution on May 21, 1920, to repeal the war against Germany and Austria. Though Wilson vetoed it, the resolution was eventually approved in 1921. President Harding then submitted to the Senate a treaty for a separate peace with Germany, made possible by the Knox Resolution. Three weeks later, on October 12, 1921, Knox died suddenly of a paralytic stroke in Washington, D.C.

Knox enjoyed a deep friendship with President Taft before and during his tenure as secretary of state. Their relationship began when Knox was a senator and Taft was the secretary of war under President Roosevelt. His friendship with Taft and Taft's confidence in his friend provided Knox with much influence in the administration. Taft regarded Knox as the head of the cabinet and responsible for state affairs. Knox held no special interest in foreign policy prior to his appointment as secretary of state and was not Taft's first choice, as both Elihu Root, Theodore Roosevelt's last secretary of state, and Senator Henry Cabot Lodge declined Taft's offer.

Knox began his tenure by reorganizing the Department of State into regional divisions. This novel idea sought to organize U.S. relations with different groups of countries under officials who had previously acquired an expertise in those countries through Foreign Service. Another added benefit of this structure was the rotation of Foreign Service employees between service in a foreign country and Washington. Knox believed that such a system would enlarge personnel interchange between State and the Foreign Service, thereby preventing Foreign Service personnel from losing touch with the home viewpoint. Though he relied on subordinates to run the day-to-day details of the department, Knox maintained a firm control over policy. Because Knox regarded his role as similar to a prime minister, even the president found it necessary to justify to Knox his decision to mobilize troops on the Mexican border in 1911.

In the Far East, Knox continued the Open Door policy of his predecessors, John Hay and Elihu Root. The Open Door policy was based on the idea of equal opportunity of all foreign firms to conduct business in China as a means of ensuring China's territorial integrity and sovereignty. Specifically, the United States sought the equal opportunity for U.S. firms to compete in mining and railroad business in China on a level playing field with firms from Japan, Russia, Great Britain, France, and Germany. However from 1905–1909, there were no U.S. financial interests that sought mining and railroad construction projects. Though the other major powers would voice support for it, they ignored it in practice. Knox realized that the Open Door would continue to exist more as theory unless the United States moved to enforce it. The Taft administration believed that the U.S. government should more actively enforce the policy by aggressively promoting U.S. investments in China. This new aggressive role by the U.S. government is what distinguishes Dollar Diplomacy from the Open Door policy.

Another of the principal goals of the U.S. government's Chinese foreign policy was to maintain China's territorial integrity and sovereignty. President Taft and Secretary Knox believed that China's sovereignty could be best protected if the special railway concessions made by the Chinese government to Russia, Japan, France, and Great Britain were reversed. Knox reasoned that if China's government owned the railways, the special advantages these countries had in China could be neutralized. Knox's China policy was based also on the belief that the best hope of promoting U.S. influence in China was by introducing a large amount of American capital into the area. Knox believed that the presence of American capital would help to protect China's political integrity because it would provide greater diplomatic leverage for the United States when dealing with the other powers. Foreign diplomats had been critical of U.S. efforts to play a role in China that was beyond its economic interests.

Knox attempted to create a loan agreement to be backed by Japan, Russia, France, Great Britain, Germany, and the United States for China to purchase the northern Manchurian railways from Russia. It was hoped that later China could purchase the southern Manchurian railways from Japan. As part of the agreement, Japan and the Great Powers of Europe would share in its management for a period. The goal of this plan, called the Neutralization Plan, was to neutralize the commercial advantages of the Japanese and Russians, along with the latter's French ally, built around their control of Manchuria's transportation system. Additionally, Knox believed that by promoting international financial cooperation, the new policy could realize the goals of the Open Door policy. If this failed, then the United States and Britain would implement the Chinchow–Aigun Agreement, which they had just negotiated with the Chinese government. Under this agreement the United States would arrange the financing of a railway that would parallel the Manchurian lines and be constructed by the British.

Unfortunately, Knox's neutralization proposal and the Chinchow–Aigun project were failures. Not only were Russia, Japan, and France unwilling to give up their special commercial positions in China, but the British, who had formed a previous alliance with Japan to counter growing German imperialist designs, acquiesced to Japan's opposition to neutralization. In addition, the Russians would not allow the proposed new lines under the Chinchow–Aigun Agreement to cross its border with China and a section of the Manchurian line it controlled.

With the failure of the neutralization plan, Knox pursued other initiatives to obtain equal opportunities for American business interests in Manchuria and China proper while preserving China's territorial integrity. For the duration of his tenure, Knox pursued a policy of international cooperation when dealing with the Chinese as a way to protect China's sovereignty and to open China for U.S. capital. Knox's cooperation policy promoted the coordination of policy by the major powers through the International Consortium. The Consortium consisted of banking groups from the United States, Britain, France, and Germany to be joined by Japan and Russia later. Knox organized two loans to China using Consortium capital designed to reform the Chinese currency, promote industrial development in Manchuria, and strengthen Chinese conservatives in their struggle for control over China. However, neither loan initiative was fully implemented, and the Consortium broke down. Knox's reluctance to extend U.S. diplomatic recognition to the revolutionary government of the Republic of China stymied China's efforts at shoring up its international credit standing, causing greater instability in the region. President Wilson abandoned Knox's international cooperative policy toward China and recognized the Republic of China on May 1, 1913.

Problems associated with Latin America occupied Knox's attention from the very beginning of his term. Beginning in the 1890s, American intervention in the Caribbean basin had become the common response of the United States whenever it felt that its interests were jeopardized. Critics of intervention argued that U.S. military operations were at the behest of large American financial interests seeking to protect their investments. It is in this context that the United States developed its dollar diplomacy in the region.

Through dollar diplomacy, President Taft and Secretary Knox sought to promote order and stability throughout Central America and the Caribbean and to strengthen the Monroe Doctrine. Knox believed that injecting American capital into the region would decrease the need for direct military intervention by the U.S. and European governments. As such, Dollar Diplomacy in Latin American sought to promote a different set of objectives than in China. However, because public opinion in the United States did not make a distinction between the administration's failing China policy and Caribbean basin policy, there was little popular support for dollar diplomacy.

Knox's solution for the problems in the region was to develop a plan similar to the Santo Domingo Convention for both Nicaragua and Honduras. As with the Santo Domingo Convention, Knox sought an agreement with Nicaragua and Honduras that pledged their customs revenues to repay private sources of financial assistance from American bankers. In the case of Honduras, Knox was able to negotiate the Knox–Paredes Convention.

The Knox–Paredes Convention was composed of two components, a loan arrangement and a customs collection treaty. Unfortunately for Knox, neither the U.S. Senate nor the Honduran Congress ratified the convention. The loan agreement was opposed by the Honduran Congress and was never approved. American detractors claimed that the loan arrangement was a bailout for certain American special interests.

Jose Santo Zelaya, the Liberal dictator of Nicaragua, fomented much of the political instability of the region that faced Knox. Because Zelaya openly defied the United States, Knox believed that regional stability in Central America could only be achieved if the Nicaraguan leadership was neutralized. To achieve his goal, Knox broke diplomatic relations with the Zelaya regime and adopted a firm response to Zelaya's military movements in the region. Knox recognized the nascent rebellion led by Juan J. Estrada as the representative of the Nicaraguan people.

With the accession of Dr. Jose Madriz as Nicaragua's president after the resignation of Zelaya, the Nicaraguan government's conflict with the Estrada rebels intensified. The United States intervened with 100 marines to keep open the Bluefield port and to protect U.S. interests. This action by the United States essentially protected Estrada because his forces were trapped in Bluefields by Nicaraguan government forces. Knox then allowed Estrada to consolidate his hold, keeping the Bluefields customs office, thereby ensuring Estrada's control of Nicaragua's primary source of income. Soon the Madriz government collapsed, and Estrada accepted the Dawson Agreement between Nicaragua and the United States. Under this agreement, the new Nicaraguan government pledged that it would seek rehabilitation loans in the United States, which were to be secured by customs receipts. The agreement also called for the prosecution of the murder of two U.S. citizens in Nicaragua by the Zelaya government during the revolution, abolishment of monopolies, and the creation of a claims commission to resolve disputes with Nicaragua's creditors. The Knox–Castrillo Treaty of June 6, 1911, linked secured loans from U.S. banks with a customs receivership agreement. However, it suffered the same fate as the convention for Honduras because the U.S. Senate would not consent to the creation of financial protectorates.

Because approval of the Knox–Castrillo Treaty by the U.S. Senate became increasingly unlikely, American bankers refused to release additional money to the Nicaraguan government from completed loans. The ensuing collapse of Nicaragua's finances led to a short-lived revolt by pro-Zelayist Liberals, and it is against this backdrop that American troops intervened in Nicaragua. Officially, the U.S. intervention of 1912 was to protect the lives and property of its citizens. However, Knox was under pressure to provide protection to the U.S. bank syndicate that had loaned Nicaragua money for currency reform. If he failed to protect U.S. investors, the dollar diplomacy framework would have collapsed.

The main intervention force that Taft sent to Nicaragua consisted of 2,500 marines and eight warships. A contingent of marines moved into the interior of Nicaragua to open the railroad lines and fought rebels at Barranca-Coyotope in a coordinated campaign with Nicaraguan federal troops. After the defeat of the Liberal rebels the United States maintained a Legation Guard in Managua that supported the Conservative Nicaraguan government of Adolfo Diaz and trained the Nicaraguan National Guard. The 1912 intervention marked the first use of U.S. troops to suppress a revolution in Central America.

In the remaining months of the Taft administration, Knox was able to negotiate a canal option with Nicaragua that provided Nicaragua with three million dollars of U.S.-backed collateral for more loans. It also stipulated that the United States would have an option to lease sites for naval bases. This clause strengthened the Monroe Doctrine by preventing foreign naval bases in Central America. Though the treaty was submitted to the Senate for ratification, the Taft administration ended before its approval in 1916 under the name of the Bryan–Chamorro Treaty.

Dollar diplomacy was designed to substitute dollars for bullets by encouraging private companies and banks to conduct business in the Caribbean basin. It was made possible by the surplus of U.S. capital for overseas investment created by the rebounding U.S. economy that President Taft and Secretary Knox had inherited. Critics of the time argued that dollar diplomacy was used to force on the peoples of the region loan contracts that benefited a coterie of Wall Street bankers. The ultimate effect, they argued, was military intervention by the United States in the internal affairs of these countries. Bernard C. Nalty provided a more sanguine account of the official purpose of dollar diplomacy when he stated that it was to have U.S. diplomats encourage foreign states to borrow or buy from American banks and manufacturers "[to] relieve the chronic financial burdens of friendly nations, raise their standards of living, and by providing markets for American goods, ensure continued domestic prosperity."

Soon after taking office, the Taft administration was faced with the problem of Mexico's revolution. Unlike the Nicaraguan revolutions, Knox and Taft officially adopted a strict noninterventionist policy toward Mexico's internal conflicts. It is unclear why Taft did not order armed intervention of Mexico after he mobilized troops and naval power at the beginning of the 1910 revolution. However, it is generally recognized that such action by the United States would have united all the Mexican factions against the invaders. Though the United States did not adopt a policy of outright support of Fransisco Madero's revolt against the Porfirio Diaz government, it did allow U.S. arms and money to cross into Mexico in support of the revolution. Instability continued after Madero's ascension to the presidency, though Taft had placed an embargo on private arms shipments into Mexico.

Although Taft's embargo of arms shipments aided Madero's effort to stay in office by keeping arms out of his rivals' hands, he was overthrown and killed five days later in a palace revolt by General Victoriano Huerta. President Taft and Knox's tenure ended before the United States took any action to recognize the Huerta government.

BIBLIOGRAPHICAL ESSAY

The primary source of Knox's official correspondence is located in the Manuscript Division of the Library of Congress, Washington, D.C. Other sources include the James M. Beck Papers located at the Seeley G. Mudd Manuscript Library, Princeton University Library. The Beck papers consist of correspondence, articles, addresses and scrapbooks that document Beck's career as lawyer, Assistant United States Attorney, United States Attorney, Assistant Attorney General, Solicitor General of the United States, a Republican member of Congress, author, and public speaker. It contains Knox materials from 1902–1903 and 1913–1921. Knox's Memos and instructions can be found in the official records of the State Department in the National Archives. Additional sources of relevant items may be found in the papers of Theodore Roosevelt and William Howard Taft.

An excellent study of Knox's dollar diplomacy is Paige Elliott Mulhollan's *Philander C. Knox and Dollar Diplomacy, 1909–1913* (1966). This work also provides an exhaustive compilation of newspaper accounts about Knox's personal life and policy initiatives. For a polemic of dollar diplomacy at the time of its inception, see Juan Leet's *United States and Latin America: Dollar Diplomacy* (1912). Gerald Richbook's *The Relations of the United States with China During the Taft-Knox Administration* (1953) provides a good in-depth examination of Knox's Far East policy.

See Bernard C. Nalty, *The United States Marines in Nicaragua* (1968) for a concise chronological narrative of the role of the U.S. Marines in the American interventions in Nicaragua between 1910–1913. This work was prepared by the Historical Branch, G-3 Division Headquarters, U.S. Marine Corps as part of the Marine Corps Historical Reference Series. Herbert F. Wright provides a good introductory work on Knox and his policy initiatives in *The American Secretaries of State and their Diplomacy*, ed. Samuel Flagg Bemus (1958). However, Wright tends to be overly gratuitous in his assessment of Knox as a person and his policies.

Michael Sanchez

ROBERT LANSING (1864–1928)

Served 1915–1920
Appointed by President Woodrow Wilson
Democrat

Robert Lansing served as secretary of state for President Woodrow Wilson from 1915 to 1920. Born on October 17, 1864, in Watertown, a small city in northern New York, he was the eldest child of John and Maria Lay Dodge Lansing. John Lansing, Robert's great grandfather, was a member of the New York legislature and a delegate to the Philadelphia Constitutional Convention. Another paternal ancestor, Jacob C. TenEyck, served as Judge of the State Court of Common Pleas and was prominent in the American Revolution. Both his grandfather and father were distinguished lawyers. His maternal grandfather, Edwin Dodge, served as land agent for Gouverneur Morris and as a member of the state legislature and a judge in the New York Court System.

From the beginning, young Robert "Bert" Lansing seemed destined for a legal and public-service career. After graduating from Amherst College in 1886, he read law in his father's offices and, in 1889, was admitted to the New York Bar. After a trip to Europe, he became the junior partner in the Lansing and Lansing firm of Watertown, an affiliation he kept until his father's death in 1907.

Although not brilliant, Lansing was hard-working and well read in law as well as U.S. history, international relations, and psychology. He was shy and disliked dealing with strangers, and he was reluctant to appear in court, preferring to prepare cases and then turn them over to his father for presentation.

Lansing married Eleanor Foster the eldest daughter of John Watson Foster in 1890, and in so doing took his first real step toward a career in foreign affairs. Foster, a veteran U.S. diplomat who was Minister to Mexico, Russia, and Spain, served as secretary of state during the presidency of Benjamin Harrison (1892–1893) and had an extensive legal practice representing foreign governments in Washington. Lansing assisted in Foster's practice and in 1892 was himself appointed associate counsel for the United States at the Bering Sea Fur Seal Arbitrations.

From 1892 to 1907, Lansing alternated between assisting his father in Watertown and the international law practice of his father-in-law. Over the years, his involvement in international law increased. He served as American Counsel before the Bering Sea Claims Commission in 1896–1897, at the 1903 London sessions of the Alaskan boundary tribunal, at the 1908–1910 arbitration of the North Atlantic coast fisheries at The Hague, at the 1911 North Atlantic Fisheries and Fur Seals Conference, and at the 1913–1914 arbitrations before the British-American Claims Commission. By 1914, Lansing had as much experience in international arbitration tribunals as any other American.

During those years, he also served as counsel for the Chinese and Mexican legations and for private individuals in the Venezuelan asphalt disputes in 1905. His daily contact with his father-in-law further improved his knowledge of international relations. Foster continued his own activities, serving as special advisor to the Chinese delegation to the peace conference to end the Sino-Japanese War and then, in 1907, representing China at the Second Hague Conference.

Lansing did much in addition to practicing law, including coediting a textbook on American government, helping to found the American Society of International Law, and assisting Dr. James Brown Scott in establishing the *American Journal of International Law*. From 1889 to 1907, Lansing also became politically active, serving as a delegate to the 1892 National Convention and as Democratic county chairman. In 1902, he was defeated in the Watertown mayoralty race, his only venture as a candidate. Within the party, he sided with the Grover Cleveland faction and opposed William Jennings Bryan.

By 1913, Lansing had developed a philosophy of government based on political and diplomatic conservatism. In the area of foreign policy, he was a realist who believed in serving the national interest and protecting national prestige. As he wrote, "Force is the great underlying actuality in all history," and "No nation at war, whose national safety is menaced should be expected to permit obligations of justice, morality, humanity or honor to interfere with acts it considers necessary for its self-preservation."

On June 23, 1915, Woodrow Wilson appointed Lansing secretary of state. Lansing had served as counselor for the Department of State from April 1, 1914, until June 9, 1915, when he was named secretary of state *ad interim*, with William Jennings Bryan's resignation.

Over the years, Lansing had clearly come to enjoy his international legal activities; with Wilson's election in 1912, he sought the position of assistant secretary of state. He was not successful, and in fact the position was abolished in a departmental reorganization. With John Bassett Moore's resignation as counselor in 1914, Lansing again sought high office in the State Department. Elihu Root, then Republican Senator from New York and a former secretary of state, supported his bid. Root, who served with Lansing on several international commissions, wrote Wilson about Lansing: "I have formed a very high opinion of his ability and industry. He is earnest, single-minded, and faithful to his work and has rather unusual experiences in international law." No doubt smarting about charges of Bryan's inexperience, indeed, some said incompetence, and his patronage activities, Wilson saw Lansing as someone who could bring stability to the department. Lansing was quickly nominated and confirmed and began his duties as counselor on April 1, 1914.

From that date until his appointment as permanent secretary in June 1915, Lansing was in charge of daily activities. Bryan was frequently absent from the department and even when there he remained aloof from everyday details, giving Lansing the opportunity to learn the department thoroughly. This period also was one of intense activity as Lansing became immersed in the three geographical areas that were to dominate his State Department years: the Caribbean, where Lansing believed U.S. security was firmly at risk; Europe, where Lansing sought to preserve a balance of power favorable to the United States; and East Asia, where Lansing sought stability as the best means of countering Japanese advances in the area.

Initially, Lansing's interim and permanent appointments were not assured. Wilson appeared to want someone other than Lansing as a replacement for Bryan, but remarked that "he had canvassed the field and could not hit upon a satisfactory outside man." The president ruled out Colonel Edward M. House, his special adviser, for health reasons and to preserve House's special status. He was considering Secretary of the Treasury William Gibbs McAdoo and Secretary of Agriculture David F. Houston, both of whom desired the permanent appointment, as well as Chicago lawyer Thomas Jones. Yet, due to the European war and the resulting crises that involved the United States, Wilson realized he needed an experienced diplomat, rather than another political appointment like Bryan. He had come to rely on Lansing's technical advice, and because Lansing was familiar with the work of the department and understood the Wilsonian approach to foreign policy, Wilson overcame his doubts that Lansing "was not a big enough man" and "did not have enough imagination."

Many supported Lansing's candidacy, including the press. The *New York Times* noted that such a nonpolitical appointment would meet with the satisfaction of most Americans. House's support proved critical. House wrote the president: "The most important thing is to get a man with not too many ideas of his own and one that will be entirely guided by you without unnecessary argument, and this, it seems to me, you would find in Lansing." Both Wilson and House were to learn that they had underestimated Robert Lansing.

World's Work observed that "those who know the Department know that Mr. Lansing has been carrying it since August, 1914." Such good press relations, in contrast to Bryan's, continued throughout much of Lansing's term as secretary. In June 1918, *Current Opinion* called him the "most likeable" secretary in history. His relations within the State Department and with the Foreign Service also were good. He stressed merit and efficiency, was himself accessible, conferring every day with his principal advisers, and worked to increase morale in the department.

The Rogers Act of 1924, a major reorganization that merged the consular and diplomatic corps into a single Foreign Service, was in part the result of Lansing's work. He also was generally well received by the Washington diplomatic corps, who considered him experienced and a man of integrity, though Lansing had had his share of problems with the German and Austrian ambassadors, Count Johann Heinrich von Bernstorff and Dr. Constantin Theodore Dumba, respectively. Questioning Lansing's influence with Wilson and House, Bernstorff had written Berlin: "Since Wilson decides *everything*, any interview with Lansing is a mere matter of form." This was an overstatement and showed more than anything else Bernstorff's lack of understanding of Lansing's role.

Lansing's relations with his government associates in the cabinet and Congress were equally harmonious and correct, though not intimate. He formed no close friendships with cabinet colleagues, and some of his contemporaries no doubt agreed with Secretary of the Navy Josephus Daniels' description of Secretary Lansing as being "capable, meticulous, metallic and mousy." He worked hard at improving relationships with Congress and had much better contacts with Republican congressional leaders than perhaps any member of the Wilson administration.

Lansing's key relationships with House and the president were awkward at best, though House had come to give Lansing his due. After detailed conversations with Lansing, House noted: "I feel that I have a working partner in the State Department who will carry his full share." Lansing also respected House's relationship with Wilson. House was to comment that "my position was unusual and without precedent, and it would have been natural for him to object to my ventures in his sphere of activities. He never did. He was willing for me to help in any way the President thought best."

With Wilson, the relationship was difficult. Wilson was idealistic, moralistic, and intuitive, whereas Lansing was realistic, practical, skeptical, and analytical. The president never really trusted Lansing, in part because of his antipathy for lawyers, and Lansing was certainly a lawyer's lawyer.

Nonetheless, Lansing learned how to deal with Wilson. As Daniel Smith has noted: "He submitted long memoranda to the President which could be studied without a feeling of pressure, avoided references to public opinion as compelling a course of action, clothed policy advice in moralistic and idealistic terms, and worked closely with Colonel House and others in trying to sway Wilson to his point of view."

Lansing continued to keep the president's goals in mind and served as secretary of state with enthusiasm until the Paris Peace Conference, when his differences with the president became great. Firmly committed to democracy, Lansing was still able to recognize the legitimacy of the various forms of government that existed throughout the world and believed that national sovereignty was a most important concept underpinning the relations between countries. As such, he stood at a distance from President Wilson's goals for democratic foreign policies.

In 1924, responding to a biographical data form, Robert Lansing listed 49 principal questions that came up during his incumbency as secretary of state, from the *Lusitania* crisis and the "rights of neutrals and belligerents with respect to neutral trade in time of war" to "the difficulty of transacting the business of the Department of State without free access to the President" and "the decision to resign during the President's illness when it became evident that the President was willing to assume the responsibility for the retirement." These questions fell into the general areas of the European war; Latin America, especially the Caribbean; East Asia, particularly relations with Japan; the Russian Revolution; the Paris Peace Conference; and finally, Lansing's departure from Wilson's Cabinet.

Perhaps the area where Lansing had his greatest influence—the European war— would lead to the area of Lansing's least influence—the Paris Peace Conference. Neutrality, with a leaning toward the Allies, was the United States' initial policy in Europe, largely as a result of Lansing's suggestions. Arms trade, allowing the arming of belligerent merchant ships, extending private commercial credits for the Allies, and overturning Bryan's "loan ban" of August 1914 and holding the Germans to "strict accountability" for the loss to submarines of American ships and lives were all policies Lansing championed. He also worked to protect legitimate U.S. interests when dealing with the Allies, especially the British, but never to the point of threatening Anglo-American relations.

Underlying Lansing's views, which he was able to convert into policies supported by President Wilson, was a belief that Germany threatened American security, especially if it proved victorious in the European conflict. Indeed, as Lansing took over as secretary, he became obsessed with German absolutism and worried about the absolutist powers—Germany, Japan, and even Russia—coming together. He sought to mark time "until the indignation . . . of the American people against Germany could be sufficiently aroused." That process took longer than Lansing expected, with missteps over the sinking of the *Arabic* in 1915 and the *Sussex* in 1916. There was a formal protest in October 1915 about the Allied blockade, but the blockade continued, and Wilson and Lansing seemed satisfied not to press further. Wilson tried for peace, proposing to mediate between the belligerents in 1916, but his efforts failed. In February 1917, with the German announcement of unrestricted submarine war, Wilson was prepared to sever diplomatic relations with Germany. By April, Wilson finally called for war, using arguments that Lansing had been putting forward for months, thus constituting the high water mark of Lansing's influence on Wilson concerning European affairs. The war itself, however, saw Wilson increasingly rely on Colonel House as a diplomatic agent and as a confidant in planning the peace.

Meanwhile, Lansing was forced to devote much of his attention to both Latin America and East Asia. In Latin America, Lansing walked into a very difficult situation. The Mexican Revolution caused many difficulties for Washington, prompting Wilson to send troops to occupy Veracruz in April 1914, an action Lansing supported. Lansing hoped to smooth Mexican-American relations, given his worries about German influence there with the outbreak of war in Europe in the summer of 1914. As Lansing wrote: "Our possible relations with Germany must be our first consideration and all our intercourse with Mexico must be regulated accordingly." In 1915, he called a conference of representatives of Latin and South America, out of which came *de facto* recognition of the government of Venustiano Carranza. Thus, Mexican-American relations took a temporary turn for the better.

Lansing also worked to purchase the Danish West Indies in the Caribbean, again in deference to his concerns about Germany; made it clear that the Caribbean was an American sphere of interest, supporting interventions in Haiti in 1915 and the Dominican Republic in 1916; and supported further intervention in Mexico over the activities of Pancho Villa, including threatening war with Mexico in 1919 over the arrest of Consular Agent William O. Jenkins.

The problem with Lansing's policy toward Latin America was that it was built on two somewhat inaccurate beliefs. First, throughout the period 1914 to 1918, he overemphasized the German threat in Latin America, perhaps symbolized by the row over the Zimmermann telegram, which, though it proved to be helpful in his crusade against Germany, was vastly overplayed. Second, he believed that the Caribbean was an American lake, with the United States free to do whatever it believed necessary to preserve its interests. This led to frequent intervention (Mexico, Haiti, the Dominican Republic) and a legacy that leaves little fond memories in Latin America of either Lansing or Wilson. Not until the Good Neighbor policy of Franklin D. Roosevelt in the 1930s would American relations with Latin America substantially improve.

In the Far East, Wilson practiced "missionary diplomacy," stemming from many years of contacts between Chinese and Americans ("China hands"), particularly

U.S. missionaries. President Wilson had come to believe that the United States had a special role in China to spread democratic ideals, teach Christian morals, and help the Chinese in the quest for stability and progress. He had developed a warm attitude toward the efforts of the Chinese for self-government and liberty. He realized the importance of the Open Door, which guaranteed American interests in China, while understanding the limits of U.S. policy regarding China, knowing that the American people would not support a war on behalf of China. China, in other words, was at the center of Woodrow Wilson's East-Asian world.

For Lansing, China was incidental. Japan was the real potential problem in the Far East for the United States and the democratic world. He knew, of course, that Britain and the United States could control Japan; but Britain, especially British seapower, was unavailable after 1914, and the United States alone stood in opposition to Japanese expansionism. The Japanese had seized German holdings in the Shantung Province of China and forced the so-called "Twenty-one Demands" on China in 1915. Lansing urged negotiations and moderation concerning Japan with the president. Thus, while the United States publicly opposed any interference with sovereignty in China, Japan and China signed an agreement in May 1915 through which Japan gained large concessions.

While being willing to recognize Japan's "special interests" in Manchuria and the two countries' "special and close relations, political as well as economic," Lansing hoped to get Japan to publicly state its acceptance of the Open Door and its commitment not to interfere in China proper. These points were the basis of the Lansing–Ishii Agreement of November 2, 1917. Still, the agreement was interpreted in different ways, not only by the United States and Japan but also by Lansing and the president, with Wilson being unable to accept the realistic concessions that Lansing thought necessary.

This division between the president and the secretary of state became evident again at the Paris Peace Conference, when the Japanese pressed for the German rights in Shantung, recognition of a paramount position in Eastern Asia, acceptance of wartime treaties with China, a declaration of racial equality, and control of the German islands in the North Pacific. The Japanese failed, in the end, to get the statement on equality and gained only mandate control, through the League of Nations, of some of the German islands. The big stake was Shantung and a general solution to the Chinese problem. After difficult negotiations, complicated by earlier treaties between Japan and France and Great Britain as well as a Japanese threat to boycott the treaty and the League, the Japanese won control of German economic rights in Shantung. Wilson had opposed the claims but was forced to accept them.

Another factor complicating Japanese-American relations was the Russian Revolution. Lansing at first hailed the overthrow of the Tsar in March 1917. When the commission headed by Elihu Root returned from Russia, he began to worry about the Provisional Government. Although the commission believed the Provisional Government stable and capable of continuing the war effort, Lansing predicted that the Russian Revolution would "far surpass in brutality and destruction of life and property the Terror of the French Revolution." Thus, he was not surprised when the Bolsheviks came to power and withdrew Russia from the war. He immediately recommended a nonrecognition policy toward the Bolsheviks, which President Wilson accepted.

From the beginning, Lansing was far more alarmed than Wilson about Bolshevism and its possible implications. He quickly came to the view that the United States should support military intervention. He convinced Wilson to support financial aid to Great Britain and France to help Russian opponents of the Bolsheviks, but was unable to deter Wilson from permitting all forms of contact with the Bolsheviks.

The president soon learned that any Wilsonian negotiation with the Bolsheviks would have to take place against the active opposition of Lansing and the State Department. Eventually, Wilson gave in, with U.S. troops going to North Russia and Siberia with a large contingent of Japanese troops in Siberia. The intervention was doomed to failure, if for no other reason than that the differences between Wilson and his advisers and the British, French, and the Japanese on its objectives were so great. The intervention succeeded only in getting Soviet–American relations off to a very poor start, especially when combined with the continuing policy of nonrecognition. Lansing's influence here left a legacy that was to continue into the 1930s and beyond.

By autumn 1918, Lansing's alarm about Bolshevism had grown, and he worried that a harsh peace would only aid the spread of Bolshevism to Germany and its allies. He also had become concerned with President Wilson's call for a League of Nations, which raised the questions of collective security and self-determination. Any such league, Lansing believed, should remain simple and practical.

In many ways, Lansing represented traditional diplomacy and Wilson a radical departure from the past, and the war months proved to be very frustrating for Lansing. At the peace conference, Lansing found his differences with President Wilson's views about peace and the postwar world fundamental and growing. The practical Lansing believed that many of Wilson's hopes and ideas ignored the basic selfishness of countries. The president also clashed with Lansing over the composition of the peace delegation, with Lansing recommending against Wilson's personal participation and advocating the appointment of Elihu Root. On both counts, Wilson rejected the secretary's advice.

Lansing remained part of the team and served as a member of the U.S. delegation in Paris; but the president, aided by House, made the important decisions, ignoring Lansing as well as General Tasker Bliss and Henry White, the other U.S. delegates to Paris. At Paris, Lansing was part of the Council of Ten, but Wilson soon began to meet with the other Allied leaders—David Lloyd George of Britain, Georges Clemenceau of France, and Vittorio Orlando of Italy—and it was that group that made the real decisions. Further, Wilson and House dominated the work on the League of Nations, with Wilson ignoring Lansing's suggestions for revisions to the League proposal. Lansing was so frustrated that, on several occasions, he considered resigning both from the delegation and as secretary of state.

Lansing became more critical of Wilson as the conference continued, especially as Lansing's fear of Bolshevism grew. He opposed the harsh treatment proposed for Germany, predicting that reparations would never be collected. But he fought a losing battle, as Wilson was willing to compromise on this issue to secure British and French support for the League, though Lansing and Wilson did agree on opposing any dismemberment of Germany. In other areas at Paris, such as Japan, Lansing's influence was equally limited. Thus, Wilson came to view Lansing as conservative and obstructionist.

In the end, Lansing signed the Treaty of Versailles on June 28, 1919, because he believed, more than anything else, that Europe needed peace, even if an imperfect one. Back home, with Wilson's stroke and serious incapacitation in October 1919, Lansing worked actively for Senate ratification of the treaty, while trying unsuccessfully to draft reservations to the treaty that would be satisfactory to Wilson, the Republicans, and the Allies. Obviously, the tense relationship between Lansing and President Wilson could not continue indefinitely, and in February 1920, showing some evidence of recovery from his stroke, the president demanded Lansing's resignation.

Ostensibly the reason was because Lansing had presided over unauthorized meetings of the cabinet during the President's illness. The cabinet had met a number of times between October 1919 and February 1920, but Lansing was not the only cabinet member who felt that such meetings were necessary. The president also received memoranda of the discussions at the cabinet meetings. Wilson, however, came to object to Lansing's role, accusing him of an "assumption of Presidential authority" and stating that he would be relieved if Lansing "would give your present office up and afford me an opportunity to select some one whose mind would more willingly go along with mine."

Lansing immediately complied, given that he had already considered resigning as early as January 1919 when, as he noted to the president, it became apparent that "you no longer were disposed to welcome my advice in matters pertaining to the negotiations in Paris, to our foreign service, or to international affairs in general." Wilson accepted the resignation on February 13, 1920. Bainbridge Colby succeeded Lansing as secretary of state.

Lansing, as Daniel Smith has noted, "has emerged as one of those fortunate public men who have grown in stature with the passage of time." Although able and quite experienced in diplomacy, Lansing was for many years eclipsed by Wilson and Wilson's special adviser, House. In recent years, however, Lansing's contributions have been recognized and put in proper perspective.

In Latin America, Lansing had been able to preserve U.S. interests, though not making much progress in encouraging Pan-Americanism. In East Asia, he had worked with some success to control Japanese expansionism, while at the same time preserving stability for China. In the European disaster, he had worked, with ultimate success, to get Wilson to side with the Allies to defeat Germany. Although the Treaty of Versailles and the League of Nations in particular posed difficulties for Lansing, taken in perspective he had contributed to a successful European policy. Finally, by initiating the nonrecognition policy toward Bolshevik Russia, he had set the course for American-Soviet relations for the next 15 years. Nevertheless, as Smith has written, "although Lansing was an able Secretary of State, he fell short of greatness, partly because of his own conservative limitations and partly because of the conditions under which he worked."

After his resignation, Lansing returned to the practice of international law. With Lester H. Woolsey, also a former State Department official, Lansing established the firm of Lansing and Woolsey, with offices close to the State Department. Over the next several years, the firm represented a number of foreign governments, including China, Poland, Persia, and Finland. In 1923, the firm served as counsel for Chile in the Tacna–Arica arbitration with Peru.

In the remaining years of Lansing's life, he was quite active in other areas, including the Presbyterian Church, the American Red Cross, the Carnegie Endowment for International Peace, and the Archaeological Society of Washington. His spare time found outlets in sketching, fishing, golf, as a baseball fan, and as a dutiful husband.

Lansing's long life in public service came to a close in his Washington home when, after a brief illness, he died on October 30, 1928.

BIBLIOGRAPHICAL ESSAY

Numerous manuscript collections are indispensable to understanding Lansing's term as secretary of state. They begin, of course, with the Lansing Papers themselves, deposited in the Manuscripts Division of the Library of Congress, which is a large collection—62 volumes of correspondence, memoranda, appointment books, and daily desk diaries covering the period 1911 to 1928. There is also a small but nonetheless significant collection of Lansing Papers at Princeton University. Other important manuscript collections include the Woodrow Wilson Papers at the Library of Congress, which also houses the collections of a number of Lansing's governmental colleagues, including Newton D. Baker, Henry White, Tasker Bliss, George Creel, Breckinridge Long, Josephus Daniels, William Jennings Bryan, Ray S. Baker, Thomas W. Gregory, William G. McAdoo, John Bassett Moore, Elihu Root, Lester H. Woolsey, and Joseph P. Tumulty; the papers of Lansing's father-in-law, John Watson Foster, also in the Library of Congress; the papers of Edward M. House and Frank Polk at Yale University; and the State Department Records in the National Archives.

Among the most important published document collections are the annual volumes of the State Department from 1914 to 1920, *Papers Relating to the Foreign Relations of the United States*, especially the 13-volume *Paris Peace Conference, 1919*, and the two-volume *Lansing Papers, 1914–1920*, a selection of Lansing personal files, published after his death in 1928. *Papers of Woodrow Wilson* (1966–1994), edited by Arthur S. Link et al. and published by Princeton University Press, is also indispensable, its 69-volume collection containing virtually all primary materials about Wilson and the events of the Wilson administration, including relevant Lansing documents.

Lansing wrote extensively about his diplomacy and his view on foreign policy. The most important of his works are *The Peace Negotiations: A Personal Narrative* (1921), *The Big Four and Others of the Peace Conference* (1921), *War Memoirs of Robert Lansing* (1935), published seven years after his death and based on his private correspondence and memoranda, and Robert Lansing and Gary M. Jones, *Government: Its Origin, Growth, and Form in the United States* (1902), important for his early views on U.S. government. He wrote many articles over the years, a number of which appeared in the *American Journal of International Law*, which are also important for understanding his thoughts on diplomacy. Many of his contemporaries' memoirs, autobiographies, diaries, and letters also are useful.

Turning to secondary literature, there is as yet no published full-scale biography of Lansing. Thomas Henry Hartig's, *Robert Lansing: An Interpretive Biography* (1982) from Ohio State University, covers his entire career. There are several published treatments of Lansing as secretary of state, including Julius W. Pratt,

---

"Robert Lansing," in Samuel Flagg Bemis (ed.), *The American Secretaries of State and Their Diplomacy* (1929), 10, 47–175; Julius W. Pratt, "Robert Lansing," *Dictionary of American Biography*, 10; and Daniel Smith, "Robert Lansing," in Norman A. Graebner (ed.), *Uncertain Tradition: American Secretaries of State in the Twentieth Century* (1961). The best works on Lansing and the European war are two books by Daniel M. Smith, *Robert Lansing and American Neutrality, 1914–1917* (1972) and *The Great Departure: The United States and World War I, 1914–1920* (1965).

Other works covering this subject that should be consulted include John Milton Cooper, *The Warrior and the Priest: Woodrow Wilson and Theodore Roosevelt* (1983) and his *Pivotal Decades: The United States 1900–1920* (1990); Patrick Devlin, *Too Proud to Fight: Woodrow Wilson's Neutrality* (1974); Robert H. Ferrell, *Woodrow Wilson and World War I, 1917–1921* (1985); Lloyd C. Gardner, *Safe for Democracy: The Anglo-American Response to Revolution, 1913–1923* (1987); Arthur Walworth, *Woodrow Wilson* (1958); August Hecksher, *Woodrow Wilson;* Dragon Zivojinovic, "Robert Lansing's Comments on the Pontifical Peace Note of August 1, 1917," *Journal of American History*, 56 (1969); Daniel M. Smith, "Robert Lansing and the Formulation of American Neutrality Policies, 1914–1915," *Mississippi Valley Historical Review*, 43 (1956–1957); George Barany, "Wilsonian Central Europe: Lansing's Contribution," *Historian*, 28 (1966); and Arthur S. Link, *Wilson: The Struggle for Neutrality, 1914–1915* (1960).

Especially important are Robert W. Tucker, "An Inner Circle of One: Woodrow Wilson and His Advisors," *The National Interest* 51 (1998), which analyzes the respective roles of Lansing and House; Ernest R. May, *The World War and American Isolation, 1914–1917* (1959); Louis J. Gerson, *Woodrow Wilson and the Rebirth of Poland, 1914–1920* (1953); J. A. S. Grenville, "The United States Decision for War, 1917: Manuscript Diary of Robert Lansing," *University of Nottingham, Renaissance Modern Studies*, 4 (1960); Edward H. Buehrig, *Woodrow Wilson and the Balance of Power* (1955); Arthur S. Link, *Woodrow Wilson and the Progressive Era, 1910–1917* (1954); and Victor S. Mamatey, *United States and East Central Europe, 1914–1918* (1957).

Lansing's role in East Asian diplomacy is most thoroughly covered in Burton F. Beers, *Vain Endeavor: Robert Lansing's Attempts to End the American-Japanese Rivalry* (1962). Other treatments of value are Thomas Henry Hartig, "Robert Lansing and East Asian-American Relations: A Study in Motivation," *Michigan Academician* (1974); Burton F. Beers, "Robert Lansing's Proposed Bargain with Japan," *Pacific Historical Review*, 26 (1957); Roy Watson Curry, *Woodrow Wilson and Far Eastern Policy* (1957); Tien-yi Li, *Woodrow Wilson's China Policy, 1913–1917* (1952); Stephen G. Craft, "John Bassett Moore, Robert Lansing, and the Shadong Question," *Pacific Historical Review* 66(1997); and Russell H. Fifield, *Woodrow Wilson and the Far East: The Diplomacy of the Shantung Question* (1952).

For relations with Russia, consult George F. Kennan, *Soviet-American Relations, 1917–1920* (1956), 2 vols., and Eugene P. Trani, "Woodrow Wilson and the Decision to Intervene in Russia: A Reconsideration," *Journal of Modern History*, 48 (1976). Three recent books on the Russian question are David S. Foglesong, *America's Secret War Against Bolshevism: U.S. Intervention in the Russian Civil War, 1917–1920* (1995); David W. McFadden, "After the Colby Note: The Wilson Administration and the Bolsheviks, 1920–21," *Presidential Studies Quarterly*, 25 (Fall 1995); and Georg Schild, *Between Ideology and Realpolitik: Woodrow Wilson and the Russian Revolution, 1917–1921* (1995).

Lansing's Latin-American activities are detailed in Louis G. Kahle, "Robert Lansing and the Recognition of Venustiano Carranza," *Hispanic American Historical Review*, 38 (1958), 353–372; David Glaser, "1919: William Jenkins, Robert Lansing, and the Mexican Interlude," *Southwestern Historical Quarterly*, 74 (1971); Dmitri Lazo, "Lansing, Wilson and the Jenkins Incident," *Diplomatic History* (1985); Clyde G. Koehne, *Mexican Policy of Robert Lansing, 1915–1920* (1975); and George William Baker, Jr., *The Caribbean Policy of Woodrow Wilson, 1913–1917* (1962).

Two books that address Lansing's role at the Paris Peace Conference are Thomas Bailey, *Woodrow Wilson and the Lost Peace* (1944), and Lloyd E. Ambrosius, *Woodrow Wilson and the American Diplomatic Tradition: The Treaty Fight in Perspective* (1987). See also Dmitri Lazo, "A Question of Loyalty: Robert Lansing and the Treaty of Versailles," *Diplomatic History* (1985). Another interesting view of Lansing's notion of Realpolitik may be gleaned from Frederick S. Calthoun, *Uses of Force in Wilsonian Foreign Policy*.

Finally, Lansing's family is covered in Claude G. Munsell, *The Lansing Family: A Genealogy of the Descendants of Gerrit Frederickse Lansing* (1916), and his appointment as secretary of state in Paolo E. Coletta (ed.), "Bryan Briefs Lansing," *Pacific Historical Review*, 27 (1958). His resignation is covered in Joyce G. Williams, "The Resignation of Secretary of State Robert Lansing," *Diplomatic History*, 3 (1979), 337–44; Daniel M. Smith, "Robert Lansing and the Wilson Interregnum, 1919–1920," *Historian*, 21 (1958–1959); Gene Smith, *When the Cheering Stopped* (1964); and Daniel M. Smith, *Aftermath of War: Bainbridge Colby and Wilsonian Diplomacy, 1920–1921* (1970).

Eugene P. Trani

HUGH S. LEGARÉ
(1797–1843)

Served 1843 as Interim Secretary of State
Appointed by President John Tyler
Whig

Hugh Swinton Legaré was born on January 2, 1797, in Charleston, South Car-olina. His father, Solomon, descended from French Huguenots, whereas his mother, Mary, was descended from Scotch Presbyterians. Hugh was a healthy four-year-old when he had a near fatal reaction to a smallpox inoculation, which stunted the growth of the lower half of his body. Thereafter, he walked with a limp, seldom rode a horse, and suffered from melancholia at times.

He studied at Moses Waddle's Willington Academy and was the valedictorian of his graduating class in 1814. Determined to lead the life of a gentleman scholar, Legaré read widely in law and literature on his own from 1814 to 1817. In 1818, he traveled in Europe and studied law and language at Edinburgh University, where he came to know Washington Irving and Walter Scott.

On his return to the United States, Legaré began a highly successful law practice and was elected to the state legislature and served 1820 to 1822 and again from 1824 to 1830. Although he supported laissez-faire economics and was against fed-eral internal improvements expenditures, Legaré held Northern views on national finance. He extolled credit and the English financial system.

Legaré was closely associated with the *Southern Review*, which he helped estab-lish. He became the principle contributor, and at times editor, of the *Review*, help-ing to make it a journal of national distinction. The *Review* displayed Legaré's erudition to the fullest. He was a lifelong student of the classics and was at home in French, Spanish, Italian, German, and Greek.

His great passion was the law. He had mixed feelings about the English common law tradition, admiring it for helping to curb the civil law's caesaristic and absolutist tendencies, yet deciding that the civil law was for him more consistent than judge-made common law. At the same time, he believed fervently that law developed over time as a result of man's search for both freedom and justice within society. The law was shaped over generations by judicial decisions, honed over centuries, and aided by the ancillary legal codes. The current generation was the beneficiary of all the accumulated legal wisdom of the past. The law thus built was primarily the work of judges far above the maddening noise of a temporary popular majority, uninterested in questions of justice.

Nullification was the crisis of his adult life. When Calhoun popularized it in 1828, Legaré attacked it as unconstitutional in the *Southern Review*. However, unlike Webster and similar to Tyler, Legaré thought the states having formed the union, had the right to secede from it. In 1832 he was rescued from the nullification fray when the state legislature elected him Attorney General of South Carolina, then an apolitical office.

President Jackson appreciated his stand against nullification, however, and later in the year Legaré was given the post of chargé d'affaires in Belgium. His duties in Brussels were light, enabling him to master German and travel all over Europe, where he admired the Prussian bureaucracy, discussed law with the elderly Von Schlegel, and added to his knowledge of legal systems.

Returning home in 1836, he was elected to Congress, where Washington's rough and tumble politics were hard on his sensibilities. He managed to earn Calhoun's opposition by making an important speech against his sub-Treasury bill. Legaré was a good economist but an indifferent politician. His speech was lucid, but a political disaster. For the first time Legaré faced important opposition in his reelection campaign, and he was bitterly surprised when he suffered defeat at the hands of his closest friend, Isaac Holmes.

Legaré supported William Henry Harrison and John Tyler in 1840, and at the time of the mass resignations from the cabinet, President Tyler appointed him U.S. attorney general in 1841. This post was then a part-time job at half the pay of the rest of the cabinet, but allowed him to maintain his law practice. He rented John Bell's Washington residence, liquidated his Charleston holdings, and brought his mother, sister, and three slaves to the capital, where he grew affluent pleading private cases before the Supreme Court at one thousand dollars apiece.

As attorney general, Legaré was highly efficient, averaging one legal opinion every day. In 1842–1843 he won 7 of 11 cases before the court as attorney general and 3 of 4 private cases (the 4th being a draw). His work won high praise from Chief Justice Roger Taney and Associate Justice Joseph Storey. When the Whigs passed a small tariff in 1842 in part to preserve distribution to the states of revenue from the sale of public lands, Tyler vetoed it, and Legaré defended a legal challenge to that action in a decisive argument.

When the Virginia slave ship *Creole* was taken over by 19 mutinous slaves who ordered her into Nassau, the British freed all the slaves except the 19 mutineers, whom they refused to return, the United States having no extradition treaty with London. Legaré, an expert in international law, argued successfully that a ship entering a foreign port under duress was not subject to that port's law, and in 1853 arbitration awarded the slave owners $100,000 in compensation.

Legaré's legal work had helped move the Webster–Ashburton treaty to conclusion, after which, Webster resigned as secretary of state in 1843. When Tyler offered Legaré Webster's post as secretary of state, the Carolinian refused, knowing Tyler's probable fate and wanting to keep his position as attorney general, but then accepted the position *ad interim.*

Legaré was an advocate of manifest destiny, supporting U.S. expansion to the Pacific coast and working to make the United States an important power in the

Pacific basin. He was a strong advocate of Texas annexation and had accepted the *ad interim* appointment in part because he thought he could better accomplish that annexation as a temporary secretary. He protested the seizure of Hawaii by an unauthorized British naval squadron and hoped to break the British hold on Hawaiian trade. Further, he organized a trade mission to China, which after his death led to the first commercial treaty with China.

In June 1843, he traveled to Boston, where President Tyler and the cabinet attended the dedication of the Bunker Hill Monument. Suffering extreme abdominal pains, the Secretary of State missed the ceremonies and was moved from Tremont House to the home of his Boston friend George Ticknor.

Correctly assessing his odds, Hugh Legaré made out a will and died at his friend's home on June 19, 1843. Although he did not serve long enough as secretary of state to have a significant track record, he was certainly a brilliant lawyer and an excellent attorney general both in Columbia and Washington. Well educated, an accomplished linguist, he was also an expert in civil and international law. By the time of his death, Legaré was the acknowledged premier of the Tyler administration. Years later, Tyler commented that his political decline began when Legaré died.

BIBLIOGRAPHICAL ESSAY

The papers of Hugh Legaré are housed in a variety of locations, including, primarily, the South Carolina University Library. Other locations include Duke University Library; Historical Society of Pennsylvania; Library of Congress; National Archives; Public Record Office, England; and the South Carolina Historical Society. A useful collection of Legaré's writings can be found in *Writings of Hugh Swinton Legaré* (1846), 2 volumes, edited by Mary Legaré.

The standard biography is Michael O'Brien, *A Character of Hugh Legaré* (1985). An older but still useful biography is Linda Rhea, *Hugh Swinton Legaré, a Charleston Intellectual* (1934).

Legaré's tenure in Tyler's cabinet and his relationship with the president is ably presented by Marvin R. Cain, "Return of Republicanism: A Reappraisal of Hugh Swinton Legaré and the Tyler Presidency," *South Carolina Historical Magazine*, October 1978.

Two short studies on Legaré as a literary figure are Vernon L. Parrington's, *Main Currents in American Thought*, volume 2, *The Romantic Revolution in America 1800–1860* (1954), and Jay B. Hubbell, *The South in American Literature 1607–1900* (1954).

Alfred Sullivan

EDWARD LIVINGSTON (1764–1836)

Served 1831–1833
Appointed by President Andrew Jackson
Democrat

Misfortune, wrote the biographer of Edward Livingston, followed Livingston's footsteps from the end of his first congressional career in 1801 to the end of his life. Yet despite repeated setbacks, both personal and political, Livingston persevered to become secretary of state and minister to France under Andrew Jackson. Though not given much latitude or responsibility in foreign affairs as secretary of state by Jackson, this "Montesquieu of the Cabinet," so called because of his scholarship and Francophilia, shown most brightly in his post in Paris following his duties in Washington.

Livingston was born May 28, 1764, at Clermont, Columbia County, New York. Receiving his early education at home at Esopus, now Kingston, New York, he graduated from Nassau Hall (Princeton University) in 1781 and studied law in Albany and New York, counting among his fellow students Alexander Hamilton and Aaron Burr. He was admitted to the bar in 1785 and began a law practice in New York City. He married a merchant's daughter, Mary McEvers, in 1788, and their union produced three children.

Born into a wealthy family long powerful in the politics of New York, Livingston received his political tutelage from his brilliant brother, Robert, member of the Continental Congress, secretary of foreign affairs during the Confederation, and envoy to France. Livingston early on met important national figures, such as Lafayette, Washington, Jefferson, and of course, Hamilton and Burr and developed a wide circle of acquaintances. Livingston was a devoted defender of the Republic and often expressed strong nationalistic views. Yet, guided by the example of his brother (17 years his senior), he developed a cosmopolitan view of the world that included a healthy respect for France and a disdain for Britain (due, in part, from British troops having burned the family's home during the Revolution).

After serving in Congress from 1795 to 1801, where he was one of the leaders opposing Jay's Treaty, Livingston was appointed federal district attorney and, later, mayor of New York. Livingston served admirably during an epidemic of yellow fever, helping to dispense quick and efficient aid, but his loose and inefficient management permitted a clerk appointed by him to the district attorney's office to remove over $44,000 earmarked for federal taxes. Taking the responsibility for the theft, Livingston was directed to pay the federal government $100,000. His political career shattered and his law business declining, Livingston, who had become a widower in 1801, left New York for New Orleans in late 1803.

Livingston married a young Creole widow two years after his arrival and soon assumed a commanding place among political and social leaders in opposition to Governor W. C. C. Claiborne. During his career as a Louisiana attorney, Livingston opposed the introduction of common law into the territory, contributed to new territorial codes, and most importantly, drafted a new criminal code for Louisiana that eliminated capital punishment, prevented most corporal punishment, and established reform schools and penitentiaries. For this achievement, he won plaudits from scholars and politicians around the world. His political activity included a controversy with President Jefferson over a parcel of land in the Mississippi, serving as aide-de-camp to Andrew Jackson during the Battle of New Orleans, and representing New Orleans in Congress, 1822–1828, and Louisiana as junior senator, 1829–1833. He finished repaying the government the $100,000 owed from his New York days by 1826.

As a congressman and senator, Livingston, along with most of his colleagues, focused more on domestic affairs than foreign, and he supported internal improvements and veterans' pensions. A firm Jackson champion, he was offered the position of minister to France by a grateful Jackson after the election of 1828 but after careful consideration refused the president in May 1829. Although he wanted the position badly, he could not accept it due to his financial resources. In Paris, where diplomats were expected to entertain heavily and the United States provided but a meager salary for its envoy, only a man with available personal wealth could hope to represent the country adequately, and as real estate made up the bulk of Livingston's assets, he had little ready cash.

Jackson's break with his vice president, John C. Calhoun, in the spring of 1831 caused the president to ask for the resignation of his entire cabinet to preserve a sense of political impartiality, because half the members supported Calhoun. Secretary of State Van Buren wrote Livingston on April 9, 1831, asking him to come to Washington immediately to see the president. Van Buren had persuaded Jackson to ask Livingston, recognized by all political factions as a man of integrity, to become Van Buren's successor. In short, Jackson selected Livingston for the post for reasons of domestic political harmony, rather than for Livingston's experience in foreign affairs. Livingston, happy as a senator, reluctantly agreed in a letter to the president, April 20, 1831. Following a brief confirmation skirmish in which Jackson's enemy, Henry Clay, embarrassed the administration by demanding an investigation into the means by which Livingston had paid back his debt to the government, Livingston received Senate approval in January 1832. The Louisianan, deeply humiliated by Clay's antics, briefly considered legal action and remained embittered about the episode.

As secretary of state, Livingston dealt with questions of boundaries and commerce, issues unresolved from Van Buren's two years as secretary. They remained largely unsettled when Livingston left office two years later. Although the 68-year-old attorney was able, his was little more than a caretaker secretaryship, in part because Jackson acted as his own secretary in foreign affairs and in part because the president never trusted Livingston in the State Department, preferring the advice of his trusted confidant, Van Buren. Nevertheless, Livingston made the best of his situation and aided the president in domestic matters, as well as in affairs in Europe, Central and South America, and the Orient.

The most immediate problem facing Livingston was the northeastern boundary dispute between the United States and Britain. The Convention of 1827 provided that King William of the Netherlands act as arbiter and submit a report suggesting a fair boundary. The king having given his report by 1831, American officials had to decide whether to accept his findings. The British seemed disposed to accept, as was Jackson, but the administration had to face fierce opposition from the states of Maine and Massachusetts. Jackson, in a decision he later regretted, listened to his advisers and sent the king's report to the Senate without recommendation, where-upon the Senate rejected it in July 1832 and urged the president to embark on new negotiations with Great Britain.

Meanwhile, Livingston held conversations with state officials in Maine and hammered out an agreement in which the state forsook all claims north of the St. John and east of the St. Francis rivers in exchange for other disputed territory and, if necessary, the funds arising from the sale of a million acres of land in Michigan. But by March 1833, when the new British chargé, Sir Charles Vaughan, arrived in Washington, the agreement with Maine had broken down, for the state legislature declared all international agreements not binding unless submitted to and approved by the people of Maine in town meetings. Disappointed but undaunted, Livingston suggested a new boundary to the British, using the head of the St. Croix River as a marker and drawing a line from it to the heights that divided the waters that flowed into the St. Lawrence River and those that emptied into the Atlantic. The line was similar to that suggested by the king, though somewhat less generous to the Americans. Lacking the support of Maine, however, success eluded the administration. Yet, it is interesting to note that the Webster–Ashburton Treaty of 1842 incorporated Livingston's proposed boundary.

Commercial matters dominated the conversations directed by Livingston between the U.S. and European nations. Spoliations resulting from seizures of American shipping during the Napoleonic wars had been a source of irritation and stalled negotiation between the United States and a few European nations for years before Jackson made their settlement a top priority. The American minister to Paris, William C. Rives, concluded a treaty with France on July 4, 1831, by which France agreed to pay $4.6 million in claims to the United States in six annual installments from which one-twentieth of the amount would be deducted to pay French claims against the United States. In addition, the French would reduce duties on long-staple cotton in exchange for reduced American duties on bottled and casked wine. The president approved of the treaty, but Livingston worried that the reciprocal trade agreement might be of doubtful constitutionality and that the French claims coming out of the American settlement might be too high. Van Buren and Rives, in close touch with each other and with the president, convinced Jackson that Livingston's fears were groundless. Jackson sent the treaty to the Senate, where it was ratified unanimously in January 1832. In February 1833 Secretary of the Treasury Louis McLane presented a bill to the French minister of finance, after prior notification, for the first installment of the funds. The French refused to pay, for the Americans had overlooked one detail: the Chamber of Deputies had not approved the treaty and appropriated the money. In 1832 a cholera epidemic shortened the annual parliamentary session, and in 1833 a pending Greek treaty was given precedence over the American. A furious Jackson could not understand French procrastination, but despite his displeasure and determination to resolve the matter, nothing more came of the treaty while Livingston remained secretary.

The United States had better luck with its negotiations with Naples and Russia. After threatening to recall the U.S. envoy, John Nelson, and send in the frigate *United States* to encourage cooperation in settling claims, King Ferdinand in Naples agreed to negotiations, and a treaty was concluded October 8, 1832. James Buchanan, envoy to Russia, succeeded, in turn, in wringing a treaty of commerce and navigation from St. Petersburg, although he could not persuade the Russians to agree to a treaty protecting the rights of neutrals in war.

Livingston, overridden in the French negotiations and having had little to do with the dealings in Naples and Russia, also exerted little influence in the mission of the U.S. emissary, Edmund Roberts, to the Orient that resulted in treaties with Siam and Muscat. Similarly, he had little to do with the treaty with Turkey ratified in February 1832 or with claim negotiations with Spain and Portugal.

He exerted more influence in hemispheric affairs. In May 1832 New Granada, under British pressure, rescinded a treaty permitting reciprocal trading rights and abrogated an agreement from 1824 granting the United States most-favored-nation status. Livingston, in strong terms, upheld the Monroe Doctrine for reasons commercial, rather than political. In the Falkland Islands, Argentines, having occupied the islands, seized three U.S. ships engaged in fishing and sealing. After a U.S. warship visited the islands and removed their inhabitants, a U.S. representative was sent to deal with Buenos Aires. The Argentines refused to concede any points, and the envoy withdrew, but not before the British seized the Falklands and settled the issue of their sovereignty. The Jackson administration, on Livingston's urging, did not protest this action as a violation of the Monroe Doctrine, presumably because the islands were of not great importance. Finally, regarding Texas, Livingston informed the U.S. representative, Anthony Butler, that his proposal that the United States loan Mexico five million dollars, for which the United States would receive the mortgage for Texas was unconstitutional. Butler, Livingston wrote, should stick to settling remaining details of two proposed treaties of limits and commerce.

Perhaps remembering his own situation in having to decline the post in Paris, Livingston attempted a large-scale reform of the Foreign Service by seeking from Congress appropriation for a consular salary structure, with restrictions against engaging in commerce, and a fee scale for consular duties. For diplomats he asked housing, money for filing and office supplies, and clerks. But Congress did not act on either recommendation, and in the end, Livingston had to be content with issuing a standard sheet of instructions for consuls regarding communications, duties, and behavior.

Six months after Livingston took office, Jackson wrote Van Buren that he did not plan to keep the Louisianan in office long. Jackson decided by October 1832 to send Livingston to Paris to replace Rives, though he chose to wait until after the presidential election and, later, until after the tumultuous congressional session in the spring of 1833. Livingston resigned from office May 29, 1833, and the same day was appointed minister to France.

As secretary of state, Livingston did not exert great influence. Jackson so dominated the handling of foreign affairs that Livingston could not even hire his own clerks without risking presidential scolding on his selections. In conducting foreign affairs, Livingston consistently concerned himself with legal matters, such as the constitutionality of reciprocal trade agreements, and, like Jackson, proved an ardent nationalist, willing to go to great lengths to protect U.S. commerce and honor. Yet, during his tenure, Livingston demonstrated more strength and power in domestic affairs, perhaps because of his greater knowledge and experience in these matters and because the president granted him more leverage in this realm than he did in foreign relations. Livingston indirectly opposed Jackson over the recharter of the Bank of the United States, perhaps helping shorten his stay as secretary, and he greatly aided the president in the nullification issue with South Carolina by rewriting and polishing Jackson's Nullification Proclamation of December 1832.

Livingston had a better chance to demonstrate his diplomatic skills at his post in Paris because he had more freedom of action, although facing the French as Jackson's representative during the height of the spoliation-claims crisis proved difficult. Through his patient persistence and excellent relations with the French, except at the height of the crisis, when he was *persona non grata* at the Quai d'Orsay because of unhappiness with Jackson's hard-line stand, Livingston aided greatly in achieving settlement of the claims. He returned home in June 1835 and retired to his country estate, Montgomery Place, in New York, where he engaged in scholarship and a small law practice. He died at home May 23, 1836, just before his 72nd birthday.

BIBLIOGRAPHICAL ESSAY

The first place to check for the activities of Edward Livingston as secretary of state is in Francis Rawle's "Edward Livingston," in Samuel Flagg Bemis (ed.), *The American Secretaries of State and Their Diplomacy*, vol. 4 (1928). Rawle provides a fine, balanced survey of Livingston's diplomatic achievements, while underscoring the secretary's limited power. Although almost five decades old, William B. Hatcher's biography, *Edward Livingston, Jeffersonian Republican and Jacksonian Democrat* (1940), remains the standard account of the life of this unlucky and courageous man. Hatcher gives little space to Livingston's diplomatic activities, preferring to focus on his involvement in domestic affairs while secretary of state, especially in the bank and nullification issues. Jackson's relations with all four of his secretaries of state are depicted in John S. Basset, *Life of Andrew Jackson*, 2 vols. (1931), one of the first scholarly biographies of Old Hickory; a more recent, detailed comparison is provided in John Belohlavek's handy *"Let the Eagle Soar!" The Foreign Policy of Andrew Jackson* (1985).

Two nineteenth-century works provide anecdotes and personal glimpses of Livingston. See Charles Havens Hunt, *Life of Edward Livingston* (1864), and Louise Livingston Hunt, *Memoir of Mrs. Edward Livingston* (1886), about the second Mrs. Livingston by her grandniece. For some provocative insights into the relationship between Martin Van Buren and Livingston, see J. C. Fitzpatrick (ed.), *Autobiography of Martin Van Buren*, in the Annual Report of the American Historical Association, II (1918).

A fine collection of diplomatic documents for this period is included in Adelaide R. Hasse, *Index to United States Documents Relating to Foreign Affairs, 1828–1861* (1914). Bassett's edited *Correspondence of Andrew Jackson* (1926–1935) includes some of the important correspondence between Jackson, Van Buren, and Livingston, especially that regarding the president's appraisal of and plans for Livingston. The full correspondence may be found divided between the Van Buren papers and the Jackson papers, both located in the Library of Congress and on microfilm.

Richard W. Fanning

JAMES MADISON (1751–1836)

Served 1801–1809
Appointed by President Thomas Jefferson
Democratic-Republican

James Madison was born on March 16, 1751, into the landowning class of the Virginia piedmont. His father, James Madison, Sr., was the wealthiest planter in developing but still provincial Orange County. James, Jr. was the eldest of 10 siblings, 7 of whom lived to adulthood. His father happily supported his eldest son's academic and political endeavors. In 1769, he sent James to the College of New Jersey (later Princeton University), a more expensive but superior alternative to the College of William and Mary—where most planters' sons went.

Madison soon became a protégé of John Witherspoon, the college's Scottish-born president. Under Witherspoon's guidance, he first began to think of America as a future continental empire. The young Virginian read broadly and intensively, particularly in the political and economic theories of the Scottish Enlightenment. He graduated in two years, nearly studying himself to death in the process. After college, Madison spent several months reading law, pondering a career, and fretting over his health—the latter remaining a lifelong tendency.

Like many young men, Madison found an opportunity to distinguish himself in the American Revolution. Small and sickly, he proved too frail to serve in the military. Instead, he put his intellect to work for the cause. He served first as a delegate to the Virginia Constitutional Convention, where he began his lifelong friendship and political partnership with Thomas Jefferson. In 1778 and 1779 Madison labored on the Virginia Council of State, where he helped coordinate Virginia's contribution to the war effort. Impressed with young Madison's intelligence and tenacity, the state's leaders sent him to represent Virginia in the Continental Congress.

Madison arrived at the Continental Congress in early 1780. At the time, American prospects appeared grim. The states had yet to ratify the Articles of Confederation, the French essentially controlled the Continental Congress, and British forces were amassing in the vulnerable South. Madison played an important role in reinvigorating the Congress. He focused on provisioning the army and asserting

U.S. claims in the West. In particular, he pushed for American access to the Mississippi River. He knew the river was the key to attaching the trans-Appalachian West to the new nation. Maintaining access to the Mississippi and control over the West remained an important focus of Madison's attention throughout his career.

Following the war, Madison served in the Virginia state legislature. His experience in the Continental Congress had instilled in him a national perspective that often clashed with powerful local interests—particularly the faction led by Patrick Henry. Like many other American leaders, Madison quickly became disillusioned with the Articles of Confederation. Under that system, the central government lacked financial stability, military clout, and the power to regulate commerce. In essence, it could neither maintain order nor defend the nation's interests abroad.

The weakness of the national government became painfully clear when, beginning in 1783, London closed its colonies to U.S. trade. The following year, Spain revoked U.S. rights on the Mississippi, threatening American prosperity and settlement in the West. Madison viewed these developments as grave threats to the young republic. He believed true independence required territorial expansion and freedom of commerce.

By the mid-1780s, he had become completely disillusioned with the dominance of the state governments. The 13 former colonies followed different and often contradictory commercial policies, which proved easily manipulated by foreign powers. Moreover, many state legislatures refused to fulfill their obligations to the central government, making it impossible for the Articles Congress to press U.S. interests abroad. Like many other American leaders, Madison had decided that a vigorous foreign policy required a stronger central government.

Two crises in 1785 and 1786 confirmed Madison's conclusions. The first was the Jay–Gardoqui treaty, which U.S. Secretary of Foreign Affairs John Jay negotiated in response to the Spanish closure of the Mississippi. The agreement opened Spanish colonial markets to U.S. trade whereby the United States would forbear the use of the Mississippi for 30 years. Though Congress failed to ratify the treaty, Jay's negotiations infuriated Americans in the West and South, who accused Eastern interests of selling them out. The second crisis was Shays' Rebellion in western Massachusetts, which revealed the inability of the central and state governments to maintain order in the American interior. These incidents convinced Madison of the need for a new system that could balance sectional interests, regulate the settlement of the West, and protect American commercial rights.

In 1786–1787, along with New Yorker Alexander Hamilton, Madison pushed for efforts to reform the national government. First came an abortive meeting in Annapolis, then the Constitutional Convention in Philadelphia. Madison spent the months before the gathering in Philadelphia studying the history and political theory of republics, and he arrived at the convention better prepared than any other delegate. Indeed, his plan for the new government set much of the agenda for the convention. Although Madison wanted a central government stronger than the new Constitution provided, he supported the final product in the difficult campaign for ratification by the states in 1787–1788.

To promote ratification, especially in New York, Madison, Hamilton, and John Jay cooperated in the writing of the *Federalist* essays. Of these, the most famous is Madison's *Federalist* #10, which distilled his innovative thoughts on the American republic. Previous political theory had maintained that republics must remain small to guarantee liberty. In contrast, Madison argued that the principal danger to republican liberty stemmed not from expansion but rather from different economic factions. In a large republic, however, factions could not easily gain control of the government. Hence, he concluded, "Extend the sphere and you take in a greater variety of parties and interests; you make it less probable that a majority of the whole will have a common motive to invade the rights of other citizens." Madison had come to believe that only expansion could guarantee republican freedoms. Indeed, he considered the U.S. Constitution a blueprint for continental empire. Of course, like other men of his background, he ignored the theft of African and American Indian liberty that such an American empire would entail.

In addition to territorial expansion, Madison hoped the Constitution would bring commercial freedom. Once the new federal government began operating in 1789, he pressed Congress to impose discriminatory commercial taxes on British commerce. In doing so, he collided with the policies of Secretary of the Treasury Alexander Hamilton, who planned to use customs receipts from British imports to fund his national financial system. Madison considered commercial policy the key to gaining respect abroad, and he was flummoxed by the Washington administration's refusal to use that power. By 1790 he found himself opposing much of Hamilton's plan and worrying about the direction the federal government was headed.

Secretary of State Thomas Jefferson shared his friend's concerns. Like Madison, Jefferson unsuccessfully opposed Hamilton's economic plan. By 1791, Madison and Jefferson had gone public with their criticism. Their break with the Washington administration led to the formation of the nation's first party system. Soon supporters of Jefferson came to call themselves the "Democratic-Republicans" and identify their enemies as "Federalists."

Beginning in 1793, foreign affairs became the principal concern of the U.S. government and helped solidify the two-party system. In that year, the French Revolution engulfed Europe in a general war. For most of the years 1793–1815, conflict raged across the continent that brought opportunities and dangers for the new republic. The opportunities came from the weakened European imperial presence in North America and expanded outlets for American commerce. The danger lay in the possibility of being drawn into the conflict. The Washington administration sought to avoid that possibility by declaring U.S. neutrality in the conflict. However, Hamilton's financial plan ensured that the United States leaned toward Britain.

Both Madison and Jefferson criticized administration policy. They believed not only that the United States had an obligation to France under the 1778 treaty but also that Americans ought to support the triumph of republicanism over monarchy. Although the plotting of Citizen Genet in 1793 embarrassed them, they refused to reverse their position. The disagreement led to both Jefferson's resignation and Madison's increased opposition to the administration. Ironically, despite Washington's favorable neutrality policy, British seizures of U.S. ships in the West Indies nearly led to war in 1794. Madison again urged retaliatory commercial legislation. Instead, the president sent John Jay to negotiate with London. The resulting November 1794 Jay Treaty sent shock waves throughout the nation. The treaty provided for British evacuation of forts in American territory and ended most seizures of U.S. ships. But it granted few concessions to American commerce, contained no recognition of neutral rights, and required the United States to renounce retaliatory commercial legislation.

Madison condemned the accord as an "attempt to Prostrate us to a foreign & unfriendly nation." He accused the Federalists of abandoning both commercial interests and "the most sacred dictates of National honor." Even more importantly, he believed the renunciation of commercial retaliation deprived the United States of a crucial diplomatic lever. Contrary to his predictions, however, U.S. commerce thrived under the Jay Treaty. In addition, Anglo-American rapprochement spurred Spain to sign the Treaty of San Lorenzo in October 1795, which guaranteed Americans free access to the Mississippi. Indeed, Federalist diplomacy had brought a modicum of stability to both U.S. commerce and Western settlement.

Unconvinced, Madison continued his efforts to build an opposition party. Both he and Jefferson increasingly distrusted the tendencies of the federal government in the domestic and foreign spheres. In particular, they feared that the Washington administration's repression of the Whiskey Rebellion in 1795 represented creeping militarism and that the Jay Treaty would lead to war with France.

Events confirmed those fears. Following Jefferson's loss to John Adams in the 1796 election, the United States became embroiled in naval hostilities with France. That conflict, in turn, brought political repression at home in the form of the Alien and Sedition Acts. Jefferson and Madison responded by penning the Kentucky and Virginia Resolutions, respectively, which asserted the rights of states to oppose the federal government. In a complete reversal of his earlier views, Madison now held that the federal government, particularly in matters of diplomacy, posed the greatest threat to liberty. Indeed, he had concluded that the "management of foreign relations appears to be the most susceptible of abuse of all the trusts committed to government."

Madison and Jefferson weathered the storm of persecution and readied their party for the 1800 contest. Both men feared that Adams would lead the nation into full-scale war with France, to the benefit of Britain. Yet, to everyone's surprise, Adams moved to make peace with France, setting himself at odds with Hamilton. The resulting divisions within the Federalist Party facilitated Jefferson's electoral triumph.

In November 1800, on his way to Washington, Jefferson stopped at Madison's home, Montpelier. Madison had the pleasure of informing his visiting friend that he would be the next president. (Of course, the bizarre deadlock with running mate Aaron Burr left Jefferson unsure of his final victory until February 1801.) In the same visit, Madison accepted Jefferson's offer of the position of secretary of state.

The position held little glamour in 1800. Jefferson planned to cut the State Department budget by closing overseas delegations. Madison would have only a few clerks to assist him with the office's heavy correspondence. Moreover, he would be responsible for pushing Jefferson's ambitious foreign policy goals without the benefit of either military power or unified public opinion. Madison knew that divisions over foreign policy had divided the nation throughout the 1790s. Reducing those divisions would be a difficult and thankless job.

Still, he was the logical choice. He had devoted much of his public career to questions of foreign relations, and despite the partisan bile of the 1790s, he remained widely respected. Nevertheless, Madison was much less cosmopolitan than most of his peers. He had never traveled outside the country. Perhaps partly for this reason, he remained a confirmed Anglophobe throughout his life. In the British Empire, he saw a power dedicated to obstructing American economic independence. Happily for Madison, that view coincided with Jefferson's own ideas.

The election of 1800 was a pivotal point in the young nation's history. For Jefferson, the Republican triumph represented a democratic "revolution." He had campaigned on a promise to safeguard the nation's republican virtues, which he believed the Federalists had tainted with their devotion to commerce, public debt, and military power. Jefferson argued that the nation's strength lay in the agrarian virtue of yeoman farmers, and he vowed to protect their interests.

Madison never espoused Jefferson's mystical faith in the people. But over the course of the 1790s, he had come to agree with Jefferson on the dangers of federal power. Consequently, although he dedicated himself to protecting agrarian virtue, he also retained a skepticism of the general public that Jefferson never quite managed. Indeed, they were very different men. Jefferson was the democratic philosopher, Madison the analytical thinker.

Despite, or perhaps because of, these differences, no president and secretary of state have cooperated more harmoniously than Madison and Jefferson. Most importantly, they always agreed on foreign policy objectives. Unlike the Federalists, they believed the United States could force other nations to respect American interests. Because both men adhered to the vision of an agrarian republic, they concentrated their efforts on territorial expansion. Nevertheless, they understood the relationship between agrarianism and the need for foreign markets. Paradoxically, although both Jefferson and Madison deplored the effects of commerce on the republic, they also placed excessive faith in the power of U.S. commercial policy to coerce other nations.

Historians have largely focused on Jefferson when studying the diplomacy of this period. The president took great interest in diplomatic affairs, and consequently scholars have often ignored Madison's central role in Jeffersonian diplomacy. Always a backroom operator, Madison seemed content to shape policy while letting Jefferson dominate the spotlight. Nevertheless, the president had unlimited confidence in his secretary of state.

After Madison, the most important member of the cabinet was Albert Gallatin, the Swiss-born secretary of the treasury. Gallatin acted as the administration's realist, often questioning policy he found too aggressive or expensive. Madison supported Gallatin's efforts to shore up the nation's finances, and the two men rarely disagreed. When Madison became president, he kept Gallatin at the treasury post. Madison also worked cooperatively with Secretary of War Henry Dearborn and Attorney General Levi Lincoln, both from New England. Some tension did arise with Secretary of the Navy Robert Smith, whose brother, Senator Samuel Smith, proved an incessant schemer. Nevertheless, Madison's close relationship with Jefferson left him ascendant in the cabinet.

Madison was able to forge good relations with the heavily Republican Congress. For most of his tenure as secretary, the Federalists remained too weak to oppose his policies. He did have problems, however, with the "Old" Republicans, led by John Randolph of Virginia. They remembered Madison's earlier advocacy of a stronger federal government, distrusted his enthusiasm for commercial sanctions, and feared his influence over Jefferson. Despite these critics, Madison's supporters in Congress usually won out.

Madison's interaction with foreign diplomats was less congenial. Foreign emissaries usually underestimated him due to his frail physique and quiet manner. Over time, however, most came to respect, if not resent, his insistent promotion of U.S. interests. Spanish Minister Don Carlos Martinez d'Yrujo eventually refused to speak to Madison, whereas British Chargé Edward Thornton and Minister Anthony Merry often found themselves subjected to Madison's complaints on British maritime policy. Madison had a friendlier relationship with the young French Chargé Louis Pichon. Indeed, the secretary of state often reasoned so effectively with Pichon that the chargé became a mouthpiece for U.S. policy. This dynamic changed when a wilier French minister, Louis Marie Turreau, arrived in 1804. Overall, foreign diplomats admired Madison's intellect but resented his tendency both to ignore other nations' interests and to equate American ambitions with morality.

In his inaugural address, Jefferson characterized his foreign policy with the noble sentiment: "Peace, commerce, and honest friendship with all nations, entangling alliances with none." Still, he and Madison proved quite willing to risk war, prohibit commerce, manipulate "honest friendship," *and* consider alliances when it suited their purposes. Like Jefferson, Madison viewed U.S. national interests moralistically. Indeed, the two men often seemed to think in syllogism: The United States embodies liberty; to survive, the United States needs territorial expansion and commercial freedom; therefore, whoever opposes U.S. expansion and commercial rights opposes liberty.

Such reasoning led Madison to focus on two ambitious objectives: first, to safeguard agrarian virtue through territorial expansion; second, to establish expansive neutral rights for American ships. Like Jefferson, he considered all of North America a U.S. patrimony, temporarily held by savages and effete Old World empires. He was confident that all of it would eventually fall to the American empire, but British, French, and Spanish colonial ambitions worried him, nonetheless. Of even greater concern during his tenure was the issue of neutral rights. Madison thought American merchants should be able to trade anywhere, especially in the "most natural and valuable commerce" of the West Indies.

But how could the United States force the European powers to respect its territorial and commercial ambitions? Surely not through military spending and war, both of which Madison and Jefferson deplored. Herein lay the paradox of Republican diplomacy: Jefferson and Madison espoused more expansive foreign policy goals than their Federalist predecessors while reducing the nation's military power.

Madison believed that U.S. commercial and strategic importance would resolve that dilemma. The European powers could not afford to alienate the United States, he reasoned. Great Britain would bend to U.S. sanctions because it could neither maintain its manufactures nor feed its West Indies colonies without American products. True, the severance of trade with Britain would deprive Americans of British manufactured goods. But "household manufactures" in the United States might take their place. In support of the 1807 embargo, he noted, "We shall be deprived of market for our superfluities. They will feel the want of necessaries." In essence, he believed commerce sanctions offered a means to coerce other nations while avoiding the pitfalls of military spending and warfare.

Madison did not eschew the threat and use of force, however. Both he and Jefferson often warned the European powers of future conflict if U.S. "rights" were not respected. Indeed, he exhibited even less pacifism than Jefferson in the face of European provocations. In addition, both men proved quite willing to use force against nonwhite peoples such as American Indians and the Barbary pirates.

Since 1783 the Barbary powers of northern Africa had harassed U.S. merchant ships in the Mediterranean. Like the European nations, the Washington and Adams administrations had paid protection money to the pirate states. Adams had built a small navy to defend against attacks, but the ships ended up fighting the French. Despite their misgivings about naval power, Jefferson and Madison had long advocated a more aggressive stance toward the pirate states. Both men viewed the conflict with the Barbary powers as part of the struggle to free U.S. commerce from foreign interference and defend national honor.

Tensions in the Mediterranean were escalating in 1801. The Pasha of Tripoli had threatened hostilities against the United States. In response, Jefferson sent four warships to the Mediterranean to protect American merchant ships. Madison believed the show of force would chasten the Pasha and deter the other Barbary powers from following Tripoli's example. On May 20, 1801, he informed U.S. Consul to Tunis William Eaton of this policy of containment, explaining that he hoped the "contagion" of Tripoli's aggression "will not have spread either to Tunis or Algiers; but should one or both of them have followed the perfidious example, their corsairs will be equally repelled and punished."

Before the naval expedition arrived in the Mediterranean, Tripoli declared war on the United States. In response, from 1801 to 1803 the American fleet attempted both to blockade the port of Tripoli and to maintain peace with the other Barbary powers. That effort experienced a major setback when the U.S. frigate *Philadelphia* ran aground while chasing pirates. Forces in Tripoli captured the crew of 300—precipitating the United States' first overseas hostage crisis. The Jefferson administration was further mortified when U.S. diplomats in Europe requested assistance from the European powers. The president complained to Madison of "this sordid disposition to throw upon the charity of others." After all, the objective of the naval mission had been to display the power of the United States to defend its rights.

Instead of negotiating through Europe, Madison and Jefferson increased military pressure on Tripoli. They sent more ships to punish the pirates and approved an invasion led by Eaton across the Libyan desert. The motley expedition, along with naval pressure, encouraged the Pasha of Tripoli to negotiate. In 1805, U.S. diplomat Tobias Lear signed a peace that ransomed the crew of the *Philadelphia* for $60,000 and freed U.S. merchants from Tripolitanian harassment. However, the treaty did not end U.S. troubles in the Mediterranean. Algerian corsairs began attacking American commerce on the withdrawal of U.S. naval units in 1807, and the Barbary powers continued to harass U.S. ships and extort money until 1815.

From 1801 to 1803, Europe enjoyed a rare period of peace. During these years, the United States remained largely free from commercial disputes. Instead, Madison and Jefferson focused on promoting U.S. territorial ambitions and rebuilding relations with France. To their surprise, they found the two goals incompatible.

In October 1800 French First Consul Napoleon Bonaparte had forced Spain to cede the vast territory of Louisiana to France in the Treaty of San Ildefonso. He planned to rebuild the French Empire in the Western Hemisphere. The centerpiece of his scheme was the rich French sugar colony of Saint Domingue—present-day Haiti. Saint Domingue was the wealthiest slave colony in the world, but the island depended on the United States for food imports. Napoleon believed that the development of Louisiana under French control would wean Saint Domingue from its dependence on the United States and help reestablish French power in the Western Hemisphere.

There was a problem with this scheme: France did not control Saint Domingue. Since 1791, a slave rebellion led by the brilliant ex-slave Toussaint L'Ouverture had rocked the island and moved it toward quasi-independence. In the same period, U.S. merchants had developed a thriving trade with the former bondsmen. By 1797, approximately 600 U.S. ships traded regularly with Saint Domingue, with exports totaling more than $5,000,000. Napoleon desperately wanted to reestablish French control over the colony. However, a French expedition to reconquer the colony would succeed only if the United States agreed to stop trading with Toussaint and supply only the French army.

Initially, American assistance seemed assured. In July 1801, Jefferson told French Chargé Pichon that once France made peace with Britain and sent a force to occupy Saint Domingue, "nothing would be easier than to furnish your army and fleet with everything, and to reduce Toussaint to starvation." Pichon received no such assurance from the secretary of state. Unlike Jefferson, Madison immediately grasped the connection between Saint Domingue and the rumored transfer of Louisiana. Instead of promising to starve the Haitian rebels, Madison informed Pichon that the importance of U.S. trade with the island meant "the administration could not risk falling out with Toussaint." He then warned the French diplomat of the dire consequences of French possession of Louisiana.

Indeed, the president and the secretary of state initially differed on this issue. As Napoleon had hoped, Jefferson viewed the Haitian revolution through the prism of slavery and Franco-American relations. The president feared the effects of the revolution on American slaves, and he realized U.S. help in reconquering the island could improve relations with Paris. In contrast, Madison's approach to the Haitian revolution hinged on his goals of commercial and territorial expansion.

Madison had little inclination to curb the flourishing trade with the ex-slaves. Even more importantly, he understood the importance of the Treaty of San Ildefonso to American expansion. Both he and Jefferson feared that the territorial transfer from Spain to France included both Louisiana and the Floridas. Unlike the decrepit Spanish Empire, France under Napoleon presented a very real threat to U.S. ambitions. French control of those territories would obstruct American trade and expansion on the Gulf Coast. Madison realized that only Toussaint's revolutionaries stood in the way of French occupation of Louisiana.

To forestall that nightmare, Madison turned to his favored foreign-policy weapon: commerce. He simply refused either to halt U.S. commerce with Toussaint or to promote trade with the large French force that arrived in Saint Domingue in early 1802. The French expedition, commanded by Napoleon's brother-in-law, Victor-Emmanuel Leclerc, engaged in a bloody conflict with the Haitians throughout 1802 and 1803. Despite continuous appeals from Leclerc and Pichon, Madison refused to honor Jefferson's promise to "starve out Toussaint." Indeed, by spring 1802, Madison had concluded that Saint Domingue would form "a very powerful obstacle" to French occupation of New Orleans.

The Louisiana crisis intensified in October 1802, when Spanish officials in New Orleans revoked American commercial rights on the Mississippi. The river provided the principal trade outlet for Americans living in the West. Its closure threw American politics into turmoil. To the U.S. minister in Madrid, Madison lamented the "sensibility of our Western citizens to such an occurrence. . . . The Mississippi is to them everything. It is the Hudson, the Delaware, the Potomac and all the navigable rivers of the Atlantic States formed into one stream."

Both Jefferson and Madison believed, incorrectly, that Paris had ordered the closing of the river as a prelude to French occupation. Several months before the closure, Jefferson had attempted to warn Paris that French possession of New Orleans would force the United States to "marry ourselves to the British fleet and nation." Now, in response to the Spanish action, he forcefully removed Indians in the region and increased American forces near the Mississippi. These idle threats of alliance with Britain and invasion of Louisiana had little impact on Napoleon. Instead, the matter hinged on Saint Domingue, and Jefferson, too, now pinned his hopes on that struggle. In late 1802, he appointed James Monroe to negotiate the possible purchase of New Orleans and the Floridas from France. In his instructions, he emphasized that "St. Domingo delays their taking possession of Louisiana, and they are in the last distress for money for current purposes." He hoped that the failure of the Leclerc expedition, along with escalating Franco-British tensions, would encourage Napoleon to sell at least part of his North American empire.

He sold it all. In April 1803, on learning of the destruction of Leclerc's army, Napoleon decided to sell not only New Orleans but also all of Louisiana—for the bargain price of $15 million. Jefferson was elated by the unexpected windfall. Among other things, the sale meant that the upcoming Lewis and Clark expedition would now be exploring U.S. rather than Spanish territory—as was originally planned. But the president also worried that the purchase of foreign territory was unconstitutional. Madison had no such qualms. He believed that the advantages of adding to the American empire justified the means of obtaining it.

The Louisiana Purchase convinced both him and Jefferson of the success of their carrot-and-stick diplomatic strategy. On the one hand, they had threatened conflict and alliance with Britain if France kept New Orleans. On the other hand, they had offered friendship and money if France proved willing to part with it. Both men seemed to forget that the Haitian revolutionaries were largely responsible for their success.

The years following the triumph of the Louisiana Purchase brought only frustration and disappointment. By early 1804, French forces had abandoned Saint Domingue, and Toussaint's successor had declared the independent Republic of Haiti. For two years, Madison resisted French Minister Turreau's demands that he curb U.S. trade with the ex-slave state. In 1806, however, he supported a congressional bill prohibiting commerce with the island. Although many Southerners embraced the bill out of fear of slave rebellion, Madison's shift can be attributed, once again, to territorial ambitions. U.S. trade with the Haitians had helped him pry Louisiana loose. He now hoped that prohibiting that trade would encourage France to support American claims to West Florida.

Because Spain had not ceded the Floridas to France, Napoleon could not sell them. But that did not stop the Jefferson administration from claiming West Florida as part of the Louisiana Purchase. The claim was flimsy, but both Madison and Jefferson convinced themselves of its "rightness." Their self-delusion stemmed largely from their desire for the strategically and commercially important territory. In early 1803, before the Louisiana Purchase, Madison had submitted a report for Congress emphasizing that "The Floridas and New Orleans command the only outlets to the sea [for the American West] and must become a part of the United States, either by purchase or conquest." He tried both, first claiming purchase, then threatening conquest.

In 1804, Congress and the administration pushed U.S. claims to West Florida with the Mobile Act. The virulent Spanish protest to the legislation surprised Madison and Jefferson. They had assumed that U.S. threats of force, along with French pressure on Madrid, would force Spain to back down. Yet, even after Spain entered the war against Britain in December 1804, Madrid resisted the U.S. claims. American offers of bribery also failed to sway Spanish officials. Indeed, to his infinite frustration, Jefferson left office without having annexed West Florida.

Overall, the Jefferson administration experienced a troubled second term. In 1803, Europe had again descended into war. Madison would have to grapple with the ramifications of that war, as secretary of state and then as president, until 1815. The conflict brought carnage to the continent and unprecedented prosperity to the United States. The U.S. commercial fleet filled the void left by the warring navies, becoming the largest merchant marine in the world. Yet in the midst of that prosperity, British restrictions on U.S. commerce continued to frustrate Madison. He had spent the previous 20 years arguing for economic retaliation against Britain. Now, with the president's support, he would test his theories of commercial coercion.

The dispute centered on two key issues: the carrying trade and impressment. Of the two, the carrying trade was by far more important. Madison had long championed an expansive definition of neutral rights, and after 1805 he took up the cause as a personal crusade. In that year, tensions increased dramatically with the British admiralty's *Essex* decision, which outlawed the American reexport (or broken voyage) trade. The British were engaged in a desperate struggle to isolate Napoleon on the continent. Their wartime strategy depended on their naval effort to isolate France from overseas trade. The American carrying trade undermined that strategy by claiming neutral rights to trade with the continent. U.S. merchants had also expanded their trade within the British Empire, which English merchants vehemently resented.

Madison consistently criticized British policy and defended the neutral rights of American merchants. In January 1806 he published a long pamphlet that traced the history of British commercial restrictions. In it, Madison rejected London's assertions of wartime exigencies. Instead of blockading France, Madison argued, British policy aimed to strangle American trade and to hold the United States in a position of dependence.

In April, the Jefferson administration attempted to alter British policy by passing the Non-Importation Act, which prohibited a limited number of British imports. Madison disliked the measure. Arguing that Britain's real weakness lay in its dependence on American products, he urged a prohibition of U.S. exports. Jefferson became increasingly receptive to Madison's argument between late 1806 and late 1807, when both sides of the European war increasingly targeted American commerce. Napoleon's Berlin Decree in late 1806 and Milan Decree in 1807 declared neutral ships that cooperated with British policy subject to seizure. In late 1807, a

British Order in Council proclaimed that neutral ships could trade with Napoleon's holdings only after obtaining licenses in British ports. Essentially mercantilist in nature, these restrictions made a mockery of American independence.

At the same time, Anglo-American tension over impressment—the British practice of seizing suspected deserters aboard U.S. ships—reached its height. London had a legitimate complaint against American merchants. Large numbers of British seamen had deserted the British navy for higher paying jobs in the U.S. merchant marine. However, British commanders had an unfortunate tendency to impress American seamen as well as British deserters. Not surprisingly, the practice offended American national pride. A particularly egregious attack on the U.S. frigate *Chesapeake* by a British warship in June 1807 resulted in 3 deaths, 18 injuries, and the removal of 4 seamen. The *Chesapeake* affair galvanized American public opinion against Britain just as the increased restrictions on commerce were becoming apparent. Madison protested the "indignity offered to the sovereignty & flag of the nation, and the blood of Citizens so wantonly and wickedly shed." War fever ran high, but Madison and Jefferson still hoped for a nonmilitary solution.

After negotiations with London stalled, they decided to pass an embargo on U.S. exports and the carrying trade. The embargo lasted from late 1807 to early 1809. Madison assumed it would work in tandem with Napoleon's continental system to starve Britain into acknowledging neutral rights. To his surprise, the embargo proved an unmitigated disaster. The loss of exports and carrying trade devastated the U.S. economy. Ironically, before the embargo, American commerce had flourished despite British and French offenses. Only federal commercial policy proved capable of stifling U.S. trade.

The ensuing economic catastrophe split the Republicans and revived the Federalist Party. Still worse, the embargo failed to bring London to heel. The British found new markets and substitutes for American products in Latin America, which was moving toward independence. Even more frustrating, many Americans defied the embargo and smuggled their products through Canada. The widespread resistance forced Jefferson to implement draconian measures of enforcement that far exceeded the executive powers claimed by his Federalist predecessors. Even then, Canadian naval stores and smuggled American goods found their way to the British navy and West Indies—the embargo's two principal targets. By early 1809, with the economy prostrate and New England threatening secession, the Republicans agreed to end the embargo.

Madison found far greater success in his quest for territorial expansion than he did in commercial policy. His tacit support of the Haitian revolutionaries, along with Napoleon's European concerns, helped produce one of the greatest triumphs in U.S. history. With the Louisiana Purchase, Americans gained a continental empire. Yet even with that empire, the United States remained a pigmy in a world of giants. Like Jefferson, Madison never fully accepted that cold, hard fact. He consistently overestimated the importance of the United States to the European powers. Moreover, he misunderstood the mentality of wartime Great Britain. He assumed that London, locked in mortal struggle with Napoleon, would renounce its crucial naval power to avoid American economic sanctions.

The failure of the embargo starkly revealed Madison's flawed reasoning. Since the 1780s, he had maintained that the European powers, particularly Great Britain, were dependent on American products. Yet the embargo revealed that the United

States needed Britain much more than vice versa. Indeed, Madison both overestimated the importance of the United States to Europe and underestimated the impact of his commercial policies on the U.S. economy. That mistake ensured that the next president would inherit a discredited commercial policy, a weakened economy, and a divided ruling party. Unfortunately for Madison, he was the next president.

The embargo ended on March 4, 1809—the day Madison assumed the presidency. Unlike Jefferson, he proved incapable both of avoiding war with Britain and of controlling the Republican Party. His failures stemmed partly from the election of a hawkish Republican Congress in 1810. But the increased military adventurism and fractiousness of the era owed much to Madison's leadership. Indeed, much of his administration seemed an effort to avenge the foreign-policy frustrations he had suffered during his years as secretary of state.

In October 1810, Madison forcefully annexed Spanish West Florida. In early 1812, he secretly supported a filibustering attempt in East Florida. Even more importantly, he moved toward war with Britain. In 1810 Congress passed Macon's Bill Number 2, which opened trade to Great Britain and France but pledged to close trade with one nation if the other renounced its commercial restrictions. Napoleon seized the opportunity to stoke U.S.–British tensions by announcing the removal of sanctions on U.S. ships. In mid-1812, in response to Napoleon's dubious claim and continued British depredations, Madison requested that Congress declare war on Britain.

The following conflict found the nation neither prepared nor united. The New England Federalists, whose commercial interests lay with the British Empire, refused to support the war effort. Still worse, 11 years of Republican leadership had left the military establishment woefully inadequate. Madison pinned his hopes on the conquest of Canada, which he assumed would easily fall to U.S. forces. Instead, the American forces suffered humiliating setbacks throughout 1812 and 1813. The British navy blockaded the U.S. coast, and in August 1814 British troops burned Washington, D.C.—forcing James and Dolley Madison to flee.

In the last half of 1814, the United States miraculously snatched a stalemate from the jaws of defeat. An American victory on Lake Champlain halted a British invasion while Andrew Jackson's repulsion of a British force in New Orleans secured the nation's vulnerable underbelly. Even before these victories, London had decided to negotiate an end to the costly conflict. The resulting Treaty of Ghent, based on the principles of *status quo ante bellum*, resolved none of the issues that had led to the conflict. Yet, the end of the Napoleonic Wars freed the United States from most British commercial restrictions. Even more important, Andrew Jackson's campaigns broke Indian resistance in the Gulf Coast region and laid the groundwork for Spanish cession of East Florida.

Despite the humiliating experiences of the war, American victories in late 1814 largely erased the memory of Madison's incompetent wartime leadership. Most Americans considered the conflict a second War for Independence, and the appearance of victory enabled Madison to claim vindication for his three-decade struggle against the British Empire. The end of the conflict enabled him to focus on domestic matters for the first time in his presidency. He successfully pushed for a renewal of the Bank of the United States and called for federally funded internal improvements. Critics suspected he was finally revealing his Federalist colors.

In March 1817, Madison retired to Montpelier, where he dabbled as gentleman farmer and elder statesman for nearly 20 years. He maintained his close friendship with Jefferson until the latter's death in 1826. To his surprise, the sickly boy from Orange County outlived all his fellow Founding Fathers and spoke of even "outliving myself." He enjoyed his life with his extended family and continued to offer advice on diplomatic and constitutional issues until his death in 1836 at the age of 85.

BIBLIOGRAPHICAL ESSAY

Though James Madison left few private papers, the public record reveals much about this very public man. The newest edition of his papers is William T. Hutchinson, William M. E. Rachal, Robert A. Rutland, et al. (eds.), *The Papers of James Madison* (1962–). So far 17 volumes down to 1801 have been published. The same series is also publishing *The Papers of James Madison: Secretary of State Series* (1986–), an excellent collection of diplomatic correspondence. Five volumes down to 1803 have appeared. For later years, see Gaillard Hunt (ed.), *The Writings of James Madison*, 9 vols. (1900–1910). A wonderful recent contribution, especially for Madison's relationship with Jefferson, is James Morton Smith (ed.), *The Republic of Letters: The Correspondence between Thomas Jefferson and James Madison, 1776–1826*, 3 vols. (1995). For other diplomatic correspondence and affairs of state, refer to the useful but limited *American State Papers, Foreign Relations* (1982). The most complete collection of official documents can be found at the National Archives.

A good, concise account of Madison's life is Jack N. Rakove, *James Madison and the Creation of the American Republic* (1990). The best single-volume biography is Ralph Ketcham, *James Madison: A Biography* (1971). The most detailed, if uncritical, portrait of Madison is Irving Brant's *James Madison*, 6 vols. (1941–1961). Also indispensable is Henry Adams's classic, *History of the United States during the Administrations of Jefferson and Madison*, 9 vols. (1889–1891).

Reginald Horsman's *The Diplomacy of the New Republic, 1776–1815* (1985) is a brief but excellent overview of early U.S. foreign relations. For a stimulating critique of Jefferson's and Madison's diplomacy, see Bradford Perkins, *The Creation of the Republican Empire, 1776–1865* (1993), chapter 5. A good introduction to Madison's ideas on commercial policy is Drew McCoy, "Republicanism and American Foreign Policy: James Madison and the Political Economy of Commercial Discrimination, 1789 to 1794," *William and Mary Quarterly*, 3rd ser., 31 (October 1974). For a fascinating critical reinterpretation of Republican foreign policy, see Robert W. Tucker and David C. Hendrickson, *Empire of Liberty: The Statecraft of Thomas Jefferson* (1990). Also useful is Lawrence S. Kaplan, *Entangling Alliances with None: American Foreign Policy in the Age of Jefferson* (1987).

U.S. policy toward the Barbary pirates is examined in Louis B. Wright and Julia H. Macleod, *The First Americans in North Africa: William Eaton's Struggle for a Vigorous Policy against the Barbary Pirates, 1799–1805* (1945); and Ray W. Irwin, *The Diplomatic Relations of the United States with the Barbary Powers, 1776–1816* (1931). The standard treatment of the Louisiana Purchase is Alexander DeConde, *This Affair of Louisiana* (1976).

For U.S.–British relations, see Bradford Perkins, *The First Rapprochement: England and the United States, 1795–1805* (1955), and *Prologue to War: England and the United States, 1805–1812* (1961); and Burton Spivak, *Jefferson's English Crisis* (1979). U.S. policy toward France is examined in Clifford L. Egan, *Neither Peace Nor War: Franco-American Relations, 1803–1812* (1983).

For an analysis of commercial disputes as the principal cause of the War of 1812, see Reginald Horsman, *The Causes of the War of 1812* (1962). Two other excellent works that examine Republican diplomacy and war are J. C. A. Stagg, *Mr. Madison's War: Politics, Diplomacy, and Warfare in the Early Republic, 1783–1830* (1983), and Steven Watts, *The Republic Reborn: War and the Making of Liberal America, 1790–1820* (1987).

Jason Colby

WILLIAM L. MARCY (1786–1857)

Served 1853–1857
Appointed by President Franklin Pierce
Democrat

"To the victor belong the spoils" is a phrase that has long been cited as the ultimate expression of a partisan, patronage politician. That it was uttered by someone who for most of his political career sought to be a voice of moderation is even more of a surprise, for William L. Marcy was indeed such a figure. His long and distinguished career, which included service as governor of and senator from New York, secretary of war under President James K. Polk, and finally secretary of state to President Franklin Pierce in the years 1853 to 1857, would prove that he was far more a statesman than a mere machine politician.

Born in Southbridge, Massachusetts, a son of farm parents, Jedediah Marcy and Ruth Learned, Marcy attended various village schools before being admitted to Brown University, from which he graduated in 1808. After graduation, he moved west to Troy, New York, where he studied law and was admitted to the bar in 1811. One year later, he married Dolly Norvell, who was to bear him three children before her death in 1821. When the War of 1812 broke out, Marcy enlisted in the state militia. Although seeing limited combat service, he rose through administrative ranks to become adjutant general by 1821.

Ever since his youth, Marcy had been an ardent admirer of Thomas Jefferson and so became active in Democratic Republican politics, writing for the *Northern Budget* in Troy and the *Argus* in Albany, both anti-Federalist publications. The party's success on the national level made it possible for Marcy to advance in New York politics. He became friendly with Martin Van Buren, and together they wrote a pamphlet promoting Rufus King's campaign for the U.S. Senate. With King's election, Marcy's political stock rose, and he increasingly began to play a more active role in state politics as a member of what became known as the Albany Regency. In 1823, he moved permanently to Albany and was named state comptroller. In 1824, he took as his second wife Cornelia Kramer, with whom he had three children; in 1827, he was appointed a justice on the state supreme court, where he rendered close to 200 opinions and presided over a very controversial case involving the anti-Mason movement.

As a result of this presence in state politics, Marcy was elected by the Democratic state legislature to the U.S. Senate, where he served from December 1831 to January 1833, when he resigned to take over the duties of governor. As a three-term incumbent, 1833–1838, Marcy became embroiled in the aftermath of President Andrew Jackson's veto of the Second Bank of the United States bill, and despite his best efforts to keep his party from splintering, he failed and was defeated for a fourth term. However, as governor he was able to expand the state's court system; settled a New Jersey border dispute; established school libraries, teacher training academies, insane asylums, and a women's prison; and authorized the first geological survey of the state. He also began to speak out against the activities of abolitionists, whom he believed threatened to destroy the fabric of the union.

In the years after leaving state office, Marcy first accepted appointment on a commission examining claims of U.S. citizens against Mexico, and in 1854, newly elected President James K. Polk named him as his secretary of war. Almost immediately he became enmeshed in Polk's expansionist policies and subsequent war with Mexico. He defended Generals Winfield Scott and Zachary Taylor as leaders of the major campaigns against Polk's efforts to replace them with Democrats. Although he had little faith for the success of a campaign into the Mexican interior, once the decision was made to proceed, he worked diligently to see that the armies received adequate reinforcements and supplies. In addition, he urged the president to accept the peace treaty, which special envoy Nicholas Trist had negotiated in defiance of Polk's order to break off talks and return to Washington.

In the aftermath of the Mexican War, the issue of the extension of slavery into the federal territories caused significant dissension within the Democratic Party, and Marcy sought to heal these wounds both in New York and at the national level. Although he considered slavery morally wrong but sanctioned by the Constitution, he sought some common ground with the Free-Soilers, who wanted the territories free of slavery. This question, along with other issues from the election of 1844, had weakened party morale in the Empire State. With the enactment of the Compromise of 1850, open warfare now existed between the more conservative Democrats led by Marcy, and the Free-Soiler phalanx, led by Martin Van Buren and his close ally, John A. Dix. In 1852, after the Democrats regained the White House, the new president, Franklin Pierce, was determined to end all political rivalries in Albany. As part of his plan to keep New York in the Democratic column, Pierce nominated Dix for a ministerial post and named Marcy secretary of state. If these maneuvers only temporarily solved New York's factional problems, they did at least place the country's foreign affairs in diligent, conscientious, and energetic hands.

As head of the State Department, Marcy, who had never traveled outside the United States, assumed control of a small, overworked bureaucracy both at home and abroad. President Pierce, who had expansionist plans for his administration, insisted that Marcy appoint Southern extremists to the most influential diplomatic posts. One such appointment went to Pierre Soulé of Louisiana, who had always eyed Spanish Cuba for possible annexation to the United States. Soulé's mission resulted in his joint authorship, along with James Buchanan and John Y. Mason, ministers to Great Britain and France, respectively, of the Ostend Manifesto, which declared that Spain should be compelled to give up Cuba by force if necessary. Although released in 1854 and later repudiated by Marcy, the fact that it had been issued during his tenure was a source of embarrassment to him and to the country. It did, however, hasten his efforts to resolve satisfactorily Cuba's seizure of the slave ship *Black Warrior*. Although Marcy's moderate stance on the slavery issue obviously contributed to his initial acquiescence in the actions of Soulé and the other pro-Southern expansionists, his refusal to endorse their actions moderated a potentially explosive diplomatic situation.

During the four years of Marcy's tenure, the secretary negotiated 24 treaties, the largest number ratified by any administration up to that time. Four deserve special attention: the Gadsden Treaty, 1853, which added nearly 30,000 square miles to the United States so as to facilitate the construction of a transcontinental railroad; the Marcy–Elgin Treaty, 1854, which related to trade and fisheries in Canada and the Maritime provinces; a treaty with the Netherlands, 1855, which first opened ports in the Dutch colonial settlements to American consuls; and a treaty with Denmark, 1857, which ended the long-standing dispute over charges for using the Danish Sound. Eleven of the treaties involved extradition issues as well as provisions for expanding U.S. trade and diplomatic opportunities with Latin America and the Far East, most notably the Townshend Harris mission to Japan in 1855.

With the end of the Pierce administration in March 1857, Marcy's years of public service came to an end. Four months after leaving office, he died suddenly while vacationing at Ballston Spa, New York. He was buried in a cemetery five miles north of the city of Albany, where he had spent many of his early years and which he considered the home of his main political base.

His death at age 70 brought to a close a long and distinguished career as a public servant. Although an able senator, governor, and secretary of war, Marcy's greatest accomplishments clearly came during his years with the State Department. In an otherwise undistinguished presidential administration, he managed to negotiate many important treaties and conventions that opened up new areas of trade, commerce, and influences outside the continental United States. He was, as he had been so often in the past, a moderating influence in a time of growing passion. Rather than leaving a legacy as a spoilsman politician, a stereotype with which he is often associated, Marcy has a record of accomplishments in every period of his public career. Yet, despite being involved with foreign policy problems for only four years, he nevertheless deserves to be ranked as one of the leading secretaries of state of the nineteenth century.

BIBLIOGRAPHICAL ESSAY

Marcy's papers are in the Library of Congress, but most of the documents pertain to New York state politics and have little relevance to his policies as secretary of state. There are also some manuscript sources in the Department of State records in the National Archives.

Bibliographical sources on Marcy are very limited. There is only one lengthy biography of Marcy, Ivor Spencer, *The Victor and the Spoils* (1959) and a shorter study in Samuel Flagg Bemis (ed.), *The American Secretaries of State and Their Diplomacy*, Vol. 6 (1928).

Additional information about Marcy may be found in Paul H. Bergeron, *The Presidency of James K. Polk* (1987), and in Larry Gara, *The Presidency of Franklin Pierce* (1991).

John Muldowny

GEORGE C. MARSHALL (1880–1959)

Served 1947–1949
Appointed by President Harry S. Truman
Democrat

George Catlett Marshall, soldier and statesman, was born in Uniontown, Pennsylvania, December 31, 1880, to George Catlett, Sr., a prosperous coking coal manufacturer and entrepreneur, and Laura Bradford, whose children already included Marie Louise and Stuart Bradford. The Marshalls had Virginia and Kentucky roots and were distantly related to U.S. Chief Justice John Marshall. The only member of the family born north of the Mason-Dixon Line, George spoke with a lifelong western Pennsylvania accent.

Uniontown was a manufacturing town during Marshall's childhood, closely tied to the coal, coke, and steel industries. The family lived in the last house in town on West Main Street, which was a portion of the historically important National Road. In addition to instructing his younger son in the outdoors life of hunting and fishing, which remained Marshall's hobbies throughout his life, his father introduced him to history of the area, which included such French and Indian War sites such as George Washington's Fort Necessity and General Edward Braddock's defeat and grave. An abiding interest in history and its lessons was also one of Marshall's enduring characteristics. He was close to his mother, from whom he apparently acquired his taciturn but optimistic and tolerant disposition and Episcopalian Church affiliation.

In 1890, Marshall's father sold a large portion of his properties and invested the funds in land and facilities at Luray, Virginia. When the speculative land boom collapsed in western Virginia in the early 1890s, the family was plunged into unaccustomed financial straits. Only his mother's modest income from some Pittsburgh property prevented serious hardship.

Marshall's early education had been somewhat informal, and his father was embarrassed by his son's scholastic weaknesses when he transferred to public school in 1889 for four years. When it came time to consider young Marshall's educational future in 1897, the enticing free education at the U.S. Military Academy was clearly beyond his reach scholastically and physically. (Marshall was right-handed, but his right elbow had been injured and healed improperly.)

Marshall matriculated at the Virginia Military Institute (VMI) in September 1897 and immediately became enthusiastic about the regimen there. Having already developed, somehow, the knack for systems analysis, he quickly understood the key elements in the VMI system, such as the relatively modest importance of scholastic as opposed to military achievement, character education, and upholding the honor code. Being of a rather stoic temperament, Marshall was little exercised by various absurdities and irritants in military school life, accepting them as merely part of the system to be endured while pursuing higher goals. A tall, slender, hard-working, and ambitious youth, Marshall pursued the goal of military authority with vigor, managing to hold the highest cadet office available. He graduated in civil engineering in 1901.

The idea of making a career in the U.S. Army was stimulated in Marshall by the Spanish-American War. Given the low status of the army, his parents did not encourage his interest. Moreover, the Virginia Military Institute was essentially a state technical school, and few of its cadets desired to make a career of military service. Despite the army's recent expansion, by the time Marshall was ready to graduate in early 1901, few officer billets were available for civilian applicants. Marshall had to receive permission to take an entrance examination, but such hurdles were of minor consequence to him once he decided his course. In addition to his VMI connections, he brashly used his parents' political connections in Washington and even managed, without an appointment, to barge in to see President McKinley. He easily passed the test, but had to wait for his 21st birthday to be commissioned. He also had to receive his commission before marrying his fiancée, Elizabeth Carter Coles, whom he had met at VMI.

Theodore Roosevelt signed Marshall's commission as second lieutenant of infantry on January 18, 1902, with rank to date from February 2, 1901. After a brief honeymoon, he was sent to join Company G of the 30th Infantry Regiment in Mindoro, later in Manila in the newly acquired Philippine Islands. His nine months in Mindoro, which was isolated by weeks from communication with higher headquarters, made Marshall virtual "governor" of a large swatch of the island and was the first of numerous instances in the early decades of his career where he was able to exercise command far beyond that normal to his rank.

In the Philippines, Marshall demonstrated three traits that would appear repeatedly and be crucial to his development as a leader. The first was his ability to assert control of a situation where his leadership was improperly, at least in his eyes, or inadvisably challenged and to do it in a manner that seemed reasonable to most participants. Second, and related to the first, was his willingness to stand up to persons in authority when he considered them in the wrong. Third, was his determination to seize opportunities to learn things that appeared to be useful only in the long term.

Despite its new colonial responsibilities and increased size, the U.S. Army prior to World War I was essentially a constabulary force, disbursed in scores of small isolated garrisons, mainly in the Western United States. Between December 1903 and August 1906, Marshall had tours of duty at Fort Reno, Oklahoma Territory, and on the Texas-Mexico border. Good fortune permitted Marshall to matriculate at the Infantry and Cavalry School at Fort Leavenworth, Kansas, in August 1906.

The highest-ranking students in each class were retained for a second year, which was considered the gateway to General Staff and War College assignments. Overhearing some students dismiss his chances, Marshall resolved to study efficiently and rigorously. He finished first in the class both years and was retained for two additional years as an instructor for students who far outranked him. As an instructor, Marshall served as an assistant editor of the *Infantry Journal*, and although he published but a single essay himself, he significantly enhanced his editing skills. Marshall became known for the clarity and conciseness of his writing, traits generally emulated by his later subordinates.

When school was out for the summers, Marshall was assigned to duty with various National Guard unit camps. Although he recognized the weaknesses of the Guard system, Marshall respected the National Guard, and this respect was reciprocated. This was particularly valuable during the 1940–1942 mobilization period, when large numbers of unacceptable Guard officers had to be relieved of command without creating a political uproar. Summer Guard duty also permitted Marshall to experiment in the field with units far larger than he could hope to command for decades. As a planner and operations officer, Marshall was quick, thorough, and forceful. By 1911, the Adjutants General of Pennsylvania and Massachusetts were competing for Marshall's services.

By the time he returned to the Philippines in August 1913, Marshall had a wide circle of friends, admirers, and former students in the army, although he was still only a first lieutenant. Marshall was assigned to prepare plans for the 1914 Philippine Department maneuvers. By luck (and some arrangement), Marshall became *de facto* commander of the 4,841-man attacking force that overwhelmed the defenders south of Manila. To recover from the near physical breakdown these duties provoked, Marshall vacationed in Japan and visited Russo-Japanese War sites in Manchuria. Major General Hunter Liggett made Marshall an aide-de-camp to preclude his relegation to the low-level tasks befitting his rank. He returned to the United States as a captain in 1916, and Major General J. Franklin Bell made him an aide to help plan and coordinate significant parts of the army's mobilization as it was organized into the Allied Expeditionary Force (AEF) By now, Marshall had become adept at interpreting and anticipating his commander's desires, protecting his best interests, and using his authority to accomplish the job.

As the head of the Plans and Operations section of First Division staff, Marshall was the second American ashore with combat troops in France on June 26, 1917. For the next year, he would consider and wrestle with the impact of America's lack of preparedness for war. The First Division's problems occupied him until mid-July 1918. He was denied a combat command and retained on the staff because, as his commanding general, Robert L. Bullard, noted, Marshall probably had no equal in the Army in the teaching and practice of war. AEF commander John J. Pershing, who had experienced then Major Marshall's displeasure in early October 1917 over Pershing's seeming lack of appreciation for First Division's problems, had him moved to a planning job at General Headquarters.

Marshall found the view from General Headquarters far different from that at First Division; the staff at GHQ dealt not with companies and regiments but with ocean tonnage, ports of debarkation, dock construction, tank manufacture, methods of training divisions, and the complexities of inter-Allied politics. His previous "localitis" (i.e., the presumption that one's own problems are the organization's or the country's most pressing) was made clear, and thereafter he sought to make certain that he was considering the "big picture" and not merely pressing daily minutiae. This search for clear, concise, yet broad-based intelligence and advice from subordinates manifested itself later in his reorganization of portions of the U.S. Army in early 1942 and the State Department in early 1947.

Marshall supported Pershing's determination to train and command a separate American army in France, rather than see individual units used as replacements in French and British commands. Marshall's relations with the French were excellent, in part because of his respect for their fighting prowess and their assistance in helping the woefully unprepared Americans learn fighting skills and in part because of the good relations he had with the ubiquitous French liaison officers. His contact with the British was limited until after the war, but there is no evidence that he developed the antagonism that many AEF officers did toward the British officer class—for that matter, Marshall did not appear to dislike the Germans as a people, although he sought to destroy their field forces.

Historically, warfare by coalitions was fraught with difficulties and opportunities for a unified enemy; thus Marshall considered Ferdinand Foch's elevation to Supreme Allied Commander in 1918 to be a good idea. In subsequent years, Marshall developed a philosophy that valued unity of command, which included a single commander over all Allied armed forces in the same theater. A corollary was his belief that the country contributing the most forces should command the theater. Marshall largely got his way in this respect in World War II, NATO, and the Korean War. Fixing the lack of unity of command in the State Department in 1947 was one of the first reforms he implemented.

In May 1919, Marshall became one of General Pershing's three aides-de-camp, a position he held until departing for troop duty in China in mid-1924. These five years—helping General Pershing wind up AEF affairs and then serving as Chief of Staff Pershing's office manager—constituted a postgraduate education in national and War Department politics for Marshall. Although they were not a new but a recurring pattern in American history, the post–World War I congressional hearings and investigations, the general lack of public interest in ground forces, and the consequent excessive defense budget cuts also taught Marshall important lessons about handling Congress and dealing with army public relations and the National Guard.

At Tientsin, China, with the Fifteenth Infantry Regiment between 1924 and 1927 guarding the supply line to the foreign legations in Beijing, Marshall learned to speak the local Chinese dialect. He also witnessed warlord fighting and some of the effects of the Nationalists' drive to unify China. In 1927 he was assigned to teach at the Army War College, but his wife died shortly after the semester began. Given the opportunity to command the academic department of the Infantry School at Fort Benning, Georgia, Marshall made the school the fountainhead of army reform. Quietly and gradually, so as not to arouse opposition, Marshall brought into the faculty open-minded men recently returned from troop duty such as Omar N. Bradley and Joseph W. Stilwell. "We bored from within without cessation during my five years at Benning," Marshall said after he left in 1932. He hammered incessantly on the theme of simplicity. He was particularly aggrieved by "colorless pedantic form" used in army manuals, insisting on clear, concise language. Some 200 future generals passed through the Infantry School as instructors or students during Marshall's tenure.

The Infantry School period was a happy one for Marshall, and in October 1930 he married Katherine Tupper Brown, a vivacious widow with three young children. In 1932 he was pleased to return to commanding troops, as he hated desks and paperwork. Between 1934 and 1936, he was detailed to Chicago as senior instructor for the Illinois National Guard. He undertook to reform Guard training, improve its morale, reeducate the Guard's officer corps, improve the organization's image among the middle class, and use his three years in Chicago as a proving ground for his citizen-soldier training ideas.

In October 1936, Marshall finally received his general's star and was given command of the Fifth Brigade of the Third Division at Vancouver Barracks, Washington. In July 1938 he was recalled to the War Department to head the War Plans Division. In October 1938 he became the army's deputy chief of staff, and by April 1939, President Roosevelt had decided to name him the next chief of staff. His first foreign assignment was to visit Brazil in May and June 1939 on a goodwill military mission that sought to offset a pro-German and Italian bias in the ruling political and military elite. Marshall was particularly successful in making friends with Brazil's Army Chief of Staff, General Pedro Monteiro, thereby laying the groundwork for that nation's participation as an ally in World War II.

Marshall was sworn in as chief of staff of the U.S. Army on the morning of September 1, 1939, a few hours after the news reached Washington of Germany's invasion of Poland. Significant progress in mobilizing American military and economic power began only with the shocking German victories in the spring of 1940.

President Roosevelt's gauging of the public's mood between 1939 and 1941 was generally accurate and his cautious foreign policy frequently justified, Marshall believed. The chief of staff was determined to operate as a member of a political-military team and not to adopt the traditional expedient of attempting to compromise the president's organizational and appropriations decisions via friends in Congress. It was important for Marshall to demonstrate his nonpartisan role to both the executive and legislative branches. He was successful in his efforts to ensure cordial relations between the War Department and Congress; he was an effective witness, profoundly informed on military matters, and better acquainted than most professional soldiers with the political difficulties besetting a legislator, and appreciative of the public's anxieties at the time. He appeared 48 times before various House and Senate committees between the summer of 1939 and the autumn of 1941. Many in Congress trusted Marshall more than "that man in the White House."

The chief of staff's role between late 1939 and late 1941 was to modernize an army traumatized by penury and isolation for nearly a generation, a role for which Marshall was probably uniquely qualified. Between the fall of France in June 1940 and the attack on Pearl Harbor, the army's air and ground forces increased 750 percent, threatening the army's antiquated organizational structure with overload and collapse. Marshall responded to the period's unique challenges with enormous energy and activity. Not only was he frequently before Congress, but he was also constantly on the move, visiting new cantonments, witnessing new weapons demonstrations, inspecting training facilities, observing maneuvers, and seeking effective leaders to promote. He frequently and unequivocally put officers on notice that he expected them to pay close attention to the quality of their troops' morale.

Prior to the end of World War II Marshall was generally loath to express ideas about foreign policy in public or even personal correspondence Of course, as the chief military strategist in the war, Marshall's strategic ideas had foreign policy implications such as his insistence on landings in north and south France in 1944 and the decision not to drive for Berlin or into Czechoslovakia in 1945, but he did not feel the necessity of offering Roosevelt foreign policy advice. Indeed, he and the other military advisors played relatively little role in the Yalta or Potsdam conferences, as these were mainly concerned with political settlements.

His interest in air power began when he was a student at Fort Leavenworth. After 1938 he aggressively used the transport plane as a tool to manage the army; he was constantly flying and required his staff officers and inspectors to fly. Marshall's belief in a balanced air-ground force, however, did not appeal to many strategic bombing enthusiasts, who were determined to create a separate air force. Marshall was certain that the pilot-dominated air service was far from ready to operate as an independent bureaucracy, so he made an informal agreement with his friend, Air Forces Chief of Staff Henry H. ("Hap") Arnold. Arnold would suppress the independence enthusiasts; Marshall would see to it that airmen gained the experience necessary to run a postwar independent organization.

Three weeks after Pearl Harbor, Marshall convinced the reluctant British to create the American–British–Dutch–Australian Command in the Pacific under Britain's Sir Archibald Wavell. This short-lived command established the precedent for a single Allied commander in such theaters as Europe (Dwight D. Eisenhower) and the Mediterranean (Sir Harold Alexander). Indeed, one of Marshall's most constant and successful policies during World War II was strengthening the Anglo-American alliance, despite differing strategic interests.

Strategically, Marshall was a staunch supporter of the Germany-first strategy, which implied holding the line against Japan—although after the Pearl Harbor attack, he approved far more aggressive operations in the Pacific than prewar plans had anticipated. He was reluctant to commit the United States to lengthy and expensive campaigns in the Mediterranean, as many British leaders preferred. Although political necessity and military opportunism in 1942 and 1943 necessitated major Allied operational commitments to North Africa, Sicily, and Italy, Marshall rebelled at further investments in what he called the "suction pump" in the Mediterranean and forced a commitment to a spring 1944 invasion of Normandy.

As late as the Cairo Conference of December 1943, Marshall was presumed by most British and American leaders to be the likely choice as supreme allied commander for Europe, but given political and personality issues in other theaters that required Marshall's touch (especially the Pacific and China), the high regard in which he was held in the United States, and especially President Roosevelt's reluctance ("I feel I could not sleep at night with you out of the country"), Dwight D. Eisenhower was named to the post. Marshall was disappointed at losing this opportunity to lead the army he had created, but he accepted the decision as he always did—without further comment. He was pleased with Eisenhower's performance. Marshall's philosophy was to pick good leaders (and he was rather proud of his success in this), protect them from outside interference (especially from Washington), but relieve them quickly if they failed.

Given his confidence in his subordinates, Marshall's focus tended to be six months ahead of the current battle. For example, at the time of the Battle of the Bulge, December 1944–January 1945, Marshall was concerned with occupation problems, Pacific strategy, and the coming massive movement of troops there, demobilization, and postwar military organization. U.S. planning throughout the war had aimed at keeping its own casualties low. As a result the United States accepted aerial bombardment as an acceptable component of its military strategy. In consequence, Marshall had little difficulty accepting the use of atomic bombs on Japanese cities, particularly after the fierce Japanese resistance on Okinawa and Iwo Jima.

In his final biennial report as army chief of staff in September 1945, Marshall expressed his optimism about the usefulness of the United Nations as a force for peace, conviction that the nation was no longer capable of simple hemispheric defense but had world responsibilities, and determination that the country maintain a military reserve capable of deterring potential aggressors. In his last speech as chief of staff at Princeton University, November 26, 1945, he asserted that Americans should learn from the military and foreign policy mistakes of the past, from their relations with other nations, and of their new role in the world. The United States, he said, had to assume its responsibilities as a world power and not turn inward and unilateralist.

Following V-J Day, Marshall was anxious to retire after nearly 44 years of active duty, 6 as army chief of staff, but the army had many demobilization problems to solve. Marshall was not permitted to retire until mid-November 1945. On November 27, less than 24 hours after his retirement ceremony, President Harry Truman—who was an ardent admirer—called him back to duty for the thankless task of attempting to mediate between the Nationalists and Communists in China.

The precipitating factor was Ambassador to China Patrick J. Hurley's sudden resignation and public denunciation of the Truman administration's China policy and the alleged undermining by disloyal State Department professionals of his efforts in China. Truman needed someone to offset Hurley and to deflect criticism of administration policy. Marshall had little time to prepare for the mission, however, as a special congressional committee was preparing to call him to testify on the Pearl Harbor attack, which was being used by some members of the Republican Party as a club to beat Franklin D. Roosevelt's legacy as well as the Democratic Party.

Marshall demanded and received written policy guidance and unity of command in China (i.e., nearly complete control of all aspects of U.S. involvement in policy, negotiations, embassy issues, finances, and official reporting). Executive departments were instructed to seek Marshall's approval on anything they did with regard to China.

Marshall was aware that his chances of success were slim, but he was undismayed and determined. Neither side was anxious to have him (or any other outsider) attempt to mediate the growing civil war, but both feared to oppose his mission and hoped to manipulate it to their own ends. Initially the results were encouraging, and some important written agreements were reached in January and February 1946. By spring, however, the cease-fire agreement was breaking down, and by midsummer both sides had decided that their best hope lay in military victory. Marshall was able to delay the onset of all-out war, but in the end he could not achieve a political settlement. He ended his mission by writing a lengthy report in late 1946. Marshall's criticisms of the Nationalist government and his subsequent opposition to significant American military involvement in the Chinese civil war were major factors in causing him to be branded, in the eyes of such conservatives as Senators William Jenner and Joseph McCarthy, as a Communist dupe or even an outright traitor.

It is not clear exactly when President Truman decided to appoint Marshall secretary of state. Some comments by Albert Wedemeyer, commanding general of the China Theater, following a mid-February 1946 meeting, imply that the subject had already been broached to Marshall, but Truman was waiting for the general to complete the China mission, presumably in the summer. Secretary Byrnes was aware that Marshall would succeed him. When Army Chief of Staff Dwight Eisenhower visited Marshall in Nanking on May 9, he reiterated the president's desire that Marshall accept the post. Marshall's continued hope for some kind of settlement and the pleas of various Chinese that he stay, however, extended his mission months beyond what he had expected.

The November 1946 congressional elections were a disaster for the president's party, and the Republicans took control of both houses. Truman desperately needed a neutral figure of high public standing and good rapport with Congress and the press to take charge of foreign affairs. By December the rumors were widespread that Marshall would end his China mission and might become secretary of state.

His nomination was announced on January 7, 1947. That same day, Senator Arthur Vandenburg, head of the Foreign Relations Committee, put the nomination through his committee and the full Senate. Nevertheless, Vandenburg was worried, Marshall's staff knew, that Marshall might harbor presidential ambitions. Thus within minutes of arriving at Union Station in Washington on January 21, Marshall told reporters that he would not be a candidate for office at any time in the future. He took the oath of office that same day.

A team player and loyal subordinate, Marshall never called Truman anything but "Mr. President," and he did not take liberties with Truman's admiration for him. He was not interested in personal publicity, empire building, or poaching on others' turf. Moreover, he tried to understand other leaders' problems and to work with them. The dominating presence in Truman's cabinet, he had few detractors in Washington or the press.

As a military leader—and most people continued to refer to him as "General" rather than "Mr. Secretary"—Marshall was not stereotypically "military" in his thinking, as Dean Acheson observed. He was not swayed by military claims of superior knowledge or understanding of foreign issues. He admitted the inevitability of military downsizing, favoring balanced air-ground-sea forces and Universal Military Training to give the United States a reserve force of military significance. He was opposed to saber rattling unless the United States was prepared to act forcefully if its bluff was called, believing that foreign military professionals could easily see through empty posturing. He was also strongly supportive of the idea of civilian control of the military, including atomic energy—which the army had been making an effort to control. Marshall was reluctant to flaunt the United States' monopoly of atomic weapons.

Marshall's relations with members of Congress of both parties were generally good, and he was careful to cultivate Arthur Vandenburg, a power in the senate and the Republican Party, a reformed prewar isolationist, and now leader of the party's internationalist wing. When Marshall went to Moscow in March 1947 on his first foreign assignment as secretary—and at a number of subsequent international conferences—he took with him the Republican "shadow" secretary of state, John Foster Dulles.

Marshall generally asked his predecessor's staff to remain, slowly bringing in a few people for key positions and transferring people he did not want. When he became secretary of state, Marshall convinced Will Clayton, Assistant Secretary of State for Economic Affairs, and Dean Acheson, Under Secretary, to stay on for a few months.

Acheson was told he was to be Marshall's chief of staff and that all issues for the secretary were to come through Acheson's office. Marshall then brought in Robert A. Lovett to train as Acheson's replacement. He also had the department's secretariat reorganized along lines similar to that in the War Department, which gave him firmer control. Marshall ended the old system whereby numerous department officials brought projects and ideas directly to the secretary for approval, creating enormous confusion at times. He also eliminated the old "clearance" system that required every interested section in the department to sign off on an idea, which encouraged delays and stifled initiative. Finally, he created an in-house "think tank": the Policy Planning Staff. Its job was to enable the department to anticipate problems rather than merely reacting to them; members were directed to think ahead and not to become involved in routine operations. Although not every Marshall innovation was lasting, many continued long after he left office. Marshall made the State Department once again a major player in Washington policy circles.

Marshall reiterated his belief in the necessity of assuming a world role in his first public speech as secretary of state, again at Princeton on February 22, 1947. Although these sentiments were unexceptional among the Eastern foreign policy elite, they were still not widely accepted among the public, and Marshall quickly found himself in the role of "selling" them throughout the country.

Western Europe remained the focus of U.S. foreign policy during Marshall's two years at State. East Asian problems, however, were temporarily displaced to third place behind those involving the eastern Mediterranean (Greece and Palestine). Concern with Latin American problems was a distant fourth in intensity. Nevertheless all problems were viewed by foreign policy makers as being related to Soviet power and Moscow's perceived control over communists everywhere.

Marshall's first priority was preparing to attend the Moscow Foreign Ministers Conference, scheduled to open in mid-March 1947, which would be dominated by issues relating to the status of Germany. Marshall was thus not heavily involved in the February crisis over Great Britain's desire to reduce its expenses in supporting the governments of Greece and Turkey, although he supported the general Truman administration consensus that the United States had to assume portions of Britain's mantle in the region. When he received the final draft of the Truman Doctrine message in Moscow, Marshall's reaction was that the anti-Soviet rhetoric was excessive and the extensiveness of the proposed mandate, that all countries threatened by communism could call on the United States for aid was too broad, but he did not insist that the message be modified.

One result of his mediation mission to China was to inure Marshall to drawn-out negotiations that crawled toward a series of small compromises that potentially would result in a significant settlement. Marshall's assumption that Joseph Stalin was a hardheaded realist who ultimately would agree to a compromise settlement was worn away over weeks of meetings, and he ultimately concluded that the communists desired social and economic chaos in Europe—as they had in China the previous year—on the presumption that they would benefit. By the time the conference ended on April 24, its chief accomplishment was the firm establishment in Marshall's mind that the Soviet Union had no desire for an early restoration of order in Germany. Moreover, his numerous talks with the French and British foreign ministers and his personal observations on the way to and from the conference convinced Marshall that Europe's economic plight was severe and that the United States had to do something quickly to prevent the complete breakdown of West Europe's societies. The patient was sinking, he told a nationwide radio audience on April 28, while the doctors deliberated.

Marshall directed that the Policy Planning Staff be activated immediately with George F. Kennan as chairman. Kennan and Will Clayton were particularly important in generating the ideas that Marshall put together for a brief, consciously low-key speech at Harvard University on June 5 that warned of Europe's plight, asserted that the United States could successfully help economically, but insisted that the initiative come from a coordinated Europe (a political requirement for congressional acceptance, as Marshall knew). Meanwhile, Marshall worked carefully to reassure Senator Vandenberg that the program's costs would not bust the budget.

By the time European Recovery Program legislation was submitted to Congress in December 1947, President Truman and the press had taken to calling the idea the "Marshall Plan." Typically, Marshall never used the term, because he thought it unseemly to confer on one person credit for a collective accomplishment. In addition to testifying, at which Marshall was always effective, he launched a major public relations campaign to support the plan by giving speeches to key groups. Throughout his first year in office, Marshall had been careful to avoid overheated rhetoric regarding the Soviet threat, but as the struggle for passage intensified in the spring of 1948 and Soviet power in Europe seemed to grow (evidenced by the Communist coup in Czechoslovakia), he increasingly claimed in speeches that the choice was between good and evil and that the United States had to lead the forces of good. In retirement, he was somewhat apologetic about his excesses here, but at the time he thought them justified by the circumstances.

Germany's status in Europe was a constant issue during Marshall's tenure, and he spent considerable time trying to overcome understandable French worries about it. At the November–December 1947 London conference of the Council of Foreign Ministers, Marshall was again prepared to spend as long as necessary to arrive at a solution, but those meetings were a greater failure than the Moscow session and merely highlighted East–West divisions. British-American determination to address the economic and political problems in their occupation zones in Germany, even if the Soviets did not cooperate, swiftly escalated into the Berlin crisis and airlift of April 1948 to May 1949. Marshall's role during the airlift period was mainly in working to keep the Western Allies unified and urging a firm stance against the Soviets while demonstrating a willingness to use the United Nation's (UN) machinery to seek a solution. He opposed the United States' taking provocative stands and asserted his willingness to negotiate the basic legal issues once the blockade was lifted.

Although Marshall was a vigorous supporter of the UN and spent considerable time at its meetings, he was also pleased to take a significant portion of the credit for establishing the North Atlantic Treaty Organization (NATO) and picking its first military leaders. As had become his methodology, Marshall vigorously courted

Senator Vandenberg, finally overcoming his reluctance to seek a congressional resolution favoring regional defense agreements.

While he was in China, Marshall was well aware of the severe reductions in deployable U.S. ground forces and of the grave risks of significant direct U.S. involvement in other people's civil wars. He was unalterably opposed to anything beyond sending a few advisors and some materiel. He manifested this same caution regarding the Greek civil war, although he found Greek government leaders more amenable to American military and political advice than the Chinese government had been. Marshall recommended an aggressive American military mission head, General James A. Van Fleet and, when he visited Athens in October 1948, an American-financed increase of the Greek army.

One of the more controversial and uncomfortable situations Marshall found himself embroiled in was the status of Palestine, especially whether it should be partitioned between Jews and Arabs. It was not sufficient for the United States to support partition, Marshall thought; it had to be prepared to use force to enforce partition in the face of Arab hostility. Marshall had the U.S. delegation to the UN call for a special session of the General Assembly and a temporary trusteeship under the UN. In May 1948, Truman's political adviser, Clark Clifford, wanted the president to announce, even before Israel declared its independence, that he would recognize the new state. Marshall opposed this as damaging to U.S. prestige in the UN, as the U.S. had a resolution pending in the UN for a truce, and the borders of a new state were undecided. Marshall was incensed—and told Truman so—that the president would follow staff advice so blatantly motivated by domestic political considerations. In the end Marshall accepted Truman's decision to recognize Israel.

Marshall sought to improve ties with Latin America, but his efforts were hurt by his admission that there was little the United States could do for the region economically, given U.S. commitments in Europe. He twice went for lengthy meetings: to Rio de Janeiro in August 1947, when he needed to devote considerable effort to preventing displays of anger among the delegates at the lack of a Latin American Marshall Plan; and to Bogota in April 1948, when he signed the agreement creating the Organization of American States.

The November 1948 elections made final Marshall's retirement plans. Truman's surprise victory and the Democratic Party's resumption of control of both houses of Congress meant that Marshall's nonpartisan status was no longer essential to get foreign policy items through Congress. Moreover, just as the Berlin crisis was heating up in May 1948, Marshall was found to need a kidney operation; he postponed the procedure until December. Truman reluctantly accepted Marshall's resignation, which was to coincide with the president's inauguration on January 20, 1949.

Marshall was clearly one of America's greatest secretaries of state. He brought to the office a unique blend of skill in military and international relations, managerial expertise, bipartisan values, and lack of personal ambition. He was cautious and not given to promising more than he could deliver. He was usually thoughtful toward and understanding of his subordinates; he had what the military termed "loyalty down." He was loyal to his commander-in-chief in a period when other leaders, even in the president's own party, saw Mr. Truman as a temporary officeholder who ought to be replaced on the Democratic ticket in 1948 or, for Republicans, as one who certainly would be repudiated in the November election. Marshall's solid support, even when he vigorously disagreed with Truman, as over the recognition of Israel, was a source of great comfort and strength to the president.

If he had a weakness, it was in occasionally insufficient appreciation of political considerations; not everyone had the luxury of his degree of nonpartisanship. After he reorganized the State Department, Marshall was initially inclined to expect the department's bureaucracy to work like a wartime military organization that enjoyed unified popular support and politicians' trust of their technical expertise. Marshall had to learn that the Truman administration's political interests had to be considered at every stage of policymaking and that he could not maintain his wartime expectation that subordinates should bring him relatively comprehensive recommendations for solving various problems that he could accept or veto.

As the former chief of staff of the U.S. Army and *de facto* leader of the wartime Joint Chiefs of Staff, Marshall was not easily manipulated by the Pentagon or military proconsuls abroad. He recognized the limits of American military power and the need to calculate realistically the degree of influence that such power could have in international relations. He was not generally given to inflated or overly excited rhetoric about the surpassing evil of the enemy—and thus the futility or foolishness in seeking negotiations with it—even if he did sometimes feel the need to talk tougher than he should have.

One-third of his two years in office was spent in international conferences and the rest in juggling multiple crises. He genuinely tried to understand other leaders' viewpoints and to negotiate small agreements that might lead to improved relations and thus to more significant agreements. His skill with Congress was legendary, and he rarely clashed with other Washington department heads. He even got along, generally, with working reporters.

He deserved being named *Time* magazine's "Man of the Year" for 1947 and the award of the Nobel Peace Prize in 1953 for his part in perhaps the most effective foreign policy ever implemented by the United States, the Marshall Plan.

In October 1949, President Truman named Marshall head of the American Red Cross. The job was hardly a sinecure. The organization had been riven with high-level strife and continued to suffer from the antipathy of many veterans. Marshall worked hard and traveled around the country seeking to heal the organization's rifts, improve its morale, and raise its public image.

On September 21, 1950, to end Secretary of Defense Louis Johnson's conflict with the president and the State Department, because of the outbreak of the Korean War, made Marshall's resumption of a military role useful, and despite Marshall's warning that his China mission increasingly made him a lightning rod for conservative critics of the administration, the president named him secretary of defense. Marshall promised to stay six months to oversee U.S. mobilization for the war. China's intervention, the need to relieve General MacArthur from office, and the demands of a coalition war, however, forced him to remain longer. He retired from national public service for the last time on September 12, 1951.

In real retirement at last, he and his wife lived in Leesburg, Virginia, and Pinehurst, North Carolina. He maintained his ties to the Virginia Military Institute, but he generally avoided public affairs. George C. Marshall, age 78, died on October 16, 1959, at Walter Reed Army Hospital. He is buried in Arlington National Cemetery.

BIBLIOGRAPHICAL ESSAY

While he was in public office, Marshall endeavored to prevent people writing about him. He did write a World War I reminiscence, *Memoirs of My Services in the World War, 1917–1918*, ed. James L. Collins, Jr. (1976), but he decided against publication during his lifetime. After World War II he refused to write a memoir, despite being offered sums reported to run as high as one million dollars. In the mid-1950s, however, he permitted an authorized biography; Forrest C. Pogue's excellent *George C. Marshall* (1963–1987), is still the standard against which all writing about Marshall must be measured. Two excellent single-volume biographies are: Mark A. Stoler, *George C. Marshall: Soldier-Statesman of the American Century* (1989) and Ed Cray, *General of the Army: George C. Marshall, Soldier and Statesman* (1990).

Two specialized volumes are also valuable. Thomas Parrish has written *Roosevelt and Marshall: Partners in Politics and War, the Personal Story* (1989). Robert H. Ferrell's *George C. Marshall as Secretary of State, 1947–1949* (1966), volume 15 in the *American Secretaries of State and Their Diplomacy* series is still valuable, despite the author's not having access to the enormous repository of documents and information about Marshall that Forrest Pogue created and that is now at the George C. Marshall Foundation in Lexington, Virginia.

A key primary source for understanding Marshall is *George C. Marshall Interviews and Reminiscences for Forrest C. Pogue*, ed. Larry I. Bland, 3rd ed. (1996). Four of the seven volumes of a documentary edition have been published as of this writing and cover the period 1880 through 1944: *The Papers of George Catlett Marshall* (1981–), ed. Larry I. Bland and Sharon Ritenour Stevens. Mrs. Marshall's autobiography, which covers the years 1930 to 1945, is also of some value: *Katherine Tupper Marshall, Together: Annals of an Army Wife* (1946).

Larry I. Bland

JOHN MARSHALL (1755–1835)

Served 1800–1801
Appointed by President John Adams
Federalist

John Marshall will always be remembered as one of the great figures in American history. His tenure as Chief Justice of the U.S. Supreme Court helped shape American law. By acclamation, he is regarded as the greatest embodiment of the U.S. Constitution. However, his influence on American history encompasses much more than his tenure as chief justice.

Marshall was born in 1755 in Fauquier County, Virginia. John was the first of 15 children. His father, Thomas, was a self-made man. He began as a planter before accumulating great personal wealth as a land speculator. Thomas Marshall also held a variety of elective offices during John's childhood. When the revolution began, Thomas Marshall, along with his sons, served under long-time friend George Washington. John Marshall served as a lieutenant in the Culpepper Minutemen at the age of 19, eventually rising to the rank of captain. He saw action at the battles of Brandywine and Germantown and was with Washington at Valley Forge.

After the revolution, Marshall studied law at the College of William and Mary for less than a year before going into private practice in 1780. He specialized in civil law, primarily land and estate issues. Like many lawyers of his day, Marshall became active in politics. His early government positions all dealt with state and local political issues. He served in the Virginia legislature and was a delegate to the state convention that approved the new Constitution.

Marshall first became enmeshed in international affairs as part of a diplomatic mission to France. Marshall accompanied Elbridge Gerry and Charles Pinckney to Paris in 1797 in an attempt to head off impending hostilities between the two nations. However, things did not go as planned. Upon their arrival, French foreign minister Talleyrand refused to meet with them, eventually sending three anonymous men to their hotel requesting numerous concessions and large bribes. Ultimately, the American diplomats refused to meet the French demands. Marshall, reporting the French demands, referred to the mysterious men as Mr. X., Y., and Z.

Upon his return to the states, Marshall received a hero's welcome as public sentiment in the country was outraged at the so-called XYZ affair.

His reputation enhanced following his handling of the XYZ affair, Marshall moved on to national politics. He won his first national office, a seat in the U.S. House of Representatives in 1798. In this capacity, his nationalist tendencies became clear, as he argued for broad presidential power in extradition under the Jay treaty, contending that the president is the "sole organ of the nation in external relations." Two years later, Marshall was chosen by President Adams to be secretary of state. He served in this capacity from May 13, 1800, until March 4, 1801.

Adams originally retained the entire cabinet of his predecessor, George Washington. However, nearing the end of his presidency, Adams removed key members of his cabinet that he felt were loyal to Alexander Hamilton. After first refusing the position of secretary of war, Marshall was chosen by Adams to be secretary of state, replacing Timothy Pickering. This restructuring split the Federalist Party in two. Among those remaining loyal to Adams, the choice of Marshall was well received.

The job of secretary of state in the early days of the republic was defined more broadly than it is today. Marshall not only had to deal with international issues, but also with many administrative tasks at home. Marshall was responsible for granting patents, copyrights, and passports, conducting the census, recording land patents, overseeing the U.S. Mint, printing and delivery of the laws of the United States, preparation and delivery of commissions, and supervision of U.S. territories and the oversight of the construction of all new federal buildings in Washington. He even took charge of speech writing, including penning Adams's farewell address.

On the international side, Marshall, as secretary of state, dealt with issues and negotiations involving France, England, Spain, and the Barbary Pirates. The main thrust of the Marshall tenure was an emphasis on neutrality. In negotiations with each of these nations, he insisted that the relationship of the United States with the other nation had no bearing on U.S. relations with any other. In each instance, Marshall was able to avoid war, perhaps the most important international accomplishment of a secretary of state in this era. Though only in office for nine months, Adams was generally pleased with the Marshall's performance as the last Federalist secretary of state. His term as secretary was efficient, if unremarkable. During his nine months in office, no major crisis occurred, and upon leaving office, no major conflicts were eminent.

During the last month of the Adams administration, Marshall served concurrently as secretary of state and chief justice of the Supreme Court. Certainly, his career after serving as secretary of state was far more distinguished. Although Marshall had served in virtually every level of government, it was not until his appointment to the nation's highest court that his legacy was formed. In his years on the court, he ruled on many areas of international affairs that he had been directly involved with in his previous position. His court would reach important decisions on issues such as neutrality, impressment, prize cases, piracy, and extradition. Marshall gained perspective in all of these areas as secretary of state.

However, his most notable contribution as secretary of state may have come from the failure to perform one of his administrative duties, namely the failure to deliver a commission appointing William Marbury to the position of justice of the peace. Before yielding control of the government to Thomas Jefferson and the Democratic Republicans in 1801, outgoing President Adams and the Federalist

Congress created a number of new judicial offices. Among those nominated by the president and confirmed by the Senate was William Marbury. However, during the hectic final days of the Adams administration, Marshall neglected to deliver Marbury's commission. When James Madison took over as the new secretary of state, he refused to honor the commissions left over from his predecessor. Thus, when Marbury went to court seeking to have his appointment honored, his case came before newly appointed Chief Justice John Marshall.

Marshall skillfully used this opportunity to fulfill his Federalist vision and to create the greatest asset of the judicial branch: the power of judicial review. This power gives the courts the ability to review any action of government to determine whether or not it is constitutional. Stemming directly from Marshall's failure to deliver the commission, this single decision allowed him to make the judiciary a coequal branch in our federal system and cement his legacy as one of the major figures of American history.

BIBLIOGRAPHICAL ESSAY

An annotated edition of Marshall's papers is in the process of being published. Herbert A. Johnson, Charles T. Cullen, and Charles F. Hobson have successively edited 10 volumes of *The Papers of John Marshall* (1974-), documenting Marshall through 1827. The volumes include judicial opinions, newspaper articles, speeches, and correspondence. Still helpful editions of his letters include Charles C. Smith (ed.), "Letters of Chief Justice Marshall," *Proceedings of the Massachusetts Historical Society*, 2nd ser., 14 (1900); and Charles Warren, "The Story–Marshall Correspondence 1819–1831," *William and Mary Quarterly*, 2nd ser. 21 (1941). See also John Stokes Adams (ed.), *An Autobiographical Sketch by John Marshall* (1937).

A vital source for understanding Marshall's political ideas is his *The Life of George Washington*, 5 vols. (1804–1807). An excellent guide to Marshall's writings is Irwin S. Rhodes, *The Papers of John Marshall: A Descriptive Calendar*, 2 vols. (1969).

Although dated, Albert J. Beveridge's *The Life of John Marshall*, 4 vols. (1916–1919), is still the standard biography. A shorter work is Francis N. Stites's superb biography, *John Marshall: Defender of the Constitution* (1981). Two older works that are still valuable for their understanding of Marshall's jurisprudence are James B. Thayer, *John Marshall* (1901), and Edward S. Corwin, *John Marshall and the Constitution* (1920).

For analyses of the Marshall Court and his jurisprudence, see George Lee Haskins and Herbert A. Johnson, *Foundations of Power: John Marshall, 1801–1815* (1981); G. Edward White, *The Marshall Court and Cultural Change, 1815–35* (1988); Robert Kenneth Faulkner's excellent *The Jurisprudence of John Marshall* (1968); Thomas C. Shevory (ed.), *John Marshall's Achievement: Law, Politics, and Constitutional Interpretations* (1989); Richard J. Brisbin, Jr., "John Marshall and the Nature of Law in the Early Republic," *Virginia Magazine of History and Biography* 98 (1990); and G. Edward White, *The American Judicial Tradition: Profiles of Leading American Judges*, rev. ed. (1988).

On Marshall and judicial review, see Gordon S. Wood, "The Origins of Judicial Review," *Suffolk University Law Review* 22 (1988); J. M. Sosin, *The Aristocracy of the Long Robe: The Origins of Judicial Review in America* (1989); Kermit L. Hall's brief but effective *The Supreme Court and Judicial Review in American History* (1985); Elizabeth McCaughey, "*Marbury v. Madison:* Have We Missed the Real Meaning?" *Presidential Studies Quarterly* 19 (1989); Christopher Wolfe, *The Rise of Modern Judicial Review* (1986); Leslie Friedman Goldstein, *In Defense of the Text* (1991); Robert Lowry Clinton, *Marbury v. Madison and Judicial Review* (1989); Sylvia Snowiss, *Judicial Review and the Law of the Constitution* (1990); Thomas Gorey, "Origins of the Unwritten Constitution: Fundamental Law in American Revolutionary Thought," *Stanford Law Review* 30 (1978); and Suzanne Sherry, "The Founders' Unwritten Constitution," *University of Chicago Law Review* 54 (1987).

For Marshall's diplomatic career, see Andrew J. Montague's essay, "John Marshall," in Samuel Flagg Bemis (ed.), *The American Secretaries of States and Their Diplomacy* (1958), and Frances Howell Rudko, *John Marshall and International Law* (1991).

Paul Weizer

LOUIS MCLANE (1786–1857)

Served 1833–1834
Appointed by President Andrew Jackson
Democrat

Louis McLane was born on May 28, 1784, in Smyrna, Delaware. Circumstances for the young McLane in Delaware were fortuitous, claims his biographer, because he was "of Scottish and English descent, Methodist in religion, Federalist in politics, son of a military hero, and a Wilmington lawyer of downstate birth." These factors provided the basis for his success.

McLane's father paved the road for his son's advancement because of his role as a leading citizen of Delaware. Allen McLane served in several major battles during the Revolutionary War, including Yorktown, by which time he had been commissioned a captain. During the 1790s the elder McLane supported the Federalist Party and in 1797 was appointed customs collector at Wilmington by President Washington. McLane would retain his collectorship into the 1820s, all the while establishing political contacts that helped clear a path for his son.

The young McLane also inherited some of his father's personality traits: "a choleric temper, a vigorous spirit, and an ardent ambition." He has been variously described by historians as "intelligent and able," "clear minded and efficient," "volatile, opinionated, one who loved power and the wielding of it, a tactful person who was skillfully diplomatic, and a manager of men."

McLane enjoyed a varied education. It began with a brief enrollment in the Friends School in Wilmington. Not long after, McLane's father obtained a commission for him as a midshipman in the Navy. He was assigned to the *Philadelphia* under the command of Stephen Decatur, and at 15 years of age set sail for the West Indies. Although it was an exciting voyage, a naval career was not congenial to his aspirations, so he enrolled in the Newark Academy, Delaware, on his return. He eventually settled on the law, and once again his father's influence was significant. The elder McLane was friends with one of the most famous Delaware lawyers and politicians, James Bayard. It was to Bayard's law office in Wilmington that Louis McLane began his apprenticeship in about 1804. After surviving a duel with another of Bayard's apprentices, John Barratt, McLane was admitted to the bar in 1807.

Like his father and his mentor, Bayard, McLane became a member of the Federalist Party. Delaware was predominantly Federalist and would remain so into the Jackson presidency. Even though Delaware remained Federalist, on the national level, McLane, like other Federalists such as the famous chief justice Roger B. Taney of Maryland, had to make accommodations if they were to advance in the political world. Because McLane remained attached to many of his Federalist beliefs throughout his career, his relations with the Jacksonians were invariably strained. Although he served in Jackson's cabinet, his grand aspirations, the presidency and, if offered, an appointment to the Supreme Court, never materialized, nor did he gain as much influence as he might have otherwise.

McLane's political career began when he was elected to the House of Representatives in 1816. By the end of 1822 he had become chairman of the Ways and Means Committee. As the nation moved toward the election of 1824, the party system was in disarray. The Republicans splintered into factions in the absence of a strong Federalist Party. Five "Republicans" vied for the presidency, and McLane committed himself to William Crawford of Georgia. The election of 1824 was decided in the House of Representatives, where the choice was between John Quincy Adams, Andrew Jackson, and William Crawford. McLane had deep reservations about Adams, and after hearing news of the latter's bargain with Clay, he believed it to be politically unwise to support Adams. On the other hand, while questioning Jackson's character, McLane did not reject the possibility of ultimately voting for him. When it was his turn to vote, McLane, sole representative for Delaware, voted for Crawford.

McLane became a Jackson supporter by 1828. This transformation was achieved by his close association with another Crawfordite, Martin Van Buren, with whom he shared quarters for several years when Congress was in session. Van Buren, like McLane's father earlier, provided a number of opportunities for success, and even though the friendship between the two was an uneasy one, McLane greatly benefited from his support. Other factors that led McLane to finally cast his support with the Jacksonians include the influence of his other associates, many who were Crawford men and saw their political advancement greatest in the Jackson camp. McLane also may have been influenced by the fact that he gained Jacksonian support in his election to the Senate Ways and Means Committee, placing second to Samuel Smith of Maryland.

In giving his support to Jackson, McLane expected a cabinet position in return. Van Buren encouraged McLane's appointment to strengthen the former's influence in the Jackson cabinet. Circumstances, however, worked against McLane's appointment. He had lost control of Delaware to his opponents, who kept Delaware out of the Jackson fold in the election of 1828. Jackson preferred that McLane remain in the U.S. Senate (elected in 1827), where support was needed, and he wanted to avoid giving the Delaware opposition the opportunity of replacing McLane in the Senate if he ascended to the cabinet. McLane's aspirations were briefly put on hold.

Although McLane was not appointed to Jackson's cabinet, he did obtain a diplomatic assignment in which he attained a stunning success. Jackson appointed him as Envoy Extra-ordinary to Britain in 1829 in an effort to erase the tension between the two nations as a result of the Adams administration. McLane successfully negotiated the removal of British restrictions on American trade to the West Indies, opening the ports to American commerce, which had been a national goal since the Jay treaty. This was a phenomenal achievement for McLane and demonstrated his considerable diplomatic skills.

President Jackson reorganized his cabinet in 1831 as a result of the Margaret (Peggy) Eaton affair, and McLane was named secretary of the treasury. Despite his Federalist proclivities and his "choleric temper," McLane had impressed the Jackson insiders, and he enjoyed the firm support of Martin Van Buren to gain entrance into the fold.

The new secretary of the treasury played a small role in the tariff crisis of the early 1830s. The South was in an uproar over the high tariff rates established in 1828 and 1832, which many interpreted as not being beneficial to the region. The state of South Carolina, behind John C. Calhoun, refused to allow the tariffs to be collected in her port and threatened to secede from the nation, if necessary. Under Jackson's prompting, McLane drafted a measure that was introduced in Congress by Gulian C. Verplanck and was known as the Verplanck bill. Essentially the bill significantly reduced the tariff rates in an attempt to make them more palatable to the South. McLane also contributed to the drafting of the Force Bill, giving the president military authority to intervene in South Carolina. Henry Clay's compromise tariff ended the tariff crisis and made it unnecessary to implement either of McLane's measures.

The chief dilemma facing the new treasury secretary concerned the future of the Bank of the United States (BUS). Secretary McLane believed, like a good Hamiltonian, that the BUS served the well-being of the country and should be rechartered. He knew that Jackson was not pleased with the BUS but believed the president could perhaps be persuaded otherwise.

McLane proposed to pay off the national debt prior to the end of Jackson's first term and sell the government's stock in the bank, knowing that the president would welcome such viewpoints. Meanwhile, McLane met with Nicholas Biddle, president of the BUS, to convince him to delay seeking recharter during the 1832 election, especially since Jackson wanted no interference in his bid for reelection.

The rechartering of the BUS became the significant issue of the election of 1832, and it hurt McLane's chances for future advancement under Jackson's aegis. Biddle, pressured by presidential aspirant Henry Clay and other friends of the bank, ignored McLane's advice and sought immediate recharter. A number of Jackson supporters were also dissatisfied with the secretary of treasury's position on the bank in his report to Congress in December 1831. Not only did his report support rechartering the BUS, but also many Jacksonians feared that the administration might be led off the "old Republican track" by McLane's federalism. According to Van Buren, the treasury report brought him "pain and mortification." In fact, McLane's biographer argues that the treasury report severely restricted McLane's upward mobility. In reality, McLane's career had nearly reached its peak, and his conspicuous federalism seemed to have been an underlying factor.

The reelection of President Jackson marked the demise of the BUS and the eclipse of McLane's influence in the cabinet. The administration wanted to reduce the influence of the bank by removing federal deposits before the charter expired in 1836. McLane supported recharter and opposed removal whereas the president relied heavily on the Attorney General Roger B. Taney to articulate his position. As Taney's stare shone brighter, McLane's began to wane. Once again a cabinet reshuffle took place. McLane was appointed secretary of state, and William Duane filled the treasury position. McLane had supported the appointment of Duane to prevent his enemy, Taney, from gaining the post. Several months later the strategy went awry as Duane was fired for refusing to remove the deposits. McLane's involvement in the appointment of Duane did nothing to help his tarnished image. Taney was eventually selected to fill the treasury post, and the deposits were removed as Jackson wished

A combination of factors led to McLane's appointment as secretary of state. The present secretary, Edward Livingston, expressed an interest in another diplomatic post. Because Livingston supported improved Franco—U.S. relations and also spoke the language, he was sent as the new minister to France to replace William C. Rives, who desired to return home. Notwithstanding their differences on treasury matters, Jackson had been impressed with McLane's diplomatic mission to England and therefore appointed him as the new secretary of state.

In May of 1833 McLane embarked on his duties. His first task, once again at the urging of Jackson, was to restructure the State Department. He was successful in this endeavor, bringing about a more orderly department. McLane's plans started with a chief clerk, whose responsibility as undersecretary was to supervise eight bureaus. The bureaus were divided into the diplomatic, which contained three subsections comprising all the European nations, Russia, and North and South America; a consular bureau; a home bureau; a bureau of archives; a bureau of pardons and copyrights; a superintending bureau; a translating bureau; and a Patent Office

After reorganizing the department McLane attended to several matters that had gone unresolved for years. The northeastern boundary between Maine and Canada dated back to 1783 and had been a constant thorn in diplomatic negotiations between Britain and the United States. Adding to the problem was that any boundary line consented to by the United States could not take away land from a state. Maine insisted on this stipulation. Unfortunately, during his tenure as secretary McLane was unable to attain a permanent resolution to this boundary question

The chief dilemma facing McLane during his term in the State Department was the French indemnity controversy. In July 1831, the American minister to France, William C. Rives, negotiated a treaty whereby the French agreed to pay 25 million francs as an indemnity for the seizure of American vessels under the Napoleonic decrees leading to the War of 1812. The French also agreed to lower tariff duties on imported American cotton. In return the United States agreed to a reduction of American duties on imported French wine. The controversy began when the French Chamber of Deputies omitted authorization of the first installment of the indemnity. It seems that some of the deputies believed that the repayment figures were excessive and offensive to the French people. Paying the Americans might also establish a bad precedent whereby other nations would demand reimbursement for alleged injuries. Another justification for refusing the indemnity was the opposition forces' attempt to embarrass the king and government.

Jackson sought the advice of his cabinet to deal with the French crisis. The president proposed a policy of reprisal against French shipping. Livingston, serving as minister to France, advised the president to send a forceful message to the French by placing an embargo on all French commodities. Secretary of State McLane supported the president's proposal because the Chamber of Deputies were procrastinating and avoiding payment to prevent unpopularity with the French people. Taney, on the other hand, was alarmed at Jackson's proposal and McLane's corroboration. Taney feared that forceful action would precipitate war. He even enlisted the support of Vice President Van Buren to try and convince Jackson to maintain a patient stance. Jackson eventually abided by the counsel of Taney and Van Buren, which only infuriated McLane. Ambitious, proud, jealous of his "domain," McLane was indignant at Jackson's failure to heed his counsel for the second time. Jackson had failed to use McLane's counsel regarding the bank deposits issue and now sided with Taney, who McLane carried ill feelings toward, on the French spoliations question. McLane submitted his resignation in June 1834.

The resignation of McLane from the State Department was perhaps inevitable. His relations with Van Buren, who actually served as his mentor in Jackson's cabinet, had always been uneasy. At the time he submitted his resignation McLane faulted Van Buren for his lack of support in the French indemnity question. McLane was so upset with Van Buren that he refused to inform him about his resignation, the latter having to ask the president to confirm the story. In addition to McLane's troubles with Van Buren, he also recognized the weakness of his political circumstances. Under Jackson, the secretaries of state conducted foreign policy with a minimum of influence. Furthermore, McLane was restricted in the control of appointments in his department, leading him to exclaim to one office seeker "that the appointment properly belonged to his office—but as matters were—He thought that the New York delegation . . . would determine on the individual."

Although McLane now returned to private life, it was not an inactive one. He was selected as president of the Morris Canal and Banking Company in May 1835. The company worked out of the northeast New Jersey area with ties in New York and Pennsylvania. Under McLane the company gained respectability and profitability during his short tenure as director

In December 1836, McLane was lured away from the Morris Canal and Banking Company to serve as president of the Baltimore & Ohio railroad. Again his business acumen brought success to his company. In his 12-year reign the railroad doubled in length, especially westward. He also made it possible to use the telegraph with the B&O railroad and began a workers compensation system.

McLane briefly reentered public office in 1845 when President James K. Polk appointed him to negotiate the Oregon boundary with Britain. While in Polk's service McLane was mentioned as a possible secretary of state, but nothing came of it. In August of 1846 he returned home, reclaiming his B&O position. On October 7, 1857, several years after retiring from his position with the B&O, Louis McLane died in Baltimore.

BIBLIOGRAPHICAL ESSAY

For an exhaustive but delightful treatment of Louis McLane, the biography by John A. Munroe is indispensable: *Louis McLane: Federalist and Jacksonian* (1973). The same author provides a wealth of information on McLane's home state of Delaware in *Federalist Delaware* (1959). Robert V. Remini's comprehensive and masterful three-volume biography of Andrew Jackson, in which the final two volumes detail McLane's service in that president's cabinet, is extremely valuable: *Andrew Jackson and the Course of American Freedom* (1981), *Andrew Jackson and the Course of American Democracy* (1984). There are brief descriptions of McLane, particularly his relationship with Van Buren, in John Niven's meticulous biography, *Martin Van Buren and the Romantic Age of American Politics* (1983). The Federalist Party in its declining years is admirably recounted by Shaw Livermore, Jr., in *The Twilight of Federalism* (1962).

Lester Brooks

JAMES MONROE (1758–1831)

Served 1811–1817
Appointed by President James Madison
Democratic-Republican

Early in 1811 a door opened, and a previously maligned diplomat was invited at long last to the grand stage. After a tentative dance relying on crafty letters and go-betweens, two powerful old friends were reunited. James Monroe—soldier, states-man, politician, diplomat—accepted the call to service by President James Madison and became secretary of state as the most tenuous diplomatic crisis yet confronted by a fledgling nation exhausted the avenues for peaceful resolution. From his service in this vaunted post, Monroe would go on to become the fifth president, the last of the "Virginia Dynasty" (whereby four of the first five presidents were from that state) and the third statesman whose service as secretary of state would help to launch him to the presidency (his own secretary of state, John Quincy Adams would follow suit). As president, Monroe would preside over many successful diplomatic negotiations and would issue the foreign policy doctrine that bears his name. More than any president before him, Monroe dedicated his life service to pursuing sound diplomatic relations between the United States, a nation he saw arise from the shadows of a colonial mother England, and the world powers of the time. His service as secretary of state, therefore, provides an excellent case study of American diplomacy.

James Monroe was born in Westmoreland County, Virginia, on April 28, 1758. Monroe's father, Spence Monroe, oversaw a farming plantation of some 500 acres, enough to qualify him as an esteemed plantation owner, though he was a basement resident of this social class. (By comparison, the renowned Washingtons owned upwards of 6,000 acres). The family traced its lineage to a Scotsman, Andrew Monroe, who had settled in the colony in 1650 and established a farming stead of about 200 acres. Monroe's mother was the former Elizabeth Jones, whose Welsh-born father had acquired land in King George County. Elizabeth Jones inherited a portion of the property.

Prior to Spence, the Monroe forebears had been unable to afford a college education for their children. James attended Campbell Academy starting at age 11, where he was exposed to drills in arithmetic and Latin. At 16, he entered William and Mary College in Williamsburg, the colonial capitol, where he was immediately accepted to the upper division. At William and Mary, Monroe established a friendship with John Marshall that lasted until political animosities of the 1790s would put a wedge between them.

Spence Monroe had died early in 1774 and, after attending to the financial obligations of his father, James had been encouraged by his uncle, Judge Joseph Jones, to continue his academic studies. Jones was a member of the House of Burgesses and would be involved in the call for the First Continental Congress. While at college, Monroe became embroiled in the deteriorating relations between England and the colonies. By the spring of 1776 he and several classmates had enlisted in the Third Virginia Infantry, and in time Monroe would find himself in New York as part of General Washington's main forces. Monroe took part in the crossing of the Delaware River and was subsequently wounded during the Battle of Trenton. The injury to his shoulder was life-threatening and required months of convalescence. Upon his return to the army, Monroe was made an aide-de-camp to one of Washington's brigade commanders, William Alexander, Lord Stirling. Although he found an officer's regimen boring and unfulfilling as compared to the excitement of being in the field, Monroe would later describe the knowledge of military affairs gained in his service to Lord Stirling as invaluable during his tenure as secretary of war to Madison (during the War of 1812, he would assume this post in addition to maintaining the State office). After wintering with Washington at Valley Forge in 1778, Monroe received a recommendation from the General that would empower him to return to the fighting as a field officer. The state of Virginia conveyed the rank of Lieutenant Colonel on Monroe and empowered him to raise a regiment of volunteers. However, Monroe's military career came to an end, as he was unable to raise the troops. Throughout his lifetime, however, close friends often referred to him as Colonel Monroe, and Monroe would become the last Revolutionary War hero to become president.

Monroe did not give up his military career easily. He remained bitter for some time that circumstances kept him from the fray. One of the people he unburdened himself to was the governor of Virginia, Thomas Jefferson, whom he had met in Williamsburg. The two developed a fast friendship that would, but for a few instances of political and personal turbulence, last a lifetime. It was Jefferson who encouraged Monroe to return to William and Mary and to take up the study of law, under the tutelage of the governor, no less. In 1782 Monroe was elected to the Virginia House of Delegates as a representative from King George County, and following the spring session, he was named to the Governor's Council (essentially the governor and eight councilmen wielded the executive power of the state). In short order, Monroe found himself elected to the Congress of the Confederation in 1783, serving until 1786. Politically he was attuned to the majority of young politicians of the time. He maintained a vested interest in the rights of individual states and believed in limited powers for the federal government. In 1786 Monroe married the former Elizabeth Kortright, and within a year she had given birth to a daughter, Eliza. Another daughter, Maria, followed, as did a son who died in infancy.

Though he opposed the ratification of the Constitution in Virginia, he was chosen to serve as U.S. Senator in 1790. Monroe exhibited a distinct interest in diplomacy, believing that nations could settle their differences through rational discourse much like enlightened men. A fierce supporter of the rights of individuals and of sovereign nations, Monroe, like Jefferson and the other emerging Republicans, had taken a concerted interest in the revolution in France. President Washington appointed Monroe as the Minister to France in 1794 as warfare between the French Republic and the European monarchies was at a peak. This would result in the first diplomatic failure to weigh heavily on the young statesman. Some historians have suggested that the appointment of Monroe, an enthusiastic French sympathizer, was inappropriate at the time. In the midst of complicated diplomatic maneuverings, Monroe was expected to appease the French government should John Jay be able to reach an acceptable treaty with the British. Instead, the administration believed that Monroe had acted in bad faith by his overtly cordial relations with the French. When he neglected to make use of the administration-provided justifications in defense of the Jay Treaty in his dealings with the French government, incoming Secretary of State Timothy Pickering recalled Monroe at once. Monroe returned to the United States the next year to publish a bitter account of the foreign affairs difficulties in France. His "View of the Conduct of the Executive in Foreign Affairs of the United States" leaves no doubt that Monroe believed he had been unjustly treated by the administration.

He reentered politics in Virginia, serving as governor from 1799–1802 (three terms). As a politician, Monroe was often affiliated with the conservative faction concerned that the federal government not be empowered to the point of denying individual liberties, typical of his uncle, Judge Jones, and his friend, Jefferson. During the administrations of Washington and John Adams, Monroe found himself still aligned with his friend, as part of the evolving Jeffersonian movement that would dominate national politics for more than a quarter century. Jefferson, elected president in 1800, called Monroe back to the national stage to address another diplomatic situation with France in 1803.

Monroe's charge was to assist the minister to France, Robert Livingston, in establishing access to the Mississippi River. Initially, the hope was to purchase New Orleans, and perhaps the Floridas, though by the time Monroe arrived, Napoleon had already informed Livingston of his astonishing offer to sell the entirety of Louisiana. The treaty arranging for this unprecedented transfer of land would begin the dispute over the Floridas, a dispute that Monroe would revisit throughout his service as a diplomat and as president. Despite denials from Spain and France, Monroe and Livingston proclaimed that the Louisiana Purchase entitled the United States to lands in Western Florida lying east of the Perdido River, including Mobile Bay, in addition to the vast territory of Louisiana west of the Mississippi River.

In 1804 Monroe was directed to Madrid to assist Charles Pinckney in efforts to purchase the eastern, larger portion of Florida from Spain. There were also diplomatic efforts to obtain these lands from Spain as part of long-standing damage claims by the United States against that country. After months with no progress, Monroe found himself directed to another European hot spot.

The Jefferson administration ordered Monroe to London, where he would join William Pinckney of Maryland in efforts to resolve continuing economic and sovereignty difficulties with Great Britain (essentially the issues that Monroe would confront as secretary of state as he and President Madison concluded that diplomatic avenues had been exhausted and that a second war for independence was inevitable). The presence of Pinckney is intriguing, as it provided an opportunity for John Randolph, an avowed anti-Jefferson Virginian, to promote Monroe as a viable alternative to the current administration. Randolph was desperate for a way to derail the ascension of James Madison, serving as secretary of state and Jefferson's heir apparent, to the presidency. First he suggested to Monroe that the administration had little faith in him, thus Pinckney's assignment.

Monroe and Pinckney approached the British government with instructions to resolve two primary issues: impressment of sailors from U.S. vessels on the seas and the prohibition of U.S. ships trading goods between France and Spain (and the French and Spanish colonies). Essentially, the latter reflected an attack on the U.S.'s economic viability as a neutral nation. The British control of the seas made it easy for ships to patrol the Atlantic and deny U.S. ships access to certain trade ports, for both perceived military and economic advantage. On the issue of impressment, the huge size of the British navy made it a challenge to adequately man vessels. This difficulty was compounded by the harshness of life at sea for British sailors, many of whom jumped at the opportunity to defect. As a result, it was long-standing British policy to stop ships suspected of carrying escaped sailors and put such men back into service of the Crown. The opportunities for abuse, particularly in regards to an English-speaking former colony, were rampant. The administration objected to this practice as an attack on U.S. sovereignty.

When the British agreed to resolve the trade issue and to redirect orders regarding impressment though they would not end the practice, Monroe and Pinckney were forced to decide whether to concede this long-standing issue or leave the negotiating table. Agreeing to a treaty, Monroe was very hurt when Jefferson and Madison refused to submit it to the Senate, primarily because of the impressment omission. This caused a rift politically and personally among the Virginians, as Monroe heard circulating rumors that the treaty was rejected to establish Madison's place ahead of Monroe as Jefferson's successor. Jefferson's concern about the rift allowed the two men to make a slight reconciliation in short time, but Monroe remained distant toward Madison, believing that he had been poorly advised by the secretary of state and also that Madison should have defended the merits of the treaty to Jefferson.

Throughout his life Monroe believed that he had acted appropriately in his relations with Great Britain. He consistently claimed that the concessions he and Pinkney accepted were dismissed prematurely by the administration without taking into account the positive impact the treaty could have had on the country. Still, in 1806 he found himself in an unenviable position. Monroe had been repudiated for his diplomatic efforts in two important instances, by two separate administrations, including that of his mentor, Jefferson. In the first instance, he was called back for his inappropriately concessionary attitude toward France, and then under similar circumstances, his attempt at a treaty with Great Britain was rejected.

President Madison began 1809 preparing his administration for the difficult road that lay ahead. During his tenure as secretary of state to Jefferson, he had participated in the frustrating diplomatic efforts that were the product of perpetual abuse by both France and Great Britain, particularly the latter. It had escaped both Jefferson and himself as to how a neutral country could, through diplomacy, protect its sovereign rights in the face of global belligerents who recklessly disregarded them.

In his cabinet, Madison had settled on a compromise candidate in Robert Smith to serve as his secretary of state. Smith's brother was Senator Samuel Smith of Pennsylvania, part of a Senate faction that harshly opposed Madison in part because of a hatred for the Swiss-born secretary of the treasury, Albert Gallatin. Gallatin admirably served the previous administration and was initially considered for the state post until Madison realized he would not be confirmed. Most historians have denigrated Smith as an incompetent afforded a much higher station in life than his skills warranted. It took Madison two years, as he and his country moved steadily toward armed aggression with Great Britain, to finally rid himself of Smith.

Though the two men had grown further apart when Monroe allowed himself to be championed by a faction led by Virginian John Randolph as an alternative to Madison in the 1808 presidential campaign, Jefferson had been encouraging each of them to close the rift during Madison's first term. Both seemed to genuinely recognize the value of the other and the depth of their friendship. Once back in the fold, the two would remain dear friends until Monroe's death in 1831. But at this tenuous moment in 1811, a catalyst appeared necessary to fully restore relations. It has been suggested that Madison appointed John Tyler, then governor of Virginia, to a federal judgeship to free up that position for Monroe's return to the top of Virginia politics. In fact, Monroe had been appointed to the governor's office when the offer came to enter the Madison administration.

In a revealing exchange of letters, the formerly close friends, in the vague language of political prudence, felt each other out regarding a possible reconciliation. Monroe's response to Madison's invitation to join the latter's cabinet expressed two main worries. Having recently assumed the governor's post in Virginia, he wanted to ensure that his leaving this important state office could be couched in terms of the utmost national interest. In other words, Monroe had to be represented as the great diplomatic hope at this time of crisis. Secondly, he requested assurances that American policy toward the British was not so wholly committed as to deny him any real influence on the ultimate resolution. Then, after mentioning his failed negotiations with France, Monroe wrote, "I was sincerely of the opinion that it was for the interest of our country to make an accommodation with England, the great maritime power, even on moderate terms, rather than hazard war, or any other alternative." Monroe concluded that he remained convinced of the soundness of his opinions and that his views generally were unchanged. That is, nations should consider war a last and costly resort if avenues remained to protect rights through tact and diplomacy.

Monroe referred to the incidents surrounding his failed negotiations with both European powers, though his letter clearly suggested that he still maintained reservations about pursuing war with Great Britain. Madison's cautiously cryptic response did not explicitly address specific positions of the current State Department; however, he acknowledged the sincerity of Monroe's efforts to negotiate. The president's response satisfied Monroe that he had in no way overstepped his orders in 1806. This last hurdle cleared the way for reconciliation, and Monroe became the secretary of state.

Thus Monroe entered the administration with a view toward diplomatic reconciliation with Great Britain. In short time, he would become invaluable to the Madison administration as the point person in guiding the war effort through the Congress of 1812. This transition gives wonderful insight into Monroe's impressions of Great Britain and the limits of diplomacy with the European powers.

Two weeks after Monroe had entered the State office, Madison passed on the views of the administration to Joseph Gales, editor of the unofficial administration newspaper, *The National Intelligencer*, during a private dinner. The subsequent editorial, written by Gales, focused heavily on the idea that the Twelfth Congress might need to resort to measures stronger than economic coercion if the new British minister, Augustus Foster, brought no orders exhibiting a shift of British policy. Monroe was alarmed to read the tone of the editorial and initially assumed that it was a sabotage attempt against the administration by Robert Smith's former clerk.

With the arrival of Foster in May, the picture began to clear for Monroe. At first, Foster described Monroe as having a "mild and conciliatory" manner about him. Once aware of Foster's instructions for negotiation (confirming a harsher shift, not a conciliatory one). Monroe fully examined the State office files and became aware of the increased rigidity of the British since he had left Washington. Although many historians belittle Madison's abilities as a war leader, in fact the president can be shown to have guided war measures in a consistent manner. His intimacy with the Constitution and its duly established separation of powers provided Madison with hesitancy regarding his legal right to direct Congress down the path to war. However, his trust in Monroe as the administration mouthpiece allowed him to overcome many of these reservations. Through Madison's arguments, the information in the State files, and Foster's inability to resolve the diplomatic issues deemed of highest priority by the United States, Secretary of State James Monroe soon moved to support the administration's stance completely, which by the summer of 1811 had evolved into an ultimatum: Without a relaxation of the restrictive British orders against the neutral United States, a declaration of war to defend the rights of this nation must proceed.

During the fall of 1811 Madison, in Virginia and in continual contact with his trusted Monroe, called Congress to convene a month early and prepared his initial address. This address has been widely viewed as a call to military preparedness in the face of British aggression. Throughout the war session, Monroe acted as the official administration liaison with Congress on matters regarding the war effort. In this capacity, his recognition of the need to challenge Britain's views of the United States as a second-tier nation becomes evident. Monroe worked particularly closely with the House Foreign Affairs Committee, made up of the dramatic figures most historians have labeled as the "War Hawks."

From the beginning of the congressional session that would culminate in a declaration of war, Monroe, on behalf of the administration, worked with the new congressional leadership in an effort to implement a preparedness plan. This suggests that the administration's main thrust during the session was preparing for a war. If the administration were dedicated to continued diplomatic negotiations, it would have targeted the main body of Republicans, who seemed to prefer a continuation of the failed economic coercion policies. Monroe quickly became the pivotal link between the president and the congressional leadership. Monroe commanded respect from the new congressional leaders and was on good terms with men like Henry Clay and John Calhoun. From the opening of the session through the end of November Monroe worked closely with the House Foreign Affairs Committee to hash out the program that would be advanced. He continued his close relations up through the war vote.

Monroe's leadership at this trying time is evident in many of his communications with the Foreign Affairs Committee. Also, Monroe stressed that the administration was pledged to a war by the end of the session if relations with Britain did not improve. Monroe summarized the administration's position by saying that "The United States has not however resorted to war . . . (which) dreadful as the alternative is, could not do us more injury than the present state of things, and it would certainly be more honorable to the nation."

As an embargo was debated as a last step before the war declaration, Monroe again, just as he had throughout the session, provided direction to the Committee. John Randolph recorded on March 31, 1812, that: "The President thought we ought to declare war before we adjourn, unless Great Britain recedes, of which there was no prospect." The congressional leadership looked to the administration for a guiding hand throughout the war session. They had requested that the administration provide formal commentary on the boldest actions of the session. The Committee asked Monroe, in his official capacity, if the administration would put forth a message of request for the embargo. Monroe assuredly replied that Madison would put forth the request, assuming the House would find it acceptable. The next day Madison suggested the embargo, which was supported by a bill Gallatin had designed for that Committee at its request.

Monroe's role in acting as a voice of leadership for the war Congress has caused much speculation about the authorship of many documents pertaining to the Foreign Affairs Committee. It is widely held that the committee's report of November 29, 1811, which parroted the president's opening address, was a committee product (with both Monroe and Clay active members and possible authors). The war manifesto that was presented following Madison's eventual war message of June 1, 1812, was originally thought to have been written by Calhoun, though certainly it was also largely a product of the committee as a whole and thus, again, benefited from Monroe's guidance. Joseph Gales speculated that Monroe was the author, offering as proof that the draft presented to Congress was in the handwriting of Monroe's personal secretary. This is hardly definitive, but it is a fact that the manifesto was presented to Congress within a day of Madison's war message, and it had obviously been prepared well in advance in anticipation of the war request. The piece that it undoubtedly resembles is the House Foreign Affairs Committee report of November 29, 1811. Although the authorship will forever be in doubt, there is no question that Monroe was instrumental in the deliberations surrounding the first of these two documents and likely played a large role in the formulation of the second.

Following the Senate debate to include France in the war declaration, the Congress announced a state of war with Great Britain on June 17. Secretary of State James Monroe played a vital role in the process. As this young nation faced a declaration of war, his service shifted from diplomatic overtures to a deaf Great Britain to communicating the concerns of the administration to the Congress that would ultimately declare war. Monroe, however, arrived at this ultimate war declaration with some guilty misgivings. He wrote his friend John Taylor: "You thought that I might contribute to promote a compromise with Great Britain, and thereby prevent a war between that country and the United States . . . I own to you that I had some hope . . . that I might aid in promoting that desirable result. . . . Nothing would satisfy the present Ministry of England short of unconditional submission, which it was impossible to make. This fact being completely ascertained the only remaining alternative was to get ready for fighting, and to begin as soon as we were ready." It only seems natural that a secretary of state would feel some disappointment at such a result. Particularly a statesman of the order of James Monroe, groomed as a Jeffersonian Republican ideologue, would find it difficult to give up the belief that the reasonable and enlightened leaders of nations could prove unable to resolve conflict without a resort to warfare.

The other major issue that Monroe confronted as secretary of state involved efforts to acquire Florida from Spain. The Floridas had been of vital interest to the United States for years because of their strategic importance to the developing nation. As for Monroe's involvement with this issue as secretary of state, the Madison administration had already established rather clandestine efforts prior to Monroe's arrival in Washington.

In 1810, political turmoil raged in Spain as France and Britain continued their epic conflict. Spanish impotence held out the threat that another European power might pursue the occupation of strategic Florida. Additionally, Madison was advised that much of the region's wealth would be found west of the Pearl River, in an area primarily inhabited by Americans. This territory, though disputed, had been claimed by the United States as a result of Monroe's and Livingston's negotiations for the purchase of Louisiana.

With the Floridas so vital to the southeastern seaboard, opinion in the United States held that it was but a matter of time before they became part of the nation. Any other European power establishing a presence there would be disastrous. Madison became involved in efforts to annex this disputed portion of West Florida at the request of local residents. With veiled encouragement from the administration, these residents established a revolutionary government, claimed independence, and requested that the United States annex the area. The administration responded by occupying this area. At the beginning of 1811, Congress provided President Madison with the authority to assume custody of Florida in its entirety, should the threat of occupation from any power other than Spain emerge, or at the request of local inhabitants, as had occurred in West Florida. This was the situation Monroe inherited on his arrival in April of 1811. By that summer, as thoughts of war with Great Britain intensified, the United States had stretched its western occupation east to the Perdido River. The majority of Western Florida was thus in American control, excepting Mobile, where the Spanish maintained a garrison to protect the mouth of the Mobile River.

In response to these perceived aggressions, Spain, whose unrecognized volatile government left her without a minister in the United States, turned to her British ally to dispute the actions. Monroe received as his first contact with the British Minister Augustus Foster a protest against the occupation of Florida. However, Monroe had continually maintained since 1803 a U.S. claim to the lands extending east from the Mississippi River to the Perdido River. Hence Monroe refused to entertain any suggestions that the occupation was in any way improper. In fact, as Foster pressed his concerns that Eastern Florida might also fall to U.S. usurpations, he recorded as Monroe's response laughter and dismissal. From this, Foster surmised that indeed Eastern Florida might expect the same type of faux revolutionary occupation.

Just prior to adding Monroe to his cabinet, Madison did sponsor efforts in East Florida that suggest an intrigue of sorts. General George Mathews, formerly a governor of Georgia, was provided instructions from Secretary of State Robert Smith (therefore, Madison) to determine if the governor of East Florida, or the existing local authority, saw fit to turn those lands over to the United States. Mathews received his charge on a visit to the capital in January 1811, and it is likely that he met not only with Madison himself, but with other members of the administration as well. Upon determining that the governor of East Florida would not entertain thoughts of American occupation, Mathews embarked on his remarkable plan to incite a revolutionary uprising that would.

This event played out primarily after Monroe had replaced Smith in the State office, though it began under the latter's watch. Therefore, Monroe may have been unaware of Mathews's actions upon entering the Cabinet, and possibly even when he issued orders in June 1811 that Mathews proceed with his mission in East Florida. However, it would make perfect sense for Madison to have informed Monroe of the venture. Shortly, no doubt, Monroe was fully apprised as he received correspondence from Mathews regarding the General's intentions. In two letters during the summer of 1811, Mathews advised that the residents of East Florida were primed for revolution. He requested military assistance from the United States that would enable the people to overthrow the existing government. Although his initial orders may have suggested support for a revolutionary upheaval if necessary, Mathews's letter, requesting both U.S. military support and guidance, received only silence. The ugly nature of the venture eventually prevented the administration from acknowledging it.

Mathews, however, interpreted the lack of response as silent support and proceeded as best he could. Through Senator William Crawford of Georgia, he requested that Secretary Monroe reassign him should his actions stray from the intent of the administration. By September of 1811, the British Minister Foster got wind of the developments and demanded of Monroe that the incursion be halted. The poor relations between Britain and the United States as the latter moved toward a war declaration allowed Monroe to avoid responding to Foster for two months, and then by repeating the interests of the United States in this vital area. How to read the lack of response to Mathews is a difficult matter. Historian Julius Pratt suggested that the administration "wished the plan to proceed, but preferred to avoid committing itself in any way, so that it might disavow the action of its agent should that course prove expedient."

In April 1812, reports emerged of Mathews establishing a revolutionary party in East Florida. In truth, it consisted primarily of Georgia militia and other opportunists willing to cross the border and wear the guise of dissatisfied residents. Still, Mathews managed to enlist the help of the U.S. Navy in controlling the Spanish city of Fernandina and Amelia Island. His supposed "insurgents" then turned the acquisitions over to Mathews and, by extension, the United States. Securing additional help from the U.S. military in the area, Mathews then embarked on a similar plan to take St. Augustine, the capital of East Florida. From an entrenched position outside the city, Mathews eventually reported to the administration that all of East Florida had been ceded to the United States.

The embarrassment brought about by these final actions proved too much for the administration to bear, though the end result gives insight into the diplomatic skills Monroe wielded on behalf of his country. Either the bogus revolutionaries, the compromising involvement of the U.S. military, or both sealed Mathews's fate.

In a letter from Monroe, he was dismissed and his actions were repudiated by the administration that refused to accept East Florida in this dubious manner. Monroe emphasized in his letter to Mathews that the General had widely digressed from the course of action the administration intended for him to follow. Monroe then proceeded to advise the Spanish government that Mathews had been disavowed, and that the seized territories would be immediately returned. Governor D. B. Mitchell of Georgia took on Mathews's command and was empowered to negotiate with the Governor of East Florida for a return of the occupied territory.

The chapter was not yet closed, however. While Monroe formally assured Foster of the return of the lands, he advised the French Minister Serurier that, though Mathews had overstepped his authority, "now that things had reached their present condition, there would be more danger in retreating than advancing." The occupation was maintained with Mitchell encouraged to not remove troops without the safety of the insurgent population ensured. This gave Mitchell ample diplomatic opportunity to delay resolution with the Spanish Governor. The occupation was still in full force as the summer of 1812, and the war with Spain's ally Britain, arrived.

Once the War of 1812 had begun, Monroe perceived a lack of purpose in his office. True, there were immediate and ongoing overtures of a peaceful settlement, but Britain continued to refuse a shift on the issue of impressment. The Department of War now reigned as the vital office of state affairs. Feeling useless in Washington, Monroe entertained thoughts of his revolutionary youth and demanded military assignment. Madison was able to fend off the request by making Monroe the interim Secretary of War after removing the ineffectual William Eustis because of early incompetence in running the war effort. However, Madison's Senate opponents rose up to the opportunity to embarrass the president and refused to confirm Monroe in this capacity. The eventual replacement, John Armstrong, engaged Monroe in an ongoing dialogue regarding the course of the war, each commenting on the other's shortcomings in a cabinet skirmish fueled to some degree by presidential ambitions. After the successful British attack on Washington, and amidst criticism for numerous errant decisions, Armstrong eventually resigned from the cabinet in the summer of 1814, and Monroe again became the acting Secretary of War. He would maintain the State and War Departments throughout the rest of the war effort. After several dismal defeats, the prospects of the American forces enjoyed an unlikely reversal shortly after Monroe took on the War Department, though how much of a role he played is much debated.

As early as May of 1813, the Madison administration had dispatched commissioners to Europe to negotiate a peaceful resolution to the War of 1812, based on Monroe's instructions. The Treaty of Ghent ultimately addressed none of the aggrieved issues announced by the United States in her declaration of war. However, the widely held perception, both domestically and abroad, was that the United States had achieved its place as a nation of standing. Some of this perception no doubt resulted from the commendable actions of the commissioners, who refused to entertain British requests for land concessions. Of note, commissioner Albert Gallatin refused to entertain Monroe's suggestion that the question of Florida as a spoil to the United States be included in the deliberations. Fighting essentially to a draw, the United States had succeeded in its war to protect neutral rights. James Monroe, through the diplomatic efforts of the State Department, then the coalition building with the war Congress, and through his management of the last year of the war, played a vital role in this success.

Any discussion of James Monroe's service as a diplomat must, of course, extend to his presidency. Monroe followed Madison into that office in 1817. With the successful culmination of the War of 1812, the nation entered a time of economic growth and perceived political cooperation. The Federalist Party essentially disappeared as a viable force in American politics after the war. However, there were still factions within the Republican Party that would eventually emerge to liven up the Monroe presidency.

The lack of an overt political conflict and the general contentment of the nation following the war created the "era of good feelings" that is associated with Monroe's tenure. This unique set of political circumstances allowed Monroe to achieve reelection without opposition in 1820, a feat only achieved by one other president—George Washington. To retain Washington on his pedestal as the only president to win the Electoral College unanimously, one elector cast a vote in opposition to Monroe.

With domestic affairs in relatively good order (the Missouri Compromise was the most important national issue during his tenure), Monroe's legacy as president would naturally emerge in the arena of foreign relations. Despite the failures he had endured as a diplomat, this seems particularly fitting for a statesman so dedicated to the relations of his nation to other powers. Monroe's foreign affairs legacy would involve recognition of the new Latin American republics, establishment of a boundary with Russia, the negotiations with Spain over the Louisiana Territory and the Floridas, and the statement of U.S. foreign policy that has come to bear his name, the Monroe Doctrine.

Monroe brought into his cabinet one of the most widely acclaimed statesman in the annals of U.S. history, John Quincy Adams. The situation he inherited as president was altogether different from that faced by each of his predecessors. For Monroe, the essential focus on protecting the rights of the United States as a sovereign power, a problem faced to some degree in each of the previous presidencies, had been removed for the most part. The problems that Monroe would face as president were created almost entirely by the continuing collapse of Spain's empire in the Americas. Along with establishing a northwest boundary with Russia, these events would dominate foreign affairs for the Monroe presidency and would each play some role in his statement of policy in 1823.

The acquisition of Florida remained extremely important to President Monroe. Despite disappointment that the war effort had not resulted in a transfer of the Floridas to the United States, Monroe believed that only a minimal diplomatic exertion would be required to finish the job. In fact, Monroe's administration became embroiled in a situation that made the Mathews affair seem of no consequence. General Andrew Jackson, the war hero of the Battle of New Orleans, was appointed the task of quelling Seminole Indian advances from Florida. Jackson sent a message to Monroe that was painfully direct in its explanation of how Florida could be forcibly obtained without implicating the U.S. government. Similar to Mathews, Jackson's message received no reply.

Not one to be bothered by the lack of directives, Jackson in short order had coerced cooperation from the U.S. Navy, occupied an abandoned Spanish fort in Florida, executed two Indian leaders, and moved on a Seminole village on the Suwanee River. Finding the village deserted, he headed farther inland, capturing and executing two English prisoners (as inciters of the Indian attacks), shelling the Spanish Governor into surrender near Pensacola, and then naming one of his colonels as civil and military governor of that city. The diplomatic wrangling that followed would take time to resolve, but ultimately these events led to the acquisition of Florida and to the establishment of a very favorable southern and western boundary of Louisiana recognized by the United States and Spain in the Transcontinental Treaty of 1819.

In this instance, and in general, Monroe has suffered unfairly in comparison to his secretary of state. Most likely this has occurred because the exhaustive diaries kept by John Quincy Adams are not countered by similar accounts on the part of the president. Monroe's written record is mostly in the form of letters and correspondence, though his edits and notations appear throughout Adams directives in the State Department. This would bolster the tendency for presidents for receive credit, or blame, for the events of their administration. Undoubtedly, despite Adams's adroit skills, President Monroe was the ultimate spokesperson on matters of foreign affairs during his administration. During the Florida crisis, Adams described Monroe as deliberate and slow to take action. Throughout his administration, Monroe made a habit of allowing the counsel of his cabinet members percolate as he considered an appropriate course of action. This would seem the product of prudence more than anything else.

The Monroe Doctrine, comprised of passages from Monroe's annual address to Congress in 1823, has been perpetually misapplied and misinterpreted by both historians and statesmen alike over the past 175 years. Its exact meaning, intent, and continued usefulness have been continually debated. Historians have also scrambled to determine the authorship (and perhaps, more importantly, intellectual origin) of the report, with passionate supporters of both Monroe and Adams promoting their respective candidate. This exhaustive debate cannot be rehashed here. In fact, the passages were a practical application of and reemphasis of American policy that had been established as far back as the Washington administration, which should further cloud attempts to establish the original formulator. Recently emerged from a war with its former imperial mother, the United States in 1823 was confronted with fledgling attempts at independence by the colonies of Latin America. On the European stage, the Holy Alliance had put forth its view of the divine right of monarchy and its refutation of any republican form of government. Whether President Monroe crafted each word of the Doctrine or not, and almost surely he did not, he was responsible for the passages being a product of his administration. And he is further responsible for the forethought that necessarily attends such expressions of policy.

In determining the content of his annual address near the end of 1823, Monroe faced a number of issues on the global stage. After carefully maintaining a neutral stance toward the burgeoning republics in South America, his administration had been freed to recognize the nations the year before after resolving diplomatic issues with Spain. However, the members of the European Holy Alliance had reiterated their stance in favor of monarchical governments and denying the validity of republican ones. To underscore this point, French troops had reinstated King Ferdinand VII on the Spanish throne. Fears that European powers might have designs on the new Latin American republics seemed real to most American statesmen, excepting John Quincy Adams. And the Russian Tsar, Alexander, had announced his intention to populate the Oregon coast and to deny American fishing access in that region. Then, completely unexpectedly, Great Britain came calling with an invitation to issue a joint declaration regarding the colonial Americas in an effort to prevent any future annexations by European powers. In and of itself, the suggestion was remarkable. Great Britain, which was a dominant world power and against whom the United States had recently fought a war over neutral rights, was ready to proceed in concert with a nation whose own independence it had scarcely recognized, by action if not by word, for over 20 years.

Monroe, initially inclined to accept the invitation for a joint declaration was so surprised by the offer that he immediately contacted his Virginia friends and predecessors, Jefferson and Madison, to solicit their advice. With Adams, a future president, in the cabinet, it has been noted that this diplomatic overture from the British likely received the immediate attention of more presidents than any single foreign policy issue in American history. Both Madison and Jefferson recommended to Monroe that he embrace this opportunity. But he had already begun to have doubts, and Adams discouraged such a declaration as well, most colorfully with this comment: "It would be more candid, as well as more dignified, to avow our principles explicitly to Russia and France, than to come in as a cock-boat in the wake of the British man-of-war.

During his second term, Monroe had often considered the possibility of making a formal statement of policy regarding European powers and their possible designs on the New World. Initially flattered that mother England would see fit to invite the United States to the world stage, Monroe considered the options (and the advice from Jefferson, Madison, and Adams) for about one month prior to bringing the matter to the full cabinet's attention. In the first meeting in November of 1823, he announced his own reservations about such a declaration, concerned about perceptions of the United States acting as subordinate to England. The impact of such a joint statement on national pride had weighed on Monroe during his personal deliberations. The lessons of the War of 1812, and its preceding diplomacy, died hard indeed.

Ultimately, the passages that would comprise the Monroe Doctrine were compiled and enunciated by the administration alone. In fact, to deny that England was among those warned against aggression in the West would be to miss the tone of the message. True, the opportunistic statement was designed specifically to encourage South American independence, to warn European aggressors (particularly the French and Russians) that transgressions in the New World would not be tolerated, but undeniably the drawing of these, to use Jefferson's phrase, "two spheres," excluded Great Britain from influence as well. Although Monroe denied any pretense that his statement amounted to a promise of war with any country that overstepped these guidelines, the Doctrine was a blatant challenge to the European powers, including mother England.

In many ways, the passages of Monroe's annual message that would come to be called the Monroe Doctrine serve as an exclamatory proclamation of the status achieved by this nation through the War of 1812. The concerns of national pride and abuse of sovereignty that had guided Secretary of State Monroe as he worked in the leadership of the war movement surely resounded in these statements of autonomy. As stated in one of the principal passages: "We owe it to candor and to the amicable relations existing between the United States and those powers (European) to declare that we should consider any attempt on their part to extend their system to any portion of this hemisphere as dangerous to our peace and safety."

The difficult election of 1824 concluded with John Quincy Adams chosen in a bitter House of Representatives fight (in truth, the lack of an electoral college winner seemed to remove Monroe as a target for the candidates). During the campaign, aspirants had pushed the president for support, if not of them personally, at least of their view of various political events that had become part of the propaganda. William Crawford, a carryover in Monroe's administration, had been playing politics with Monroe throughout his second term, convinced that the president sought to deny him that high office. Following his predecessors' lead, Monroe noted that it was inappropriate for former presidents to enter such political fray (a practice he seemingly tried to maintain as president as well). Still, Jackson's bitter supporters continued to repaint events surrounding Jackson during the Monroe administration, often placing the former president in a position of having to defend his version of these actions. In 1828, Adams and his supporters actually made a proposal to bring Monroe back as his vice presidential running mate. This was ultimately rejected, and Jackson ensured that Quincy Adams would follow in his father's footsteps as the only two presidents of the first seven to serve but one term.

Monroe's life after the presidency was a fairly difficult one. Indeed, the stress of his financial difficulties, which forced him to confront the loss of his plantation holdings, coupled with the crises of personal tragedy would prevent Monroe from living even 10 years after leaving office. The most positive component to his life after the presidency was the intense renewal of his friendship with Madison. The two wrote frequently and saw each other several times each year.

Heavily in debt, he managed to pay off some of the most pressing obligations tied to the management of his plantation at Oak Hill. An interesting footnote to his political service emerged when, facing continued financial ruin, Monroe pressed the U.S. government for reparations dating back to his earliest diplomatic services. In carefully detailed accounts, Monroe offered that he had not been properly compensated throughout his service to this nation. Ultimately, this would consume him for many years with the government finally supplying him with approximately $60,000. Varied congressmen debated whether this was because of the validity of the claims (some dated back 20 years) or out of charitable feelings for a former president fallen on hard times.

Monroe's last public service came in 1829 as a member of Virginia constitutional convention. Madison, John Marshall, and John Randolph were also called to serve. Monroe, in fact, was chosen as president of the convention. He served for over two months, giving infrequent speeches, before his health forced him to resign in December.

In 1830, though bolstered somewhat by the second approval of funds from the federal government, Monroe was staggered by the death of his son-in-law, George Hay, and then of his wife just days later. Shaken by the loss of his wife, Monroe was moved to New York by his daughter, where he lived with her family. By December of that year, Monroe was essentially an invalid, confined to his quarters. He would linger until July 4, 1831, before joining Jefferson and Adams as presidents whose day of death would commemorate the birth of a nation.

James Monroe served his country at a time when public service was seen to create a remarkable breed of statesman. It is no wonder that Monroe and other presidents of the era cultivated a diplomatic education through their subordinate roles to previous leaders. Monroe served his country ably as a soldier, a legislator, an ambassador, and an executive leader. As secretary of state he was exposed to the machinations of ambitious nations as they struggled through the awkward dance of foreign relations. This exposure served him well as president. Monroe was afforded the opportunity, by national standing and personal resolve, to pronounce and apply long-standing American foreign policy principles in a manner that was both prudent and forceful. After his successes as secretary of state and secretary of war during the United States' second war for independence, this pronouncement bore the unalterable weight of U.S. diplomatic custom. Some of its intended audience may have ignored the proclamation as presumptuous or galling. But none soon challenged it. Thus Monroe's presidency began the phase of American growth and development of this continent.

BIBLIOGRAPHICAL ESSAY

The definitive biography of Monroe is Harry Ammon's *James Monroe: The Quest for National Identity* (1991). Two older biographies with some continued value are George Morgan's *The Life of James Monroe* (2003) and W. P. Cresson's *James Monroe* (1971). For an important overview of Monroe as secretary of state see "James Monroe" by Julius Pratt in *The American Secretaries of State and Their Diplomacy*, edited by Samuel Flagg Bemis (1963), and *The Jeffersonian Democracy: James Monroe* by Daniel C. Gilman (1972).

For broad representations of the Monroe era, two books by George Dangerfield are valuable: *The Awakening of American Nationalism: 1815–1828* (1965) and *The Era of Good Feelings* (1986).

For solid discussions of U.S.–British relations and other perspectives on early U.S. foreign relations see H. C. Allen's *Great Britain and the United States: A History of Anglo-American Relations (1783–1952)* (1955), A. L. Burt's *The United States, Great Britain, and British North America: From Revolution to the Establishment of Peace after the War of 1812* (1940), Norman K. Risjord's *The Old Republicans: Southern Conservatism in the Age of Jefferson* (1965), Rudolph Greenfield Adams's *A History of Foreign Policy of the United States* (1924), and Paul A. Varg's *Foreign Policies of the Founding Fathers* (1970).

For information on the coming of war and the diplomatic efforts prior and after see Henry Cole's *The War of 1812* (1966), Reginald Horsman's *The Causes of the War of 1812* (1962), Roger Brown's *The Republic in Peril: 1812* (1971), Clifford L. Egan's "Origins of the War of 1812: Three Decades in Historical Writing," *The Mississippi Valley Historical Review*, 28:2 (1941), and two books by Bradford Perkins: *The Causes of the War of 1812* (1962) and *Prologue to War: England and the United States 1805–1812* (1974).

The definitive study of the Monroe presidency is Noble E. Cunningham, Jr.'s *The Presidency of James Monroe* (1996). Monroe's writings are compiled as *The Writings of James Monroe*, edited by Stanislaus Murray Hamilton (1902, 1998). *James Monroe, 1758–1831: Chronology-Documents-Bibliographical Aids* (1969), edited by Ian Elliot provides a brief overview of important Monroe documents and a timeline of his life. Studies on the Monroe Doctrine are too numerous to reference in detail, but the following merit review: Frank Donovan's *Mr. Monroe's Message—The Story of the Monroe Doctrine* (1963) and Dexter Perkins's *The Monroe Doctrine, 1823–26* (1932).

Monroe's service as secretary of state also gets treatment in Irving Brant's *The Fourth President—A Life of James Madison* (1985). Discussion of the authorship of the war reports can be found in "Documents Section," *The American Historical Review*, 13:2 (January 1908), and Charles Wiltse's "The Authorship of the War Report of 1812," *The American Historical Review*, 49:2 (January 1944). Good introductions to the era include Henry Adams's *The United States in 1800* (1955) and *A History of the United States 1801–1817* (1969).

Bryan McAuley

EDMUND S. MUSKIE (1914–1996)

Served 1980–1981
Appointed by President Jimmy Carter
Democrat

Edmund Sixtus Muskie was born in Rumford, Maine, on March 28, 1914, the son of Polish immigrants Stephen and Josephine (Czarnecki) Muskie. Stephen Muskie's name was shortened from Marcizewski by U.S. immigration officials. Rumford, a paper mill town, served as the humble backdrop of Muskie's working-class upbringing. Muskie graduated cum laude with a Bachelor's degree from Bates College in 1936. He then studied law, receiving his degree in law from Cornell University in 1939. He started his law practice at Waterville, Maine, in 1940. With the outbreak of World War II, Muskie joined the Navy in 1942, serving on destroyer escorts in both the Atlantic and Pacific theatres. He left the service in 1945 at the rank of lieutenant to resume his law practice. He married Jane Frances Gray on May 29, 1948. The couple had five children.

Muskie began his political career as a Democrat and State Representative in the Maine House of Representatives from 1948 to 1951, the latter two years of which he served as the Democratic floor leader. Muskie served on the Democratic National Committee from 1952–1955. In 1955 he became Maine's governor, and only the second Democrat and the first Roman Catholic elected to serve in that capacity in the state's history. He served as governor until 1959. In that year he won his bid to become Maine's first Democratic senator, a position he held until named secretary of state in 1980 by President Jimmy Carter.

Muskie, an imposing man with a lanky six-foot-four frame and rugged facial features reminiscent of the mountains in his home state, was also a gifted orator with a strong moral sense and a legendary temper, leavened by a dry sense of humor and warm personal charm. He also developed a capacity for consensus building, a necessity for a Democrat attempting to carve out a political career in a predominantly Republican state. These personal attributes enabled Muskie to become one of the country's most effective legislators. After challenging the Southern Democrats and the Senate seniority system they dominated in his first vote as a senator, Muskie was relegated to committees then considered less consequential. But through his innovative work on housing, the environment, and the New Federalism, each of the committees to which he was assigned grew in prominence. He served as Chairman of the Government Operation's intergovernmental relations subcommittee, of the Public Works environment subcommittee, and of the housing subcommittee of the Senate Banking, Housing and Urban Affairs Committee. His work on the environment is considered one of his most important legacies as a U.S. senator, winning him the apt title of "Mr. Clean."

In time Muskie sought appointment to the Senate Foreign Relations Committee. He served on it twice, once in the early 1970s when the important War Powers Resolution was being fashioned in Congress to restore some balance between the executive and the legislature in connection with the use of U.S. military forces abroad during foreign conflicts and crisis. Muskie was a voice of moderation during the 1960s in regard to the country's most significant foreign policy issue, the Vietnam War. He supported President Lyndon Johnson's policy in Vietnam and reverted to criticism of President Nixon's Vietnam policy. Despite the partisan dimension of this shift, Muskie avoided the labels "hawk" and "dove" and was viewed as a principled participant in the national debate on Vietnam.

Muskie gained wider national prominence in 1968, when Vice President Hubert Humphrey chose him as his running mate in the 1968 presidential campaign. The Humphrey–Muskie ticket lost to Richard Nixon and Spiro Agnew, but Muskie emerged as a colorful, almost Lincolnesque figure as Humphrey's running mate and as a conciliatory voice in the truculent debates concerning Vietnam. When the 1972 campaign season came around, Muskie was one of the leading contenders for the Democratic nomination. But while campaigning in New Hampshire, Muskie wept after denouncing a press story that had been critical of his wife. Although Muskie won the New Hampshire primary, the incident cast doubt on his toughness, and his fortunes began to slide as the primary season advanced. He lost the nomination to Senator George McGovern.

In subsequent years Muskie confounded critics by championing both liberal causes, including strong advocacy for tough environmental legislation, and conservative ones, such as the need for budgetary and fiscal responsibility in Congress. He was one of the most distinguished and widely respected members of the U.S. Senate, when in the last year of the Carter administration, he was called on to fill the post of secretary of state following the resignation of Cyrus Vance over the Iran hostage controversy.

Ed Muskie joined Jimmy Carter's foreign policy team in late April 1980. Secretary Vance, who alone among Carter's advisors had opposed the rescue operation aimed at freeing American hostages held in Iran, resigned in the wake of that mission's failure. Carter offered the job to Muskie, not so much because of his experience in foreign affairs, but because of his knowledge of the American political system and his sterling reputation as a senior American statesman in the Senate. Carter wrote in his diary that this was the role he expected Muskie to play as secretary of state, "a senior statesman and spokesman for our country on foreign policy." The expectation was that Warren Christopher, who stayed on as deputy secretary of state, would assume a larger role in the day-to-day operations of the department, in which Vance had hitherto been deeply engaged. Christopher was Carter's second choice for the secretary of state position in case Muskie declined. But, to the surprise of many of his colleagues, Muskie readily accepted the offer and embraced the senior statesman role Carter had in mind for him.

In nine months, there was little time for Muskie to make a large mark on the course of U.S. foreign policy. He might have had more time to demonstrate his skills had Carter won a second term. Instead he became a lame-duck secretary of state in a lame-duck administration. In most areas of policy, Muskie served in a caretaker capacity, although many credit his personal style and capacity for consensus building as important factors in the ultimate resolution of the hostage crisis in Iran. Working with and through the Algerian government, Muskie's State Department finally reached agreement on terms for the return of the hostages in the waning weeks of the Carter administration.

U.S.–Soviet relations, especially in the aftermath of the Soviet invasion of Afghanistan in December 1979, remained very cool. Muskie met with his Soviet counterpart, Alexei Gromyko, in May 1980, soon after taking up his new post, in what was the first high-level meeting between U.S. and Soviet government officials since the Soviet invasion of Afghanistan. Muskie rejected as cosmetic a Soviet offer to withdraw from Afghanistan in return for U.S. recognition of the new Soviet-backed regime in Kabul. Little headway could be made in superpower relations in light of Moscow's intransigence in Afghanistan and its ongoing military buildup.

Relations with allies in Europe proved to be an ongoing source of tension as disagreements over how to handle the Soviet threat persisted, especially on the question of deployment of nuclear weapons. Muskie proved to be a soothing presence in the heated exchanges with European leaders during the economic summit of June 1980, at which numerous foreign policy matters were discussed.

In the Middle East, where Carter was fresh from his Camp David success, many problems still persisted, including a proposed arms sale to the government of Saudi Arabia, which was eventually postponed for decision by the next administration. In the final three months of the Carter administration, energies turned to the necessary task of transition. Otherwise, the main preoccupation in the last months of the administration centered on reaching a deal with the Iranians on release of hostages. Diplomacy eventually prevailed, although the Iranians deprived Carter and his secretary of state the pleasure of greeting the hostages back home during their tenure. The Iranians waited until Ronald Reagan assumed office, inflicting one final insult on the beleaguered Carter presidency.

Upon his departure as secretary of state in 1981, Muskie went into retirement from political life as a widely respected elder statesman. He joined the law firm of Chadbourne and Parke in Washington, D.C., in 1982, a position he held until his death. He contributed several chapters to books on various aspects of foreign policy, and coauthored books, including the *President, the Congress and Foreign Policy* in 1986. He served on the president's special review board in 1986–1987 that investigated the Reagan administration's involvement in the Iran-Contra affair. Muskie occasionally reentered the policy fray, as he did in 1995 on matters relating to the environment. He died of heart failure two days before his 82nd birthday, on March 26, 1996, in Washington, D.C., and was warmly eulogized by his many admirers from across the political spectrum.

BIBLIOGRAPHICAL ESSAY

Ed Muskie, unlike so many prominent political men of our time, left no memoirs. He did write occasionally on foreign policy concerns, including reflections on the role of the presidency and Congress in foreign policy on matters of defense. A useful book that details the calming influence he exerted in the much-battered presidency of Jimmy Carter is Hamilton Jordan's *Crisis: The Last Year of the Carter Presidency* (1982). Jimmy Carter's memoirs of his presidency, *Keeping Faith* (1982), offer further insight into Carter's appreciation of Muskie as a senior statesman, as does Burton I. Kaufman's *The Presidency of James Earl Carter, Jr.* (1993). Cary Sick, *All Fall Down: America's Tragic Encounter with Iran* (1985), recounts Muskie's role in the resolution of the Iran hostage crisis.

Robert F. Gorman

RICHARD OLNEY
(1835–1917)

Served 1895–1897
Appointed by President Grover Cleveland
Democrat

Richard Olney served as secretary of state in the difficult last two years of Grover Cleveland's second administration. Born in Oxford, Massachusetts, on September 15, 1835, he was the son of Wilson Olney and Eliza Butler. His grandfather, an ambitious, demanding entrepreneur, had founded the small town's first textile mill and bank. The family descended from Thomas Olney, a follower of Roger Williams in the seventeenth century. Richard was most profoundly influenced by his Rhadamanthine and disciplined grandfather and his ambitious and proud mother in making his career choices.

Olney was educated at Leicester Academy, Brown University (1851–1856), and Harvard Law School (1856–1858). Admitted to the bar in Massachusetts, he found employment in the law firm of Judge Benjamin F. Thomas. In 1861, he married the judge's daughter, Agnes, and inherited the lucrative law practice at the death of the judge in 1876. The Olneys had two children.

Olney cultivated the friendship of Boston's upper-class corporate community. Increasingly, his hard-nosed negotiations on behalf of corporate clients and his penchant for tireless work established him in the highest reaches of Boston society. Encouraged by friends in the Democratic Party, he ran successfully for one term in the state legislature in 1873. However, his cold demeanor, forbidding mien, and stern dark eyes restricted his appeal to many voters. He was defeated for reelection and henceforth concentrated on corporate law, especially on railroad law. In the early 1880s, he forged the legal groundwork for the Eastern Railroad Company's near monopoly over rail traffic in the northern half of the state. In the latter half of the 1880s, he served as general counsel for the Chicago, Burlingame and Quincy Railroad and successfully fended off state efforts to regulate and control rates.

To represent New England in his second administration's cabinet, Cleveland appointed Olney to be his attorney general in 1893. During his two years as attorney general, Olney's command over details and driving ambition to master the details of diverse events led him to know the issues in other cabinet departments.

As such, he became indispensable to Cleveland and a bit of an irritant to competing cabinet officials. Olney's inflexible pro-business, antilabor positions, evinced in his work for the railroads, continued into his years as attorney general. In addition, his concern for social stability, the protection of property, and the value of the currency, and his growing conviction that access to foreign markets would be a key to future American prosperity, were constants throughout his career.

The onset of the deep and prolonged depression of 1893–1897 corresponded to Cleveland's second term in office. Olney, the staunch Democratic conservative, deplored social disorder and the growing challenges by the growing ranks of the unemployed to business as usual. Active on a host of fronts, Olney validated Cleveland's preference for not annexing the newly independent Hawaiian Republic and for not restoring the native Queen; assisted Cleveland in his message to Congress requesting the repeal of the inflationary Sherman Silver Purchase Act of 1890 (repealed 1893); provided federal protection of Western railroads by seizures from dissident marchers; and broke the 1894–1895 Pullman strike by the use of federal injunctions and troops to keep the interstate mails running. This latter action led to the American Railway Union's boss Eugene V. Debs being jailed and led to charges of an unholy alliance between business and the courts that greatly weakened the Cleveland administration. The next year, Olney argued the case before the Supreme Court. The Court upheld his position and in effect outlawed strikes against railroads carrying either mail or general interstate commerce. The opinion held for the next quarter century.

Upon the untimely death of Secretary of State Walter Q. Gresham in 1895, Cleveland appointed Olney to that post. Olney had become indispensable to Cleveland and had already pontificated on a range of foreign policy concerns even during Gresham's term. Commissioned on June 8, 1895, Olney's two-year term as secretary of state was marked by several bellicose outbursts with foreign diplomats and imperious orders to subordinates in the department. He rarely saw ambiguity or shades of gray between differing positions and treated his opponents as he had once treated opponents in court.

As secretary, Olney enjoyed a reputation as a master of details and an ergophile. He expected the same of his subordinates. Typically, he was a linear thinker and concentrated on one problem at a time. As a lawyer, he gathered copious information and then made a prompt disposition of a decision. He tended not to see ambiguity in a situation, and his policy decisions were often imperiously announced without feel for the politics or the nuances of a situation. He relied heavily on the able Assistant Secretary of State Alvey A. Adee for correct diplomatic procedure and language and on President Cleveland for occasionally softening his often acid and unilateral policy notes. He was seldom viewed as indecisive or vacillating once he had reached a decision. Olney took office in the midst of rapid economic change.

Between the end of the Civil War in 1865 and the end of the century, the United States became one of the world's great economic powers. Due in part to considerable government aid and high protective tariffs during and after the Civil War, the United States experienced astonishing, if uneven, economic growth. The population more than doubled to 71 million, which provided a dynamic internal market for finished goods. Wheat production tripled, coal production increased eightfold, steel and rail manufacturing and oil production increased 20-fold. Total imports of goods jumped from $354 million to $1.03 billion. By the end of the century, Americans challenged

Europeans for world markets in iron, steel, oil, cotton, and wheat. Indeed, starting in 1874, the country's exports regularly exceeded imports, which created more efficient technology at home and surplus capital for investment overseas. The U.S. share of world trade rose from 6 percent in 1868 to 11 percent in 1913.

The rapid expansion came at a price. In 1873, a financial panic marked the beginning of a 23-year-long depression that, with only a few brief upturns in the 1880s and early 1890s, threatened the well-being of the industrial labor and farmers alike. The lingering depression was due to the same high productivity of factories and farms that made the United States a major economic competitor in world markets. Despite the growth of the domestic market, Americans produced more than they could consume. Hence, persistent deflation characterized the era. To compensate, farms and factories increased production, thereby aggravating the deflationary spiral. The period was, in addition, marked by recurrent unemployment, strikes, and riots in many large cities and the questioning of industrial capitalism's ability to allocate resources and capital fairly.

The Gilded Age's inability to find solutions to recurrent economic dislocation was due to the lack of experience and understanding of the rapid internationalizing of the economy. Even as the domestic market expanded, key sections of the economy required overseas markets to sustain profits. By the end of the nineteenth century, for example, the iron and steel industry exported 15 percent of its goods, sewing machine makers 25 percent, and oil refineries 57 percent of their illuminating oil. Once self-sufficient farmers now depended on unpredictable foreign markets to take 20 percent to 25 percent of their wheat production and between 70 percent and 80 percent of their cotton crop. Moreover, growing competition from foreign wheat and cotton growers in Russia, Argentina, Egypt, and India forced domestic growers to lower their prices while finding ways to sell more abroad.

In this difficult socioeconomic context, Olney had reached two fundamental conclusions. Influenced by his conservative Eastern Democratic background, he believed the depression begun in 1893 to be the result of the maturing of the industrial revolution, high rates of productivity, and a lack of adequate domestic demand to absorb industrial surpluses. Without new sources of demand, the dramatic labor challenges to the capitalist order could, he felt, devastate the American republic. Secondly, he also believed that America had, by the end of the nineteenth century, concluded its long period of internal development and had emerged as a new world power with important interests abroad. His goal was to assist the country in clearing obstacles to international expansion by using all instruments of power at his disposal. He denied that Washington's Farewell Address, which cautioned against international involvement, had been intended as a permanent strategy. As he saw it, Washington was giving the proper advice for a young country but had always intended for the United States to engage the world when it was ready. For Olney, as for Gresham and Cleveland, this meant primarily commercial access to Latin America and secondarily to Asia. Access to markets under terms favorable to America's industry and commerce was the key to social peace and economic prosperity. Colonies, for him, as for Gresham and Cleveland, were not necessary and might endanger the goals of the United States to maintain peace and the free flow of goods. Olney's goal was to secure a free hand in world affairs and to take advantage of European rivalries to obtain commercial advantage. The blunt, aggressive, and stubborn Olney was often checked by Cleveland, who softened his occasional threats and outbursts with leading powers such as Britain. Nevertheless, Cleveland backed Olney as they agreed on the ultimate objectives of a newly aggressive and energetic United States in the international arena.

In this context, Olney continued the aggressive posture that the United States evinced in Hawaii in 1893, Brazil in 1893, and Chile in 1891. To maximize access to Latin American markets and to also retain a free hand in dealing with potential trade partners there, Olney would, with the approval of Cleveland, challenge Britain's traditional authority in the region and greatly expand the understanding of the Monroe Doctrine. The occasion for this was the long-smoldering Venezuela boundary dispute with British Guiana.

Since the 1840s, British diplomats had claimed large stretches of territory lying between the newly independent country of Venezuela and the colony of British Guiana. The dispute lay dormant for decades as the territory in question seemed of minimal value. However, in the 1890s, the British began to press their claim more vigorously as rumors of mineral wealth in the region circulated. More important to the United States, the disputed land claims surrounded the entry into the Orinoco River, a long waterway that was a key to additional trade with South America. Cleveland had, by 1895, determined that the growth of U.S. trade interests in the region combined with the emergence of a viable U.S. naval force made a more forceful approach toward Britain possible. By the mid 1890s, Britain had increased its claims in the area from 76,000 square miles to 108,000 square miles, and a nearly bankrupt, unstable Venezuela had broken off diplomatic relations with Britain and begged the United States to intercede. In February of 1895, and under some pressure to act from Congress, Cleveland formally announced his opposition to Britain's vast claims and urged negotiation on them. Britain, occupied with Germany's rise to power and conflict in South Africa, ignored the plea.

After Olney's succession to the position of secretary of state in the summer of 1895, the British faced a more stubborn and blunt negotiator. Though Cleveland softened the initial draft of the note to Britain of July 20, 1895, it nonetheless was a forceful statement of U.S. interests in Latin America and a broadened view of what the Monroe Doctrine implied for the region. Specifically, Olney argued that the "infinite resources [of the U.S.] combined with its isolated position render it master of the situation and practically invulnerable as against any or all other powers." For Olney, the Monroe Doctrine was an accepted keystone of policy toward Latin America and gave the United States broad powers to intervene to protect its vital interests there. For Olney, the safety and welfare of the United States were endangered when commerce was hindered or if Latin American stability and democracy were threatened by outside powers. The note ended by demanding peaceful arbitration as the only mode of determining the disputed boundaries.

Caught by surprise and concerned about more pressing challenges by the French and Germans to British interests elsewhere in the world, Prime Minister Lord Salisbury replied on December 7, 1895. He denied that the Monroe Doctrine was recognized as international law and further charged the United States with trying to make a protectorate of Latin America. Decrying the moralistic undertone to the Olney note, Salisbury described the U.S. effort as one driven by America's need to expand commercially. Accepting U.S. interests in seeking expanded markets, however, Britain agreed to arbitrate the dispute. Olney's demands, which had been kept secret from the Venezuelans as well as the American public, were announced in

December 1895. Most industrialists and merchants supported Cleveland, although critics of the president, particularly those with banking ties to Britain, felt that Olney's note was too blunt and risked war with an old trading partner. Most, however, saw it as a rational response to the defense of expanding U.S. commercial and strategic interests. Many Latin Americans were pleased with the protection against British aggression and paid homage to Cleveland when he died in 1908. By enforcing an expanded interpretation or corollary of the venerable Monroe Doctrine, Olney and Cleveland had denied Britain additional influence in the Caribbean and control of the vital Orinoco waterway. Most significantly, they had displayed an aggressiveness on behalf of trade interests and the Monroe Doctrine against the very country that had, for so many decades, provided the navy that, in effect, kept other European powers at bay. Final arbitration of the dispute in 1899 allowed Venezuela to retain control of the entrance to the Orinoco River while giving Britain much of the rest of the territory in dispute. With the matter behind it, both countries had laid a basis for a lasting accord, which served both well in World War I and beyond.

No less troubling to Olney was the resumption of civil war in Cuba in 1895. Precipitated by economic collapse in Cuba's sugar and tobacco industry due to the tariff protection afforded U.S. crops in the Wilson–Gorman Tariff of 1894, the rebel's war against colonial Spain enjoyed considerable support from Cuban leagues and American labor. Cleveland and Olney, both conservative anticolonialists, were limited in their range of options. On June 12, 1895, Cleveland issued a neutrality proclamation in the Cuban war. This recognition of a state of insurgency required Olney to protect American lives and property in Cuba in addition to enforcing the rules of neutrality. In this initial stage, Olney clearly hoped that Spain would restore order while making minimal reforms to placate Cuban insurgents.

However, with the formation of a provisional government by the insurgents and their growing base of popular support, Olney sought to break with the cautious initial neutrality proclamation. In late 1895, Olney urged Cleveland to become more proactive in urging a quick solution on Spain. The war, he argued, concerned the United States because American trade and prosperity was at stake, along with the traditional American sympathy with those fighting for freer political institutions. By the fall of 1895, Olney advised Cleveland that Spain would not succeed in ending the revolt by military means and therefore Cleveland should recognize the belligerent rights of the insurgents or ask Congress for outright recognition of Cuban independence. Although allowing Olney to send an investigator to Cuba to gather facts, the more cautious Cleveland declined to act on his recommendations.

With growing support in Congress for strong action against Spain and in the face of reports of Spanish atrocities under the new military governor General Valeriano Weyler y Nicolau, Cleveland and Olney issued an offer to assist Spain in negotiating the end of hostilities and encouraged Spain to make immediate reforms. Spain quickly rejected this April 4, 1896, note and openly accused the United States of interfering in a purely domestic concern. Moreover, just as Cleveland's conservative gold standard wing of the Democratic Party was repudiated in the Democratic convention of 1896, Spain denounced Olney's broad and aggressive interpretation of the Monroe Doctrine in the Venezuela matter and asked for help against the United States in Europe. No European country was in a position to respond favorably, and the outgoing Cleveland administration was reduced to issuing warnings to Spain to give Cuba autonomy. Unwilling to do more, Olney and Cleveland departed from Washington in March 1897, turning over the intractable issue to the McKinley administration. Though Cleveland and Olney had restrained American intervention in Cuba, they had laid the groundwork for the Spanish-American War of 1898 by defining how the conflict endangered vital U.S. interests and providing the rationale for the use of force to defend those interests.

Olney was never as active in Asia as he had been in Latin America and the Caribbean, but he did approve of the rapid growth of trade with Japan and China in the 1890s. Although occupied elsewhere, he was active in assisting U.S. businessmen to receive trading concessions in the region, and aggressively protected U.S. missionaries, paving the way for economic, social, and religious penetration of China. Access to reliable markets and regional stability, not the acquisition of a problematic empire, were Olney's goals.

After leaving the State Department in 1897, Olney shared in the disrepute that his wing of the party suffered at the hands of the Bryan silverites. He never held public office again, but did comment extensively on his view of the world. In 1897, he resumed his lucrative corporate law practice in Boston and served on a host of prestigious organizations. Among these were the Peabody Education Fund, the Smithsonian Institution, the American Society of International Law, and the Franklin Union. At age 78, he was offered the ambassadorship to Great Britain by President Woodrow Wilson as well as a governorship of the new Federal Reserve Board. He refused both due to advanced age. Olney died of cancer on April 8, 1917.

His diplomatic legacy is relatively slight and is perhaps more a reflection of the changed geopolitical and economic circumstances of the country than anything else. Nonetheless, his actions were resolute and anticipated, in broad outline, the more active foreign policy stance in subsequent administrations.

BIBLIOGRAPHICAL ESSAY

Most of the personal papers of Olney are in the Richard Olney Papers and the Grover Cleveland Papers, both in the Manuscript Division of the Library of Congress. Professional correspondence is in the Olney and Charles E. Perkins collections of the Burlington Railroad Archives, Newberry Library, Chicago. His official correspondence while serving in the Justice and State Departments are in the files of those departments in the National Archives. The best single explanation of his view of the Monroe Doctrine as well as an explanation of his interpretation of economic events in the United States is found in his article, "International Isolation of the United States," *Atlantic Monthly* 81 (May 1898): 577–88; and "Growth of our Foreign Policy," *Atlantic Monthly* 85 (March 1900): 289–301. Two full-length biographies both view Olney as an active shaper of events in the second Cleveland administration. They are Henry James, *Richard Olney and His Public Service* (1923), and Gerald G. Eggert, *Richard Olney: Evolution of a Statesman* (1974). Sympathetic portrayals of Olney as a defender of traditional U.S. political values and interests can be found in the sketch of Montgomery Schuyler in S. F. Bemis (ed.), *The American Secretaries of State and Their Diplomacy*, vol. VIII (1928), and A. L. P. Dennis, *Adventures in American Diplomacy* (1928). Much of contemporary scholarship sees

Olney in the context of changing economic and political circumstances related to the acquisition of foreign markets. A representative example of this approach is Walter LaFeber, *The New Empire: An Interpretation of American Expansion 1860–1898* (1963) and Ernest R. May, *Imperial Democracy: The Emergence of America as a Great Power* (1961). Also helpful in placing Olney in the broader context of ideology, economics, and domestic politics are Robert L. Beisner, *From the Old Diplomacy to the New, 1865–1900* (1986), and Walter LaFeber, "The American Search for Opportunity, 1865–1913," in *The Cambridge History of U.S. Foreign Relations* (1995), edited by Warren Cohen. An assessment of Olney's relationship to Cleveland and the cabinet is found in Richard Welch, Jr., *The Presidencies of Grover Cleveland* (1988).

Alfred Castle

TIMOTHY PICKERING (1745–1829)

Served 1795–1800
Appointed by President George Washington
Continued in office under President John Adams
Federalist

Timothy Pickering, Jr., was born in the coastal community of Salem, Massachusetts, July 17, 1745, the eighth of nine children from the union of Timothy and Mary Wingate Young Pickering. A deacon in the Congressional Church, the elder Pickering was an unpleasant character who antagonized townsfolk. Unfortunately, son Timothy inherited his father's abrasiveness, self-righteousness, and ability to make enemies.

Whatever his deficiencies of personality, father Pickering prospered in prerevolutionary Salem. Thus, son Timothy was one of the few colonials to obtain a college education, graduating from Harvard in 1763. Timothy then studied the law and was admitted to the Massachusetts bar in 1768; he never enjoyed his profession. Pickering spent most of his life on the public payroll; one is tempted to render the judgment that he had no other recourse; ineptness, incompetence, or plain bad luck hobbled him in what would now be called the private sector. Consequently, after finishing at Harvard, Pickering became an assistant to the register of deeds in Essex County, Massachusetts. The politically ambitious Pickering was soon elected town clerk and register of deeds. From his perch, Pickering observed firsthand the hothouse politics that preceded the American Revolution.

Given Pickering's inherent conservatism, it is understandable that he was a Loyalist—a Crown sympathizer—in the early stages of the events that led to the revolt against Britain. Of course, Pickering's role in the Massachusetts government was another factor in his loyalist leanings. Further, Governor Francis Bernard had appointed the youthful Salem native a lieutenant in the provincial militia in 1766. Yet Pickering abandoned the Loyalist cause and joined the Whigs or patriots. Why Pickering made the shift is unclear. Cynics believed that he followed the lead of fellow Salemites. Needless to add, he was assailed from various quarters for being a political turncoat.

Pickering was involved in the American Revolution from start to finish. As the British staged a desperate, fighting retreat back to Boston after the battles at Lexington and Concord, Pickering, now a colonel, totally mishandled his regiment, permitting the British to make good their escape. Perhaps humiliated, Colonel Pickering returned to Salem for several months. Early in 1776, Pickering, who maintained a sincere interest in military affairs, led 90-day volunteers to join General George Washington and his tiny army encamped at Morristown, New Jersey. Not long afterward, Washington asked Pickering to serve as adjutant general of the army. Pickering filled the position, served on the Board of War from 1777–1780, and was then Quartermaster General of the Army, from 1780 to 1785. In these noncombatant roles, Pickering witnessed the squabbling, bickering, and corruption that accompanied the revolution. He also witnessed Washington's rising fame. In the crusty New Englander's mind, the Virginian was not deserving of the demigod status accorded him.

Pickering, still technically Quartermaster General, settled in Philadelphia in 1783, determined to make his fortune. Alas, ventures as merchant and land speculator flopped. By 1787 he was back in politics, moving his growing family to Pennsylvania's frontier, where Pickering helped organize Luzerne County, named for a French Minister to the United States. Shortly thereafter he was a delegate to the Pennsylvania State Convention to ratify the Constitution. But as the decade ended and the new government was established in New York, Pickering was on the brink of financial catastrophe.

President Washington came to Pickering's rescue, permitting him to climb the ladder of power to important positions. More precisely, Pickering's friends persuaded the president to appoint the Pennsylvanian to a federal position: negotiating with Seneca Indians unhappy with the encroaching settlers. Pickering sympathized with natives, and he tried to be fair with them. To his credit, he managed to obtain the neutrality of the Senecas and other groups of the Six Nations at a time when the American army had been humiliated in battles beyond the Ohio River. The praise that Pickering reaped was music to his ears. It also led to Washington naming him Postmaster General of the United States. The Pickerings could move to a big house in Philadelphia, now the seat of government.

Pickering served the Federalist administrations of Washington and John Adams throughout the decade of the 1790s, first as postmaster general, then briefly as secretary of war in 1795, and finally as secretary of state from 1795 to 1800. It was a critical period; the new government had to be established, the frontiers had to be secured, the economy righted, and unity promoted. Complicating and hindering Washington's and Adams's goals was the French Revolution, a domestic upheaval that began in France in 1789 but soon alienated all Europe. War followed between France, Austria, and Prussia in 1792. In February 1793, Britain and France went to war. Suddenly America faced the question: Should it honor its 1778 alliance with France if France requested, should it declare neutrality, or should the new nation align itself with the hated but economically powerful former mother country?

Strong emotions and angry rhetoric swept the country. France was America's ally; Louis XVI's kingdom had been the first nation to recognize the independence of the United States of America. Many citizens looked to France as a counterweight to Britain's enormous economic power and cultural influence. The revolution frightened others, especially Washington and his circle. They were appalled when Louis was executed in January 1793, and they were upset by the rising tempo of violence that engulfed France. Sacrosanct institutions and traditions were assaulted or swept aside. Vice President Adams wondered where the revolutionary zealots would stop. Meanwhile, the American economy was recovering from the doldrums of the 1780s. No small part of the improvement was linked to the expansion of international commerce, and Britain was by far the nation's major trading partner.

President Washington consulted his cabinet—the postmaster general was not then considered part of that organization. On April 22, 1793, he issued a Proclamation of Neutrality, setting a precedent followed by administrations into the twentieth century but also upsetting French partisans in America. Regardless of memorials, complaints, and the appearance of the French Republic's first envoy, the youthful Edmond Charles Genet, the proclamation remained intact.

Within a year of the neutrality proclamation, the United States was poised on the brink of war with Britain. From the American vantage point, there were ample reasons for hostilities: the capture of American merchantmen in the West Indies; noncompliance with the 1783 peace treaty, most glaring in the continued British occupation of forts along America's northern border; and the question of British complicity with the natives in the territory north of the Ohio River.

Washington chose negotiations instead of war. He ordered John Jay, an Anglophilic New Yorker then serving on the Supreme Court, to negotiate in London. The resulting Treaty of London or Jay's Treaty of November 19, 1794, infuriated the French, enraged Anglophobes in America, and helped promote the rise of political parties. Although the treaty was signed in November 1794, it did not become law until late April 1796. By the latter date, Timothy Pickering was secretary of state.

Pickering's rise had been meteoric and owing to luck rather than any particular skill. From the postmaster generalship, he succeeded Henry Knox as secretary of war in 1795. In August 1795, the incumbent secretary of state, Washington's friend and fellow Virginian, Edmund Randolph, fell victim to a cabinet lynching in which Pickering played a part. The Royal Navy had intercepted dispatches from the French envoy in the United States. Of course, His Majesty's representative in Philadelphia wanted to help the American government, so the captured documents were given to the United States. The messages seemed to show Randolph to be a French sympathizer, in essence a French mole in the American government. Confronted by Washington, the flustered Randolph resigned.

Timothy Pickering succeeded Randolph, becoming the nation's third secretary of state. There are at least two ironies in Pickering's promotion. First, he believed the job might be beyond his capabilities. Second, he was not on Washington's list to succeed Randolph. Able men spurned the job for a variety of reasons, leading Washington to turn to Pickering. The 50-year-old secretary of war overcame his reservations and accepted the appointment. Despite his considerable public service, Pickering was unqualified to be secretary of state. He was too provincial, too partisan, too vindictive, and too narrow minded. In a famous letter to Benjamin Waterhouse in 1811, John Adams opined that a secretary of state should comprehend the universe. An Adams might have had that ability; Pickering could comprehend only New England. Worse, Pickering, who at one time had been extremely critical of Britain, was by 1795 a near fanatical foe of France and the French Revolution. He never lost his hatred for that nation. On the Senate floor 16 years later, he referred to France as the "whore of Babylon."

Serving under Washington, Pickering's primary goal and preoccupation was the approval and implementation of the Jay Treaty. In his single-minded pursuit, Pickering was not above misstatements or dereliction of duty. For example, he denied that Jay's Treaty conflicted with various clauses of America's 1778 pact with France, when in fact it did. He also ignored or brushed aside for months the correspondence of Pierre Adet, the French minister in Philadelphia. The treaty became law in April 1796, not because of Pickering's activities, but rather because Washington threw his immense prestige behind the measure.

Pickering stayed in office when Adams succeeded Washington in 1797. By that time, Franco-American relations were on the verge of collapse: the French had refused to receive Charles Cotesworth Pinckney as America's new representative. French corsairs were pillaging American Caribbean shipping. Adet had interfered in the 1796 presidential election, supporting Jefferson against Adams. The French meanwhile complained that the United States had subordinated the concept of freedom of the seas to the whim of King George III's admiralty. They were also incensed by America's trading with the black rebels of Haiti. In short, each nation had serious grievances.

Taking office, Adams chose to negotiate with the French government known as the Directory. Just after his inauguration, he named a three-man delegation to rendezvous in Paris for resolution of outstanding differences. The three Americans were rebuffed in October 1797, by underlings of the French Foreign Minister, Charles Maurice de Talleyrand-Perigord; the French demanded a bribe or loan as a prerequisite to serious discussions. Pinckney, speaking for his colleagues John Marshall and Elbridge Gerry, rejected the French demands. This was the famous XYZ affair.

News of the attempted shakedown created a sensation in the young republic. Forgotten was the fact that bribery was an integral part of French diplomacy. Overlooked also was the concurrent payoffs of the Barbary pirates of North Africa. Perhaps anger reached a fever pitch because it was America's erstwhile ally, France, making the demand. Certainly the era's riotous politics played a role in whipping up hysteria.

It seemed that a French war was imminent in the late spring and summer of 1798. The Congress created a navy department and approved naval expansion. Plans were made for a drastic expansion of the army in wartime with Washington as commander; the Franco-American 1778 treaty was unilaterally terminated; and four measures collectively known as the Alien and Sedition Acts became law. All that was needed was President Adams to request a declaration of war from the Congress. Pickering supported these actions to put the country on a war footing, and he was pleased that Anglo-American relations improved. The United States cooperated with Britain in the West Indies, promoting trade with Haitian rebels; American ships were sometimes safeguarded by His Majesty's vessels. The United States also either overlooked or minimized continued British infringements on the nation's neutrality, and the British continued impressing Americans. Small wonder that new British envoy Robert Liston and Pickering got along so well.

The now very popular Adams hesitated taking the country into a war. He knew from many sources that France did not want hostilities with the United States. Adams was also wary of his nemesis, Alexander Hamilton, whom Washington had insisted should serve in his stead until war was a reality. In February 1799, the president decided to try negotiations again. Pickering, who was not consulted by Adams about another mission, was aghast. It seemed to him that the United States had just cause for war. He sensed also that war would enhance Federalist chances of victories in upcoming elections. Throughout the year 1799 Pickering tried to subvert Adams's peace initiative.

The second round of negotiations did not get underway until March 1800. By that time the French government associated with the undeclared war, the Directory, had been swept from office in a coup d'état staged by a young Corsican artillery officer, Napoleon Bonaparte. Fighting the Austrians in Italy, Napoleon's absence retarded negotiations. Meanwhile, Adams had wearied of the roadblocks to his peace policy erected by dissident cabinet members. He first sacked Secretary of War James McHenry. Suspicion then fell on Pickering. The president believed the secretary of state was linked to Hamilton, and he requested Pickering's resignation. Pickering, who needed the salary, refused. The president then summarily dismissed his secretary of state in May 1800. Although Pickering and Hamilton shared certain interests, Pickering was in no way controlled by the former secretary of treasury.

Pickering should never have been secretary of state. It was not that he was an incompetent, incapable of growing while in office. Rather, Pickering could not put the national interest ahead of his prejudices. Further, his relationship with Adams was poor. Perhaps if the frequently absent Adams had spent more time in Philadelphia he might have been more aware of Pickering's shortcomings and removed him earlier. Instead, Pickering was around to hinder Adams's every step. Had Pickering prevailed, the United States would have fought France, and Timothy Pickering would be remembered as a sinister figure, reviled for undermining peace. In fairness to Pickering, he knew that he was not the person to be secretary of state. Washington should have kept searching for a worthy replacement for Randolph.

Pickering moved back to Pennsylvania following his dismissal. Dogged by failure, he was saved by friends and admirers who bailed him out of a disastrous economic situation and persuaded him to return to Massachusetts. In the Bay State Pickering was elected to the U.S. Senate. He watched with disgust and dismay Jefferson's and Madison's administrations, opposing almost everything the Virginians sought. He fought the Louisiana Purchase and damned the Embargo while welcoming the disgraced British Minister to the United States, Francis James Jackson, to Boston.

Turned out of office by the Republican-controlled legislature in 1811, Pickering was back in Washington as a Representative in 1812. Of course, he opposed the War of 1812. He flirted with opponents of the war and welcomed the Hartford Convention of 1814–1815, though he was not a delegate to the controversial assemblage. Rejected for office in 1816, Pickering returned to Salem to engage in farming and polemical pursuits. Filled with hatred of the deceased Adams, he supported Andrew Jackson's presidential bid against John Quincy Adams in the election of 1828. He died on January 19, 1829, five weeks before Jackson's inauguration.

BIBLIOGRAPHICAL ESSAY

Timothy Pickering remains a secondary or tertiary figure in American historiography. Perhaps this is only fitting; in his long and active life, Pickering was never a figure of overwhelming importance. Gerard Clarfield, *Timothy Pickering and the American Republic* (1980) is smoothly written, well-researched, and almost definitive biography. Clarfield has also written the standard *Timothy Pickering and American Diplomacy 1795–1800* (1969). A much older and naturally friendlier account is Octavius Pickering and Charles W. Upham, *The Life of Timothy Pickering* 4 vols. (1867–1873). Douglas Southall Freeman et al., *George Washington*. 7 vols. (1948–1957) treats Pickering from Washington's viewpoint. Alexander DeConde, *The Quasi* War (1966) has written the best account of the undeclared war with France. Anyone with a serious interest in Pickering should read his sometimes amazing and usually prolix letters available in a microfilm edition from the Massachusetts Historical Society.

Clifford Egan

COLIN POWELL (1937–)

Served 2001–
Appointed by President George W. Bush
Republican

On December 16, 2000, President-elect George W. Bush nominated Colin L. Powell as secretary of state. The U.S. Senate unanimously confirmed the nomination. On January 20, 2001, Powell was officially sworn into office as the 65th secretary of state and the first African American to hold this position.

Prior to this appointment, Powell was a professional soldier for 35 years. During his military career, Powell held a host of command positions and rose to the rank of four-star general and Chairman of the Joint Chiefs. After his stellar military career, he was the chairman of America's Promise: The Alliance for Youth, which is a national nonprofit organization dedicated to helping build character and competence of young people.

Colin Luther Powell was born in New York City on April 5, 1937. Powell's parents, Luther Theopolis Powell and Maud Ariel Powell, were immigrants from the island of Jamaica. Powell's parents left Jamaica to pursue the American dream. Powell lived in Harlem, New York, until he was three years old, when the family moved to the Bronx, New York. Powell's parents instilled in him and his sister, Marylin, a strong faith and a respect for the Anglican Church. His parents also instilled a hefty respect for formal education. Despite his parents' lectures on the virtues and benefits of formal education, Powell showed very little promise as young student. As a result of Powell's indifference to education, he was placed in a class for students who performed poorly academically. He continued to approach education indifferently throughout his middle school and high school academic careers.

In 1954, Powell graduated from Morris High School. Powell's parents insisted that he attend college. Though Powell did not hold any particular desire to pursue higher education, out of a deep sense of obedience and devotion, he applied to two institutions of higher learning in the New York area: New York University and City College of New York. Despite Powell's lackluster grades, he was accepted to both schools but chose City College of New York because it was the cheaper of the two. At City College of New York, Powell enrolled in the engineering program. He was fairly successful initially, until he took a mechanical drawing class. During the mechanical drawing class, he realized that he did not have an interest in engineering. After his experience in that class, Powell decided to become geology major because he thought it would be an easy major. Powell was wrong in his assessment, and his grade point average dropped into the "C" range.

One day while walking on the City College of New York's campus, Powell noticed the Army Reserves Officers' Training Corps (ROTC) marching on campus. This resonated with Powell, who decided he liked the way the ROTC drill team, "The Pershing Rifles," performed. He was also fascinated with the ROTC's decorative uniforms and their no-nonsense appearance in public. With his interest awakened, Powell joined the ROTC and became affiliated with "The Pershing Rifles." At this stage in his life, Powell did not have any plans on making the military a career, but soon realized that military life suited him well. He liked the discipline, camaraderie, and physical challenges that the ROTC program demanded. With ROTC, Powell had finally found something that grabbed his interest and fueled a newfound desire to succeed.

Another lasting impression that fueled Powell's desire to succeed was a brush with the South's "Jim Crow" laws. Powell enrolled in a military training program at Fort Bragg, North Carolina, one summer. After returning to City College, he became a catalyst for success by pushing his fellow cadets to pursue excellence. He became the head of "The Pershing Rifles" and during his senior year was tapped as cadet colonel, the ROTC's highest rank. In 1958 Powell graduated from City College of New York, first in his ROTC class.

After graduation, Powell was commissioned as a second lieutenant in the U.S. Army. As a young army officer, Powell moved frequently. During his first assignment, he was stationed at Fort Benning, Georgia, which is the home of the army's Infantry School, where he studied classes that specialized in the airborne infantry and the "Rangers" unit. After completing his training at Fort Benning, he headed for West Germany, where he joined other U.S. soldiers monitoring the Warsaw Pact nations. He became a platoon leader and then ascended to the position of commander of a rifle company. By 1960, Powell had risen to the rank of first lieutenant and had made such a good impression on his superiors that he took over as battalion leader in an infantry battalion at Fort Devens, Massachusetts. This position held great responsibility, as it gave him responsibility for all the decisions regarding the battalion's personnel. Powell's quick ascension to battalion leader was no small accomplishment; it was usually granted to higher-ranking officers. Being a people person, having wisdom beyond his years, and always being proactive helped Powell succeed in his duties as battalion leader.

In 1962 while Powell was still stationed in Massachusetts, he went on a blind date with Alma Johnson, a speech pathologist from Birmingham, Alabama. Although Powell knew that he would soon be deployed to Southeast Asia to fight in the Vietnam conflict, the two decided to get married. Colin Powell and Alma Johnson were married on August 25, 1962, but the couple did not get a chance to honeymoon long, because he left for Vietnam at the end of 1962. Alma moved back to Birmingham, Alabama, to live with her parents while Powell was serving overseas. In 1963, Alma gave birth to the couple's first son, Michael. Because of his tour of duty in Vietnam, it was more than six months before Powell saw his son.

During his first tour in Vietnam, Powell displayed the courage and valor that has become synonymous with his name. Powell and his men were wading through a

Vietnamese rice paddy field when he stepped on a sharpened stake that was hidden underwater. The stake went through his left foot and exited through the top of his combat boot. He was shipped to the city of Hue to recover, and just a few weeks later, he returned to combat duty. For his combat injury, he was awarded the Purple Heart. Powell's first tour of duty in Vietnam ended in November 1963.

Having acquired a thirst for knowledge and having not forgotten his parents' push for formal education, Powell requested permission to attend the army's Command and General Staff College at Fort Leavenworth, Kansas, in 1964. One year later, Powell's second child and first daughter, Linda, was born. At about the midpoint through his course work at the Command and General Staff College, he sought permission from the army to allow him to pursue a master's degree. He was denied permission because his superior thought he had not been a top-notch undergraduate and therefore was not worth the risk of investing the army's resources in a mediocre student. This insult served as a motivating factor in Powell's decision to apply himself academically. Powell proved his superior wrong and graduated second in his class of 1,244 at Leavenworth. Believing that his lofty class ranking would change the thinking of his superior, Powell thought surely that he would be granted permission to attend graduate school. He was not granted permission; instead, the army sent him on a second tour of duty in Vietnam.

In 1968 Powell began his second tour in Vietnam. By then, he was an infantry battalion executive officer and an assistant chief of staff with the 23rd Infantry Division. Shortly after Powell's tour began, a military publication ran a story about the year's top five Leavenworth graduates. The commander of the 23rd Infantry division read the article, saw that he had the number two graduate under his command, and decided that he wanted Powell on his staff. This action pulled Powell out of constant combat duty, though he would still occasionally go on combat missions. On one such occasion, Powell went on a mission with a helicopter unit, and the pilot attempted to land in a small space. The blade of the helicopter hit a tree, and the helicopter crashed and began to burn. Powell pulled the pilot from the burning aircraft wreckage. He was awarded the Soldier's Medal, which is awarded to individuals who voluntarily risk their life in a noncombat situation. In July 1969, Powell's second Vietnam tour ended.

After Powell's second Vietnam tour, he was finally granted permission to pursue graduate education. In the fall of 1969, he enrolled in George Washington University to pursue a Master of Business Administration (MBA), because he believed that the Department of Defense needed good business managers. In July 1970, Powell was promoted to the rank of lieutenant colonel. Powell had ascended through the ranks of the military at a pace faster than most of his peers. In 1971 he completed graduate school, obtaining the MBA degree that he had long sought. Also in 1971, his third child, Anne, was born.

In 1972, the Army's personnel department urged Powell to apply for the highly coveted position as a White House Fellow, which sponsors promising military officers to serve as an assistant for a one-year duration in various executive branch departments. Powell applied, interviewed, and was selected from among more than 1,500 applicants. During the internship, Powell served as the assistant to Frank Carlucci, the deputy secretary from the Office of Management and Budget, who assists the president in preparing the nation's budget for the fiscal year and provides the president with performance analysis of each government program. In assisting

Carlucci, Powell also had the opportunity to work with Casper Weinberger, which would be the beginning of a long working relationship. Through his industrious work ethic, Powell made an indelible impression on both Carlucci and Weinberger.

After Powell's White House Fellowship ended in 1973, he took command of the First Battalion of the Second Infantry Division's 32nd Infantry Regiment. This regiment faced several internal problems, and it was Powell's aim to clean up the regiment. In a few short months, Powell's forceful command style had yielded the desired result, a disciplined and cooperative regiment. In 1974, he returned for a second stint at the Pentagon and served as an operations research analyst in the assistant defense secretary's office.

In 1975, Powell was accepted into the National War College at Fort Lesley J. McNair in Washington, D.C. His 10-month study there provided Powell with an education on national security policy, specifically how to plan and implement national security strategies. In February 1976, Powell was promoted to the rank of colonel and was made brigade commander of the 101st Airborne Division, which is based at Fort Campbell, Kentucky. Although this new command interrupted his National Air College education, he did graduate with distinction in 1976. After serving as a brigade commander, he returned to the assistant to the deputy defense secretary in the Pentagon, but this time Powell would be serving a Democratic administration. By 1979, Powell had served in the Pentagon for three presidents, Richard Nixon, Gerald Ford, and Jimmy Carter. In June 1979, Powell was promoted to the rank of brigadier general.

In 1980, California governor Ronald Reagan soundly defeated Jimmy Carter in the presidential election, and among Reagan's initial cabinet appointments was Casper Weinberger to the post of secretary of defense. Wienberger asked Carlucci to serve as his deputy. In turn, Carlucci remembered Powell's dutifulness and industrious work ethic during his days at the Office of Management and Budget, and asked him to serve as his assistant. Powell accepted the position and began work once again in the Pentagon. Although, Powell agreed to serve as Carlucci's assistant, his heart was still in the military field, and he longed to return to his old position as a field commander.

In 1981, Powell returned to the field when he was appointed assistant commander to the Fourth Infantry Division at Fort Carson, Colorado. He would spend the next two years in that position. In 1983, Powell was made the deputy commander general of the Army Combined Arms Combat Development unit at Fort Leavenworth, Kansas. His tenure in this position would be short because in the spring of 1983, Casper Weinberger began searching for a new senior military assistant and tapped Powell as his choice to fill the position. Before long the Weinberger and Powell one-two punch was a formidable force in the Pentagon. Powell became Weinberger's trusted confidant and right-hand man. He traveled extensively with the secretary of defense, logging many hours while visiting numerous countries. Because of Powell's excellent service, he was promoted to the rank of major general. By this time, Powell had earned the trust of senior officials in the White House, and he was solicited to help the Reagan administration to reshape foreign policy. In particular, Powell was asked to help plan military actions for the war in Grenada in the fall of 1983.

After the Iran-Contra scandal, Frank Carlucci replaced John Poindexter as the national security advisor. President Ronald Reagan wanted Carlucci to help rectify and restore the image of the National Security Council. Again, Carlucci turned to Powell for assistance in the yeomen's task of resurrecting the damaged image and low morale of the National Security Council. At first, Powell turned down Carlucci's request for service. However, after three attempts and a telephone call from President Reagan, Powell accepted Carlucci's offer. He began work in the Pentagon in 1987. On occasion, Carlucci would allow Powell to give presidential briefings, and this would be the beginning of a great working relationship with President Reagan.

In November 1987, Casper Weinberger resigned as secretary of defense, citing his wife's poor health as the cause. Consequently, Frank Carlucci became the new secretary of defense, a move that left Carlucci's old position as national security adviser vacant. Powell was the overwhelming choice to replace Carlucci, and his nomination had few objections. In December 1987, the 50-year-old Powell officially took over duties as the national security advisor. His tenure was marked by an occasional squabble with George Shultz over foreign policy issues, such as the best method for removing Panamanian dictator Manuel Noriega from power. These policy squabbles helped Powell form his philosophy for the use of military action. Powell also found himself at odds with African American leaders, who perceived Powell as being too loyal to President Reagan and the Reagan administration's policies. Before President Reagan left office, he promoted Powell to the rank of four-star general and commander and chief of the U.S. Forces Command at Fort McPherson in Atlanta, Georgia.

Around this time, Powell was so popular that whispers swirled that Vice President George H. W. Bush, who was running for president, would ask him to become his running mate on the Republican ticket. However, the invitation never materialized. Vice President Bush asked Dan Quayle to be his running mate and won the presidential election in 1988. Shortly after taking office, President Bush offered Powell the position of director of the Central Intelligence Agency. Powell declined.

In 1989, Secretary of Defense Dick Cheney asked Powell to accept an offer to become the Chairman of the Joint Chiefs of Staff. Cheney, who had served on the House Intelligence Committee, remembered Powell's diligence as national security advisor. Cheney also held Powell in high regard and therefore recommended Powell as the replacement to retiring Joint Chief of Staff Chairman William Crowe, Jr. Powell officially took over the reins as Joint Chief of Staff in October of 1989. Within the first few months of office, Powell was quickly thrust into the spotlight when tensions escalated in crises in the Philippines, Panama, and El Salvador. Remembering the horrors of his two tours of duty in Vietnam, Powell was reluctant to use military force in these situations. However, once the decision was made to use military force, Powell organized decisive, quick, clean, and successful missions.

In August 1990, Iraqi troops invaded Iraq's southern neighbor, Kuwait. Under the leadership of Iraqi President Saddam Hussein, Iraqi troops took control of Kuwait's precious oil resources and positioned military forces for further invasions of Iraq's neighbors. At the time, Iraq held the most powerful military in the Middle East, and there were fears that it would gain a monopoly on the world's oil market and gouge the world with astronomically high oil prices.

Powell knew that a strong show of force would be needed to make Saddam Hussein back down and abandon his invasion of Kuwait. President Bush decided to remove Kuwait from the control of Iraq by military force and requested that Powell draw up the war plans for "Operation Desert Shield." At the time, this was the largest deployment of U.S. forces since the Vietnam War. By November 1990, 180,000 U.S. soldiers were poised and ready to remove Kuwait from the hands of the Iraqis, and an international standoff ensued. Always believing that war should be the last resort, Powell favored pursuing further economic sanctions against Iraqi. Neither the buildup of U.S. troops nor the sanctions levied by the United Nations caused Hussein to flinch; therefore additional troops were deployed as the U.S. military readied itself for war.

Despite his personal reservations, Powell began implementing the plan to exercise the full force of military power. The United Nations Security Council set January 15, 1991, as a deadline date for Iraq's withdrawal from Kuwait or else face war. Hussein's troops did not retreat, and less than 24 hours after the deadline passed, Persian Gulf War I began. A little more than a month later the Iraqi military had suffered greatly, and few days later Saddam Hussein agreed to withdraw from Kuwait and submit to the dictates of the United Nations by signing Resolution 1441.

With the end of Persian Gulf War I, Powell publicly outlined his philosophy for efficient and decisive military action. Although not a formal document, it has become known as the "Powell Doctrine." The Doctrine expresses that military force should be used only as a last resort and only if it is clear that national security is at risk. If national security is at risk, then a disproportionate and overwhelming force should be used against the enemy. The Powell Doctrine further requires that there should be strong public support for military actions and there must be a clear exit strategy from the conflict.

With the great success of Persian Gulf War I, whispers began to circulate that he would replace Vice President Dan Quayle on Bush's 1992 ticket for the presidency, but Powell assured all that he had no desire to run for political office. Instead, he agreed to serve as Chairman of the Joint Chiefs of Staff for an additional two years. After Persian Gulf War I, Powell and Dick Cheney began to restructure the military because of federal budget cuts. Among their plans in searching for cost-cutting measures, they looked for domestic military bases that could be consolidated or closed without severely impairing the role of the military. Powell retired from the military in 1993. After his military career, he pursued a career as a public speaker and author, publishing a best-selling autobiography in 1995.

In November 2000, Texas Governor George W. Bush defeated Vice President Al Gore in one of the most contested and controversial presidential elections in U.S. history. In putting together his cabinet, President Bush called on Powell to lead the State Department. Within the Bush Cabinet, Powell was seen as a moderate in comparison to the other members of the president's cabinet. Some cabinet members have viewed Powell as being too moderate because of his centrist views, which included support of affirmative action and abortion rights. He has often been described as an amazing package of superior leadership skills, unlimited analytical skills, and linear thinking skills. He is considered a well-prepared and confident warrior with an abundance of self-control. Having spent most of his career in the executive branch, Powell was adept at bureaucratic combat. His bureaucratic combat style was patient and discreet. He usually gave interviews on the record so that he could not be accused of undermining those with whom he disagreed in the administration.

These diplomatic and bureaucratic skills were put to use in defusing warlike tensions between India and Pakistan. The relations between these two nuclear neighbors deteriorated after two deadly attacks in Srinigar and the Kashmir regions. Both countries stationed troops at the India–Pakistan border and were poised for war. Powell diplomatically cooled tensions in the region. After Powell visited India, he traveled to Nepal, which was the first U.S. cabinet-level visit since former Vice President Spiro Agnew's trip in 1971.

After the events of September 11, 2001, Powell's comforting diplomatic skills were placed at a premium. However, Powell was pushed into the background in the administration and among U.S. foreign policy heavy hitters. He seemed to have diminished influence on the administration's direction in foreign policy. He suffered several minor defeats in policy disputes with cabinet members over North Korea and global warming, as well as other issues. Powell clashed on almost every aspect of American foreign policy with the more "hawkish" cabinet members, in particular Secretary of Defense Donald Rumsfeld, Vice President Dick Cheney, and Deputy Secretary of Defense Paul Wolfowitz. These titans of foreign policy clashed on policies in dealing with Afghanistan, China, North Korea, and Russia.

Powell did not back the neoconservative cabinet members' "unilateralist" approach to U.S. foreign policy, believing that the United States should work in concert with its allies and the United Nations. As a second war with Iraq loomed, the schism on how best to implement U.S. foreign policy grew deeper. Wolfowitz pushed for an aggressive campaign to overturn the government of Iraq, despite opposition from France, Germany, Russia, and China. Many of the "hawkish" members viewed Iraq as unfinished business and the events of September 11 as providing an opportunity to topple the Iraqi regime. Powell urged that such a policy would destroy the antiterrorism coalition and infuriate Arab allies. Powell maintained that the United States should focus on al-Qaeda because it would be easy to rally and sustain international support for such a policy. Powell warned that an international coalition against terrorism would not hold up if the United States targeted Iraq. Powell believed that although Iraq was engaged in saber rattling, it was a fairly weak nation and could be contained with minimum effort.

Powell urged the administration not to place Iraq at the top of the list of foreign policy concerns unless there was compelling evidence and a smoking gun to link Iraq with al-Qaedea. He also warned that any war campaign in Iraq would be drawn out, multifaceted, and could last for several years. Powell worked to convince the president of the need to build a strong coalition similar to the one used during Persian Gulf War I and to gain support through the United Nations' Security Council. Powell's blueprint for U.S. foreign policy included dealing with al-Qaeda, Osama bin Laden, the Taliban, and other terrorist networks that execute terrorism through seizing their assets around the world.

As the drumbeat for war grew louder, Powell made an attempt to convince the administration to revamp United Nations Resolution 1284, which set a deadline for Iraq to allow United Nations' weapons inspectors into the country or face military action. With Powell's failure to convince the administration to slow the momentum for war, he then persuaded the president to first present the case to the U.S. public, the Congress, and the United Nations.

Powell's tenure as secretary of state was made difficult by nondiplomatic snafus and continued internal battles of the Bush administration, which alienated the

United States from many of its traditional allies. These squabbles also alienated Powell from the rest of the president's cabinet, which often showed up in contradictory policy statements by administration officials. Powell publicly stated that President Bush wanted weapons inspectors to return to Iraq to continue to look for weapons of mass destruction. However, Vice President Dick Cheney contradicted Powell by stating that inspections were not the primary goal of the U.S.'s policy in Iraq. Vice President Cheney stated that the advantages of attacking Iraq far outweighed the risk of inaction. In a clash with Donald Rumsfeld, Powell urged the Pentagon officials to hasten the process by which investigators decide the fate of prisoners held at a base in Guantanamo Bay, Cuba. Rumsfeld countered with the insinuation that Powell was not speaking on behalf of the nation. Rumsfeld and Powell also disagreed over policy in Iraq. Rumsfeld echoed Cheney's sentiments that inactivity in Iraq was not a policy choice. In another clash, Rumsfeld stated that the decision to invade Iraq would be made by the administration's leadership and not by consensus, which was seen as an apparent swipe at Powell.

A decade after the Persian Gulf War I, Powell found himself dealing with old foes but this time the issues and the mandate for war were not as clear cut. Although he favored further United Nations' sanctions and weapons inspections, on February 5, 2003, Powell gave an hour-long indictment of Iraq to the United Nations Security Council. Powell's vivid multimedia presentation attempted to provide evidence to prove that Iraq was violating United Nations Resolution 1441. Powell's presentation began with evidence purporting to show that Iraq systematically evaded and deceived United Nations weapons inspectors. Powell also raised questions on the status and location of inventory of stocks of biological and chemical weapons that were unaccounted for under the United Nations provisions. Powell then offered an argument pointing to Iraq's nuclear weapons program and an alleged link to al-Qaeda. With Powell's presentation, the United States hoped to secure a United Nations resolution authorizing the use of force on the basis of Saddam Hussein's refusal to disarm under the terms of Resolution 1441. A United Nations mandate would also provide political cover for European and Arab states to cooperate with an invasion that was deeply unpopular with their citizens.

Powell's presentation resonated with the U.S. public, but not with most members of the world community. Members of the United Nations Security Council, in particular China, France, Germany, and Russia were skeptical about moving toward war. These countries, among others, called for expanded weapons inspections by United Nations weapons teams. The United States did not secure enough votes to gain a United Nations resolution, and Persian Gulf War II began on March 19, 2003, with the U.S. launching missiles in an attack on Iraqi President Saddam Hussein's headquarters.

During Persian Gulf War II, Powell heard criticism from both the liberal and conservative segments of society. Actor Harry Belafonte criticized Powell's stance on the Bush administration's push for war. Belafonte likened Powell to a "house slave" in the Bush administration. Powell called Belafonte's comments "unfortunate" and "a throwback to another time." Powell also reiterated that he was proud to be serving the nation and the president. Former Speaker of the House of Representatives, Newt Gingrich, was also critical of Powell, citing the latter's "diplomatic failures." Specifically, Gingrich cited the failure of the State Department to apply its diplomatic muscle to persuade Iraq to disarm and comply with United Nations resolution. He also cited the inability to convince Turkey to allow U.S. troops to base there prior to the war, although the Turkish government heeded its citizen's public outcry opposing the war. Gingrich went so far as to call for a "bold, dramatic, change" at the State Department. However, the White House disagreed, expressing its confidence in Powell by stating that he had done an excellent job in promoting the president's views and advancing his agenda. Some speculated that Powell was embarrassed by the failure to find substantial evidence of chemical, biological, or nuclear weapons in Iraq. Powell maintained that he had no regrets about his presentation to the United Nations Security Council. He has argued that the presentation holds up if it is read carefully.

On May 1, 2003, President Bush landed on the deck of the aircraft carrier, the USS *Abraham Lincoln* and in a dramatic fashion declared, "Major combat operations in Iraq have ended." However, the mission was not completed, and the reconstruction has proven to be far more difficult than the administration originally predicted. Sporadic guerilla attacks have hampered reconstruction in Iraq. Two leaders of the governing council of Iraq have been assassinated. Also killed in Iraqi resistance attacks was the United Nations chief administrator in Iraq, Sergio Vieira, who was killed in a car bomb explosion outside the United Nations headquarters. As the civilian and military casualties continued to grow during the reconstruction effort, many of the United States' traditional allies, specifically Germany and France, refused to take an active role in the rebuilding efforts. Russia has refused to assist until a United Nations resolution has been secured. Powell has played a large role in soliciting countries to deploy troops or make financial contributions to the Iraqi reconstruction efforts, spending time in talks with United Nations Secretary-General Kofi Annan and the foreign ministers of Britain, France, Germany, and Russia, hoping to forge a more unified global front.

Powell brokered a deal with Poland to take an active role in reconstruction of Iraq. A Polish multinational division took over security responsibility for south-central Iraq. Among the countries represented in the Polish-led force were Hungary, Nicaragua, Bulgaria, Latvia, Slovakia, Fiji, Lithuania, the Philippines, Dominican Republic, Romania, Ukraine, Honduras, Mongolia, Thailand, Spain, Slovenia, Tonga, and Kazakhstan, which totaled only about 9,000 soldiers.

When the reconstruction began in Iraq, the Bush administration again turned to Powell to draft and introduce a resolution that would authorize a multinational force for peacekeeping in Iraq. The proposed resolution would give the United Nations a greater role in the political and economic reconstruction of Iraq. In consultation with other countries, Powell worked on the proposed resolution's language, and initial responses were positive. The new resolution built on United Nation Resolution 1483, which recognized the United States and Great Britain as the occupying powers in Iraq. The resolution also urged member states "to assist the people of Iraq in their efforts to reform their institutions and rebuild their country." The new resolution would provide political cover for those governments who wanted to participate but whose hands were tied by public opposition and anti-American sentiments in their countries.

Also in 2003, Powell made an attempt to launch President George Bush's "Roadmap to Peace in the Middle East" between Israel and the Palestinians. Powell met with Israeli Prime Minister Ariel Sharon and Palestinian Authority Prime Minister Mahmoud Abbas to pursue cease-fire initiatives with both sides. The

Palestinian State would be carved out of the West Bank and Gaza. However, terrorist attacks and retaliations by both parties hampered Powell's attempts to execute the "roadmap to peace." Mahmoud Abbas resigned after an internal power struggle with Palestinian Leader Yasser Arafat. Powell was later replaced as chief representative of the United States in the "road map to peace" by National Security Advisor Condolezza Rice, which many believed was a prelude to Rice replacing Powell if he stepped down as secretary of state. To put it mildly, the roadmap process reached a dead end.

In July 2003, rumors surfaced that Powell would step down in 2004. Powell publicly asserted that he had no plans of leaving and reiterated that he served at the pleasure of the president. However, those close to Powell stated that if he were to leave office, "he would have done a Herculean job of contributing in his term as Secretary of State." Powell remains one of the most popular political figures in Gallup Poll history. Many believe that he is the first African American who would have a legitimate chance to win the presidency. Some have continued to call for Powell to run for the highest office in the land.

BIBLIOGRAPHICAL ESSAY

Colin Powell's autobiography, *My American Journey* (1996), which was coauthored with Joseph E. Perisco, provides the most comprehensive account of Powell's life and career. *The Leadership Secrets of Collin Powell* (2003), authored by Oren Harari, provides excellent insight into Powell's core beliefs on leadership, negotiations, and self-knowledge. Harari used his monthly column in *Management Review* to distill many of Powell's speeches into 18 leadership principles that can be applied by the public. *Colin Powell: A Biography* (2003), by Richard Steins, establishes a timeline of events in Powell's life and traces his rise through the military ranks to becoming secretary of state.

F. Erik Brooks

EDMUND RANDOLPH (1753–1813)

Served 1794–1795
Appointed by President George Washington
Federalist

Edmund Randolph, the scion of the most prominent family in Virginia's capital city of Williamsburg, was born August 10, 1753. Edmund's grandfather, father, and uncle had all served as attorney general for the Virginia colony. After attending the College of William and Mary, Edmund himself went on to serve as attorney general first of Virginia, then of the newly formed federal government under the Constitution of 1787. Ironically, he detested the practice of law. It was only the first of many contradictions that plagued the life and career of Edmund Randolph.

Edmund began his law career in 1774. With the outbreak of the American Revolutionary War, and under Randolph's prodding, influential relatives and friends wrote George Washington, successfully requesting that he make Randolph an aide. Randolph felt a particular need to prove his loyalty because although his uncle, Peyton Randolph, was a prominent, if moderate, leader in the revolutionary movement, his father was a loyalist who took Edmund's mother with him into exile in England.

Edmund served only a few months as Washington's aide. With the sudden death of his Uncle Peyton, Edmund escorted his widowed aunt back to Williamsburg and stayed on to accept ever more responsible offices. In November 1776, he became mayor of Williamsburg. He was Virginia's delegate to the Continental Congress in 1779, served as Virginia's attorney general through most of the 1780s, and succeeded Patrick Henry as governor in November 1786.

Despite Randolph's concern with state affairs, he was a vocal supporter of a stronger federal government. As governor, he headed Virginia's delegation to the Constitutional Convention of 1787 and formally presented the Virginia Plan. Yet, Randolph was always an individualist who had a difficult time coordinating his views with others to form an effective coalition. He broke with Madison's Virginia Plan to support a plural executive; when that failed, he sought to limit the president to a single term. He proposed that all navigation acts require passage by two-thirds of each house rather than a simple majority. He looked to the Senate to control the

416

excesses of democracy, and he was very disturbed when the Great Compromise reduced the influence of the large states by eliminating proportional voting in the Senate.

Randolph was not the only delegate to object to certain parts of the Constitution as it emerged from the Philadelphia convention. Yet, he was one of only three to refuse his signature at the end. Randolph's concerns were sincere and understandable, but his actions exemplified the weaknesses that would plague and ultimately destroy him. He did not have the ability to go to the heart of a matter like a Hamilton, Jefferson, or Washington. He became bogged down in detail and sacrificed major goals for peripheral concerns. He placed excessive importance and also his reputation and honor on trivial matters. Despite his imposing physical presence and oratorical skill, he had an opaque writing and thinking style that did little to clarify his concerns to others or, one suspects, to himself. Thus, many of his fellow delegates to the Philadelphia Convention believed his refusal to sign the Constitution was his way of covering himself in case it proved unpopular.

Randolph insisted he was following a "middle line" on the Constitution. He wanted the state ratifying conventions to submit amendments to a second national convention before ratification. Madison finally convinced him that his stance was aiding those who wanted to scrap the entire document, and Randolph came around to accept the idea of ratifying the Constitution before amendments were added. Randolph's conversion was a significant factor in the Virginia convention's decision to ratify.

Randolph informed Madison in a convoluted letter that he was not in a financial condition to accept a federal office but would appreciate the offer of one so he could decline it. Randolph believed that such an offer would demonstrate to those who had criticized his course on the Constitution that he was still a significant figure. Madison ignored the tortured reasoning and prose in this letter, assumed Randolph truly wanted a federal office, and may have helped influence President Washington to appoint Randolph the first U.S. attorney general. Initially, this office was a minor part-time job, but as the cabinet split between Hamilton and Jefferson, Washington increasingly turned to Randolph for more impartial advice on foreign and domestic as well as legal affairs. Jefferson was not as happy with Randolph's "middle way" as Washington was. He called it a "half-way system between right and wrong" and said Randolph was "the poorest chameleon I ever saw having no colour of his own, and reflecting that nearest him."

Randolph had sided with Jefferson on the first significant issue for which Washington solicited his opinion by arguing that a national bank would be unconstitutional. But when war broke out between Great Britain and France in 1793, Randolph backed Hamilton in advocating an immediate Proclamation of Neutrality and in warning about the power and danger of pro-French sympathies in the nation.

Jefferson was thoroughly chagrined at what he considered Randolph's desertion of the republican cause. Jefferson and his partisans argued against an immediate proclamation of neutrality because they thought the United States should use the diplomatic leverage provided by Britain's war with France to win British concessions on America's neutral rights and past grievances. They thought the British would pay a considerable price to ensure that the United States did not join the war on the side of America's ally, France, especially if the United States made use of the threat of commercial retaliation against Great Britain and its colonies. Yet, the Jeffersonians continually ran afoul of Hamilton's contrary belief that a confrontation with Great Britain would be disastrous because tariffs on the voluminous British trade provided most of the federal revenue that supported Hamilton's elaborate financial plans for the United States.

Randolph did not go as far as Hamilton in advising cooperation with England, however. Randolph supported Jefferson's argument that neutrality should not be interpreted to require the breaking of the perpetual Treaty of Alliance the United States had signed with France during the American Revolution. Randolph even ensured that in drafting the Proclamation of Neutrality, the actual word *neutrality* was omitted from the text.

By the end of 1793, Jefferson, concerned that his advice was seldom taken by Washington and troubled by his support of antiadministration politicians while a member of Washington's cabinet, resigned as secretary of state. When Jefferson and Washington could not agree on a worthy successor, the former suggested Randolph as an interim appointment. Washington admitted the possibility, but he was afraid that Randolph might expect to keep the office, "and I do not know that he is fit for it nor what is thought of Mr. Randolph." Jefferson was unenthusiastic about his own suggestion, noting that Randolph's straitened financial circumstances might compromise his independence, but in the absence of a better-qualified candidate, Washington appointed Randolph as secretary of state on December 24, 1793.

The most significant issue to face Randolph as secretary of state was Jay's Treaty with Great Britain. The United States and Great Britain were on the brink of war as Randolph took office because British ships had suddenly captured more than 250 American vessels engaged in the trade with the French West Indies. This, on the heels of a year of disputes over neutral rights, several years of conflict over British occupation of the Great Lakes forts on the American side of the Canadian Border, and Britain's continuing refusal to open its West Indies to American trade, brought even pro-British Federalists like Hamilton to threaten war.

Naturally, Jeffersonian Republicans and Hamiltonian Federalists differed in their approach to the crisis. Jefferson and Madison argued for commercial retaliation. Hamilton and the Federalists argued for military preparations to be followed by negotiations unaccompanied by commercial retaliation or threatening language. Washington chose the Federalist approach. He appointed a Federalist, John Jay, as a special envoy to Great Britain and looked on silently as Jay helped derail Republican proposals for commercial retaliation in Congress.

Randolph was involved only peripherally in this vital debate. He had initially suggested the appointment of a negotiator, but had played no part in the debate on commercial retaliation or in the appointment of Jay. Even Jay's instructions were written more by Hamilton than by the secretary of state. Still, Randolph showed some leanings toward the Jeffersonian view by unsuccessfully opposing the part of Jay's instructions that permitted him to sign a trade treaty with England. The secretary realized that Jay might trade away the weapon of commercial retaliation in return for British concessions. Randolph managed to add to Jay's instructions a suggestion for a different sort of approach and leverage. He pointed out that Jay might approach other neutrals who were forming a League of Armed Neutrality, and that the British might make some concessions to keep the Americans out of such a League.

Randolph was totally unsuccessful in putting his imprint on the Jay Treaty. Jay made no approach to the League, and Hamilton undermined the weapon by revealing to the British minister in the United States that the United States had no intention of joining any such league. Jay instead dealt with the British in a friendly and open fashion, avoiding all threats except the implicit one of the American arms buildup. He eventually traded a 10-year commitment to avoid interference with British commerce for a basic minimum of British concessions. Great Britain promised to surrender its forts on U.S. territory in 1796, to permit a neutral commission to award compensation for the 250 American ships captured in the latest British sweep, and to open the British West Indies to small U.S. ships under extremely strict conditions. The British made no further concessions to U.S. neutral rights, refused compensation for the slaves they had carried away at the end of the Revolution, said nothing about their practice of impressing American seamen, and were able to convince the Americans to submit the debts they owed the British to a neutral commission.

Randolph was disturbed by Jay's preliminary treaty draft and wrote him a long list of suggested improvements, but Jay concluded the treaty before Randolph's suggestions reached him. Randolph loyally suppressed his critique and at Washington's order submitted the treaty to the Senate for its advice and consent. After the Senate eliminated the article on the West Indies trade because of the stringent restrictions contained in it, that angry and divided body consented to the treaty by a vote of 20 to 10, precisely the two-thirds vote needed.

As Washington was considering his own ratification, the British resumed their captures of American merchant ships carrying foodstuffs to the French West Indies. Randolph advised Washington to withhold his ratification until the British stopped this practice. Washington agreed, had Randolph inform the British minister of his determination, and set off for Mount Vernon leaving the treaty in limbo.

The Federalists in Washington's cabinet and in the Congress were aghast at the delay in ratification and blamed Washington's action on Randolph. They soon had an instrument of revenge. A British cruiser had recently captured a French ship, aboard which were several dispatches from Joseph Fauchet, the French minister to the United States. One of those dispatches spoke of "precious confessions" made by Randolph to Fauchet. The dispatch also implied that Randolph had requested money from Fauchet for nefarious purposes. The British sent these dispatches to their minister in the United States who turned them over to Randolph's opponents in the cabinet. Without telling Randolph of their secret, they convinced the secretary of state to write Washington requesting his immediate return to Washington. Upon the president's arrival, the conspirators informed him of Randolph's alleged treachery. Washington angrily decided to defy Randolph's advice and ratify the treaty immediately. He then confronted Randolph with Fauchet's dispatches and demanded an explanation. Randolph defiantly resigned on August 19, 1795.

The ruined secretary tried desperately to clear his name with a testimonial from Fauchet and in a long and convoluted pamphlet that spent as much time accusing Washington of prejudice as it did vindicating Randolph's own conduct. Fauchet supplied him with other dispatches that showed the "precious confessions" to have been rather innocuous, if indiscrete, comments on America's internal politics. Randolph's request for money did not involve a bribe for himself but advance payments to flour merchants who supposedly owed debts to the British and whose politics might be more independent if they were relieved of those obligations.

The effect was not what he had hoped. James Madison summarized the impact of the secretary's pamphlet: "His greatest enemies will not easily persuade themselves that he was under a corrupt influence of France, and his best friends can't save him from the self-condemnation of his political career as explained by himself."

Randolph returned to the private practice of law and regained a position of leadership at the Virginia bar. He wrote another pamphlet defending himself and attacking the Jay Treaty during the 1796 debate in the House of Representatives over funding the treaty. He took time in 1798 to write a careful treatise for James Madison on the nature and power of the states as expressed in the Constitution and the Virginia Resolution Madison had authored. In 1807 he again appeared briefly on the national stage as one of Aaron Burr's defense counsels during Burr's famous trial for treason.

Yet, he continued to be plagued by the problems generated during his service as secretary of state. He was found personally liable for some discrepancies in the State Department accounts, and the judgment left him destitute. His brother-in-law paid off the debt in four installments, and Randolph, with his health rapidly declining, was reduced to a physical and financial dependent. Death released him on September 12, 1813.

BIBLIOGRAPHICAL ESSAY

The most complete collection of Randolph Manuscripts is the Edmund Randolph Papers at the university of Virginia. Moncure D. Conway's *Omitted Chapters of History Disclosed in the Life and Papers of Edmund Randolph* (1888) represents the most complete set of printed Randolph papers. Randolph himself wrote two separate defenses of his conduct. Randolph's first vindication is in Peter V. Daniel (ed.), *A Vindication of Edmund Randolph, Written by Himself, Published in 1795* (1855). His second defense is in a more elaborate pamphlet titled *Political Truth or . . . an Inquiry into the Truth of the Charges Preferred Against Mr. Randolph* (1796).

The standard biography of Randolph is John J. Reardon, *Edmund Randolph: A Biography* (1974). Reardon's work has superseded H. J. Eckenrode, *The Randolph's: The Story of a Virginia Family* (1946), an outdated family biography that emphasizes the importance of blood, and Jonathan Daniel's *The Randolph's of Virginia* (1972), a good family history.

Two works are critical to an understanding of Randolph's vindication. Irving Bryant's "Edmund Randolph, Not Guilty," *William and Mary Quarterly* (April 1950), is an important analysis of Randolph's vindication. Jerald L. Comb's *The Jay Treaty: Political Battleground of the Founding Fathers* (1970) provides some new information on Randolph's vindication.

Jerald A. Combs

WILLIAM P. ROGERS (1913–2001)

Served 1969–1973
Appointed by President Richard M. Nixon
Republican

William Pierce Rogers, the 55th secretary of state of the United States, had the misfortune of serving in the cabinet during the first term of President Richard M. Nixon. Because of the actions of Nixon and his national security adviser, Henry A. Kissinger, Rogers experienced an extremely frustrating and disappointing four-and-one-half years in office. The prominent Cold War historian John Lewis Gaddis, writing in 1982, referred to Rogers as "little-remembered" in his role of secretary of state.

Rogers was born in the small upstate New York town of Norfolk on June 23, 1913, the son of Harrison A. Rogers and Myra Beswick Rogers. When his mother died when he was 13, he moved to the nearby town of Canton, New York, to live with his grandparents. He graduated from Canton High School and then earned a B.A. degree from Colgate University in 1934, followed by a law degree from Cornell University in 1937. For the next year he worked for a Wall Street law firm, followed by four years as an assistant district attorney under Thomas E. Dewey, the district attorney for New York County and later the Republican presidential candidate in 1948.

In 1942, in the wake of the Japanese attack on Pearl Harbor, Rogers entered the U.S. Naval Reserve as a lieutenant junior grade. During his wartime service he served on the aircraft carrier *Intrepid* during the invasion of Okinawa. When he left the Navy in January 1946, he returned to the New York County district attorney's office, where he stayed until moving in April 1947 to Washington as counsel, and later chief counsel, of the Senate Special Committee to Investigate the National Defense Program (later the Senate Permanent Investigating Committee). During this period, he and Representative Richard M. Nixon of California became friends. Rogers worked with the committee in the effort to prosecute the "five-percenters" who had fixed federal contracts for private firms and also advised Nixon to accept Whittaker Chambers' accusations against Alger Hiss, a State Department official.

Nixon then pushed the case that resulted in the perjury conviction of Hiss and put Nixon in the limelight.

Rogers joined the Washington office of the New York law firm Dwight, Royall, Harris, Koegel & Caskey, later named Clifford, Chance, Rogers & Wells, in March 1950 and stayed with this firm until his death, except for periods of federal service in the Eisenhower and Nixon administrations. He became a prominent lawyer whose clients included influential firms, among them *The Washington Post.*

His friendship with Richard Nixon drew him into politics in 1952, when Nixon was the Republican vice presidential candidate on the ticket of Dwight D. Eisenhower. He worked at the 1952 Republican Convention on behalf of Eisenhower, and during the ensuing campaign he advised Nixon, especially when it became known that some of his California supporters had set up a private slush fund for him. Rogers helped Nixon prepare the famous "Checkers" speech that saved his place on the ticket and led to his election as vice president in 1952.

On Nixon's recommendation, Rogers on January 27, 1953, became a deputy attorney general in the Department of Justice, serving as the department's chief liaison officer with Congress and the press. When Attorney General Herbert Brownell, Jr., resigned in October 1957, President Eisenhower chose Rogers to succeed him, and he served until the end of the Eisenhower Administration in January 1961. He played a major role in the crisis over the attempt to integrate the Little Rock, Arkansas, High School in the fall of 1957. He strongly supported the Supreme Court's *Brown v. Board of Education of Topeka* decision of 1954 and as attorney general supported the enforcement of integration. He also led a fight against syndicate crime and instituted antitrust cases against large corporations, including General Electric and Westinghouse. On occasion, such as President Eisenhower's first heart attack in 1955, he counseled Vice President Nixon. In January 1961, when the Democrats took over the presidency, he returned to the practice of law, working out of his firm's New York office. Richard Nixon also practiced law in New York for some years in the 1960s; he and Rogers saw each other frequently during this period.

Although Rogers was not extensively involved in foreign affairs during the 1960s, his law practice did involve some international law cases. In 1965 he was a member of the U.S. delegation to the United Nations General Assembly, and two years later he was a special U.S. representative at a 10-week meeting of the Ad Hoc Committee on Southwest Africa. Rogers was not President-elect Nixon's first choice to be secretary of state in 1969; Nixon selected him because of his successful prior experience in the federal government and his experience as a negotiator. Also, Rogers and Nixon were personal friends, and Rogers frequently had served as his adviser on various issues. The Senate confirmed Rogers as secretary of state on January 20, 1969, and he took the oath of office two days later.

Rogers's term as secretary of state, lasting more than four and one-half years, was chaotic almost from the beginning. His problem had nothing to do with his own competence or leadership of the State Department, but rather with the personalities and methods of operation of Nixon and his national security adviser, Henry A. Kissinger. Nixon had a deep interest in foreign affairs, and his intention from the beginning was to maintain personal control in that area, with the close assistance of Kissinger. Nixon expected Rogers to manage the State Department and the Foreign Service, which the president disliked and degraded, and to handle foreign policy matters that the president did not reserve to himself and Kissinger.

At the start of his term Nixon adopted a system for handling foreign policy designed by Kissinger, aimed at concentrating decision making, and indeed negotiations in the important areas, in the hands of the national security adviser and the president himself. Nixon and Kissinger worked out this plan without any direct participation of Secretary Rogers. The national security adviser gained the power to order preparation of National Security Study Memoranda (NSSMs), which would determine the work of the State and Defense Departments and other agencies involved in foreign affairs. Within this system policy papers came up through numerous panels chaired by Kissinger. The president made final decisions on matters considered by the panels, sometimes in National Security Council (NSC) meetings and on other occasions solely by himself and Kissinger. Often the result was a decision in which the State and Defense Departments had little opportunity to participate. Kissinger also chaired a Senior Review Group that replaced the Senior Interdepartmental Group dominated by the State Department during the preceding Johnson administration. Although the NSC staff included numerous members brought over from the State Department, they were under Kissinger's control and had little direct relationship with the State Department while at the NSC.

Kissinger's system also excluded Secretary of Defense Melvin R. Laird in much the same way as it pushed Rogers aside, but Laird resisted more, had ways that Rogers did not have to learn what was going on in the White House, and also, as a former influential congressman, had important contacts in Congress. Nixon and Kissinger considered Laird, like Rogers, as a thorn in the side of their efforts to maintain exclusive control of foreign and military policy. Nixon, who operated frequently through back channels, occasionally issued military orders without going through Laird's office. The National Security Agency, an agency of the Defense Department, secretly provided Laird with many of Nixon and Kissinger's back channel communications, and the Joint Chiefs of Staff, independently of Laird, received copies of many White House documents through a Navy yeoman attached to the White House staff. Nixon and Kissinger left to Rogers and the State Department issues and areas that they did not want to control—trade, foreign aid, cultural, scientific, and information programs, United Nations affairs, and low-priority regions—Latin America, Africa, and for a time early in the administration, the Middle East.

Kissinger, strong-minded, insecure, jealous, and vindictive, soon came to dislike Rogers intensely, and spent much of his time subverting Rogers's work and his efforts to play the traditional role of secretary of state. An epic struggle occurred between Kissinger and Rogers, lasting until Rogers finally resigned in the fall of 1973. The published diaries of H. R. Haldeman, Nixon's chief of staff, chronicle the almost daily disputes between the two—with Kissinger the chief protagonist. Haldeman notes that he headed a "Henry-Handling" committee, on instructions from the president, to deal with Kissinger's problems with Rogers. Kissinger, for example, did not want Rogers to have any private contacts with Soviet Ambassador Anatoli Dobrynin, and the president approved this approach. Kissinger wanted to deal with Dobrynin privately without input or interference from Rogers. On occasion Rogers did meet with Dobrynin, but the Soviet ambassador had been told to make his approaches directly to Nixon and Kissinger, and he knew Rogers was not important in the U.S.–Soviet relationship. Another Kissinger ploy was to use translators provided by foreign officials rather than State Department translators to keep his activities and important information secret from Rogers. He once proposed that Rogers not be allowed to make speeches unless Kissinger cleared them in the White House in advance, but Nixon did not approve this proposal.

Kissinger's jealousy showed up frequently. Because Rogers and the president were old friends, Nixon sometimes would invite him to dine privately at the White House, but never invited Kissinger to do so. This greatly agitated Kissinger. He blamed Rogers for planting stories in the press about his relationship with the actress Jill St. John. Kissinger's usual response to disagreements with Rogers was to threaten to resign. Nixon assigned Haldeman the task of calming Kissinger and persuading him to stay on. The Kissinger–Rogers rivalry bothered Nixon very much, and more than once he considered asking one or the other or both to leave the administration.

The one important area of foreign policy that Nixon relegated to Rogers in 1969 when the administration came into office was the Middle East. Nixon thought that Kissinger being Jewish would affect the latter's approach to the Middle East conflict, and in Nixon's mind this was one of the less-important foreign policy issues at the moment. The 1967 Six-Day War between Egypt and Israel had ended in a cease-fire, with Israel in possession of most of Egypt's Sinai Peninsula. In April 1969, Egyptian President Gamel Abdel Nasser abrogated the 1967 cease-fire. Thereafter, in 1969–1970, the Egyptians and Israelis engaged in a war of attrition. Late in 1969, after meetings with the Arabs, Israelis, Soviets, and others, Rogers proposed a peace plan calling for Israel to return almost all the Sinai area to Egypt. When Rogers first presented it, Nixon and Kissinger did not like it, but they let it stand as a way of gaining time for later initiatives. Kissinger, jealous of the publicity Rogers got in this instance, secretly let Israeli Prime Minister Golda Meir know, on Nixon's authority, that the White House did not favor the plan, cutting the ground out from under Rogers. Ultimately both Israel and Egypt rejected the Rogers plan.

The State Department continued to lead on Middle East policy for most of the next year. Rogers put forward another initiative, calling for a 90-day cease-fire to allow negotiations on the dispute; both Egypt and Israel accepted, and the cease-fire became effective on August 7, 1970. Although it did not end for long the rivalry between the Arabs and Israelis in the Middle East, the Rogers initiative received recognition at the time as timely and important. By the end of 1970, Nixon and Kissinger in effect took the Middle East away from Rogers and the State Department.

The ongoing conflict in Southeast Asia was perhaps the most important foreign and military policy issue the Nixon administration confronted when it took office. Nixon and Kissinger thought that the Vietnam War could not be won by the United States and its allies, but they favored keeping the pressure up in the hope of getting concessions from North Vietnam. Although essentially excluded from dealing with this issue, Rogers opposed U.S. initiatives that might escalate the war and favored negotiations to end the conflict.

Nixon's "Vietnamization" program, begun in 1969, included reducing U.S. troop levels, training the South Vietnamese forces, and turning the fighting over to them. The troop withdrawal program proceeded at a slow pace, lasting over three years. Also in 1969, the "Nixon Doctrine" emerged—applied first to Asia and then globalized: Asian nations should increasingly handle their own problems on internal security. The United States would help train their forces, which would do the fighting. Rogers generally agreed with Vietnamization and the Nixon Doctrine, but he objected to aggressive acts in Southeast Asia undertaken secretly by Nixon and Kissinger. The first example was the secret bombing of Cambodia, starting in March 1969. The Ho Chi Minh Trail ran in part through Cambodia, North Vietnamese sanctuaries were located there, and the United States assumed that COSVN—the Communist Central Office for South Vietnam—was located in Cambodia. Nixon decided in February 1969 to bomb the Fishhook area of Cambodia when the North Vietnamese began an offensive from that location. The decision to bomb and the related planning were kept from Rogers until the operation began in mid-March 1969. He opposed and argued against bombing a neutral country. The bombing, which lasted until the spring of 1970, remained secret, because neither North Vietnam nor the Cambodians acknowledged it publicly.

In January 1970 the North Vietnamese began an offensive in north central Laos. The Nixon administration considered bombing the area, but Rogers opposed, and the bombing did not take place then. The next month the Laotian prime minister requested B-52 bombing missions, which began then and continued for three years. Rogers objected to Nixon's decision to bomb, but the president rejected his arguments.

In March 1970, Prime Minister Lon Nol overthrew the Cambodian government, headed by Prince Norodom Sihanouk for nearly 30 years. Lon Nol declared Cambodia's neutrality and ordered the North Vietnamese and Viet Cong to leave the country, but they instead launched an attack on Lon Nol's government. Nixon reacted by planning for an invasion of Cambodia against these enemy troops, using U.S. and South Vietnamese forces. Rogers argued strongly against this plan, stressing that the invasion would cause a storm of protest in the United States. When the invasion, involving 31,000 U.S. and 43,000 South Vietnamese troops, began on May 1, 1970, the widespread and violent protest that Rogers had predicted indeed took place. Some 250 Foreign Service officers in the State Department protested the invasion in a petition sent to Rogers, who subsequently refused a White House demand for the names of the petitioners.

Again, after the North Vietnamese in late March 1972 began a major offensive in the northern area of South Vietnam, Rogers opposed Nixon's response—a major U.S. bombing campaign in mid-April against enemy oil storage depots near Hanoi and Haiphong. These strikes were successful, but the North Vietnamese offensive continued, leading Nixon to order the mining of Haiphong harbor, North Vietnam's largest seaport. Rogers argued that this operation should at least be postponed until after a U.S.–Soviet summit scheduled for late May 1972, but Nixon rejected his advice.

By the summer of 1972 the fighting in Vietnam remained furious, but the competing sides had become more amenable to a compromise settlement. Negotiations had begun in Paris as early as 1968 and had continued sporadically since then, with Rogers participating occasionally on the U.S. side. In the meantime Kissinger and Le Duc Tho, North Vietnam's representative in Paris, engaged in secret talks, unknown even to Rogers. A tentative agreement in October 1972 broke down because of the opposition of Nguyen Van Thieu, South Vietnam's leader. A bombing campaign against North Vietnam in December 1972 took a heavy toll, after which the North Vietnamese agreed to resume negotiations. In late January 1973 the United States and North Vietnam reached a settlement, including the withdrawal of all U.S. troops and the return of U.S. prisoners of war from North Vietnam. Rogers, although not a significant participant in the talks leading to the agreement, signed for the United States on January 27, 1973.

An incident involving North Korea early in the Nixon administration made clear the policy and action differences between Kissinger and the president on one hand and Rogers on the other. On April 15, 1969, the North Koreans shot down an unarmed EC-121, a U.S. reconnaissance plane on an intelligence mission over international waters about 90 miles from the coast of North Korea. Kissinger, perhaps recalling candidate Nixon's criticism in 1968 of the mild U.S. reaction when the North Koreans seized the *Pueblo*, favored retaliatory bombing, and Nixon considered this possible response. Rogers, backed by Laird, the JCS, and CIA director Richard Helms, opposed this action, fearing it might lead to a wider conflict over what was probably a North Korean error.

Eventually Nixon backed away from such retaliation and relied on verbal criticisms of North Korea, along with the movement of two U.S. aircraft carriers to the Sea of Japan. Kissinger and Nixon were furious because Rogers and the others had opposed the bombing, and the EC-121 incident convinced them that Rogers should be kept out of such issues. Kissinger subsequently established the Washington Special Action Group (WSAG), which he chaired. Its other members included the second-ranking officers at State, Defense, the CIA, and other agencies. Nixon later said he regretted not following his own instincts in the EC-121 matter, saying he relented because both Rogers and Laird threatened to resign.

In August and September 1970 there was alarm in the administration when it discovered Soviet construction activity at Cienfuegos, Cuba. The United States feared that the Soviets intended to establish a nuclear submarine base in Cuba. When the NSC discussed the matter on September 23, 1970, Rogers opposed any action that would cause a crisis between the United States and the Soviet Union. The administration then resorted to diplomacy, but Rogers played no role in the settlement of the issue in October 1970. Kissinger and Soviet Ambassador Dobrynin exchanged diplomatic notes that included a Russian pledge not to establish a submarine base in Cuba.

In September 1970, Salvador Allende, a Marxist, captured a plurality in a three-candidate election for the presidency of Chile. Although Kissinger and the NSC paid little attention to Latin America, Kissinger was very concerned about the possibility that the Chilean Congress, which had to select the new president, would choose Allende. He was angry with the State Department, which had done nothing, in his view, to oppose Allende. Kissinger, using the CIA but excluding the U.S. embassy in Chile, made various efforts to keep Allende out of office, including encouraging a coup and influencing members of the Chilean Congress. All these efforts failed, and the Chilean Congress in October 1970 chose Allende for the presidency. The Nixon administration remained cool to Allende's administration, rejecting the advice of the U.S. ambassador in Chile to try to work with Allende. Rogers played no significant role in this affair, excluded by Nixon as he was in many other instances during his term as secretary of state.

The involvement of the United States in another crisis, involving Pakistan and India in 1971, further demonstrated the policy differences between the State Department and the White House. When India won independence from Great Britain in 1947, the British detached the Muslim areas from the former colony to establish Pakistan, separated into two parts by a thousand miles of Indian territory, with West Pakistan the dominant part. In elections in December 1970, the vast majority in East Pakistan favored autonomy. Civil war began three months later when West Pakistani forces moved in and began a bloody military campaign to control the eastern section. State Department officers in Islamabad, West Pakistan, recommended that the United States not intervene in favor of East Pakistan, whereas other foreign service officers in Dacca, the East Pakistan capital, criticized the reluctance of Washington to protest against the bloodshed in East Pakistan. India's November 1971 military intervention to assist East Pakistan broadened into a bloody war between India and Pakistan. Kissinger and the White House favored Pakistan, in part because they were using its government as a back channel for secret contacts with the Chinese government.

Reacting to the brutality of Pakistan's army against East Pakistan, Rogers and the State Department believed that the United States should move closer to India. Kissinger disagreed; the Soviet Union and India had signed a friendship treaty in August 1971, and he feared that the Soviets might intervene in the conflict on India's side. As it turned out, neither the Soviet Union nor China intervened. In mid-December 1971 Pakistan and India agreed to a cease-fire. Subsequently East Pakistan became independent as the nation of Bangladesh. The severe Kissinger–Rogers clash over this crisis further delineated the deep differences between the two on major foreign policy issues.

The successful effort of Nixon and Kissinger to open normal relations with China provided another example of the exclusion of Rogers from a very important diplomatic initiative. When Kissinger received a secret invitation to visit China in June 1971, Rogers was not told about it. Just before Kissinger left Washington early in July 1971 to visit China on what was announced as a fact-finding tour of Asia, Rogers learned of the matter. Kissinger arrived in Beijing on July 9, 1971, after a secret trip on a Pakistani aircraft from Islamabad. Kissinger and Chinese Premier Zhou Enlai agreed on a final communiqué stating that President Nixon would visit China early in 1972 to discuss normalization of U.S.–China relations. Nixon announced this plan publicly on July 15, 1971. Kissinger made another preparatory trip to China in October 1971, again without any significant involvement by Rogers.

Nixon visited China for seven days late in February 1972. Nixon and Kissinger excluded Rogers, who made the trip, from the important meetings with Mao Zedong and Zhou Enlai. The draft communiqué for this summit, prepared by Nixon, Kissinger, and the Chinese leaders, contained an affirmation by the United States of its alliances with Asian nations, including South Korea, Japan, Australia, and New Zealand, but made no mention of the Republic of China on Formosa. Rogers complained directly to Nixon about this omission, angering both the president and Kissinger. At the moment Nixon talked of firing Rogers. Ultimately Nixon agreed to a change in the communiqué: there was no reference in the final document to U.S. defense arrangements in Asia, but Kissinger in his final briefing on the China meetings did acknowledge that the defense treaty with Taiwan remained active. Rogers' intervention resulted in this compromise, but he had little to do with the U.S. agreement to recognize and establish formal diplomatic relations with the People's Republic of China.

Another important issue during the Nixon administration was the strategic arms competition with the Soviet Union. In 1968 the Johnson administration had agreed to have strategic arms limitation talks with the Soviet Union, but it was left to the Nixon administration to go forward with them. It did so during 1969, its first year in office, when talks with the Soviet Union began in Vienna. Although Rogers was somewhat involved in internal Nixon administration discussions on the issue, neither Nixon nor Kissinger was receptive to his views, and they excluded him from any meaningful role. Kissinger again used back channels to deal with Ambassador Dobrynin, exclusive of the U.S. SALT delegation involved in the Vienna talks. Thus Rogers was surprised when Nixon and Soviet leader Leonid Breznev announced on May 20, 1971, that they had decided to work toward an agreement that would include an antiballistic missile system provision as well as limitations on offensive weapons.

On a secret trip to Moscow in April 1972, Kissinger and Breznev discussed several outstanding issues, on which they made progress. Typically, Rogers knew nothing of Kissinger's trip until after the NSC advisor had left Washington. In late May 1972, Nixon went to Moscow for a summit meeting. Rogers was along on the trip, but he and his State Department colleagues were not involved in the important matters discussed in Moscow. Two U.S.–Soviet agreements emerged from this summit—an interim agreement on limitation of strategic offensive arms and a treaty on the limitation of antiballistic missile systems. Both entered into force on October 3, 1972. Although Rogers had been involved in initiation of the talks in 1969 that led to these agreements, Nixon and Kissinger often ignored his advice and kept him from an active role in the negotiation and drafting of the agreements, one of the most important international accomplishments of the Nixon administration.

Perhaps reflecting his exclusion from most important matters, Rogers chose to travel extensively during his term as secretary of state. Between 1969 and mid-1973, he visited 66 nations, 20 of them more than once. The countries he visited most frequently were Belgium—eight visits, mainly on NATO affairs, the United Kingdom (8 visits), France (7 visits), and Germany (5 visits). Significantly his only trip to the Soviet Union was with Nixon at the May 1972 summit meeting.

Because of the almost constant disagreements between Rogers and Kissinger during Nixon's first term, the president occasionally considered firing one or both of them, and Kissinger repeatedly threatened to resign because of his conflicts with Rogers. After his reelection in 1972, Nixon wanted to make some cabinet changes, including replacing both Kissinger and Rogers, but by this time the Watergate affair had become the dominant issue for the Nixon administration. Rogers had handled selected political questions for Nixon during the 1972 campaign, and as Watergate heated up in late 1972 and early 1973, Nixon consulted with Rogers, a lawyer, on issues related to that matter. When Nixon forced E. R. Haldeman and John Ehrlichman, his closest aides, to resign in April 1973 over the Watergate scandal, Rogers advised them and helped them write their letters of resignation.

Pressured to resign shortly after Nixon's reelection, Rogers proposed to stay on until at least June 1, 1973, to complete certain work at the State Department and to avoid giving the impression that Kissinger had forced him out. Nixon considered both Kenneth Rush and John Connally to succeed Rogers, but ultimately decided to add the position of secretary of state to Kissinger's already heavy schedule as national security adviser. By the time Rogers finally agreed to resign, Nixon decided, because Watergate had become the dominant issue, to keep Kissinger in a prominent place in his administration. When he announced Kissinger's appointment in late August 1973, Nixon said Rogers had wanted to leave at the end of his first term but had been prevailed upon to remain in office for a time to complete unfinished business in the State Department. Rogers's term officially ended on September 3, 1973.

After leaving the Department of State, Rogers returned to the law firm of Clifford, Chance, Rogers & Wells, with offices in New York and Washington. Rogers performed one additional public service in the post–State Department years, as chairman of the presidential commission to investigate the Space Shuttle Challenger accident in 1986. The result, after a long investigation, was a report sharply critical of the National Aeronautics and Space Administration for its management of the space exploration program.

Rogers lived in Bethesda, Maryland, and continued the practice of law until his death at the age of 87 on January 2, 2001. His wife, four children, 11 grandchildren, and four great grandchildren survived him. When former President Nixon died in 1994, Rogers graciously described him as "a great world leader" who would gain stature in later years as memories of Watergate receded.

BIBLIOGRAPHICAL ESSAY

William P. Rogers left no personal account of his work as secretary of state and thus far there is no full-length published biography of him. The published literature on the Nixon administration, specific foreign policy events during the period, and on Nixon himself is extensive. Among the most detailed are Stephen E. Ambrose, *Nixon*, vol. 2, *The Triumph of a Politician, 1962–1972* (1989), and Ambrose, *Nixon*, vol. 3, *Ruin and Recovery, 1973–1990* (1991). Other selected studies include Seyom Brown, *The Crises of Power: An Interpretation of United States Foreign Policy During the Kissinger Years* (1998); William Bundy, *A Tangled Web: The Making of Foreign Policy in the Nixon Presidency* (1998), an excellent account by a seasoned State Department and Defense Department official; John Ehrlichman, *Witness to Power: The Nixon Years* (1982), by a top Nixon aide; John Lewis Gaddis, *Strategies of Containment: A Critical Appraisal of Postwar American National Security Policy* (1982); H. R. Haldeman, *The Haldeman Diaries: Inside the Nixon White House* (1994), an inside account providing much information on the Kissinger–Rogers relationship; George C. Herring, *America's Longest War: The United States and Vietnam, 1950–1975* (1985), a detailed history, including the Nixon period; Seymour Hersh, *The Price of Power: Kissinger in the Nixon White House* (1983); Walter Isaacson, *Kissinger: A Biography* (1992), a comprehensive account; U. Alexis Johnson with Jef O. McAllister, *The Right Hand of Power: The Memoirs of An American Diplomat* (1984), by Rogers's under secretary of state; Jeffrey Kimball, *Nixon's Vietnam War* (1998); Henry A. Kissinger, *White House Years* (1979), Kissinger's personal account; John Prados, *Keepers of the Keys: A History of the National Security Council from Truman to Bush* (1991); Barry Rubin, *Secrets of State: The State Department and the Struggle over U.S. Foreign Policy* (1985); Robert D. Schulzinger, *Henry Kissinger: Doctor of Diplomacy* (1989); Melvin Small, *The Presidency of Richard Nixon* (1999); Gerard Smith, *Doubletalk: The Story of SALT I* (1980); and U.S. Department of State, *Foreign Travels of the Secretaries of State, 1866–1990* (1990).

Roger R. Trask

ELIHU ROOT (1845–1937)

Served 1905–1909
Appointed by President Theodore Roosevelt
Republican

Elihu Root, secretary of state from July 7, 1905, to January 27, 1909, was a major figure in American law, politics, and foreign relations during the greater part of his long life. His first cabinet office was that of secretary of war, from 1899 to 1904. Upon resignation as secretary of state in 1909, he became a senator from New York. As secretary of state, as senator, and as an ex-senator, he was the foremost American exponent of the judicial approach to the development of international institutions and organizations to maintain peace.

Elihu Root was born February 15, 1845, in Clinton, New York. His father, Oren Root, was then a young teacher moving from school to school; in 1849 he became professor of mathematics at Hamilton College in Clinton, a position he would hold until near the end of his life. The family was proud of its descent from English families that had settled in New England and New York during the seventeenth century. Root's mother, Nancy Whitford Buttrick, was a granddaughter of Major John Buttrick of the Massachusetts Minute Men who commanded them at Concord Bridge on April 19, 1775. Elihu Root graduated from Hamilton College in 1864 and taught for a year at an academy in Rome, New York. He then entered New York University, from which he received a bachelor of law degree in 1867.

Admitted to the New York bar in 1867, Root had considerable success almost from the first. In 1873 he won the favorable attention of other lawyers when he served as one of the defense counsel for the notorious Tammany boss, William Marcy Tweed, then on trial for larceny, forgery, and other offenses. One result of this experience was association with a senior member of the defense, David Dudley Field. In Field's office Root read the *Draft Outlines for an International Code*, which Field had written the year before; Root's interest in international law began at that time. Marriage to Clara Wales, daughter of a prominent Republican, Salem Wales, editor of the *Scientific American*, soon opened to Root opportunities to work with Republican leaders. When President Chester A. Arthur appointed him to a two-year term as U.S. attorney for southern New York in 1883, Root's influence in legal and political circles greatly increased. The position also gave him an opportunity to develop his interest in international law, for he prosecuted ships outfitted to aid insurgents in Haiti and Colombia. He became an authority on the neutrality laws of the United States.

Root's interest in international law notwithstanding, his legal career was primarily that of a corporation lawyer. Wealthy men, among them, Frederick W. Vanderbilt, Thomas Fortune Ryan, and William C. Whitney, retained him, and he also acted as counsel for the federal government and the state of New York. When Theodore Roosevelt's gubernatorial candidacy nearly ended in 1898 over discovery he had listed Washington as his residence to avoid New York taxes, Root found a way out of that embarrassment. By the mid-1890s Root was regarded as one of the greatest American lawyers, the peer of such lawyers as former President Benjamin Harrison and Joseph Hodges Choate, later an ambassador to Great Britain.

At the beginning of his administration, President William McKinley offered Root an appointment as minister to Spain, believing Root's conciliatory abilities could avert war. Root refused. McKinley offered to raise the Madrid post to an embassy, and Root refused again. Nearly a year after the Spanish-American War McKinley asked Root to accept appointment as secretary of war. Victory had brought with it enormous problems. The Philippines, Guam, and Puerto Rico became American possessions, and the United States army was occupying Cuba. Filipinos who had rebelled against Spain were now rebelling against the United States. The War Department, which was trying to govern the new empire, was in disarray. There had been notable battles in Cuba during the recent war, and American soldiers had fought with valor, but it was common knowledge that the army had been badly managed. The press and politicians blamed Secretary of War Russell A. Alger, who resigned. McKinley at once asked Root to succeed him. Root became secretary of war on August 1, 1899.

Root's service as secretary of war under Presidents McKinley and Roosevelt was arguably as important in the history of American foreign relations as his later career as secretary of state. As McKinley hoped, Root laid the foundations of civil government in the Philippines, Cuba, and Puerto Rico, developing policies that were ably implemented by William Howard Taft in the Philippines, General Leonard Wood in Cuba, and Charles H. Allen in Puerto Rico. The Philippines were Root's greatest problem, for the army had to battle the guerrilla forces of Emilio Aguinaldo until April 1902. An especially severe test of Root's management came in 1900, when the Boxer Rebellion raged in northern China, for the secretary had to send army units from the Philippines to join the international expedition to rescue the besieged legation quarter in Peking. From these experiences and from intensive reading Root gained a unique perspective on the problems of personnel, organization, and supply, which had caused his predecessor's downfall.

Beginning with his first annual report in 1899, he advocated important reforms. McKinley and Roosevelt gave him full support, and Congress was responsive. Congress, in the Dick Act of January 21, 1903, transformed the state militia or National Guard into an "Organized Militia," which became an effective reserve system. Three weeks later, on February 14, Congress abolished the office of commanding general, replacing it with a general staff corps. Root meanwhile had established a new army school system, founding special schools at a number of army posts, the most important of which was Ft. Leavenworth, Kansas. By general orders he established the Army War College on November 27, 1901. Root's work in the War Department was much admired by other civilian leaders of military establishments during the early twentieth century. Richard Burden Haldane, British war minister from 1905 to 1912, said that Root's five annual reports were "the very last word concerning the organization and place of an army in a democracy." Newton D. Baker, American secretary of war during World War I, said that Root's service as secretary of war had been "the outstanding contribution" made by any holder of the office and that without it American participation in World War I would have been "a confused, ineffective and discreditable episode."

Both McKinley and Roosevelt called on Root for assistance with matters outside the usual sphere of the secretary of war. During a critical moment of the Boxer Rebellion, Secretary of State John Hay was absent from Washington, and Root administered the State Department as well as his own department. In 1903 Roosevelt asked him to serve as a member of the Alaska Boundary Tribunal to determine the location of the boundary between the Alaska Panhandle and Canada, in dispute since discovery of gold in the Yukon in 1896. Roosevelt agreed to refer the matter to a tribunal only when it was agreed that the president and King Edward VII would each appoint three "impartial jurists of repute." With that arrangement, Roosevelt reasoned, the United States could not lose. Roosevelt's appointment of Root, together with Senator Henry Cabot Lodge of Massachusetts, and ex-Senator George Turner, of Washington, was severely criticized, for it seemed highly unlikely they could be "impartial." In fact, they joined with the British Lord Chief Justice, Lord Alverstone, in upholding the American contentions, but they awarded some territory to Canada. Root, in particular, was praised for his judicial bearing in this episode.

Root resigned as secretary of war on February 1, 1904, and returned to the practice of law in New York. His resignation came at a critical moment in American foreign relations. Events of large consequence for the future foreign policies of the United States were in progress. War began between Russia and Japan after a surprise Japanese attack on Port Arthur on February 8. The threat of European interventions in the Americas was another problem. The blockade of Venezuela by the Germans, British, and Italians in late 1902 and early 1903 to force Venezuela to honor its financial obligations had aroused alarm in the United States. What if a European power should use debt collection as a pretext for establishing a permanent foothold in the Americas?

The Dominican Republic, in 1904, defaulted on payments on its foreign debt, and Roosevelt decided to announce a policy to forestall European creditors planning another armed expedition into the Americas. Root, as a private citizen, proved to be an effective spokesman for the administration. Addressing a Cuban dinner in New York on May 20, 1904, he read what Roosevelt called a "joint letter" in which the president made one of his first statements of the Roosevelt Corollary to the Monroe Doctrine. He declared that no American nation need fear intervention by the United States if it acted "with decency in industrial and political matters" and paid its obligations, but "Brutal wrong-doing, or an impotence which results in a general loosening of the ties of civilized society" might "require intervention by some civilized nation, and in the Western Hemisphere the United States cannot ignore this duty." Roosevelt, in his annual message on December 6, 1904, stated a revised version.

Root was quick to give support. In an address to the New England Society on December 22, he explained the corollary's reasonableness, but at the same time repudiated another famous corollary, that which Secretary of State Richard Olney had announced in 1895 during the Venezuelan Boundary crisis between the United States and Great Britain. Olney had announced that "Today the United States is practically sovereign on this continent, and its fiat is law upon the subjects to which it confines its interposition." Olney's corollary, Root realized, offended Latin American pride. He hoped that Latin Americans would recognize that the Platt Amendment in regards to Cuba and the Roosevelt Corollary, which could apply to any part of Latin America, protected the Latin American republics as well as the United States. Within a few days Roosevelt acted in the Dominican Republic. U.S. warships entered Dominican ports, and American and Dominican officials signed a protocol giving the United States temporary control of the Caribbean country's customshouses. The Senate declined ratification, but after an Italian cruiser arrived in Dominican waters on March 14, Roosevelt acted without the Senate's approval. He negotiated a modus vivendi with the Dominican government by which an American citizen took control of its customs. The Roosevelt Corollary was firmly in place.

While Root was absent from Washington, Secretary Hay's health declined, and he died July 1, 1905. Root had long been Hay's choice as his successor, and the president, too, wished to have Root as secretary of state. Root accepted the appointment on July 7 and on July 19 took the oath of office. Besides the implementation of the Roosevelt Corollary, much diplomacy was in progress as he assumed his new responsibilities. The Russo-Japanese War overshadowed everything else, but a crisis over Morocco was nearly as dangerous, and there was fear it could lead to war between Germany and France. The president was actively engaged in efforts to secure settlement of the Russo-Japanese War and resolution of the Moroccan crisis, and he kept full control of these initiatives.

Although Roosevelt had applauded the Japanese military performance, he feared the consequences of a too great Japanese victory. He thought it best that Russia remained a Far Eastern power, and he hoped to achieve a balance of power in eastern Asia. He offered good offices—perhaps one should say he pressed them on Russia and Japan. The two belligerents accepted, and Roosevelt arranged a conference at the Portsmouth naval base in New Hampshire and Maine. The conference met from August 8 to September 5. The two powers had little difficulty agreeing on what was essentially a division of Manchuria. Japan received Port Arthur and other concessions in the Liaotung Peninsula and the South Manchurian Railroad. The Russians kept the Trans-Manchurian Railroad and also agreed not to interfere in Korea. The sticking point was the Japanese demand for an indemnity. The Russians refused to budge. Roosevelt suggested that the Russians cede the southern half of Sakhalin Island in lieu of an indemnity. Finally, the Japanese and Russians accepted this suggestion, and the treaty was signed on September 5, 1905. The Peace of Portsmouth was the greatest single achievement of Theodore Roosevelt's personal diplomacy. When it was announced in 1906 that he had won the Nobel Peace Prize, spokesmen of peace organizations in the United States and Europe applauded, but neither the president nor his secretary of state had any illusions about Portsmouth.

New incidents threatened continued Japanese-American friendship. When it was learned that Japan would receive no indemnity from Russia, thousands of Japanese, blaming the U.S. president, rioted in Tokyo and other cities of the island empire. In 1906 there came another unpleasant episode: the San Francisco school segregation crisis. As the people of San Francisco struggled to reconstruct their city after the great earthquake of April 13, 1906, their school board segregated Japanese students in public schools. In October the Japanese government protested vigorously, and the president and secretary of state admitted the justice of that protest. The president persuaded the school board to rescind its segregation order but only after agreeing to take steps to limit Japanese immigration. Root recognized that here was a problem that had to be resolved in such a way as not to offend Japanese sensibilities, and suggested that the Japanese themselves take steps to stop the immigration. The Japanese ambassador on February 24, 1907, presented a note in which his government promised to withhold passports for laborers planning to enter the United States, but that promise could solve only part of the problem. Many Japanese immigrants had passports to America's insular possessions or to other countries, and Japan recognized the right of the United States to deny admission to these people. Congress enacted legislation specifically giving the president that authority, and he promptly made use of it, issuing the necessary proclamation. Another Japanese note in February 1908 provided a firm basis for ending the immigration. Root's agreement with Japan—the so-called Gentlemen's Agreement—seemed a considerable achievement. Roosevelt, however, believed that the time had come for a display of American power. In December 1907 he ordered the U.S. battle fleet to begin a voyage round the world. The president's main purpose was to demonstrate the might of the U.S. navy to the Japanese.

Secretary Root, meanwhile, negotiated with Ambassador Takahira along the lines of the Taft–Katsura conversations of more than three years before, which gave Japan a free hand in Korea and recognized U.S. control of the Philippines. Root and Takahira exchanged notes on November 30, 1908, declaring that their governments respected the "existing status in the Pacific and the territorial possessions of each other." They pledged respect for the principles John Hay had made so important in Far Eastern diplomacy—maintenance of the Open Door in regards to the trade of China and respect for the independence and integrity of that country. They declared themselves "firmly resolved" "to respect" the territorial possessions of each other in the Pacific and pledged themselves to communicate with each other should any threat to the status quo occur. Root had secured reaffirmation of adherence to the Open Door policies and a promise to respect the American interests in the Philippines. The Japanese had also secured recognition of their interests in the Chinese Empire—and there was nothing in the agreement to interfere with their activities in Korea. Dropping pretenses, the Japanese annexed Korea in 1910.

Despite the traditional policy of nonentanglement, there was considerable American involvement in Europe during the Roosevelt administration. As noted, when Root became secretary of state, the president had in-hand negotiations in regards to Morocco. His initiative led to a conference in Algeciras, Spain, in January 1906. Root took a larger part in the Algeciras negotiations than in those at Portsmouth, drafting instructions for the U.S. delegate, Henry White, ambassador to Italy, and corresponding with him on several occasions before the conference closed. Apparently, though, the secretary had doubts about American involvement, for he wrote, "our interests are not sufficient to justify us in taking a leading part." The United States, voting with all the powers except Germany and Austria-

Hungary to give France and Spain everything they wanted in Morocco, contributed to German fears of diplomatic isolation. Thereafter, the Germans would resist any move that they thought would leave them in a position as embarrassing as the one in which they found themselves at Algeciras.

Root and Roosevelt in 1905 and 1906 brought many secretarial positions and the consular service under civil service rules, and this meant that examinations became necessary for appointments; it also meant that knowledge of international law became a necessary part of a candidate's preparation. Root was very interested in two conferences, both of which were scheduled for 1906, the third Pan-American Conference and the Second Hague Peace Conference. Both were concerned with international law and United States policy in the Americas, matters of special interest not only to Root but also to the new men he was bringing into the State Department, such as Chandler P. Anderson; Robert Bacon, who became assistant secretary of state on September 5, 1905; and James Brown Scott, who became solicitor of the department in 1906.

The Pan-American Conference was scheduled to meet in Rio de Janeiro in July 1906. Root was especially anxious that the United States take a conspicuous stand for hemispheric harmony at the conference, for there had been much criticism of the administration's actions in the Caribbean and of the Roosevelt Corollary. Root decided that it was necessary to make a strenuous effort to demonstrate the goodwill of the United States toward the Latin American republics and to secure from European powers significant gestures of respect for them. He thought that the United States should accept as far as possible a statement of Foreign Minister Luis M. Drago of Argentina—the "Drago Doctrine"—that collection of debts did not justify violation of a nation's sovereignty, and he thought the United States should secure admission of all the Latin American states to the Hague Conference (only Mexico and Brazil had been invited to the 1899 Conference and only Mexico attended). Breaking with the tradition that a secretary of state should not leave U.S. territory, Root went to Rio. The conference was a gala affair. More than most Latin Americans, the Brazilians approved American policies. They even built a meeting hall for the conference and named it the Monroe Palace. Root was feted everywhere. Despite ceremonies and celebrations, the secretary of state found time for the diplomatic initiatives that were his primary objectives. On July 31 he told the conference that he hoped all independent countries of the Western Hemisphere would attend the second Hague conference. There was considerable discussion of the Drago Doctrine. The conference adopted a cautious recommendation that the Second Hague Conference study the debt question.

The Second Hague Peace Conference was a more complicated matter than the Rio Conference, for it was to continue discussions begun at the Hague Conference of 1899, and it was to take up legal questions raised by the Russo-Japanese War. The Hague Conferences had begun with a famous invitation issued in 1898 by Nicholas II, czar of Russia. The only results of the Russian armaments proposal were three declarations. One forbade dumdum bullets; one prohibited using poison gas—still in an experimental stage—for five years; and another forbade throwing projectiles or explosives from balloons or kites for five years. The conference achieved more when it turned to codification of the laws of war. It concluded a convention on the laws of land warfare that gave the international law of land warfare wider sanctions and extended the Red Cross Convention to cover naval warfare. It was in regards to arbitration that the conference did its most conspicuous work, and the arbitration convention still ranks as one of the great projects for furthering peaceful settlement of international disputes in modern times. The convention declared that offers of mediation and good offices should never be considered unfriendly acts and established the Permanent Court of Arbitration, which was really only a panel of jurists from which nations could choose arbitrators.

At the Hague, the Roosevelt administration warmly endorsed the arbitration convention and the Permanent Court. Roosevelt arranged in 1902 to submit the first case to the court, a dispute with Mexico about claims, the case of the Pious Fund of the Californias, and he arranged in 1904 to have the court settle the question of whether or not Britain, Germany, and Italy—the three powers that blockaded Venezuela—should be paid before other creditor powers. In 1904 he told the visiting Interparliamentary Union that he would call another conference.

Root entered into office as secretary of state expecting to begin work on the program for the new conference. On September 13, 1905—eight days after signature of the Peace of Portsmouth—the Russian ambassador, Baron Rosen, called on the president. Awkwardly he told of the czar's special connection with the Hague Conference and of his continuing interest. Roosevelt told Rosen he was quite willing for the czar to take the initiative. Roosevelt believed this development gave the United States a freer hand, but he was mistaken. The Russians now had control of the program, and they soon announced that armaments would not be on the agenda. Yet, Roosevelt and Root had no difficulty in regards to including the Latin American republics. The Russians agreed to invite them, and then agreed to postpone the conference until 1907, when Root informed them that the Latin Americans would have difficulty finding enough experts in international law for two conferences in the same year.

The exclusion of armaments from the program of the Second Hague Peace Conference gave the impression of failure before the conference met. Root was prepared for inconclusive negotiations and warned the American delegates not to expect too much, but the conference negotiated 13 conventions, 11 of them concerned with the laws of war. Critics charged that the term "Peace Conference" was a misnomer, for the conference spent far more time trying to regulate warfare than in its consideration of peaceful means for settling international disputes. The conference revised the 1899 land warfare convention and the convention extending the Red Cross to the sea. A new convention concerned rights and duties of neutral powers and persons in land warfare. Another new convention required a declaration of war before beginning hostilities—a result of widespread disapproval of Japanese surprise attack on the Russian fleet in 1904. The conference differed from its predecessor in its far-reaching consideration of maritime warfare. Britain's opposition had prevented such a discussion in 1899. When the American delegation, acting in accord with instructions based on a tradition dating back to the American Revolution, asked acceptance of the doctrine that private property not contraband should be immune from capture at sea, the conference listened but did nothing more. Roosevelt and Root, although doubtful that this "small-navy" idea suited the interest of the United States as a great naval power, instructed the American delegates to reintroduce the proposal. Again there was a rebuff, but the British and other naval powers were, nonetheless, as anxious in 1907 for discussion of maritime laws of war as they had been uninterested in 1899. Maritime aspects of the Russo-

Japanese War had raised troubling questions, and naval authorities in many countries wanted answers. The 1907 conference negotiated seven new naval conventions. Convention XII, in the opinion of many delegates, was an achievement of great importance. It provided for an international prize court. Based on British and German proposals, this convention received strong support from the American delegates. Unfortunately, the conference could not agree on rules for capture at sea, and such an agreement was necessary before establishment of the court. The British began quiet consultation with other naval powers. In this way began a series of negotiations about naval warfare that would continue at the London Naval Conference of 1908–1909 and was still in progress when World War I began in 1914.

The American delegates at The Hague exercised more leadership in regards to arbitration than the laws of war at sea. Root had told them to do their best to bring about "a development of The Hague Tribunal into a permanent tribunal composed of judges who are judicial officers and nothing else." He wanted them to have adequate salaries and no other occupations, and he wanted them to be chosen from countries with different systems of law. The head of the American delegation, Joseph Hodges Choate, ably assisted by James Brown Scott, almost achieved Root's great objective. The conference agreed on a project for a Court of Arbitral Justice, which would indeed have been a court always in existence, in contrast to the Permanent Court of Arbitration. Unhappily, Choate and Scott were denied success from an unexpected quarter: the Latin Americans. Led by Ruy Barbosa of Brazil, they objected to any plan in which all nations could not be represented. Because 44 countries were represented in the conference, the court would have had to have 44 judges to please the Latin Americans. How could a court with so many judges be the kind of court lawyers wanted? There were long discussions of systems of representation, but every plan presented to the conference brought Latin American objections. Finally, the conference conceded defeat. It merely expressed the wish that when the problem of representation could be worked out the court would come into existence.

When it became apparent that the court convention could not be concluded, the U.S. delegates proposed a separate obligatory arbitration convention. The Americans recommended a convention that would have included a stipulation that the special agreements arranging arbitration be negotiated in accord with the constitutional needs of the concerned parties. Delegates from several countries favored the plan, but the German delegates, insisting they favored obligatory arbitration, found so much fault with every proposal that agreement became impossible. This disappointment, notwithstanding, the conference agreed on some slight changes in the arbitration convention, and a revised version became Hague Convention I, the Convention for the Pacific Settlement of International Disputes. Despite the failures of the arbitral court project and obligatory arbitration, the latter concept proved of value to the American delegates as they endeavored to secure action on contract debts. Hague Convention II forbade use of force to collect debts until arbitration had been offered and refused.

One of the most important negotiations of the conference of 1907 concerned future conferences. It required little effort to reach agreement. Although the Hague conferences were never declared a permanent institution the agreement on this point meant that in effect it was to be a permanent part of diplomatic machinery. The third conference was to convene after eight years, just as the second conference had convened eight years after the first. An International Preparatory Commission was to begin preparation of the program two years in advance of the third conference. To the satisfaction of the Americans, this meant that the Russians would not again control the program. American participation in the agreement for another conference was a conspicuous one and seemed to foreshadow a larger American role in Europe, but the American delegates disabused anyone of such an impression. Acting on Root's instructions, they repeated the reservation made by their predecessors in 1899 that in signing the Convention for the Pacific Settlement of Disputes:

> Nothing contained in this Convention shall be so construed as to require the United States of America to depart from its traditional policy of not intruding upon, interfering with, or entangling itself in the political questions of policy or international administration of any foreign state; nor shall anything contained in said Convention be construed to imply a relinquishment by the United States of its traditional attitude toward purely American questions.

There was little in the conventions to excite fears of senators; ratifications were easily secured. Root now asked the president to reconsider his attitude toward the Hay arbitration treaties. Roosevelt had withdrawn the treaties from the Senate rather than accept amendments requiring submission to it of special agreements under the treaties. Root advised meeting the Senate's objections by adding to the Hay treaties a requirement that special agreements be sent to the Senate for advice and consent. Only in this way could senatorial approval be secured, and Root thought that even such awkward treaties would have value. They would at least proclaim the interest of the United States in the peaceful settlement of disputes. Roosevelt saw Root's point, and the secretary began negotiations. Root and the French ambassador, Jean Jules Jusserand, signed the first treaty, on February 10, 1908. Ultimately, 24 such treaties were signed and ratified.

Root was quick to adapt the recent Hague experience to the Americas. Upon the invitation of the United States, representatives of the Central American states gathered in Washington in late 1907 to consider ways of maintaining peace. Root persuaded them to adapt the draft convention for a court of arbitral justice to their often-troubled region. They established such a court at Cartago, Costa Rica. Andrew Carnegie, upon Root's suggestion, provided funds with which to build a meeting hall for the court. As the Roosevelt presidency neared its end, the New York legislature elected Root a U.S. senator, and he resigned as secretary of the state on January 26, 1909. As he left the State Department the nation's press and political leaders lauded his service. No one was more lavish in his praise than President Roosevelt, who wrote that to "deny Root credit for what the Department of State has done because it has been done under me as President is a good deal like denying credit to Sherman and Sheridan because they were under Grant." The president gave him full credit for policy in Latin America and for the promotion of peace in the Western Hemisphere. Root also provided leadership in the advancement of international law and the idea of world court.

Moving from the State Department to the Senate meant no interruption in Root's efforts to further the Hague ideas. Shortly before leaving the department he drafted instructions for the American delegates at the London Naval Conference and had the satisfaction of learning, only a month after he became senator, that the Declaration of London had been signed. Root believed the declaration would make certain that the International Prize Court, which he had called the most important achievement of the Second Hague Peace conference, could at last be established, and he had hoped that court could be used to advance the world court idea. Root suggested that the prize court be vested with the powers of an arbitral court, but this was not done. (There were greater disappointments in regards to the declaration for Root and other proponents of codification of international law. The House of Lords blocked British ratification, and other nations delayed. The declaration was never ratified but was the subject of many controversies during World War I.)

Root, meanwhile, was actively involved with the Permanent Court of Arbitration at The Hague. On his last day as secretary of state, Root and Ambassador James Bryce signed an agreement under the terms of the Anglo-American arbitration treaty of 1908 to refer the controversy over the North Atlantic Fisheries to The Hague. Upon President Taft's request, the senator in 1910 served as U.S. counsel before the Permanent Court of Arbitration. The court's award was a series of compromises that seemed to favor Britain rather than the United States, but Root and the president both decided the award really was quite satisfactory. Root believed the conflict essentially a dispute between two groups of fishermen rather than governments, and the settlement promised an end to their squabbling.

The fisheries arbitration was only one of several events that made 1910 a banner year in Root's life. President Taft appointed him a member of the Permanent Court of Arbitration, and a new organization for peace came into existence, which Root was to head for 15 years, the Carnegie Endowment for International Peace. At once the Endowment began an active campaign for peace and justice under the direction of the indefatigable James Brown Scott, its secretary.

Secretary of State Philander C. Knox negotiated arbitration treaties with Britain and France, which provided for arbitration of all justiciable disputes. Root decided that it was again time for restraint and proposed an amendment withdrawing from arbitration "the traditional attitudes of the United States concerning American questions or other purely governmental policy." Other amendments followed; the Senate voted ratification. Taft decided not to ratify after hearing of British and French objections. In 1913 Root served as president of the Permanent Court of Arbitration in a case involving Britain, Spain, and Portugal, and at the close of that year the Norwegian Storthing awarded him the Nobel Peace Prize for 1912.

Despite constant involvement in matters pertaining to peace and international law, Root was an influential spokesman for the conservative viewpoint in the Senate. As chairman of the Republican National Convention in 1912 he held the convention in line for President Taft and watched the Roosevelt delegates walk out. The party split virtually ended his friendship with Roosevelt and made possible the election of Woodrow Wilson. Root kept a watchful eye on diplomacy during the Wilson administration. He gave the president support in one of his first diplomatic controversies—his successful campaign to persuade Congress to repeal discriminatory tariffs on the Panama Canal as violations of treaty obligations, campaign promises notwithstanding. Thereafter, he was often a severe critic of Wilson in regards to both the Mexican Revolution and the European War. When the United States declared war in 1917, Root gave loyal support. Later that year, on the president's request, the 72-year-old former senator and secretary of state headed a special mission to revolutionary Russia, which traveled across North America, the Pacific Ocean, and the Eurasian landmass to Petrograd. It is one of the best-remembered moments of the diplomacy of World War I, but it accomplished little.

At no time during the war did Root lay aside for long his advocacy of courts, conferences, and international law. Early in the Wilson administration he prodded Secretary of State William Jennings Bryan into initiating negotiations to establish the International Preparatory Commission to prepare for the Third Hague Peace Conference and to renew the Root arbitration treaties. The outbreak of the war in Europe made the ideas of the Hague System seem inadequate to Root for a moment, but he did not long think in this vein. On February 11, 1915, he wrote to Charles Francis Adams that events were "tending irresistibly to Tennyson's Parliament of Man, and the Federation of the World." When an American organization called the League to Enforce Peace formed later in the year under Taft's presidency and began calling for a new world order that would use force if necessary to maintain peace, Root was interested but declined invitations to join.

The framing of the Covenant of the League of Nations at the Paris Peace Conference in January and February 1919 immediately caused contradictory reactions among American political leaders, and the leaders of the Wilson administration were especially interested in Root's opinions, for they knew they could have an important effect on ratification of the Versailles Treaty with the League Covenant attached. In late March 1919 while President Wilson was for a second time en route to Paris, Acting Secretary of State Frank Polk asked Root to suggest amendments to the League Covenant. Root at once complied. One amendment called on signatory powers to obligate themselves to refer all disputes "of a justiciable character" to the Permanent Court of Arbitration or to the Court of Arbitral Justice "when established, or to some other Arbitral Tribunal." Root's most important amendment concerned the Monroe Doctrine. It noted that the United States would accede "to the wish of the European states that it join its power to theirs for the preservation of the general peace," but the United States would sign only with the understanding that nothing in the document be construed as a relinquishment by the United States "of its traditional attitude towards purely American questions," or to require submission of its policies toward such matters (including immigration) "to the revision or recommendation of other powers."

Root opposed the idea of collective security expressed as a guarantee of independence and territorial integrity in Article X of the Covenant, but did foresee large benefits from the League. In a letter to Will H. Hays, chairman of the Republican National Committee on March 29, 1919, he fully explained his position. There were a multitude of "justiciable" disputes—financial claims, fishing rights, some boundary problems, and so on. Arbitral tribunals had been dealing with them successfully for many years, and an improved court system could do even better. On the other hand, there were political questions no court could touch. Although he was not willing for the new organization to have the kind of authority Wilson wanted it to have he stressed that:

> The great and essential thing about the plan contained in the "Constitution for a League of Nations" is that it makes international conferences on political questions compulsory in times of danger; that it brings together such conferences upon the call of officers who represent all the powers, and makes it practically impossible for any nation to keep out of them.

Root's suggestions were an important factor in Wilson's decision to ask the conference to amend the Covenant, and this the conference did. Root testified before the Senate, urging stronger reservations, including exclusion of Article X—the guarantee article—but tried to convince Republicans to support the League. He himself in 1920, accompanied by James Brown Scott, went to The Hague on the invitation of the League of Nations to consider plans for the new world court. Root and Scott and a small group of international jurists were able to complete the work of the Second Hague Peace Conference. The Permanent Court of International Justice was founded by the League on the basis of the Court of Arbitral Justice project of 1907. Root looked forward to its early establishment but believed that American participation in the court made American membership in the League necessary. He became one of the 31 pro-League Republicans who signed a declaration that the best way to ensure U.S. membership in the League was to elect Warren G. Harding.

Root served as a delegate to the Washington Conference of 1921–1922 on Naval Armaments and Far Eastern questions, doing good work with a submarine convention and sometimes recommending caution as the conference under American leadership transformed the Open Door into a multinational treaty. When it was learned that a nation could belong to the World Court while remaining out of the League, Root and other prominent Americans urged ratification of the world court protocol. Harding was willing, but the proposal met with obstacles in the Senate. Calvin Coolidge had the same difficulties. On his 84th birthday, February 15, 1929, Root again set sail for The Netherlands and there helped negotiate changes in the court statute to facilitate U.S. entry. President Herbert Hoover had no more luck with the court matter than Harding and Coolidge. President Franklin D. Roosevelt had no greater success than his Republican predecessors. When Root died on February 7, 1937, the matter was still unresolved. Eight years later, on July 28, 1945, the Senate voted ratification of the United Nations charter and the attached statute for the International Court of Justice. The ideals and arduous labor of Elihu Root, Woodrow Wilson, and other men of goodwill of the early part of the twentieth century were integral parts of the great documents the Senate approved that day.

BIBLIOGRAPHICAL ESSAY

The most important unpublished materials pertaining to Elihu Root's career are in the Elihu Root papers in the Library of Congress. The papers of William McKinley, John Hay, Theodore Roosevelt, Chandler P. Anderson, Robert Lansing, William Howard Taft, and Woodrow Wilson, also in the Library of Congress, contain many Root documents, as does the James Brown Scott collection in the Georgetown University Library. The files of the War and State Departments in the National Archives also include important records concerning Root's service as secretary of war and secretary of state.

The Root documents include dispatches and instructions in the *Papers Relating to the Foreign Relations of the United States* and numerous letters in Elting E. Morison (ed.), *The Letters of Theodore Roosevelt* (8 vols., 1951–1954). Robert Bacon and James Brown Scott edited eight volumes of Root's addresses and papers, which they published at Harvard University Press. They are: *Addresses on Government and Citizenship* (1916); *Addresses on International Subjects* (1916); *The Military and Colonial Policy of the United States* (1916); *Miscellaneous Addresses* (1917); *North Atlantic Coast*

Fisheries Arbitration at The Hague (1917); *Latin America and the United States* (1917); *The United States and the War, The Mission to Russia, Political Addresses* (1915); and *Men and Policies* (1925).

Philip C. Jessup, *Elihu Root* (2 vols., 1938) is a distinguished study of the entire Root career based on Jessup's interviews with Root as well as intensive research in his papers. Richard W. Leopold, *Elihu Root and the Conservative Tradition* (1954) is a brilliant interpretation of Root's career in both domestic politics and international relations.

There have been a number of brief biographies. James Brown Scott, long a close associate and friend of the former secretary, published "Elihu Root: Secretary of State July 7, 1905 to January 27, 1909" in Samuel Flagg Bemis (ed.), *The American Secretaries of State and Their Diplomacy* (vol. IX, 1928). Philip C. Jessup published a brief sketch of Root in the *Dictionary of American Biography* (vol. 22, Supplement Two, 1958). Charles W. Toth's "Elihu Root (1905–1909)" is in Norman Graebner (ed.), *An Uncertain Tradition: American Secretaries of State in the Twentieth Century* (1961).

Books of particular importance for Root's career in international relations include the following: Russell F. Weigley, *History of the United States Army* (1967); Warren F. Kuchl, *Seeking World Order: The United States and International Organization to 1920* (1969); Calvin D. Davis, *The United States and the Second Hague Peace Conference: American Diplomacy and International Organization 1899–1914* (1976); and Sondra R. Herman, *Eleven Against War: Studies in American Internationalist Thought. 1898–1921* (1969).

Calvin D. Davis

DEAN RUSK (1909–1994)

Served 1961–1969
Appointed by President John F. Kennedy
Continued in office under President Lyndon B. Johnson
Democrat

Dean Rusk probably never read a poem written by the Nobel Prize winning Polish author Wistawa Szymborska that begins—"After every war someone has to tidy up. Things won't pick themselves up, after all." These few lines arguably describe the role that Rusk sought to fill as a major participant in the conduct of U.S. foreign policy from 1945 to1968. Out of the chaos created by the Second World War, the future secretary of state wanted a world order in which Hitlerian aggression, later expanded to include its communist cousin, could not reoccur. Reasoning statesmen, working with a United Nations bolstered by the rule of law, would form the first Wilsonian bulwark. If that battle line did not hold, than a coalition of Western, democratic governments would stop aggressive acts, preferably by collective security, but failing that, by unilateral American actions. No mistaken Munichs, let alone unacceptable Dunkirks, would mark the path to peace if only resolute leaders would defend the borders of democracy and freedom against transgressors.

Born on February 9, 1909, to farm parents down on their financial luck in Georgia, but highly educated and possessed of good instincts, Rusk prospered in his intellectual development. His father, trained in the ministry, contributed a foundation of strong southern Presbyterianism and an even stronger work ethic to his son. A southerner to his core, Dean admired and came to share many of the ideas and principles of his fellow southerner, Woodrow Wilson. At Davidson College in North Carolina, he further imbued even more of the moral approach when he attended his father's alma mater. His religious and political beliefs grew so important that he considered becoming a missionary to China. Although he finally followed the path of worldly rather than religious internationalism, a crusading, missionary zeal and a continued interest in Asia always remained.

His scholarly bent led the young Phi Beta Kappa to the Rhodes scholar competition and then successfully to Oxford University in 1932. There his attraction to international law and its promise of an orderly world blossomed. World events at the time strongly influenced his development as he watched the rise of Germany,

Italy, and Japan. He not only came to oppose their aggressive actions but also criticized the Western powers' policies of appeasement. Never a pacifist, and enhancing the traditional southern admiration for the military, he had hoped that the democracies would take active roles and even go to war, if necessary, to stop the tides of aggression. Here, then, was a young man who had come to important decisions about world affairs at an early point in his intellectual growth and in essence held to those convictions, aided by rationalizations, for the remainder of his life.

After graduation in 1934, he made a failed attempt to join the Department of State. Accepting a position at Mills College in California, he became a professor and specialized in classes on foreign relations. Munich and the failure of the League of Nations to halt aggression greatly affected him, and he left academic affairs to join the U.S. Army as a captain in 1940. By 1941 he held a position in military intelligence in Washington, D.C., rose to become a major, and even more important, established himself as an expert on South Asia, Southeast Asia, China, and the Western Pacific. This led, in turn, to important contacts with Generals George Marshall and Joseph Stilwell. By 1944 he was deputy chief of staff for the China-Burma-India theater. It is sufficient to state that the war reaffirmed his beliefs in the U.S. mission to save the world from chaos and led him to make his mark by joining that crusade.

In the last days of the Second World War, in July 1945, Rusk was posted to the War Department's Operations Division, where a combination of hard work, knowledge, and chance placed him in a position to share in a decision of great importance for the future of Korea. The Soviet Union and the United States had agreed that they would jointly, from the north and the south, liberate Korea, but had not yet decided on the division line between their respective military occupations. When the Soviets asked for a recommended line, Rusk and his colleagues suggested the 38th parallel. It became, of course, one of the most famous and controversial temporary borders of the entire twentieth century, and one that Rusk defended with a passion.

By 1947 Rusk had earned the full support of George Marshall, who appointed him director of the Office of Political Affairs in the Department of State. The young Georgian now entered into a very competitive institution that included such luminaries as George Kennan, Dean Acheson, and Robert Lovett along with Paul Nitze. His area of specialization, Asia, placed him at a disadvantage in that Europe was at the center of U.S. policies and the aforementioned Europeanists were thus in the seats of power. Further, although Rusk was not an international lawyer, he also represented a legalist approach that with the rise of the Soviet threat took a second chair to those who believed that a military buildup might attract more Soviet attention than appeals to the rule of law. And finally, although Truman respected Rusk, he was far more open to the realist Europeanists than to the more idealistic camp. Rusk, in a lower position of power, did not push his opinions once a policy decision was made and then wisely displayed support and loyalty to a president to whom loyalty was important. Indeed, that value was also highly prized by Rusk.

Rusk left the Department of State in 1952 to become president of the Rockefeller Foundation. Although he had many Republican supporters, such as John Foster Dulles, as a political appointee, Rusk doubted that the expected Republican administration would retain him in the Department of State. This new position in New York not only provided him with a much needed financial boost but also kept him in the public view in a city whose interest in foreign affairs was second only to that of Washington. The Foundation's international programs fulfilled his desire to do good for others in the world. His report on U.S. foreign policy in 1959, calling for an active, dynamic president, struck a chord with many members of the prestigious and influential Council on Foreign Affairs, also housed in New York.

By November 1960, when the victorious Kennedy was looking for a secretary of state, Rusk represented a known quantity in the U.S. foreign policy establishment. His qualities of maturity, experience, and substance, may have appealed to a pragmatic John F. Kennedy. The president's first choice, however, was not Rusk but Robert Lovett, who declined but recommended Rusk. Although Rusk was probably among the top half-dozen candidates, it is clear that Rusk was not well known by Kennedy, who is reputed to have remarked, "Who the hell is Dean Rusk?" The Georgian, however, had few enemies, important contacts with Southern congressmen, and the reputation of being a loyal subordinate. The latter was an important asset. Kennedy, a man who excelled in the making of images and wanted to be known as *the* leader, did not want any foreign policy competitors in the area he planned to dominate himself. The hard-working, competent, unassuming Rusk may well have seemed the perfect choice for Kennedy. The president would be the famous architect and the secretary of state would be the hidden builder.

The extent of the builder's contributions were to be even more obscured by the secretary's working methods. Rusk claimed that he had private talks with Kennedy and later with Johnson, and that it was on those occasions that he gave the bulk of his advice to the presidents. Much later, he wrote, "Documents are surrounded by much discussion among those handling policy, and those discussions are, of course, nowhere on the record." He also stated that over 2,100,000 cables went out from the Department of State with his signature on them and, "of these I personally saw fewer than one percent." Even on the available Cuban missile crisis tapes, Rusk is a somewhat shadowy figure, often absent. Others, such as Robert Kennedy, Robert McNamara, and McGeorge Bundy, also had the president's ear on foreign policy issues. Rusk was not in the inner circle; in the Johnson administration, he was. All of this means that it is not an easy task to pin down what advice Rusk gave, when he gave it, and whether it was followed. The president, of course, left few records of those discussions. Nor did Rusk, who placed a high value on confidentiality, so the exact extent of the secretary's influence is thus unclear.

The first major crisis of the Kennedy administration involved a substantial failure at the Bay of Pigs in Cuba. Kennedy, who was informed in November of this top-secret U.S. attempt to use Cuban refugees to overthrow Fidel Castro, could have stopped this Eisenhower administration initiative, but chose to continue the project. He did not, however, mention it to his secretary of state until January 22. Rusk, who had doubts about the plan, found that the president was working through one of Rusk's subordinates. Mortified that Kennedy would follow such a procedure, Rusk held his tongue, and it was not until the first week in April that Rusk told the president that he opposed the operation. By that time the president had already decided to go ahead; the events began to unfold on April 15. Kennedy decided to cancel a second air strike, and the Cuban brigade went forth to its doom on the morning of April 17. Kennedy, although he publicly accepted the responsibility, believed his advisers had failed him, and Robert Kennedy agreed. The best and brightest had stumbled. Rusk loyally accepted the rebuke and vowed to look at military proposals much closer in the future.

It is arguable that the initial failure in Cuba led to a series of events and consequences that might well not have occurred had the administration either not gone forward with the project or not bungled it so badly. First, in the conference between Kennedy and Khrushchev at Vienna in June, the Soviet premier was harsh and intimidating with the new president. Perhaps he judged him as weak and inexperienced at the Bay of Pigs; indeed, he taunted Kennedy about the failure. Secondly, as a result of the Kennedy's obsession with Castro, a covert operation, Operation Mongoose, was designed to eliminate Castro, and a series of military exercises were held in the Caribbean. And, last, and most important, the Cuban Missile Crisis of October 1962 had its beginnings in these prior events.

The Cuban Missile Crisis, of course, was the single most important foreign affairs crisis of the Kennedy administration. Human intelligence reports began to surface in August that Soviet missiles were being sent to Cuba. Rumors were confirmed on August 29 with photos taken by U-2 planes. The president decided that something had to be done and formed an Executive Committee of his leading advisers to discuss options. The meetings of the ExComm group have become the source of lore and legend, but it is important to note that many substantial discussions took place outside the confines of its rooms and tape recorders. The recorders were not voice activated as they were in the Johnson administration, but were started, and ended, only when the president pushed the secret buttons. The book, *The Thirteen Days*, by Robert Kennedy (actually written by Ted Sorenson) is not always a reliable source nor are the tapes. Nevertheless, although the voice of Rusk on the tapes is usually that of one who was well prepared and had given thought to what he was going to say, he was clearly not one of the leaders of the discussions. Speaking with greater authority were McNamara, George Ball, Llewellyn "Tommy" Thompson, McGeorge Bundy, Robert Kennedy, and of course, the president.

Rusk, at the initial meeting on September 24, called for "immediate and appropriate action." He, like others, feared Soviet threats in Berlin in response to any U.S. actions. At first the secretary saw only two options: a quick air strike without warning against the missile sites or immediate approaches through the Organization of American States and the United Nations, but characteristically soon swung to the latter stance. He then favored a full examination of the use of some sort of blockade against Cuba. When Adlai Stevenson suggested that the United States propose an exchange involving the withdrawal of U.S. missiles from Turkey and a U.S withdrawal from Guantanamo Bay, in exchange for the removal of the Soviet missiles in Cuba, the president immediately rejected that recommendation. Rusk now focused on the blockade and suggested that the term *quarantine* might be a better choice, probably because the term *blockade* had certain legal connotations in international law that limited U.S. actions whereas *quarantine* did not.

Kennedy, on the evening of October 22, delivered his address to the nation and the world in which he called on the Soviet Union to immediately cease and desist. He also promised that if any of the missiles were launched from Cuba against any nation in the Western Hemisphere, it would be considered an attack by the Soviet Union requiring a full retaliatory response on the USSR itself. To state that many people in the world were extraordinarily frightened by that message would be an understatement. Critics have argued that a nonpublic negotiation with the Soviet Union might have been a wiser alternative to the public showdown that the president's address created. Such a route might have been usually suggested by a secretary of state; the tapes do not reflect that Rusk proposed that method at that time.

As the quarantine tightened, the ExComm group concentrated on its workings. When the news came in that some of the Soviet ships were either stopping or even turning around, Rusk, in an aside to Bundy, made his famous remark that "We were eyeball to eyeball, and I think the other fellow just blinked." Despite the apparent success of the quarantine in preventing additional Soviet materials from entering Cuba, there was still the problem of how to get the already situated missiles out. Thoughts again turned to air strikes and what to do about the U.S. missiles in Turkey. After considerable tension, the U.S. government decided to accept the first letter that Khrushchev had sent, and not the second one, as a basis of agreement with the Soviet Union. It was Rusk, perhaps prepped by Ambassador Raymond Hare in Ankara, who proposed that the United States tell the Soviet leader that although no public deal could be made involving the U.S. missiles in Turkey, the president would, in fact, remove them as soon as possible after the present crisis was resolved. The actual public arrangement provided that the United States would not invade Cuba if the Soviet Union would remove its missiles from Cuba. A further secret deal, not revealed to the U.S. public for almost 17 years, involved a Kennedy promise to remove the missiles from Turkey. Kennedy, apparently, according to Soviet sources, feared that a public release of such a deal might adversely affect his political future.

The Cuban Missile crisis was over. Many years later, Rusk claimed that he had made approaches through the United Nations to have the organization settle the dispute, but the details remain sparse.

Despite Rusk's loyal support of President Kennedy's policies, other insiders complained among themselves that he was not strong enough in debating the military's influence, especially on Vietnam. Some evidence exists that if Kennedy were reelected in 1964, he planned to replace Rusk with Robert McNamara. Like all the plethora of reports about what Kennedy would have done had he only lived, this one, too, dramatic though it would have been, did not happen, and Rusk continued as secretary of state.

With the occupation of the Oval Office by Lyndon Johnson, however, Rusk not only was not asked to leave, but both his status and influence increased. Rusk found in the new president a fellow southerner who both respected his abilities and listened to his advice. The secretary moved from the outer circle of advisors into the inner ring. It must have been a gratifying moment, as Johnson's outlook was quite similar to his own. Although Rusk always supported the president in public, he often disagreed and differed from Johnson on many issues. He was not a "yes" man, but once a decision was made, he carried out Johnson's policies.

Under both Kennedy and Johnson, Rusk opposed any sort of accommodation with Communist China. In private he might admit that U.S. policies were too rigid, but neither he nor the two presidents he served wanted to stir up potential political struggles with right-wing supporters in Congress. Neither had a profile of courage on that issue; it took Richard Nixon and different circumstances to achieve that goal. Besides, it is doubtful that Rusk could ever have moved away from his visceral dislike of the Communist Chinese, which stemmed, in large part, from his memory of them killing U.S. soldiers in the Korean War. He also regarded them as unworthy rulers of the China he had known. Although he held a degree of respect for the Nationalist Chiang Kai-shek in 1949, he had supported the Truman administration's decision not to intervene in the Chinese civil war because he believed that the corruption and inability of the Nationalist regime to solve China's problems had caused it to lose the support of the Chinese people. Yet, he also could not support the Communists or their leader Mao because to Rusk, they did not represent the Chinese people but a foreign (Soviet) ideology. Mao was regarded as a major villain, certainly the equal of Hitler and Stalin. The Chinese Communist support of North Vietnam intensified Rusk's belief in the importance of saving South Vietnam from the power of Communism. He was careful, however, to caution Johnson against the use of unlimited military power in Vietnam lest the Chinese use it as an excuse to openly enter the war against the United States.

It is Vietnam, of course, that is the core issue with Rusk's critics. During the Kennedy administration he supported the escalation of U.S. military advisers from 1,600 to 16,000. Some years later, in retirement, he lamented with considerable hindsight that he had not suggested to Kennedy, ever indecisive on Vietnam, that the United States show its determination and get the job done by sending not just 15,000 more troops but 98,000 troops. Rusk, also, along with Kennedy, Henry Cabot Lodge, and others, shares the responsibility for the coup that led to the overthrow and assassination of Ngo Dinh Diem in 1963. Few today would argue it was a wise decision. The secretary of state also stands at the very center of a historical controversy over whether Kennedy, if he had lived, would have withdrawn the United States from Vietnam. Rusk unequivocally stated, again and again, that the president had at no time indicated to him that he intended to withdraw the United States from Vietnam.

Under President Johnson, Rusk continued to support the escalation of U.S. troops into Vietnam. He believed that sooner or later North Vietnam would back down. Johnson himself searched for new strategies, but could find no other course of action that did not involve either an admission of U.S. failure or the end of an independent South Vietnam under Communist control. Rusk displayed even less enthusiasm than Johnson for hopes that successful negotiations with North Vietnam might occur. He agreed, in general, with the advice of the so-called wise men, senior advisers like Dean Acheson, that the United States must continue its policies. Even Rusk's closest friend in the Department of State, George Ball, could not change the secretary's mind. The secretary was convinced that biased media coverage at the time of the Tet Offensive in 1968 was influencing public opinion against the war effort and unsuccessfully advised the president not to give in to the press criticisms by beginning new negotiations. Stubborn as ever, he was prepared to stay the course.

In his most important postsecretarial statement, he admitted that he had made two major mistakes on Vietnam. First, he had underestimated the tenacity of the North Vietnamese. Second and even more importantly, he had overestimated the patience of the American people. If the first was largely but not completely unforeseeable, because the North Vietnamese fight against the French might have given an indication of their resolve, the second was not. The Korean War experience, which had impacted him in so many other ways, might have warned him about the impatience of the U.S. public with long drawn out, inconclusive wars.

If failure were written all over Johnson and Rusk with regard to Vietnam, one cannot make the same argument with respect to Europe. Johnson used his old

"Master of the Senate" skills with caution and wisdom to effectively lead the Western Alliance. Thomas Alan Schwartz argues that Johnson's "conduct of policy toward Europe deserves consideration as one of the most important achievements of his administration." In the single most important relationship, that of the United States and the Soviet Union, there were, unlike the Kennedy administration, no dramatic crises or marches to the brink of war, or overheated calls to defend the frontiers of civilization. Johnson and Rusk avoided that kind of rhetoric and worked patiently for détente with the Soviet Union and a relaxation of tensions within the central area of conflict, Europe. Johnson did not try to forge a special personal relationship with the Soviet leaders. However, Rusk and the Soviet ambassador to the United States, Anatoly Dobrynin, worked very effectively with each other. Rusk and Johnson were very proud of their accomplishments in Europe and were especially pleased with the Nuclear Nonproliferation Treaty.

There were the usual ups and downs between the United States and its major allies, Great Britain, Germany, and France. It was, of course, U.S. relations with the latter and its leader, Charles de Gaulle, that led to the greatest fissure within the alliance. To state that de Gaulle had illusions of grandeur and resented American power in Europe is an understatement. Rusk and most of Johnson's other advisers wanted the president to take a tough stance against de Gaulle's designs. Relations were so strained at one point that in a famous conversation between de Gaulle and Rusk, the former stated that he wanted every U.S. soldier out of France. The secretary, known for his bon mots, asked if that included dead Americans in military cemeteries. Johnson, much wiser in this case, ignored his advisers, treated de Gaulle with respect, and let the French leader become the victim of his own ambitions. Although the French did withdraw from the alliance, this action did not, as expected by many observers, lead to a break between the United States and France.

Rusk left office in 1969. He had served longer than any other secretary of state in U.S. history with the exception of Cordell Hull. Until 1984 he was a professor of law at the University of Georgia. Ten years later in 1994 he died at age 85. In 1995 the United States resumed diplomatic relations with Vietnam.

BIBLIOGRAPHICAL ESSAY

The best work on Rusk is Thomas W. Zeiler's *Dean Rusk: Defending the American Mission Abroad* (2000). Still useful is *Waging Peace and War: Dean Rusk in the Truman, Kennedy, and Johnson Years* (1988), by Thomas J. Schoenbaum. Rusk did not write any formal memoirs, but a book with his son, Richard Rusk, *As I Saw It* (1990), offers limited recollections. Only George Ball, among all of the Kennedy/Johnson advisers, offers important observations on Rusk in his *The Past Has Another Pattern* (1982). Thomas Alan Schwartz's *Lyndon Johnson and Europe* (2003) presents a positive image of the president's policies in Europe.

Thomas H. Buckley

WILLIAM H. SEWARD (1801–1872)

Served 1861–1869
Appointed by President Abraham Lincoln
Continued in office under President Andrew Johnson
Republican

William Henry Seward was born in the hamlet of Florida, Orange County, New York, on May 16, 1801. Samuel Sweezy Seward, Henry's father, was of Anglo-Welsh descent, whereas Henry's mother, Mary Jennings Seward, was of Irish descent. Samuel Seward was a doctor, merchant, and land speculator who invested his money shrewdly, so at his death in 1849, he left his family over $300,000. Mary was a kind person and loved by her family and neighbors. A few years before her death in 1843, William Seward responded to a letter written by a man who had disagreed with Seward's defense of the Irish in the United States. Seward defended the character of Irish Americans and said he could do no other without dishonoring his mother.

With the strong support of his father, Seward received the best schooling in Orange County and at the age of 15 entered Union College in Schenectady, New York, graduating in July 1820. Seward had begun to read law in 1819 and was admitted to the New York bar in October 1822. Early in 1823, Seward became a law partner of Judge Elijah Miller in Auburn, county seat of Cayuga County. Seward married Frances Adeline Miller, the daughter of his law partner, on October 20, 1824. In the late summer of 1823, while traveling through Rochester, New York, Seward met Thurlow Weed, then editor of a local newspaper. Their political partnership did not begin until late 1827, but once established, it was the cornerstone of Seward's career until the complete triumph of the Radical Republicans in New York State in 1866.

Seward was attracted to politics early. Politics in the 1820s were confused and largely built on personalism and factionalism. Seward condemned the Federalists for their carping during the War of 1812 and did not support DeWitt Clinton for president in 1812. During the early 1820s Seward supported Martin Van Buren, who was building up his political machine, the Albany Regency. Yet in 1824, Seward supported John Quincy Adams for president and DeWitt Clinton for governor. The reasons for this shift are not plain. Seward denounced the corruption of the Regency in 1824, and he lived in a community that favored education and internal improvements, both strongly supported by Adams. Seward's father-in-law was a National Republican and a strong supporter of Adams. Finally, the Regency did not dominate Cayuga County and there was resentment over Van Buren's increasingly authoritarian rule.

Seward was elected chairman of a National Republican convention in 1828, but hitched his wagon to the rising star of anti-Masonic political activity that was sweeping New York. Thurlow Weed was one of the leaders of a new statewide anti-Masonic party. The defeat of Adams's bid for reelection in 1828 demonstrated the decline of the National Republicans in New York State, whereas anti-Masonry continued to grow in strength. Weed, soon to be known as "The Dictator," had begun to broaden the anti-Masonic political platform to include a protective tariff and internal improvements. Seward helped Weed in the nomination of anti-Masonic candidates in the 1830 party convention, and Weed secured Seward's nomination of the anti-Masons for the state senate in the seventh district. Seward won the election by 2,000 votes.

Seward's actions in the senate prefigured his work on behalf of the Whig party. He argued for penal reform, attacked monopolies, supported railroad charters, and wanted railroads and canals to be owned by the state. Seward strongly supported the rechartering of the Bank of the United States but voted for resolutions supporting President Jackson in the nullification crisis of 1833. Seward and Weed worked together to form a state Whig party organization in 1833–1834. The new party was held together by a dislike of Jackson and his policies and a strong animosity toward Van Buren and his political machine. Although the new Whig party was split by anti-Masonic and National Republican factions and faced a very strong and veteran Democratic party, Seward enthusiastically accepted the Whig nomination for governor in 1834. Although he was defeated, he ran well and thus became a leader of the New York State Whig party.

Seward was elected the first Whig governor of New York in 1838 as a result of the continuing effects of the Panic of 1837. He and Weed worked as a team to organize and run the state government. As governor, Seward supported the enlargement of the Erie Canal, the building of three railway lines, the establishment of a state board of education, schools for immigrant and Negro children, and prison reform. Further, Seward refused to remand three black seamen who had tried to help a slave escape from Virginia. Seward found himself in a similar situation in regard to Georgia and South Carolina. These controversies identified Seward as a leader of the antislavery movement, and his battle over education for the children of immigrants established him as an opponent of nativism.

Seward was reelected in 1840 as part of the Harrison landslide and soon was embroiled in a controversy with President John Tyler, Secretary of State Daniel Webster, and British Minister of Foreign Affairs Lord Palmerston over the New York murder trial of Alexander McLeod, a Canadian official involved in the attack on the U.S. ship, the *Caroline*, which had been carrying supplies to Canadian rebels. Seward insisted that the trial take place, yet cooperated with the federal government to keep the Canadian–United States border peaceful.

Seward decided against running for a third term but still pushed the legislature to support his internal improvements program. He was ignored, as the Democrats regained both houses of the New York legislature in the elections of 1841 and went on to win the governorship in 1842. Seward witnessed his successor's inauguration and wished him well publicly, which broke precedent and shocked the assembled audience.

This respite from politics was timely because Seward had not given sufficient time to either his financial affairs or his legal practice. In 1842, he owed $200,000. Seward developed his law practice and devoted himself to paying off his debts. He was able to derive a handsome income from real estate investments, and his legal retainers continued to grow, to the point that he was debt-free and able to give up his law practice by the mid-1850s.

By the mid-1840s Seward was convinced that slavery was the great political issue. To his mind, the United States needed to begin instituting manumission, with compensation and without revolutionary upheaval. This would benefit both slaves and masters and the country as a whole. Seward was a pragmatic moderate. That is to say, he thought slavery a moral wrong—for he deemed it impossible for a human being to be converted into property by any law or constitution—yet he wanted slavery to end with the least possible damage to the country.

Seward had been against the Mexican War but had advised congressional Whigs to vote for war appropriations. He was dubious of General Zachary Taylor as the Whig nominee, but campaigned for him vigorously once Taylor was nominated and was happy to see the old general victorious in November 1848. Weed worked for months to get Seward elected to the U.S. Senate, and Weed had his way when the New York legislature elected Seward to the post on February 6, 1849.

From the beginning Seward was seen to be a leader of the antislave forces in the U.S. Senate. What was worse, from the Southern Whig point of view, Seward soon became a trusted advisor to President Taylor and strongly supported the president's plan to admit California as a free state. Seward gave his famous "Higher Law" speech, in which he denounced Clay's proposed compromise in 1850. This speech, and his "Irrepressible Conflict" speech of 1858, marked Seward as a radical on the slave question in the eyes not only of Democrats but of conservative Whigs and Republicans as well. This was ironic, given his belief that Emancipation, though inevitable, should occur constitutionally and slowly, with compensation to the slave owners.

With Taylor's death in 1850, Millard Fillmore, an opponent of Seward and Weed, became president of the United States. Fillmore wholeheartedly supported Clay's compromise, and under the stewardship of Illinois Senator Stephen Douglas the Compromise of 1850 was passed and signed into law. Seward supported the law and with the deaths of Clay and Webster became the leader of the Whig party, just as the party was disintegrating beyond hope. General Winfield Scott's presidential nomination by the Whigs and his defeat in the general election was blamed on Seward by most Whigs.

The passage of the Kansas–Nebraska Act in May 1854 drove the final stake through the heart of the Whig party. Seward, though, was unsure whether any new party would be viable, and he and Weed wanted to keep the New York State Whig party functioning so that Seward could at least be reelected to the Senate. Weed was able to secure Seward's reelection by the state legislature on February 6, 1855. In the summer 1855 Weed made contacts with Republicans throughout the state, and in late September 1855 Seward and Weed and the New York State Whig party moved as a body into the Republican Party.

Seward led the Republican fight in the Senate against President Franklin Pierce's Kansas policy, the goal of which was to make Kansas a slave state. This and other actions made Seward one of the national leaders of the new Republican Party. He wanted the Republican presidential nomination, but Weed was concerned that if Seward obtained it, his opposition to the nativists would cost Seward the election. Bowing to the judgment of Weed and other advisors, Seward refused to allow his name to be put in nomination. John C. Frémont received the nomination and went down to defeat in November 1856, losing to James Buchanan.

Seward fought the Buchanan administration over its support of the Dred Scott decision, its attempt to acquire Cuba for the United States, and especially over Buchanan's insistence on admitting Kansas as a slave state against the wishes of the vast majority of Kansas settlers. Seward undercut his attempt to create a moderate image once again in his campaign speech in Rochester, New York, on October 25, 1858. Seward presented the United States as resting on two incompatible political systems, one slave and one free. Hence, he argued, there would be an "irrepressible conflict," which would leave the country either entirely free or entirely slave. Southerners and Northern conservatives condemned the speech as violent and destructive.

The reaction to the speech cast a shadow over Seward's and Weed's hopes for the former's nomination for president at the Republican Convention at Chicago in May 1860. Many held Seward responsible for John Brown's raid on Harper's Ferry in October 1859. Many in the Middle West considered him too radical to carry the Lower North, whereas in the East, Know-Nothingism was still alive and hostile to Seward's work against nativism. And Horace Greeley, editor of the *New York Tribune*, constantly suggested that Seward was too weak to be a Republican candidate. In the end, Seward, lost the nomination to Lincoln because the bosses and delegates decided that Seward's "radicalism" and antinativism would cost the Republicans the election.

Swallowing his disappointment and bitterness, Seward campaigned hard for Lincoln throughout the North, including his home state of New York, and helped Lincoln win the election of 1860. In response, South Carolina soon seceded, followed by Mississippi, Florida, Alabama, Georgia, Louisiana, and Texas. Seward's commitment to representative government and his nationalism caused him to view this as a disaster.

Seward believed in an evolutionary, economically driven, nonviolent Manifest Destiny for the United States. The Union would endure because of the cement of the Mississippi River system, railways, canals, telegraph lines, the citizens' sense of the superiority of American political institutions, and the growth of national pride. This Union, this nation, was based on the ideal of political and civil equality in the form of a federal republic. The central government in this federalism would promote national power by the use of the tariff, subsidies to industry, and internal improvements. Agriculture, industry, and commerce together would be the engines of national prosperity. The federal government could oil these engines by land grants to settlers and schools, improvement of patent laws, a protective tariff, and government aid to transportation and communications.

The U.S. economy would benefit—and had benefited—from immigration, for it was immigrants who provided the labor for the farms, factories, railroads, and canals. Immigration should be encouraged and the new inhabitants should be given their civil liberties and rights. Slavery, like nativism, hindered the development of the United States, was morally wrong, and challenged the American claim to world leadership. Hence, it should be abolished, but gradually, so as not to destroy the United States as an important member of the family of nations.

Seward argued that the United States was destined to be a world leader due to its wealth, its population, and its representative form of government enshrined in the Constitution. The success of American political institutions would move other countries to emulate them and, combined with economic expansion, this ideological influence would lead to the peaceful expansion of the United States. Seward eschewed war as an instrument for this territorial expansion. Instead, he envisioned a gradual and peaceful expansion of the country as Canada, Hawaii, Mexico, Central America, and the islands of the Caribbean, having changed their institutions to the U.S. model and being tied economically to the United States, would seek admittance into the American Union. In his mind's eye, Seward foresaw a North American federated empire based on representative government, the abolition of slavery, and an expanding continental economy. This vision was threatened by secession and the rise of the Confederate States of America.

Lincoln formally offered Seward the State Department on December 8, 1860, citing his leadership in the party and his integrity, intelligence, and experience. Seward, although initially inclined to accept the post, wavered after hearing of other proposed cabinet choices, but accepted on December 28. Intraparty fighting over the cabinet waxed heavy in January and February 1861. On March 2, 1861, Seward asked Lincoln to permit him to withdraw his acceptance of the State Department, in an attempt to force Lincoln to compose the cabinet to Seward's liking. Lincoln and Seward talked on March 4. No record of the conversation exits, but Lincoln did propose Seward for U.S. Minister to Britain and William Dayton as his second choice for State. The next day, Seward withdrew his resignation.

In the eyes of many, and in his own eyes, Seward was the real leader of the Republican Party. This put a burden on him in the Senate because Lincoln remained powerless until his inauguration. Seward was appointed to the Senate Committee of Thirteen designed to fashion compromises to overcome the succession crisis. Seward's policy was to delay action so that Southern passions could cool and Southern Unionism could reassert itself. To these ends, Seward suggested dividing New Mexican territory into two halves and allowing the southern half to come in as a slave state. Yet he established communications with some of the strong Unionists in Buchanan's cabinet and urged the governors of New York and Massachusetts to begin organizing their states' militias.

Seward hoped that in the absence of rash or violent acts Unionism would reassert itself, and the seceded states would, one by one, return to their old place in the Union. Yet at times Seward seemed to believe that more than a pacific domestic policy was needed. Then he argued that a foreign war against Britain, France, or Spain would reunite the country in an explosion of patriotic feeling. In truth, Seward, along with most other supporters of the Union, was groping his way the whole time before Sumter. In late January 1861, in a speech to the Senate, he pledged his support of the Union by force of arms if necessary, but likewise pledged his support for the Washington Peace Convention, which met throughout February 1861.

Seward was on the spot because he was expected to act as leader of the party, and as such, he not only led in formulations of policy vis-à-vis secession but also presented plans for the composition of Lincoln's cabinet, introduced the president-elect to members of Congress, and edited a draft of Lincoln's inaugural address.

Thus, his attempt to force cabinet changes by his threat to resign. It was fortunate for Lincoln and the country that Seward withdrew his resignation and joined Lincoln's official family.

In the beginning, Seward viewed himself as the premier of the Lincoln administration. He had doubts about both Lincoln's administrative ability and the president's decision to hold and resupply Fort Sumter. Further, Europe was beginning a militant policy in the Americas while European diplomats were recommending recognition of the Confederacy by their governments and threatening Seward with the same. Seward told Lincoln of the developing intervention crisis and Lincoln ignored him. In response, Seward wrote his infamous "Some thoughts for the President's Consideration" on April 1, 1861. In it, Seward made a bid to become the *de facto* head of the government with Lincoln's acquiescence. Lincoln shared Seward's memo with no one, and instead wrote a firm but polite reply to Seward. Lincoln argued against precipitate action, defended his policy to resupply Sumter, and said that whatever policy was to be implemented, "I must do it." Seward never challenged Lincoln's overall command of policy again and, over the next four years, became one of Lincoln's most trusted friends and advisors.

Lincoln gave Seward free reign in foreign policy, only occasionally modifying dispatches and instructions to U.S. ministers abroad. As time went on Lincoln came to rely more and more on Seward's judgment and ability in matters ranging from White House procedures and protocol to more substantive matters, such as Secretary of War Cameron's temporary closing of Baltimore newspapers and General Frémont's military proclamation freeing the slaves of Missouri. Lincoln postponed issuing the preliminary Emancipation Proclamation on Seward's advice that it would be best to issue it after a Union military victory.

By the autumn of 1861, Lincoln had developed the habit of visiting Seward's home in the evening to enjoy Seward's conversation, anecdotes, and, over time, friendship. Secretary of the Navy Gideon Welles, jealous of this growing bond between the two, observed that Seward had "a wonderful facility for adapting himself to situations over which he had no control." There was more to the relationship than that. Both men had a keen sense of humor, an ability to get along with difficult people, the ability to conciliate their opponents, and an absence of vindictiveness. Moreover, both were in fact moderates on the race question, defenders of fundamental black liberties, and slowly coming around to limited Negro suffrage.

Seward's relations with his fellow cabinet members were uneven—Secretary of the Treasury Salmon P. Chase, a radical, tried to remove Seward from his post throughout 1862, an effort culminating in the December 1862 attempt. Secretary of War Edwin Stanton and Seward were friends throughout the war, but their friendship suffered after Johnson removed Stanton from the cabinet. Secretary of the Navy Welles was always jealous of Seward and fought him over what Welles argued were issues within the province of the Navy Department. Montgomery Blair, although a conservative, attacked Seward for his influence with Lincoln, over Seward's alleged weakness early in the war, and for not having a sufficiently forceful Mexico policy.

The Congressional Radicals never trusted Seward and attacked him for his "undue influence" over Lincoln. Senator Charles Sumner, especially, attacked Seward's "warmongering" because the Senator coveted Seward's job. (More than anyone else, Sumner was responsible for convincing British statesmen in 1861 that

Seward was bent on war and heartily disliked the British.) Representative Henry Winter Davis attacked Seward's Mexico policy throughout 1864 and 1865 and opposed Seward's strong support of Lincoln's moderate reconstruction policy. In fact, all Radicals opposed that support and wanted Seward's removal for it—their anger grew as they witnessed Seward's unfailing loyalty to Johnson.

Richard Pemell, Lord Lyons, and Henri Mercier, the British and French ministers to the United States, respectively, at first distrusted Seward, viewing him as a warmonger intent on starting a war between their countries on any flimsy pretext. Yet, by the time Mercier was transferred to Madrid in 1864, he had developed a deep respect for Seward's tact and diplomacy. Lyons, utterly convinced of Seward's moral depravity in 1861 for his alleged desire for a unifying war against Britain, grew to like Seward and to see in him the best hope for peace between the two countries. Mercier described the overall sentiment of the European diplomatic corps at the end of 1863 by saying of Seward, "Il est trés sage."

Due to the uniqueness of the situation in which Seward found himself from 1861 to 1865, he was unable to put his foreign policy vision of U.S territorial and economic expansion into action. With U.S. military power directed toward the suppression of a major rebellion, it could not be used to protect interests in Mexico and the Caribbean. In fact, there was a very real danger that European governments, especially Britain and France, would grant the Confederacy diplomatic recognition and then intervene with force to ensure Confederate independence.

Seward's dream of the United States creating a federated North American republic literally covering the whole continent was giving way to a nightmare of Spain recolonizing the Caribbean, France turning Mexico into a monarchical puppet, and Britain recognizing the Confederacy and joining the fight against the North, thereby crippling the power of the United States forever. To maintain the dream and stave off the nightmare, Seward repeatedly asserted the inviolability of the United States and insisted that the rebellion was an internal, domestic affair, beyond the jurisdiction of any foreign country. This assertion, repeated constantly, was the basis of Seward's refusal to ever officially hear an offer of mediation from the European powers. For even to entertain an offer of mediation would be an implicit acknowledgment that the Confederacy was a government in control of territory sufficient for it to be welcomed into the family of nations. Such an acknowledgment by Seward would have destroyed the official position of the United States against granting belligerent status to the South, against diplomatic recognition of the South, and against allowing ships for the Confederacy to be built in Britain and France. Seward always argued from the inviolability of the United States in the face of the interests, often pointed, of the European powers.

Although he never referred in his correspondence or public statements to the Monroe Doctrine, Seward was guided by it in his policies. His public reticence on the Doctrine stemmed from his belief that mentioning it would only antagonize the European powers against whom it was supposedly directed. He would, however, sometimes refer to the traditional policy by which the United States opposed European interference in the Western Hemisphere.

Seward adhered to the Doctrine in his protests, increasingly sharp after the war was over, to France for its interference in Mexico and to Spain for its recolonization of the Dominican Republic and its war with Bolivia, Chile, Ecuador, and Peru. In a way, Seward's protests against British actions vis-à-vis the Confederacy can be viewed as an extreme application of the Doctrine to protect the territorial viability not of a Latin American state, but of the United States itself.

Seward's dream of American territorial expansion had to wait until after a Union victory, which many times during the Civil War did not seem likely. Nonetheless, that dream undergirded his subsequent efforts in Samoa, Hawaii, Alaska, and the Caribbean. Seward attempted outright annexation in the Caribbean, while in the Pacific his policy was designed to increase commercial possibilities for the United States, thereby providing the basis for future territorial expansion.

The situation Seward faced as secretary of state was unprecedented. Even before the Civil War began, but after the first seven states had seceded, many Europeans were toasting the "immortal smash" and predicting that the United States could never be cobbled together again. Seward, aware of European opinion, thought that the United States could indeed be cobbled together if war between the United States and a European power threatened. This was one reason that underlay Seward's April 1, 1861, memo to Lincoln suggesting demands be sent to some European countries to explain their policies vis-à-vis the United States and offering to head the government himself. A greater reason was the news of the dispatch of French and Spanish warships to U.S. and Caribbean waters and threats from European ministers that their countries would intervene in the United States to secure cotton. Seward threatened hostilities with European states throughout March and April before receiving the news that Britain and France had recognized the belligerent status of the Confederacy—in response to the battle of Fort Sumter and Lincoln's blockade proclamation—by their respective neutrality proclamations.

When Lyons and Mercier attempted to make an official, joint presentation of the belligerency recognition, Seward refused to see them together and told them that he would never consent to see them together officially. Seward held to this throughout the war. He also refused to receive officially the notification of the British and French recognition of Confederate belligerency, and worked throughout the war to have it rescinded. By refusing to receive the notice officially, Seward was able to keep the issue "alive" for the whole four years of the war. Busy defending the belligerency proclamations to Seward, Lyons and Mercier had neither time nor justification for subsequent diplomatic relations with the Confederacy. Seward's persistent challenges of the proclamations even became bellicose at times, especially in 1861 and 1862.

Even before the attack on Sumter, and throughout the first two years of the Civil War, Seward repeatedly warned of the possibility of war if Britain and/or France extended diplomatic recognition to the Confederacy. British or French diplomatic recognition of the Confederacy, he made clear, would be viewed by the United States as an "unfriendly act" with the deepest consequences for future Anglo- and Franco-American relations. Lyons thought it possible either that Seward would push Britain and the United States inadvertently into war, or that Seward would instigate a war as a matter of policy, especially if Britain and/or France extended diplomatic recognition to the Confederacy.

Wanting to protect their countries from the first scenario, Lyons and Mercier trod very carefully in their communications with Seward, especially during the first two years of the Civil War. Many times they would postpone a meeting with Seward so as to free themselves from having to present him with the contents of an unpleasant diplomatic dispatch. Other times they would soften the language of a dispatch or couch it within the framework of friendly concern. Most importantly, they became, in effect, Seward's advocates in their communications with their home governments. Regularly, Lyons and Mercier would warn their respective governments of the dire and violent consequences of granting the Confederacy diplomatic recognition. By doing so, they forced their governments to face the difficult but absolutely necessary question: How would granting diplomatic recognition to the Confederacy advance the material interests of their countries? They were forced to answer that it would not, unless they forcibly broke the Union blockade of the Confederacy, which would have been an act of war.

This understanding, tied to knowledge of Seward's war threats and the realization that the cotton famine—so hurting their countries—was caused by a Confederate cotton embargo, caused Britain and France, especially Britain, to adhere to their original policy of withholding diplomatic recognition of the Confederacy. Each day that diplomatic recognition was not granted made it less likely that it would be granted, because fundamentally the situation in the United States had not changed. When it did look like the military situation was changing dramatically in the Confederacy's favor, with General Robert E. Lee's invasion of Maryland in September 1862, British Prime Minister, Lord Palmerston, decided to schedule a cabinet meeting for late October, at which he would support diplomatic recognition of the Confederacy. When the news reached Britain of Lee's defeat at Antietam on September 17, 1862, however, Palmerston recoiled from this position, and the British government refused to change its policy.

This was the closest that Britain came to diplomatic recognition of the Confederacy. The Union victory at Antietam was a real turning point in the war, for with it Lincoln was able to issue the preliminary Emancipation Proclamation of September 22, 1862, followed by the final Emancipation Proclamation of January 1, 1863, which made the slaves in the areas still in rebellion forever free. This act put the British promoters of Confederate independence on the defensive, a position from which they were unable to free themselves for the rest of the war.

Emancipation, coupled with increased cotton supplies, the Polish revolt, rising tension over Schleswig-Holstein, and increased distrust of Emperor Louis Napoleon of France—due to his activities in Mexico—made it impossible for the British government to extend diplomatic recognition to the Confederacy. Louis Napoleon, deeply embroiled in Mexico, did not want to antagonize the United States further by recognizing the South and certainly did not want to do so without the British. He also was inhibited from taking any action vis-à-vis the United States by the confused situation in Europe in 1863 and 1864. When the South was without hope in late 1864, it tried the bribe of gradual emancipation to entice European recognition. Britain, aware of the condition of the South, refused. Seward had thus delayed diplomatic recognition until changed conditions made it impossible for the British and French to grant such recognition.

Before Seward received the news of Queen Victoria's Neutrality Proclamation, he decided to begin negotiations with Britain and France on the United States entering into the Declaration of Paris. The Declaration, signed by the Great Powers of Europe, abolished privateering and agreed to the principle that a neutral flag made neutral goods, save war contraband. It established that neutral goods under enemy flag were free from capture, and that blockades, to be recognized, must be effective. Seward's purpose was to remove a potential cause for European states to recognize Confederate belligerency.

Actual negotiations on the Declaration were delayed for about two months due to confusion over which diplomats, Lyons and Mercier on U.S. soil, or Charles Frances Adams, U.S. minister to Britain, and William Dayton, U.S. minister to France, had authorization to negotiate on the Declaration. After it was clear that the negotiations would take place in Britain and France, they ran aground over the privateering clause. Britain and France wanted American acceptance of the Declaration minus the privateering clause, whereas the United States was insisting on the complete Declaration. Britain and France then countered with an addendum to the Declaration, specifying that U.S. acceptance of it in no way changed the British and French neutrality proclamations. By accepting this, the United States would have recognized Confederate belligerency. Seward refused to have the United States sign the Declaration under these circumstances, and the negotiations ended.

The negotiations over the Declaration of Paris had the unfortunate consequence of increasing the distrust between the United States, on one side, and Britain and France, on the other. The European governments were convinced that Seward was trying to "trap" them into an unneutral stance toward the Confederacy by tricking them into agreeing to the privateering section of the Declaration. (Jefferson Davis, President of the Confederacy, had on April 17, 1861 offered letters of marque to shipowners who wanted to privateer; Lincoln had followed with a proclamation blockading Confederate ports on April 19, 1861.) The antiprivateering section would force the Europeans to be unneutral in the American conflict. Seward, on the other hand, was convinced that the initial delay in negotiations was planned and not due to any confusion over authorization; Britain and France played the United States along, knowing the negotiations were not serious, just to lull the United States into a false sense of security.

This mutual distrust was well in place by the time the Trent Affair began. Captain Charles Wilkes, of the USS *San Jacinto*, stopped the HMS *Trent* off the coast of Cuba on November 8, 1861. A boarding party removed two Confederate commissioners, James M. Mason and John Slidell, and their secretaries from the British ship, but did not take the *Trent* in as a war prize. The Confederacy had sent Mason and Slidell to act as diplomatic agents in Britain and France and so, Wilkes argued, they were contraband of war.

When the news of Mason's and Slidell's capture reached the United States on November 16, 1861, the Northern press and public unanimously supported the act. Seward said nothing public about it. The British government quickly responded, and the British press and public opinion strongly supported their government. Palmerston's government demanded the release of Mason and Slidell and an apology from the U.S. government. Although the British note did express the hope that Wilkes had acted without orders, a second note gave the United States seven days in which to respond. Russell, in his instructions, said that an apology was not absolutely necessary if the U.S. government acknowledged that Wilkes acted without orders.

Lyons presented the British demands unofficially to Seward on December 19 and agreed to Seward's request for a delay until December 21, and then again to December 23. Lincoln and the vast majority of the cabinet, in a meeting on December 25, were against complying with the demands, wanting instead to suggest arbitration to adjudicate the dispute. Seward argued against this, being helped by the French government's support of Britain and by Senator Sumner, who read letters from British friends describing the war sentiment and preparations for war in Britain. The cabinet met again the next day and agreed with Seward to release the prisoners and accepted, with minor revisions, Seward's draft of the official explanation for the release.

By Seward's behavior during the crisis and his public note explaining his government's action, he was able to placate both the British government and U.S. public opinion. Lyons told his government how moderate and concerned for peace Seward had been in the crisis and how it had been Seward above all others who had been responsible for the peaceful outcome. Seward's note placated the U.S. public by explaining that, by releasing the prisoners, the government was not kowtowing to the British but rather upholding international legal principles against impressment defended by the United States since the administration of Thomas Jefferson.

This changed British attitude toward Seward aided his diplomacy in 1862 and 1863 because his war threats in those years were viewed, not as the ravings of a half-mad and unscrupulous politician, but as a reflection of the seriousness to the United States of foreign diplomatic recognition of the Confederacy and of permitting the building of warships for the Confederacy in Britain. After the British turned away from the idea of extending diplomatic recognition to the Confederacy in the autumn of 1862, the gravest war threat came from the British government, which allowed the Confederacy to have warships built for it in British ports.

The two most famous were the *Florida*, which left Liverpool in March 1862, and the *Alabama*, which left in July 1862, after orders had been issued by the British government to detain her. The British had applied a narrow interpretation of the Foreign Enlistment Act, which made illegal the construction and arming of warships within Britain for a belligerent, and they were slow in issuing the detention order. The *Florida* sank 38 U.S. merchant vessels before her capture in October 1864, while the *Alabama* sank or captured 64 U.S. merchant ships before her destruction in June 1864. Seward had Adams regularly lodge formal complaints with the British for the destruction caused by the *Alabama* and the *Florida* and show proof that they were engaged in war for the Confederacy.

With Seward's prodding, the House and the Senate passed a bill that Lincoln signed in March 1863 that allowed the president to authorize privateers. When Lyons protested the law, Seward replied that British law did not stop the British from building Confederate privateers in Britain. In March 1863 Lyons wrote to Russell that Seward had warned that without British assurances of no new *Alabamas*, and even in the face of war with Britain, the United States would authorize privateers. As a direct result of this, the British government seized the *Alexandria*, which was being built in Britain for the Confederacy, in April 1863.

A new group of armor-plated ships, the Laird rams, continued to be built in Britain for the Confederacy from July to September 1863. Adams, following Seward's instructions, protested their construction throughout the summer. When Russell informed Adams in early September that the British government could not interfere with those ships, Adams replied that if the rams escaped, "this is war." Russell had ordered the seizure of the rams before Adams's war threat but had failed to inform him until September 8. Russell acted as he did because of the threat of U.S. privateers and the severe deterioration in Anglo–U.S. relations. This was a major victory for Seward's diplomacy and finally pushed Britain into a "neutral" neutrality and away from one that had leaned toward the Confederacy.

Seward's foreign policy successes contributed to the strengthening of his relationship with Lincoln. The two also grew closer together after Lincoln defended Seward masterfully during the 1862 cabinet crisis. By withstanding the onslaught of attacks from the Congressional Radical Republicans, Lincoln was able to keep both Seward and Secretary of the Treasury Salmon P. Chase in the cabinet, thereby strengthening his government. Seward, on the other hand, was politically weakened by the attack, and from that point on more dependent than ever on Lincoln. This is not to say that the two were simply or always friends. Lincoln had refrained from drawing a sword over Seward's wound, but he had also prevented Seward from achieving his overriding goal—the presidency. Seward always harbored some bitterness over his defeat by Lincoln and had the sense that Lincoln did not quite measure up to himself. This caused petulant outbursts by Seward as late as 1868 about Lincoln's failings. Yet, they admired and liked each other, and it was understood that Lincoln would support Seward for the Republican nomination in 1868. This was strengthened by Seward's support of the moderate Reconstruction policy that Lincoln was forming in 1864 and 1865. By Good Friday 1865, Seward and Lincoln were close friends, linked by bonds of affection forged by their work together during the sad, strange time of the Civil War.

The tragedy on Good Friday shocked Seward and left him confused as to his place in the cabinet. He had had friendly relations with Vice President Andrew Johnson throughout the war years and Seward had helped Johnson receive the vice presidential nomination of the Union party in 1864. But Johnson was not an easy man with which to get along. The new president was a states' rights Democrat who supported Emancipation because slavery benefited the Southern aristocracy. To Johnson, blacks were and always would be inferior to whites. Further, Johnson was stubborn, unable to compromise, and thought that the formation of Reconstruction policy was the prerogative of the president.

Johnson listened to many people in the late spring and summer of 1865. Seward agreed with the general outline of Johnson's Reconstruction policy and even defended it in the autumn of 1865. But relations between the two cooled owing to Seward's belief that Congress had a constitutional role to play in formulating a Reconstruction policy. Seward tried to play a conciliatory role but Johnson's contempt for Congress and his refusal to compromise, when combined with the Radical Republicans' distrust of Johnson and the desire to push their own program, made Seward's position almost untenable. With Johnson's veto of the Civil Rights Act of 1866 and Congress's override of the veto in April 1866, the breach between the Johnson and Congress became permanent.

Seward found himself having to walk a political tightrope. On the one hand, he needed good relations with the president or risk being dismissed and seeing his plans in foreign affairs come to naught. On the other hand, he wished to placate Congress and compromise where Johnson was stubborn, and he needed some kind of good relations with Congress if any of his plans were to bear fruit. Seward was against a radical reorganization of the parties, instead hoping for the success of a moderate Reconstruction policy. This was not to be, as Radicals swept the 1866 midterm elections.

Although Johnson ignored Seward's advice on domestic issues, Seward was assailed by both Radical Republicans and Democrats for being the power behind the throne and setting Johnson's Reconstruction policy. Seward always tried to cultivate important Radicals such as Stevens and Sumner in order to protect his foreign policy plans. But when Johnson fired Secretary of War Edwin Stanton and removed General Philip Sheridan from his position as military governor in August 1867, he asked Seward to stay in office, which Seward did. Seward did enjoy political power and had influence over Johnson in foreign policy matters. He thought U.S. acquisitions were possible in the Caribbean, and even some Radicals wanted him to remain. He may also have realized that resignation now could mean the end of his public career, a prospect he was not yet prepared to accept. In any event, Seward stayed in the Cabinet, maintained contact with the Radicals, presided over the president's legal defense fund campaign—made necessary by the House's impeachment of Johnson—and pleased the president with his support. In the view of most scholars, Seward gave Johnson more loyalty than he deserved.

Although Seward did not use the term "Monroe Doctrine" in his diplomatic correspondence, because the European powers refused to accept it as a principle of diplomacy, he was motivated by it and used it as a foundation for his policies dealing with European actions in the Western Hemisphere. In 1861 Seward was forced to back down from a threat against the Spanish for their recolonization of Santo Domingo, and so he was careful thereafter simply to record U.S. interest in European actions in the Americas without either threatening or accepting them. Yet the knowledge that the end of the Civil War would free the United States to reissue its protest caused Spain to relinquish the colony in July 1865. Further, the Spanish were involved in a war with Bolivia, Chile, Ecuador, and Peru in 1865 and 1866. Seward informally showed the Spanish minister to the United States a dispatch Seward had sent to the U.S. minister to Spain, which warned that if Spain continued the war, the United States could not remain neutral. Spain stopped the war.

Seward's greatest triumph in upholding the Monroe Doctrine was in helping to convince France to leave Mexico. In one of his more quixotic gestures, Louis Napoleon of France had decided to establish a French protectorate in Mexico under the cover of a joint British, French, and Spanish military expedition to occupy Veracruz in October 1861 in retaliation for Mexican suspension of debt payments to these three powers. In 1862, the British and the Spanish withdrew, and the French increased their military force in the country, leading to the French occupation of Mexico City in June 1863. Archduke Maximilian of Austria accepted the Mexican crown, and the Juarez government was forced to flee to the countryside. The U.S. government refused to recognize Maximilian's government, but did not protest the French troops in Mexico. Seward feared that too strong a protest might lead to French recognition of the Confederacy. Hence the United States, from 1863 to mid-1865, simply expressed its friendly interest in the intent of the French government.

After Appomattox, Seward expressed the serious concern of the United States over French intentions, and in February 1866 Seward demanded that the French set a time limit for their evacuation of Mexico. The United States sent 50,000 troops under General Philip Sheridan to the Mexican border. In April 1866 the French Foreign Minister Drouyn de Lhuys announced that the French army would leave Mexico by November 1867, and in fact the last French troops left in March 1867. Seward interceded on behalf of Maximilian, but he was executed in June 1867 by the reinstated Juarez government. The established policy of the United States, which opposed European interference in the Western Hemisphere, was vindicated.

Seward was a committed expansionist but his attempts at territorial expansion had to await the successful conclusion of the Civil War and then had to face a Congress opposed to his moderate Reconstruction policy and to territorial expansion. Seward proposed the U.S. annexation of the Dominican Republic, but the cabinet refused to support it. He worked with Congress to authorize the United States to extend a protectorate over both Haiti and the Dominican Republic, but the House voted down a resolution authorizing this. He signed a treaty with Denmark, purchasing the Virgin Islands, but the Senate never voted on it. The Senate rejected a commercial reciprocity treaty with Hawaii, which Seward had hoped would lead to its annexation by the United States. The Senate also refused to act on a treaty Seward had negotiated with Samoa, which would have given the United States a naval base in Pago Pago, one of the best harbors in the Pacific.

The only gains of territory under Seward were the Midway Islands, occupied September 1867, and Alaska, the acquisition of which Seward secured by pushing the Senate to consent to the purchase treaty a mere two weeks after its signing on March 30, 1867. The House debated the $7.2 million appropriations bill, but the sense that this would help lead to the annexation of Canada, and gratitude to the Russians for the fleets they sent during the Civil War as a goodwill gesture, prompted the passage of the appropriations bill in 1868, soon after President Johnson's acquittal by the Senate.

Seward's support of Johnson and the massive decline in Johnson's popularity destroyed Seward's political hopes. Although the Radicals failed to remove Johnson from office, they controlled the national Republican Party and were able to bring General Ulysses S. Grant into their ranks. Further, Seward's political base in New York State disappeared when Weed lost control of the Republican Party to the Radicals in the 1866 election. With Grant's election to the presidency in November 1868, Seward's career was soon over.

Most historians judge Seward to be the second-best secretary of state in U.S. history, after John Quincy Adams. He was able to forestall diplomatic recognition of the Confederacy, and his protests led to the British moving to true neutrality and to the British prohibiting Confederate shipbuilding. His protests of this activity formed the basis for the successful U.S. claims for damages that the United States won in 1871. Further, Seward was able to vindicate the Monroe Doctrine and to protect the sovereignty of a sister American republic without war by his astute Mexican policy. Although he was unsuccessful in most of his attempts at territorial acquisition, Seward's policy concerning Samoa, Hawaii, and the Caribbean anticipated U.S. policy by over 25 years. Further, Seward laid the basis for the United States to be a true Pacific power by his successful attempts to move the United States to acquire the Midway Islands and Alaska. In some ways, given the consequences of failure, Seward's accomplishments were greater than Adams's. Had Adams failed, the fundamental territorial integrity and power of the United States would not have been threatened. Had Seward failed, the United States could have broken apart into competing confederacies, which could have been manipulated by the European powers to the detriment of all within this potential Disunited States of America.

In the little less than four years left to him after he left office, Seward returned to Auburn, worked on his autobiography, and traveled throughout the world, visiting Canada, Alaska, Mexico, Cuba, Japan, China, India, Egypt, Syria, the Holy Land,

Turkey, Greece, Italy, Austria, and France. Seward died quietly and quickly on October 10, 1872.

BIBLIOGRAPHICAL ESSAY

The most important primary source for Seward's life is the collection of his papers in Rhees Library at the University of Rochester, which contains 150,000 items, including thousands of letters to Seward and drafts and copies of letters written by him. Other collections in Rhees Library are the Thurlow Weed Papers and the George Washington Patterson Papers, both of which house many letters from Seward and Weed.

Fredrick W. Seward's *Seward at Washington, as Senator and Secretary of State* (1891), contains hundreds of Seward's letters. Because Frederick edited the letters, they have to be used with caution; the dates he gives for the letters are often incorrect, and there are many errors in his biography. See also his *Reminiscences of a War Time Statesman and Diplomat* (1916). *The Works of William H. Seward*, 5 volumes (1884), edited by George E. Baker, contains Seward's principal speeches and public writings. *Papers Relating to the Foreign Affairs of the United States, 1861–68*, 19 volumes (1862–1869) includes much of the diplomatic correspondence of the United States. Seward was the first secretary to submit this to Congress annually, beginning in 1861. He included only some of the correspondence and removed passages from some letters.

The definitive biography of Seward is Glyndon G. Van Deusen's *William Henry Seward* (1967). An older but still useful biography is Frederic Bancroft's *The Life of William H. Seward*, 2 volumes (1900, reissued 1967). Also consult John M. Taylor, *William Henry Seward: Lincoln's Right Hand* (1991), which in some ways may be more satisfying than Van Deusen. See also Henry W. Temple's "William H. Seward" in Samuel Flagg Bemis (ed.), *The American Secretaries of State and their Diplomacy*, Volume III (1958). Biographies of two other participants in Civil War diplomacy that have a good deal of material on Seward are Martin B. Duberman, *Charles Francis Adams, 1807–1886* (1961), and Daniel B. Carroll, *Henri Mercier and the American Civil War* (1971).

For Seward's liberal nationalism, see Joseph G. Whelan, *William Henry Seward, Expansionist* (1959), one of the best unpublished dissertations on Seward; and Ernest Paolino, *The Foundations of American Empire* (1973).

For Seward's relationship with Lincoln and policy positions in 1860–1861, see Glyndon G. Van Deusen, "Seward and the Secession Winter of 1860–61, *Canadian Historical Association Papers* (1966); William Baringer, A *House Dividing: Lincoln as President-Elect* (1945), which deals with Seward's negotiations with Lincoln over the composition of the Cabinet; Patrick Sowle, "A Reappraisal of Seward's Memorandum of April 1, 1861 to Lincoln," *Journal of Southern History*, 32 (1967); and Kinley J. Brauer, "Seward's 'Foreign War Panacea': An Interpretation," *New York History* 55, no. 2 (1974), which questions the common understanding of Seward's infamous memo to Lincoln. Richard N. Current, *Lincoln and the First Shot* (1963), discusses Seward's role in the debates and negotiations concerning Fort Sumter; Norman B. Ferris's *Desperate Diplomacy* (1976) and *The Trent Affair* (1977) are both sympathetic to Seward's tactics and strategy in 1861; and Gordon H. Warren, *Fountain of Dis-*

content: The Trent Affair and Freedom of the Seas (1981), is a bit more critical of Seward than Ferris.

Many fine works cover the diplomacy of the Civil War, including Kinley J. Brauer, "Seward, American Politics and Anglo-American Relations: The British Perspective," *American Chronicle*, I (February 1972), which ably presents the anti-Seward opinions of British statesmen; Stuart L. Bernath, *Squall Across the Atlantic* (1970); David Paul Crook, *The North, the South, and the Powers: 1861–1865* (1974); Ephraim Douglass Adam's classic *Great Britain and the American Civil War* (1925); Lynn M. Case and Warren F. Spencer's fine study, *The United States and France: Civil War Diplomacy* (1970); Henry Blumenthal, *A Reappraisal of Franco-American Relations: 1830–1871* (1959); Brian Jenkins, *Britain and the War for the Union* (1974); and Frank Lawrence Owsley King, *Cotton Diplomacy* (1931).

Edward S. Mihalkanin

JOHN SHERMAN (1823–1900)

Served 1897–1898
Appointed by President William McKinley
Republican

John Sherman was born on May 10, 1823, at Lancaster, Ohio, to Charles Robert and Mary Sherman (née Hoyt). John was the eighth child of the family and a younger brother to William Tecumseh Sherman. Their father moved from Connecticut to Ohio and in 1811 established a law practice, rising to a seat on the state supreme court before his untimely death in 1829.

The death put the family in straitened circumstances, and the children were sent to different relatives and friends for their care and educations. Although raised for the most part in different households, John and Tecumseh were bound together by ties of deep affection that lasted their whole lives. John was educated in Lancaster and in Mt. Vernon, where he lived for four years with an extended family member. Sherman learned surveying, quit school at 14, and joined a crew working on canal improvements. By the age of 16 he was the foreman overseeing the construction of a dam. Sherman was dismissed from his job after the Democrats won the elections in 1839 due to the spoils system.

In 1840 he began the study of law under his uncle, Judge Jacob Parker, and his oldest brother, Charles Taylor Sherman, at Mansfield, Ohio, with such self-discipline that people soon forgot Sherman's earlier indifference to education and his boisterous behavior. He was already practicing law by the time he was admitted to the bar on May 10, 1844. Sherman became a partner in a lumber company and began to invest in real estate shrewdly. Sherman married Margaret Sarah Cecilia, the only child of an important Mansfield lawyer, Judge James Stewart, on August 31, 1848. The Shermans never had biological children; they did adopt a daughter.

Sherman attended the national Whig conventions of 1848 and 1852 and in 1854 won election to the U.S. House of Representatives as part of the anti-Kansas Nebraska Act electoral avalanche. Against the spread of slavery into the federal territories, Sherman was a moderate within the new Republican Party on questions of both race and finance. He drafted the majority report of the committee sent to investigate the troubles in Kansas, which the Republicans used effectively in the 1856 presidential campaign. Due to his hard work, the Republican caucus nominated him for Speaker. Due to his endorsement of Hinton Rowan Helper's antislavery book *The Impending Crisis*, which he had not read, Sherman fell short of the necessary votes. Yet, in the new Congress he became chair of the Ways and Means Committee. Sherman campaigned vigorously for Republican candidates in 1860. After President Abraham Lincoln successfully nominated Senator Salmon P. Chase to the Treasury secretaryship, Sherman was selected to fill the vacancy. From the beginning Sherman was a member, then by 1863, chair, of the Senate Finance committee and supported both the Legal Tender Act of 1862 and the National Banking Act of 1863—the latter law providing the basis of the U.S. banking system, which lasted until the Owens–Glass Act of 1913 created the current Federal Reserve System.

Sherman was a moderate on the slavery issue when the Civil War began, but events of the war pushed him toward the radical faction of the Republican Party. He supported the Emancipation Proclamation and the Thirteenth Amendment abolishing slavery. With the war over, Sherman was inclined to support the Lincoln–Johnson moderate program of Reconstruction. Yet, Sherman's strong devotion to party loyalty, President Andrew Johnson's unwillingness to compromise and his aversion to any Congressional role in Reconstruction policy, and a hardening of Northern public opinion in favor of the Radical Reconstruction policy in reaction to Johnson's intransigence—all led Sherman to support the Radical program. Specifically, Sherman voted for the Fourteenth Amendment, the extension of Negro suffrage to the District of Colombia, the Reconstruction Acts, the Tenure of Office Act, and Johnson's removal from office.

Sherman was very active in securing the Republican presidential nomination for Rutherford B. Hayes in 1876. After the election became contested, the senator was part of a delegation that visited Louisiana to investigate the elections on behalf of the Republican ticket and in general unofficially represented Hayes in discussions concerning the disputed election, which Hayes finally was certified as having won.

Hayes tapped Sherman for the Treasury due to the latter's experience in financial matters, his knowledge of the Senate, and his work for Hayes throughout the election year. Sherman proved to be the strongest and most important cabinet member. The president soon developed the habit of having Sherman accompany him on carriage rides where they could discuss political issues in private.

National financial issues dominated Sherman's agenda. Although at first in favor of allowing Civil War greenbacks to be used in payment of government bonds, he is credited with the passage of the Specie Resumption Act of 1875, which required redeeming the bonds in coin at face value. As Treasury Secretary, it was Sherman's task to implement the terms of the law. It is a mark of his skill that he was able to resume specie payments without a run on the banks and in the face of hostile Democrats, who controlled the House for four years and the Senate for two. Sherman also negotiated bond sales on very advantageous terms to the United States. Due to Sherman's acceptance of the Bland–Allison Act's limited coinage of silver while opposing the free coinage of silver, the United States was still on the gold standard when he left the Treasury Department.

Sherman believed that his adroit handling of national fiscal policy and the resultant prosperity earned him the Republican Presidential nomination in 1880. The Ohio delegation however, was badly divided, and the Republican nomination went to James A. Garfield who, ironically, was leading the Sherman forces at the convention. Overall, Sherman failed to receive the nomination throughout the 1880s because his support of the gold standard embittered the silverite West, while his acceptance of the use of some silver as currency disturbed the gold bug East.

Sherman returned to the Senate in 1881 and remained there until 1897. He was able to hold onto his seat throughout this time even though the Democrats won the state three times. He was a Senator's senator, able to work for legislative compromises, knowledgeable about Western Republican preferences, and a shrewd judge of potential political fallout from congressional actions. Although he did not support wholeheartedly in 1890 the Anti-Trust Act and Silver Purchase Act, both of which bore his name, they became law because of his ability to compromise to keep the Republican Party together.

In 1897, in what later became one of his most controversial actions, Sherman accepted the office of secretary of state in the new administration of William McKinley. This appointment has been denounced through the years mainly due to Sherman's incapacity for the office and McKinley's supposed motives in offering Sherman the post. There is enough blame to go around.

It was an open secret that Sherman's mental powers had declined and, specifically, he suffered from memory lapses. McKinley had heard talk of Sherman's decline but had also been told that the senior Ohio Senator was fine mentally. After talk continued about Sherman, McKinley angrily defended the appointment by saying that Sherman was in perfect physical and mental health.

Still, it appears that McKinley failed to fully investigate Sherman's capacity for office. Neither Sherman nor his family informed McKinley of the extent of the old senator's decline. Part of the reticence of Sherman's family may have been due to the senator's desire to leave the Senate for the State Department. Sherman endured a hard-fought election campaign in 1892 and anticipated either retirement or a tough race in 1898. Sherman was delighted with McKinley's offer of the cabinet post.

Anyone attempting to ascertain McKinley's motives in proffering the offer to Sherman (or his motives for many other actions) is faced with a task similar to having to trace the outline of a shadow cast by a ghost. The president did not take anyone into his confidence. Most of his close friends admitted that they did not feel that they really knew him. McKinley's public persona was a mask carefully crafted over many years, and he could be disingenuous when caught in the middle of competing demands and interests. His public papers betray very little of the private man. McKinley was the first president to make extensive use of the telephone for official business, so much of the evidence of his direction of policy is missing. In fact, Fred Greenstein's concept of the "hidden hand presidency" applies to McKinley as much as, if not more than, it does to Eisenhower.

McKinley apparently accepted Sherman for the post, although he was not the president elect's first choice, because Sherman's selection solved some pressing political problems, and McKinley intended to be his own secretary of state in any case. Although Marcus Hanna, national chairman of the Republican Party wanted to be a senator, McKinley preferred Hanna to be a subordinate and so offered him the office of postmaster general in mid-November.

Hanna declined. He instead suggested approaching Sherman to ask the senator if he were interested in the State Department. McKinley, who more than most politicians did not like to say no, agreed to have Hanna explore the subject with Sherman. Shortly after meeting with Hanna, Sherman informed Hanna that he would accept the State Department if asked by McKinley. McKinley's response was to send an emissary to Senator William Boyd Allison of Iowa to ask if he would accept state if asked. Allison was not interested in the position and said he would not accept it if it were offered.

Although McKinley preferred Hanna in the cabinet, he was not against a possible Senate appointment. McKinley simply did not want it to appear that he had nominated Sherman to make a vacancy for Hanna. McKinley was sensitive to the appearance of impropriety in his relationship with Hanna. McKinley nevertheless was content with Sherman at State due to the senator's stature in the party and his knowledge of the Senate. Given his intention to control his administration's diplomacy, McKinley planned for an old friend, William R. Day of Ohio, to take the position of first assistant under Sherman.

Factional infighting among Ohio Republicans quickly sullied the choice of Sherman. The retiring senator requested that Governor Asa A. Bushnell appoint Hanna to replace him. Bushnell and Senator Joseph B. Foraker, a former governor, headed a faction bitterly opposed to Hanna. Foraker protested Sherman's appointment directly to McKinley before it was made. After the appointment became public, Bushnell and Foraker fought against Hanna's appointment for six weeks, with Bushnell even offering the Senate seat to Congressman Theodore E. Burton, who turned it down. Not withstanding the offer to the congressman, Bushnell wanted the seat for himself. In the end Bushnell did not acquiesce in the naming of Hanna until McKinley sent Day as his personal emissary to request the governor's support for the appointment.

The chief casualty of the Foraker–Hanna feud was Sherman. The Foraker forces made the charge that a deal had been made between Hanna and McKinley to force Sherman out of the Senate and into the cabinet and further that Sherman was not up to the job. These rumors had the effect of drawing attention to any misstep Sherman made once he took office and caused people to put the worst possible construction on them. Also, the more obvious it was that Sherman was having difficulty at State, the more people were convinced that, in fact, a deal had been made in the first place.

Sherman's tenure at State, from March 1887 to April 1898, was troubled from the beginning. McKinley asked Sherman for suggestions on his inaugural address. Sherman's memo advised that the use of U.S. military force would be inevitable to resolve the Cuban issue. McKinley did not use anything from Sherman's memo for his inaugural.

Soon after Day was appointed first assistant secretary at State, he was given authority over all the important diplomatic issues facing the administration, including negotiations for the annexation of Hawaii. Sherman was not informed of the negotiations and in response to an official inquiry from the Japanese minister, denied that such negotiations were taking place. Soon thereafter, the treaty was signed on June 16, 1897, and the Japanese could not help but think that the U.S. government had acted in bad faith on this issue.

The episode had unfortunate consequences for the McKinley administration. It was then that Sherman began to convince himself that his appointment had been designed all along to make room for Hanna in the Senate and that McKinley had never intended for him to play a role in the formation of foreign policy. For Sherman, this state of affairs was confirmed as McKinley's old friend, Day, increasingly look over the day-to-day administration of the department and oversaw the diplomacy of all the most important issues facing the government.

Sherman held two interviews with the press in the late summer that exacerbated the controversies over his appointment and his relations with McKinley and Day. In the interviews, especially in the second, Sherman had made very indiscreet comments about Hawaiian annexation, Britain, and Spanish control of Cuba. Sherman was severely criticized in the public press and apologized to McKinley for his comments. The president agreed that Sherman should not grant any more interviews but did not ask for his resignation.

Although Sherman continued to treat McKinley with respect during their meetings, he began to criticize the president constantly behind his back. Members of Sherman's extended family also began to criticize McKinley and repeated the charge that the secretary of state had been appointed to the cabinet against his will only to make a way to the Senate for Hanna. Sherman began to see himself as the victim, brooding over his impotence and increasingly angry at Hanna for having put himself in this condition. The gossip made the newspapers by late 1897, and the press was demanding that McKinley ask for Sherman's resignation by early 1898. Sherman's family, in its desire to hurt McKinley, ironically delivered a blow to Sherman's reputation from which it has never recovered.

By the end of 1897, McKinley was directly controlling the foreign policy of his administration and had begun inviting Day to the cabinet meetings, an additional affront to Sherman's sensibilities. The negotiations with Spain over Cuba in 1898 were conducted by Day following the direction of McKinley. Sherman lingered on as the situation over Cuba reached a crisis stage with the publication of the De Lôme letter and the sinking of the USS *Maine* in February 1898.

Sherman resigned his office on April 25, 1898, in response to a request from McKinley. According to John Hay, the immediate need to replace Sherman "was precipitated by a lapse of memory in a conversation with the Austrian Minister of so serious a nature that the President had to put in Day without an instant's delay . . . "

Even in the face of Sherman's general weaknesses and inconsistent policy statements, it may have been possible for Sherman's tenure to have been less contentious and less damaging to his reputation if he had been willing to conform to the general foreign policy objectives of the McKinley administration and had been content to be more of a figurehead rather than a driving force in policy formulation.

Sherman's policy differences and different expectations about his role aggravated, rather than ameliorated, the problems caused by the waning of his strength and memory. Sherman was against the annexation of any territory not on the U.S. mainland, and that opposition included both Cuba and Hawaii. For all of his bellicose statements about the Spanish presence in Cuba, moreover, Sherman was totally opposed to war with Spain as a way to end the dispute over the island. More inferentially, Sherman may have expected to be the guiding light of the McKinley administration as he had been in the Hayes presidency. However unrealistic those hopes were, the failure to meet them would account for the increasingly sour mood of Sherman as he opposed McKinley's direction of policy. If Sherman had been content to serve out his appointment as a figurehead (Lewis Cass in the Buchanan administration comes to mind), his time at State would not have dishonored his reputation as much as it did.

In retirement, Sherman became a caustic critic of McKinley and particularly resented Hanna as the instrument of his public humiliation. Sherman visited Washington, D.C., when the Senate was in session. He made a point to avoid Hanna but became increasingly friendly with Foraker. Sherman's wife of over 50 years died, adding to his gloom. He remained a bitter critic of the McKinley administration to the end, which came on October 22, 1900. At the time of Sherman's resignation, Secretary of the Navy John D. Long observed that it was "rather a sad termination of one of the most useful careers of American Statesmen."

BIBLIOGRAPHICAL ESSAY

The Sherman papers are in the Library of Congress. Sherman's *Recollections of Forty Years in the House, Senate, and Cabinet*, 2 volumes (1895), does not include material on his service as secretary of state. Also of interest is Rachel Sherman Thorndike (ed.), *The Sherman Letters* (1894), which include the correspondence between Sherman and his brother William Tecumseh Sherman from 1837 to 1891 and for 1894. Two old but still useful biographies of Sherman are Theodore E. Burton, *John Sherman* (1906) and Winfield S. Kerr, *John Sherman, His Life and Public Service*, 2 volumes (1908). See also Louis Martin Sears, "John Sherman," *in The American Secretaries of State and Their Diplomacy*, ed. Samuel Flagg Bemis (1958).

For McKinley and his administration see Margaret Leech, *In the Days of McKinley* (1959); Howard Wayne Morgan, *William McKinley and His America* (1963) and his *America's Road to Empire: The War with Spain and Overseas Expansion* (1965); and Lewis L. Gould, *The Presidency of William McKinley* (1980).

Edward S. Mihalkanin

GEORGE P. SHULTZ (1920–)

Served 1982–1989
Appointed by President Ronald Reagan
Republican

George Pratt Shultz was born in New York City on December 13, 1920, the son and only child of Birl E. and Margaret Shultz. At a young age, Shultz's family moved to Englewood Cliffs, New Jersey, where he spent a happy childhood. His father worked at the New York Stock Exchange, where the young George often spent Saturday mornings while his father worked. Shultz lived with his parents until his college years at Princeton, where he pursued a major in economics and a minor in public and international affairs.

Upon receipt of his bachelor's degree in 1942, Shultz applied for graduate school in economics at the Massachusetts Institute for Technology (MIT). He was accepted into the program of Industrial Economics, but instead joined the marines and after training was shipped to the South Pacific, where he saw action during 1943–1945. After the war, he began graduate studies at MIT and was married. He completed his Ph.D. in industrial economics in 1949 and stayed on at MIT, where he coauthored three books on labor and wage issues. He taught at MIT until 1957 and served for a year in 1955–1956 on President Dwight D. Eisenhower's Council of Economic Advisers under Chairman Arthur Burns. In 1957, Shultz took a professorship in industrial relations at the Graduate School of Business at the University of Chicago. While authoring additional books at Chicago, Shultz also served as Dean of the Graduate School of Business from 1962–1968 and as a fellow at the Center for Advanced Study in Behavioral Sciences from 1968–1969. After two decades in academia, Shultz was tapped by President Richard Nixon, to serve as secretary of labor in 1969, launching his first tour in government service.

Shultz was well prepared to become secretary of labor, where he undertook a reform of the Job Corps and addressed the oil import control system. His noninterventionist policies in handing a major longshoreman's strike, which began under the Johnson administration and continued into that of Nixon's, proved successful in putting pressure on labor and management to resolve that dispute through collective bargaining. With several successes at the department of labor under his belt, it was not long before his talents as a manager drew the further attention of the Nixon administration, which had undertaken a reorganization of the executive office budget process with the creation of the Office of Management and Budget (OMB). Nixon tapped Shultz as OMB's first director, giving Shultz an opportunity to gain valuable White House executive experience dealing with both domestic and national security issues. In 1972, with the international monetary system in disarray following the breakdown of the Bretton Woods system of fixed exchange rates and dollar convertibility, Shultz was called on to become Nixon's secretary of the treasury, an office he occupied during a time when international monetary policy was a high-profile issue for governments around the world. He had significant contact with foreign leaders in this capacity, providing him with international experience and exposure that would prove valuable during his later service as secretary of state.

In 1974, Shultz left government to become executive vice president of the Bechtel Corporation. He continued to serve, however, during President Ford's tenure as the chairman of the Council on Economic Policy's East-West Trade Policy committee. From 1975 to 1977 he served as president of Bechtel Corporation and later, from 1977 to 1981, as vice chairman of the company. He also served as director and president of the Bechtel Group in 1981–1982. While gaining this significant private-sector experience, Shultz also served as a professor of management and public policy at Stanford University from 1974 to 1982. The second call to public service for Shultz came in June 1982, when President Ronald Reagan tapped him to become successor to Alexander Haig as secretary of state.

George Shultz became secretary of state at a time of great global turmoil and of disarray within the Reagan foreign policy team. Outgoing Secretary of State Haig was on record as declaring that the National Security Council (NSC) staff had been engaged in guerrilla warfare against his efforts to run foreign policy from the State Department, whereas Reagan appeared reluctant himself to take charge either of the NSC staff or of foreign policy generally. Shultz realized that he would need to be seen as the clear and steady captain of foreign policy formulation and execution, but understood that his boss would be Reagan. By gaining Reagan's confidence in his loyalty, Shultz hoped to be able to avoid internecine NSC/State bickering. At the same time, he did not view the State Department bureaucracy as an enemy to the Reagan foreign policy agenda. He hoped to bring his talents as a manager and as an energetic leader to the position of secretary of state and thus also to gain the loyalty and support of the professionals in the Department, despite their reputation for leftward political leanings. During his six-and-a-half-year tenure as secretary of state, Shultz largely succeeded in this delicate balancing act, through a calm, steady, and honest handling of his duties as occupant of the third-highest office in the executive branch.

Shultz established immediate credibility with Congress prior to and during his confirmation hearings by resigning all positions with the Bechtel Corporation, ending his other organizational and business ties, and placing his financial assets in a blind trust. He assembled a capable and experienced team of deputies from his own coterie of acquaintances, including Ken Dam and Allen Wallis; from holdovers of the Haig period, notably, Lawrence Eagleburger, who would later become secretary of state under George Bush; and from other State Department insiders. His attitude of respect toward career State Department personnel was generally appreciated at Foggy Bottom, and he cultivated open and honest relations with the press, which gave him credibility when he testified before Congress on the Iran-Contra scandal during Reagan's second term.

Shultz believed, as an economist and businessman, that the Communist system had proved to be a failure, both as an economic model and as a political reality. Upon assumption of his duties as secretary of state, he believed that the United States needed to reassert itself on the world stage at a time of global turmoil and after a long period of national self-doubt. In these basic assumptions, he was in complete agreement with President Ronald Reagan.

Corollaries to these basic assumptions included the idea that the United States must be ready to stand up against Communist threats and expansionism, to promote a free enterprise version of national economic development throughout the world, and to maintain a patient resolve to negotiate long-standing and ticklish regional disputes such as those in the Middle East, Southern Africa, and Central America. A crucial factor in the Reagan/Shultz perspective was the notion that although the Soviet Union was bankrupt economically, it nonetheless was a major military threat. Thus, they agreed that Soviet leaders must be made to understand that they could not win the arms race or rely on conventional military strength to spread their influence or undermine the stability of pro-Western regimes.

Consequently, Shultz supported the Reagan military buildup, the resuscitation of American military morale, and a robust policy of support to opponents of Communism throughout the world. Shultz was on record both before and during his tenure as secretary of state that only a persistent, strong, and patient application of U.S. economic, political, and military power could restore American credibility and leadership of the free world and ensure the defeat of the Soviet menace.

From the very start of his tenure as secretary of state, Shultz faced problems in the Middle East, in particular the Israeli/Palestinian battles over control of Lebanon. Like secretaries of state before him and since, Shultz grappled with the complexities of the Arab–Israeli conflict throughout his tenure, during which diplomatic and political successes and failures were in evidence. Low points included the bombing of the U.S. Marine barracks in Lebanon in 1984 and the violence surrounding the *Intifada* in the West Bank and the Gaza in 1988–1989. But Shultz was also successful in negotiating a Palestine Liberation Organization (PLO) withdrawal from Lebanon and later engineered a peace agreement between Israel and Lebanon. He also oversaw the reflagging of tankers in the Persian Gulf in 1987, as a means of protecting commercial oil trade in a region destabilized by the Iran–Iraq war. Toward the end of his tenure, Shultz saw an opportunity for the United States and the Soviet Union to work together toward peace in the troubled region, but all efforts significantly to advance the peace process failed, including the Shultz initiative that called for a process of connecting (or "interlocking") issues that could be dealt with quickly with those more difficult questions that would be essential to the final status of Israeli–Palestinian relations and the creation of a Palestinian state. The *Intifada*, which prompted the Shultz initiative, emphasized more strongly that peace in the region would prevail only when the conflicting parties became serious about achieving it. A patient negotiator by style, Shultz persisted throughout his tenure to advance the Middle East peace process.

Perhaps the most controversial decisions and policies of the Reagan administration centered on Central America. In Afghanistan, support for the *mujihideen* forces against Soviet invaders evoked little criticism. Support for Jonas Savimbi in Angola elicited louder cries in opposition, but the loudest opposition to U.S. aid came in Central America, where U.S. support for the Nicaraguan contras and for the right-wing government of El Salvador in its civil war with Marxist guerrillas met with determined and vitriolic criticism. Yet, Reagan and Shultz held firm in their support for anti-Communist governments and "freedom fighters," despite withering criticism from the media and Congress. This persistent position, coupled with a redoubling of U.S. military spending and a global offensive to demand that Third World governments privatize and democratize, ultimately bore fruit in the collapse of the Sandinista government in Nicaragua and eventually the collapse of Communism in the Soviet motherland. Emblematic of both the controversy and the ultimate success of this get-tough policy promoted by Reagan and Shultz was the invasion of Grenada. Though Grenada posed no major direct threat to U.S. security, it offered a symbolic opportunity to reverse a leftist coup d'état, demonstrate U.S. resolve, and flex U.S. military muscle.

The central strategy for Shultz and Reagan was containment of the Soviet Union, which was consistent with the general policy of all previous U.S. administrations since the beginning of the Cold War in the late 1940s. However, after the failure of the United States in Vietnam, and the years of détente and decline in military capacity that marked the Nixon, Ford, and Carter years, Shultz was eager to follow through with Reagan's gut instinct that the Soviet Union, if tested with resolve, would collapse from a combination of internal rot and external pressure. The testy U.S.–Soviet relationship was best symbolized in the nuclear arms area, where Shultz, in keeping with Reagan's overall policy, promoted nuclear expansion, including the new strategic defense initiative, while leaving the door open to nuclear arms negotiations. This carrot-and-stick strategy eventually convinced the youthful Soviet leader, Mikhail Gorbachev, that the United States was seriously committed to the arms race and would spend what it took to win it. With the Soviet economy rapidly disintegrating, its invasion of Afghanistan turning into an unending financial drain; its other foreign investments in Ethiopia, Angola, and Central America going sour; and unable to stop the pressures for reform in Poland and other parts of Eastern Europe, the Soviet leadership eventually bowed to the pressures and the realities.

Dealings with European allies centered largely around East-West policy, arms control initiatives, and strategies for dealing with East European states, where reform movements, such as the Polish Solidarity movement, served as harbingers of Communism's death knell. Although relations with North Atlantic Treaty Organization (NATO) members were often tense, Shultz effectively cultivated ties with numerous foreign leaders and their foreign ministers, most notably those of the United Kingdom and Germany.

In Africa, Shultz embraced the Reagan administration philosophy of constructive engagement with South Africa, preferring to use political and diplomatic means of persuasion instead of confrontation to move the white minority regime toward reform of its widely detested apartheid regime. This policy received a setback with the congressional override of Reagan's veto of the South African sanctions bill in October 1986. Persistence paid off in that region, as patient negotiations to secure withdrawal of Cuban forces from Angola and of South African withdrawal from Namibia gained steam in 1988–1989. This was eventually followed by significant reforms in South Africa in the early 1990s under the Bush administration. The 1980s also saw many countries in Africa reluctantly bowing to the new U.S. insistence on tying its aid to reform and privatization of national economies. Under Shultz, the United States remained a major player in humanitarian and refugee assistance to Africa.

Asian affairs demanded Shultz's attention as well, especially in cultivating ties with Japan as a strategic ally and in moderating the sometimes tense U.S.–Japanese trade relationship. Shultz sought to maintain and deepen ties with China, to ensure the peaceful economic reform of the world's largest country while keeping moderate and quiet pressure on the country's nondemocratic regime to improve its human rights record. Nonproliferation concerns called for monitoring of China's transfer of nuclear technology. U.S. support for Taiwan continued on Shultz's watch, which predictably proved to be a constant irritant in U.S.–Chinese relations. Basically, Shultz hoped to lay the groundwork for the eventual reform of China's communist government by encouraging its efforts toward free enterprise reforms, based on the conviction that Communist political ideology could not long withstand a budding capitalist approach in economic policy. In dealing with another Asian authoritarian regime, the Philippines under Ferdinand Marcos, Shultz chose the path of encouraging democratic reforms and demonstrated critical support for opposition leader Corazon Aquino, who eventually emerged victorious in 1986 after more than a year of very tense turmoil.

In dealing with terrorism, Shultz pursued a get-tough attitude of retaliation against known terrorist supporters, as in the bombing of Libya after terrorist attacks on U.S. military personnel in Germany. Shultz insisted on a no-negotiation policy where hostage taking was involved. He opposed the Iran-Contra policy of arms for hostages, and his testimony before Congress made clear that the arms for hostage policy was the result of a maverick operation at the NSC. His generally forthcoming testimony in the midst of that crisis deflected criticism from President Reagan and pointed to the need for future methods of preventing such operations in defiance of legislative statutes. Shultz emerged from the major setback of the Reagan administration as a forthright loyalist.

With the victory of George H. W. Bush in 1988, George Shultz began to prepare for his departure from government, which took place on January 20, 1989, as he handed over the reigns to a new Republican administration with James Baker as secretary of state. Shultz left the State Department with a legacy of which to be proud. Shultz had experienced both setbacks and successes, but on the whole, his vision of a world marked by greater freedom in both the political and economic spheres, was on the brink of realization that would have seemed impossible at the time he assumed the office. Many problems beset the world, but real progress toward peace in Southern Africa, Central America, South and Southeast Asia was already manifest. The collapse of Communism was already well underway in Eastern Europe and the Soviet Union. On the whole, the world was both a more peaceful and a freer place, owing at least in part to the policies George Shultz pursued as secretary of state.

George Shultz returned to academia and the private sector upon his retirement from government service. He has served as a distinguished fellow of the Hoover Institution at Stanford University since 1989 and as a member of the Board of Directors of Charles Schwab and Company and of the Bechtel Group. He published memoirs of his tenure as secretary of state in 1993 and was a visible supporter of Condoleeza Rice's candidacy as potential National Security Advisor during the George W. Bush's presidential campaign of 2000, a nomination eventually made by President-elect Bush in December of that year. He is a visible elder statesman on a variety of national and international issues and served on the California Governor's Economic Policy Advisory Board from 1995–1998. During his retirement years, Shultz has enjoyed the satisfaction of seeing many of his diplomatic efforts come to fruition, including the peaceful transition to democracy and majority rule in South Africa, the widespread achievement of peace and democratic rule in Central America, and the final and complete collapse of Communism in the former Soviet Union.

BIBLIOGRAPHICAL ESSAY

The most detailed account of George Shultz's tenure as secretary of state is found in his own memoirs, *Turmoil and Triumph: My Years as Secretary of State* (1993). Comparing Shultz's memoirs with those of other major international players of the time illustrates both his importance to many of the great issues of the day and the respect with which he was held by other major actors. As related in his *The Future Belongs to Freedom* (1991) Eduard Shevardnadze, Soviet Foreign Minister, and later President of Georgia, developed a deep admiration and friendship with Shultz and worked effectively with him to achieve common causes in U.S.-Soviet relations. General Secretary Mikhail Gorbachev spoke highly of Shultz's calm and collected demeanor and referred to him as on old friend and colleague in his *Memoirs* (1995). Shultz is given credit by the two former Soviet leaders for helping to develop and nurture "New Thinking" in foreign affairs among the two superpowers. This opinion is underscored by academic studies concerning U.S.–Soviet relations. See, for instance, Peter G. Boyle's *American-Soviet Relations: From the Russian Revolution to the Fall of Communism* (1993).

Lou Cannon's biography of Ronald Reagan, *President Reagan: The Role of a Lifetime* (1991) provides an interesting insider account of the struggles within the Reagan administration between conservatives and moderates, such as Shultz, to influence the foreign and national security policy of the U.S. government. Shultz won the begrudging respect of Lawrence Walsh, the special prosecutor named to investigate the Iran-Contra affair. Walsh, in his *Iran-Contra: The Final Report* (1993) claimed that Shultz's testimony in the hearings was in certain respects inaccurate and misleading. However, in his *Firewall* (1997), Walsh claimed that he didn't pursue litigation against Shultz because he was one of the few Reagan associates who had attempted to oppose the Iran-Contra arms for hostages deal and who attempted to be honest and not be part of a cover-up, thus serving as a lone "voice of courage and reason" among Reagan aids. Shultz's political adversaries, at both the international and national level alike, thus describe him in positive terms, albeit with reservations.

Robert F. Gorman

ROBERT SMITH (1757–1842)

Served 1809–1811
Appointed by President James Madison
Democratic-Republican

Robert Smith was born in Lancaster, Pennsylvania, November 3, 1757, the youngest of John and Mary Buchanan Smith's five children. Less than two years later, the Smiths moved to the small but flourishing port city of Baltimore, Maryland; two of the five Smith children, sons Robert and Samuel, played significant roles in the history of Baltimore and Maryland.

As the American Revolution commenced, Robert attended the College of New Jersey, today Princeton University, where he graduated with the class of 1781. In striking contrast to his older brother Samuel, who became an illustrious soldier of the Revolution, Robert saw but limited service, participating in the Battle of Brandywine. Throughout their very long lives, Samuel Smith always overshadowed his youngest brother.

As the new American Republic was launched, Robert Smith's career flourished. He studied law, becoming an attorney. He speculated in Virginia and Kentucky lands, laying the foundation of his future fortune. In 1789, Robert was chosen to be a Maryland presidential elector, casting a vote for the nation's first leader, George Washington. From 1793 to 1798, Smith was in Maryland's Senate. Between 1796 and 1800, he served in Maryland's House of Delegates; concurrently, he was a member of Baltimore's City Council for the three years ending in 1801. As the new century dawned, Robert Smith was a prominent citizen of Baltimore and Maryland.

As businessmen and merchants with far-ranging interests, the Smiths were Federalists, that is, supporters of President Washington and the economic policies advanced by Secretary of the Treasury Alexander Hamilton. Hamilton left office in 1795 as Washington did in 1797. Under the new president, John Adams, the United States found itself in an undeclared war with France. Adams and the Federalists put the country on a war footing, increasing taxes and undermining civil liberties in the notorious Alien and Sedition Acts of 1798. Samuel Smith, then in Congress, voted against this legislation; soon he and his brother were targets of Maryland Federalists in the vicious political atmosphere that marred the decade.

The two Smith naturally gravitated to the Republican faction led by Thomas Jefferson and James Madison opposing Federalist policies. In the closely contested election of 1800, the Smiths rendered yeoman service helping the Republicans garner half of Maryland's electoral votes. A grateful Jefferson offered Samuel Smith the post of secretary of the navy, which Smith rejected. When the new president was rebuffed by two more Republicans, Samuel Smith reluctantly agreed to occupy the office until a permanent secretary could be found. The search ended in July 1801, with Robert Smith agreeing to be secretary of the navy. Presumably, Samuel Smith influenced Jefferson in the selection. On the other hand, the 43-year-old Robert was a loyal Republican, a successful businessman, and a man with expertise in admiralty law.

Smith served Jefferson and the country loyally and effectively until Jefferson left office in 1809. It was not an easy job: he was somehow expected to oversee the downsizing of the navy while the infant fleet suppressed Barbary pirates preying on American commerce in the Mediterranean. Despite the budgetary ax, the Marylander managed no only to keep a small force on station thousands of miles from American shores, but he helped select and promote outstanding leaders in the officer corps. Smith also cooperated with Jefferson; after consulting with Smith, Jefferson named Jacob Crowninshield Smith's successor as navy secretary at the start of Jefferson's second term. The plan was for Smith to move to the attorney general's post, and technically Smith was the nation's chief legal officer for five months. When Crowninshield's health prevented him from joining the government, the ever-compliant Smith moved back to his old job. Jefferson was comfortable enough with Robert Smith to pen his underling a very famous letter in which the president admitted a youthful flirtation with a neighbor's wife. In short, although Smith was never the intimate of Jefferson that Madison or Treasury Secretary Albert Gallatin was, he was a trusted lieutenant.

All was not well in Jefferson's political family, however. Considerable friction developed between Senator Samuel Smith and Jefferson in 1805–1806; Senator Smith objected to presidential maneuverings to secure West Florida. Then he was disturbed by Jefferson's selection of William Pinckney, a Maryland Federalist lawyer, to join James Monroe in delicate diplomatic negotiations in Britain. Finally, Samuel Smith faulted the administration's weak response to infringements on the country's neutrality during the Napoleonic Wars. To say that Robert found himself in an awkward situation would be an understatement.

Then there was Robert Smith's feud with Gallatin. Difficulties between the two centered on Gallatin's relentless penny-pinching. Even the smallest expenditures attracted the eagle-eyed Gallatin, who was fanatically committed to curbing public spending and extinguishing the national debt. Smith became increasingly frustrated with Gallatin's oversight, chafing at the treasury secretary's demands for explanations about Navy Department costs. The two men were bitter enemies by the end of Jefferson's presidency.

Jefferson's friend and neighbor, Madison, swept to victory in the 1808 presidential election despite political infighting in Republican ranks and sectional unhappiness with the ban on American exports in American ships known as the embargo. The Federalists aided Madison's march to victory with their political ineptitude. So James Madison took the oath of office as the nation's fourth president on March 4, 1809.

Madison found himself in a witches' cauldron of troubles domestically and internationally. On the home front, the learned chief executive cobbled a cabinet together that included Gallatin and Robert Smith. Instead of naming his first choice, Gallatin, to run the Department of State, the new chief chose Smith. Two centuries later it remains an interesting question: Why Smith instead of Gallatin? The Smiths had supported Madison's election after a fashion. Smith, of course, enjoyed support from his brother and others in the Senate. Conversely, Gallatin was disliked by more than a few Republicans for his tightfistedness at the Treasury. Some Republicans and most Federalists despised the Swiss-born Gallatin as a foreigner. Madison knew of Jefferson's regard for Smith. Further, the new president was familiar with Smith's competence in handling the Navy Department. He also knew that Smith had been exceedingly cooperative with Jefferson as evidenced by the Crowninshield episode. Finally, Madison, having served eight years as secretary of state, probably thought that Smith could busy himself administering the department while he, Madison, crafted the nation's foreign policy. Whatever the reasons for Smith's appointment, he became the sixth secretary of state of the United States.

Robert Smith became secretary of state with no clear vision for American policy. Most likely he shared the beliefs of some Republicans from the middle states that a more vigorous defense of the national interest was in order. Whatever Smith's views, the inescapable conclusion one reaches is that Madison was the chief architect of American policy; Robert Smith was secretary in name only.

Smith acceded to office at a most difficult moment. For six years, two titans, Great Britain and France, had been struggling for victory in a great conflict that actually had its origins in the French Revolution. With France invincible on land and Britain dominant on the oceans, stalemate had resulted. In this environment, both nations had implemented commercial restriction with the intention of damaging the other's economy. Caught between the Goliaths was the United States of America. Under Jefferson, the nation had followed the neutrality policies first enunciated by President Washington in 1793. As Washington and President John Adams discovered, neutrality did not exempt American commerce from interference or American sailors from being snatched from American flagged vessels. Jefferson learned the same lesson. English warships hovered off the eastern seaboard of the United States, screening America's commerce; they also kidnapped American sailors, an act the British called impressment. France was hardly an innocent. Trade with France and French-controlled Europe was hindered by complex rules, and French corsairs captured American merchantmen on the high seas. If France were not as guilty as Britain in offending the United States, it was merely because of Britain's maritime hegemony.

Within days of Madison's inauguration, missions were sent to Britain and France seeking revocation of onerous edicts affecting the United States with promises of a favorable response. Sadly, these undertakings failed. At home, however, a breakthrough seemed to have taken place in Anglo-American relations in the Erskine agreement of April 1809. David M. Erskine, His Majesty's Minister to the United States, had signed an accord with the U.S. government in which Britain would not enforce trade restrictions as they pertained to the United States in return for the suspension of the embargo's successor, the nonintercourse act, against Britain. It seemed for a few months that France had been isolated, that Anglo-American relations had been put on a new level of cooperation, and that Madison would succeed where Jefferson had failed. The euphoria lasted until July 1809, when George Canning, Britain's Foreign Minister, disavowed Erskine's agreement. Erskine left America amid outbursts of rage and frustration. It should be remembered that the Erskine debacle was the president's responsibility; talks leading to the measures started under Madison. Although Smith was in office when agreement was inked, he had little or nothing to do with it.

The Erskine fiasco was soon eclipsed by the flap caused by Francis James Jackson, Erskine's successor. Jackson has been described as "an able, if flawed product of the diplomatic patronage system." In America his abilities were totally outshone by his flaws. Like many Englishmen of his station, Jackson simply despised the United States. He believed the Americans to be crude, bumptious upstarts manipulated by demagogic politicians. It is one thing for a diplomat to hold such beliefs; it is quite another to make one's sentiments known, which is precisely what Jackson did. In short order, Jackson made himself wildly unpopular and unwelcome.

A year into Madison's presidency, the United States was arguably worse off than when Madison had taken the oath of office. The British continued their impressments and violations. With the French, the situation was little better. Napoleon kept signing new decrees, the net result being ever greater dangers for those American merchantmen voyaging to French-dominated ports. Attempts to negotiate with the French were as fruitless as those with the English. About the sole bright spot for Madison was the so-called West Florida revolution of September 1810, when American settlers seized the area around modern-day Baton Rouge, Louisiana. Spain, which occupied the region, had been fending off American diplomatic inquiries about inclusion of the area in the Louisiana Purchase. By 1810 the Spaniards were fighting Napoleon at home and coping with independence movements in their vast New World empire. Thus a generation before the term Manifest Destiny was coined, American settlers brushed aside Spanish authority, creating the short-lived Republic of West Florida, and then joined the American Union. Secretary of State Smith's role in all this was that of a conduit of messages between Madison and the settler-revolutionaries; he fully approved the takeover of the Baton Rouge District.

In the winter of 1810–1811, Madison began developing plans to escape the continued humiliations heaped on the United States; the groundwork for a second war with Britain was laid. Madison's plan included better relations with France. Hence, he accepted Napoleon's word that two measures, the Berlin and Milan decrees, were no longer applicable to America. With the British adamant that the Napoleonic move was fraudulent, the president invoked the appropriate clauses of a law called Macon's Bill #2 and imposed nonimportation on Great Britain. Building on Napoleon's action, the president planned to cement better relations with France through negotiations with a new French minister in Washington and a new American envoy, his friend, Joel Barlow, in Paris.

Meanwhile, strong political winds were sweeping Washington. The continuing Gallatin–Smith feud came to a head in the brawl over the rechartering of the Bank of the United States. Gallatin favored the rechartering; Senator Samuel Smith did not. Smith alluded to the overwhelming foreign ownership of bank stock. He did not comment on his investments in Maryland banks that would be enhanced with the demise of the Bank of the United States. Once again, Robert Smith found himself linked to his brother's politics.

481

Gallatin decided to force the president's hand: either Madison dismissed Smith or he, Gallatin, would resign. Forced to choose, Madison opted to ask Smith for his resignation. To make the demand more palatable, Smith would be offered an appointment as Minister to Russia, a spot already occupied by John Quincy Adams. Smith's replacement in the cabinet would be James Monroe, a popular Virginian, who had been at odds with Jefferson and Madison since the two had rejected a treaty he and Pinckney had negotiated in December 1806.

Late in March Madison summoned an unsuspecting Smith to a meeting. How long the discussion between the two ensued is uncertain, but Madison's April "Memorandum on Robert Smith" covers almost nine printed pages. The president offered a laundry list of Smith's shortcomings: he questioned Smith's loyalty; he found Smith's diplomatic correspondence wanting; he had been indiscreet in conversations with the British; and he had opposed the restrictive system. Apparently Smith was bewildered by these and other charges leveled by Madison. He was particularly hurt when, after requesting the London mission instead of St. Petersburg, Madison blandly replied that other arrangements had been made and "that it was a place of discussions & negotiations calling for appropriate talents & habits of business." In Madison's mind, that made Smith ineligible.

Although the meeting ended on a civil note, Smith grew furious as he reflected on what had transpired. He would leave his post, but he also decided to write an exoneration of himself in what came to be called *Robert Smith's Address to the People of the United States*, a critical account of Madison and the foreign policy of the United States. Smith should have listened to his brother who counseled him not to vent his anger publicly. In a pamphlet duel with the president, Samuel Smith knew that Robert would lose. Soon criticisms rained on Robert and by summer's end, public interest in the affair had evaporated.

Smith served as secretary of state under trying circumstances. He did not enjoy Madison's confidence. He was a bystander to political warfare not of his own making, tarred by brother Samuel's Senate activities. Internationally, even if he had had a free hand, Smith faced the same vexing problem that Madison had as secretary of state under Jefferson: how to protect and secure American neutral rights while a life-and-death struggle was being waged by the great Continental powers. Madison was unsuccessful under Jefferson. Smith, who enjoyed none of the powers and influence of Madison, could hardly have succeeded. Instead, he had to content himself running his department while more or less ignored by the president. He was neither the shortest serving secretary of state nor the first one removed. Certainly he was not a major figure in the history of the prestigious office.

Smith returned to Baltimore, where he lived the rest of his life engaged in various businesses, intellectual, and religious pursuits. Brother Samuel, meanwhile, added to his Revolutionary War laurels with a stalwart and successful defense of Baltimore during his latter stages of the War of 1812. While Samuel basked in the limelight, his businesses began to deteriorate; brother Robert refused to become involved in an economic resuscitation of Samuel, who died in 1839. Three years later, on November 26, 1842, Robert died in Baltimore, the last surviving presidential elector from 1789.

BIBLIOGRAPHICAL ESSAY

Robert Smith has attracted scant historical attention. Thom M. Armstrong, *Politics, Diplomacy and Intrigue in the Early Republic: The Cabinet Career of Robert Smith*,

1801–1811 (1991) is the published form of a dissertation done at the University of California at Santa Barbara. The late, controversial scholar Charles Tansill wrote a useful sketch of Smith's tenure at the state department, "Robert Smith," in Samuel Flagg Bemis (ed.), *The American Secretaries of State and Their Diplomacy* (10 vols., 1927–1929). Some insight about Robert can be gleaned in two biographies of Samuel Smith. Frank A. Cassell, *Merchant Congressman in the Young Republic: Samuel Smith of Maryland, 1752–1839* (1971) and John Silas Pancake, *Samuel Smith and the Politics of Business: 1752–1839* (1972). Critical mention of Smith abounds in the historiography of the origins of the War of 1812. See, for example, Henry Adams, *History of the United States during the Administrations of Jefferson and Madison* (9 vols., 1889–1891); Irving Brant, *James Madison: The President, 1809–1812* (1961); Clifford L. Egan, *Neither Peace Nor War: Franco-American Relations, 1803–1812* (1983); Bradford Perkins, *Prologue to War: England and the United States, 1805–1812* (1961); and J. C. A. Stagg, *Mr. Madison's War: Politics, Diplomacy, and Warfare in the Early American Republic, 1783–1830* (1983). An outstanding account of cabinet government under Jefferson with favorable treatment of Smith is Noble E. Cunningham, *The Process of Government under Jefferson* (1978). Finally, Stagg et al., *The Papers of James Madison: Presidential Series* (1992, 1996), Volumes 2 and 3 contain very useful material concerning Smith's two years as secretary of state.

Clifford Egan

EDWARD R. STETTINIUS, JR. (1900–1949)

Served 1944–1945
Appointed by President Franklin D. Roosevelt
Continued in office under President Harry S. Truman
Democrat

Edward Reilly Stettinius, Jr., served as secretary of state for exactly seven months during one of the most crucial periods in American history. His only biographer characterized him as "the secretary who was not secretary of state." Eminent diplomatic historian Samuel Flagg Bemis dismissed him for being "a figurehead in policy behind whose handsome visage was Franklin D. Roosevelt who really controlled our diplomacy." Yet, Joseph Grew, a veteran of 40 years service in the Department of State, observed that Stettinius "was the best chief I ever had." Although he had many shortcomings a secretary of state, Stettinius was more than a mere figurehead. In his brief tenure, this talented administrator reorganized the Department of State, served as a spokesman for U.S. interests at the Yalta Conference, and played a vital role in the creation of the United Nations, only to be removed by President Harry S Truman at the moment of his greatest accomplishment.

Born in Chicago on October 22, 1900, Stettinius grew up in comfortable circumstances as the son of a partner in the Wall Street banking house J. P. Morgan & Company. Upon his graduation from the exclusive Pomfret School in Connecticut, Edward went on to the University of Virginia, where much to the chagrin of his family, he managed to earn only six credits in three and one-half years.

Stettinius took a job with General Motors after company vice president John Lee Pratt convinced him that his creative and humanitarian instincts could be fulfilled through a business career. He rose through the company rapidly. In 1933 Stettinius worked with the New Deal's National Recovery Administration, drafting codes designed to bring about economic recovery. The next year he accepted a position with United States Steel. Within four years he became chairman of the board, just in time to deftly handle a Justice Department investigation of monopolistic practice and steer the company through a major recession.

Rather than fighting the New Deal, as did so many in the corporate world, Stettinius endorsed much of it. His friendship with Roosevelt's advisor, Harry Hopkins, led the president to appoint him as head of the newly reconstituted War Resources

484

Board, which was quickly scrapped. In June 1940 the president asked him to serve on the Advisory Commission to the Council of National Defense as Commissioner of Industrial Materials. Early the next year he was named Director of Priorities in the Office of Production Management. The assignment in both jobs was the same: increasing production as the government prepared for the worst, a difficult task considering the shortages of raw materials, the reluctance of many businessmen to switch over to defense work without a declaration of war, and endless wrangling among labor, business, and New Dealers.

After eight months of mixed success, Stettinius replaced Hopkins as the head administrator of the Lend-lease Administration, although it was understood that important policy decisions with regard to aiding antifascist forces would continue to come from inside the White House. By all accounts he did an excellent job, streamlining the bureaucracy to the point that the time to process a request for materials dropped from three months to three days. When the United States entered the war in December 1941, the supply vehicle for fighting a global war was firmly in place. Roosevelt restricted Stettinius's responsibilities to nonmilitary supplies during World War II. His efficient handling of the Office of Lend-Lease won him plaudits from Congress and the press. Public relations skills learned in the world of business helped to sell people on what had been a very controversial program.

After Roosevelt accepted Sumner Welles's resignation, due to an ongoing struggle between Secretary of State Cordell Hull and Welles, the administration settled on Stettinius as undersecretary of state. Although he lacked diplomatic experience and critical thinking skills, Stettinius brought to the job strong administrative and public relations abilities, the admiration of congressional conservatives, good liberal credentials, and a firm friendship with Hopkins.

Stettinius set to work quickly, lobbying the Senate in support of a resolution strongly endorsing a new United Nations organization based on the accord that Hull had reached with the Soviet Union and Great Britain at the Moscow Conference. The undersecretary attempted a major departmental reorganization to eliminate overlapping jurisdictions, to better coordinate policy with the White House, and to bring about better public relations. The hasty shuffling did not improve matters much but at least boosted the president's confidence in the department. In April 1944 the president entrusted Stettinius with an important diplomatic mission, sending him to London to sound out the British about postwar policy in advance of the approaching D-Day landings. Churchill did agree that the Allies should put the UN together in advance of military victory but remained convinced that regional security was the best insurance against Soviet domination of Europe.

The climax of Stettinius's work as undersecretary came at the Dumbarton Oaks Conference near Washington, August 21 to October 7, 1944, where representatives of the Big Four met to hammer out details of a new international security organization. The ailing secretary of state put Stettinius in charge of the U.S. delegation. The American proposals, as drawn up by State Department personnel, tried to correct the flaws that made the League of Nations less an instrument of collective security than a debating society. Real power was reserved for the executive council where the great powers would keep the peace and be afforded veto power. An economic and social office would foster international cooperation. Embittered by its expulsion from the League in 1939, the Soviet Union demanded an absolute veto. Wary of being the only communist nation in an otherwise capitalist organization, the Soviets also wanted votes for each of their 16 republics, a demand that so alarmed the Americans that it was referred to in all correspondence only as "the X-matter" for fear of leaks to the press. Unable to agree on these issues, they were papered over in the hope that the Big Three leaders could settle them later, although the powers achieved a remarkable degree of unanimity on other matters. As chairman of the Conference, Stettinius demonstrated ample diplomatic skills.

The largely successful conclusion of the conference came in time to help Roosevelt win an unprecedented fourth term as president. With Hull ill and Roosevelt still insisting that postwar territorial considerations be postponed, American foreign policy drifted through late 1944. Following Hull's resignation, which finally came in November over differences on the postwar treatment of Germany, Stettinius emerged (as he had after the ouster of Welles) as the compromise choice pushed by Harry Hopkins. Roosevelt favored either Welles or Henry Wallace for the job, but Hull detested both men. The president also passed over James Byrnes, who had the right experience and a high standing with Congress because, as Stettinius noted "Jimmy might question who was boss." Stettinius was unlikely to challenge FDR and Hopkins or upset the president's bipartisan approach to foreign policy. Public opinion polls revealed strong support for Stettinius. His quick Senate confirmation yielded only one dissenting vote.

Although it was widely understood that FDR would continue to manage wartime policies from the Map Room in the White House and communicate directly with Stalin and Churchill, Stettinius managed to make his own contributions to U.S. foreign policy. Stettinius recast the outmoded Foggy Bottom bureaucracy. He named Charles Bohlen as a special liaison between the department and the White House to foster better communications. The secretary formed the State-War-Navy coordinating committee as a top-level clearinghouse of information. Accepting the resignations of all the assistant secretaries, save Dean Acheson, Stettinius (with Hopkins's approval) nominated Nelson Rockefeller, William R. Clayton, and Archibald MacLeish for the posts and secured approval for two additional assistants. The nominations drew fire from Senate liberals who believed that, with the exception of the liberal poet MacLeish, the new team was too conservative and pro-big business, but after Roosevelt interceded all won confirmation. Stettinius almost doubled the staff of the secretary's office. His reorganization plan of December 1944 proved more successful than his first attempt as undersecretary, especially in the streamlined routing of reports and the creation of top-level committees on policy and postwar programs.

Stettinius spent more time at international conferences during his brief tenure than he did in Washington. After meeting with British Foreign Minister Anthony Eden at Malta, Stettinius accompanied the president to the Yalta Conference (February 4 to February 11, 1945), one of the most controversial diplomatic gatherings in modern history. As expected, Roosevelt did most of the talking. Yet the secretary's explanation of the U.S. position on UN Security Council voting procedures brought praise from Stalin and Churchill as well as Charles Bohlen, who later called it "the best presentation of all our positions at Yalta." The Soviets agreed to the U.S. compromise that the permanent council members have limited veto power in cases that involved them and settled the "X-matter" of additional UN votes. The American delegation thus obtained what it wanted most: a Big Three agreement on the UN, an organization that could settle problems resulting from an imperfect peace. With Stalin determined to have Poland in hands friendly toward Moscow and the Red Army driving across Eastern Europe, the best Roosevelt and Stettinius could do was a nebulous agreement to reorganize the Soviet-backed regime in Warsaw. A Declaration on Liberated Europe committed the great powers to recognize the right of peoples, freed from fascist tyranny, to democracy. Stettinius did not take part in a secret agreement between Roosevelt and Stalin on the Far East. At least for a time, Stettinius received a share of the credit for his part in the Yalta Agreement.

After Yalta, Stettinius faced the task of convincing Latin American diplomats to support the United Nations. Many delegates to the Mexico City Conference on Problems of Peace and War of the American Republics, held from February 21 to March 5, supported a regional approach to collective security. Under Stettinius, the United States endorsed a regional security proposal, the Act of Chapultepec, which created a military alliance, to be put in effect should aggression occur against any signatory as long as the war lasted. Once the war had been won, the parties involved would reconvene to consider extending the arrangement. Mexico launched a movement to amend the Dumbarton Oaks Proposals on the UN to make the world body more democratic. As a compromise the secretary of state agreed that the concerns of the conference would be taken into consideration at the founding conference of the UN to be held in San Francisco. Finally, Stettinius backed away from the administration's determination to punish Argentina for pro-Axis activities, convincing Roosevelt that a few token acts of contrition by the Peron regime would make the Argentines "good neighbors" deserving of admission to the UN.

Stettinius chaired the U.S. delegation to the San Francisco Conference on the United Nations, but Roosevelt's death on April 12, 1945 numbered Stettinius' days as secretary of state, for President Harry S Truman did not have much faith in him. Yet, with the UN Conference just two weeks away, Truman asked the secretary of state to stay on amid rumors that he would soon be replaced. The conference, April 25 to June 27, 1945, took place at a time of increased suspicions among the members of the Grand Alliance. American officials, including Stettinius, tried to "get tough" with the Russians. The United States blocked a Soviet bid to seat Poland while working behind the scenes to admit two of the Soviet Republics and Argentina, maneuvers that angered internationalists including Cordell Hull. Stettinius fought long and hard against the impulse felt by both sides to preserve regional security arrangements at the expense of a strong world organization as envisioned just a few months earlier. Regionalists (led by Assistant Secretary Rockefeller and Senator Arthur Vandenberg) gained momentum as the conference wore on to the point that Article 51 of the UN Charter provided the base from which to buid political blocs of "collective self-defense."

Stettinius found himself allied briefly with Soviet Ambassador Andrei Gromyko when the smaller nations rebelled against the great power veto arrangements agreed to at Yalta. Gromyko's assertion that the veto could be used to block the discussion of issues, as opposed to Security Council action, an interpretation rejected by the U.S. and Britain, put the conference at a dead end. Following a suggestion from the British ambassador, Stettinius wired the U.S. Ambassador to Moscow, Averell Harriman, asking Harry Hopkins, then in the Soviet capital, to intercede directly with Stalin. The Soviet leader's acquiescence in the Anglo-American interpretation allowed the conferees to finish their work. More than any one else, Stettinius worked at San Francisco to preserve as far as possible the structure hammered out at Dumbarton Oaks. He managed the heterogeneous U.S. delegates well, winning over their respect through hard work and by hewing to his convictions.

In his absence from Washington, though, undersecretary Joseph Grew had handled the management of foreign policy without consulting Stettinius closely. President Truman had not kept him abreast of plans to send Hopkins to see Stalin. On June 27, 1945, the president accepted Stettinius's resignation submitted following the death of Roosevelt. The president had given the job to James Byrnes after Roosevelt's funeral, effective at the conclusion of the UN Conference. The choice made sense for several reasons. Stettinius had never held public office, but was next in the line of presidential succession, and Truman wanted a man who had faced the electorate. The president also thought the appointment "might help balance things up" from the summer of 1944 when Roosevelt and the Democratic National Convention had chosen him for the vice presidency rather than Byrnes, the more qualified candidate. Most importantly Stettinius was a Roosevelt-Hull man at a time when Truman had decided to move away from their universalist policies.

Serving only seven months in office under presidents who wanted decision making kept at the White House, Edward Stettinius had neither the inclination nor the opportunity to become a major force in U.S. foreign policy. Truman privately assessed his first secretary of state as "a fine man, but never an idea new or old." Stettinius did have the wisdom to choose experienced, forceful people as his subordinates and the talent to make them work together harmoniously. He managed many of his major tasks well, especially the administrative restructuring of the Department of State and the establishment of the United Nations.

Truman tried to let Stettinius down easily by making him the head of the American delegation to the UN Prepatory Commission, which was to meet in London. He attended the first UN General Assembly and Security Council sessions in London and New York in early 1946 as chairman of the American delegation. On June 2, 1946, shortly after the resolution of the Iran crisis, Stettinius resigned, never to return to public service.

Edward Stettinius spent the remaining years of his life pursuing the interests of his formative years. As Rector of the University of Virginia he organized foreign policy seminars and fund-raising campaigns. Mixing humanitarian concerns with capitalism, the former secretary of state created Stettinius Associates—Liberia, Inc., a system of privately controlled economic aid to the African nation of Liberia. The chief legacy of this scheme turned out to be a new system of ship registrations under the Liberian flag designed to help shipowners evade taxes, health and safety laws, and union wages. Stettinius spent the last months of his life collaborating with Professor Walter Johnson on a book defending American actions at Yalta. On October 31, 1949, three days after the publication of *Roosevelt and the Russians*, Stettinius died of a coronary thrombosis at the age of 49.

BIBLIOGRAPHICAL ESSAY

The University of Virginia houses the papers of Edward R. Stettinius, Jr., a well-organized collection of some 500,000 items including material from his business career, the NRA, the War Resources Board, the National Defense Advisory Commission, the Office of Production Management, the Lend-Lease Administration, the Department of State, conferences and missions he attended, and the United Nations. Microfilm copies of guide cards are available for loan. The Papers of the Department of State, National Archives and Records Service (Washington, D.C.) contain much information on his government service. Manuscript collections in the Franklin D. Roosevelt Presidential Library (Hyde Park, NY) and the Harry S. Truman Presidential Library (Independence, MO) will yield material on Stettinius. Other collections of papers of individuals who worked closely with him include Cordell Hull, Breckinridge Long, Leo Pasvolsky, and Robert P. Patterson (Library of Congress, Washington); James Forrestal (Princeton University Library); Joseph Grew (Houghton Library, Harvard University); Henry L. Stimson (Yale University); and Arthur H. Vandenberg (Clements Library, University of Michigan).

The Department of State series Foreign Relations of the United States for the years 1943 to 1946 (Washington, D.C., 1963–1969) are a readily accessible source of information on Stettinius. Papers concerning the founding of the United Nations have been published by that organization as *Documents of the United States Conference on International Organization* (1945) and *Security Council, Official Records, First Year, First Series*, Supplement, No. 1 (1946).

Published biographical and autobiographical material on Stettinius is thin. For an excellent, brief summary of his life, see *American National Biography*, Vol. 20 (1999), pp. 687–689. Thomas M. Campbell and George C. Herring (eds.), *The Diaries of Edward R. Stettinius, Jr.* (1943–1946), material culled from the Stettinius Papers and connected with a narrative, is the best single source on his public service. Richard L. Walker, "E. R. Stettinius, Jr., 1944–45," in *The American Secretaries of State and Their Diplomacy*, Vol. 14 (1969), Samuel Flagg Bemis and Robert Ferrell (eds.), is an 87-page treatment that covers the basics. Walter Johnson, who collaborated with Stettinius on a book, analyzes his brief tenure as secretary of state in Norman A. Graebner (ed.), *An Uncertain Tradition: American Secretaries of State in the Twentieth Century* (1961) and summarizes his life in John A. Garraty and Edward T. James (eds.), *Dictionary of American Biography*, Supplement Four (1946–1950), pp. 776–778. Stettinius wrote two books, neither of which reveals much of the man: *Lend-Lease: Weapon for Victory* (1944) and *Roosevelt and the Russians* (1944).

Although Stettinius did not live long enough to write his memoirs, many of his colleagues did—or left behind papers, which have been published. Those that contain significant material on him include Dean Acheson, *Present at the Creation: My Years in the State Department* (1969), which is very critical of the Stettinius style; Joseph Grew, *Turbulent Era: A Diplomatic Record of Forty Years, 1904–1945*, 2 vols. (1953), who admired his "chief"; W. Averell Harriman and Ellie Abel, *Special Envoy to Churchill and Stalin, 1941–1946* (1975); and W. Averell Harriman, *America and Russia in a Changing World, A Half Century of Personal Observation* (1971), works that express a certain appreciation of the secretary. Also, see Cordell Hull, *The Memoirs of Cordell Hull*, 2 vols. (1948), who praises his former undersecretary's work; Robert E. Sherwood, *Roosevelt and Hopkins: An Intimate History* (1948), who discusses the friendship between Hopkins and Stettinius; and Henry L. Stimson and McGeorge Bundy, *On Active Service in Peace and War* (1948), who mute the blunt criticism of Stettinius so evident in Stimson's diary. Harry S Truman, *Memoirs*, 2 vols. (1956), and Robert H. Ferrell (ed.), *Off the Record: The Private Papers of Harry S. Truman* (1980) explain the president's lack of faith in his first secretary of state; and Arthur

H. Vandenberg, Jr., and Joe A. Morris (eds.), *The Private Papers of Senator Vandenberg* (1952) traces the senator's growing admiration for Stettinius.

The diplomacy of World War II and the early Cold War has been covered in numerous monographs. James Macgregor Burns, *Roosevelt: The Soldier of Freedom, 1940–1945* (1990) discusses Roosevelt's relationship with Stettinius. The best monographs on Stettinius's work in creating the United Nations are Thomas M. Campbell, *Masquerade Peace: America's UN Policy, 1944–1945* (1973) and Ruth B. Russell, *A History of the United Nations Charter: The Role of the United States, 1940–1945* (1958). Graham H. Stuart, *The Department of State* (1949), examines the departmental reorganizations undertaken by Stettinius critically. Rodney Carlisle, "The American Century Implemented: Stettinius and the Liberian Flag of Convenience," *Business History Review* 54 (1980): 175–91 details the former secretary of state's postwar business dealings.

Peter Buckingham

HENRY L. STIMSON (1867–1950)

Served 1929–1933
Appointed by President Herbert Hoover
Republican

Henry Lewis Stimson was one of America's most distinguished public servants, ranking with such other statesmen in the twentieth century as John Hay, Elihu Root, and Charles Evans Hughes. His important contributions spanned almost a half century—a period during which the United States passed from a newly acquired status of world power, barely beyond having a Western frontier, to the dominant world power, albeit briefly, with a monopoly of atomic weapons. It was Stimson's hope that the United States would assume responsibilities of world leadership, and before he died in 1950 there was evidence that America had accepted a major international role.

Stimson's family history in America goes back to the seventeenth century. His ancestors fought in the colonial wars and the Revolution; his father served in the Civil War. When young Henry was almost four, his father left his business on Wall Street to study medicine in Europe, eventually becoming a prominent New York surgeon. Thus, at an early age, Henry was introduced to the world beyond America. Henry's mother, after a progressive illness, died when he was eight. He and his sister went to live with grandparents and were reared under the particular care of a loving unmarried aunt.

Stimson attended small private schools in New York City before his father determined a more rigorous education was necessary and sent him to Phillips Academy at Andover. From there he went to Yale, where he was elected to Phi Beta Kappa and Skull and Bones, a prestigious senior society. Stimson believed that the latter was the most important educational experience of his life. Harvard law school, an editorship of the *Harvard Law Review*, and intellectual contact with George F. Palmer, Josiah Royce, and John Fiske followed. Leaving Cambridge after two years and returning to New York, Stimson came under the strong influence of his father, who arranged a position with Root and Clarke, a law firm that within a few years admitted Stimson as a partner. Thus began a long association with Elihu Root whose example, advice, and favor supported Stimson in his rise in private and public life. Years later Stimson would note that many people relied on Root, considering his advice the most valuable they could receive.

Stimson emerged in American public life during the Progressive Era, and he supported many of the changes the reformers sought. During these years he was U.S. attorney for the southern district of New York, unsuccessful candidate for governor of New York in 1910, and President Taft's secretary of war. In the first of these positions he brought together a group of excellent young lawyers who successfully matched wits with corporate attorneys. Stimson's only major attempt at elective office failed because he was a poor campaigner, and the Republican Party was splitting. The Republican rift confronted Stimson even more starkly when he served in Taft's cabinet. Stimson admired Roosevelt; the two men had much in common from their enjoyment of frontier life to regulating trusts to their natural sympathy for the military. Yet Stimson's cabinet position, undertaken with Roosevelt's blessing, necessitated Stimson's loyalty to Taft and his pleas to Roosevelt for party unity. Roosevelt professed to understand, but the campaign heat strained their friendship, at least for a time. By 1915 they came together again in confronting a world at war.

The year 1915 was a watershed for Stimson's interests. Before that year, as perhaps with other progressives, Stimson focused on domestic issues, but by 1915 the war compelled Stimson to consider preparedness, Prussianism, and America's worldview. From this time until the end of his career, international affairs dominated his public life.

Stimson feared that America's voice was muted because there appeared little strength to support the nation's rights. Who doubts, he asked, that Wilson's note to Germany would receive more attention if it were known that America's navy was in readiness and its people disciplined and trained in arms? Fearfully, he saw a comparison with Jefferson and Madison's disastrous peace-at-any-price policy of a century earlier. He opposed woman's suffrage, for he foresaw in the nation's preparation for self-defense that women, ignorant of forceful methods, might align themselves with well-meaning sentimentalists to oppose measures of national insurance. This conclusion came from the tortured reasoning that the question of giving any class of people the vote should be decided solely by the effect their voting would have on the general welfare of the community, including themselves; otherwise, he said, by conferring a privilege we might destroy real rights. Nor did his interest in military training wane when the war was over. Stimson believed that universal military training was important for imparting American ideals of citizenship, initiative, and rules of personal hygiene. These were benefits even if there were no wars.

Important in Stimson's view of America's emerging world role was President Wilson's proposal for a League of Nations. On this issue Elihu Root guided Stimson. Stimson believed that the time was coming when one nation's aggression against another nation would be considered an offense against all, and he believed that the United States should encourage this development. For this reason he supported the idea of a League of Nations, but he thought Wilson's proposal moved too fast, particularly with Article 10 of the League Covenant. Stimson, along with Root, favored a gradual development that would move people in the right direction but not create obligations that would be disregarded. The League would be a forum where the United States would learn to assume world responsibilities.

The Senate's failure to accept the League disappointed Stimson. He blamed both Wilson and the president's opponents, but his major regret was his self-deception that Warren Harding, if elected president, would support America's membership in a world organization. Harding did not, but Stimson also made little effort in this direction either.

Calvin Coolidge promoted Stimson's return to public service when he called on Stimson to resolve a nasty situation developing in Nicaragua, the scene of recurrent U.S. intervention for many years. A revolution supported by Mexico was on the verge of successfully challenging a regime of questionable constitutionality but recognized by the United States. Stimson's frank discussions threatening the use of force against the revolutionaries convinced most of them to end their fighting. The threat plus promises to supervise that next presidential election ended the immediate crisis, but the opposition of a little-known Nicaraguan nationalist, Augusto C. Sandino, led to guerrilla warfare that involved the United States until the end of Stimson's term as secretary of state.

President Coolidge's satisfaction with Stimson's ready handling of the revolutionary crisis in Nicaragua made the emissary acceptable when Chief Justice Taft and Philippine leaders recommended him to succeed Leonard Wood as governor general of the Philippines. As in his brief service in Nicaragua, Stimson's tenure in the Far East revealed the patrician striving to work fairly, sympathetically, and honestly with those he was supervising, but not believing them ready for independence. For Stimson, the United States had assumed a responsibility not yet fulfilled. Without supervision there was, Stimson believed, "the Malay tendency to backslide."

As Stimson's first year in the Philippines neared its end, he talked of staying another year or more to finish what he considered the most important work ever placed in his hands. There were great changes coming in the Far East, and America's influence on those changes depended on its accomplishments in the Philippines. Stimson believed that the United States was showing the way for such colonial powers as Great Britain and the Netherlands.

In the midst of these thoughts on American's role as an imperial leader, Stimson learned from his law partner George Roberts that President-elect Hoover was considering the governor general for a post in the cabinet—secretary of state or attorney general. Stimson expressed willingness to head the State Department, and Hoover, encouraged by Charles Evans Hughes and Elihu Root, made a formal offer after two other candidates refused the position.

The new president and his secretary of state were not well acquainted at the time of Stimson's appointment. Stimson now came to appreciate the president's broad knowledge, but as the administration developed there were differences that made Stimson's years as secretary of state not the happiest of his public service. Long a proponent of a strong presidency, the secretary came to believe that Hoover failed to exercise leadership to the fullest. The two men came to differ on policy. Stimson believed the United Sates should exercise strong influence in deterring aggressors, whereas the president favored abstaining.

During Stimson's tenure as secretary of state, Far Eastern questions played prominent roles in his work. Two episodes, both involving Manchuria, posed particular problems. They also represented challenges to treaty obligations that Stimson believed were important for developing world order. Although the United States had refused membership in the League of Nations, the American people's interest in disarmament and peace was manifest in the Washington Conference treaties and the Pact of Paris (the Kellogg–Briand Pact of 1927). In Washington there had been agreement to respect China's sovereignty and independence, and in Paris there was renunciation of war as an instrument of national policy. Both of these agreements were at issue as Stimson tried to sort out differences between China and the Soviet Union and between China and Japan.

The issues in Manchuria in the 1920s were not easy to define, and Stimson's handing of the Russo-Chinese dispute over the Chinese Eastern Railroad (C.E.R.) in 1929 reflects a newly seated secretary of state with little knowledge of Far Eastern history acting too impulsively. The Russian-built and controlled C.E.R. had been lost by the Russians during the American and Japanese intervention in Siberia, and revolution-weakened Russia was slow to reassert its dominance until 1924, when a reinvigorated Bolshevik diplomacy regained preponderant influence in the railroad. Chinese nationalism increasingly resented such foreign intrusion, and in 1929 the Chinese seized the Russian-managed telephone and telegraph systems in Harbin and the C.E.R. The two nations seemed headed for serious conflict; by August Secretary Stimson feared war, and in October and November there were Soviet incursions into Manchuria.

Between July and November Stimson tried various tactics to defuse the situation. His first concern was the vitality of the Kellogg–Briand treaty signed just the year before and not even proclaimed when the first news of trouble arrived in Washington. Complicating Stimson's efforts was America's lack of direct diplomatic contact with the Soviet Union. He talked directly with the Chinese, communicated through the French with the Soviets, and encouraged signatories of the Kellogg–Briand Pact to pressure the contending powers to reach a peaceful settlement. The Chinese were evasive until the situation became grave; the Soviets distrusted the United States and thought Washington was pro-Chinese (not the case in this affair): the Japanese wanted no international interference in Manchuria; the British and French were more sympathetic but not overly concerned. Finally the principals settled the dispute bilaterally. Stimson later admitted that his efforts may have had little influence on the outcome but noted that peace was kept.

The second Far Eastern episode, involving China and Japan, was the most important foreign policy issue confronted by Secretary Stimson. The triggering event was a mysterious explosion along the South Manchurian Railroad a little after 10:30 on the night of September 18, 1931. The Japanese army in Manchuria responded to the alleged Chinese provocation by occupying Mukden and eventually all of Manchuria. The broader picture included Chinese nationalism, declining Japanese foreign trade, growing Japanese social and economic inequalities, increasingly assertive Japanese militarism, and weak governments in Tokyo and Nanking, which encouraged Japanese officers of the Kwantung Army in Manchuria to act independently.

Henry Stimson noted the direct line from that fateful September evening in 1931 to the attack on Pearl Harbor. As Japanese troops moved out from their zone along the South Manchurian Railroad and appeared to violate the Covenant of the League of Nations, the Nine Power Treaty, and the Kellogg–Briand Pact, Stimson recognized that the United States would have to respond. Hoover and Stimson were both concerned about not having the tar baby placed on Washington's doorstep. The United States supported a League resolution in October calling for Japanese evacuation of Chinese territory, and when that had little effect Stimson approved the appointment of a commission to investigate the Manchurian problem. In the meantime Stimson was exerting quiet but direct pressure on Japan. Resolutions, appointment of a commission, and diplomatic pressure did not stop the Japanese occupation of Manchuria. Chinchow fell on January 1, 1932.

Stimson decided on a policy of nonrecognition of the fruits of Japanese aggression. Stimson fashioned with his advisers the note that went to the Chinese and Japanese on January 7, 1932. The note specifically mentioned the rights of U.S. citizens under the Open Door policy and the covenants and obligations of the Pact of Paris.

Early in the crisis Washington sought to avoid responsibility for the problem, but with Stimson's note, historically honored as his doctrine, the United States was out front and alone. It required no further action but it hardened U.S. policy toward Japan.

Although American preference after the Great War was to avoid collective security arrangements, there was strong support for peace through disarmament. The United States had taken the lead in naval disarmament in 1922. Efforts to expand the limitations of the Washington Naval Conference failed in 1927, but by 1929 the United States and Great Britain—Herbert Hoover and Ramsey MacDonald now heading these governments—moved toward accommodation.

At the beginning of his tenure as secretary of state Stimson worked for naval disarmament, and in January 1930, he led the American delegation to the London Conference. The Americans and the British, encouraged by their leaders, worked out differences on numbers and weights of cruisers and the sizes of guns. The Japanese won outright a ratio of 10–10–7 for small cruisers and destroyers and in practice, if not principle, did the same for heavy cruisers because the United States agreed to delay building up to its allotment.

The conference also had its recurring political problems. The French were not interested in naval limitation without provision for French security, and the Americans and British would not provide a meaningful security arrangement. At one point Stimson seemed ready to accept consultation on French security problems if the British would meet French demands. However, Stimson retreated from consultation after receiving from Hoover instructions not to accept what he called a camouflaged obligation. In the long run the treaty probably meant little in international relations. National rivalries remained, and leaders emerging in the Far East and in Central Europe would pose dangers to the status quo. Nonetheless, for Stimson the important result was improved Anglo-American relations.

Disarmament confronted Stimson again in 1931–1932. During this time he talked with major European leaders and exchanged views on disarmament and security, but little was accomplished. He attended the Geneva conference where the familiar issues were debated once again. Unshackled by public opinion and political constraints, Stimson would have agreed to consult with France in the event of a threatened war, joined the World Court, and cooperated closely with, if not joined, the League of Nations.

Stimson and Hoover also resisted repeated demands to send U.S. troops to a number of Latin American states experiencing turmoil from the Great Depression. In the face of the Sandino revolt in Nicaragua, President Hoover and Secretary Stimson decided that intervention was too costly—there were limits to the protection American citizens could expect in Nicaragua. While not forswearing intervention, Hoover and Stimson withdrew U.S. forces from Central America and established a foundation for a policy of nonintervention formalized under the good neighbor rubric of Franklin Roosevelt's administration.

Stimson often noted the overwhelming somber effect of the Depression on the president, whose attention understandably focused on the economy. Stimson's one success was his policy to end intervention in Latin America and improve relations with neighbors south of the border. Naval disarmament and efforts to support the Open Door seemed to have little effect in allaying distrust of nations and preserving Chinese independence and territorial integrity. Stimson would aver that his and Hoover's policies improved Anglo-American relations and would have done more to improve relations with Europe had the president followed his advice on reduction of war debts. Stimson stands out as a transition figure between an America that rejected the League of Nations and one that was a prime mover for the United Nations and assumed responsibilities of the Truman Doctrine and the Marshall Plan.

When Hoover was seeking reelection and seeking strong support from his cabinet, there was a note of discord. Stimson, as secretary of state, thought he should avoid aggressive partisan politics. Hoover was disappointed in what he felt was Stimson's mild and nonpartisan contribution. Stimson thought he had gone too far and wished he "wasn't in it." If reelected, Hoover would not have retained Stimson in the cabinet.

Seven years later Roosevelt, hoping to moderate partisan criticism, called on 72-year-old Stimson to enter public service again as secretary of war. In the War Department he oversaw development of the draft, mobilization of the army, and near the end of his career, use of the atomic bomb. These years also revealed that U.S. foreign policy had become what Stimson had envisioned when he was in the State Department. The United States had accepted world responsibilities and those disturbers of international peace—those violators of the League Covenant, the Nine Power Treaty, and the Kellogg–Briand Pact—were defeated and their leaders punished. Stimson could retire in 1945 with a feeling of accomplishment not only in seeing policies he advocated in place but also in seeing the emergence of a new generation of leaders cut in his mold and supportive of a broad role for the United States in world affairs. Stimson died in 1950.

BIBLIOGRAPHICAL ESSAY

In a 1937 conversation with Stimson, Ramsey MacDonald complained of his memory and of the fact that he had not kept diaries or records of his personal experiences. When Stimson told him what he had done with his diary, the former prime minister was envious. Scholars can be thankful for Stimson's sense of duty to the historian. His diaries and papers are in excellent order and well indexed. The originals are housed at Yale, but microfilm editions are available in major libraries around the country.

Stimson also authored numerous books and essays. Completing his mission to Nicaragua for President Coolidge, he published *American Policy in Nicaragua* (1927). Concerned about the problem of U.S. cooperation with the League of Nations in developing effective methods to prevent war, he wrote *The Far Eastern Crisis: Recollections and Observations* (1936). In his Stafford Little Lectures, *Democracy and Nationalism in Europe* (1934), he argued again for American responsibility in world affairs. Important for Stimson's views is his and McGeorge Bundy's *On*

Active Service in Peace and War (1947), written as a pilot biography while Stimson's memory of important events was still alive.

Elting E. Morison's *Turmoil and Tradition: A Study of the Life and Times of Henry L. Stimson* (1960), was supported by a grant from the Stimson estate and is a friendly biography emphasizing Stimson's strong qualities as gentleman, lawyer, and public servant. Robert Ferrell has written the best account of Hoover's and Stimson's foreign policy in *American Diplomacy in the Great Depression* (1957). See also Ferrell's volume on Stimson in *The American Secretaries of State and Their Diplomacy* series (volume XI, 1963). Richard N. Current's *Secretary Stimson: A Study in Statecraft* (1954), is critical. In *Herbert Hoover's Latin American Policy* (1951), Alexander DeConde sees the beginning of a good neighbor policy during the Hoover years. Armin Rappaport's *Henry L. Stimson and Japan, 1931–33* (1963), describes Stimson's desire to halt Japanese aggression and his lack of support at home or abroad to do so. Whether Stimson's policy was appropriate remains open. For the influence of Stimson as part of a chain of individuals from Theodore Roosevelt and Elihu Root to Dean Acheson, Averell Harriman, George Kennan, and others of the post–World War Two generation, see Walter Isaacson and Evan Thomas, *The Wise Men: Six Friends and the World They Made* (1986).

William Kamann

ABEL P. UPSHUR (1790–1844)

Served 1843–1844
Appointed by President John Tyler
Whig

Abel Parker Upshur (1790–1844), an aristocratic planter, slaveholder, and judge from Virginia's eastern shore, served briefly as secretary of state during John Tyler's presidency. Despite his short tenure at the helm of the State Department—less than a year—Upshur left his mark on U.S. diplomacy by opening the way for the nation's surge of territorial expansion in the 1840s. Texas was the prize coveted by Upshur and his fellow Virginian, Tyler. The two longtime friends very nearly succeeded before Upshur's tragic death in an explosion aboard the USS *Princeton* on February 28, 1844. As secretary of state, Upshur had skillfully and resolutely negotiated a Texas annexation treaty and believed he had garnered the necessary votes for quick Senate ratification. Ultimate success crowned the Virginian's efforts when Texas was annexed by joint resolution of Congress little more than a year after his death. The 1846 settlement with Great Britain of the lengthy Oregon territory dispute had its roots in Upshur's diplomacy as well. In confronting the Texas and Oregon issues and the other diplomatic issues of his day, Secretary Upshur invariably had one eye on Great Britain, the only nation that seriously challenged the United States' continental expansion, commercial ascendancy, and national destiny.

Upshur's wariness of Britain and his distrust of the former mother country's designs for world commercial and economic hegemony did not come naturally. The son of a moderately well-to-do planter with Federalist leanings and pro-British sympathies, he was taught at the parental knee to question the Jeffersonian values and beliefs prevalent in early nineteenth-century Virginia. After a brief stay at Yale, Upshur transferred to Princeton, but failed to graduate because he was dismissed for his part in a student protest against the repressive discipline of Princeton President Samuel Stanhope Smith. Undaunted, the young rebel returned to Virginia to pursue legal studies with the renowned Richmond lawyer William Wirt. As a fledgling attorney he mixed with other members of Virginia's elite in the highly charged political atmosphere of the state capital, establishing friendships with several of the state's future leaders, including John Tyler. Among his conservative colleagues, Upshur gained widespread respect as a successful lawyer, state legislator, and judge and for his strict adherence to states' rights, the sanctity of property, and the virtues of the South's "peculiar institution."

In 1829–1830, Upshur represented his eastern shore district at the Virginia constitutional convention, where he emerged as a leading opponent of democratic reform. Rejecting the theory of natural rights and denying the existence of any original or prior principles of government, Judge Upshur claimed the interests of property outweighed the interests of the majority. His eloquence at the convention helped maintain the status quo and defeat the efforts of the reformers who sought expanded manhood suffrage and increased representation for the state's western counties. A decade later, when the institution of slavery was under heavy fire from Northern abolitionists, the reactionary judge again pleased his fellow conservatives by publishing a vigorous defense of the South's besieged domestic institution. Black slavery was essential to white freedom, maintained Upshur, and accordingly was "a great positive good, to be carefully protected and preserved." The future secretary of state's proslavery credentials were honored throughout his home region, but in some political circles his extremist states' rights views, which accompanied his defense of slavery, raised suspicions that he was an incipient disunionist.

In September 1841 when John Tyler appointed Upshur secretary of the navy in his newly reorganized cabinet, many political observers perceived him as a competent provincial judge from the Virginia backwater who owed his appointment to a personal friendship with the president. The Whig press vigorously denounced Upshur's appointment, angered at what they labeled Tyler's betrayal of Whig principles since his elevation to the presidency on the death of William Henry Harrison in April 1841. One New York City editor, James Watson Webb, called for Tyler's impeachment because he had placed an alleged disunionist at the head of the Navy Department. Upshur ignored the political clamor over his appointment and energetically tackled his new duties, hoping to quiet his critics and win much-needed public approval for the beleaguered Tyler administration.

Upshur's stint as head of the Navy Department brought him national prominence and fathered the expansionist foreign policy he later pursued as secretary of state. What established the conservative Virginian as a statesman to be reckoned with was his first annual report as secretary of the navy, submitted in early December 1841. The report was a blueprint for naval expansion, modernization, and administrative reform that would alleviate the nation's vulnerability to attack and project American naval power into the Pacific basin. Upshur adhered to the traditional belief that one of the navy's primary functions was to protect the nation's commerce and far-flung economic interests. For the navy to fulfill that mission, he recommended a fleet that would be at least "half the naval force of the strongest maritime power in the world," which of course was Great Britain. Beyond that, the United States clearly needed naval bases to guard its Pacific trade and whale fisheries, preferably located on the west coasts of North and South America and in the Hawaiian Islands, "a central point" in trans-Pacific commerce. The report also called for the conversion of the fleet from sail to steam, enlargement of naval ranks to include vice-admiral and admiral, a substantial increase in the Marine Corps, and the creation of a naval academy.

Upshur's comprehensive naval plan drew support from the nation's leading newspapers, many of which published the report verbatim. Yet, political objections to the secretary of the navy's recommendations arose almost immediately, primarily focusing on the program's cost. In addition, abolitionists such as Joshua Leavitt, editor of the *Emancipator*, decried the proposed naval buildup's emphasis on strengthening coastal defenses as another scheme to employ federal power to protect the South's institution of slavery. They pointed out that Upshur had justified a larger navy to protect America's shores from attack with the argument that a foreign invasion might spark a slave insurrection and pit "hostile elements of our social system against one another." In defense of his proposals, Upshur waged his own press campaign urging public and Congressional support for naval expansion and modernization through several anonymously published editorials in the *Madisonian*, a mouthpiece of the Tyler administration. In the end, partisan sectional rivalries sidetracked much of Upshur's visionary program, although the navy did prosper during the Tyler years.

As navy secretary, Upshur's resentment of Great Britain's economic and political predominance throughout the world fueled an anti-British nationalism that came to dominate his foreign policy outlook. Britain seemed to block every U.S. territorial and commercial aspiration. Evidence of Britain's meddling to thwart an American imperial ascendancy appeared to exist in Texas and the Pacific Northwest, in Mexico and the Caribbean, in the Hawaiian Islands and throughout the Pacific Rim. Duff Green, an executive agent who twice journeyed to Britain as Tyler's "ambassador of slavery," apparently confirmed Upshur's fears. Green contended that Britain's universal hostility to slavery and the slave trade cloaked a scheme for control of the world's markets and raw materials. Counseled in a similar vein by his friend and sometime mentor, John C. Calhoun of South Carolina, it was small wonder that Upshur identified Great Britain as the most serious threat to the "peculiar" interests of his region and to the destiny of his nation.

Nearly two years of highly visible and successful service in the Tyler cabinet made Abel P. Upshur one of the president's most trusted advisors. Tyler and Upshur shared similar conservative views on slavery and states' rights, and both distrusted the British. As a cabinet member, Upshur had participated in the formulation of foreign policy and knew something of its day-to-day execution. He also favored the annexation of Texas, which not surprisingly had become the administration's number one priority. When the post of secretary of state became vacant on the death of Acting Secretary Hugh S. Legaré in June 1843, Tyler asked his loyal friend to head the State Department. Upshur resisted the shift to State, doubting his worthiness for the premier cabinet post. He briefly served ad interim, retaining his position as navy secretary until July 24, 1843, when he became secretary of state outright. Confirmed by the Senate without opposition, a tribute to the widespread respect he now enjoyed, Upshur quickly activated diplomacy geared to bringing Texas into the Union as a slave state.

The Texas annexation issue virtually obsessed Upshur during his seven-month tenure as secretary of state. He spent his first weeks in office planning an expansionist strategy. The situation was deemed critical by the ever alarmist Duff Green, then in Britain on his second mission as Tyler's special envoy. In a dispatch to Upshur, Green warned of an Anglo-American antislavery conspiracy, supported by none other than the British Foreign Secretary, Lord Aberdeen, to abolish slavery in Texas and irretrievably place the Lone Star Republic in Britain's economic and commercial orbit. Despite his awareness that Duff Green's information frequently was unreliable, Secretary Upshur uncritically accepted his analysis and employed it to justify immediate annexation, lest Great Britain succeed in the first phase of its global antislavery campaign. After consulting Tyler and seeking Calhoun's advice, Upshur opened secret treaty negotiations with Texas's minister in Washington, Isaac Van Zandt.

There were a number of obstacles facing Upshur and Tyler in their quest to annex Texas. The first were Texans, who fearing that they might again be the bride left at the altar by the fickle American groom, played coy for several months. The Texas government of Sam Houston sought guarantees against Mexican retaliation that caused Tyler and Upshur serious concern about the constitutional implications of promising military protection to a foreign nation without direct congressional approval. Opposition to annexation existed at home as well, and not solely among abolitionists. Many Northerners, troubled by the abolitionist argument that annexation of a sovereign republic was unconstitutional, questioned a policy that would add new slave territory to the Union in this seemingly extralegal fashion. Hesitation about the merits of Texas annexation among the U.S. public in turn made Secretary Upshur's task of securing a two-thirds majority in the Senate quite formidable. The secretary of state began his campaign by cajoling the Texans, hoping he could change the policy of Sam Houston's government. To overcome Northern resistance, Upshur shrewdly linked a settlement of the Oregon boundary dispute with Texas annexation, a scheme later employed by James K. Polk in his successful 1844 presidential race. Finally, to mold public opinion and gain popular support, Upshur placed a series of anonymous editorials in the *Madisonian* urging annexation and outlining the serious consequences for the Union if Texas slipped permanently under British influence. Throughout his campaign to add Texas to the Union, Upshur the juggler attempted to maintain a delicate diplomatic balance. While exploiting anti-British sentiment to gain support for Texas annexation, he also pursued a negotiated settlement of the Oregon dispute with archrival Great Britain.

Abel P. Upshur was surprisingly effective as secretary of state before death cut short his diplomacy of annexation and expansion. The terms he offered Lord Aberdeen in late 1843 for a settlement of the Oregon controversy stipulated a boundary at the 49th parallel—the boundary line accepted in 1846 when the Polk administration successfully negotiated an agreement with Great Britain that resolved the dispute. Throughout the fall and early winter of 1843, Secretary Upshur tirelessly courted votes for annexation among reluctant Senators and apparently had lined up the necessary two-thirds by mid-January 1844. The day before he was killed aboard the *Princeton*, Secretary of State Upshur completed a draft treaty with the help of Isaac Van Zandt, the negotiator for the Texas republic. Upshur died believing his treaty would win Senate approval and that he had attained, as he earlier had confided to good friend and fellow defender of southern rights, Nathaniel Beverley Tucker, "the great object of my ambition," the annexation of Texas to the Union.

As secretary of state, Abel Parker Upshur was an adroit diplomatist, a persuasive lobbyist, and a skillful manipulator of public opinion, although his concrete diplomatic achievements were marginal because of his brief tenure in the office. Upshur's major foreign policy initiatives, the annexation of Texas and the resolution of the Oregon controversy, were brought to fruition by John C. Calhoun and James Buchanan, his successors at the State Department. Perhaps Upshur's major contribution was as a leading statesman of the Old South, dedicated to using the nation's diplomacy as a means to preserve southern dominance of the Union. After a flirtation with disunionist ideas, Upshur came to believe that an extensive republic incorporating Texas as a slave state was the only foreseeable hope for the South and its "peculiar institution." Ironically, his devotion to the territorial expansion of slavery as an epoxy of union proved to be a misguided and counterproductive faith, because it stirred a sectional backlash that in the long run doomed slavery and the Old South.

BIBLIOGRAPHICAL ESSAY

The most useful manuscript source for a study of Abel P. Upshur is the Tucker-Coleman Papers collection at Swem Library, College of William and Mary. This rich collection has a number of important letters from Upshur to his friend Nathaniel Beverley Tucker pertaining to politics, slavery, the Tyler administration, and foreign relations. The Upshur Family Papers, also at Swem Library, provide genealogical data on the Upshur family, but nothing bearing on his career. Both the John Tyler Papers in the Library of Congress and the Tyler Family Papers at William and Mary contain valuable correspondence and documents relating to Upshur's service in Tyler's cabinet as secretary of the navy and secretary of state.

Two published collections of correspondence are important: Lyon G. Tyler's *The Letters and Times of the Tylers*, 3 vols. (1884–1886), which provides helpful information on the Tyler-Upshur relationship, and Clyde N. Wilson (ed.), *The Papers of John C. Calhoun*, vols. 16–20 (1984–1991), which contains valuable Upshur and Calhoun correspondence. For additional Upshur-Calhoun letters, see J. Franklin Jameson (ed.), "Correspondence of John C. Calhoun," *Annual Report of the American Historical for the Year 1899*, 2 vols. (1900).

Among the most helpful published collections of documents are William R. Manning (ed.), *Diplomatic Correspondence of the United States: Inter-American Affairs, 1831–1860* 12 vols. (1932–1939), and George P. Garrison (ed.), *Diplomatic Correspondence of the Republic of Texas*, 3 vols. (1908–1911). The pertinent volumes in the Manning collection are VII, VIII, and XII, all of which contain correspondence to and from Upshur during his tenure as secretary of state. The most important letters in the Garrison collection are in volume II. Upshur's two reports as secretary of the navy are indispensable as background for an understanding of his foreign policy outlook. See "Report of the Secretary of the Navy," Senate Document No. 1, 27th Cong., 2nd Sess. (December 4, 1841), 367–494; "Report of the Secretary of the Navy," House Document No. 2, 27th Cong., 3d Sess. (December 7, 1842), pp. 529–727. See also the following documents of the 28th Cong., 1st Sess.: Senate Documents 37 and 341 and House Document 271 for Upshur correspondence on Texas; Senate Documents 135 and 210, and House Executive Document 162 for correspondence with Britain.

Although published 40 years ago, Claude H. Hall's *Abel Parker Upshur: Conservative Virginian, 1790–1844* (1964), remains the definitive biography of Upshur. A number of scholarly studies provide insightful evaluations of Upshur's foreign policy, including Justin Smith's outdated but still useful *The Annexation of Texas* (1911); Frederick Merk's highly critical *Slavery and the Annexation of Texas* (1972); and David Pletcher's *The Diplomacy of Annexation: Texas, Oregon, and the Mexican War*

(1973), which offers a thorough overview of the Tyler administration's diplomacy and a balanced assessment of Upshur's contribution as secretary of state. For a provocative interpretation of the expansionism of the 1840s and a perceptive analysis of Upshur's beliefs and actions, see Thomas R. Hietala, *Manifest Design: Anxious Aggrandizement in Late Jacksonian America* (1985, rev. ed. 2003). Two works that shed light on Upshur's naval strategy are Kenneth J. Hagan's *This People's Navy: The Making of American Sea Power* (1991), and John H. Schroeder's *Shaping a Maritime Empire: The Commercial and Diplomatic Role of the American Navy, 1829–1861* (1985).

Edward Crapol

MARTIN VAN BUREN (1782–1862)

Served 1829–1831
Appointed by President Andrew Jackson
Democrat

When historians evaluate the formation of the second political party system in the 1820s, Martin Van Buren, the "Little Magician," emerges at the vortex. In fact, Van Buren often receives greater praise for his activities in New York and Congressional politics, than his higher profile roles as secretary of state (1829–1831) and president (1837–1841). Van Buren's career in the State Department was brief, but marked by notable successes. No risk taker, the "Red Fox of Kinderhook" was a dedicated, competent administrator who aspired to the White House and loyally followed the lead of President Andrew Jackson. He chose a course that served him well.

Van Buren was born in upstate New York, near Albany, in 1782 to respectable tavern-owning parents of Dutch ancestry. He ceased his formal schooling at the age of 14 and apprenticed with a local Federalist lawyer. Although he learned the law—and practiced with considerable success in both New York City and upstate—his true passion was Jeffersonian politics. For the next two decades, Van Buren shrewdly maneuvered his way through the Byzantine world of Empire State Republicanism.

With considerable dexterity, he moved among factions led by legendary figures such as Aaron Burr and George Clinton. Elected to the state senate (1812–1816), chosen as attorney general (1816–1819), U.S. Senator (1821–1828), and governor (1828) he emerged as the leader of a clique labeled the "Albany Regency." The Regency dueled throughout the decade with the forces of popular Governor DeWitt Clinton. In the presidential election of 1824, Van Buren backed the ill-fated candidacy of Secretary of the Treasury William H. Crawford of Georgia. The nationalistic bent of the John Quincy Adams administration repulsed Van Buren, a supporter of limited government, and he soon joined the camp of a more likely states' rights prospect, Andrew Jackson, who was gathering allies for his victorious 1828 campaign. Van Buren's energies in promoting the Jacksonian cause did not go unrewarded. When, in February 1829, "Old Hickory" invited him to join the cabinet as secretary of state, he promptly accepted. Van Buren had not acquired a reputation for detailed knowledge of foreign affairs during his Senate tenure. Preferring to focus on related domestic politics such as the tariff, he viewed noncommercial international relationships (i.e., the Panama Congress of 1826) with a jaundiced eye. Instead, Jackson brought the able Van Buren to Washington, D.C., for his affable personality, facile mind, and knowledge of the machinations of Congress.

When Van Buren arrived in the Capital in the spring, he found that the president had already chosen several critical appointees—Senator Littleton Tazewell of Virginia to Great Britain, Senator Edward Livingston of Louisiana to France, and Representative Thomas Moore of Kentucky to Colombia—without consulting his new secretary.

When Tazewell and Livingston rejected the nominations, Van Buren could rejoice in the selection of old allies—Louis McLane of Delaware and William Rives of Virginia—to replace them. Van Buren, who adopted the wise habit of accompanying the president on his frequent horseback rides into the Virginia countryside, negotiated two other key appointments with Jackson. Their choices proved regrettable—the quixotic Virginian, John Randolph of Roanoke, for Russia and William Pitt Preble of Maine for the Netherlands. As biographer John Niven has noted, Van Buren developed a "direct, open, and conciliatory" style of diplomacy. This tact proved beneficial, both in dealing with his own appointees and foreign agents. The secretary quickly cultivated the diplomatic community in Washington and ensured, too, that the president met with ministers and chargés, dispelling notions of provincialism and anti-European hostility. He also developed very positive relations with the Democratic-controlled Congress, although his rivalry with Vice President John C. Calhoun manifested itself throughout official Washington. Van Buren became a confidant of the president and a leading light in an unexceptional cabinet that was infrequently assembled for counsel. The cabinet did, however, serve as a battleground during the Peggy Eaton affair, and, when Jackson purged his advisors in the spring of 1831, Van Buren was among the few to depart and still retain presidential favor.

Although many of the problems that Van Buren would encounter and resolve during his term were dealt with by the Adams administration, perhaps none was as nettlesome as the issue of Great Britain and the West Indian trade. Commerce between the United States and the islands had been sharply limited by the Jay Treaty of 1794 and worsened during the 1820s. The frustrating failure of Adams and Henry Clay to settle the question created a diplomatic issue in the 1828 campaign. As a result, Jackson made the resolution a high priority and, together with Van Buren, developed a conciliatory strategy to offer the British. The Americans would agree to accept Crown restrictions on trade and work to settle the question by statutory law rather than convention or treaty. Unfortunately, discussions between Louis McLane and Foreign Secretary Lord Aberdeen (for the Ministry of Earl Grey) disintegrated in the fall of 1829 as the English awaited anticipated revisions in the high American protective tariff of 1828. When repeated efforts by both Jackson and McLane were met with silence from the British, the minister took a different tack. McLane encouraged merchants Senator Samuel Smith (MD) and Congressman C. C. Cambreleng (NY) to promote legislation aimed at encouraging reciprocity. In May 1830, Congress passed a measure allowing the president to open U.S. ports to British ships at his discretion. Soon thereafter, Congress also reduced the duties on West Indian produce. Jackson endorsed the bills and fixed October 5 as the date for opening U.S. ports. In mid-August the British yielded.

Aberdeen informed McLane that U.S. trade would be restored on the basis of the Act of 1825. In practical terms, the result was a victory for common sense on both sides of the Atlantic. Reciprocity meant that the British would revoke their restrictive Orders in Council of 1826 and allow U.S. vessels into their Canadian and West Indian ports, although the Crown reserved the right to tariff colonial goods that competed with American products. The Jackson administration agreed that American vessels must trade only in American goods and sail directly to the colonial ports. The United States would also admit English ships carrying their colonial products on a most-favored-nation basis. Although the Jacksonians offered little more in substance than had the Adams administration, the new American initiative, based on flexibility, cooperation, and patience, proved triumphant. The National Republicans protested mightily, but their voices were drowned out by the widespread accolades of approval. Jackson, Van Buren, McLane, and the Democrats had scored an initial impressive triumph in foreign affairs.

The other major issue with Great Britain—the Maine–New Brunswick boundary—proved more difficult to resolve. The border had been a problem since the two nations failed to settle the issue at the Peace of Paris in 1783. The British wished to build a military road in the disputed 100-mile area, whereas the Americans contemplated the agricultural possibilities for farming and timber. The resulting stalemate was complicated by the admission of Maine as a state in 1820. Finally, in 1827 both nations signed an agreement to gather evidence and present their respective claims to the King of the Netherlands for arbitration. When Jackson assumed office two years later, the monarch still awaited the submission of the materials. The U.S. position, based largely on prerevolutionary land grants, claimed ownership of the highlands between the St. Lawrence and St. Johns Rivers. The British followed a more definable route along the regional river system. American commissioners involved in the negotiations and leading politicos in the capital, including Van Buren, recognized the U.S. position was flawed. This realization did not abate the determination of the "downeasters" in Maine to obtain a lion's share of the territory.

Unfortunately, Van Buren dispatched the wrong man to the Netherlands to manage such a sensitive issue. William Pitt Preble, a native of Maine, had worked with Albert Gallatin to define the American position in 1826–1827. Preble arrived in the Netherlands in the spring of 1830 and soon thereafter presented his evidence to King William. Although the King did not deliver his opinion until January 1831, Preble became increasingly anxious about the outcome. When the verdict was delivered, William rejected the U.S. "highland claim," but awarded the United States almost 8,000 of the 12,000 disputed square miles. Preble, furious at the territorial cost to Maine, returned to the United States, denouncing the monarch as a tool of the British. In the United States patriots of all stripes held a similar view of William's duplicity. Although emotions ran high, especially in New England, Jackson realized that the compromise would not damage either U.S. security or agricultural interests. Conversely, prolonging the controversy could possibly lead to an unwanted and unnecessary border war. The president also understood the sensitive nature of the situation and that Maine would have to be cajoled rather than forced into accepting a surrender of the disputed property. Jackson decided by August 1831 to first obtain British acceptance of the proposal in an effort to strengthen his hand strategically. Van Buren, resigned from the cabinet and now in the role of minister-designate to Britain, functioned as the point man with Foreign Secretary Lord Palmerston and obtained the needed assurances.

While taking no public position, Jackson attempted to finesse the settlement through the Maine legislature and the Senate. Maine seemed open to a resolution, as long as the state could influence the final Anglo-American agreement and it received territorial compensation for sacrificed lands, but the Senate was not as amenable. Not only did the Senators reject the nomination of Van Buren as Minister to England (by the tie-breaking vote of Vice President John C. Calhoun) in January 1832, but six months later they also sent the Maine proposal to a crashing election-year defeat. Talks reopened the next year on the boundary, and new proposals proffered during the remainder of Jackson's term, but the situation remained contentious and unresolved until the Webster–Ashburton Treaty of 1842. Ironically, that agreement yielded 1,000 fewer square miles than the settlement tendered by King William a decade earlier.

Although Jackson and Van Buren failed to maneuver the Maine boundary through the maze of American politics, they were considerably more successful resolving the claim for commercial violations against several European nations. These grievances dated back to the Napoleonic Wars (1793–1815), when Denmark, France, and the Kingdom of the Two Sicilies captured numerous neutral American vessels. The prompt settlement of these claims with a reasonable financial remuneration was a matter of national honor for Jackson. A breakthrough of sorts had begun with chargé d'affaires Henry Wheaton's negotiations with the Danes in 1828. Jackson wisely kept Wheaton, a National Republican, in this post at a sensitive time. After months of dealing, however, the frustrated chargé, a renowned international lawyer, relayed the paltry offer of $230,000, not quite the $1.7 million requested by the United States. Jackson and Van Buren had hoped to use this treaty as a model for other such arrangements and were disturbed by Wheaton's lack of progress. By early 1830, Jackson threatened a trade war, and the Danes caved in. On March 28, a treaty was signed allocating a $650,000 settlement—a sum far off the amount desired, but still enough to bring joy to the hearts of northeastern merchants.

Disappointingly, the resolution did not spill over into negotiations with France. Minister William Rives found the French willing to discuss the matter, but slow to seek a determination. Van Buren felt the pressure from both sides of the Atlantic. A string of missives crisscrossed the ocean as the two men struggled to establish a workable strategy. Meanwhile, nervous claimants wished to spur the talks on by "assisting" Rives; no surprise, because the total sum demanded approximated $6 million. The aid would likely come in the form of bribing certain French deputies, a strategy that Van Buren categorically rejected. Rives fought off the meddling merchants and proceeded to offer a compromise on American wine duties to induce Minister of Foreign Affairs Prince Jules Polignac to settle the naval claims. In May 1830, when the French offered only $1 million, Rives felt insulted and despondent. No end seemed in sight, when the French Revolution of July 1830 occurred, placing Louis Philippe on the throne (replacing Charles X) and Count Louis Molé as Foreign Minister. In spite of the very positive relations that Rives developed with the French court, concessions to the United States by the new regime would have been financially draining and politically unpopular. The government felt obliged to appoint another committee in October to examine the claims. Van Buren recognized the economic difficulties faced by the French and urged a patient approach that would entertain any "fair proposal" offered.

The foreign ministry experienced several shake-ups and, as no new deals were forthcoming, Rives moved toward a harder line in April 1831. He threatened commercial retaliation and rejected successive offers of $3 and $4 million. The French wanted neither a commercial conflict nor arbitration of the issue and by June 1 increased the sum to $4.6 million. Rives accepted the settlement that included duty adjustments on French wine and American cotton. The treaty, signed on July 4, received the endorsement of Van Buren, who believed it was both financially fair and politically acceptable. The Red Fox knowingly told Rives that the treaty would pass—there was simply too much money at stake—much of it belonging to the opposition. His prediction proved correct—the Senate unanimously approved the treaty in January 1832. Rives, who returned to the United States in the autumn, joined Van Buren and the president in taking credit for this popular agreement. Unfortunately, dark days lay ahead as the euphoria of agreement yielded to the reality of payment, as the French heaped delay upon delay, catapulting the two nations to the brink of war.

As the Jackson administration sought to advance American commerce around the world, the Ottoman Empire appeared as a logical entry point into the Middle East. Yankee ships had been trading—especially in rum and cotton cloth for opium—with the Sublime Porte through Smyrna since the 1780s, but without a formal treaty. Britain and France controlled commerce in the region and did not welcome a rival. Consequently, any American overtures would have to be made quietly. Adams's agents had failed to secure a treaty, but Jackson, who envisioned a trade in American manufactures to the area, made it a high priority.

In September 1829, the president selected a team of David Offley, longtime resident and consul at Smyrna, Commodore James Biddle of the Mediterranean Squadron, and New York businessman Charles Rhind as agents. Fearing European interference in the talks, Van Buren kept the relevant papers in his private rooms. Nonetheless, the British discovered the mission and intrigued against it—unsuccessfully. Rhind began the negotiations in Constantinople (while Offley and Biddle lingered in Smyrna) in February 1830 and reached agreement with the Turks before his compatriots arrived in May. The treaty provided for generous terms regarding most-favored-nation status and for extraterritoriality. Although Rhind may have been persuasive, the real reason for the Sultan's quick concession rested with a secret provision to provide American timber and shipbuilding expertise to help reconstruct the Turkish navy destroyed by a European fleet at Navarino in 1827. The Senate approved the treaty in February 1831, but not without first removing the controversial shipbuilding provision and criticizing the president for unconstitutionally appointing a commission without Congressional approval. The secretary of state received part of the blame. A Virginia correspondent informed Nicholas Trist, a clerk in the State Department, "The Turkish mission has injured Van Buren greatly. . . . Before that he stood exceedingly high in this state."

Despite the embarrassment caused by the secret provision and Rhind's acceptance of four Arabian horses as a gift from the Sultan (an unconstitutional move from a government servant), the administration pushed ahead with the revised agreement. Jackson dispatched navy veteran Commodore David Porter, Consul-General of the Barbary States, as chargé and State Department linguist William B. Hodgson to accompany him to smooth the Sultan's ruffled feathers. Arriving in August 1831, Hodgson sailed for New York three months later with a newly ratified treaty, leaving Porter behind to advise, informally, of course, the construction of a new Turkish navy. Within the year, U.S. carpenters using U.S. wood were building frigates in Turkish shipyards. A new era in American–Ottoman relations had begun.

Jackson had similar residual commercial problems with Mexico—as well as a lingering boundary dispute. The Adams administration, represented by Minister Joel Poinsett in Mexico City, had negotiated new treaties resolving trade and border problems, but both languished in a suspicious Mexican Congress. Mexican intransigence had been heightened partially because of perceived Yankee avarice. Poinsett offered $1 million for Texas at the Rio Grande border; a deal refused by the Mexican government. Simultaneously, the minister had meddled in internal Mexican politics with very negative effects.

When the Jackson–Van Buren tandem assumed office in the spring of 1829, they advanced the same expansionist agenda as their predecessor. However, they decided to increase the offer for Texas to $5 million. The Democrats wanted to secure New Orleans, the Mississippi River, a "natural boundary" between Texas and Mexico, the Western frontier, and gain potential land for either Indian removal or a possible territory for "free people of color." They did not, however, realize that Poinsett's stock had fallen dramatically and maintained him at his post. Word reached Washington in the fall of 1829 of the minister's indiscretions concurrent with a request for his recall from the Mexican government. Jackson quietly brought Poinsett back to the Capital, replacing him with an old colleague from the Battle of New Orleans, Colonel Anthony Butler. Butler and Jackson had engaged in extensive and enthusiastic discussions about Texas annexation, and although he had no diplomatic experience, Butler was entrusted with the purchase.

Butler arrived in Mexico City in December 1829 amidst extensive political turmoil. His mission did not go unnoticed by the British. Minister Charles Vaughn met with Van Buren in Washington in March 1830 to discuss U.S. intentions regarding Mexico. The Red Fox feigned outrage that the Crown should suspect American territorial designs upon its neighbor and urged that the British use their considerable influence in Mexico City to promote harmony between Mexico and the United States. Vaughn, fully apprised of American goals from Mexican newspapers, was likely unconvinced by Van Buren's evasiveness and denials. British concern was justified. Although many Mexicans were intensely nationalistic and there was a rising tide of anti-Americanism, the country was politically divided and the leadership uncertain. By the spring of 1830, Mexico had recently experienced a failed Spanish invasion, a revolution that replaced Vicente Guerrero with Anastacio Bustamante, and the revolt of eight states against the central government.

Van Buren, aware of the anti-American feeling, confided to Butler that his task would be magnified. Yankees were increasingly perceived, not as an ally to aid and protect against invading Europeans, but as a greedy and grasping neighbor. Not surprisingly, rather than sell Texas, the Mexican government moved to secure the province and restrict American immigration. Butler remained hopeful in spite of the warning signs. After all, Foreign Minister Luís Alaman wanted U.S. support in the event of another Spanish invasion and seemed agreeable to discussing a commercial treaty. In April 1830, however, Van Buren ordered Butler to shelve the Texas issue and focus on the boundary and commercial problems. The strategy worked. By December, he had succeeded in garnering a treaty that provided for most-favored-nation status, no discriminatory duties, and neutral rights in time of war. The pact was signed in April 1831. Concurrently, Butler inked the Poinsett boundary agreement that had been drawn up in 1828. The line was set at the Sabine River—not the Rio Grande, which would no doubt displease the president.

Jackson hoped that Butler's trade triumph would augur well on the Texas front. It became increasingly imperative that the diplomat move quickly because rumors were mounting of an impending revolt of Americans in Texas. "Old Hickory" knew that with antislavery sentiment rising in the North, it would be much more difficult to annex an independent Texas Republic than purchase a province from Mexico. He preferred the Jeffersonian Louisiana model. Jackson also feared growing British influence in Texas that might produce either annexation or independence.

American designs on Texas were not realized—at least not under Van Buren. Butler soon revealed himself to be a blustering, grasping opportunist, who managed to overstay his mission in Mexico City by several years. Jackson finally replaced him in 1835, but by then Texas had drifted into a war, which would end at San Jacinto in March 1836. As Jackson predicted, antislavery feeling would keep the Lone Star Republic out of the Union until 1845. Van Buren departed the administration in April 1831 with a sense of genuine accomplishment. Under his guidance commercial treaties with Great Britain, Turkey, and Mexico had been negotiated, spoliations claims resolved with Denmark and France, and a border agreement tentatively reached with Mexico. The failure of the administration to resolve the Maine boundary rested with that state and recalcitrant senators. A parallel failure to obtain Texas was largely the result of Mexican nationalism. As his former law partner confided to Van Buren, "The moment also at which you are to withdraw is particularly propitious. You have held the office just long enough to show that you were fully equal to its duties, but not so long as to be exposed to the prejudices which of late years are so intimately associated with the long possession of this office."

Surviving his rejection as Minister to Great Britain, the Fox triumphed over rival John C. Calhoun, replacing him as vice president in Jackson's second administration (1833–1837). He emerged as the Democratic Party's natural choice for the nomination to succeed "Old Hickory" and won a narrow popular (but commanding electoral) victory over several Whig candidates in 1836. His presidency was immediately troubled, however, by the Panic of 1837, an economic collapse that consumed his term in office. In foreign affairs, Van Buren's major problems involved Great Britain, particularly the unresolved problem of the northeastern boundary, exacerbated by the Canadian rebellion of 1837.

He anticipated the defeat that awaited him in his reelection bid in 1840 and retired to his homestead, "Lindenwald," in upstate New York. Van Buren unsuccessfully sought the Democratic Party's nomination in 1844 that went to the victorious James K. Polk. When Polk offered Van Buren the London mission, the Fox declined. Instead, Van Buren became seriously involved in antislavery politics in New York and was chosen by the new Free-Soil Party as its presidential candidate in 1848—receiving a credible 10 percent (290,000) of the popular votes. He supported the Compromise of 1850 and returned to the Democratic Party in 1852, supporting its candidates for the presidency as the best hope to preserve the Union. The advent of Civil War shocked and depressed Van Buren, who died on July 24, 1862, after suffering through months of asthma attacks.

BIBLIOGRAPHICAL ESSAY

An extensive collection of Martin Van Buren Papers (in his almost indecipherable script) can be found at the Library of Congress, Massachusetts Historical Society, and New Public Library, and New York State Library. Fortunately, *The Autobiography of Martin Van Buren*, edited by John C. Fitzpatrick (1920) covers his life into the vice presidency, providing insights into his tenure in the State Department.

For many years the standard biography had been the sympathetic study by Holmes Alexander, *The American Talleyrand: The Career and Contemporaries of Martin Van Buren* (1935), supplemented by the chapter on Van Buren in Samuel F. Bemis, *American Secretaries of State and Their Diplomacy* (1927–1929). In the 1980s, however, a Van Buren renaissance provided several even-handed biographies, including John Niven, *Martin Van Buren: The Romantic Age of American Politics* (1983) and Don Cole, *Martin Van Buren and the American Political System* (1984). The Peggy Eaton affair and the cabinet crisis of 1831 that led to Van Buren's resignation is most recently covered by John Marszalek, *The Petticoat Affair* (1997). Van Buren's diplomatic career is treated generally in John M. Belohlavek, *Let the Eagle Soar!: The Foreign Policy of Andrew Jackson* (1985) and Don Cole, *The Presidency of Andrew Jackson* (1993).

Specific problems are dealt with in (Great Britain) F. Lee Benns, *The American Struggle for the British West Indies Carrying Trade, 1815–1830* (1923), Henry Burrage, *Maine in the Northeastern Boundary Controversy* (1919), Howard Jones, *To the Webster–Ashburton Treaty: A Study in Anglo-American Relations, 1783–1843* (1977, (Denmark) Soren Fogdall, *Danish-American Diplomacy, 1776–1920* (1922), (France) Richard McLemore, *Franco-American Diplomatic Relations, 1816–1836* (1941), (Turkey) David F. Long, *Nothing Too Daring: A Biography of Commodore David Porter* (1970), Thomas Bryson, *American Diplomatic Relations with the Middle East, 1784–1975* (1977), and (Mexico) James Callahan, *American Foreign Policy in Mexican Relations* (1932); Gene Brack, *Mexico Views Manifest Destiny, 1821–1846* (1975); and J. Fred Rippy, *Joel R. Poinsett: Versatile American* (1935).

John Belohlavek

CYRUS VANCE (1917–2002)

Served 1977–1980
Appointed by President Jimmy Carter
Democrat

Twentieth-century American statesmen—indeed, statesmen in any century or nation—share common attributes that distinguish them as benefactors of their countries and of their world. Diplomatic and negotiating skills lead the list of talents necessary to such men. Other important qualities include modest self-effacement, a large dose of nonpartisanship in matters of state, and an optimistic faith in the ability of even the most intransigent belligerents to find some common ground based on mutual self-interest. Most of all, statesmen possess an abiding hope that, with reason, guidance, and dogged perseverance, political leaders can be shown a path from hostile bloodletting to peaceful accommodation. The United States has been blessed with a handful of such men in the last century. Among them, there is no better example than Cyrus Vance, a man who dedicated his life to a belief in negotiated settlements and earned the title "the Ultimate Troubleshooter" from Strobe Talbott.

Cyrus Vance was born the second son to Amy Roberts and John Vance in Clarksburg, West Virginia, on April 27, 1917. In the next year, the family moved to Bronxville, New York, so that John could commute to his lucrative insurance business in Manhattan. Cyrus was never to know his father beyond his seventh year, when the elder Vance died unexpectedly. In grief, the family traveled to Switzerland for a year where Cyrus and his brother learned French at the Institute Sillig in Vevey.

John Vance's death threw the burden of raising two sons on Amy Vance. Vance's mother was a thoughtful woman who inculcated a sense of moral values to her children. These characteristics transferred to her son. To fill part of the paternal void, Cyrus turned to his uncle, the famed Constitutional lawyer and previous ambassador to England, John W. Davis. In 1924, Davis became a candidate for president at the Democratic convention that had to cast 105 ballots before obtaining a majority. As Vance's mentor, Davis quizzed the young man on points of law on Sundays when Cyrus went to his home.

With the tempering provided by this rarefied political and legal atmosphere, Vance was sent to the Episcopalian Kent School in Connecticut, where students were expected to take responsibility for many aspects of the school's operation. Vance headed the school government as a senior and was an outstanding athlete. Early on, Vance was noted for the propriety that was to be admired by associates and friends thereafter.

Vance entered Yale University as an economics major in the fall of 1935. Like Vance, classmates William Bundy and Stanley Resor were to go on to serve in the Kennedy administration. Vance's continued academic and athletic success and his membership in fraternal and honor societies at Yale contributed to his leadership credentials. Vance developed empathy for the plight of the poor as a result of his summer work at the Grenfell Mission in Labrador. He seems to have retained this empathic perspective in his later duties as a diplomat and foreign policy formulator.

Next came Yale Law School and graduation with honors in 1942. Vance met Gay Sloan at Yale, but their marriage was deferred until 1946, until after his service as a Navy officer in destroyers in several major Pacific battles. Also in 1946, Vance passed the New York bar exam and accepted a position offered by the prestigious Wall Street firm of Simpson, Thatcher, and Bartlett. Ascription as well as hard work and achievement counted in initial employment and subsequent promotion to partner in the firm.

Private practice from 1947 to 1957 enhanced litigation and negotiation skills, but did not turn Vance from his support for the Democrats or his developing liberal values. The firm encouraged political involvement, and Vance became a member of the Council on Foreign Affairs (he became a director in 1968 after his first period of service in government). In 1957, he accompanied a senior partner to Washington to work on the creation of the National Aeronautics and Space Commission as a staff member of Lyndon Johnson's Senate Preparedness Investigation Committee. Vance's work with Johnson's committee and friendships with McGeorge Bundy and Sergeant Shriver resulted in his appointment as General Counsel in Robert McNamara's Department of Defense in 1961. Vance admired McNamara, and evidently the feeling was reciprocated. Vance became the head of the Office of Management Planning and Organization Studies, which was responsible for McNamara's attempt to increase the efficiency of the mammoth Defense establishment. From there, Vance became the secretary of the army in 1962 and deputy secretary of state from 1964 until he retired in 1967 because of a painful back ailment. Vance's close association with McNamara is important; the two shared several elements of style and temperament. Both men were cautious rationalists dedicated to self-effacing public service. Neither depended on ideology or a well-defined view of the world to interpret reality. Each favored the lawyerly case-by-case approach to problem solving rather than risking the danger of forcing the facts into a preconceived picture. Although by 1967 both McNamara and Vance had come to oppose the costs of the Vietnam War, they refused to voice their opposition publicly. Instead, they expressed their concerns to the president directly. Both men were pragmatists within broad but strict boundaries of morality and decency. Even though they ran the world's largest military establishment, neither had great faith in exclusively military solutions to foreign policy problems. Both tended to believe that economic and political factors overshadowed applied force in the long run. Thus, with a beginning at the Defense Department during the Vietnam War,

Vance gained an insight of the limitations and dangers of reflexive military action, which shaped his action as secretary of state

Vance may well have been the most qualified and experienced crisis negotiator to assume the position of secretary of state in this century. During his tenure in the Defense Department, Vance had gained a reputation as a skilled arbitrator. Twice in 1965 Vance served in this capacity, first in Panama and then in the Dominican Republic. Responding to rioting over the flying of the U.S. flag in Panama, Vance assisted in defusing the tension and, foreshadowing later events, came to understand the anti-American sentiments that infected U.S. relations with Latin America. In the Dominican Republic crisis, Vance was involved in the complex and ultimately unsuccessful negotiations to obtain a political settlement between the right and the left in the wake of Johnson's dispatch of Marines.

After his resignation in 1967, Vance was recalled by the Johnson administration to decide on the procedures to be taken by federal troops in response to the June riots in Detroit. Following this, Vance was off to Cyprus to obtain a settlement, which prevented a Turkish invasion of that divided island. In the spring of 1968, Johnson set Vance to South Korea to forestall any military action by the Park government against North Korea in the wake of alleged attacks and the seizure of the *Pueblo*. Then, in April 1968, Vance was appointed Deputy Chief Negotiator to the Paris Peace talks under Averell Harriman. After difficult haggling to obtain apparent agreement to include the National Liberation Front in the negotiations, Vance was frustrated by Saigon's last-minute refusal to agree to such an arrangement.

This extraordinary record of diplomatic activity evidently solidified Vance's belief that political solutions are ultimately preferable to attempts to project national interest on the battlefield. This became a characteristic response style for Vance as secretary of state.

Vance's support for Sergeant Shriver in the 1976 presidential election ended when Shriver withdrew from the campaign. In the interim years, Vance had been active in the Trilateral Commission, where he met Governor Jimmy Carter of Georgia in 1971. Work on the Commission brought contact with Zbigniew Brzezinski as well. Brzezinski had become Carter's foreign policy instructor, and his relationship with Carter was strong by 1976. When Vance's name was mentioned as the likely person for secretary of state, Brzezinski approved.

Vance reports that he found Carter's principled approach and his centrist perspective to foreign affairs agreeable. In October 1976, he sent Carter a memo, sketching out his overall views on the foreign policy needs of the next several years and the regional and topical requirements that flowed from them. The document is particularly revealing of Vance's thinking and dispositions. In cautioning against allowing U.S.–Soviet relations to dominate foreign policy, Vance cited the growing importance of energy, environmental, population, and nuclear proliferation issues to relations between the industrial and nonindustrial nations. Perhaps because of Carter's commitment to human rights, Vance strongly endorsed vigorous activity in international forums and in foreign policy decisions but then added the caveat that the United States should do so, "without unrealistically inserting itself into the internal operations of other governments." Vance argued for the United States to "keep its mind focused on long-term general objectives, not just the crises of the moment." Ironically, it was just such events—the Iran hostage crisis and the Soviet invasion of Afghanistan—that resulted in the discrediting of the Carter administration foreign policy by 1980.

The memo was followed by an invitation to Plains, Georgia, in late November after Carter's election. There, the two men met informally and shared thoughts on the conduct of foreign policy over the next four years. Both men agreed that the second round Strategic Arms Limitation Treaty (SALT II) was the highest priority. They agreed that arms reductions should not be linked to Soviet behavior in other areas of the world. Vance expressed his strong belief that the problems of Third World nations should be treated independently of the U.S.–Soviet relationship.

In the Middle East, Vance favored a comprehensive settlement, which addressed the problem of a Palestinian homeland. Other positions taken by Vance included early normalization of relations with the People's Republic of China and a Panama Canal Treaty, which Vance thought would put U.S. relations on a more "realistic" plane in this hemisphere. Carter expressed again his strong feeling about promoting human rights and shaping policy with that in mind. Vance agreed in principle, but told Carter that strategic considerations should take first priority in some instances. For example, he argued that Carter should reconsider a withdrawal of U.S. troops from South Korea as a protest of human rights violations. Overall, Vance's memo and these conversations became the foreign policy agenda for the first three years of the Carter administration. At this general level, both men were in basic agreement.

On the evening of November 30, 1976, Carter asked Vance to become his secretary of state, and Vance agreed promptly. There is no doubt that he wanted the job. There was, however, some opposition to Vance from Carter loyalists, particularly Hamilton Jordan. The loyalists looked on the Carter victory as a mandate for the outlanders and a rejection of the traditional establishment. Vance, with his education, career, and background epitomized that establishment. In spite of this opposition, Carter opted for experience and credentials. In doing so, he recognized the need for continuity that is especially important in foreign policy. Zbigniew Brzezinski was named National Security Advisory two weeks later.

All new administrations face two basic kinds of foreign policy situations. First, there are the initiatives that the administration plans to begin or continue. Second, there are the issues and problems that develop unforeseen, often requiring prompt handling. Planned initiatives for Carter and Vance included a second nuclear arms treaty with the Soviets, normalization of relations with China, a Panama Canal Treaty, and a peace settlement in the Middle East. Unforeseen problems included Soviet activities in Angola and the Horn of Africa and the invasion of Afghanistan; the Chinese incursion into Vietnam; the overthrow of the Shah in Iran and the subsequent taking of U.S. hostages; and myriad other matters that erupted on a daily basis. Any secretary of state at any point in office must be able to handle several of these two kinds of issues simultaneously.

Vance and Carter had high hopes for real arms reductions rather than just a limitation in deployment. The lengthy and often frustrating SALT II negotiations lasted two and one-half years and ended in failure because the Soviet invasion of Afghanistan gave opponents within the administration and in the Senate the necessary ammunition to ensure its defeat.

The SALT II process demonstrated many of the major obstacles that faced Vance in the Carter years. Initially, Carter's idealistic desire to obtain a comprehensive arms reduction agreement was rejected by Leonid Brezhnev because the Soviets were taken by surprise by the proposal. Fortunately, Vance had a second proposal, based on the 1974 Vladivostok agreements obtained by the Ford administration that was more agreeable to the gradualist approach of the Soviets. As negotiations proceeded, the Europeans, led by Chancellor Helmut Schmidt of West Germany, became increasingly alarmed. They feared their security interests were being ignored in light of Soviet deployment of intermediate range missiles targeted at NATO countries. A promise of U.S. deployment of cruise and Pershing II missiles within three years, assuaged these concerns.

Senator Henry Jackson, the Democratic Chair of the Subcommittee on Arms Control, was suspicious of any nuclear arms deal with the Soviets. He and Republican conservatives were alienated by Carter's difficult decision to suspend B-1 bomber construction. In addition, the approval of the Panama Canal treaty had been portrayed by opponents as a strategic defeat.

Within the administration, Brzezinski used Soviet and Cuban activities in Africa as a justification for linking SALT II to Soviet activities in the Third World. Vance disagreed. He argued that nuclear arms negotiations were too important to be made conditional on events that had little logical relationship to them. This debate clearly reflected the differing worldviews that increasingly divided the Carter administration between Brzezinski's NSC and Vance's State Department after 1977.

Despite these problems, the final version of SALT II was signed by Carter and Brezhnev on June 18, 1979, and the struggle moved to the Senate ratification process. After divisive debate, the Senate Foreign Relations Committee voted 9–6 to recommend ratification to the full Senate. The Soviet invasion of Afghanistan on Christmas Day 1979 ended two and one-half years of negotiation, compromise, and agreement.

Vance's critics in the administration later charged him with failing to take a tough stand against Soviet activity in Africa. They attributed the Afghan invasion to an unwillingness to link SALT II to Soviet behavior. It is unlikely, however, that the Soviets would have accepted this conception of détente. Their conception of it did not link SALT II to activities in other parts of the world, and they did not recognize that sentiments to make such a linkage had grown in the U.S. They viewed Afghanistan as a critical buffer state between the Islamic underbelly of the Soviet Union and the radical Shiite forces gathering strength in Iran.

In any case, the most significant element in the Carter–Vance foreign policy package was dead. Perhaps Vance should have been more accommodating to opponents in the administration and in the Senate, but it is difficult to find fault with him for not foreseeing a Soviet invasion of Afghanistan becoming the final act in the struggle for SALT II.

Negotiations on a treaty to return the Canal Zone to Panama resumed in February 1977. By May, Vance had decided to divide the treaty into two: one that would transfer the Canal Zone to Panama by the year 2000, and another that would give the United States the right to ensure the Canal's security in perpetuity. The treaties were submitted to the Senate in September 1977. After extensive negotiations and compromises both with the Torrijos government in Panama and dubious senators, the treaties were signed and, on two barest majority votes (68–32) approved by the Senate in March and April, 1978.

From the beginning, Carter and Vance knew that a treaty to turn the Canal over to the Panamanians would arouse emotional opposition. The canal symbolized U.S. dominance of the Western Hemisphere, just as control over Gibraltar and the Suez Canal had symbolized British imperial power. Consistent with his views on Third World problems, Vance saw the issue from the Latin American perspective as well as from U.S. interests. For Vance, long-term stability in that area of the world would be better served by the treaty, even given short-term opposition with the United States. It is evident that Carter and Vance expended much of their reservoir of support in this effort. Now, opponents more easily labeled the administration as weak and too willing to sacrifice U.S. vital interests. Yet, undertaking the treaties and bringing them to completion required great strength and courage because it was so easy for opponents to take advantage of the symbolism and emotionalism that surrounded U.S. possession of the Canal.

If any foreign policy event is remembered from the Carter–Vance years it is likely to be the dramatic negotiations that resulted in the withdrawal of Israeli troops from the Sinai and the treaty between Israeli and Egypt, which brought about the first diplomatic recognition of Israeli by an Arab country. Although much of the credit can be attributed to the enormous risk taken by Anwar Sadat of Egypt (he eventually paid the price in his own life), the persistence of Carter and Vance deserves the bulk of it.

The Egyptian–Israeli peace treaty was a victory for Carter's and Vance's persistent negotiating styles. Although Carter and Vance initially planned for a comprehensive agreement that would provide the Palestinians with a homeland either in Gaza or on the West Bank, that plan was defeated after Menachim Begin's government refused to halt Israeli settlement in those areas. Sadat's dramatic trip to Jerusalem in December 1977 isolated him in the Arab world and ensured that no more than an Israeli–Egyptian accord to settle the 1967 war between them would be possible. Persistent and shrewd negotiations by Vance with Foreign Minister Moshe Dayan in July 1978 made possible the Camp David meeting between Begin and Sadat in September of that year. Carter demonstrated what could be achieved by direct and dedicated participation in a negotiating process. Carter's success with the able assistance of Vance and a specially chosen State Department–NSC team achieved the most impressive foreign policy accomplishment of the Carter administration.

Other issues of major significance in the Carter administration include the normalization of relations with China, the transfer of political power from a white Rhodesia to a black Zimbabwe, the Soviet–Cuban involvement in Ethiopia, and the ousting of the Somoza government in Nicaragua. Each of these events was important beyond the immediate circumstances.

Zbigniew Brzezinski took an increasingly important role in the normalization of relations with the People's Republic of China. This became a major source of irritation with Vance because Brzezinski saw China as a "card" to be played in the U.S. global struggle with the Soviet Union. Vance was caught off guard when Brzezinski convinced Carter to a hasty announcement of normalization of relations on December 15, 1978. The formal abrogation of the U.S. relationship with Taiwan, including the defense treaty, had not yet been fully worked out with Congress where resistance among conservatives was considerable. Deng Xiaoping's visit to the United States in February 1979 and his anti-Soviet remarks made matters even more difficult from Vance's perspective. China's abortive attack on Vietnam on February 17 demonstrated that a neutral policy between the USSR and the PRC was more prudent than leaning toward the Chinese.

Throughout 1978 and 1979, Vance was involved in negotiations that ultimately led to a peaceful transition in Rhodesia (consequently renamed Zimbabwe) from the white government of Ian Smith to black political control. These efforts resulted in the eventual constitutional changes that allowed the peaceful elections that brought to power a new, black-dominated parliament in April 1979 and the election of one of the former rebels, Robert Mugabe, in March 1980.

Elsewhere in Africa, Soviet and Cuban activities resulted in unfavorable U.S. domestic consequences for Vance's philosophy of and approach to global foreign policy. When Cuban troops came to the aid of the Ethiopians in their war with Somalia in February 1978, Vance came into direct conflict with Brzezinski, who went public with a statement that this Soviet-inspired move would disrupt the SALT talks. Privately, Brzezinski pushed for a show of military force in support of the Somalis and in opposition to Vance's typical desire to reach a negotiated settlement without jeopardizing the SALT talks. Vance was incensed by Brzezinski's public statement. He went directly to Carter with the reminder that the secretary of state was to be the president's foreign adviser. Carter failed to give an unambiguous denial of this attempt by Brzezinski to link Soviet behavior in the Third World with the SALT talks. The result was that the administration appeared confused and indecisive on the important question of whether U.S. participation in strategic arms depended on Soviet behavior in other parts of the world. The incident reflected Carter's unwillingness to commit to one or the other of his two primary advisors. It represented a turning point in the process of increased suspicion and alienation between Vance and Brzezinski and their very different perspectives on global politics.

The human rights emphasis of Carter–Vance foreign policy was put to the test in Nicaragua and the Somoza dictatorship. Neither Carter nor Vance were willing to seek to overthrow that admittedly corrupt government before the violence beginning in September 1978. Vance sought the intervention of the Organization American States when all-out fighting began, but the OAS governments rejected direct U.S. intervention—legacy of American activity in Latin America haunts any U.S. involvement there. So, despite the administration's position on human rights, inconclusive action in Nicaragua resulted in a continuation of formal U.S. support for Somoza's regime up to his resignation in July 1979. Critics found further evidence of confusion and vacillation in the administration's reactions to these events.

Despite Vance's philosophy that local conditions would determine U.S. foreign policy, he does not seem to have treated Iran in this fashion as the protests and then fighting led by the Shiite mullahs began in 1978. Brzezinski (reflecting Kissinger's and Nelson Rockefeller's support for the Shah) would have favored a military coup or even U.S. military intervention, if necessary, to support the Shah's regime. He, like Kissinger before him, could see little but strategic location as the premise for action.

It is safe to say that no one in the highest reaches of the government recognized the strength of religious fundamentalism prior to the final departure of the Shah on January 16, 1979. Both before and after the Shah's fall, Vance supported attempts to replace his authoritarian rule with a moderate alternative, Shapour Bakhtiar. The Ayatollah Khomeini returned to Tehran from his exile in France in February 1979. The disorganization in the Iranian Army, itself divided between Shah loyalists and Khomeini supporters, meant that there was no effective resistance remaining. Bakhtiar resigned, and Khomeini appointed Mehdi Bazargan to head a provisional government.

Vance favored an attempt to establish some sort of relationship with Khomeini through the Bazargan government, but the refusal to accept a U.S. ambassador indicated that Khomeini was not going to permit it. The problem of allowing the ailing Shah to enter the U.S. was the central focus of demonstrations in Tehran directed at the embassy. Vance was under pressure from Brzezinski and Kissinger to allow admission. The decision to let him enter in October 1979 for medical treatment led to Khomeini's call on students to step up the anti-American demonstrations, and on November 3, the embassy was overrun and the U.S. hostages were taken. On November 6, the Bazargan government fell, and power gravitated to the Revolutionary Council under control of Khomeini and the other mullahs.

When the Soviets launched their invasion of Afghanistan on December 25, the damage to the Carter administration was complete. Brzezinski now finally eclipsed Vance's leadership in foreign policy in the administration. Vance's submission of his resignation to Carter following the decision to attempt a military rescue of the hostages in April 1980, was the first time a secretary of state had resigned on a policy question since William Jennings Bryan did so in 1915. Much to his credit, Vance remained consistent to the ethical standards he had pursued throughout his three years in office. When he was no longer Carter's key foreign policy assistant, he could not remain. Also to his credit, he never exploited his opposition to the failed rescue attempt.

Although Vance retired from government service, he did not retire as a negotiator. During the early 1990s, he served as a personal envoy for two United Nations Secretaries-General—Javier de Cuellar and Boutrous Boutrous-Ghali. Between 1991 and 1993, he was dispatched on a fact-finding mission to Nagorno-Karabahk (March 1992), to South Africa (July 1992), and to Greece (May 1993) to negotiate a Greek settlement with Macedonia that prevented the turmoil in the Balkans from expanding into the Aegean.

Most noteworthy during these years, Vance paired with Bosnian Serbs and Muslims to fashion a political solution to the ongoing ethnic warfare in the disintegrating Yugoslavia. The result was a complex federal government that divided Bosnia into 10 ethnically based federated states. Initially, the agreement was criticized by the newly elected U.S. President Bill Clinton because it left unpunished the leaders who had conducted the "ethnic cleansing," which had already led to much bloodshed. Bosnian Serbs, led by Radovan Karadzic who were heavily implicated in ethnic brutality, rejected the proposal because it split the Bosnian Serbs into two separate geographic regions. Also, the plan was too complex with its many distinct and hostile federated states cobbled together in the name of maintaining one Bosnian entity. The proposal was moribund even before its formal introduction in June 1993. Nevertheless, the Vance–Owen scheme did pave the way for the Dayton Accords in 1995 that provided at least an enduring restoration of peace if not a political settlement.

Cyrus Vance died at age 84 on January 12, 2002. If a definition of a statesman is one who seeks to achieve what is possible within a specific historical and political context, then Cyrus Vance was an exemplar of it in the last third of the twentieth century. What is even more admirable, he served with no desire for power or personal gain, and, most importantly, he maintained his integrity and ethics, even at the expense of his position as secretary of state. To be sure, he had his critics among conservatives and those who interpret foreign policy in terms of hard-edged and narrowly defined national interest. Yet, he can hardly be faulted for the half of a lifetime that he spent in the cause of peaceful settlement of international conflicts.

All new administrations start with great hopes for accomplishment and success. Few of them end with the same degree of optimism. With the fresh start of the

Carter election, Cyrus Vance had good reason to be optimistic. He felt he had a carefully reasoned foreign policy plan that enjoyed the support of the president. He also felt that he had an agreement that he would be the president's principle foreign policy advisor.

There can be little doubt that there were notable successes in the Vance years. The Egyptian–Israeli peace treaty opened new possibilities for solutions in the Middle East. The Panama Canal Treaty demonstrated to the Latin American countries that the United States was capable of acting in a nonimperialistic fashion in that area of the world. Vance's efforts in the Rhodesian settlement enabled a peaceful transfer of power where most predicted protracted and bloody warfare. All these successes vindicated his faith in negotiations and political settlement rather than more belligerent alternatives.

The failures of the Carter–Vance–Brzezinski era are instructive because they characterize persistent problems in the making and implementing of U.S. foreign policy since the Kennedy administration. The overlapping roles of the secretary of state and the national security advisor, where both assert their positions as policy advisors and where there are significant differences between them, became a serious problem in the Carter administration. President Carter never did make a definitive choice between the two until most of the damage to his reputation had been done.

Despite the failures of the Carter–Vance years, it may well be that Vance's conception of the proper principles for U.S. foreign policy will serve as a more lasting model for the future than the Cold War and balance of power mentalities that have dominated since the late 1940s.

BIBLIOGRAPHICAL ESSAY

Not quite memoirs, Cyrus Vance's *Hard Choices: Critical Years in American Foreign Policy* (1983) reflects on the main events of his period as secretary of state. The book reveals the character of the man because of the absence of criticism where it would be easy to resort to it. Vance is the statesman and diplomat even here.

David McLellan's *Cyrus Vance* (1985) summarizes some of the major Carter–Vance foreign policy questions and difficulties but is somewhat short on analysis and is obviously friendly.

Bernard Gwertzman's article, "Cyrus Vance Plays it Cool," *New York Times Magazine* (March 18, 1979) does an excellent job of describing Vance's temperament and the consequences of it for Washington politics. It is also a good summary of Vance's philosophy.

Like other memoirs of former presidents, Jimmy Carter's *Keeping Faith: Memoirs of a President* (1982) is essential reading for a perspective on the foreign policy of the era but does not shed much light on the key controversies that divided the administration internally—particularly the Vance–Brzezinski tension.

Zbigniew Brzezinski's memoir, *Power and Principle: Memoirs of the National Security Adviser, 1977–1981* (1983), on his years as NSA is an essential companion to Vance's. It accurately reflects Brzezinski's power politics, bipolar geopolitical struggle conceptions so opposed to Vance's outlook.

Strobe Talbott's *Endgame: The Inside Story of SALT II* (1979) is the exhaustive, complete story of the negotiations and politics leading to the signing of SALT II.

John Norton

ELIHU B. WASHBURNE (1816–1887)

Served 1869
Appointed by President Ulysses S. Grant
Republican

Elihu B. Washburne, the secretary of state with the shortest tenure on record, five days, was born on September 23, 1816 in Livermore, Maine, to a poor family. Washburne had intermittent schooling and a variety of jobs until he settled on the law as his career. Washburne received his law degree from Harvard Law School and was admitted to the bar in 1840, the same year he set up his practice in Galena, Illinois.

Washburne was elected to the U.S. House of Representatives in 1853 as an anti-slavery Whig and joined the new Republican Party as it formed in Illinois. During his terms in the House, Washburne acquired a reputation for his knowledge of the budget and economic matters. From Fort Sumter on, Washburne was a staunch Unionist and the chief sponsor of the then unknown Ulysses S. Grant. Although some accounts differ as to the precise role Washburne played in Grant's early Civil War career, the congressman was the main sponsor of Grant, supporting the latter's succession of appointments and promotions and defending the general against his detractors, especially after the battle of Shiloh. Washburne served as chairman of the Committee of the Whole during President Andrew Johnson's impeachment proceedings and vigorously advocated Johnson's removal from office.

There has been disagreement by historians as to the reasons Grant offered Washburne the post of secretary of state. Fuller says that Grant made the offer to give Washburne prestige for a diplomatic post and as a personal compliment. McFeely, Grant's latest biographer, characterizes the prestige argument as "silly" but does support the argument that Grant offered the position in a moment of gratitude and extreme happiness as he heard the 1868 presidential election returns in Washburne's home.

The moment passed. In the face of criticism over the Washburne appointment and Washburne's advice against pushing Grant's nomination of Alexander T. Stewart for secretary of the treasury, Washburne submitted his resignation as head of the state department. Grant promptly nominated Washburne for U.S. minister to

France, which the Senate quickly and gratefully confirmed. Washburne took no action as secretary.

The most important event during his ministerial tenure was the Franco-Prussian War (1870–71). Washburne stayed in Paris throughout the conflict, including the German bombardment of Paris and the time of the Commune. Washburne was equally firm with both the French and North German governments on issues arising from the war and at the time of his resignation in 1877, he was held in high esteem by the German and French governments.

During Washburne's retirement, he wrote his diplomatic memoirs and tried for the Republican presidential nomination in 1882, an act for which Grant, trying for a third term, never forgave him. Washburne died in Chicago in 1887.

BIBLIOGRAPHICAL ESSAY

Washburne's papers are in the Library of Congress. Grant's letters to Washburne are housed in the Illinois State Historical Society, Springfield, Illinois. They have been published in part in Ulysses S. Grant, *General Grant's Letters to a Friend, 1861–1880*, introduction and notes by James Grant Wilson (1897); and John Y. Simon (ed.), *The Papers of Ulysses S. Grant* (1967–).

There is no biography of Washburne. Washburne wrote about his diplomatic experience in *Recollections of a Minister to France*, 2 vols. (1889). Washburne's correspondence relating to his ministerial service was published with the title *Franco–German War and Insurrection of the Commune* (1878). See also Joseph V. Fuller's biographical sketch, "Elihu B. Washburne," in *The American Secretaries of State and Their Diplomacy*, edited by Samuel Flagg Bemis (1958). William McFeely's *Grant* (1981) discussed the events of Washburne's appointment in a few pages.

Edward S. Mihalkanin

DANIEL WEBSTER (1782–1852)

Served 1841–1843; 1850–1852
Appointed by President William Henry Harrison
Continued in office under President John Tyler
Reappointed in 1850 by President Millard Fillmore
Whig

Although historians usually associate Daniel Webster with the politics of the "Great Triumvirate" (the other two were John C. Calhoun and Henry Clay) and the conservative legal principles he expounded in numerous court cases, he also demonstrated an expertise in foreign affairs that has likewise earned him a respected place in history. Two times Webster served as secretary of state, from March 5, 1841, to May 8, 1843, and from July 23, 1850, to his death on October 24, 1852. In both instances he advocated a strong foreign policy based on the law and property rights; recognized the intimate relationship between domestic and foreign affairs; opposed territorial expansion as divisive, injurious to the national interest, and conducive to war; sought to spread American commerce into the Pacific and East Asia; and resisted intervention in the internal concerns of other nations—unless the source of trouble directly affected the American interest. His most outstanding achievement was the Webster–Ashburton Treaty of 1842 with England, for it resolved many long-standing irritants between the nations and laid the basis for a midcentury rapprochement that permitted the United States to concentrate on westward expansion.

Webster came from a New England Puritan background that emphasized religious faith, hard work, responsibility, drive and ambition, personal loyalty, and patriotism to country. Born on January 18, 1782, on a frontier farm in Salisbury, New Hampshire, the young Webster was of frail health, but he attended Dartmouth College, where he excelled in English, history, and philosophy. While studying law with a local attorney in Salisbury, he taught school to pay debts and to help a brother in college. Webster was admitted to the bar in Boston in 1805 after a clerkship under the prominent international lawyer, Christopher Gore. By Webster's 30th birthday, he was practicing law in Portsmouth, New Hampshire, and had married Grace Fletcher in 1808, who would be with him for almost 20 years until her death.

Webster soon became a congressman, an eminent lawyer, an expert on constitutional principles, and a well-known orator. He was elected to the House of Representatives in 1812 and again in 1814 as a Federalist opposed to the War of 1812. His legal practice had meanwhile spread into the federal courts, and in a change that caused his congressional duties to lag, he moved from Portsmouth to Boston. Between 1817 and 1823, he defended the principle of national supremacy in three pathbreaking cases: *Darmouth College v. Woodward; McCulloch v. Maryland;* and *Gibbons v. Ogden.* Webster also won recognition as an orator in the Plymouth speech of December 22, 1820. As a member of the Massachusetts constitutional convention of that same year, he fought against the move to democratize control of the state senate and judiciary.

Webster's fame continued to grow. He was elected to Congress from the Boston district in 1822 and remained there for two terms. His law practice rapidly expanded, primarily due to fees garnered from Spanish claims before the commission established under the Adams–Onís Treaty of 1819. As a congressman he called for a national program of internal improvements and in 1824 argued in vain against a protective tariff while presenting a comprehensive statement of the doctrines of free trade. He served as chair of the Committee on the Judiciary, where he drew on the ideas of Joseph Story of the U.S. Supreme Court in working for an expanded and reformed federal judicial system and for increased federal jurisdiction over crimes. On foreign matters, Webster called for broad executive powers during the controversy surrounding the Monroe Doctrine, and he gave a speech in early 1824 that expressed widespread popular interest in the Greek Revolution. He hoped that President John Quincy Adams would offer him an appointment as minister to England, but this never came. In the meantime, Webster delivered the first Bunker Hill oration in 1825 and gave eulogies on John Adams and Thomas Jefferson in 1826, both of which further enhanced his reputation as a speaker.

In June 1827 Webster was elected to the U.S. Senate, where for over two decades he made several unsuccessful bids for the presidency while becoming a leading exponent of national conservatism. He worked with national Republicans in opposing Andrew Jackson and then became a Whig. The new party was largely under the control of Henry Clay, who also sought the executive office. When the idea of the national convention became standard procedure, Webster, who refused to be a party regular, alienated numerous Whigs and was never able to win the nomination. His wife's death in early 1828 drove him into a state of despondency that was finally relieved by his second marriage to Caroline Le Roy in December 1829. From the late 1820s to the early 1840s, he helped to formulate national policy relating to financial matters, tariffs, slavery, territorial expansion, nullification, secession, and nationalism. In his great debate with Robert Hayne of the early 1830s, Webster made his position clear on states' rights and sectionalism: "Union and Liberty, one and inseparable, now and forever!" His devotion to the Union led him to support legislation establishing federal supremacy during the South Carolina nullification crisis of that same decade.

Webster continued to work against the Jacksonians through the Martin Van Buren administration. In the last days of this presidency, Webster's knowledge of international affairs, particularly in regard to England, persuaded a number of people to support sending him to London in 1839 as a special emissary to resolve the northeastern boundary problem. Even though Congress approved an appointment and Webster wrote a long and learned treatise setting out proposed treaty terms, Van Buren chose to work through the U.S. minister in London, Andrew Stevenson. Webster nonetheless visited England in a private capacity, where he met many public figures and became convinced of the necessity of establishing good relations between the Atlantic countries.

After the election in 1840 of Whig William Henry Harrison to the presidency, Webster became secretary of state. Harrison died after only one month in office, leaving John Tyler as president—the first time succession to that office had fallen to the vice president. A Virginia slaveholder and states' rightist, Tyler had little in common with most Whigs, either in political principles or in personal relations. Serious difficulties ensued as political and personality clashes meshed with both domestic and foreign issues. Although the other cabinet members resigned, Webster offered to remain as secretary of state because, he declared, of his interest in resolving Anglo-American problems. He also liked the position and the prestige it offered, and he thought his chances better for undercutting Clay and seeking the presidency. By now 59 years old and in good health, Webster had black hair and a dark complexion, stood nearly 5'10" tall, and possessed a huge chest and shoulders that exuded a sense of power and presence that was accented by a large head, heavily furrowed eyebrows, and deeply set, intense eyes. These characteristics combined to produce what some called the "Godlike Webster."

As secretary of state, Webster upheld the law and national honor in dealing with a range of issues that involved several countries. In a minor squabble with Portugal over tariffs, Webster maintained the right of the United States to levy ad valorem duties on imported goods, and under his lead, the United States for the first time (in a case involving Syria) extended the nation's diplomatic protection to its missionaries outside the country. Grievances continued with Mexico over Texas and border claims matters, and irritants developed with Spain over the *Amistad* affair. Threats to the independence of the Sandwich Islands (Hawaii) led to the declaration of the Tyler Doctrine, which (as a forerunner to the Open Door Note of 1900) upheld the territorial rights of a weaker people against European imperialists. Webster expressed opposition to intervention in other countries' affairs, and he resisted westward expansion as dangerous to the nation's republican principles. His biggest problem was a long series of disputes with England: the northeastern boundary and related border issues; the African slave trade and the status of slaves in British ports; and visit and search and impressment.

Webster's most immediate problem was a legacy of the Van Buren administration: the animosities stemming from the *Caroline* crisis of 1837–1838 and the related issue involving Alexander McLeod. In late 1837, during the course of the Canadian rebellions against the British crown, U.S. citizens violated the Neutrality Act of that year in using the privately owned steamer *Caroline* to transport both war materiel and men into Canada to support the revolution. On the night of December 29, a group of Canadian militiamen attacked the steamer on the American side of the Niagara River. During the melee, several of the crew were wounded, an American was killed, and the vessel was set afire, left to sink in flames just above the falls. Although the furor dissipated the following year and negotiations dragged over whether the *Caroline*'s destruction was self-defense, excitement built again in 1840 when a Canadian deputy sheriff named Alexander McLeod was arrested in New York for murder and arson during the raid. The British foreign secretary, Lord Palmerston, instructed his minister in Washington, Henry S. Fox, to demand McLeod's release. Even if McLeod had participated, Palmerston declared, individuals were not responsible for public acts ordered by the governments involved. His argument repeatedly rejected by the government in Washington, the peppery secretary warned that "McLeod's execution would produce war; war immediate and frightful in its character, because it would be a war of retaliation and vengeance." Van Buren's secretary of state, John Forsyth, rejoindered that the issue fell under the jurisdiction of the state of New York, not the government in Washington, and the trial was set for March 1841. In the meantime Webster became secretary of state.

Webster had to defuse the McLeod crisis before he could work toward improving relations with England. He first reversed his predecessor's stand and agreed with the British government's acceptance of responsibility for the *Caroline* attack; but like his predecessor, he was unable to secure McLeod's release because of the doctrine of states' rights. Webster next sought to bring the case before the New York Supreme Court on a writ of habeas corpus, thinking the procedure would result in McLeod's release. But the court refused to free the prisoner and set a later court date, albeit with a change of venue. Webster then prepared to bring the case before the U.S. Supreme Court on a writ of error; but McLeod persuaded him against this course in preference for a quicker trial. Although Governor William H. Seward of New York refused Webster's request to order a *nolle prosequi* (a move not to prosecute on a indictment), he offered private assurances that evidence in the trial would establish McLeod's innocence. Furthermore, Seward implied that even if the jury voted to convict, he as governor would grant a pardon and prevent an execution. Despite the excitement and threats of war, in October 1841 McLeod established an alibi and in less than a half hour the jury returned an acquittal.

A change of government had meanwhile taken place in England that augured for goodwill between the nations. The new prime minister, Sir Robert Peel, and his foreign secretary, Lord Aberdeen, both wanted peace, and Webster and Tyler were anxious to comply. The secretary of state had earlier assured Fox that the United States would be willing to resolve the central issue—the northeastern boundary dispute—by accepting a conventional line in exchange for equivalent concessions. Stevenson had left his post in London, and his successor, Webster's friend Edward Everett, had established an excellent rapport with the British court. The most important development, however, was the Peel ministry's decision to send a special emissary to the United States. In the fall of 1841 Lord Ashburton (Alexander Baring) was appointed special minister, authorized to resolve all disputes between the nations. Ashburton was elderly, married to an American lady, wealthy (from the Baring Brothers banking house), and a friend of Webster's since their meeting in England two years before. Ashburton joined Webster in recognizing the importance of good Anglo-American relations.

Webster and Ashburton entered negotiations in Washington during the summer of 1842, fully expecting to settle all problems within a few days. But even though they agreed to engage in open, honest diplomacy, numerous difficulties arose that severely tested each man's patience. The most exasperating matter was the northeastern boundary. Although the two men decided to dispense with the weary arguments over maps and documents purporting to give the location of the Canadian–American boundary, they found these noble objectives impossible to achieve. Like earlier diplomats dealing with the boundary issue, Webster and Ashburton soon found themselves mired in detailed discussions regarding land and water configurations in the American northeast.

Both negotiators quickly fell into the traditional patterns of resolving international disputes. Before Ashburton's arrival in April, Webster had come into the possession of two "red-line maps" supposedly stemming from the Paris peace proceedings of 1782–1783 and delineating the boundary between Maine and New Brunswick. Yet, they contained markings that awarded the British more territory than that given by an arbitral decision of 1831 by the King of the Netherlands. Webster kept them both from Ashburton. The British emissary likewise engaged in secret diplomacy when, without authorization from his superiors in London, he privately sought the views of New Brunswick on the boundary. To his dismay, the leaders of that government dispatched a delegation to Washington, which made more stringent demands than the Peel ministry had authorized in the talks with Webster. Meanwhile, Webster had privately asked a politician from Maine, Francis O. J. Smith, to circulate newspaper articles in that state warning that failure to agree on a boundary compromise could lead to war with the British. Furthermore, Webster got authorization from President Tyler to draw from the "secret-service fund" (an annual congressional allotment for the president's use in foreign affairs) to send a Harvard history professor, Jared Sparks (who had earlier located one of the red-line maps in Paris), on a secret mission to the capital of Maine with the two maps to convince the state's leaders of the necessity of a rapid settlement before other similar maps were uncovered that would substantiate England's extreme claims to the disputed territory. Finally, to smooth the way to settlement (a treaty with England, of course, would require a two-thirds vote of the senate), Webster arranged what he called the "grand stroke"—having Maine and Massachusetts send commissioners to the talks in Washington. Ashburton, however, considered it improper for a diplomat to meet with representatives of American states and refused to do so.

Patience and personal relationships ultimately prevailed, however, for in July, the two diplomats agreed to a compromise. The United States received 7/12 of the territory in dispute but land that comprised 4/5 of the assessed value of the area (including the greatly contested Aroostook Valley), whereas the British got what they wanted: a strip of land in the northeast that would permit the construction of a military road below the St. Lawrence River and allow access to their interior Canadian possessions. The United States also received Rouse's Point, an important strategic position at the top of Lake Champlain. To placate Maine and Massachusetts, the government in Washington agreed to compensate each state $150,000 for land conceded to England. Americans also won free navigation of the St. John River, which wound through Maine and New Brunswick before emptying into the Atlantic Ocean. For another disputed territory, the northwest boundary from Lake Superior to the Lake of the Woods (upper Minnesota), the two men drew a line that (unknown in 1842) awarded the United States vast deposits of iron ore in the Vermilion and eastern Mesabi ranges. On the third of the territorial questions, that of Oregon (which included territory stretching from southern Alaska to Spanish California), both men decided that in view of more pressing matters, it was advisable to postpone an attempted settlement.

The negotiations also focused on maritime issues that southerners feared would jeopardize the institution of slavery. Longtime disagreements over the African slave trade had become entangled with slavery as well as with Britain's claims to the right of search and impressment. The entire question had become explosive because of the *Creole* mutiny of November 1841, during which 19 of 135 slaves on an American slaver moving from Virginia to New Orleans (thus legally engaged in the interstate or domestic slave trade) led a revolt near the Bahamas. After taking command, the blacks steered the vessel into the British port of Nassau, where British officials eventually granted their freedom on the basis of the crown's emancipation legislation of the 1830s. Webster immediately recognized a conflict of laws. The British action was a violation of U.S. property rights, and yet, as he explained to Everett in a note meant for Aberdeen's perusal, "we well knew that when slaves get on British ground, they are free." But in the interests of harmonious international relations, Webster argued, a national law must not violate another nation's persons or property driven into territorial waters by forces beyond their control. Because the extradition provision of Jay's Treaty of 1795 had expired, however, Webster could only appeal in vain for the slaves' return on the basis of comity or hospitality. On the larger question of the African slave trade, even though both the United States and England had taken legal measures toward ending the practice, only the latter had attempted to enforce them. No legitimate connection existed between the *Creole* voyage and the traffic in African slaves; the first was legal, whereas the second was a violation of law. Yet, in the minds of southerners, the two had become inseparable because they both involved British intervention in a way ultimately injurious to slavery.

Thus, in a real sense the two negotiators had to quiet a rumbling slavery issue during the negotiations. Ashburton consented to Webster's joint-squadron proposal that called for cooperation in suppressing the business and, in so doing, attempted to ease the fears of Americans about British sailors boarding American ships and engaging in examinations that were reminders of search and impressment. On the *Creole*, Ashburton won Webster's agreement to refer the issue to the government in London. In the meantime the envoy promised no "officious interference with American vessels driven by violence" into British ports, and he agreed to an extradition provision that, to satisfy antislavery groups in England, did not include mutiny and revolt on the list of seven extraditable crimes. In 1853 an Anglo-American claims commission awarded compensation to owners of the liberated slaves.

Webster and Ashburton resolved other matters by exchanging notes that did not officially become part of the treaty but were nonetheless integral to the general settlement. On the *Caroline*, Ashburton expressed regret that his government had not apologized for the incident at the time of its occurrence. Concerning McLeod, both sides acknowledged the principles of a public act, and Webster lamented the lengthy delay in the judicial process. In resolving the *Caroline* and McLeod affairs, Webster set out a convincing explanation of the doctrine of self-defense. To prevent another instance like that involving McLeod, Webster supported "An Act to provide further remedial Justice in the Courts of the United States," which Congress passed on August 29, 1842. The new legislation authorized federal jurisdiction over matters involving aliens charged with criminal acts committed under government orders. As for impressment and the related right of search, Webster attached to the treaty a long exposition of America's opposition to the acts, which was intended to quiet critics of the administration. Ashburton accepted the note, believing this a small price to pay for the furtherance of better Anglo-American relations.

The Webster–Ashburton Treaty, signed in Washington on August 9, 1842, was a compromise that, probably for that reason, came under heavy attack in both countries during the ratification debates and afterward. In the midst of the controversy, an additional map was unearthed in England that supported the extreme American claim and thus balanced off those maps held by Webster (which he had shown Ashburton on the day of the treaty's signing in Washington). Despite the bitter exchanges, the truth is that neither set of maps contained boundary markings considered by the Paris diplomats of 1782–1783 to be final; they had agreed to resolve actual locations by joint commissions established after the war.

In 1846, Webster's archenemy, Charles Ingersoll of Pennsylvania, charged him with interfering with the McLeod trial and with warning Seward that unless the prisoner were released, New York City would be "laid in ashes." Unable to prove these allegations and humiliated by Webster's counterblows in the Senate that Ingersoll's mind was "grotesque" and had screws "loose all over," the Pennsylvanian brought three new charges against the former secretary of state: illegal use of the president's secret-service fund, improper deployment of the money to "corrupt party presses" in New England, and leaving the State Department in default of over $2,000. The result was a bizarre attempt to impeach Webster retroactively; he had been out of office since 1843. After a House committee heard testimony in his defense (including that of former President Tyler), it fully exonerated Webster. About Ingersoll, an embittered Webster declared, "I leave him in the worst company I know in the world—I leave him with himself." The controversy was not over. Webster later came under attack by historians, who accused him of taking money from Ashburton in exchange for a boundary settlement favorable to England. No evidence has appeared to support this charge.

Webster was not pleased to see the nation's attention turning increasingly westward after passage of the treaty with England. Aberdeen thought that the general feelings of goodwill promoted by the treaty might encourage a settlement of the Oregon boundary. When he suggested the idea in October 1842, Webster was not enthusiastic. In an informal private letter to Everett in November, Webster objected to the Columbia River as a boundary because it did little for commerce and would not allow the United States a single good harbor on the entire Pacific coast. Even though Tyler later recommended a special mission to London to deal with Oregon, to negotiate the purchase of Upper California, and to improve commercial relations, neither Congress nor the British showed interest. When Webster privately proposed a tripartite arrangement whereby the British, in exchange for a settlement of the Oregon matter, would persuade Mexico to cede Upper California to the United States for money aimed at satisfying American and British claims against Mexico, the British again expressed no interest.

Texas also caused a problem. Early in the administration, Tyler had urged Webster to seek its acquisition, but the secretary favored recognition of Texas's independence. Webster had long opposed the arguments that annexation would benefit northern shipping concerns, and that anti-slave-trade enforcement would maintain the balance between slave and free states. Annexation, he believed, would promote deeper sectional division in the United States.

While secretary of state, Webster again demonstrated his commitment to the law when he confronted problems with Spain that grew out of the *Amistad* mutiny of 1839. In July of that year, a group of blacks led by Joseph Cinqué had risen in revolt on board the Spanish slaver *Amistad* as it was engaged in a coastal voyage from Havana to Puerto Principe, Cuba. After ordering their white captives to steer the vessel back to Africa, the blacks were deceived into thinking that they were en route home, when in reality they were inching up the Atlantic coast. Two months later, off Long Island, New York, the captain of an U.S. naval vessel captured the *Amistad*, the blacks, and the cargo and took them to an admiralty court for prize adjudication. Abolitionists heard of the case and took it to civil court. After a long legal process involving a series of appeals, the case came before the U.S. Supreme Court in March 1841, where Associate Justice Joseph Story ruled that the blacks were "kidnapped Africans," illegally taken by slavers in Africa to Cuba in violation of Anglo-Spanish treaties against the slave trade. The blacks' mutiny in the Caribbean was an exercise of the natural right of self-defense against unlawful detention.

Once freed by the Supreme Court, the *Amistad* blacks became the objects of renewed damage claims by the Spanish. Webster was only mildly opposed to slavery, and he certainly did not want to lend support to the abolitionist cause. The law was his rightful refuge. He insisted that the Supreme Court had acted legally in declaring the blacks free. The Spanish had no just claims to indemnification for the vessel, its cargo, and the blacks. Yet, even while turning down the Spanish demands, he and President Tyler could find no law authorizing the U.S. government to arrange the transportation of the blacks back to Africa. With private support, the *Amistad* captives returned to their homes in January 1842.

Webster at first appeared inconsistent regarding principles of nonintervention in other countries' concerns, but his basic guideline was the American interest. He adhered to nonintervention when agents from the Sandwich Islands asked the United States to extend diplomatic recognition and negotiate a treaty. Even though American commercial interests probably had legitimate reason to fear that European countries (particularly England) might occupy the islands, Webster did not believe that recognition and a treaty were wise. However, in a communication to the major European capitals, he urged respect for the integrity of the Sandwich Islands, and the president asked Congress to authorize the dispatch of an American commissioner. In a special message to Congress on December 30, 1842, the president used Webster's words to declare what has become known as the Tyler Doctrine: the United States opposed "any attempt by another power . . . to take possession of the islands, colonize them, and subvert the native Government."

Cuba was a different matter, for it lay within the Western Hemisphere and was therefore important to America's security. Fear had grown that the British were planning to instigate a revolution on the island that would destroy slavery and leave a black republic susceptible to the guise of British protection. The United States made it known that any British use of force in Cuba would cause war and that Spain could depend on American military and naval assistance in protecting its island possession. When a dispute developed between Britain and Argentina over the Falkland Islands, Webster saw no vital American interests involved and argued that the Monroe Doctrine did not apply to issues having their origins before that pronouncement.

Webster resigned from the State Department in May 1843. His chief intention had been to resolve the northeastern boundary dispute with England, which he had done with the treaty of 1842. Perhaps more important, Tyler's insistence on the annexation of Texas and spreading the nation westward had combined with the bitter division within the Whig party to make Webster's stay within the cabinet no longer tenable. On the same day that he sent instructions to Caleb Cushing of Massachusetts as commissioner to China, May 8, 1843, Webster tendered his resignation.

Webster did not withdraw from the national scene. In the presidential campaign of 1844 he attempted to mend ties with the Whig party by campaigning for its candidate, Henry Clay, who nonetheless lost to James K. Polk and the expansionist Democrats. Webster's friends persuaded him to accept a vacated U.S. Senate seat, which became effective on March 5, 1845. Again he would play the role of opposition to the administration. When Tyler supported a joint resolution leading to the annexation of Texas, Webster argued that the move violated the treaty-making power of the president and Senate. On the Oregon question, he favored a compromise with England because even though the area in question had valuable harbors and was suitable for a naval base, it was not worth a war. When war came with Mexico in May 1846, he stood in staunch opposition. Afterward, he resisted the annexation of territory because he feared that sectional strife over slavery would destroy the Union. When the territorial issue reached a crisis level in 1850, he worked for a compromise that would avert secession and certain civil war. In his "Seventh of March Speech," he supported national principles and offered assurances to those who doubted that the Union would survive. He succeeded in arousing the animosity of both North and South.

With the Union seemingly in peril, the new chief executive, Millard Fillmore (Zachary Taylor had died in office), invited Webster in July 1850 to join his cabinet as secretary of state. Webster began his second term during the furor over the Compromise of 1850 and the growing domestic difficulties regarding slavery. Indeed, his appointment was attributable more to his reputation for compromise in resolving the crisis over slavery and new territories than to his ability in formulating foreign policy.

Weak national leaders and divisiveness over slavery ensured an ineffective foreign policy during the decade preceding the Civil War. Americans violated neutrality legislation by engaging in filibustering expeditions designed to wrest Cuba from Spain. The Central American republics were prey for powers outside the hemisphere, including England and France. Unrest persisted along the Texas border, and Mexico's lingering fears of American's expansionist intentions blocked Webster's attempt to secure railroad concessions across the Isthmus of Tehuantepec. Washington's spokesmen expressed the tone of "Young America" in seeking expansion in Latin America, debating whether to become involved in the ongoing revolutions in Europe, and expanding trade in the Far East. The most serious effort at expansion—the southern desire to build a Caribbean empire—repeatedly stumbled over the issue of slavery. Northerners were convinced that southerners wished only to spread slavery and acquire more influence in Congress. The peculiar institution and the expansion of republican principles remained in disharmonious wedlock, each blocking the other until they reached a level of emotional stalemate. Thus Webster, who revered the law and societal order, found the State Department an unbecoming place during the early 1850s.

A liberal revolution had broken out in Hungary in 1848, and the following year President Taylor had privately sent a special envoy with instructions to extend recognition and negotiate commercial agreements if the situation warranted such moves. The envoy was unable to fulfill his mission when Russia aided the Habsburg regime in Austria in putting down the revolt. When the Austrian government learned of Taylor's intentions, its chargé in Washington, J. G. Hülsemann, hotly protested. Webster, by now secretary of state, opted to use the American people's interest in Hungary to unite them in overriding their differences regarding slavery and other sectional matters.

In late 1850 he criticized Austria in the "Hülsemann Note." The developments in Hungary, Webster asserted, "appeared to have their origin in those great ideas of responsible and popular governments on which the American constitutions themselves are founded. . . . The power of this republic, at the present moment, is spread over a region, one of the richest and most fertile on the globe, and of an extent in comparison with which the possessions of the House of Habsburg are but as a patch on the earth's surface." The Austrian monarch was furious over the note and succeeding events. In 1851–1852, the exiled leader of the Hungarian rebels, Louis Kossuth, arrived in the United States to persuade it to assist his people in winning independence. At a bipartisan banquet held in Kossuth's honor and sponsored by Congress, Webster claimed to be speaking in a private capacity in hailing the "American model upon the Lower Danube and on the mountains of Hungary." Although Webster had succeeded in uniting Americans and in perhaps drawing attention to his chances for the presidency, his actions strained relations with Austria and dangerously skirted his principles of nonintervention in European affairs.

Webster encountered numerous other problems while secretary of state. French interests in the Sandwich Islands aroused concern, leading Webster to ask the government in Paris to refrain from any action threatening their independence. In Santo Domingo, prolonged unrest had endangered foreign holdings and trade and caused the United States to break with its tradition of nonintervention by sending a special agent to the island with directives to work with the French and British in restoring order. Longtime disagreement with England over the northeast fishing business erupted again in the summer of 1852. The British had relaxed their enforcement of the provisions of the Convention of 1818, by which Americans were not to fish within three miles of British holdings. In 1851 England offered to extend fishing privileges in exchange for duty-free importation of fish into the United States. The government in Washington refused to grant such concessions, and the British retaliated by strictly enforcing their fishing regulations. Informal negotiations arranged by Webster (by now in poor health) succeeded only in securing a tenuous truce. And, beginning in 1851, Webster again turned down Spain's resumed demands for indemnification stemming from the *Amistad* affair. In his last diplomatic treatise, dated August 21, 1852, Webster examined Peru's claim to the Lobos Islands (located about 20 miles off its coast and rich in guano deposits) and, in a reversal of the United States' earlier position, convinced Americans that their opposition had no legal basis. Declining health took its toll, forcing him to spend long periods out of Washington and eventually taking his life on October 24, 1852.

The greatness of a man is often marked by the length and breadth of his shadow. If so, Webster's shadow encompassed both foreign and domestic concerns. Diplomatist, constitutional lawyer, Unionist, orator, statesman—all these characteristics befitted this multifaceted and multitalented man. As secretary of state, he practiced a personal style of diplomacy that was unusual for the nineteenth century. In so doing, he worked for the spirit of compromise in resolving international disputes, helped establish a greater respect for the law in international relations, and made strong pronouncements on behalf of justice in seeking national claims. He was not above making apologies when his nation was in the wrong, and he was willing to make concessions regarding immediate issues to accomplish long-range objectives.

Webster also helped to spread the nation's commercial interests into the Pacific and Asia. Indeed, the Tyler Doctrine constituted the first important statement of concern about the Pacific area. The Cushing mission to China resulted in the Treaty of Wanghia of 1844, which established diplomatic relations with China and won American trading rights by the most-favored-nation principle. In 1851 Webster drafted the original instructions for what would later become the Matthew Perry expedition that opened Japan to trade. Despite these notable achievements, the rapprochement with England encouraged by the Webster–Ashburton Treaty overshadowed them all. And yet, ironically, Webster's greatest success promoted what he had least wanted: westward expansion.

BIBLIOGRAPHICAL ESSAY

The primary materials relating to Webster are rich. The most complete collection is the Daniel Webster Papers, edited by Charles M. Wiltse and available both on microfilm and in letterpress edition. For Webster's time as secretary of state, see Kenneth E. Shewmaker (ed.), *The Papers of Daniel Webster, Diplomatic Papers, Volume 1: 1841–1843* (1983), and Shewmaker and Kenneth R. Stevens (eds.), *The Papers of Daniel Webster, Diplomatic Papers, Volume 2: 1850–1852* (1988). Still helpful is James M. McIntyre (ed.), *The Writings and Speeches of Daniel Webster*, 18 vols. (1903). Diplomatic materials and state papers are in the General Records of the State Department (instructions, dispatches, and notes), which are available on microfilm from the National Archives in Washington, D.C.

Secondary works dealing with Webster abound in number and quality. For the best biography, see Maurice G. Baxter, *One and Inseparable: Daniel Webster and the Union* (1984). See also Irving H. Bartlett, *Daniel Webster* (1992); Robert F. Dalzell, Jr., *Daniel Webster and the Trial of American Nationalism, 1843–1852* (1975); and Richard N. Current, *Daniel Webster and the Rise of National Conservatism* (1955). Still useful are Claude M. Fuess, *Daniel Webster*, 2 vols. (1930), and George T. Curtis, *Life of Daniel Webster*, 2 vols. (2003). For detailed accounts of Webster's terms as secretary of state, see Clyde A. Duniway, "Daniel Webster" (first term), in Samuel F. Bemis (ed.), *The American Secretaries of State and Their Diplomacy*, vol. V (1928); and Duniway, "Daniel Webster" (second term), in vol. VI (1928).

The Webster–Ashburton negotiations dominate the literature regarding Webster's time as secretary of state. Albert B. Corey, *The Crisis of 1820–1842 in Canadian-American Relations* (1970), is especially strong on the Canadian rebellions and the Canadian side of the issues with the United States. Wilbur D. Jones shows that England moved close to war with the United States over the McLeod affair in *The American Problem in British Diplomacy, 1841–1861* (1974). The most complete coverage of the treaty of 1842 with England is Howard Jones, *To the Webster–Ashburton Treaty: A Study in Anglo-American Relations, 1783–1843* (1977). A defense of Webster's performance during the negotiations, the work includes analyses of the *Caroline* and McLeod affairs, *Creole* slave mutiny, and Aroostook War and northeastern boundary dispute. The most critical account of Webster's actions regarding the boundary settlement is Samuel F. Bemis, *John Quincy Adams and the Foundations of America Foreign Policy* (1949), who accuses the secretary of providing information to Ashburton and taking money for it. Webster, Bemis concludes, "achieved a diplomatic triumph—against his own country." Frederick Merk raises questions about Webster's use of newspaper articles in New England in his *Fruits of Propaganda in the Tyler Administration* (1971). From the British perspective, Kenneth Bourne places the Webster–Ashburton Treaty within the context of North American rivalries between the Atlantic nations in his *Britain and the Balance of Power in North America, 1815–1908* (1967). The overall importance of the resolution of Anglo-American differences becomes clear in Charles S. Campbell, *From Revolution to Rapprochement: The United States and Great Britain, 1783–1900* (1974). For a good overview of the boundary question within the regional setting, see Paul A. Varg, *New England and Foreign Relations, 1789–1850* (1983). The most recent work dealing with the Webster–Ashburton Treaty and the Oregon Treaty of 1846 is Howard Jones and Donald A. Rakestraw, *Prologue to Manifest Destiny: Anglo-American Relations in the 1840s* (1997).

A number of works have concentrated on specific aspects of the Anglo-American problems leading to the Webster–Ashburton Treaty. For the *Creole* issue of 1841, see Howard Jones, "The Peculiar Institution and National Honor: The Case of the *Creole* Slave Revolt," *Civil War History* 21 (March 1975). The northeastern boundary dispute became enmeshed with the problems of states' rights, as shown by Howard Jones in "Anglophobia and the Aroostook War," *New England Quarterly* 48 (December 1975). On the *Caroline,* and *McLeod* see Kenneth R. Stevens, *Border Diplomacy: The Caroline and McLeod Affairs in Anglo-American–Canadian Relations, 1837–1842* (1989). See also Howard Jones, "The *Caroline* Affair," *The Historian* 38 (May 1976). And on the politics involved in the attempt to impeach Webster retroactively for his role as secretary of state, see Howard Jones, "The Attempt to Impeach Daniel Webster," *Capitol Studies* 3 (fall 1975).

Other matters have received attention. For the domestic political difficulties of the time, see Merrill D. Peterson, *The Great Triumvirate: Webster, Clay, and Calhoun* (1987). On the *Amistad* mutiny of 1839, see Howard Jones, *Mutiny on the Amistad: The Saga of a Slave Revolt and Its Impact on American Abolition, Law, and Diplomacy* (1987). For the Hungarian involvement, see Donald S. Spencer, *Louis Kossuth and Young America: A Study of Sectionalism and Foreign Policy, 1848–1852* (1977). Three articles by Kenneth E. Shewmaker are especially helpful: "Daniel Webster and the Politics of Foreign Policy, 1850–1852," *Journal of American History* 63 (Sept. 1976); "Untaught Diplomacy: Daniel Webster and the Lobos Islands Controversy," *Diplomatic History* 1 (Fall 1977); and "Forging the 'Great Chain': Daniel Webster and the Origins of American Foreign Policy toward East Asia and the Pacific, 1841–1852." *American Philosophical Society* 129 (1985).

Howard Jones

LIST OF CONTRIBUTORS

DAVID ANDERSON
University of Indianapolis

PAUL BELLAMY
Parliamentary Library, Wellington,
New Zealand

JOHN BELOHLAVEK
University of South Florida

LARRY I. BLAND
George C. Marshall Foundation

H. WILLIAM BRANDS
Texas A&M University

KINLEY BRAUER
University of Minnesota

WILLIAM BRINKER
Tennessee Technological University

F. ERIK BROOKS
Georgia Southern University

LESTER BROOKS
Anne Arundel Community College

PETER BUCKINGHAM
Linfield College

THOMAS H. BUCKLEY
University of Tulsa

CHARLES CALHOUN
East Carolina University

ALFRED CASTLE
Samuel N. and Mary Castle
Foundation

JAMES CHACE
Bard College

KENDRICK CLEMENTS
University of South Carolina

KENTON CLYMER
Northern Illinois University

JASON COLBY
Cornell University

JERALD A. COMBS
San Francisco State University

EDWARD CRAPOL
College of William and Mary

CALVIN D. DAVIS
Duke University

KARL DEROUEN
University of Wellington

MICHAEL DEVINE
Harry S Truman Presidential Museum
and Library

CHARLES M. DOBBS
Iowa State University

JUSTUS DOENECKE
University of South Florida

CLIFFORD EGAN
University of Houston

DEAN FAFOUTIS
Salisbury University

RICHARD W. FANNING
Mississippi State University

ROBERT H. FERRELL
Indiana University–Bloomington

ROBERT F. GORMAN
Texas State University–San Marcos

NORMAN GRAEBNER
University of Virginia

THEODORE HINDSON
Texas State University–San Marcos

DAVID JACKSON
Bowling Green University

HOWARD JONES
University of Alabama

WILLIAM KAMANN
University of North Texas

WILLIAM KLUNDER
Wichita State University

ALEXANDER W. KNOTT
University of North Colorado

JEFFREY MAUCK
Texas State University–San Marcos

BRYAN MCAULEY
George Ranch Historical Park

EDWARD S. MIHALKANIN
Texas State University–San Marcos

KAREN MILLER
Oakland University

JOHN MULDOWNY
University of Tennessee

JOHN NORTON
Lebanon Valley College

AMY PORTWOOD
Rutgers University

BENJAMIN D. RHODES
University of Wisconsin–Whitewater

LELIA ROECKELL
Molloy College

MICHAEL SANCHEZ
Texas State University–San Marcos

ALFRED SULLIVAN
Texas State University–San Marcos

EUGENE P. TRANI
Virginia Commonwealth University

ROGER R. TRASK
Historical Office, Office of the
Secretary of Defense

PAUL WEIZER
Fitchburg State College

MARVIN ZAHNISER
Ohio State University

QUICK REFERENCE CHRONOLOGY OF SECRETARIES OF STATE

The American secretaries of state are listed following in chronological order with their dates of service and the administration(s) they served.

John Jay
1784–1790
Secretary under the Articles of
    Confederation

Thomas Jefferson
1790–1793
George Washington

Edmund Randolph
1794–1795
George Washington

Timothy Pickering
1795–1800
George Washington/John Adams

John Marshall
1800–1801
John Adams

James Madison
1801–1809
Thomas Jefferson

Robert Smith
1809–1811
James Madison

James Monroe
1811–1817
James Madison

John Quincy Adams
1817–1825
James Monroe

Henry Clay
1825–1829
John Quincy Adams

Martin Van Buren
1829–1831
Andrew Jackson

Edward Livingston
1831–1833
Andrew Jackson

Louis McLane
1833–1834
Andrew Jackson

John Forsyth
1834–1841
Andrew Jackson/
    Martin Van Buren

Daniel Webster
1841–1843
William Henry Harrison/
    John Tyler

Hugh S. Legaré
1843 (Interim Secretary)
John Tyler

Abel P. Upshur
1843–1844
John Tyler

John C. Calhoun
1844–1845
John Tyler

James Buchanan
1845–1849
James K. Polk

John M. Clayton
1849–1850
Zachary Taylor

Daniel Webster
1850–1852
Millard Fillmore

Edward Everett
1852–1853
Millard Fillmore

William L. Marcy
1853–1857
Franklin Pierce

Lewis Cass
1857–1860
James Buchanan

Jeremiah S. Black
1860–1861
James Buchanan

William H. Seward
1861–1869
Abraham Lincoln/
    Andrew Johnson

Elihu B. Washburne
1869
Ulysses S. Grant

Hamilton Fish
1869–1877
Ulysses S. Grant

William M. Evarts
1877–1881
Rutherford B. Hayes

James G. Blaine
1881
James Garfield/
    Chester A. Arthur

Frederick T. Frelinghuysen
1881–1885
Chester A. Arthur

Thomas F. Bayard
1885–1889
Grover Cleveland

James G. Blaine
1889–1892
Benjamin Harrison

John W. Foster
1892–1893
Benjamin Harrison

Walter Q. Gresham
1893–1895
Grover Cleveland

Richard Olney
1895–1897
Grover Cleveland

John Sherman
1897–1898
William McKinley

William R. Day
1898
William McKinley

John Hay
1898–1905
William McKinley/
    Theodore Roosevelt

Elihu Root
1905–1909
Theodore Roosevelt

Robert Bacon
1909
Theodore Roosevelt

Philander C. Knox
1909–1913
William Howard Taft

William Jennings Bryan
1913–1915
Woodrow Wilson

Robert Lansing
1915–1920
Woodrow Wilson

Bainbridge Colby
1920–1921
Woodrow Wilson

Charles Evans Hughes
1921–1925
Warren G. Harding/
    Calvin Coolidge

Frank B. Kellogg
1925–1929
Calvin Coolidge

Henry L. Stimson
1929–1933
Herbert Hoover

Cordell Hull
1933–1944
Franklin D. Roosevelt

Edward R. Stettinius, Jr.
1944–1945
Franklin D. Roosevelt/
    Harry S Truman

James F. Byrnes
1945–1947
Harry S Truman

George C. Marshall
1947–1949
Harry S Truman

Dean Acheson
1949–1953
Harry S Truman

John Foster Dulles
1953–1959
Dwight D. Eisenhower

Christian Herter
1959–1961
Dwight D. Eisenhower

Dean Rusk
1961–1969
John F. Kennedy/
    Lyndon B. Johnson

William P. Rogers
1969–1973
Richard M. Nixon

Henry Kissinger
1973–1977
Richard M. Nixon/
    Gerald R. Ford

Cyrus Vance
1977–1980
James Earl Carter, Jr.

Edmund S. Muskie
1980–1981
James Earl Carter, Jr.

Alexander M. Haig, Jr.
1981–1982
Ronald Reagan

George P. Shultz
1982–1989
Ronald Reagan

James Baker III
1989–1992
George H. W. Bush

Lawrence S. Eagleburger
1992–1993
George H. W. Bush

Warren Christopher
1993–1997
William Clinton

Madeleine Albright
1997–2001
William Clinton

Colin Powell
2001–
George W. Bush

INDEX

pean affairs and, 144; family background of, 141; Far East and, 145; Latin America and, 145–46; marriage to Anne Ahlstrand Ely, 147; Progressives for Wilson and, 142; strengths and policies of as secretary of state, 143, 146

Colby, John Peck, 141

Cold War, 234; Alexander Haig and, 235; Bush-Baker years and, 44; Dean Acheson and, 3, 6, 15; end of, 180; enlargement and, 117; James F. Byrnes and, 88; Reagan administration and, 475

Coles, Elizabeth Carter, marriage to George Marshall, 352

Colhoun, Floride Bonneau, 98

Commerce and Alliance treaties (1778), and France, 288

Communism, 260

Communist expansion: John Foster Dulles's tactics against, 169, 170, 171–73, 174, 175, 177; U.S. covert activities and, 170, 171

Comprehensive Test Ban Treaty, 37

Compromise of 1850, 349, 452, 531; Hamilton Fish and, 192; Henry Clay and, 131; Martin Van Buren's support for, 510; William Evarts and, 182

Confederate States of America: Britain withholds diplomatic recognition of, 458, 460; rise of, 454

Congo, Christian Herter and, 251

Conkling, Roscoe, 63, 65, 184

Constitutional Convention, 277; Edmund Randolph and, 416; James Madison and, 335; Timothy Pickering and, 401

Continental Congress, 105; Edmund Randolph's attendance at, 416; James Madison's contributions to, 334–35; John Jay and, 273, 274; Thomas Jefferson as delegate to, 280

Contras, U.S. support for, 475

Convention for the Pacific Settlement of Disputes, 437, 438

Convention of 1818, Canadian-American border settlement and, 24

Convention of 1827, 330

Coolidge, Calvin, 441; Charles Evans Hughes as secretary of state under, 254, 261; Frank B. Kellogg appointed by, 293, 294; Henry Stimson and, 493

Cortlandt, Mary Van, 273

Costa Rica, 111

Council on Foreign Affairs, 445, 513

Counterinsurgency, John Foster Dulles and, 170

Covert actions: Bay of Pigs and, 445–46; in Guatemala, 171; in Iran, 170–71; John Foster Dulles and, 170, 177; in Latin America during Reagan administration, 236

Cowdin, Martha Waldron, marriage to Robert Bacon, 41

Cox, James, 257

Crawford, William H., 23, 126, 369, 381, 504

Creole mutiny, slavery issue and, 527–28

Crimean War, 139

Crittenden, John J., 137

Croatia, 48

Crowninshield, Jacob, 479

Cuba, 109; Alexander Haig and, 235–36; Christian Herter and, 251–52; Daniel Webster and, 530; Edward Everett and, 189–90; Hamilton Fish and, 196–97; Henry Clay and, 129–30; John Hay and, 240, 241; John Sherman and, 469, 470; Ostend Manifesto and, 86; Richard Olney and, 397–98; William R. Day and, 152–55, 158; William Rogers and, 426

Cuban Missile Crisis: Dean Acheson and, 3, 15; Dean Rusk and, 446–47

Cuban War, 152–55

Cuellar, Javier de, 519

Cyprus crisis, Henry Kissinger and, 302–3

Dallas, George M., 83

Dam, Ken, 473

Dana, Francis, John Quincy Adams and, 20

Daniels, Josephus, on Robert Lansing, 316–17

Dardanelles, Dean Acheson and Soviet designs on, 4, 8–10

Davis, Cushman Kellogg, 293

Davis, Henry Winter, 456

Davis, Jefferson, 459

Davis, John W., 512

Davis, Norman H., 143

Dawes Plan, 294; Charles Evans Hughes and, 259

Day, Luther, 149

Day, William R., 149–61, 469, 470; appointment to and service on Supreme Court, 160–61; birth of, 149; China trade and, 156; Cuba policy and, 152–55, 158; death of, 161; education of, 149; family background of, 149; Hawaiian annexation treaty and, 151; marriage to Mary Schae-

Nicholas II (czar of Russia), 435
Nicholson, Alfred P., 108
Nicolay, John G., history of Abraham Lincoln by, 238
Niebuhr, Reinhold, 14, 165
Nine Power Treaty, 259, 494, 496
Nitze, Paul, 444
Niven, John, 505
Nixon, Richard M., 248, 304, 305; Alexander Haig's service under, 235; Alger Hiss case and, 421–22; "Checkers" speech and, 422; Dean Acheson and, 3, 16; election of, 179; George Shultz and, 472, 473; Henry Kissinger and, 299, 300, 301; James F. Byrnes and, 95; normalization of U.S. relations with China and, 300, 427; SALT I negotiations with Soviet Union and, 427–28; Vietnam War and, 390, 424, 425; Watergate scandal and, 301, 428; William Rogers and, 421, 422, 423, 424, 428
Nixon Doctrine, 424, 425
"Nixon shocks," Henry Kissinger and, 302
Noncolonization, John Quincy Adams and, 30, 31
Non-Importation Act, 343
Nonintervention principle, John Quincy Adams and, 30
Nootka Sound crisis, 282, 284–85
Noriega, Manuel, U.S. removal of, 47–48, 410
North American Free Trade Agreement (NAFTA), Warren Christopher and, 118–19
North Atlantic Fisheries and Fur Seals Conference, 315
North Atlantic Treaty Organization (NATO): Alexander Haig as Commander of, 235; Bosnian war and, 121; Clinton administration and, 118; Dean Acheson and, 1; George Marshall and, 360; George Shultz and, 475; James Baker, III, and, 48
Northern Ireland, Warren Christopher and, 121
Northern Securities Company, 41; Philander Knox's antitrust suit against, 308
Northern Securities Co. v. United States, 161
North Korea: Colin Powell and, 412; nuclear weapons drive in, 119; William Rogers and, 426
Northwest Ordinance of 1784, Thomas Jefferson and, 280

Norvell, Dolly, marriage to William Marcy, 348
"No-Transfer" rule, 130
NSC. *See* National Security Council
NSSMs. *See* National Security Study Memoranda
Nuclear arms race, George Shultz and, 475
Nuclear Nonproliferation Treaty, 449
Nuclear technology, John Foster Dulles, deterrents to Soviet advancement and, 170
Nuclear Weapons and Foreign Policy (Kissinger), 300
Nullification crisis, 99, 100, 107; Hugh Legaré and, 326; John Forsyth and, 200; William Seward and, 451
Nullification Proclamation, 332
Nuremberg trials, 298
Nye, Gerald P., 266
Nye Committee, 267

OAS. *See* Organization of American States
Obregon, Alvaro, 260
Office of Economic Stabilization, 91
Office of Strategic Services, Ho Chi Minh and, 171
Office of War Mobilization, 91
Oil embargo (1973), 302
Oil import control system, George Shultz and, 472
Olney, Richard, 152, 232, 393–98, 433; appointed as secretary of state, 394; Asia and, 398; as attorney general, 393–94; birth of, 393; broadened view of Monroe Doctrine by, 396; Cuba and, 397–98; death of, 398; education of, 393; Great Britain and, 396–97; Latin America and, 395, 396; legal career with railroads and, 393, 394; marriage to Agnes Thomas, 393; socioeconomic conditions during tenure of, 395–96; Spanish-American War and groundwork of, 398
Olney, Thomas, 393
Olney, Wilson, 393
Olney's corollary, 433
Onís, Luis de, 26, 27, 125
OPEC. *See* Organization of Petroleum Exporting Countries
Open Door notes, 242–43, 525
Open Door policy, 145, 146, 319; influence of, 434, 441; Philander Knox's continuation of, 309
Operation Desert Shield, 411